THE GREAT NORTH

THE GREAT NORTH

A COLLECTION FROM
HARPER'S MAGAZINE

GALLERY BOOKS

Gallery Books
an imprint of W.H. Smith Publishers, Inc.
112 Madison Avenue
New York, New York 10016

This volume first published in 1990 by

The Octopus Group Limited
Michelin House, 81 Fulham Road, London SW3 6RB

This edition published in 1990 by Gallery Books
an imprint of W.H. Smith Publishers Inc.
112 Madison Avenue, New York 10016

ISBN 0 8317 4255 0

Printed in Great Britain

CONTENTS

ANTELOPE HUNTING IN MONTANA

OF all the numerous species of large game to be found in the far West, there is none whose pursuit furnishes grander sport to the expert rifleman than the antelope (*Atilocapra americana*). His habitat being the high open plains, he may be hunted on horseback, and with a much greater degree of comfort than may the deer, elk, bear, and other species which inhabit the wooded or mountainous districts. His keen eyesight, his fine sense of smell, his intense fear of his natural enemy, man, however, render him the most difficult of all game animals to approach, and he must indeed be a skillful hunter who can get within easy rifle range of the antelope, unless he happens to have the circumstances of wind and lie of ground peculiarly in his favor. When the game is first sighted, even though it be one, two, or three miles away, you must either dismount and picket your horse, or find cover in some *coulee* or draw, where you can ride entirely out of sight of the quarry. But even under such favorable circumstances it is not well to attempt to ride very near them. Their sense of hearing is also very acute, and should your horse's hoof or shoe strike a loose rock, or should he snort or neigh, the game is likely to catch the sound while you are yet entirely out of sight and far away, and when you finally creep cautiously to the top of the ridge from which you expect a favorable shot, you may find the game placidly looking for you from the top of another ridge a mile or two farther away.

But we will hope that you are to have better luck than this. To start with, we will presume that you are an expert rifleman; that you are in the habit of making good scores at the butts; that at 800, 900, and 1000 yards you frequently score 200 to 210 out of a possible 225 points. We will also suppose that you are a hunter of some experience; that you have at least killed a good many deer in the States, but that this is your first trip to the plains. You have learned to estimate distances, however, even in this rare atmosphere, and possess good judgment as to windage. You have brought your Creedmoor rifle along, divested, of course, of its Venier sight, wind-gauge, and spirit-level, and in their places you have fitted a Beach combination front sight and Lyman rear sight. Besides these you have the ordinary open-step sight attached to the barrel just in front of the action. This is not the best arm for antelope hunting; a Winchester Express with the same sights would be much better; but this will answer very well.

We camped last night on the bank of a clear, rapid stream that gurgles down from the mountain, and this morning are up long before daylight, have eaten our breakfasts, saddled our horses, and just as the gray of dawn begins to show over the low, flat prairie to the east of us we mount, and are ready for the start. The wind is from the northeast. That suits us very well, for in that direction, about a mile away, there are some low foot-hills that skirt the valley in which we are camped. In or just beyond these we are very likely to find antelope, and they will probably be coming toward the creek this morning for water.

We put spurs to our horses and gallop away. A brisk and exhilarating ride of ten minutes brings us to the foot-hills, and then we rein up, and ride slowly and cautiously to near the top of the first one. Here we dismount, and, picketing our ponies, we crawl slowly and carefully to the apex. By this time it is almost fully daylight. We remove our hats, and peer cautiously through the short, scattering grass on the brow of the hill.

Do you see anything?

No; nothing but prairie and grass.

No? Hold! What are those small, gray objects away off yonder to the left? I think I saw one of them move. And now, as the light grows stronger, I can see white patches on them. Yes, they are antelope. They are busily feeding, and we may raise our heads slightly and get a more favorable view. One, two, three— there are five of them—two bucks, a doe, and two kids. And you will observe that they are nearly in the centre of a broad stretch of table-land.

"But," you say, "may we not wait here a little while until they come nearer to us?"

Hardly. You see they are intent on getting their breakfast. There is a heavy frost on the grass, which moistens it sufficiently for present purposes, and it may be an hour or more before they will start for water. It won't pay us to wait so long, for we shall most likely find others within that time that we can get within range of without waiting for them. So you may as well try them from here.

Now your experience at the butts may serve you a good turn. After taking a careful look over the ground, you estimate the distance at 850 yards, and setting up your Beach front and Lyman rear sights, you make the necessary elevation. There is a brisk wind blowing from the right, and you think it necessary to hold off about three feet. We are now both lying prone upon the ground. You face the game, and support your rifle at your shoulder by resting your elbows on the ground. The sun is now shining brightly, and you take careful aim at that old buck that stands out there at the left. At the report of your rifle a cloud of dust rises from a point about a hundred yards this side of him, and a little to the left, showing that you have underestimated both the distance and the force of the wind—things that even an old hunter is liable to do occasionally.

AN EARLY MORNING CALL.

We both lie close, and the animals have not yet seen us. They make a few jumps, and stop all in a bunch. The cross-wind and long distance prevent them from knowing to a certainty where the report comes from, and they don't like to run just yet, lest they may run toward the danger instead of away from it. You make another half-point of elevation, hold a little farther away to the right, and try them again. This time the dirt rises about twenty feet beyond them, and they jump in every direction. That was certainly a close call, and the bullet evidently whistled uncomfortably close to several of them. They are now thoroughly frightened. You insert another cartridge, hurriedly draw a bead on the largest buck again, and fire. You break dirt just beyond him, and we can't tell for the life of us how or on which side of him your bullet passed. It is astonishing how much vacant space there is round an antelope, anyway. This time they go, sure. They have located the puff of smoke, and are gone with the speed of the wind away to the west. But don't be discouraged, my friend. You did some clever shooting, some *very* clever shooting, and a little practice of that kind will enable you to score before night.

We go back to our horses, mount, and gallop away again across the table-land. A ride of another mile brings us to the northern margin of this plateau, and to a more broken country. Here we dismount and picket our horses again. We ascend a high butte, and from the top of it we can see three more antelope, about a mile to the north of us; but this time they are in a hilly, broken country, and the wind is coming directly from them to us. We shall be able to get a shot at them at short range. So we cautiously back down out of sight, and then begins the tedious process of stalking them. We walk briskly along around the foot of a hill for a quarter of a mile, to where it makes a turn that would carry us too far out of our course. We must cross this hill, and after looking carefully at the shape and location of it, we at last find a low point in it where by lying flat down we can crawl over it without revealing ourselves to the game. It is a most tedious and painful piece of work, for the ground is almost covered with cactus and sharp flinty rocks, and our hands and knees are terribly lacerated. But every rose has its thorn, and nearly every kind of sport has something unpleasant connected with it occasionally; and our reward, if we get it, will be worth the pain it costs us. With such reflections and comments, and with frequent longing looks at the game, we kill time till at last the critical part of our work is done, and we can arise and descend in a comfortable but cautious walk into another draw.

This we follow for about two hundred yards, until we think we are about as near our quarry as we can get. We turn to the right, cautiously ascend the hill, remove our hats, and peer over, and there, sure enough, are our antelope quietly grazing, utterly oblivious to the danger that threatens them. They have not seen, heard, or scented us; so we have ample time to plan an attack. You take the standing shot at the buck, and together we will try and take care of the two does afterward. At this short distance you don't care for the peep and globe sights, and wisely decide to use the plain open ones. This time you simply kneel, and then edge up until you can get a good clear aim over the apex of the ridge in this position. The buck stands broadside to you, and at the crack of your rifle springs into the air, and falls all in a heap, pierced through the heart.

And now for the two does. They are flying over the level stretch of prairie with the speed of an arrow, and are almost out of sure range now. You turn loose on that one on the right, and I will look after the one on the left. Our rifles crack together, and little clouds of dust rising just beyond tell us that, though we have both missed, we have made close calls. I put in about three shots to your one, owing to my rifle being a repeater, while you must load yours at each shot. At my fourth shot my left-fielder doubles up and goes down with a broken neck; and although you have fairly "set the ground afire"—to use a Western phrase—around your right-fielder, you have not had the good fortune to stop her, and she is now out of sight behind a low ridge.

But you have the better animal of the two, and have had sport enough for the first morning. We will take the entrails out of these two, lash them across our horses behind our saddles, go to camp, and rest through the heat of the day; for this September sun beams down with great power in mid-day, even though the nights are cool and frosty.

And now, as we have quite a long ride to camp, and as we are to pass over a rather monotonous prairie country *en route*, I will give you a point or two on flagging antelope, as we ride along, that may be useful to you at some time. Fine sport may frequently be enjoyed in this way. If you can find a band that have not been hunted much, and are not familiar with the wiles of the white man, you will have little trouble in decoying them within rifle range by displaying to them almost any brightly colored object. They have as much curiosity as a woman, and will run into all kinds of danger to investigate any strange object they may discover. They have been known to follow an emigrant or freight wagon with a white cover several miles, and the Indian often brings them within reach of his arrow or bullet by standing in plain view wrapped in his red blanket. A piece of bright tin or a mirror answers the same purpose on a clear day. Almost any conspicuous or strange-looking object will attract them; but the most convenient as well as the most reliable at all times is a little bright red flag.

In the fall of 1881 I was riding down the Yellowstone River in company with my friends Huffman and Conley, on our return from a hunting expedition to the Big Horn Mountains. While passing over a piece of high table-land overlooking a portion of the valleys of the Yellowstone River and Big Porcupine Creek we met a couple of hunters, who told us that a large herd of buffaloes were grazing on the Big Porcupine about fifteen miles from us; and knowing that antelope are nearly always found hanging on the outskirts of every herd of buffaloes, we at once began to scan the country with our glasses in search of them. We were soon rewarded by seeing a number of small white specks on the dead grass away up the Porcupine that seemed to be moving. We rode toward them at a lively gait for perhaps a mile, and stopped to look again. From this point we could easily identify them, although they still seemed to be about the size of jack-rabbits. We again put spurs to our horses, and rode rapidly to within a mile of them, when we picketed our animals in a low swale, took out our "antelope flag"—a piece of scarlet-colored calico about half a yard square—attached it to the end of my wiping stick, and were ready to interview the antelopes.

I crawled to the top of a ridge within plain view of the game, and planted the flag. The breeze spread it out, kept it fluttering, and it soon attracted their attention. This bit of colored rag excited their curiosity to a degree that rendered them restive, anxious, uneasy, and they seemed at once to be seized with an insatiable desire to find out what it was. Huffman went to the top of another ridge to my right, and some distance in advance, and Conley crawled into a hollow on the left, so that we three formed a half-circle, into which we intended, if possible, to decoy the game.

When they first discovered our flag they moved rapidly toward it, sometimes breaking into a trot. But when they had covered about half the distance between us and their starting-point they began to grow suspicious, and stopped. They circled around, turned back, and walked a few steps, then paused and looked back at the, to them, mysterious apparition. But they could not resist its magic influence. Again they turned and came toward us, stopped, and gazed curiously at it. The old buck that led the herd stamped impatiently, as if annoyed at his inability to solve the mystery. They walked cautiously toward us again down an incline into a valley which took them out of sight of the flag.

This, of course, rendered them still more impatient, and when they reached the top of the next ridge they were running. But as soon as the leader caught sight of the flag again he stopped, as did the others in turn when they came in sight of it. They were not more than a hundred yards from me, and were still nearer to my friends. There were seven in the band—two bucks, three does, and two kids. Their position was everything we could wish, and though we might possibly have brought them a few yards nearer, there was a possibility of their scenting us even across the wind, which, of course, we had arranged to have in our favor, and I decided that rather than run the risk of this and the consequent stampede, I would open on them where they were. It had been arranged that I was to begin the entertainment, and drawing a fine bead on the white breast

of the old buck, I pulled. Huffman's and Conley's rifles paid their compliments to the pretty visitors at almost the same instant, and for about thirty seconds thereafter we fanned them about as vigorously as ever a herd was fanned under similar circumstances. The air was full of leaden missiles, and the dry dust raised under and around the fleeing quarry. Clouds of smoke hung over us, and the distant hills echoed the music of our artillery, until the last white rump disappeared among the cottonwoods on the river-bank. When the smoke of battle cleared away, and we looked over the field, we found that we had not burned our powder in vain. Five of the little fellows, two bucks and three does, had fallen victims to their curiosity. The two fawns had, strangely enough, escaped, probably because they, being so much smaller than their parents, were less exposed.

I once saw a coyote sneak from behind a hill toward a herd of antelope. Instantly there was a grand rush of all the adult members of the band, male and female, toward the intruder, and when they had gotten in front of the kids they stopped, with bristles erect, ears thrown forward, and heads lowered, presenting a most warlike and belligerent appearance. The coyote, when he saw himself confronted with this solid phalanx, suddenly stopped, eyed his opponents for a few moments, and then, apparently overawed at the superiority of numbers and warlike attitude of his intended prey, slunk reluctantly away in search of some weaker victim. When he was well out of sight, the older members of the band turned to their young, caressed them and resumed their grazing.

The speed of the antelope is probably not excelled by that of any other animal in this country, wild or domestic, except the greyhound, and in fact it is only the finest and fleetest of these that can pull down an antelope in a fair race.

In the little village of Garfield, Kansas, there lived a man some years ago—the proprietor of a hotel—who had two pet antelopes. The village dogs had several times chased them, but had always been distanced. One day a Mexican came to town who had with him two large, handsome greyhounds. Immediately on riding up to the hotel he saw the antelopes in the yard, and told the proprietor, gruffly, that he had better put "them critters" in the corral, or his dogs would.

kill them. The proprietor said he guessed the "critters" were able to take care of themselves, especially if the dogs did not spring upon them unawares. This aroused the Mexican's ire, and he promptly offered to wager a goodly sum that his dogs would pull down one or both of the antelopes within a mile. The challenge was accepted, the stakes deposited, and the antelopes turned into the street, and the "greaser" told his dogs to "take 'em."

The dogs sprang at the antelopes, but the latter had soon reached a vacant lot across the street. They started off down the river. For a distance of four miles the river-bottom was an open prairie, and as level as a floor. As the quartette sped over this grand natural race-course, the whole populace of the town turned out *en masse* to see the race. Men and boys shouted, and ladies waved their handkerchiefs. Betting was rife, the natives offering two to one on the antelopes, the Mexican and the few other strangers in town being eager takers. It was nip and tuck, neither animals gaining nor losing perceptibly, and when at last the four went round a bend in the river four miles away, and were hidden by a bluff, the game was, as nearly as could be seen by the aid of good field-glasses, just about the same distance ahead of the dogs as when they left town.

Some hours later the dogs returned, so tired they could scarcely walk. The Mexican eagerly looked for hair on their teeth, and although he could find none, was confident that his dogs had killed the antelopes. A mounted expedition to search for the carcasses and settle the question was agreed upon, but as it was too near night to start when the dogs returned, it was arranged to go in the morning. But when the parties got up the next morning they found the antelopes quietly grazing in the hotel yard. The Mexican left town in disgust, followed by his lame, sore-footed dogs, and muttering that he "never seed no varmints run like them things did."

The antelope, one of the brightest and most graceful and beautiful of all our Western game animals, is fast disappearing from our broad plains, owing to the ceaseless slaughter of it that is carried on by "skin hunters," Indians, "foreign noblemen," and others who come to this country year after year and spend the entire summer in hunting. Thousands of them are killed every summer by this latter class, and left to rot where they fall, not a pound of meat, a skin, or even a head being taken from them. I have seen with my own eyes this butchery carried on for years past, and know whereof I speak.

Nearly all the Territories have stringent laws intended to prohibit this class of slaughter, but in these sparsely settled countries the provisions for enforcing them are so meagre that these men violate them day after day and year after year with impunity. This is one of the instances in which prohibition does not prohibit. And what I have said of the antelope is true of all the large game of the great West. The buffalo, elk, deer, mountain-sheep, etc., are being slaughtered by the thousands every year—tenfold faster than the natural increase. And the time is near, *very* near, when all these noble species will be extinct. The sportsman or naturalist who desires to preserve a skin or head of any of them must procure it very soon or he will not be able to get it at all.

QUEBEC

QUEBEC may be called the Poets' Corner of America, for the poet there
is most certainly buried under monastic
shadows, even while yet alive. And taking the term in a more attractive sense—
one that pleased my fancy greatly when
a child—Quebec is the mellowest nook of
this raw continent, a cozy corner filled
with materials for imagination to work
over. ⟩ It is verily a dusty, shadowy garret—where else can the poet lodge ?—furnished with intellectual rubbish and bric-
à-brac of the Middle Age; striking pictures of monk, nun, soldier, seigneur, savage; said to be actually haunted by the
devil and his spirits, and defended by God
and His angels; with miracles of daily
occurrence; the air full of legends and
superstitions, as well as of religious zeal;
peopled by the quaint folk of mediæval
times; and the whole made misty with
dust and cobwebs, comfortable with som-
nolence, and rich with the glow of social
warmth. And Nature herself draws down
the shade at candle-light to concentrate
and emphasize his feelings; for so long
as Canada is assailed by arctic winters his
nook will be an outpost in the polar wilderness, life out-of-doors will seem a bleak
adventure, and he will often turn from it
with intenser interest to the human world
of his corner, while the tempest howls in
the chimney. But the outside world also
is full of suggestions. The surroundings
of Quebec have become familiar to me by
years of observation, and still I always

look abroad with pleasure from the Citadel or the Terrace, at the great St. Lawrence Valley, walled in with mountains, cloven by a vast arm of the sea, and still watched over by primeval forests. You thus pass in a glance from the populous town through a rapid *diminuendo* of humanity on the surrounding hills to the mountain portals of the arctic wilderness. And the dome over this vast horizon of snow-drifted rivers, islands, vales, hills, mountains, is often filled with the grandest storms, the richest sunset hues, and the awful serenity and magnificence of the polar nights. Death and life here are strangely sociable; the surrounding mountains of arctic desert have many pathetic touches of human warmth, and the compact, cozy town has many marks of arctic snow and monastic austerity—a penetration of desolation into the very heart of man. The Citadel is not an inappropriate crown to the rock of Quebec, bearing in mind its historic military importance; at present it is peaceful enough in its winter whiteness and stillness; guns, mortars, and pyramids of shot peep innocently up above the snow, and the trenches are partly filled with drifts, reaching often to the parapets. But the Citadel should be crowned by a lofty monastery—the emblem of the city's birth, of its growth, and of its decay. As you leave the fortress to descend into the town you pass through a suggestive gate of chains into a little walled and cloistered city half buried in snow. You hear with relief the shouts of children on the glacis, building their own tiny forts, or "tobogganing" on the slopes, or you see young couples snow-shoeing and scaling the fortifications, with no other arms than the shafts of Cupid. And thus you are soon recalled from feeling the inexorable dominion of an arctic desolation to enjoy the warmth and cheer of human life.

Quebec occupies a high narrow promontory, Cape Diamond, between the St. Lawrence and the St. Charles rivers. It is a populous cliff, crowned with a fortress. The lower part of the town is a narrow strip of wharves and stores running about the foot of the cliffs; the upper part, enclosed by a fortified wall, covers the end of the promontory; the Citadel crowns the very summit, with bastions and parapets, and various streets and steps mount in zigzags from the Lower Town

to the Upper Town. The St. Lawrence shore, Champlain Street, is devoted to the "Coves," where the Irish part of the population live, and load vessels with lumber and timber; the Lower Town, St. Peter Street, is given up to banks, offices, shipping business, and wholesale houses; and along the St. Charles are to be found the Princess Louise Basin, with its coasting vessels, and the French wards of St. Roch and St. Sauveur. A large part of the Upper Town is occupied by Catholic institutions, many of them founded in the early part of the seventeenth century, almost before the colony contained people enough to man them: the Laval University, the Ursuline Convent, the Hôtel Dieu, the French cathedral, are prominent objects. As nine-tenths of the 62,000 inhabitants are French Catholics, and as they give the city its most original features, the most of my observations have been confined to the French Canadian population.

Outside the walls, at the rear of the Upper Town, the plateau is occupied by the Houses of Parliament, the rink, the Plains of Abraham with their martello towers, Wolfe's Monument, and the jail. The country near by is converted into a parklike region by the Gubernatorial residence, named Spencerwood, and many other country-seats. Beyond all these in every direction you find a great number of interesting resorts—lakes, falls, streams, valleys, and mountains; and the villages excel the city in quaintness and in the patriarchal character of their domestic life. In wandering along the foot of the cliffs you find some exceedingly picturesque nooks, as "Sous-le-Cap" alley; and the steeps of the town are full of quaint little nests—porches, back stairs, terraces for plants, vine-clad angles of rock. But these cliffs now are in places covered with masses of ice and snow that often come down as avalanches, and sometimes injure houses and people. When, after winding up the hill, you reach the Dufferin Terrace on top of the walls, you look down on a broken mass of roofs, dormer-windows, gables, and chimneys peeping up out of the snow, you peer into the honeycombed mass and speculate on the doings inside as you used to watch an ant-hill when a child. The houses of Quebec have two principal features—a high steep roof pierced with dormer-windows gives them a hovering, sheltering effect, and their crowning triumph is the great stone chimney, so earnest, capacious, and steadfast. The houses offer not one bit of ornamentation, the most of them are low little houses of honest stone, often clapboarded to protect the mortar from fierce winter storms. Here and there you see a long, low, French farm-house in the streets of St. Roch, and now and then a two or three storied warehouse rises above its fellows. The picturesqueness of the city depends much on these broken sky lines, simple forms in large masses of low roof, high gables, quaint dormers, and huge chimneys, all seen along winding streets running up and down the steep hills. As you struggle on through the snow and piercing wind, the houses frankly turn you the cold shoulder; their fronts, shorn of eaves, bay-windows, steps, stoops—even the doors and windows are flush with the wall—present all down the street as bare a front as that of the fortress, and give you not a niche for lodging even a sentiment of welcome. But if you get a glimpse through some porte cochère you peep into courts full of shadowy nooks, angles, galleries, and piles of good birch cord-wood for the long winter. When at last you come to the appointed place, and pull open the outer door, you enter a cozy little porch just big enough for two young elastic souls. Close the door after you, and then in due time, on opening the inner door and entering the warm hall, you feel that the house now turns the cold shoulder not to you, but to the winter gusts, and bars them out with double sashes, double doors, and a double hospitality. You can even relish the warm shadowy gloom of the average house, due partly to the small windows proper to this climate, but also in large part to the lack of lightsome artistic effects in the pervading baldness and stiffness of the arrangements, and to the overshadowing presence of the monastic spirit. You feel this on seeing the crucifixes, the common pictures of saints, and the demure, staid courtesy, which, however, welcomes you very cordially.

After a heavy snowfall Quebec seems to be a hoary city of the dead; it just peeps out of its snow-drifts; in many side streets the snow, not being carried away, is shovelled off the walks onto the road, where it forms a causeway sometimes on a level with the eaves of the houses; people on opposite walks are invisible to one another, and the horses seem in danger of

wandering from the road onto the roof. In the chief streets hundreds of men with horses and box-like sleds haul away the superabundant snow; indeed this labor in some cases costs as much as all the taxes on a property, and these are exceedingly high. The white, silent city seems at such times like a dream, for Quebec is a singular capital in having no street cries, the noises of the city being reduced to the murmur of voices, the faint shrill creaking of snow, and the tinkling of sleigh-bells; no rude sounds break upon the keen still air; no foot-falls are heard from the crowd, nor rattle of passing vehicles, nor the tramp of horses; and so the men shovelling snow might be phantoms mining for lost treasure. But the work is extremely practical, as any one will acknowledge after wallowing about canal-like streets in April or May, getting from the roofs an avalanche of snow and ice down the back of his neck. In the suburbs the lawns and gardens are covered with domesticated alps; fences, hedges, even some roofs, are covered with snow-drifts; you can snow-shoe anywhere, even up to some chimney-tops; all that breaks the white desert is a smoking chimney veiled by the exquisite tracery of bare trees against the blue sky. And yet the scenes are not always blank and white. On your early morning walk along the Ste. Foye Road you may chance to see only the gables and chimneys of St. Roch and St. Sauveur sticking up through the mist, as if these lower parts of the town were a fleet of queer craft floating on a purple sea; often a sunset over the St. Charles hills floods the magnificent arctic desert with a tropical wealth of color.

Quebec offers so many interesting topics to the student of human life that I scarcely know which to choose; it is the capital of a theocracy overgrowing a democracy, a centre of Roman Catholic education, the source of French Canadian literature—the mould, in short, of every part of a very peculiar civilization. But as these topics are too extensive for the limits of a descriptive paper, I am constrained to devote my space to scenes and customs which require no lengthy discussions, and which give glimpses of the national character and of the external life of the city. The out-door life of Quebec surprises a stranger from a more southern climate. Having in mind the furious tempests of a Canadian winter, when very often neither man nor beast is safe out-doors, he fears that suffering or even death is frequently met here when one leaves the house. And certainly nature looks into Quebec with uncommon free-dom; the entire dome of the sky, rising from a vast expanse of waters, plains, and mountains, is visible from many parts of the town; so that when the sun shines in this exceptionally clear Northern air he beams on everything, in a great rustic ef-fusion rare in a city sun; you almost take the firing of the mid-day gun for his universal guffaw, rolling through the cloudless sky. Then when a gale swoops down it bears in upon you familiarly, even with a terrible eagerness and feroci-ty; and I fancy too that the moon and stars hover close about Quebec, for when I go out on a clear night they stare with large-eyed wonder—as well they may, at a near view of such a creature! But the Canadian winter, excepting during a tempest, is a season full of comforts and enjoyments; for business sleeps, the Low-er Town seems empty, and life turns ei-ther to frolicsome out-door sports—for which the good air furnishes abundant vigor—or to warm and intimate social pleasures. Even if the thermometer be as low as ten degrees below zero, you will often find the children out-doors—cherubic bundles of fur and wool wallowing in the snow as if it were hay, the babes in their little sleds, and people out snow-shoeing, skating in the rink, or driving in their cozy "carioles"; the horses may be sil-vered over with frost, and your own eye-lashes laden with globules of ice, or now and then you may have to rub your nose with snow to warm it after freezing; but, as a rule, everybody is very comforta-ble in furs, with the help of moderate ex-ercise. This French people in America seem to have overcome the dependence of their blood on a warm, sunny climate; they walk the streets in any weather with a comfortable, moderate, often perhaps a mincing gait, while their English friends stride over the snow with a martial ear-nestness. The poor hackmen have the hardest experience; in fur caps, and long buffalo coats with collars coming up to the top of their heads, they look like bears masquerading as men, they tighten the national red sash about their waists, stamp their feet, swing their arms, and keep up a continual scuffling and joking to shorten the tedium of their long hours;

and I should not omit to add that their rubicund noses promise well to defy the frost. In braving the gloom and feroci-ty of a winter storm the city has a certain savage as well as pathetic aspect; a north-east gale comes up the St. Lawrence in bounding gusts, and scaling the cliffs of Cape Diamond, throws the snow back de-fiantly into the sky; and the battlements shake out hoary manes from their crests. But the human elements of the scene are more timid; the little houses crouching down into the snow-drifts look like tatter-ed toques with tassels of white smoke floating out on the wind: mercy on any poor soul that cannot escape the snow-laden gusts, cutting as a sand-blast! with bowed heads, and occasional turning about to catch a breath, even the well-clad hurry on, and like silent phantoms soon flit out of sight into the white obscurity. When the brooding gloom settles over the city at twilight the bugle throws its cheery notes into the arctic silence of the glacis; as you struggle along the ramparts the Angelus rings from over the monastery wall, while the cannon point to the night approaching over the mountain-tops.

In winter the shipless port of Quebec is a great valley of arctic snows, crossed hither and thither by roads marked with bushes; the deserted wharves at low tide rise up like the walls of icebergs; and when it blows, the wind seems a blast di-rect from the pole. But notwithstanding all this, the river in winter is a park of amusement, and the city spreads out tri-umphantly over the deep swift tide. On a fine afternoon you may see the artillery wend its way from the citadel down the declivities of the town and out on the ice, lines of foot-passengers, city carioles and *habitants*, market sleds passing between Levis and Quebec; crowds of people stand-ing about the race-track, the open-air skating-rink, the slide built for coasting, the booths for the sale of cakes and liq-uor, and the gamblers with cards and wheels of fortune. You consider the peo-ple daft for mistaking the day for a day in June. And on Sunday afternoon the river is more populous than the streets of the town; the crowds are merry, but not rough, for both sexes are present. A snow-shoe race is the most popular event of the winter life; it calls out the English socie-ty as well as those of the wealthy French Canadians who follow the English styles. The Saint Louis Road is filled with fine equipages set off with rich furs; the sidewalks, the high snow-covered city walls, and the glacis are diversified with stamping and stirring crowds. In spite of the snow, the cold, the death-like aspect of nature, the scene has a singular suggestion of the balmy sportive ceremonies of warmer climates; the crowds joke, talk, display their finery much as they would do elsewhere; the athletes struggling toward the goal are dressed in tights, but they find the race warm work. Mingling sympathy with enthusiasm for manly effort, the spectators cheer heartily for the victor, then shake themselves in the cold, and move off with a quick step. A snow-shoe club came from Montreal to visit the Quebec clubs, and the event showed very often the strong social propensities of the French Canadian people. The hotels were full of the guests and the hosts, all in their bright flannel costumes, and the town had the air of giving up business for a day or two, and devoting its best talent to enjoyment; all classes of men entered heartily into the boyish hilarity that prevailed everywhere—gray-haired judges, politic members of Parliament, corpulent merchants, bankers, editors; everybody who had a body worth counting, gave it up to singing, moderate drinking, joking, "bouncing," and gadding about town. On Sunday morning they all met at the rink, and marched with their band to the cathedral to hear mass; the gay costumes had a singular effect in the dim religious light. And when they departed we marched to the river with them: the cold was intense, but it did not check the general merriment. While waiting—during what would have been to many assemblages an age—for the ferry-boat, they stood about contentedly in their thin blanket suits, sang, scuffled, and talked cheerily; at last the boat, mounted by a gigantic, writhing spectre of black smoke, loomed through the fog, and landed; they embarked amid exuberant leave-taking, and as the boat stole away into the misty, sombre twilight, and among the crushing fields of ice, they still sang, and filled all that chill and gloomy air with the warmth of the Gallic nature. Snow-shoeing becomes a favorite pastime with almost everybody. I often went on long walks, even alone, over the Plains of Abraham, the wide St. Lawrence, about the suburban villages and lakes; and I always found several others abroad, often ladies. It is

a new, buoyant locomotion, each winter to pass over private gardens, fences, tree-tops, even some roofs, where without the snow-shoe you would wallow hopelessly. And you gather also an inward buoyancy from the free long swing of the step, the spring of the shoe on the snow, the pure, bracing air; secretly your self-esteem is high as you walk away to the woods, in spite of the cold and wind, and enter them for an hour of intimacy with Nature in her untrodden and silent retreat.

Sometimes a snow-shoe club invites ladies to an afternoon walk from the town to their club-house in the suburbs, and they form a joyous, pretty company walking in pairs along the roads and fields. Once a week the clubs take an evening tramp. We met in front of the rink, amid a general buzzing of voices full of boyish exuberance, a shifting of groups of men in toques and bright jaunty costumes, the whole set off on the snow by electric light and sharp shadows. At last we fell into line, and having answered to the roll-call, marched off, a fanciful company threading its way through the social streets. All at once we seem to step from the bustling town into a silent desert. The valley was vast and solemn under the planets, the mountain-tops, and the hovering arctic spirit; the notes of a distant sleigh-bell tinkled, as it were, through the limitless silence as a star twinkles through the night; the world was dim, visionary, cold, spiritual in its purity; and we ourselves marched with noiseless tread like shadows, neither casting any shadows nor sinking into the fleecy snow. We felt the chill of this weird world, but our bits of talk, low-toned, gave us a delicious feeling of companionship under the solemnity of those arctic heavens. When we arrived at the club-house we entered a perfect hive of hilarious men, and found the "driving" members, who had come in sleighs, all heroically ready for supper; and we lead the hours a merry race, with a good meal, toasts, speeches, smoking, general chatter, and numerous songs.

It was not till after midnight that we reentered the town. The streets were now deserted, and the occasional street lamp swinging from its iron bracket brought out of the dimness here and there a quaint gable or a huge chimney smoking its best and watching over the household. Our light-footed troupe marched to the measure of songs, till one after another all had

THE CITADEL.

dropped out of the ranks, and taken his solitary way into obscurity; but somehow the strains were sung under the breath, as if in awe of the night; they seemed far off, almost lost on the starlit heights of the town, and they scarcely broke the mystery and silence any more than did the faint shrill cries of the trodden snow.

The market years ago, then held between the French cathedral and the old Jesuits' college, was a perfect picture of French life; the *habitants* wore homespun, of domestic dyeing—reds, blues, yellows, set off the scene with bits of bright color. In these days of factory cloth less homespun is worn, particularly when visiting the town; and moreover the growing severity of the Church now discourages very much any tendency to ornamentation. But the market of to-day has nevertheless some quaint figures, and a general mediæval tone interesting to a visitor. On a winter day the market-places at St. John's Gate and in St. Roch's are covered with rows of little box-like sleds and bundled-up horses; both the people and their wares have a primitive look; you feel at once that careful economy, or even pinched economy and industry of a very limited range, preside over the homes of the people; nobody brings a load of anything, everybody brings a little of everything— the superfluities from the house or the garden; the quantities seem almost infantile, served up on a piece of birch bark, a bowl, or a plate. In one single sled you may see a great variety of things: a frozen carcass of mutton stands up on the snow, leans against the sled, and looks like a headless and footless wooden toy of my childhood; a pale calf's head in beatific repose; a blood-pudding; onions; a basket of milk frozen in round cakes; little balls of parsley and other herbs preserved all winter in brine; homespun cloth; crude paper flowers; socks; mittens; maple sugar; bunches of brightly colored grasses and mosses; wild birds in a cage; two or three button-hole bouquets of scarlet geraniums from the plants on the window-sill. There may also be going on in the market-place an auction of household furniture: I saw one dimly through a piercing, snow-laden wind, when the thermometer marked six degrees below zero; a few idle laborers, hackmen, and five or six old housewives stood in a group and crouched down into their coat collars; in their midst was a cart with some chairs and a bedstead, and on the cart a doubled-up, shivering auctioneer braced himself against the gusts, and proclaimed the gospel of comfort. Some of the *habitants* drive fifty or sixty miles to sell these little sled-loads of odds and ends. To withstand the cold the woman is wrapped up till she looks like a bundle of dry-goods with a head on it, and the head is often enormous, with a wadded hood, not less than three inches thick, covering all but a little oval of ruddy flesh shaped very much like the mouth, nose, and eyes; and the man wears a long gray homespun coat, with a capuchin to draw over the head, and huge elephantine overboots of cloth. The wife often comes alone to market, and even when accompanied she generally does the business, while her husband walks about, smokes, chats, and views the town. Very many of these people still retain the large strong features of their Norman ancestors, and the market thus presents many interesting types of character.

The citizens are entirely modern in their costumes: the ladies, in fur caps, sacques, and a mass of clouds, move about leisurely, exchange greetings, and with bright eyes and fresh complexions in the keen air present a cheerful sight. No one is curt, rude, or contemptuous, and the market by its social tone thus reveals the courteous and orderly relations prevailing among all classes in this province. Holy-Saturday is the chief market-day

LOADING LUMBER.

of the year. The housewife has come
through Lent with half-rations of fish
and even two or three days of starvation
thrown in, and now her eye gleams with
a fierce carnivorous joy at the sight of
fat mutton. The hypocrisy so often found
in commercial life the world over is quite
common here. There is no pretence at
having a market price, and no mortification at retracting completely an assertion.
This patriarchal, religious, primitive people have a great love of money, shown
not only by their readiness often to get
it in questionable dealing, but also by
their reluctance to use it for improvements. Here they cherish the precious
dollar, while elsewhere they use the
mighty dollar as a power for civilizing.
But if you generally feel the lack of fixed
values and of truthfulness, this moral de-
fect should not be taken as a vicious tendency of the race; it is due rather to a
want of that intellectual acuteness necessary to estimate the value of material elements, and a want of that moral acuteness needed to feel the value of truth.
The generosity of the race is real, but it
must be sought in things that do not directly touch the pocket—in their helpful-
ness, hospitality, courtesy, and in many
other kindly relations. Honesty is a
marked trait of a certain small class of
half worldly, half religious persons.

Such a powerful and absorbing organization as the Catholic Church inevitably attracts many members of the community who are free to follow their de-
votional tendencies. In this way the parish church very often draws close about
it a small colony of old maids, who delight
to live under the droppings of the sanctu-
ary. Their zeal belongs to the Middle
Ages. Morning, noon, or night they will
leave their pressing work to go to the
church to pray, confess, attend funerals,
masses, baptisms, or weddings, and some
of them have to be restrained in their
practice of fasting and other penances.
Their traits and lives are the special results of the Roman faith. In common
with other Christian sects, it teaches the
cardinal virtues, and many individuals
possessing extraordinary spiritual gifts
and general culture it raises to the higher
planes of life. But in such cases the culture and the gifts are variables, making it
difficult to show the net results of the
faith. The class just mentioned are un-
cultivated, free from any other than Catholic influence, and peculiarly subject and
susceptible to this influence.

Although the Canadian winter is so

STREET IN LOWER TOWN.

RAMPART WITH GUNS.

wholesome, and even enjoyable, to those who like out-door life in cold weather, yet everybody sighs for the return of spring to this Northern clime; and indeed six months of sleighing, skating, sliding, snow-shoeing, curling, shooting, with the monotony of constant snow and ice, might well satisfy even the most enthusiastic lover of winter sports. The first faint hint of spring is had in April, at the maple-sugar camps; the roads then are soft, full of holes, even impassable where the snow is very deep, and country establishments are full of memorable odors, not like those of the hyacinth and the lilac; but nevertheless many people of Quebec then drive away to the woods for a first meeting with spring. The farmers who make sugar sell the sap and boil it down, while the visitors pass a merry day either in the sunshine or about the kettles and fire, frying pancakes, dipping bread, or poaching eggs in the syrup, cooling sugar on the snow, or filling with it little birch-bark cornucopias, eating "la tire," singing, and thawing their spirits in the spring sunshine. But the winter does not go without giving you some hard

nips; on the morning of Saint Patrick's Day the temperature was reported as twenty-five degrees below zero; it seemed an uncongenial atmosphere for a procession; but Champlain Street was gorgeous with bunting and evergreens, and the Irish turned out in full force for a holiday. At first it was feared that the celebration would not take place, because the Archbishop refused his sanction if the Irish insisted on carrying American flags; but the difficulty was at length overcome, it was said, by his blessing each of the flags, and thus exorcising all evil and political spirits. The procession of men and horsemen in pretty costumes, trimmed often with lace, the Fire Department, banners, bands, three large American flags—and only one English—all showed off well against the snow as they wound up the zigzags of Mountain Hill in the winter sunshine. At one of the triumphal arches I observed the motto: "God bless Parnell, the uncrowned King!" The desire for spring everywhere in the air brought people to the Terrace day after day to catch the first sight of her advent in the port.

The buoys and boats had been dug out

at the least black bugs destined to crawl over the river's face and awaken him to his duties. One Sunday morning on reaching the Terrace I saw that the event had come; the smooth ice hitherto in the port was now replaced by a jagged field that had floated down from the Chaudière River, and lodged between Quebec and Levis; it was strewn here and there with masses of deals, slabs, and logs, worth thousands of dollars, that had been washed onto it by a freshet; and groups of men with ropes, sleds, and cant-hooks labored eagerly to get the logs ashore. One solitary schooner, the first sail, worked her

of the snow on the wharf of the Marine Department, and the caulker's mallet had sounded in the ship-yards of the St. Charles, where formerly forty or fifty vessels were sometimes on the stocks at once, and now not one; but these hints did not seem a sufficient attraction for her. When the ice became unsafe, the booths, rinks, slides, hack-stands, hay-market, were all removed from the St. Lawrence, and the port looked still more cheerless. Presently the ice broke away from Point Levis, down the river, and the water showed itself once more, welcome even far away. The ferry-boats had wintered in mid-river, frozen solid in three or four feet of ice; when they fired up we kept looking to them as our deliverers, for they might be

SKETCHES OF QUEBEC.

way up to the port that day; as she could not get to the wharves she moored to the ice some distance down the river, her crew came ashore across the floe, and in a few hours she sailed away with all possible despatch. Her advent and hurried departure brought to mind the poor people of Labrador, where probably some starving households were watching for her sail with a painful eagerness. During the few days when the ice was unsafe and still impassable to the ferry-boats, travellers crossed between Quebec and Levis in long wooden canoes, dragged over the ice by crews of seven men. After the jam of ice at Croix Rouge, above the city, set adrift its masses, the river became an angry flood, filled with crushing, grinding floes running with the swift tides. However, the ferries ran, the wharves and supplies for the light-houses, schooners came up to the wharves, men sang at their work, and the port at last awakened from its long torpor.

Nowhere have I hailed more gladly the robin and the sparrow, for snow-drifts were still visible in the city in June, and the lilacs, if I remember correctly, did not finish blooming until late in July. One might say that there is no spring in Que-

MARKET SCENE.

shores soon began to lose their glacial cliffs, and the St. Lawrence became once more the one great living thing in this arctic desert; but we still sighed for the ships, those white-winged messengers from other climes. It was not, however, until a westerly wind sprang up that the river became clear, and the next morning we were amazed and delighted to see the harbor covered by a very great fleet of Norwegian barks, that had come up with an east wind, like a flock of water-fowl, in the night. The coasting craft now ventured out of their berths in the Basin, the *Napoleon III.* steamed away with buoys and bec, for the trees and grass, once started, jump in a few days from winter brown to summer green. Quebec receives considerable shipping—several lines of transatlantic steamers, occasionally French and English men-of-war, yachts, and coasting crafts; but the chief business of the port is the shipping of square timber. The Norwegians seem to monopolize this carrying trade. Their vessels are generally condemned barks that they buy at a low price, and man cheaply with their relatives or with the joint owners. The "coves" stretching four or five miles above the city, along the St. Lawrence, are areas of water enclosed by booms. The rafts of timber are towed down the St. Lawrence and stowed in these coves. The vessels lie inside the booms, and the timber is hoisted from the water, and loaded through the port-holes in the bows. With her bowsprit unshipped, davits rigged over the bows, her sails perhaps drying, her anchors hanging, she represents a ship in the most picturesque dishabille; and the stevedores, working, shouting, swearing, are much like her in disorder, if not in charms. On the wharves of Quebec you see some of the most characteristic scenes of the city. The Lower Town market-places, with their *calèches* and long-bodied French carts, are filled with the *habitants* twice a week. They embark at their parishes on the primitive-looking steam-boats with a chest or a bag or two full of garden produce, knitting, wild berries, mutton. They sleep about the decks, and in the morning early land, and establish themselves on the market-place. The hour of re-embarking comes at various times of day, for many of the landings of the St. Lawrence are accessible only at high tide. The boats whistle many times, tumultuously, multitudinously, vociferously, and call their passengers from the town; but even in this moment of excitement the slow pace of life here is scarcely quickened. People arrive with their bundles and boxes long before the boat starts. One man who had failed to sell his calf brought it in a *calèche*, his arm passed most assuringly about the creature's neck. The wharves of the city offer room for scarcely a dozen ocean vessels. Nearly all the loading and the unloading are done by lighters or barges while the vessels lie at anchor. And this singular condition of the most important seaport of the province for now about 275 years, unjustified by any serious engineering obstacles, is not inaptly mentioned in support of the expression "poor Quebec." The Princess Louise Basin, it is hoped, will remove this inability of the port, and perhaps secure a part of the commerce that now goes on to the more enterprising city of Montreal.

It is eminently characteristic of this Roman Catholic civilization that festivals in general are controlled by the Church, and made either religious or semi-religious in both their aims and their ceremonies. An intelligent priest once said to me, with a shrewd smile, "Our people don't enjoy holidays unless the Church assists them"; and his statement summarizes the national custom, but perhaps not the national desires. The chief national civic festival, the Saint Jean Baptiste, is made semi-religious; the chief religious festival, the Fête-Dieu, or Corpus Christi, is made semi-civic; and the purely political holiday, Dominion Day, the 3d of July, set apart to celebrate the federation of the provinces and the foundation of a nation, receives no hearty support from the Church nor marked attentions from her flock. On going abroad one Sunday morning I found the plain gray city bedecked in her utmost pomp to honor the passage of the body of Christ; along the streets where the procession was to pass a cloud of French and some other flags floated across the blue sky and about the broken outline of Quebec's gables and dormers; evergreen arches spanned here and there the road, and a hedge of balsams arose from the curb-stones of each sidewalk; booths for the sale of beer and cakes testified to a practical estimate of the inner man; here and there hung on a house-front a box, or cupboard, as a miniature chapel, furnished with statuettes, vases, artificial flowers, a crucifix, and an altar; strips of white muslin along the hedges served as a background for hanging various objects that are supposed to arouse religious fervor—such as the motto, "Pas de rose sans épine," the portrait of Napoleon Bonaparte, photographs of esteemed members of the hanger's family, lithographs of the Holy Family, and marine views; indeed, the ardor of some in honoring the passing of the body of Christ has to be restrained by the priest, because they bring forth, poor souls, such a cloud of household gauds as to eclipse the sun of righteousness; and one of the arches in St. Sauveur was decorated with a profusion of sporting articles and surmounted by the effigy of an Indian snowshoer.

The general effect of the decorations was somewhat confusing as to intention, because at certain points along the route zealous laymen had turned their porte cochère into a chapel or "reposoir," where the procession halted for purely religious services; the "reposoir" of Saint Roch's —a high platform built at the end of a street—was a brilliant bower of evergreens hung with lace curtains, flags, gilt balls, long streamers of red, yellow, and blue

BARGES.

or in fluttering white; each corps marched in two single files, one along each side of the street, while at the head of each society the standard-bearers walked in the centre of the road, as did many priests, to accompany and command their respective corps. There were some lay and civic societies in ordinary costumes and regalia; many religious orders, and also many of the semi-religious fraternities dating from the Middle Age, and serving the Church as long tentacles run into society; a division of little charity boys, each carrying a flag, and repeating, in response to their priest, "Priez pour nous," and of little charity girls, saying prayers with the nuns scattered along their lines; a body of college students and of university students; a corps of young women in black with long flowing white veils and blue sashes, each carrying in one hand a rosary and in the other an umbrella; and the maiden standard-bearers of this order showed well and confidently their fine figures in struggling with their banner, inscribed to the Immaculate Conception; an order of La Sainte Famille—mothers of families; young men marching with a brass band that played martial music; older men, some tottering on their last march, and leading by the hand their third or perhaps fourth generation; the firemen in red, in blue, or in purple shirts; and often the military forms a part of this remarkable procession.

flannel, lithographs of Christ, the Virgin, and the Pope, and furnished with an altar decorated with pyramids of artificial flowers, vases, candles, mirrors, and lamps with red globes. The people, including all ranks of society, were much interested in all this preparation. They walked along the streets in wonder and admiration, and gave vent freely to their decorous enjoyment of the show and of the social intercourse of a holiday. At last a murmur ran through the mass, it halted, filled the walks with a dense throng, enlivened the gray wall spaces with groups of eager outstretched figures framed in the doors, windows, and dormers; and as the procession approached, their voices fell to the tones of subdued conversation. The procession was headed by three acolytes dressed in white surplices; the central one bore a tall cross, the others a candle each; then followed a line—perhaps half a mile long—of various societies, all in sombre black,

All along the line was heard the impressive muttering of a multitude, for everybody either read a prayer-book or responded to the prayers said by the priests, and as the body moved with impressive deliberation, and nearly everybody maintained a uniform appearance of devotion, the procession itself had a more religious aspect than the gaudy decorations and the social crowds. The most picturesque group of all came last—the rich, gold-embroidered canopy for the Host, with the accompanying priests and attendants in fluttering white robes. Youthful acolytes walked backward just in front of the canopy, some scattering bits of colored tissue-paper for flowers, others swinging censers with a long graceful motion, and those priests of the file on each side of the canopy who were in advance of it also walked backward. The Host is a wafer made of wheaten flour and water; accord-

under the canopy and held the *ostensorium* up in an imposing manner as high as his head. Wherever this group passed, every one fell on his knees and bowed low; it seemed as if some magic spell swept along the street and mowed people down just where it found them—in the house, on the walk, or in the mud. At the "reposoir" the group halted for rites performed at the altar, and the entire pop-

RELIGIOUS PROCESSION IN THE COUNTRY.

ing to the Catholic Church, prayers said over it at mass induce a miracle, by which the wafer is changed, "truly, really, and substantially," into the actual body of Christ. It is carried in a little gilt circular frame, the *ostensorium*. Naturally enough, the body of Christ should command great reverence; hence the walking backward, the general kneeling, the prayers, and the vast display of flags and evergreens. The priest who carried the wafer, with an attendant priest at each elbow to support his gorgeous robes, walked

ulation bowed down in worship. The ceremony to me was a spectacular scene of much novelty—quaint streets filled with banners, evergreens, and a kneeling multitude, gray gables, and dormers flaunting brilliant flags, ramparts with cannon, cliffs crowned with monastery walls, and the still loftier citadel looking down from the blue sky, while grave chants, pealing bells, and the muttering of a multitude at prayer gave impressive voices to the mediæval scene.

But I hope the ceremony is not taken by the reader for a mockery of religion because of its mundane accessories; to those who worship in this way it is the most solemn event of the calendar, and I was glad to see many of them perfectly earnest in their devotions. When, however, the Host had passed, the people resumed freely and promptly their social recreations. A stranger is often touched in seeing how this Catholic people mingle their religion with their daily duties and pleasures; frequent visits to the church, pilgrimages to shrines, the wearing of religious charms, the asking for blessings on their possessions and enterprises, their belief in miracles, their fear of a personal devil, their enlisting the saints to combat his witcheries—all infuse a rich poetic sentiment in the picture of their lives. But after some study he finds this poetic sentiment to be chiefly in his own vision, rather than in the indiscriminating creatures standing as models for the picture: it gives him a delicious sense of the picturesque, the quaint, the primitive; but the subjects suffer—half unconsciously—in their ignorance of nature, science, art, and human life. A worship full of rituals enters easily among other common duties of life; and to a stranger this familiarity seems in many cases to breed, if not contempt, at least an unfortunate indifference to the spirit of religion. My first view of this Corpus Christi procession was given me in a country parish below Quebec. It had been decided by the priest not to have the out-door procession that year; but when it was brought to his notice that a stranger studying the country desired to see it, he good-naturedly consented to have the ceremony performed. He even entered into the project of my taking a photograph of the scene—discussed the best moment, the point of view, and promised to give me a sign at the proper time. This willingness relieved me somewhat of a great reluctance to intrude, and above all to materialize—some would say desecrate—the chief religious ceremony of the Catholic Church. On Saturday afternoon the *habitants* hedged the village road with saplings, the nuns brought out their convent girls to the scene of the ceremony and drilled them in their movements, and I helped to drag the cannon of the village out of the woodshed and place it ready for firing salutes.

On Sunday morning the ladies of the best families brought their silver, vases, mirrors, and other trinkets, and helped to convert the piazza of a house in the village into a chapel, and decorated it prettily with plants, evergreens, carpets, curtains, pictures, and an altar with flowers and many ornaments. I felt deeply embarrassed at putting so many ladies to trouble, and turning out the priest, his assistants, and the entire parish in a vast display, in the honor of which circumstances forced me into partnership with the Almighty. Such a position was utterly foreign to my pretensions and my temperament, and I wished myself at home, in the quiet and reverent Friends' meeting that I often attend. But this feeling was purely gratuitous; the good-natured people, far from regarding me as an insufferable sacrilegist, were pleased with my interest in their fête. I planted my camera on the road-side opposite the altar, and awaited the events. At the close of mass the procession came out of the church, and approached with great solemnity, while the bells rang and the cannon fired. The beadle was very stately, with his staff, his black robe, his scarlet cape, and the church banner; the nuns, with their convent girls in black gowns, long white veils, and sashes, filed demurely along the sides of the road; and the *habitant* women, with umbrellas, came in a dense crowd, filling the road, as did also the men, bareheaded; they all told their beads while marching. At the end of the procession came the canopy, with its group of boys and men in white surplices, acolytes swinging censers and scattering colored papers, the choir chanting, the ostentatious wardens holding up the canopy over the gorgeous priest and the glittering *ostensorium*. The crowd, as it came near the "reposoir," parted, withdrew to each side of the way, and left the road open; then, when the wafer was brought along, they fell on their knees and bowed low. This to me was the most impressive moment, when those groups of primitive homespun peasants were kneeling and worshipping in the dust, while the priest and his attendants passed proudly on their mystic mission. It was even a startling scene, a vision far down the vista of history, a glimpse of the patriarchal ages.

When all had taken their places before the altar, the priest recited his office, and the convent girls on the upper piazza sang clearly and sweetly in response to the hard grave chants of the choir below. The decorations and bright colors, the songs of birds, the shadows of the trees flickering over the place, the sunshine and gladness of a perfect June morning, and

PROCESSION OF CORPUS CHRISTI.

the peaceful, simple, and devout spirit of the multitude, all made a charming side to this mediæval scene. Meanwhile I had awaited impatiently the priest's signal, for many striking subjects had allured me; and at last, true to his word, when he elevated the Host, and the people were all bowed and motionless, he tipped me the wink, I took my view, and the procession returned to the church as it had come.

FIRST IMPRESSIONS OF CIVILIZATION

I HAVE often been asked, Was it not wonderful to you when you first saw the lofty edifices of great cities, the locomotive, the steam-engine, and the like? Yes, it was so, in a way. Yet it is not mere immensity of structure which appears almost supernatural to the savage and overwhelms him. One reason for this may be that the natural features of our country, the gigantic granite cliffs and mountains, the wonderful walls and towers of the Bad Lands, are much grander to our minds, coupled with the idea of the Great Mystery behind them all.

Then, also, there are many painstaking animals which build so wonderfully well and artistically! Some of them are much smaller than man; for instance, the ant, the spider, the swallow, the beaver, muskrat, and others. Some dam and bridge large streams, and others suspend their homes in the air. To our simple minds the ability shown by these little creatures appears even more remarkable than the constructive genius of the white man.

In matters of observation I was as keen as a Rocky Mountain sheep, and my mind was as sensitive to impressions as the film of the camera. I had an enthusiastic love for scenic beauty. I still care little about written poetry, but the poet could scarcely enjoy more than I have always done the poetry of nature.

So far as the natural philosophy of the red man is concerned, I was well trained from childhood. But I was bewildered by the scientific, economic, social, and political systems of civilization and their practical application—the sanitation and government of great cities, their food-supply, the utilization of time and space, monetary or financial systems, and, above all of these, the phase of civilization which at first overwhelmed me most was the commerce of the paleface. To the wild Indian, his worldly occupation is a sort of play. The thing which above all else occupies his mind is the Great Mystery. Him he never forgets. In civilization, as it appeared to me at first —"Will it pay? Can I make anything on it?" seemed to be the "Great Mystery" of the white people.

When I first saw the inside of a house, it set me thinking: "Who made this house? Was it the Great Mystery?" (for my mind was trained in that manner of thinking). A powerful curiosity stirred in me—an almost irresistible desire to know just how it was done.

When my father brought me home to Dakota Territory from the wilds of Manitoba, where I had been for ten years living in exile, I was about fifteen years old, and in my own estimation already a warrior. He began to explain to me the "white man's way," and found me at first reluctant to listen.

"You must not fear to work with your hands," said my father, "but if you are able to think strongly and well, that will be a quiver full of arrows for you, my son. That is the white man's way. All of their children must go to school. Those who study best and longest need not work with their hands after that, for they can work with their minds."

I had never yet shrunk from any undertaking, for that was one of the things that I was warned against by my good grandmother as early as I could remember. "Never give up a chase," she would say to me; "never retreat from any good cause on account of danger or hardship." Already my long glossy hair had fallen under the big scissors, and my head felt cold and unprotected. I was very much in the position of the boy who is coaxed to deep water and let loose. I had to swim, and that was the end of it. I tried it, and all has turned out well, although there have been some strong currents to carry me down the stream, and at times it has taxed all my moral and physical muscle to keep afloat.

"You may plough the five acres next the river," said my father one day. "I want to see if you can make a straight furrow as well as a straight shot with the bow and arrow."

I am sorry to admit that it was poorly done. My father decided that I had no aptitude for following this particular trail. "You must go away to school," he advised me. "You will learn a great deal in two or three years. Zitkadawashta, or Good Bird (Dr. Alfred L. Riggs), has a good school, where he gathers many young men to teach them in their own tongue and in the English. Above all, he tries to establish them in a true and godly life."

I had already attended for a few months the mission day-school near our home, which was taught by Mr. Philander A. Van Nice, brother-in-law to Dr. Williamson. The latter was our missionary, through whose faithful Christian work my father had become a Christian, and whose admonishment in regard to my future possibilities assisted me throughout my student life. At this my first school I had been struck with the absurdity of having to repeat apparently meaningless words and syllables, but at last I concluded that it must have some use which I had not discovered. I learned to read a little in Dakota and English, but I absorbed very little of the "white man's way."

It may have appeared to my father that I was not receiving his advice very cordially, for he now changed his mode of argument and appealed to the strongest impulses aroused by my earlier training.

"I have no doubt," he began, "that my brother, your uncle, has brought you up with the knowledge and traditions of our tribe, especially those of our immediate band. There is no better band of the Sioux nation in bravery and self-control. Our young men are wont to dare anything. When you leave my log cabin to go away to school, you may consider yourself on the war-path. You will be seeking eagle feathers, my son. If you should not return, your father will weep proud tears.

"I have started in here with some of my people to become farmers and citizens like the white men. This is our school—ours, the old men's! I shall stick to it. I shall not go back to the reservation. I want all my sons to follow the trail which I am trying to make for you."

In a few days a neighbor of ours was on the way to Santee agency, the site of Dr. Riggs's school, and my father engaged a ride for me in his wagon. But when we got to Sioux Falls, which was then only two stores, Peter found many tracks of otter, beaver, and mink up and down the Big Sioux river. This was a temptation no Indian trapper could resist.

"I am sorry," he said to me, "but I must stop here."

I thought the matter over carefully, and finally said to him: "Tell my father that I shall not return until I finish my war-path. I am going to Santee on foot."

I took my blue blanket and extra pair of moccasins and started the next morning early from Sioux Falls. As I ascended the brow of the hill where the main part of the city is now, the sounds of the waterfall seemed to me like human cheers and war-whoops for my lonely war-path on that September morning over the sea of prairie-land. As I crossed the loop of the Big Sioux, a powerful temptation seized me to flee back at once to Canada, there to regain my freedom and wild life. But I had sent word to my father that this war-path must be completed, and I also remembered how he had said that if I did not return he would shed proud tears.

I walked the remaining 110 miles to Santee in three days. On the last day I met Dr. Riggs, whom I did not then know. I spent two years with this remarkable and godly man. Next to my own father, who in his peculiar philosophy gave me good guidance, this man has done more than perhaps any other to make it possible for me to grasp the principles of true civilization. He also strengthened and developed in me that native strong ambition to win out by sticking to what I might undertake.

Associated with him was another man who also influenced me powerfully toward honesty and right living. This was the Rev. Dr. John P. Williamson, the veteran and pioneer missionary among the Sioux.

To my mind, as soon as I began to think of these matters, there seemed to be much inconsistency in the dealings of the government with the Indians, and I could not comprehend how a great government should be dishonest, when its religion was so strongly against deceit and selfishness. It also occurred to me that the people who are favored most in this world's goods are the most ungodly kind. All these matters were confusing to me at that time. Yet I still maintained that I must finish my war-path. My father wrote to me in the Dakota language for my encouragement. Zitkadawashta had told him that I was not afraid of books or work, but rather determined to profit by them. " My son," he wrote, " I believe that an Indian can learn all that is in the books of the white man, so that he may be equal to them in the ways of the mind."

My father was very advanced in his views for a full-blooded Indian of that day, and had set the example to his fellow tribesmen in taking a homestead under the United States homestead laws.

Finally Zitkadawashta selected two of the boys to send away to higher schools among the white people. Smith Robinson and myself were the ones chosen. On the eve of my departure I received word from Flandreau that my father was dead, after only two days' illness. He was still in the prime of life and tireless in all his work. It was a severe shock to me, but I felt that I must carry out his wishes. It was clear that he who had sought me out among the wild tribes of the Northwest and set my feet in the white man's road should be obeyed. I did not return to my home, but in September, 1876, I started from Santee for Beloit College, Wisconsin, where I was to begin my serious studies.

At Yankton city I entered the cars for the first time in my life. I remember I made a careful inspection of the locomotive, and my interest in its mechanism was greatly intensified when the whole thing was in motion.

Every hour brought me new thoughts and new discoveries. I never have passed such a day, before or since. Visions came and went like the telegraph-poles as we sped by. More and more we were moving upon regions apparently too small for the inhabitants. Towns and villages grew larger and nearer together, and at last we reached a city of some little size. The streets were crowded. Everybody seemed to me to be in the greatest possible hurry. I was struck with the splendor of the shops and the brilliant show-windows, but the alacrity with which everything was done impressed me most.

As I approached the door of the college president's home, my heart almost failed me. A gray-haired and serious-looking gentleman appeared at the door. This was President Chapin, who received me kindly. He spoke to me freely, but I was scarcely able to answer him, owing to my diffidence and imperfect knowledge of English.

I was now a stranger in a strange country, and deep in a strange life from which I could not retreat. I was like a deaf-mute, with eyes continually on the alert for the expression of faces, and to find them in general friendly toward me was somewhat reassuring. Yet when I was alone in my room at last and all was still, I fancy that no prisoner in the penitentiary can have known a more nerve-trying moment. The scenes of my deliciously free and happy life in a vast wild region unfolded before my eyes, contrasted with the thought that I was now to live within limits and under rules absolutely foreign to me. More than this, I was still in the dark as to the outcome of it all.

I soon recovered my balance and set to work. I absorbed knowledge in every possible way. The more I got, the larger my capacity grew, and my appetite increased in proportion. I discovered that my anticipations of this new life were nearly all wrong. I was suddenly confronted with matters entirely foreign to my experience, which I must develop and solve by mental gymnastics. If a man had come and told me to swim a lake, or run with a message through an unknown country, I should have had some idea of the task. But this new conception of each word as having an office and a place and a specific name, and standing in relation to other words like the bricks and mortar in a house, was almost beyond my grasp. As for history and geography, they were legends and traditions to me, and I was soon able to appreciate the pure logic of mathematics. I found my greatest difficulty at this period in the study of words.

At Beloit I spent three years of student life. At the end of this time I fully realized the force of my father's simple but correct view of the future of our race—that we must adopt the ways of the white man. In some matters I was the infant of the college, but in athletics I did my full share. Other Sioux Indians were sent to Beloit Preparatory School, and as I thought it best, in order to perfect myself in English, not to hear my own tongue at all, I preferred to go where there were none to speak it. I was accordingly sent by Dr. Riggs to Knox College, Illinois, from which he himself had graduated.

Knox College is a coeducational institution. It was here that I first had to do with the paleface maidens. I must candidly confess that while I owe much to college boys in my association with them as fellow students, I owe infinitely more to the college girls.

It was here that I first began to look forward intelligently, and finally settled in my own mind that I must become a physician some day.

I had seen more than six years of civilization on the frontier and in the Middle West before I turned my footsteps toward New England. During all this time my ambitions rose higher and higher.

On one of my vacations at home in Dakota I received a letter from Dr. Riggs, who had been thus far my best friend, suggesting that I should take advantage of the Indian scholarship at Dartmouth College—a scholarship established when the college was founded as a school for Indians. This was in line with my highest aspirations, and yet I hesitated. I dreaded to cut myself off from my people, and in my heart I knew that if I did go, I should not return until I had accomplished my purpose. It was a critical moment in my life, but the decision could be only one way. I taught the little day-school at my home through the fall term, and in January, 1882, I started for Boston and Dartmouth.

Up to this time I had very little practical knowledge of the world, and in my inexperience I was still susceptible to the adventurous and curious side of things rather than to their profounder meanings. Therefore, while I was somewhat prepared, I was not yet conscious of the seriousness and terrific force of modern civilization.

It was a crisp winter morning when the train pulled into Chicago. I had in mind the Fort Dearborn incident, and the struggles of the great Black Hawk upon that very ground. It seemed to me as if we were being drawn into the deep gulches of the Bad Lands as we entered the city. I realized vividly at that moment that the day of the Indian had passed forever.

I was met at the station by friends, who took me to walk upon some of the main streets. I saw a perfect stream of humanity rushing madly along. I was surprised to notice that the faces of the people were not happy at all. They wore an intensely serious look that to me was appalling.

I was cautioned against trusting everybody, and told that I must look out for pickpockets. Evidently there were some disadvantages connected with this mighty civilization, for we Indians seldom find it necessary to guard our possessions. It seemed to me that the most dignified men on the streets were the policemen, in their long blue coats with brass buttons. They were such a remarkable set of men physically that this of itself was enough to catch my eye.

When we left Albany I found that we were in country the like of which, I thought, I would have given much to hunt over before it was stripped of its primeval forests and while deer and bears roamed over it undisturbed. I looked with delight upon mountains and valleys, and even the hamlets perched upon the shelves of the high hills. The sight of these scattered farms and little villages assured me of the presence of an earnest and persistent people.

Even the half-deserted New England village, the ruined mill, had an air of saying: "I have done what I could for the progress of civilization. Now I can rest." And all the mountains seemed to say, Amen.

For the first time I felt a great respect and reverence for the race that I had been taught to regard with suspicion and distrust.

When I reached Boston I was struck with the old mossy granite edifices and the narrow streets. Here, too, the people on the streets hurried along like sheep with the gray wolf on their trail. When I met some of them personally, their conservative ways impressed me as being cold, but I forgot that when I had learned to know them better.

I went to Dartmouth College, away up among the New Hampshire hills. The country around it was rugged and wild— an ideal place for us Indians. My mind ran back three hundred years, when all this region was full of game and the red men lived in plenty and freedom. It seemed as if I had been destined to come to view their graves and bones.

No, I said to myself, I have come to continue that which in their last struggle they proposed to take up, in order to save themselves from extinction; but, alas! it was too late. Had they followed that great Indian, Samson Occum, and kept up with the development of Dartmouth College, they would have brought forth more leaders and men of culture.

This was my ambition—that the Sioux should accept civilization before it was too late. I wished that all of our young men should at once take up the white man's way, and prepare themselves to hold office and wield influence in their native States. Although this hope has not been fully realized, I have the satisfaction to know that some Indians are now in such places, and that before many years South Dakota can be anchored politically by the balance of power held by the Sioux Indian vote between the two political parties in that State.

The staid New England civilization grew upon me gradually. A sound common sense appeared to be the basis of all their actions, whether in politics, religion, business, or love. Recognition of individual and personal worth was generous among them.

At Dartmouth College I found the buildings much older and more imposing than any I had been accustomed to see. There was a true scholastic air about them; in fact, the whole village impressed me as touched with the spirit of learning and refinement.

My understanding of English was now so much enlarged as to enable me to grasp current events as well as the principles of civilization in a more intelligent manner. At Kimball Union Academy, the little ancient institution at which I completed my preparation for college by direction of President Bartlett of Dartmouth, I absorbed much knowledge of the New-Englander and his peculiarities.

I found Yankees of the uneducated class very Indianlike in their views and habits — a people of strong beliefs, plain-spoken, and opinionated. I was much struck with the fact that the students of the academy were very frugal and saving in their habits. Nothing could have been more instructive to me, as we Indians are inclined to be spendthrifts and improvident. It is true that this hardy and moral class of men is poor in land and goods. I had been accustomed to vast fertile prairies and liberal ways. Here they seemed to count their barrels of potatoes and apples before they were fairly grown. I was told that many of the farmers' families never eat a sound apple. They always take the partly spoiled apples for their own use, and save the sound ones for market. Every little brooklet was forced to do a river's work in their mills and factories.

I finished the course here and went to old Dartmouth in the fall of 1883 to enter the Freshman class. It is true that I had associated with college students for several years before coming East, yet I must confess that Western college life is quiet compared with that of the tumultuous East. It was here that I had most of my savage gentleness and native refinement knocked out of me! I do not complain, for I know that I gained more than their equivalent.

I hardly knew what I was coming to, on the first evening we held our class meeting, when, lo! I was appointed football captain of my class. My supporters orated quite effectively on my qualifications as a frontier warrior, and I observed that some of them went so far as to predict that I would, when warmed up, scare all the Sophs off the premises! These representations seemed to be confirmed when, that same evening, after supper, the two classes met in a first "rush," and as I was not familiar with all the men, I held up the Professor of Philosophy, taking him for one of the Sophomores! This of course gave opportunity to the reporters for the Boston dailies to enlarge upon the incident.

I was a sort of prodigal son of old Dartmouth, and nothing could have exceeded the heartiness of my welcome. The New England Indian for whom it was founded had departed well-nigh a century earlier; and now a full-blooded Sioux, like a wild fox, had found his way into this splendid seat of learning! After the first excitement and novelty had worn away, I began to take, as it were, a sort of inventory of the opportunities which my wanderings had thus far brought me.

By the president and faculty I was treated with the greatest kindness, and often encouraged to ask questions and express my own ideas. My uncle's observations in natural history—for which he had a positive genius,—the Indian standpoint in sociology and political economy, were the subjects of some protracted discussions in the class-room. This became so well understood by my classmates that some who had failed to prepare their recitations would induce me to take up the time by advancing some native theory or first-hand observation upon the subject in hand.

When I had sufficiently mastered the English language, I became intensely interested in literature. Here it was that civilization began to loom up before me colossal in its greatness, when the truth first dawned upon me that nations, tongues, and civilizations, as well as individuals, have lived and died.

There were two men of the past who impressed me very much—my countryman who matriculated there a century before me, and the great Daniel Webster, who came to Dartmouth as impecunious as I was. The Indians have gone forever —no memorial of them left except the Old Pine-Tree, where it was supposed that they met for the last time to smoke the pipe of peace. The college was kind enough to keep the old tree as a relic up to my day, and under its shadow every graduating class smoked a parting pipe.

During my vacations I went to Boston sometimes, sometimes to the mountains and the seashore. My visits to Boston were always made worth while by some new discovery—some art or science of civilization brought freshly to my notice. Aside from the unique charm of old Boston, the park system, the public flower-gardens, the arboretum, the reservoirs,—each of these was a school in itself to me. My first glimpse of the ocean was an event. I looked in amazement upon the vast assemblage of vessels of all sorts and sizes. I had never even imagined the like, and it now appeared that the white man moved with as much freedom upon the water as upon dry land. The commerce of the ocean struck me as one of the most remarkable features of civilization.

I shall never forget my first night at the theatre. I was amazed by the seriousness of the actors, whose personality appeared to be entirely swallowed up in their parts, and the behavior of the audience in its freedom and abandon contrasted strikingly with the manner of those whom I had met in the churches. Here the people seemed to me to take delight in tragedy and even in crime, indifferent to the moral significance of the imaginary events which took such strong hold upon their emotions.

At the seaside hotels I met society people—people of an entirely different sort from those whom I had hitherto taken as American types. I was particularly struck with the audacity and forwardness of the women. At the summer resorts the women seemed to lead their husbands or to be independent of them. Among our people the man always leads.

I graduated at Dartmouth with the class of '87, and immediately afterward spent three years at Boston University, where I took the degree of Doctor of Medicine. Having passed in all nine years in New England, I believe I really understand and appreciate in some measure the solidity and manliness of the New England character. I have never hesitated to compare and criticise, but there has been no question in my mind for many years about the desirability of a liberal education, and the advantages of a civilized life over our earlier and primitive existence.

THROUGH INLAND SEAS

WE found waiting at the noisy dock in Buffalo a great white steamer, more like an ocean vessel than any inland boat we had ever seen — stanch, massive, rich in the appointments of luxurious travel. We boarded her and watched the hurry of night life on the wharf—the arrival of an agitated old lady with bundles, her face full of the feminine terror of being left; a little bow-legged sailor, one of our crew, who hurried into a tavern for a last cheering draught; and finally a cool gentleman in a straw hat, who had arrived in a furiously driven coupé just as the gangplank was about to be withdrawn, and who placidly stepped aboard, leaving the driver and his horse panting. Then we were off.

In the morning we were making smooth, rapid headway over Lake Erie. The shore had become a mere cloud, the vast plain of fresh water glittered blue in the sunshine, and the air was cool but soft, making mere existence a delight. On the after-deck, with its comfortable awning, from which we could look for miles over the sapphire water, a group of ladies sat at their fancy work as composedly as if they were enjoying a sunny piazza at home. The husband of one of them, spectacled and sunburned, held a skein of crimson wool while she deftly wound it into a ball. Another embroidered with birdlike movements of her plump white fingers. A lady with a silk shirt-waist and pearl beads was saying: "You know I never talk about anybody, but do you know she never answered his letter? Not one line. Did you ever hear of such heartlessness? I haven't any patience with her myself—not one bit. . . . Have you read this story? It's awfully good. It ends up just the way I like them to end—everything lovely and the goose hangs high, don't you know?" and the pearl beads danced merrily up and down with her laughter. On the port side, a stout gentleman, disturbed by the gay talk, looked up from his nap with a glare in the direction of the women, and gathering up his belongings, departed in dudgeon to the forward deck. Over in the shadow cast by the life-boats two women sat conversing in low tones.

"I never will leave them again," said the younger one with the marine glasses lying idle in her lap,—"never. I don't know how I did it this time—the darlings."

"But you never did it before, Helen," said the elder woman, soothingly, "and it's high time you did. It's better for children to be parted from their mothers occasionally, and you know it. It gives you a better chance, and them a better chance, for you to get away and take a new and broader view of things. You get into a rut, like everybody else, and it's bad for you; and you'll be home in a week or so. Oh, see that exquisite water! It is almost tropically beautiful!"

"I suppose they're just getting on their dear little afternoon dresses now," said the younger woman, plaintively. But the other was gazing at the water in temporary oblivion.

When night came it was so cool that most of the passengers withdrew to the brilliantly lighted saloon, where a round-faced young man with a tenor voice began to sing ballads. One of these had

a wistful refrain about "children on their mother's knee," and we saw the young woman with the marine glasses rise and walk out to the deck, where she stood alone in the starlight. Her older companion did not follow her, but gently handed her a handkerchief as she departed.

The following day, as we entered the beautiful Detroit River and approached the city itself, our next landing-place, a tiny steam-tug painted gray and black like a postman's uniform, and bearing the inscription "*Florence B.*—U. S. M.," came puffing out from shore, and launched a small boat, in which sat a solitary but humorous-looking man clad in a light shirt and the trousers of a mail-carrier. He rowed briskly to the side of a colossal freight-boat, tossed a rope aboard, and extended to her deck a pole bearing a small bag, which was quickly emptied by an alert sailor and refilled with outgoing mail. For this was the only marine postman in the world—"Bill" Yates, faithful servant of Uncle Sam, and probably also the only mail-carrier who risks

THE MARINE POSTMAN TRANSFERRING LETTERS

AN AFTERNOON CONCERT AT BELLE ISLE

definitely pleasant. It was on one of these that we met kindly old "Andy" Sims. He was sitting in the shadow of the warehouse, taking his lunch of bread, cheese, and something of the "soft drink" aspect out of a bottle. At his feet three cats, more or less scrubby in appearance, ate their separate meals of bread and milk, while Andy, looking blandly upon his pets, told his experiences.

his life in the performance of duty. The danger lies in making fast day and night to huge moving vessels, in being exposed to the scalding water from their exhaust-pipes, and in enduring the bitterness of the cold weather; for the *Florence B.* is on duty as long as navigation is open, from, approximately, the middle of March to the middle of December, and must keep her ropes in the water to prevent freezing, until finally the water itself can bear the cold no longer and turns to ice.

Detroit's famous park, Belle Isle, is not within the city itself, but is an island reached by a long bridge. There was a tiny but gay canal crowded with light canoes in which boys and girls laughed and chatted, the Japanese parasols of some of them lending a bizarre effect to the already foreign-looking scene; and under the tall trees sat *al fresco* luncheon parties at comfortable rustic tables provided for the purpose, with happy families clustered around them, and a general air of everybody being thoroughly at home and at ease, without either formality or undue freedom.

The waterside of Detroit is as cleanly and attractive as all watersides should be and are not, and its wharves are

"Yes," he said, finishing his cheese from one hand and stroking a purring cat with the other,—"yes, I've saved four or five lives every season fur the las' twenty-four year. I never los' but one life." He said this as one might refer to an unfortunate speculation in real estate. "Do they thank me when I save 'em? They never do. In twenty-four years not one of 'em ever thanked me. After you pull 'em out they're 'shamed of theirselves and they go away." He seemed to consider this ingratitude perfectly excusable, and we left him taking his last bite of cheese and giving the remaining bread to the cat that had clambered insistently to his knee.

One of the most interesting persons connected with the lake traffic is a sort of brother to the landlubber cowboy. He is practically the lariat-thrower of these prairielike lakes, but he does not lasso cattle or anything so trivial. His game may be a wharf or an eight-thousand-ton freighter, and he never misses his cast. He makes no pretence to anything picturesque, and it is doubtful if he would care to be so described; but picturesque he is as he swings the rope in the air from dock to vessel, or *vice versa*. He may be in trim sailor garb, member of the crew of a luxurious passenger - steamer, or merely clothed in the easy - going garments of the man who wears them merely as a means of covering.

The lariat - thrower is of no particular nationality. He may be an American, or Canadian, or Irish, or Swedish, or German, or almost anything; but after he has worked a while on these vast inland waters, the lakes put their stamp on him, and he becomes a lake man. He does his work with a certain calmness and ease, a philosophical mastery of things without excitement. If you talk with him, you will find that he knows much more than he seems to know. Sheehan, whose picture the artist has caught as he threw his lariat, discoursed upon world-wide topics.

"It's foolish for us to try to taych the Chinese annything," he said, " whin they're thousands of years old and set in their ways. Better kape our missionaries home, I say. We need 'em here, and monny of 'em, too."

The more rough-and-ready, and so more interesting, of these men are connected with the freighters and smaller steamers.

Life on the freighters in bad weather is no smooth existence, especially if they are "whaleback"—a sort of cigar-shaped iron or steel craft lying low in the water like a monitor, with fragile - looking white turrets and cabins at each end. Some of them are merely "tows," and do not travel under their own steam—"wagons" they are scornfully termed by the sailors of better craft. They are snouted forward, which has won them in addition the opprobrious name of "pig," and in more than one way the name is applicable; for these great, inert creatures have a capacity of six or eight thousand tons of iron ore or copper ingots, which is fed to them through wide mouths gaping across their brown bodies, and which they appear to consume

with greedy rapacity as it flows down to them through enormous chutes attached to the 1500-foot iron-ore docks at Duluth. Now and then a man working on the dock falls from a collapsed ore-car into the chute and down with the ore through eighty feet of terrible descent into the monster freighter yawning below. It is strange indeed that he is never killed, but is fished out from the gravel-like ore lying in the dark belly of the boat and treated for nervous shock, and is soon back at his work again.

There is a social atmosphere on these inland seas that seems quite like that of country roads. The passengers and crews of passing boats recognize each other by bows and waving of hands, hats, and handkerchiefs; and not in a perfunctory but a cordial way betokening their genuine interest. The big boats sometimes give the little ones a "lift," as country wagons pick up an overtaken pedestrian; and the revenue cutter's launch, upon which a courteous lieutenant of the service was our most kind host, gave a "lift" in this way to a tiny boat in which a government beacontender was going his rounds, caring for his various lights as a lamplighter does in the city. The lakes are almost as full of these warning lights as the city is of electric arcs. Range lights, bea-

"ANDY" SIMS

cons, fog-bells, storm-signals,—there is no end to them, nor to the brave, steady souls who keep them alight and never falter in the long and lonely performance of this duty. For the lakes are rich in capes, islands, and dangerous channels, beautiful as a dream by day—a dream of blue water and lustrous green isles wooded to their edges—but treacherous by night; and the light-keepers of the Great Lakes deserve a volume to themselves. Later, on the dock at Mackinac Island (pronounced Mackinaw), we met the light-keeper of the St. Helena light—a bronzed, squarely built man of French and Indian ancestry, who spoke excellent English with a slight roll of the *r*. His grandfather, a Frenchman, had worked for the Hudson Bay Company when he came here in a birch canoe from the north nearly a hundred years ago; and his descendant, the light-keeper, had the manners of a Frenchman, modified to a dignified gravity by his Indian heredity and perhaps the solemnity of his work. For he told us of storms—those sudden wild lake storms—and of cries in the night, and half-drowned people washed ashore, to be tenderly cared for by him and his wife until they died, or lived and went away on the next passing boat, to be nevermore heard of by the light-keeper.

The marine milkman, who supplied passing boats with milk, appeared one morning at a wharf where we tied up.

We found him interesting because he differed from his city prototype in that his customers came to him to be served. He was round and fat, and his neck was adorned with a bright red and green necktie as he sat on a bench before his island-like milk-shop, and met life with a smiling countenance and that air of one who is at ease and has plenty of room to which we of the crowded East were beginning to grow accustomed.

"Yes, I'm the marine milkman," he said, smiling broadly at the title we gave him. And when we essayed the olden

THE LARIAT-THROWER

ONE OF THE WHALEBACKS

pleasantry of which the city milkman is the immemorial victim, suggesting that he seemed amply supplied with fresh water for the purposes of trade, he laughed as if he had never heard this witticism before, and as one with a clear conscience.

After leaving Detroit we had sailed slowly and majestically out of the Detroit River into St. Clair Lake, which is like turquoise matrix with its violet and green shadows on an expanse of tender blue. The passengers were now clustered in eager groups on the forward deck, the men explaining to their womenfolk the wonders of the St. Clair Ship-Canal, which we were now approaching. Even the lady with the marine glasses seemed gathering a quiet interest, though I heard her say:

"How Robert and Dorothy would enjoy this! . . . I wonder what they're doing now? What time is it, Ellen? Two? Then I know what they're doing. They've finished lunch-

con, and Bobbity's going out to play prisoner's base. I hope he won't run too hard; it must be warm at home. And Dorothy's sitting in the window-seat up-stairs with her paper dolls and the puppy, and probably Mildred's in, and they're going to have a tea-party later for the dolls, and—"

"What a large sea-gull!" said the one she called Ellen.

"Oh yes, but it's not Dorothy and it's not Bobbity," replied her companion, mournfully.

"I should hope not," said Ellen, emphatically,—"suspended in mid-air!"

We were moving slowly, our decks drenched in sunshine. Soon we saw

A BUSINESS BOY OF "THE SOO."

ahead of us two long and narrow parallel strips of green earth, with trees growing upon them, and enclosing a midlake canal through which we must pass. This was the celebrated St. Clair Ship-Canal, eighty-two hundred feet long, a notable work of engineering. Entering this quiet slip in the midst of the lake, we passed between twin lighthouses of red brick, with green blinds and black cupolas, and homelike white palings shutting off the omnipresent water. Petunias, ox-eyed daisies, and bachelor's-buttons throve in the long, narrow gardens, and in one was a rocking-chair, and in the other a grindstone and lawn-mower; but there was a deathlike quiet everywhere, and nobody to be seen as we glided on between the scrub-willows and poplars growing as well as they could in the artificial ground. Kingfishers darted around the lighthouse towers, their orange beaks glittering in the sun, their dark-gray wings showing green beneath. At the end of the canal were more lighthouses, precisely like the others, and

there was a giant freight-boat waiting to enter the canal as soon as we passed out. Its cabin was a small railroad car without wheels, and we were told that this was the private freighter of a railway magnate. Ladies in light-hued gowns fluttered about its decks and in and out of the strange-looking cabin, and waved gracefully to us as we passed.

We entered the little Venice of the lakes—the Flats of the St. Clair River, where numbers of tiny canals intersected innumerable islands as the streets of a city intersect its blocks, and where poplars, willows, flowers, picturesque low cottages, club-houses, canoes, skiffs, and launches made up a curiously un-American scene. Occasionally there was a bit of marsh-grass in the blue water, dwindling away to thin spears; and rustic bridges spanned narrow ribbons of water and lent an air of pleasuring to the picture.

In one of the most picturesque locations stands the hospitable inn of Joe Beurrenoir. It is a rambling wooden structure, with broad verandas full of chairs, and a lawn under the trees, where there are more chairs and tables, around which Joe's guests sit for hours, drinking moderately and puffing cigars and cigarettes. On each side runs a small canal spanned by a rustic bridge, with a canoe or two waiting as carriages wait before ordinary hotels; for the inn's "stable" is a boat-house. You can step into the clear, clean water of the canals any moment for a bath. Your telephones are megaphones, through which you converse hilariously with neighboring cottages and clubs bounded by other canals, or with the occupants of innumerable passing steamers and freighters. Your waiters are Beurrenoir's pretty daughters, who are deft and given to smiling, and do not look as if they were related to

CLOSING THE GATES OF AMERICAN LOCKS ("SOO" CANAL)

HOME OF A LIGHTHOUSE-KEEPER

their round, stout, and somewhat haughty father. For Beurrenoir has made money. His frog and chicken dinners, which he cooks himself with the satisfaction of the true artist, have made him famous, and he knows it. So he wears an imperial, and twirls it with the air of one who has succeeded in his highest aims.

We were reminded, as we approached Mackinac Island, of what Harriet Martineau had said of the "wild and tender" beauty of this place; and as we came nearer, and saw at the base of its green, gently rising ascent a sail stained with Venetian red against the blue bay, it seemed to us no youthful and immature country to which we were sailing, but something old and serene and tinged with we knew not what of brooding romance and mystery. When later we had ascended the wayward roads that lead up the heights, past the ancient fort and the venerable Indian Mission, and the old white, wide-spreading hotel that used to be the headquarters of the Hudson Bay Company—and around which seven and eight thousand Indians in full regalia were sometimes assembled in former days to sell their pelts to the company, but where now great lilacs grow by the windows, and stout patrons sit complacently on the broad piazzas,—when we had passed all these and penetrated the forest of the arbor-vitæ trees that spice the air as from a million censers, but with a fragrance more freshly poignant than any incense, we found no revelations awaiting us, but only a deepening of the mystery. For here dwelt Gitchie Manitou, the Mighty Spirit, whose wigwam, when he departed from it, turned to stone, and rises now from the forest in a majestic cone for all to see. Here, too, we found the cottage where lived Constance Fenimore Woolson's "Anne"—a small dwelling half hidden in the forest shadows. Over all the island was a cloudless blue sky, and around us the brilliant water sped away league upon league into the misty distance.

DIGNITY AND IMPUDENCE

A four-thousand-ton freighter and a fisherman's boat "locking" through the American "Soo"

At the juncture of Lakes Superior and Huron lies Sault Sainte Marie, familiarly called "The Soo." Old and little, simple and significant, this town, with a manner as somnolent as the air of Irving's Sleepy Hollow, performs a magnificent part in the commerce of the world. For past "The Soo," through the immense government locks that bring the imperial Superior to the level of Huron by chaining the falls of the St. Mary's River, sails in eight months more than twice the commerce of the Suez Canal, where navigation is open all the year, and one-sixth of the entire commerce of the United States. And the work of raising and lowering millions of tons of vessels with their cargoes is accomplished with such ease and silence that the marvel of it grows hourly as the spectacle is observed.

Looking across the locks from the American side — there are three locks, two American, one Canadian — you see at your feet a strip of lush grass, then a wide flagged walk, then the clear blue water in the lock. Beyond the farthest stone flagging are the emerald and crystal rapids, and beyond them the green Canadian shore, with its clustered frame cottages, stone power-houses and pulp-mills, and still farther northward the thickly wooded hills.

Near at hand you receive an impression of colossal vessels slowly rising or sinking at your feet, of unseen machinery working its invincible will under the massive masonry, of columns and streamers of smoke against a blue sky, of occasional blowing off of steam, quiet remarks from seaman to seaman, tossing of heavy head and stern lines, and a riotous foaming of hyacinthine water as it tumbles in or out of the locks and sends the boat up to Lake Superior's level or down to that of Huron. It costs the government about five dollars each time a boat is locked up or down, whether it be a small sail-boat loaded with huckleberries or fresh eggs, or an eight-thousand-ton freighter; or perhaps a dignified vessel of many tons condescending to lock through in company with an impudent little rowboat occupied by Indian fishermen. There is no toll charged; all that the government requires is a registry of name and freightage. As you face the locks, behind you lies the little town, where you are sure that every household is taking a siesta, quite undisturbed by the fact that a steel freighter may be passing filled to the hatches with the largest load of iron ore ever taken down the lakes, the fame of whose achievement will be discussed later in a hundred smelting-works all over the country. Not that "business" is all asleep in "The Soo," where a laundry company, with a true Western sweep of view, advertises that it washes "everything from a napkin to a circus tent."

We discovered that all the small boys who inhabit the lake regions are characterized by an alert and businesslike demeanor, and a courtesy to ladies which made them seem more like men in miniature than the children they really were. The marine newsboy, who supplied the latest papers to the steamers, freighters, "tows," barges, "wagons," launches, and other craft passing perforce through the locks, climbed on and off the vessels as easily as his city brother crosses a street; was ever ready for business at the right moment, yet equally at our service to have his picture taken, or tell us, if need were, the story of his brief but active life. Another business boy of "The Soo" was halted in the street and requested to wait till our artist joined us, that we might have a picture of him seated in his tiny wagon drawn by its Newfoundland dog, and by means of which he was performing errands for the shop that employed him. He waited with perfect amiability, though we were uncomfortably aware of his inner impatience, and no sooner had the camera snapped than he was off like the wind, calling back pleasantly in response to our thanks. His was one of many real dog-wagons encountered at "The Soo." In winter the dogs are much in use for drawing sleighs, to which are harnessed from one to six or more of them, according to need.

At the edge of the town we found a small bit of Holland—a house, a strip of garden, a pond large enough for one boat to turn around in without grazing the shore, a cow and chickens, and four flaxen-haired children as reigning lords of this Lilliputian domain. Their father was one of the many lighthouse-keepers we met, and a cheerful grandmother cared for the motherless children. To get the children and the cow in proper relative position for the picture was a work of rare *finesse;* but when it was finally arranged, the little boy was more interested in the correct attitude of the cow than in his own, of which misplaced concern on his part the picture bears evidence.

From "The Soo" we crossed the river to the Canadian "Soo," and made several short excursions into Canada, including a brief railway journey that plunged us suddenly into the wildest hill-country. Here long reaches of mountain and valley were thickly grown with spruce-trees rising greenly, pinnacle after pinnacle, as far as the eye could see, and

cascades and lakes and trout-streams watered a land as romantic and untamed as was ever immortalized in song or story. The low log huts of the wood-cutters and an occasional group of miners' cabins humanized the otherwise trackless range of rich green mountain country. In its heart, far off the track of daily life, lives an elderly Englishman who has been equal to the sacrifice of every luxury except his London *Times*. At the end of each year the entire annual supply of the paper is sent to him, and every morning of the ensuing twelvemonth he reads a copy at his rude breakfast-table —a copy a year old, it is true, but bearing the day and date with a brave show of timeliness. By this simple means is he reconciled to exile in the wilderness.

But now the steamer again awaited us, and on we sailed, leaving romantic Huron for broad, majestic Superior, reluctantly passing Marquette unseen, and cutting through a tiny peninsula of Wisconsin by the Portage River, whose waters are colored by the rich copper deposits, and where the Calumet and Hecla mines radiate an Aladdin-like fame of riches. With Duluth, young, vigorous, energetic, high-perched on its windy promontory, whence it distributes grain and iron and copper to the whole world, came the end of a journey which, with its succession of natural scenes, varying from the terrible beauty of Thunder Bay to the Venetian loveliness of the St. Clair Flats, is one of which Americans may well be proud.

As we stepped ashore at Duluth, the young lady with the marine glasses followed close behind us. She was saying: "Oh yes, yes, Ellen dear, it *is* a beautiful trip, and I know it has done me a great deal of good; but you can't imagine, dear old Ellen, how I have missed Bobbity. Do you know, I—yes, I feel as if I could hardly stand it another minute. Ellen, I— *Couldn't* we go home faster by rail?"

CHICAGO

IN all probability the impecunious stranger will settle down to receive his first impression of Chicago from a street-car, because this saves money and a great deal of time in a new community. Framed for an instant by the window-sash, a myriad of things barely seen flit by in a disordered pageant of struggling people, streets bristling with chop-suey signs, great office-buildings, trolley wires, street-cars, trucks, automobiles, and Irish policemen. I open my map to see where I am heading.

"The loop," the conductor says.

"You don't mean to say so?" I look rapidly out of the window to locate the thing, fearful that I may be too late to see how the populace amuses itself.

The passengers, hanging like bananas from the straps above, pivot grotesquely about as we turn a corner. The man is still looking me over suspiciously.

"The loop," he repeats, with a dogged persistence.

"Where is it—quick!"

In my anxiety to open the car window it jams. A passing car obstructs my view.

"You're on it," he replies, dryly, withering me with a glance. "It will be five cents."

I pay my fare, and reach the cold, unsympathetic pavement, and board a car going in the opposite direction. Now we are passing through a city cañon echoing with the roar of traffic. A horde of people rushes past in the gloomy shadow cast by great walls of granite, groaning under tons of bastard ornament. This must be one of the principal thoroughfares, and I ask my neighbor where we are.

"Non capisco, Signore," is his polite reply. I bow my thanks and turn to my left.

"Could *you* tell me what street this is?"

"Bitte, ich bin nur Heute hier angekommen."

He smiles and makes some primitive signs with his hands and arms. I reply by motions more involved, occasionally moving my scalp. We are making little headway, when I spy a likely fellow sitting beside my new acquaintance. With suppressed agitation I put my question to him.

"Pardon, vat for you demande?"

He is anxious to help me. I repeat slowly, "The name of the street we are on."

"Tiens! for sure vee go on—" he replies, reassuringly; "mais lentement. Allez! Nom de Dieu, on va plus vite chez nous!"

Then I remember that Chicago is cosmopolitan. There still remains the man swinging on his strap before me. He is an American—unmistakably American—and I begin again:

"Perhaps you could tell me what street this is?"

"How's that? I didn't quite get it?"

He leans far over, holding his hand around his ear in the shape of a megaphone. I repeat my question with great emphasis, and his face brightens.

"Well," he replied, after great deliberation, "if the three-fingered Wizard is in the box, they'll make it three straight or I'm a . . ."

The end of this sentence was drowned by the explosions of a passing automobile.

"No; you've missed it," I screamed, now fully decided to make him understand. "What street are we on?"

"You think so, eh? Well, I'd like you to tell me how a man is goin' to pitch three games and be strong, and ain't all the others cripples?"

There is still my map, which I have overlooked in the excitement. I open it with a nasty grimace.

"Loop car—all out!"

And there we are again, a struggling car-load of humanity, scattering ourselves over the street. A loop victim may be easily recognized by his childish petulance and overbearing manner toward his wife or friends every time he hits the pavement where the car has dropped him. To find the loop, look for a panic-stricken group of strangers groping about in a futile effort to find the street name; for in Chicago the latter may turn up—if it does at all—in the most unexpected places: half obliterated on one of the steel posts supporting the trolley wires, or, high up somewhere, carved in weak relief on the brownstone building; again, it may be hidden beneath the cornice of a building, or the nearest basement may reveal something. If not here, the policeman will have it in his inside pocket. To find him, look for the nearest "Family Entrance."

The Chicagoan is very proud of the loop, and will glow with a sunny radiance the moment you approach the subject. "It is the greatest system on earth," he explained to me. "You see, each car, as it comes into the city from the suburbs, goes immediately into the loop when it reaches the business section of the city, and returns along parallel lines to the point it started from. Do I make myself clear?"

"Perfectly," I replied, with ill-concealed bitterness. "Suppose that you don't want to return to your starting-point, from either domestic or business reasons?"

"You don't have to; get off."

"Yes, but the loop may not be within a mile of my destination?"

His manner became somewhat intolerant, and he added: "The loop is near enough for *any* man's place of business. You can always walk."

Strictly speaking, the man who has no business in this section of the city had better look about and arrange matters so that he has, or he has no business in Chicago, and certainly none on the loop.

But it is an ungrateful pessimist who would stop to find fault with such insignificant details in this breezy city, where there is more visible, sensible independence to the square mile than in all the Eastern cities put together. You may not like Chicago—this will be because you are unfamiliar with it—but

you must love and respect the Chicagoan. He is the sanest and most rational of beings; he is contented with the city, and not anxious to persuade you to live there. If you do not like him or his city or the things contained therein, he is democratic enough to tell you what you can do. This attitude is the West, and is refreshing.

Patrick Henry, with his "Give me liberty or give me death," would have a dismal time to find employment in this happy, cosmopolitan community. I love a place where one may show one's feelings in an unmistakable manner. Chicago is the Arcadia of the man who is fortunate enough to possess his own convictions. For an indication of this latent spirit read the enormous sign conspicuously displayed in the baseball park: "The management requests the earnest co-operation of its patrons in preventing the throwing of glass bottles into the field."

Westward ho! for Gallic enthusiasm. It will be seen here that odds and ends—scrap-iron, stones, or bricks—which a high-strung, opinionated man is apt to carry with him as ballast to be gotten rid of at the propitious moment, are not included in the manifesto; but after all, a generous and liberal-minded management *must* stop somewhere.

Even in the smallest matters one's personal freedom has been safeguarded. Smoking is permitted on the front platforms of the Chicago street-cars, so that the passengers within may get the benefit of it when the car is in motion. But here again the Chicagoan is ahead of us, for we have no smoke at all. The cautious person who takes advantage of this privilege, and who knows his Chicago, will have a care to select a decent brand, or every man, woman, and child will suspect that he has been shaking dice for his cigars—lost his weekly allowance, and been reduced to the humiliating and odious stogie.

For it should be understood that in Chicago the man with the slightest drop of sporting blood in his veins never descends to the depths where he buys his cigars. He shakes dice for them with the proprietor of his store. Ask your Chicago friend about this, and he will accompany you to "his place" with the hospitable air of a man directing you to a foreign mission. Should you be friendless in Chicago, drop into the first tobacco store and look for the inevitable green baize cloth conspicuous on the counter. Here the new customer may use strong language and rattle the dice-box till his hand shakes.

So much has been said detrimental to this most maligned of communities that one comes here expecting to find a great city of slaughter-houses, breweries, and mammoth power-houses, grouped about a lake, in great disorder. It must be wild, of course, and with just a touch of that inevitable "woolliness" inseparable from the West but difficult to explain. Then comes the awakening on the morrow, when you go out to look the place over and find the Chicagoan in possession of the finest site for a city in America; an incomparable waterfront, a chain of parks unsurpassed anywhere, miles of beautiful driveways skirt-ing the lake, and the principal avenue of the city—*the* avenue of the city—with its clubs and great hotels overlooking as fair a sheet of water as you will find this beautiful land over—shimmering with faint emerald greens and blues and losing itself in a pale turquoise horizon lightly smudged by the distant train of smoke trailing behind the lake steamers. It has also the worst architecture in America, and a river, at first glance commonplace, yet revealing in its almost momentary metamorphoses a rare and exotic beauty, as it shapes its course beneath the network of bridges spanning it at every corner, or drifts past giant grain-elevators, looming vast and ghostlike above its banks, alive with longshoremen toiling at the landing. It wanders through neighborhoods where, if the artist be fortunate enough to find a motive, he had better seize it immediately and take it home with him or commit it to memory before the sun sets, for strange things happen after dark in this barren district.

Of course I did not possess this valuable knowledge when I settled down for the afternoon before a flag-tower of almost medieval character, languidly leaning over the street preparing for its final plunge into oblivion. This was my foreground, with a middle distance of shanties and a sky-line of distant towers and embattlements worthy of San Gimignano.

I had just placed a few organic lines on my copper, when a voice behind me said, "I've rayported it."

An Irish policeman towered above me.

"You've reported what?" I asked, in bewilderment.

A FLAG-TOWER OF ALMOST MEDIEVAL CHARACTER
Etched by C. H. White

"Turned in me report a week ago to Clancy at the station-house," he replied, doggedly avoiding my question.

"I don't quite understand . . ."

"Neither do I," he broke in, interrupting me. "I've said right along it ain't safe or proper to have that there tower hangin' over our wives a n d children. Say—ain't you on one of the papers?"

"No."

"Aw, gowan—quit yer kiddin'."

He gave me a playful dig in the ribs a n d chuckled. "But I've reported it just the same," he proceeded. "I says, 'Clancy,' I says, 'take it away,' I says, just like that.

"'Take nawthin' away,' says he.

"'Clancy,' says I, 'that there tower is goin' to take a tumble one of these days, and when it does there's goin' to be a procession and people movin' slow,' I says; 'and if it's a Guiney, maybe there'll be a band fer them to march with,' I says.

"'There'll be t i m e enough when we hear the music,' says he. But don't you forget it, young feller, I've reported it all right."

With that he left me and wandered s l o w l y down the street.

On the following day, after a dismal half-hour groping about in a futile effort to find the familiar tower in grotesque silhouette against the sky, I stumbled upon a small mound of earth, thinly sprinkled with sawdust.

There could be no possible doubt in

QUINCY STREET
Etched by C. H. White

my mind of the magnitude of the catastrophe that had taken place overnight. The old tower, these many years rising above the sea of weather-beaten roofs like a lighthouse to guide the weary, patient workman as he shaped his zigzag course homeward, three sheets in the wind, on Saturday nights, was no more. As I stood sadly contemplating the ruin which I in a measure was responsible for, a man in uniform waved to me from across the street.

"Didn't I tell you I'd rayported it?" he yelled, and then waving me a farewell, took a short cut through a corner lot and disappeared.

Even the affection I cherish for these homely suburbs pales into insignificance beside the memory of a delightful corner I stumbled upon by accident, right in the centre of the city, yet swept by the cool breezes of the lake. With its lions gazing stolidly at the nondescript architecture before them, and the weather-beaten, grimy façade, severe as a Florentine palace, the place itself is not particularly interesting. It is the people one meets of a midsummer's day loafing in the shade on the broad stone steps that lend an interest and variety to the day's work, found nowhere else in Chicago. Here the idler will find a sociable, warm-hearted gathering of delightful but unemployed people.

It was on these steps one morning that there was revealed to me, through the medium of a park policeman, the existence of an interest so intense in matters artistic that I may say, if he be an indication of the general trend of feeling in the street, a veritable renaissance is at hand in Chicago.

He stood silently for some time before speaking, but I felt his presence in the agitated movement among the loafers, who, awakening from their lethargy, shuffled rapidly sideways, like crabs, out of the danger zone, at his approach.

"I've never seen that kind of work done before," he began, after a long scrutiny at my copperplate; "and I've seen most of everything. I suppose that's what you call etching."

I replied that it was, and ventured a few explanations concerning the process.

"Then you ought to drop into the Institute and see the Whistlers; they have some good ones."

This was said simply, without any attempt to convey a sense of his erudition—merely a casual remark such as one amateur might make to another. He rambled along, quite innocent of the colossal impression he had made on me, occasionally jarring me with a query as to the relative merits of Düsseldorf, Munich, and Paris. Then without any warning he said:

"Of course you know Montgomery, the corn man?"

"Montgomery?"

"Yes, the corn man."

"Oh—Montgomery . . . I see . . . why, of course . . . let me think a moment. . ."

In desperation I groped about for the slightest clew to conceal my ignorance.

"I thought you'd know him," he continued, breaking in on my reverie and saving the situation. "He ain't much on apples or even backgrounds, but when it comes to corn—not on the stalk, mind you, but on the ear or off—you've *certainly* got to hand it to him. It lays over *anything* I've *ever* seen. Just set him and others before one or more ears of corn—you can even scatter it around loose—and call time, and then watch him. Why, he'll make Rubens and the rest of them in there look like pikers. No, *sir*— not an artist for miles around has anything on him, and I'd like to bet my shield he can hang it on them all."

"He must be a wonder!" I gasped.

"He *is*. I own a couple of his corn pieces and knew enough to get in when they were low. Now they bring fancy prices." He winked with profound significance. "One of them is called *Which is Which?* and has a piece of real corn tacked on the frame, and do you know it keeps you guessing to tell them apart. Even the birds fall for it."

He spoke with deep and genuine regret of his failure to follow his brother's example, who was a prosperous painter in Europe, and confessed that even now, after years on the "force," the smell of turpentine filled him with a strange and restless yearning, resulting in weeks of protracted sketching during his idle hours.

When I asked him for a memento he laughed bashfully and put me off, but when I implored of him the smallest courtesy one artist may extend to a brother, he removed his white gloves and drew with my fountain pen on the back of a visiting-card a fantastic portrait of what I believe to be a dog— executed with surprising rapidity and scarcely more than a single stroke of the pen. Pressed to sign it, he refused absolutely—in fact, did his utmost to destroy it, but failing in this he fled from the spot as if possessed.

Never again shall I find a corner with the same atmosphere as this comfortable niche with its endless variety of life and incident. Long before the officer of the law had been swallowed up in the traffic of Michigan Avenue his place was occupied by a certain Mr. Godson, whose worldly possessions at the time I had the good fortune to make his acquaintance consisted of a good suit of clothes, tobacco and cigarette papers, and a small penknife.

Barely seventeen, fully six feet tall, his small head with its piercing eyes looked ludicrously out of place on the great breadth of shoulders, and he shuffled awkwardly when he walked. He emerged from one of the studios below for a breath of fresh air, a cigarette, and anything that Michigan Avenue might offer in the way of diversion, and appeared to be on intimate terms with everything feminine within a radius of three blocks of the broad stone steps.

As he stood absorbed in my work, a dainty, chic, delightful little girl rustled past smiling, and glided down the steps, to disappear in the crowd of shoppers hurrying past.

"Gentle nature—city-broke — will eat out of the hand," he observed, breaking the ice. "We have some peaches here," he continued, flicking his ashes over the coping.

"So I see," I replied, with enthusiasm.

"Yes, there are bunches of them."

He stood lost in a reverie, looking through half - closed lids at embattlements of the new University Club across the street, but his expression led me to believe his thoughts were elsewhere. Presently he came out with it.

3rd State

White imp. -'08-

LITTLE ITALY

Etched by C. H. White

GRANT PARK
Etched by C. H. White

"Would you like me to send up a few?"

"By all means," I gasped, clasping the hand of this monarch of hospitality. Before I could recover my equilibrium his lanky frame had disappeared through the doorway. His remark was made in such a casual, offhand manner, and his disappearance was so brisk and businesslike, that I was completely at sea as to his intentions. After all, I reasoned, one does not make a consignment of females in the same manner as one might send up a basket of fruit on approval. Certainly this was a new experience, and I worked along in silence, following with my needle, to the best of my ability, the intricacies of the façade opposite.

It may have been five minutes that I sat absorbed in my work, when a light footstep at my right brought me back with a jump to our previous conversation. Two young ladies stood giggling in the shadow of the archway, very conscious of my scrutiny. Was this merely coincidence, or could it be that the inimitable Godson had . . . ? No. I dismissed the idea as preposterous. As I watched they were soon joined by a third and a fourth, forming with their great hats, fluttering with plumes, a charming group, relieved against the gray stone background. An embarrassing pause was broken by the arrival of another—a lithe little figure in a buff-colored gown, who from the nodding plumes of her picture hat to the dainty shoes with their big bows—crisp and chic—was the embodiment of grace and femininity. For a moment they stood in suppressed agitation, on the point of retreating, and I was preparing heroic measures to save the situation, when above the pretty group loomed a great pair of shoulders, topped by a small head illuminated by an infectious smile. It was Godson! And at a signal from him the squad moved forward with a flutter to join me.

When they had retired after the customary platitudes, I seized him and demanded an immediate explanation of the strange power that enabled him to accomplish miracles.

"Why, it's a cinch," he replied, modestly. "I hiked down to the studio below and said, 'You girls had better chase up-stairs and see the guy who got the only gold medal given at the last Paris Salon, working on his plate for the French government.' Those hen artists will fall for anything. You know, I'm just taking up art for an accomplishment—only been here three months, and you can bet I've not been losing any time! I leave for Dartmouth next week, but I've *certainly* been busy while I've been here. Art is *great!*"

He rolled another cigarette, and as the diminutive buff-colored figure reappeared, stopping for an instant to adjust her veil, and then moved lightly down the steps, he waved a greeting, shook my hand, pulled his cuffs down, caught up with her, and tilting his lanky frame at a perilous angle to hear what she said, drifted out of my life in the restless tide of people that flows at midday and ebbs at night along Michigan Avenue. Art, after all, has its compensations.

GAMESTERS OF THE WILDERNESS

N° Robin Hoods of legend ever lived in more complete security than those "Gentlemen Adventurers Trading in Hudson's Bay" for whom Prince Rupert had secured from his cousin, King Charles, in 1670, complete monopoly of all furs north and westward of Hudson's Bay. A thousand miles of juniper swamps and impassable cataracts cut the Hudson's Bay fur traders off from the fur traders of New France to the south. To the west was impenetrable and unknown wilderness. To the north and east for eight months of the year was an impassable barrier of ice floe and berg and those elemental frozen foes to human presence.

For fifteen years after their organization the Gentlemen Adventurers of England—the Hudson's Bay Fur Company, a company numbering among its patrons King Charles II., Prince Rupert, General Munck, the Duke of York, the Duke of Marlborough, and a host of other worthies ranging from the nobility down to the goldsmiths and merchant princes of London—slumbered in security on the margin of a frozen sea. Charles Fort with its stone bastions on Rupert's River—named after King and Prince who secured the charter—quickly sent offshoots to Moose River on the west, Albany (named after an Albany far south), and Nelson (the modern York), which drained all the furs westward to the Rocky Mountains. Rupert and Moose and Albany each yearly collected three thousand five hundred beaver-pelts, worth in modern money one dollar and a half each, not to mention twice as many pelts of otter and mink and marten and ermine and sable. To the north, Nelson (York) sent out in a single year as much as one hundred thousand dollars'

worth of beaver. "The Gentlemen Adventurers of England Trading in Hudson's Bay" had found a gold-mine rich as Spanish El Dorado.

To be sure, Radisson, the Frenchman, who had helped to found the company with Prince Rupert, had gone over to the French fur traders one year, trading Nelson (York), bag and baggage, to the French Company of the North; but Radisson had become a British subject again and traded these forts back to England. He was in the employment of the company. Radisson was safe. To be sure, the ships of the French Fur Company had continued to come to the bay; but the French fur traders demanded four beaver for a musket, where the English demanded only two; and so those French fur-ships went back to Quebec empty of cargo. Two of the French fur-ships, meeting the *Merchant of Perpetuana* trapped in the ice-floes of the north, had scuttled the Hudson's Bay ship of provisions, captured master, mate, and crew, cast all in a dungeon on bread and water for eleven months in Quebec, where Edward Humes, the captain, died, and the rest were sold to lifelong slavery in Martinique, whence only Smithsend, the mate, escaped. Sieur Peré, a gay adventurer from New France, had come down to the bay overland from the Great Lakes, with three comrades, to spy on the English fur traders for the French company; but the young seigneur had been given food and a hearty Godspeed from the English, and having deliberately let his canoe float off to sea while he slept, so that he could not be sent away, had been clapped with one comrade into the fur-fort of Albany, while the two other adventurers were put on Charlton Island

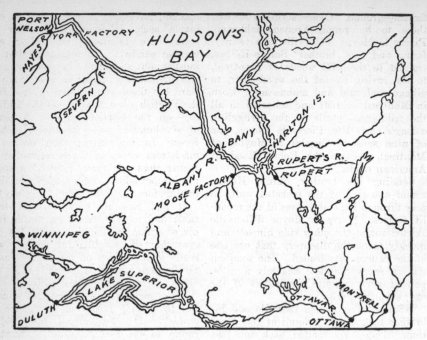

WILDERNESS WHERE THE GAMESTERS STRUGGLED
Modern chart showing the almost incredible distances and extent of the disputed territory

to earn their living hunting. The two adventurers had escaped to the mainland on a raft by night, and fleeing to Canada, a thousand miles by swamp and forest, had told a story of Peré's imprisonment that set the fire-eaters of New France in a flame. But all unknowing, the Gentlemen Adventurers of England slumbered secure on the margin of their frozen sea.

Like a bolt from the blue came the bold raiders of Pierre le Moyne d'Iberville into the midst of this security.

It was one of the long June nights, 1686, when twilight of the north merges with dawn. Fourteen cannon in all protruded from the embrasures of the four stone bastions round little Moose Factory to the southwest of the bay. The eighteen-foot pickets of the palisaded square wall were everywhere punctured with holes for musketry defence. In one bastion were three thousand pounds of powder. In another, twelve civilian soldiers slept. In a third were stored furs. The fourth bastion served as kitchen,

and across the middle of the courtyard, forty by forty feet, was the two-story stone house and residence of the chief factor. The sentinel had shot the strong iron bolts of the main gates facing the waterway; but so secure did he feel of the impossibility of attack that he had lain down to sleep, wrapped in a blanket, without even loading the cannon it was his duty to guard. Twilight of the long June night—the 18th, almost the longest day in the year—had deepened into the white stillness that precedes dawn, when two forms took shape in the thicket of underbrush behind the fort; and there stepped forth, clad in buckskin cap-a-pie, musket over shoulder, war-hatchet, powder-horn, dagger, pistol in belt, and unsheathed sword aglint in hand, two French wood-lopers, the far-famed *coureurs des bois,* whose scalping raids were to strike terror from Louisiana to Hudson's Bay. At first glance the two newcomers might have been marauding Iroquois come this outrageous distance over swamp and cataract from their own fighting-ground. Closer scrutiny showed them to be young French noblemen, Pierre le Moyne d'Iberville, age twenty-four, and his brother Sainte-Hélène, trained to the wild woods of Montreal, to the roving life of the wood-loper, to pillage and raid and ambuscade. Born in Montreal in 1661 and schooled to all the wilderness perils of the struggling colony's early life, Pierre le Moyne, one of nine sons of Charles le Moyne, of Montreal, became the Robin Hood of American wilds.

Sending his brother Sainte - Hélène round one side of the picketed walls to peer through the embrasures of the moonlit fortress, Pierre le Moyne d'Iberville skirted round the other side himself and quickly made the discovery that not one of the cannon was loaded. The tompion was in every muzzle. Scarcely a cat's-paw of wind dimpled the waters of the bay, smooth as silk.

With a quick glance Iberville and his brother took in every detail of the situation. Then they melted back into the pallid half-light like shadows. In a trice a hundred forms had taken shape in the mist—sixty-six Indians decked in all the war-gear of savage glory from head-dress and vermilion cheeks to naked, red-stained limbs lithe as a tiger, smooth and supple as satin. Sixty-six Indians and thirty-three half-wild French soldiers, gay in all the regimentals of French pomp, commanded by old Chevalier de Troyes, veteran of a hundred wars, now commissioned to demand the release of Monsieur Peré from the forts of the English fur traders. Beside de Troyes stood de la Chesnay, head of the Northern Company of Fur Traders in Quebec, only too glad of this chance to raid the forts of rival traders in time of peace. And well to the fore, cross in hand, head bared, the Jesuit Sylvie, come to rescue the souls of northern heathendom from hell.

Impossible as it may seem, these hundred intrepid adventurers had come overland from Montreal. What did the incursion of these French raiders mean? It meant that they had set out in midwinter on a voyage men hardly dared in summer. Without waiting for the ice to break up, they started from Montreal in March. No tents were carried; only the blanket, haversack fashion, tied to each man's back. Bivouac was under the stars. No provision but what each blanket carried! No protection but the musket on shoulder, the war-axe and powder-horn and pistol in belt! No reward but the vague promise of loot from the English *wigwamming*—as the Indians say—on the Northern Bay! A march of six hundred miles through trackless forests in midwinter; then down the maelstrom sweep of torrents swollen by spring thaw for three hundred miles to the juniper swamps of windfall and dank rotting forest growth around the bay!

It had been no play, this fur-trade raid; and now Iberville was back from his scouting, having seen with his own eyes that the English fur traders were really *wigwamming* on the bay. Hastily all burdens of blankets and food and clothes were cast aside and cached.

Then each man recharged his musket lest the swamp mists had dampened the powder. De Troyes led his soldiers round to the fore to make a feint of furious onslaught from the water-front. Iberville posted his Indians along each flank to fire through the embrasures of the pickets. Then with a wild yell the French soldiers swooped upon the English fort. Iberville and his brothers Sainte-Hélène and Maricourt were over the rear pickets and across the courtyard, swords in hand. Before the sleepy gunner behind the main gate could get his eyes open, one blow of Sainte-Hélène's sabre split the fellow's head to the collar-bone. The trunk of a tree had rammed in the gate. Iberville's Indians had hacked down the rear pickets, and he himself led the way into the main house. Before the sixteen inmates, dashing out in their shirts, had realized what had happened, the raiders were masters of Moose Factory. Only one other man besides the gunner was killed; and he was a Frenchman, slain by the cross-fire of his comrades over the courtyard. The cellars were searched, but there was small loot of fur. Furs were stored elsewhere; but the French were the richer by sixteen captives, twelve portable cannon, and three thousand pounds of powder. Flag unfurled, muskets firing, sod heaved in air, Chevalier de Troyes took possession of the fort for

A TYPICAL FORT OF THE HUDSON'S BAY COMPANY
From " La Potherie " (Edition of 1722)

the Most Redoubtable, Most Mighty, Most Christian King of France, though a cynic might wonder how such an act was accomplished in time of peace, when the sole object of the raid had been the rescue of Monsieur Peré, imprisoned as a spy.

Eastward of Moose, a hundred miles along the south coast of the bay, on Rupert's River, was another fort, stronger, the bastions of stone, with a dock where the Hudson's Bay Company's ship commonly anchored for the summer. Northwestward of Moose, a hundred miles, was a third fort, Albany, the citadel of the English fur traders' strength, forty paces back from the water, unassailable by sea, and the storehouse of the best furs. It was decided to attack the fort on Rupert's River first. Staying only long enough at Moose to build a raft to carry Chevalier de Troyes and his prisoners along the coast, the raiders set out by sea on the 27th of June. Iberville led the way with two canoes and eight or nine men. By the 1st of July he had caught a glimpse of Rupert's bastions. Concealing his Indians, he went forward to reconnoitre. To his delight he espied the company's ship with the H. B. C. ensign flying, that signified Governor Bridgar was on board. Choosing the night, as usual, for

attack, Iberville stationed his bandits where they could fire on the decks if necessary, and glided across the water to the schooner. Hand over fist, he was up the ship's side, when the sleeping sentinel awakened with a spring at Iberville's throat. One cleave of his sword, and the fellow rolled dead at the Frenchman's feet, Iberville stamping on the deck to call the crew aloft, and killing three men in turn as they tumbled up the hatchway, till the fourth, Governor Bridgar himself, threw up his hands in unconditional surrender of the ship and crew of fourteen. Meanwhile the din had alarmed the fort. Though the bastions were dismantled for repairs, gates were hard shut and musketry poured hot shot through the embrasures, that kept the raiders at a distance. Again it was the le Moyne brothers who led to victory. The bastions served the usual twofold purpose of defence and barracks. Extemporizing ladders, Iberville clambered to the roofs of these, hacked holes through the rough thatch, and threw down hand-grenades at the imminent risk of blowing himself as well as the enemy to eternity. " *It was*," says the old chronicle, " *with an effect most admirable*,"—which depends on the point of view; for when the sharpshooters were driven from the bastions to the main house inside, gates were rammed down, palisades hacked out, and Iberville with his followers was on the roof of the main house, throwing down more bombs. The raid became a rout. The French had Rupert, though little the richer except for the ship and thirty prisoners.

The wild wood-rovers were now strong enough to attempt Albany, one hundred miles northeast of Moose. It was at Albany that the French spy Peré was supposed to be lying panting for rescue. It was also at Albany that the English fur traders had their greatest store of pelts. As usual, Iberville led off in the canoes, de Troyes, the French fur traders, the soldiers, and the captives following with the cannon on the ship. It was sunset when the canoes launched out from Rupert's River. To save time by crossing the south end of the bay diagonally, they had sheered out from the coast, when there blew down from the upper bay one of those bitter northeast gales that at once swept a maelstrom of churning ice-floes about the cockle-shell birch canoes. To make matters worse, a fog fell, thick as night. A birch canoe in a cross-sea is bad enough. With ice-floes it was destruction. Some made for the main shore and took refuge on land. The le Moyne's two canoes kept on. The 1st of August saw his Indians and wood-lopers below the embankment of Albany. A few days later came de Troyes on the boat with soldiers and cannon.

Governor Sargeant of Albany had had warning of the raiders from Indian *coureurs*. The fort looked as shut as a locked box. Neither side gave a sign. Not till the French began trundling their cannon ashore by all sorts of clumsy contrivance, to get them in range of the fort forty yards back, was there a sign of life, when forty-three big guns inside the wall of Albany simultaneously let go forty-three bombs in midair that flattened the raiders to earth under shelter of the embankment. Chevalier de Troyes then mustered all the pomp and fustian of court pageantry, flag flying, drummer beating to the fore, guard in line, and, marching forward, demanded of the English traders, come half-way out to meet him, satisfaction for and the delivery of Sieur Peré, a loyal subject of France suffering imprisonment on the shores of Hudson's Bay at the hands of the English. One may wonder, perhaps, what these raiders would have done without the excuse of Peré. The messenger came back from Governor Sargeant with word that Peré had been sent home to France by way of England long ago. (That Peré had been delayed in an English prison was not told.) De Troyes then pompously demanded the surrender of the fort. Sargeant sent back word such a demand was an insult in time of peace. Under cover of night, the French retired to consider. With an extravagance now lamented they had used at Rupert most of their captured ammunition. Cannon they had in plenty, but few rounds of balls. They had thirty prisoners, but no provisions; a ship, but no booty of furs. Between them and home lay a wilderness of forest and swamps for one thousand miles. They must capture the fort by an escalade, or retreat empty-handed.

Meanwhile, such bedlam reigned inside the fort as might have delighted the raiders' hearts if they could have known. Sargeant, the sturdy old governor, was for keeping his teeth clenched to the end, though the larder was lean and only enough powder left to do the French some damage as they landed their cannon next day. When a servant fell dead from a French ball, Turner, the chief gunner, dashed from his post, vowing he would throw himself on the mercy of the French. Sargeant rounded the fellow back to his guns with the generous promise to blow his brains out if he budged one inch from his place. Two English spies sent out came back with word the French were mounting their battery in the dark.

For two days bombs sang back and forward through the air. There was more parleying. Bridgar, the governor captured down at Rupert, warned the company that the French were desperate—if they were compelled to fight to the end, there would be no mercy. Still Sargeant hoped against hope for the yearly English vessel to relieve the siege; but when Captain Outlaw came with word there was no more powder, the people threw down their arms and threatened to desert *en masse* to the French. Sargeant still stubbornly refused to beat a parley, so

PIERRE LE MOYNE D'IBERVILLE
(From an old print)

Dixon, the under factor, hung out a white sheet as flag of truce from the fort window. The French had just ceased firing, to cool their cannon, and had actually been reduced to pouring molten iron around wooden disks for balls, when the messenger came out with word of surrender. Bluff and resolute to the end, Sargeant marched out with two flagons of port, seated himself on the French cannon, drank healths with de Troyes, and proceeded to drive as hard a bargain as if his larders had been crammed and his magazine full of powder. Drum beating, flags flying, in full possession of arms, the governor, officers, wives, and servants were to be permitted to march out in honor, to be transported to Charlton Island, there to await the coming of the English ship. Barely had the thirty English sallied out when the wood-lopers were into the fort, ransacking house and cellar. The fifty thousand crowns' worth of beaver was found, but not a morsel of food except one bowl of barley sprouts. Thirteen hundred miles from Canada with neither powder nor food! De Troyes gave his men leave to disband on August 10, and it was a wild scramble for home—*sauve qui peut,* as the old chronicler relates, some of the prisoners being taken to Quebec as carriers of the furs raided; others, to the number of fifty, being turned loose in the desolate wilderness of the bay. It was October before Iberville's forest-rovers were back in Montreal.

The French were now in possession of the south end of Hudson's Bay. Iberville's brother Maricourt with a handful of men remained to guard the captured forts; and for ten years the inland sea became the theatre of such escapades as buccaneers might have enacted on the Spanish Main. The next year saw the indomitable Iberville back at Rupert. Over at Charlton Island, where Sargeant and his men had retired, the Hudson's Bay

Company's ship *Churchill* had been caught and frozen in the ice-floes. Iberville sent four spies to reconnoitre. Three were summarily captured by the English fur traders and thrown into the hold of the ship, manacled, for the winter. In spring one was brought above-decks to give the English sailors a hand putting masts shipshape. The fellow only waited till six of the crew were up the ratlines, when he seized an axe, brained two Englishmen on the decks, rushed down-stairs to liberate his comrades, took possession of all firearms, and at pistol-point kept the six Englishmen up the mast-poles while he steered the vessel straight to Iberville, where the cargo of provisions saved Rupert's River from famine. In vain the English sent rescue-parties south from Nelson (York), on the west side of the bay, to recapture Albany. Iberville came canoeing across the ice-floes with his Indian bandits, discovered two English ships locked in the ice before Albany, ready to attack the French in the spring, lay in ambush till he had captured half the crew of eighty-two, then took possession of both the English vessels, loaded them with furs of the fort, and sailed gayly out for Quebec, eluding two other English ships in the straits by hoisting an English flag and slipping away

COAT OF ARMS OF THE HUDSON'S BAY COMPANY

through the fog before they could send messengers across the intervening ice.

Perhaps security bred carelessness. From 1690 to 1693 Iberville was absent from the bay on the border raids of Schenectady and Pemaquid. When Captain Michael Crimmington led three Hudson's Bay Company's ships down to Albany in 1693, he found only four Frenchmen holding the fort. The other forty of the garrison were off in the woods. And in the woods they were forced to stay; for Crimmington took prompt possession of Albany for the company, finding in the cellars a ghastly form, naked, shackled hand to feet, and chained to the wall—a French criminal who had murdered first the surgeon and then the priest of the fort.

But Iberville was not the man to let go lightly what had been so hard won. It had become more than a guerilla warfare between gamesters of the wilderness. It was a fight for ascendency on the continent. It was a struggle to determine which nation was to command the rivers and waterways leading inland to the unknown West. If the French raiders were to hold their forts at the bottom of the bay, they must capture the stronghold of the Hudson's Bay Fur Company upon the west coast—Nelson, or York, at the mouth of Hayes River. Taking on board one hundred and twenty wood-rangers, Iberville sailed from Quebec on the 10th of August, 1694, with the frigate *Poli and Salamandre*. On September 24 he was disembarking his cannon below the earthworks and one hundred great guns of Nelson. Steady bombardment poured bombs into the fort from September 25 to October 14. Châteauguay, his brother, fell wounded in the fight, which redoubled the fury of the wood-lopers. While the long-range guns ploughed up the earthworks and shattered the palisades to the fore, the wood-lopers went round and in hand-to-hand fight assaulted the fort to the rear. To save the fort from utter extermination, Walsh and Kelsey, the chief traders of the English, surrendered. Of the captured, some were turned adrift in the

UNLOADING CARGO OF A HUDSON'S BAY COMPANY'S SHIP
From "La Potherie" (Edition of 1722)

woods, others carried in irons to France, because—as one of the indignant prisoners afterward complained—"*we had not the money to grease the commander's fist for our freedom.*"

And so the merry game went on between the rival traders of the Northern Bay, French and English fighting as furiously over the beaver as if each pelt had been a bar of gold. Except for one fort—Severn—half-way between Albany and Nelson, and unimportant except as a resort for the refugees driven from the other factories by the French, the Hudson's Bay Fur Company had lost all their forts on the bay. One thing favored the English adventurers. Open war had taken the place of secret treaty between France and England. The English Admiralty now furnished a convoy of frigates for the traders' supply-ships; so when Sérigny, Iberville's brother, came out from France in 1696 with provisions on the *Poli* and *Hardi* for the French at Nelson, he found English men-of-war, the *Bonaventure* and *Seaforth,* lined up for attack before Hayes River. Sérigny didn't wait. He turned swift heel for sea; so swift, indeed, that the *Hardi* split on some ice-floe and went to bottom with all hands. Without either provisions or powder, Governor de la Fôrest had no choice

but to capitulate to the Englishman, Allan, who retaliated for all Iberville's raids by carrying off his captives to England, where they lay in prison at Portsmouth for four months. Released at last, they hastened to France, where their emaciated, ragged condition spoke louder than their indignant words.

Frenchmen languishing in an English prison! Like wildfire ran the rumor of the outrage. Once before when Peré, the Frenchman, had been imprisoned on Hudson's Bay, Iberville had thrust the sword of vengeance into the very heart of the English fastness. France turned again to the same Robin Hood of Canada's rude chivalry and romance. Iberville was at the time carrying havoc from hamlet to hamlet of Newfoundland, where two hundred English had already fallen before his sword and seven hundred been captured. On the 7th of April, 1697, Sérigny, his brother, was despatched from France with five men-of-war—the *Pelican,* the *Palmier,* the *Profond,* the *Wasp,* the *Violent*—to be placed under Iberville's command at Placentia, Newfoundland, whence he was to proceed to Hudson's Bay, with orders "to leave not a vestige remaining" of the English fur trade in the north.

The squadron left Newfoundland on

JEAN BAPTISTE LE MOYNE BIENVILLE
(Brother to Iberville. From an old print)

July 8. By the 25th the ships had entered the straits amid berg and floe, with the long transparent daylight when sunset merges with sunrise. Iberville was on the *Pelican* with Bienville, his brother, two hundred and fifty men, and fifty guns. The other brother, Sérigny, commanded the *Palmier,* and Edward Fitzmaurice, of Kerry, a Jacobite, had come as chaplain. A gun gone loose in the hold of the *Wasp* had caused some damage, and forty men were disabled from scurvy on the *Pelican,* when the ships succeeded in reaching the inner side of the straits at Cape Digges. Here the ice, contracted by the straits, locked around them in an iron grip. Fog fell, concealing the ships from each other, except for the ensigns at the masts' heads, which showed all the fleet driven far southward, except Iberville's *Pelican.* For eighteen days the impatient raider found himself forcibly anchored to the ice-floes in fog, his ship crushed and banged and bodily lifted until perhaps a powder blast released pressure, or holes drilled and filled with bombs broke the ice-crush, or, unshipping the rudder, his men disembarked and, up to the waist in ice slush, towed the *Pelican* forward. On the 25th of August, at four in the morning, the fog suddenly lifted. Iberville saw that the *Pelican* had been carried back in the straits. The *Wasp* and *Violent* had disappeared; but straight to the fore, ice-jammed, were the *Profond,* and —Iberville could scarcely believe the evidence of his eyes—three English men-of-war, the *Hampshire* and *Dering* and *Hudson's Bay,* closing in a circle round the ill-fated French ship. Just at that moment, the ice loosening, Iberville was off like a bird on the *Pelican,* not waiting to see what became of the *Profond,* which escaped from the ice that night after a day's bombardment, when the English were in the act of running across the ice for a hand-to-hand fight.

On the 3d of September Iberville was before Port Nelson. Anxiously he scanned the sea during two days for the rest of his fleet. On the morning of the 5th the sails of three vessels rose above the horizon of the sea. Raising anchor, Iberville hastened to meet them and signalled them welcome. No response signalled back. The horrified watch at the masthead called down some warning. Then the full extent of the terrible mistake dawned on Iberville. These were not *his* consort ships at all. They were the English men-of-war, the *Hampshire,* fifty-two guns; the *Dering,* thirty; the *Hudson's Bay,* thirty-two—hemming him in a fatal circle between the English foe on land and their own cannon to sea.

One can imagine the wild shout of jubilation that went up from the two hundred and fifty Englishmen of the *Hampshire* to see their enemy of ten years' merciless raids now hopelessly trapped between their fleet and the fort. The English vessels had the wind, and raced over the waves, all sails set, like war-horses eager for battle. Iberville did not wait. He had weighed anchor to sail out when he thought the vessels were his own; and now he kept on his course. Of his original crew, forty were ill of scurvy. Some twenty-five had been sent ashore to reconnoitre. Counting the Canadians and Indians taken on at Newfoundland, he could muster only one hundred and fifty fighting-men. Quickly ropes were stretched to give the forces handhold over the frost-slippery decks. Stoppers were ripped from the fifty cannon, and the batterymen below under La Salle and Grandville had stripped off their shirts for the furnace of flame and powder that was to be their portion in the impending battle. Bienville, Iberville's brother, swung the infantrymen in line abovedecks, swords and pistols in hands, prepared for the hand-to-hand grapple that was bound to come against such desperate odds. De la Potherie got the Canadians to the forecastle, all ready to board when the ships knocked keels. Iberville knew it was to be like those old-time raids—a fight to the death, or victory; and on he swept, right up to the *Hampshire,* the strongest of the foe, where every shot would tell. The *Hampshire* shifted broadsides to the French, and at nine in the morning let go two roaring cannonades that ploughed up the *Pelican's* decks and stripped the French of masts naked to the hull. At the same instant the *Dering* and *Hudson's Bay,* which had circled to the left of the French, poured a musketry fire across the *Pelican's* stern. At one fell blast forty French had been mowed down, but the batterymen below never ceased their torrent of balls straight into the *Hampshire's* hull; and Iberville shouted for the infantrymen to fire into the *Dering's* forecastle, and the Canadian sharpshooters to rake the decks of the *Hudson's Bay.* For three and a half hours the three-cornered battle raged. The ships were so close, shout and countershout could be heard across decks. Faces were literally singed with the musketry fire. Ninety French were wounded. The *Pelican's* decks swam in blood. Grapeshot and grenade had set the fallen sails in flame. Railings were gone overdecks, the bridge crumbling, a gaping wound in the hull of the French ship to fore; and still the batterymen below poured their storm of fire and bomb into the English hull. The fighters were so close, one old record says, and the holes torn by the bombs so large in the hull of each ship, that the gunners on the *Pelican* were looking into the very eyes of the smoke-grimed men belowdecks in the *Hampshire.* For three hours the English had tacked to board the *Pelican;* and the mastless, splintered *Pelican* had fought like a demon to cripple her enemy's approach. The men of both decks had rushed *en masse* for the last hand-to-hand fight, when a wild shout went up from the remnants of the French. The batteries of the *Hampshire* were suddenly silenced. The great ship refused to answer to the wheel. That persistent, undeviating fire belching from the sides of the *Pelican* had done its work. The *Hampshire* gave a quick back lurch. Before the amazed Frenchmen could believe their eyes, amid the roar of flame and crashing billow, all sails set, the *Hampshire* settled and sank like a stone amid the engulfing seas. Not a soul of her two hundred and fifty men escaped. The screams of the struggling seamen had

WRECK OF THE "PELICAN"
Crew landing after sinking the "Hampshire" and capturing the "Hudson's Bay"
(From an old engraving)

not died on the waves before Iberville had turned the batteries of his shattered ship full force on the *Hudson's Bay.* Promptly the *Hudson's Bay* struck colors; but while Iberville was engaged loading his captives and taking over ninety prisoners, the *Dering* showed swift heel and gained Fort Nelson.

In the fury and heat of the fight, the French had not noticed the gathering storm that now broke with hurricane gusts of sleet and rain. The hawser that towed the captive ship snapped like a thread. Captor and captive in vain threw out anchors. The anchors raked bottom. Cables were cut, and the two ships drove along the sands before the wind. The deck of the *Pelican* was now icy with blood. Every shock of smashing billows jumbled dead and dying *en masse.* The night grew black as pitch. The little railing that still clung to the shattered decks of the *Pelican* was now

washed away, and the waves carried off dead and wounded. Tables were hurled from the cabin. The rudder was broken; and the water was already to the bridge of the floundering ship when the hull began to split and the *Pelican* buried her prow in the sands six miles from the fort. All small boats had been shot away. The canoes of the Canadians were swamped as they were launched. Tying the spars of the shattered masts in four-sided racks, Iberville had the wounded bound to these and towed ashore by the others, half swimming, half wading. Many of the men sprang into the sea half naked as they had fought. Guns and powder-horns, held high above heads, were all that was saved of the wreck. Eighteen more men lost their lives trying to swim ashore. On land, the castaways found two feet of snow. For twelve hours they had fought, without pause for food; and now, shivering round fires kindled in the bush, the half-famished men devoured moss and seaweed raw. It was at this terrible pass that the other ships of Iberville's fleet came to his rescue. They, too, had suffered from the storm, the *Violent* having gone to bottom, the *Palmier* having lost her steering-gear.

Nelson, or York, was the usual four-bastioned fur-post, with palisades and houses of white fir logs a foot thick, the pickets punctured for small arms, with embrasures for some hundred cannon. It stood some paces back from Hayes River, four miles up from the sea. The ship *Hudson's Bay* had also been wrecked, and her seamen carried to Governor Bailey of the fort word of Iberville's desperate plight. Nor was Bailey inclined to surrender even after the other ships came to Iberville's aid. With Bailey in the fort was that Smithsend who had been sold to slavery in Martinique by the French. When Iberville's messenger was led into the council-hall with flag of truce and bandaged eyes to demand surrender, Smithsend advised resistance till the English knew whether Iberville had been lost in the wreck. Fog favored the French. By the 11th they had been able to get their cannon ashore undetected by the English, so near the fort that the first intimation was the blow of hammers in erecting platforms. This drew the fire of the English, and the cannonading began on both sides. On the 12th Sérigny entered the council again to demand surrender.

"If you refuse, there will be no quarter," he warned.

"Quarter be cursed!" thundered the old governor. Then turning to his men, "Forty pounds sterling to every man who fights."

But the Canadians, with all the savagery of Indian warfare, had begun hacking down palisades to the rear. Sérigny came once more from the French. "They are desperate," he urged. "They must take the fort or pass the winter like beasts in the wilds." Bombs had been shattering the houses. Bailey was induced to capitulate, but, game to the end, haggled for the best bargain he could get. Neither the furs nor the armaments of the fort were granted him; but he was permitted to march out with his people unharmed, drum beating, flag unfurled, ball in mouth, match lighted, bag and baggage, fife screaming its shrillest defiance—to march out with all this brave pomp to a desolate winter in the wilds, while the wood-lopers led by Boisbriant ransacked the fort.

The Treaty of Ryswick put an end to the raids. Iberville sailed away to fresh glories. A seigniory had been granted him along the Bay of Chaleurs. In 1699 he was created Chevalier of St. Louis. The rest of his years were passed founding the colony of Louisiana; and he visited Boston and New York harbors with plans of conquest in his mind, though, as the Earl of Belmont reported, he pretended it was for wood and water. In the war of the Barbadoes he hoped to capture slaves for Louisiana, and had transported hundreds; but yellow fever raged in the South and Iberville fell a victim to it on July 9, 1706. He was perhaps the most picturesque type of Canada's wild wood chivalry, with all its savage faults and romantic heroism.

And his Majesty the King of France, well pleased with the success of his brave raiders, sends out a musty old despatch that reads: "*His Majesty declines to accept the white bear sent to him from Hudson's Bay, but he will permit the fur traders to exhibit the animal.*"

HUNTING THE GRIZZLY BEAR

THE bear, like man, inhabits almost every latitude and every land, and has even been translated to the starry heavens, where the constellations of the Great Dipper and the Little Dipper are known to us as well as to the ancients as *Ursi Major* and *Minor*. But North America furnishes the largest and most aggressive species in the grizzly (*Ursus horribilis*), the black (*Ursus americanus*), and the polar (*Ursus maritimus*) bears, and here the hunter finds his most daring sport. Of all the known plantigrades (flat-footed beasts) the grizzly is the most savage and the most dreaded, and he is the largest of all, saving the presence of his cousin the polar bear, for which, nevertheless, he is more than a match in strength and courage. Some specimens measure seven feet from tip of nose to root of tail. The distinctive marks of the species are its great size; the shortness of the tail as compared with the ears; the huge flat paws, the sole of the hind-foot sometimes measuring seven and a half by five inches in a large male; the length of the hind-legs as compared with the forelegs, which gives the beast his awkward, shambling gait; the long claws of the forefoot, sometimes seven inches in length, while those of the hind-foot measure only three or four; the erect, bristling mane of stiff hair, often six inches long; the coarse hair of the body, sometimes three inches long, dark at the base, but with light tips. He has a dark stripe along the back, and one along each side, the hair on his body being, as a rule, a brownish-yellow, the region around the ears dusky, the legs nearly black, and the muzzle pale. Color, however, is not a distinctive mark, for female grizzlies have been killed in company with two cubs, of which one was brown, the other gray, or one dark, the other light; and the supposed species of "cinnamon" and "brown" bears are merely color variations of *Ursus horribilis* himself.

This ubiquitous gentleman has a wide range for his *habitat*. He has been found on the Missouri River from Fort Pierce northward, and thence west to his favorite haunts in the Rockies. Individuals have been found on the Pacific slope clear down to the coast. He is found as far south as Mexico, as far north as the Great Slave Lake in British America. He not only ranges everywhere, but eats everything. His majesty is a good liver. He is not properly a beast of prey, for he has neither the cat-like instincts nor the noiseless tread of the *felidæ*, nor is he fleet and long-winded like the wolf, although good at a short run, as an unlucky hunter may find. But he hangs about the flanks of a herd of buffalo, with probably an eye to a wounded or disabled animal, and he frequently raids a ranch and carries off a sheep, hog, or calf penned beyond hope of escape. Elk is his favorite meat, and the knowing hunter who has the good luck to kill an elk makes sure that its carcass will draw Mr. Grizzly if he is within a range of five miles. He will eat not only flesh, fish, and fowl, but roots, herbs, fruit, vegetables, honey, and insects as well. Plums, buffalo-berries, and chokecherries make a large part of his diet in their seasons.

The grizzly bear possesses greater vitality and tenacity of life than any other animal on the continent, and the hunter who would hunt him must be well armed and keep a steady nerve. Each shot must be coolly put where it will do the most good. Several are usually necessary to stop one of these savage beasts. A single bullet lodged in the brain is fatal. If shot through the heart he may run a quarter of a mile or kill a man before he succumbs. In the days of the old muzzle-loading rifle it was hazardous indeed to hunt the grizzly, and many a man has paid the penalty of his folly with his life. With our improved breech-loading and repeating rifles there is less risk.

THE GRIZZLY AND HIS PREY.

The grizzly is said to bury carcasses of large animals for future use as food, but this I doubt. He hibernates during winter, but does not take to his long sleep until the winter has thoroughly set in and the snow is quite deep. He may frequently be tracked and found in snow a foot deep, where he is roaming in search of food. He becomes very fat before going into winter-quarters, and this vast accumulation of oil furnishes nutriment and heat sufficient to sustain life during his long confinement.

The newspapers often kill grizzlies weighing 1500, 1800, or even 2000 pounds, and in any party of frontiersmen "talking grizzly" you will find plenty of men who can give day, time, and place where he killed or helped to kill at least 1800 pounds of Bruin.

"Did you weigh it?"

"No, we didn't weigh 'im; but every man as seed 'im said he would weigh that, and they was all good jedges too."

And this is the way most of the stories of big bear, big elk, big deer, etc., begin and end. Bears are usually, though not always, killed at considerable distances from towns, or even ranches, where it is not easy to find a pair of scales.

The largest I have ever seen would not weigh more than 700 or 800 pounds, and I do not believe one has ever lived that would weigh 1000 pounds. The flesh of the adult grizzly is tough, stringy, and decidedly unpalatable, but that of a young fat one is tender and juicy, and is always a welcome dish on the hunter's table.

The female usually gives birth to two cubs, and sometimes three, at a time. At birth they weigh only about 1¼ to 1½ pounds each. The grizzly breeds readily in confinement, and several litters have been produced in the Zoological Gardens at Cincinnati. The female is unusually vicious while rearing her young, and the hunter must be doubly cautious about attacking at that time. An Indian rarely attacks a grizzly single-handed at any time, and it is only when several of their native hunters are together that they will attempt to kill one. They value the claws very highly, however, and take great pride in wearing strings of them around their necks.

The grizzly usually frequents the timbered or brush-covered portions of mountainous regions, or the timbered valleys of streams that head in the mountains. He occasionally follows down the course of these streams, and even travels many miles from one stream to another, or from one range of mountains to another, across open prairie. I once found one on a broad open plateau in the Big Horn Mountains, about half a mile from the nearest cover of any kind. He was turning over rocks in search of worms. At the report of my rifle he started for the nearest cañon, but never reached it. An explosive bullet through his lungs rendered him unequal to the journey.

Few persons believe that a grizzly will attack a man before he is himself attacked. I was one of these doubting Thomases until two years ago, when I was thoroughly convinced by ocular demonstration that some grizzlies, at least, will attempt to make a meal off a man even though he may not have harmed them previously. We were hunting in the Shoshone Mountains in northern Wyoming. I had killed a large elk in the morning, and on going back to the carcass in the afternoon to skin it we saw that Bruin had been there ahead of us, but had fled on our approach. Without the least apprehension of his return, we leaned our rifles against a tree about fifty feet away, and commenced work. There were three of us, but only two rifles, Mr. Huffman, the photographer, having left his in camp. He had finished taking views of the carcass, and we were all busily engaged skinning, when, hearing a crashing in the brush and a series of savage roars and growls, we looked up the hill, and were horrified to see three grizzly bears, an old female and two cubs about two-thirds grown, charging upon us with all the savage fury of a pack of starving wolves upon a sheepfold.

They were between us and our rifles

when we first saw them, and we sprang to our horses, which were picketed a few yards below, supposing, of course, that when the bears reached the elk carcass they would proceed to eat it, and pay no further attention to us. Strange to say, it was the carcass to which they paid no attention. They still came after us; we had no time for flight, and could not even release and mount our terror-stricken horses. Our only chance was to fight for our lives, and with one accord we all three grasped our hunting-knives and dashed at them. We threw our hats and yelled like Comanches, and the savage brutes, seeing themselves thus boldly confronted by equal numbers, stopped, raised on their haunches, growled, snapped their jaws for a few moments, and then walked sullenly back up the hill into the brush. This gave us an opportunity to get hold of our rifles, and then it was our turn to charge. To make a long story short, we killed the old female and one cub; the other escaped into the jungle before we could get a shot at him. The resolute front we put on alone saved our lives.

The grizzly is partially nocturnal in his habits, and apparently divides his labor of obtaining food and his travelling about equally between day and night. It is not definitely known to what age he lives in his wild state, but he is supposed to attain to twenty-five or thirty years.

Notwithstanding the great courage and ferocity of this formidable beast, he will utter the most pitiable groans and howls when seriously or mortally wounded.

Another instance of a grizzly making an unprovoked attack upon a man was vouched for by a man whom I know to be strictly truthful. Two brothers were prospecting in a range of mountains near the head waters of the Stinking Water river. The younger of the two, though an able-bodied man, and capable of doing a good day's work with a pick or shovel, was weak-minded, and the elder brother never allowed him to go any distance away from camp or their work alone. He, however, sent him one evening to the spring, a few rods off, to bring a kettleful of water. The spring was in a deep gorge, and the trail to it wound through some fissures in the rock. As the young man passed under a shelving rock, an immense old female grizzly, that had taken up temporary quarters there, reached out and struck a powerful blow at his head, but fortunate-

Drawn by J. Carter Beard.

"VIGOROUSLY BELABORING THE BEAR OVER THE HEAD WITH THE CAMP KETTLE."

ly could not reach far enough to do him any serious harm. The blow knocked his hat off, and her claws caught his scalp, and laid it open clear across the top of his head in several ugly gashes. The force of the blow sent him spinning around, and not knowing enough to be frightened, he attacked her savagely with the only weapon he had at hand—the camp kettle. The elder brother heard the racket, and hastily catching up his rifle, found his brother vigorously belaboring the bear over the head with the camp kettle, and the bear striking at him savage blows, any one of which, if she could have reached him, would have torn his head from his shoulders. Three bullets from the rifle, fired in rapid succession, loosened her hold upon the rocks, and she tumbled lifelessly into the trail. The poor idiotic boy could not even then realize the danger through which he had passed, and could only appease his anger by continuing to maul the bear over the head with the camp kettle for several minutes after she was dead.

The skin of the grizzly is one of the most valuable trophies a sportsman can obtain on any field, and its rarity, and the danger and excitement attending the taking of it, the courage it bespeaks, render it a prize of which the winner may justly feel proud for a lifetime.

The best localities in which to hunt the grizzly bear—that is, those most accessible and in which he is the most numerous— are the Big Horn, Shoshone, Wind River, Bear Tooth, Belt, and Crazy mountains, in Wyoming and Montana, all of which may be easily reached by way of the Northern Pacific road.

The best time of year to hunt for this as well as all the other species of large game in the Rocky Mountains is in the months of September, October, and November, though in the latter month the sportsman should not venture high up into the mountains where heavy snowfalls occur. There is a great deal of this class of hunting done in the summer months, but it is contrary to the laws of nature, and should not be indulged in by any true sportsman. The skins are nearly worthless then, while in the autumn they are prime; the heat is oppressive, and the flies and mosquitoes are great pests. The best arm for this class of game is a repeating rifle of large calibre, 45 or 50, carrying a large charge of powder and a solid bullet. The Winchester Express, $\frac{50}{95}$, with its new solid ball, is perhaps the best in the market, all things considered. There are several methods of hunting him, the most common being to kill an elk, and then watch the carcass. Shots may frequently be obtained in this way early in the morning or late in the evening, and on bright moonlight nights it is best to watch all night, for the immense size of the grizzly renders him an easy target at short range even by moonlight. Another method is to still-hunt him, the same as is done with deer. This is perhaps the most sportsmanlike of all, and if a coulee or creek bottom be selected where there are plenty of berries, or an open, hilly, rocky country where the bears are in the habit of hunting for worms, or any good feeding ground where bear signs are plentiful, and due care and caution be exercised, there is as good a chance of success as by any other method. Many hunters set guns with a cord running from the trigger to a bait of fresh meat, and the muzzle of the gun pointing at the meat; others set large steel-traps or dead-falls. But such contrivances are never used by true sportsmen.

Game of any kind should always be pursued in a fair, manly manner, and given due chance to preserve its life if it is skilful enough to do so. If captured, let it be by the superior skill, sagacity, or endurance of the sportsman, not by traps which close on it as it innocently and unsuspectingly seeks its food.

Grizzly bear hunting is unquestionably the grandest sport that our continent can afford. The grizzly is the only really dangerous game we have, and the decidedly hazardous character of the sport is what gives it its greatest zest, and renders it the most fascinating of pursuits. Many sportsmen proclaim the superiority of their favorite pastime over all other kinds, be it quail, grouse, or duck shooting, fox-chasing, deer-stalking, or what not; and each has its charm, more or less intense, according to its nature; but no man ever felt his heart swell with pride, his nerves tingle with animation, his whole system glow with wild, uncontrollable enthusiasm, at the bagging of any bird or small animal, as does the man who stands over the prostrate form of a monster grizzly that he has slain. Let the devotee of these other classes of sport try bear hunting, and when he has bagged his first grizzly, then let him talk!

WINTER IN CANADA

A CROWD of homespun peasants stood about me at the end of the little public hall, their sunburned faces twisting and working at drawing their pipes and emphasizing their good-humored talk. Others still came in through the door, bringing a turnip, a pair of woollen socks, or a salted eel, although the table was already piled high with such odds and ends from the farm, the house, or the sea. A clerk and a treasurer presided there, conferring and noting with the important air of public officers. The auctioneer on the platform took an astonished fowl by the legs, and holding it up to the gaze of all, opened the religious ceremony of Allsaints' Day.

"A cock for the souls in purgatory; he's fat, gentlemen, and as good as ever you tasted in your mortal lives. How much am I offered? Six sous—six sous—six. And remember, lads, he's ready for the spurs. Just look at that eye! For the souls in purgatory. A fine fat cock. How much? Twelve sous, Mr. Dubé? Yes, sir. Eighteen—eighteen—eighteen. Come, now, you fowl people, what's the matter this year? You don't seem half alive. A shilling, Mr. Gagnon—one shilling—one—one. Thirty sous, Mr. Dubé—thirty sous once, t-h-i-r-t-y sous twice, thirty sous three times. Sold to Mr. Dubé for thirty sous." And the treasurer of souls entered the item in his memorandum.

"I'm holding back for the geese," said a man at my elbow; and, as if in reply, the geese and turkeys set up a cackling that drowned every other sound. "Don't you want to buy something, sir?"

"Well, I don't know," said I. "You see, I have nobody down there to receive it; and if it went to one of your people, a Protestant turnip might disagree with a Catholic."

The sale of fowls presently ended, and the boys went off with their purchases to have a cock-fight in the barn-yard. Then a turnip was put up for sale, and raised to the price of three thirty-sou pieces.

"But that's very dear for a turnip—the price of a whole bushel."

"Yes, sir; but we don't mind the expense for a soul."

The tinsmith here struggled by me to hand in a bright tin pail.

"What's that for, Tanis?"

"Oh, it's for the souls"—only he said, "pour les *ânes*." He had assumed an air of compassionate ridicule that he thought in harmony with my feeling for this ceremony. But as I did not respond outwardly to this treatment of their convictions, he at once resumed his faithfulness.

"But," I said, seriously, "aren't you afraid the solder will melt in purgatory?"

"But, sir," he explained, earnestly, "we don't send these things to our parents—it's the money. That is, we sell whatever any one can spare from his household, and the money we give to the priest to pay for masses, at twenty-five cents apiece, to be said for the souls in purgatory. That is the way we help them out, for it's a poor place to live in."

After mass the sale was completed. And the mysterious world of souls must have rejoiced exceedingly at the high prices of geese and socks and onions.

Meanwhile a very different scene was passing in the cemetery. There on the graves were figures kneeling in silent prayer, while the cold wind moaned through the bare trees.

My winter in Canada opened with this singular scene at the Rivière Ouelle, a parish on the south shore of the St. Lawrence, about seventy-five miles east of Quebec. The village would scarcely exist without the bridge, the convent, and the church on the banks of the little winding river, for the houses are scattered along the roads leading off across the plain. And although the plain is almost treeless and bare, yet the place presents a certain picturesque effect, derived from its quaint and simple civilization. The receding lines of gables and chimneys down the roads, each with its stream of white smoke, the long low barns with great windmills striding through the air, the schooners and lumber lighters laid up on the bank, the haycocks far off on the edge of the salt-meadows along the two bays, the long fences of dark wicker-work running out over the mud-flats to catch eels, the point of rocks

A MOOSE-HUNTERS' CAMP.

and forest separating the bays, and far out in the St. Lawrence, a pound or yard made of stakes to capture white porpoises—all these details serve to interest and please the eye. But the more distant features are much more striking. Southward, about the edge of the plain, bold hills partly hide the neighboring parishes of Ste. Anne, St. Pacome, St. Philippe, and others. Northward, across twenty-one miles of the swift and turbulent currents of the St. Lawrence, the Laurentides rise to the clouds, and shelter in their deep gorges and on their high cultivated slopes St. Paul's Bay, Les Éboulements, Murray Bay, and other parishes of the north shore. This great arm of the sea, the Gulf of St. Lawrence, presents its most impressive aspect at this season. In fancy I run over again the lower Gulf, and see the exceptional phases of life along its hundreds of miles of shores. The waters are among the most dangerous and angry in the world. The belated vessels caught in October and November gales are driven about in the treacherous currents or in the blinding snow till they ground on some reef or bar far out from land. The crew escape perhaps in boats, to reach a land where an arctic winter must be passed, perhaps, in starving and freezing on some barren island. Later in the winter hunters creep over the fields of ice along shore to shoot seals, until the wind or tide changes, and threatens to carry their treacherous float out to sea. A seal-hunter, thus carried away from Ilette, drifted helplessly past the parish steeples ringing the *angelus*, till he was found frozen to death while kneeling and staring up at this pitiless arctic sky.

This polar sea has a hideous smile in winter—a chilling gleam on its black tortuous face. If you looked along the deserted Labrador coast you would see the few fishermen retired to their inland huts in the gorges of the rivers, where they find a little wood—the only luxury of the country. The mail-carriers are making one of their bi-winter trips on snow-shoes, going from twelve to fifteen miles per day along the beaches and across the gulches, and cursing the idiots who send for newspapers or books in the winter. Farther inland the Indians are wandering over the wilderness of snow, tagged at their heels by death and starvation; and wherever the forest offers good trees the lumbermen are at work cutting timber. In the

depths of the woods the moose-hunters build their camps and bring their noble game to bay. Coming farther up the Gulf we reach the inhabited regions along each shore of the river, the parishes of this quaint old French colony of Quebec. But even here this arm of the northern sea is dreaded, whether it lies still with a sinister gleam under the clear sunshine, or hides its resistless anger under the veil of a lightsome gale of snow. Those living on the islands might well make their wills, as in old times, before crossing to the main. They embark in long wooden canoes having a very wide keel shod with iron, which serves as a runner for sliding the boat over the ice. And, strange to say, the elements seem to respect these fearless boatmen, rapidly paddling over the water, or hauling their craft over the open fields of ice. But in looking across this immense flood, the waters of half a continent, I am glad to be ashore among a people living close together for shelter and warmth under an arctic winter.

The parish put on early the mourning of fall. The fields were already empty and white, the grain having but just escaped the fate of a previous crop, which had been buried under twelve inches of snow before it was even cut. The fishermen had taken up their nets and weirs along the beach to save them from the ice drifting with the tide. The cattle had been gathered into the stables, to remain for seven, perhaps eight, long months. The garden of the Abbé C——, inclosed with a high board fence, had even an unusual sentiment of seclusion about its sheltered walks; the leaves had been whirled into nooks and hollows; the statues of the Virgin and St. Joseph had left their bowers for the shelter of the house; the rustic seats were stowed in the loft of the summer-house, and the apple-trees were scaffolded with great stakes to keep their branches from breaking under the snow-drifts that will overtop them. The poor accepted the only bounty of nature in this winter snow, and banked it up about their cabins. The people collected everything into the barn and the house, put up double sashes and doors—in short, they went into their burrows to hibernate. The sentiment of the season is well told in a daily custom; for November is the "month of the dead," when this Catholic people respond to the mourn-

THE MOOSE AT BAY.

ing of nature. Every evening at eight o'clock the church bell tolls as for a funeral, while in every home the family kneels and blends a *de profundis* with the moaning night wind.

The winter brought out many quaint features of life. The people seemed to change into animals in their caps and coats of fur; the beggars all at once became more aggressive by their sharper needs, and more noticeable in their queer, cumbersome wraps; and travellers now settled down almost out of sight in the sleigh robes. The boys brought out their primitive sleds, and with their old skates showed how little practice they have on ice in this snowy latitude. Some of the girls came to the store or to evening prayers at the church on snow-shoes when the fences were covered, and many wearing buckskin moccasins walked about with the noiseless tread of Indians. As I walked the bridge in the biting air, and watched these silent motions and peculiar features of Canadian winter life, the earth seemed to be muffled, and life to go on in an underhanded, secret way. And to the eye nature was in a masquerade. For winter beyond the northern mountains often hides behind a mirror reflecting the sunny, balmy south. At sunset the heavens, glowing with gold and crimson clouds, picture the tropics; even the mountain-tops flush with the memory of summer thus revived. But the air has no poetic languor and mystery. When the vision fades, grim winter looks down from a leaden sky, and the world becomes dumb in the gray pallor of death. Then the old manor, hovering low under its great roof, and lighting up its crimson curtains, invites me to take shelter from the chill of an arctic night, and I gladly retreat from the outer world to give myself up to the warmth and cheer of social life.

The domestic life of this French-Canadian Catholic people charms me with its simplicity, contentment, and courtesy. It is a mellow civilization on this crude continent, the strongest contrast to the life of our enterprising, practical, unfinished republic. This difference between us is due very much to the aims and methods of our respective growths. The Pilgrim was a man who fled from Europe, left behind him all the old baggage of that civilization, and landed in America as an unincumbered worker to establish a self-supporting, free, eager nation: he founded a *new* England. The French colonist left Europe to extend the dominions of Rome and France, and landed here, loaded with the Catholic Church, to establish a colony modelled on the most complex and polished civilization of the Old World, and destined to be for a long while pitifully dependent on the mother country: he founded a *new* France in which there was nothing new. And such has been the weight of his Catholic burden that he has never stirred from his tracks, although within sight and sound of our loud and vigorous march. He has kept to his ancient traditions with such surprising fidelity that to-day Old France stands on the shores of the St. Lawrence, and New France on the banks of the Seine. Our civilization sprang from a new birth, and it has not outgrown the vigor, eagerness, and crudeness of youth. Canadian life began with the immigration of a completed society, and it has preserved the mellowness of its ancient existence. After the conquest in 1760 French-Canadian society was inevitably very much disorganized. But patriotic zeal and the conservative influence of the Catholic Church have kept the French-Canadians a united and separate people to this day. The only marked change that has occurred in the composition of society is the loss of the nobility and the legal suppression of the seigniors. In this parish to-day I still find virtually the classes and characters of two hundred years ago—seigniors, priests, gentlemen, peasants—and also a civilization that, in spirit at least, might take its place in a picture of the seventeenth century. For the Catholic institutions of learning avow the principle of preserving exactly the spirit and the form that governed their foundation: the world may move if it like, but they move not. The Canadian girls are all educated at convents, where the course of instruction is marked by many religious services, the routine of old-fashioned narrow instruction, the observance of etiquette, the neglect of health, and the teaching of orderly habits and good moral conduct. On coming home the young women are noticeable for their modest and extremely lady-like manners.

The gentlemen have been educated in virtually the same spirit, but they enjoy a little wider range of topics. Their college course leads chiefly through the ultra-classical and literary fields, all the time guided exclusively by the influence of the Church. They generally remain strangers to the modern discoveries in the arts, sciences, and even industries. As their minds are somewhat benumbed by a routine course of study, appealing almost entirely to the faculty of memory, they very seldom have any love of reading when turned loose in practical life. And all their habits, customs, feelings, are moulded more or less on the pattern of the unpractical, conservative, polished gentleman of old times.

Such a high and unpractical education of the gentry, and entire neglect of the peasantry, tend, of course, to sharp class distinctions, and bring about a state of society quite impossible in our democratic nation. We can not, however, fail to enjoy as well as note some of these peculiarities. For example, in every one of these parishes, without wealth and its privileges, I meet with some of the most refined pleasures. The priest, notaries, lawyers, doctors, and a merchant or two, together with the ladies of their families, form a circle that has been polished by this classical education and generations of good-breeding. Perhaps the most interesting element in this study of Canadian life is this feature—the superiority of the people over their house and furniture. For in our day of increasing luxury it is an invaluable lesson to see polished persons happy in extreme economy and simplicity of living. The situation is quite marked. In material, intellectual, and æsthetic matters no region presents fewer activities to in-

BREAD-MAKING AND WEAVING.

terest an educated mind. There are no studies to improve industries or agriculture, no public works to discuss, no reforms to agitate. The handful of newspapers coming into the parish are utterly worthless to an intelligent mind, for they are filled with trashy serial stories and politico-personal matters of incredible insignificance; even the few books in the best houses are the safe old classics, or goody-goody weaklings of newer birth. There are no lectures, no radical talkers in private circles. The only instructor of this people is the priest, and you might as well dig their fields for diamonds as search their minds for gleaming ideas. Reading is not a necessity, nor even a custom, in most of these educated families. The ladies are occupied mostly with light house-

hold labors, a little visiting, and religious services at the church mornings and evenings. They are industrious in labors of direct utility, not in artistic or intellectual accomplishments.

The gentlemen idle away the time not required by their labors. Here and there, of course, one meets a man who occupies the large leisure of this quiet life with some study. He may be a priest whose native energy has not been smothered, or an unusual professional man. Yet, in spite of the narrowness of this existence, life here is full of a certain charm that you can very seldom find, and in only small circles, in our republic. Life here is a calm success, the possession rather than the chase of happiness. I am not philosopher enough to trace this success to either the Catholic subjection of the people or to the system of a limited monarchy; but as an observer of men and manners I see that this national happiness comes chiefly from a near and homely source quite accessible to all peoples—the practice of politeness. Courtesy is the common rule of conduct here, no matter how intimate or how indifferent the relations may be between servants, friends, strangers, relatives. Your feelings are as safe as your life. French-Canadian coun-

THE OLD MANOR-HOUSE.

try society, then, differs from ours in presenting greater extremes—a peasantry that is ignorant, unenterprising, contented, devout, and a small class of gentry that is educated, polished, conservative. And all classes unite to render a humdrum existence agreeable by the arts of polite intercourse.

But I hasten to show the reader the homes of these two classes, and give a glimpse of the winter life of a Canadian parish. The old manor - house may be chosen as the representative of the homes of the gentry. The exterior is perfectly plain—low stone walls, a high steep roof pierced with many dormer-windows. It crouches down comfortably among the snow-drifts, yet keeps an open eye on the passengers. My rapping on the bright brass door-knocker brings at once the master of the house to welcome me with a manner that mingles delightfully the courtesy of France with a little of the freedom and heartiness of America. He soon unloads me of furs in the hall, while

his good-humor and wit find many pleasant little bits of talk that come through the snow shaken off my cap and coat. On entering the sitting-room the formal salutations are renewed, although I have already met the entire family once or twice to-day. But no constraint is felt in the ease and grace of habitual courtesy. Then I sit down among them, and under the charm of pleasant intercourse I almost forget to notice that the interior is as plain as the outside of the old house. There are no objects of adornment in either good or bad taste. But there is a quiet richness in the bare, unpainted walls that have changed with age to a soft misty brown hue, in the old mahogany furniture, the low ceiling, crossed by great beams casting shadows. And the whole scene is made pleasant with low lights and a peaceful spirit.

The mother and her daughters sit about the table, and knit or sew. They all are black-eyed brunettes, distinguished from the average French - Canadian peasant women by being more slender and graceful. The mother would be remarked chiefly for her shrewd intelligence in practical matters. One of the daughters, also engrossed by practical interests, is a young lady of a striking French type, a tall symmetrical person, with red cheeks and black hair, and a carriage that is stylish. Another is a dainty French miss, with a graceful figure, pale, delicate features, and large black eyes that respond to the faintest sparkle of humor. There is a girl that brightens the air with her pretty lightsome face and merry laughter, and yet subdues her child-like moods with decorum. I have had a still nearer glimpse of the character of Canadian girls by seeing the rooms of two young ladies of education. The apartments were neat, and orderly even to stiffness. They showed neither pretension nor taste in the arrangement of the plain furniture and poor draperies. But the rooms of these maidens gave me a strong impression of modesty, simplicity, and devotion. Subdued lights fell on the photographs of only their nearest relatives, on a crucifix and vial of holy water above the bed, on a prayer-bench at the foot, and on two or three framed tableaux of Biblical subjects, little porcelain figures of St. Joseph and Mary, among pebbles and moss. The girls were none the less attractive in these subdued surroundings. It all gave me a delightful impression to see the lightness and beauty of youth sheltered by reserve and simplicity. The sons of this family are college students, young gentlemen imbued with the feelings of a superior class. They generally despise manual labor. Even the poorest of them must be waited on and maintained in a style due to his rank; but, considering the constraints connected with such a position, they seem quite sensible and unaffected fellows. The head of the family is a notary, one of the chief dignitaries of this well-regulated community, organized under the laws and customs of France. He is a round-headed, muscular man, of a conservative, comfortable character. The only event that disturbs the ease and quiet of his social existence is an election.

The general life of the family may be surmised from what precedes. The ladies are generally busy with household mat-

ON THE ROAD.

ters, and a little visiting; religious ceremonies at church and at home occupy much of the time.

The gentlemen very commonly spend the evening smoking, drinking very moderately, and chatting, at one another's houses. Now and then a walk on snow-shoes, a sleigh-ride, or a hunting trip to the woods takes the young people out. But weddings, baptisms, and dinners are by no means sufficiently frequent in the small circle to afford regular entertainment. The people are thrown upon their individual resources. And although the lack of reading and the conservative tendency of intellectual life exclude new or important subjects, social life here presents many strong attractions. The people are all ready talkers in a manner that is sympathetic and somewhat dramatic. They make it a habit to be entertaining and sociable, and they inherit the cheerful and contented disposition of the French. I am surprised to see how agreeable a commonplace existence is made simply by the arts of polite intercourse, without much dependence on literature, fine arts, sciences, and set amusements.

Of course there are in the country exceptional individuals whose reading carries them beyond this narrow field. I have found two such men in this parish, the late Hon. Luc Letellier de St. Just, ex - Lieutenant - Governor of the province of Quebec, and the Abbé H. R. Casgrain. M. Letellier's removal from office in 1879 was an event of great political interest in the Dominion, involving as it did many questions of constitutional rights. His commanding presence was an assurance of the severest rectitude and most untiring energy; and he commanded my admiration by the liberality of his mind and the versatility of his information, as well as by the dignity, simplicity, and courtesy of a typical Canadian gentleman. The Abbé Casgrain is a radical priest and writer of unusual force. His stalwart figure, with strong features and eager black eyes, seems to have taken the wrong suit of clothes. But his impetuous nature has been only subdued, not subjected, by his austere religious education, and travel and varied reading have enlarged his mental horizon. He can take into fellowship even a heathen like me, and give him inside glimpses of the defects as well as the beauties of this French-Canadian Catholic life. His fruit-

ful explanations have given me a sympathy and understanding I could not otherwise have enjoyed in studying an antiquated, ultra-Catholic civilization so foreign to the spirit of our national life.

The habitants, or peasants, are widely separated from the gentry; there seems to be no democratic, average level of society. But all classes are on the best of terms, sharing as they do the national contentment and gayety. Their social life in winter presents the most characteristic features, but this unambitious people find time for their simple enjoyments at any season. The home of the habitant has been described already as the plainest and cheapest shelter demanded by comfort. But his social life presents more interesting features. In this class also one is struck by the fullness of social happiness and the meagreness of external interests; for example, Mr. D——, the most intelligent and progressive farmer of the parish, and one of the foremost men of the county, reads no paper, and gets no information on even his specialty of agriculture. He learns less than an average farm laborer among us.

"But," I said to him, "how do you keep yourself posted on the improvements?"

"Why, we don't; we don't improve; that's all. We get along well enough as our fathers did."

"I should think your long winters would be a very enjoyable season for study. What do you all do with so much time?"

"Oh, we loaf and enjoy our pipes. But we also have to work. We get up at half past five, light the lanterns, and go to the barn to feed the stock. After breakfast, at half past seven, the two principal labors of winter are begun, viz., hauling wood to keep the house warm, and threshing grain to eat. Those who go far for wood start at four or five o'clock. We used to see forty or fifty sleds in a line going up the mountain at St. Pacome to our wood lots. When the wind blows we set the windmill going, and thresh grain in the barn. After smoking the after-dinner pipe we saw wood or thresh or fan grain till the chores come again at half past four. After supper the men always go to visit a favorite neighbor—for the parish is somewhat divided into sets —until nine o'clock. The final visit to the barn, to bed and feed the stock, finish-

CUTTING AND HAULING WOOD.

es the day. And we don't make much out of reading."

"What do the women do all winter?"

"Oh, their work is never done. They, of course, keep about the same hours as the men. After making the fires and putting the breakfast and pea-soup to cook, they take the lantern and go to milk. After the breakfast, the washing of the children for school, and the sweeping are done, they sit down to spin, weave, or knit all day. Sometimes the dog may be harnessed to the little sled, and my wife rides over to a neighbor to make an evening call. But, as a rule, the women go out very seldom, excepting to the church. Of course there are days of general scrubbing—with spruce boughs for the pleasant odor they give—of washing, every three or four weeks; and seasons of special labors, as butchering before Christmas, when meats for six months are dressed, and frozen, either on the shelves of an outer room, or in boxes and barrels filled with snow. On Sunday the women must rise earlier than usual to get ready for mass at half past nine o'clock. Some families who live far from the church take their dinners with them, and eat them by a friend's stove while waiting for vespers, after which they may visit a little on the way home. Then in the fall there is the general preparation for winter, when some families move into the most sheltered end of the house, and give up the other as a store-room for wood, etc. There are also the special labors of cooking for Christmas-eve and New-Year's, the carnival season, and so on."

The habitants visit among themselves in small family gatherings now and then, most frequently just before Lent; but large public gatherings, such as balls, picnics, etc., are unknown. At these re-unions the table is loaded bountifully with meats and pastries, and the little house is filled with smoke and merriment. Cards and simple round games are the chief amusements; now and then songs are sung by each in turn without accompaniments—for pianos are extremely rare—or one of the Canadian story-

FANNING GRAIN.

masses in a Catholic community; they have no mental activity between gross materialism on the one hand and supernatural religious idealism on the other. And I find here many characters wholly given up to one or both of these opposite tendencies, who either never experience an intellectual emotion, but grovel in ignorance, or who occupy their thoughts and time with religious exaltation and mysticism, without developing the understanding. But they are a very happy people, notwithstanding the narrowness of their lives.

The chief social event of their lives is a wedding — almost the only set occasion of festivities. The priest then permits dancing among relatives, and allows unusual expenses to be incurred. But, to begin at the beginning, boys and girls generally see but little of one another, separated as they are in colleges and convents, and subsequently having but formal meetings, closely supervised by parents. The priest directs that courtship shall be very short and circumspect. It generally lasts but a few months; engagements are made very much after the pecuniary interests followed in France, and marriages generally occur at from eighteen to twenty-two years of age.

A widower of this place recently went to spend the evening with a neighbor, whose sister was an old maid whom no one had thought of marrying. When he left the house her brother suggested that he should marry her. They returned to the house, and went together to her bed, in one corner of the room, and woke her

tellers may relate some fanciful legend. The time passes pleasantly with them. But an abundant flow of hilarity in trivial chat is the chief element of their intercourse. The joker of the parish finds a delighted auditory at the village store. One can not expect much more from a people who can not read. I learn the astounding fact that many of the men who could read when boys at school actually forget the sense of printed characters. It is an ecclesiastical nation, who never read, but who derive all their instruction from the pulpit. This anti-intellectual religious education has produced here a people that are ignorant, superstitious, and poor; but one must remember also that they are courteous, orderly, and happy. There seems to be no mental democracy for the

up. Holding the candle up to his face, he said:

"Mlle. G——, take a good look at me: I'm rather worse than I seem by candle-light, and I've nine small children, and not a great deal of land. Will you marry me?"

She rubbed her eyes, still half asleep, looked him over a moment, and said, "Yes."

"Then be ready next Tuesday."

In another case, the day after the banns of marriage had been published here, the intended found his betrothed crying by the window.

"What's the matter, Maria?"

"Well, Baptist, my sister Louise wants very much to marry, because she's older, and it's her turn first. And it makes me sad to see her disappointed. Now if you would only marry her! Everything is ready, you know, and it would be such a relief."

"Well, well, don't cry about that," said he with a moment's surprise. "I don't mind if I do. Go and tell her to get ready."

The Church forbids the union of blood-relations, but it sells for a moderate price permits for even first cousins to marry, so that consanguineous unions are very common in these old parishes, where families have kept increasing and settling near the old homestead till they form clans some-times numbering several hundred of one name. Moreover, the priest permits such marriages sometimes in consideration of certain circumstances, such as the needs of

AN INTERIOR—SPINNING AND CARDING.

a family for a step-mother or step-father, the lack of beauty reducing the chances of a woman to get another offer, or the advance of age, or the poverty of a woman. All these circumstances have been abused to such a serious detriment of the population that Rome has seen fit to recommend a more rigorous enforcement of the law. The Catholic Church takes especial pains to promote marriage, and makes it a mortal sin to restrict the legitimate increase of population. This powerful influence has had a marked effect on the growth of the nation, which has increased from 60,000 in 1760 to over a million and a half. The limit of marriages seems to be only the lack of unmarried men. I rarely meet with bachelors, and they are given scarcely a moment's peace, unless they enter the priesthood. Unmarried women of the better class are condemned to a life of unusual *ennui*. In this small nation neither industry, trade, letters, arts, nor professions offer a career, education and charity are monopolized by religious orders, labor is not regarded with favor by ladies or gentlemen, and public movements are not large enough even for safety-valves. Hence very many girls enter the religious orders to escape bondage to idleness. Marriage is practically regarded as the aim of life, to be realized as a duty, and somewhat independently of sentiment. The courtship is short, the marriage contract is long and financial; then they are ready for wedlock. The bride and groom drive to church early in the morning with the parents and invited guests.

After the ceremony the string of calèches or of carioles winds along the parish roads, stopping at the houses of relatives and at other places, when the friends come out and invite them in for drinking their health. The day passes in these visits and a dinner and supper at the home of the bride and of the groom. The religious and austere tone of life here is shown sometimes by a wedding party in taking its way to the church again at sundown, where they pray, or even do penance in the *chemin de la croix*. At St. Augustin, near Quebec, some young couples, zealous in mortification of the flesh, got the permission of the priest to live together as celibates, and they finally made vows of chastity for life. In this, however, they followed not the national example, but those of Champlain and some other of the devout Catholics from whom this colony derived its spirit. The national gayety re-appears just as marked as ever at the marriage dance, beginning at six or seven o'clock, after supper. The event is the most convivial of the whole lifetime, yet an average marriage among the habitants costs in all but $20. Sometimes at supper an ancient custom is still practiced among the gentry.

The groom, who is expected to look after the material well-being of the bride, is on the alert to shield her from tricks, for he can not always count on her decorum in these circumstances. Some one drops a fork and sinks from his seat to pick it up. The groom, however, sees that he returns to his chair at once. While this is going on, another man has slipped under the table, and is crawling on all fours toward the bride.

When the guests all rise after supper the bride remains seated. "Why," they ask, "does madame remain alone at the table? Is she in ill humor already?"

"No," she replies; "but some one has stolen my slipper, and I can not walk barefooted."

They carry her in her chair to the head of the room, where she is placed in state to await farther proceedings. A loud knocking and disputing are heard at the door, and presently a ragged peddler forces an entrance into the company, calling out, "Any old boots and shoes?" The company welcome this opportune arrival, and conduct him to the bride. Here, kneeling before her, he hauls out of his great bag all sorts of old boots and shoes, and tries them on the bride's dainty foot, amid the laughter and banter of the assemblage, at the expense of the neglectful groom. At last the bride's slipper turns up, to be bought by the groom at a good round price; and the money is spent in treating the company. Sometimes even the bride is stolen, but the lover's instinct has never yet failed to find his mate.

I had not been invited to a wedding; but this social and hospitable people provide regularly for such cases by receiving a stranger as a *survenant*, or after-comer. As we drove up to the little house of M. Lévèque a crowd of bare-headed men and boys came thronging out of the door into the moonlight. The host at once welcomed us cordially, sent the horse to the stable, took us into the house, and gave me a seat on his right hand at the head of the room. For a wedding party the scene was

THE JOKER OF THE PARISH.

quite typical of this economical and simple life. The unpainted room was packed with people, the men standing in a crowd smoking and chatting at the farther end, and the women sitting on one another's knees, or on benches along the walls. Two small lamps lighted but faintly this throng of homespun peasants, dressed generally in black or dark gray; and the great shadows covering the ceiling between the beams, and the dimness of the whole scene, made it a sombre picture for the brightest moment in the lives of two young couples. For a long while I saw no brides or grooms; but finally they came out of the blackness of the adjoining room, and danced a cotillion in the small space inclosed by the crowd. The brides were distinguished from the other girls, dressed in dark linsey-woolsey, by only a little white lace about the neck. As the Church forbids round dances, they practice chiefly cotillions, quadrilles, reels, and jigs. Commonly no partners are chosen; they dance with whoever happens to stand opposite, and the movements are full of the vigor and awkwardness of peasants. The most interesting dances of the evening were the jigs by one of the brides and a burly uncombed farmer sixty-eight years old. He devoted himself seriously to the task in hand, thumping the floor, with en-

livening regularity, with feet shod in
moccasins.   Once or twice he found time
to smile on his young partner, but at once
lowered his eyes again to the floor, while
his twitching fingers beside his muscular
thighs attested the nervous earnestness of
his capering for her favor. The young lady,
meanwhile, holding her trim fine figure
erect, took her mincing steps with delicate
poise and restrained agility; she watched
his steps with downcast eyes, now and
then rejecting him with a haughty turn
of the head as she pirouetted and chas-
seyed at the changes of the tune; her
slight quick steps sent ripples of shadowy
folds down her skirts, and her youthful
comeliness and coquettish ways were well
set off by the sombre room, the rough
crowd standing about her and her burly
gray-haired partner.

But the Canadian fiddler is the most
striking feature of the dance. The one
at this entertainment was a tall, powerful
fellow in a red flannel shirt glowing beneath his black shaggy head. He is a
national, historic character, having acquired his artistic skill, his manner, his
répertoire, from a long line of fiddlers. As
a matter of fact, he is a stamping machine
with a fiddle attachment. He generally
holds the violin against his stomach, while
he sits on the very edge of his chair, leans
far back to keep his balance, and devotes
his strength to stamping with both feet,
which he raises clear of the floor from
two to six inches. And all the while he
keeps up an interesting pantomime; now
he throws his head back and regards the
ceiling, or droops his ear toward his distant instrument with a hopeless fondness.
His fervor often contorts him into ago-
nizing positions, when he turns his head
toward a far-off ideal with a wonderfully yearning stretch of the neck. And all
these affecting gestures reflect the movements of the artist's by no means invisible *sole*, for the musical phrases, having
no connection therewith, are frequently
drowned by those deafening crescendoes
of leather. The fiddler's heels thus become the real centre of the entire performance. In one of the jigs a couple

THE BALL.

who were engaged determined to monopolize the dance for some time. But soon another girl came on to the floor, and, bowing off the first, took her place. At the next change of figure another man dismissed the first in the same manner, and thus cleared the floor of the devoted pair. But these returned in the same manner at the next change, and so the contest went on for over an hour. The company were now quite excited over the endurance of the first dancers, the mischief of the meddlers, and, more than all, over the efforts of the poor fiddler. He stamped and stamped till the perspiration flowed, and the fiddle gave but feeble signs of life, while one contortion succeeded another with tragic force. But at last muscle and nerve began to flag, he lost all sense of artistic contrast, and settled down to a monotonous hard pounding of the floor. Then the by-standers came to the rescue with eager encouragement. "Give it to 'em, Louis! Come, now, more nerve. That's it; just look at 'em—the lovers are at it again! Send 'em along, now." And his frantic feet leaped again as high as ever. At midnight the old women began to yawn rather pitifully; a crusty old fellow lying on the floor behind the stove had fewer jokes to send up at the girls as they passed. One of the grooms in his shirt sleeves settled in a chair tipped back in the doorway of the dark room, and played a Jew's-harp to the weakening performance of the fiddler. Even the smoke and the laughter diminished in the farther shadowy end of the room. The carioles were soon brought to the door, and the company went off like bundles of robes down the road.

As we drove away through the moonbeams, chatting in short sentences matching the crisp winter air, the night seemed remarkably clear after the dinginess of this peasants' feast. I looked from the hill-top across the dark currents and the glistening floes of the St. Lawrence, and beyond saw distinctly the fields and woods, even some lines of fences, at Les Éboulements, twenty-five miles away, on the Northern Mountains.

Christmas and New-Year's are the culmination, though not the end, of Canadian winter life. Even the beggars are then most active and joyous in this charitable community. The housewives are busy for some days cooking meats and pastry and decorating their houses, and

secluded Canada joins the rest of the world for once in this season of rejoicing. On Christmas-eve, however, the houses are so dark and still that you wonder if the festival has been forgotten. In the convents the children are dreaming of Bethlehem and the worship of the shepherds. They hear a chorus of angels chanting as they come near and nearer; celestial light fills the world; when, suddenly opening their eyes, they find the nuns lighting the lamps, and the choir in the dormitory, chanting a Christmas carol to awaken them for the midnight mass. All over the parish, throughout Canada, and indeed in every Catholic country, the people are issuing now from their palaces or their cabins into the night, and wending their way to the temples. The bells peal out at midnight, the arched windows glow, and soon the entire parish is seen kneeling under the great dome.

In one of the lateral chapels a niche or grotto is made of spruce boughs, decorated with flowers, and brilliantly lighted with candles. The infant Jesus, dressed in a white robe, is here displayed in a manger filled with straw. The little Jesus of Tadousac is dressed in a rich silk costume of a courtier of Louis XIV., given to the chapel by a noble of that day. Here at Rivière Ouelle a devout old servant of the parsonage used to make a dramatic scene of the event. She placed beside the manger statuettes of Mary and Joseph, dressed as a priest and a nun, much smaller than their child, and a toy ass and bull.

The Infant remains on exhibition about two months, until after the fête of the Purification, and the people often say prayers before it. In the towns, at the fête of the Innocents, on the 28th December, the church is filled with little children led by their mothers or nurses. After the salut the priest takes the manger in his arms and shows it to the children passing by. The church resounds with their voices, some crying to kiss the image, others laughing with delight. After high mass, and the low mass that follows it immediately, each family returns to its home, where all sit down to a hearty Christmas supper, or at the very least to a lunch of doughnuts and liquor. In years gone by the hearty and convivial meal was more common than in these times of temperance reform. The holidays bring into the parishes here, as elsewhere, the young people from colleges and convents, but the social atmosphere does not light up much above the general monotony of this country life until New-Year's Day.

The new year begins with a patriarchal scene. Some households are on foot all night, those of grandparents preparing to receive, and those of younger couples going to visit. For there is some rivalry among the children to prove their greater respect by arriving first. In rare cases some may come as the clock strikes twelve, but generally they arrive at five or six in the morning. The Canadian year thus begins by starlight. The entire family enters at once into the room of the old couple, even though they be still abed; and there they all kneel while the old man extends his hands above their heads and gives them his blessing. Successive arrivals of the other children and grandchildren fill the house as a hive. General hand-shaking and good wishes follow, and after breakfast everybody drives to mass.

"In my childhood," said the Abbé Casgrain to me, "this ceremony always affected my mother to tears. We used to be collected by her in the parlor early in the morning, and then marched into my father's bedroom. Here we knelt before the bed while she asked him for his blessing, which he gave, after a short exhortation, to remind us of our shortcomings and duties. But we children were far more interested in the gifts lying on the bed behind him."

My own experiences during the day were quite pleasant. At an early hour I heard some of the neighbors, and also the children of the poor, knocking at the door of the inn. Some of them came in with boisterous hilarity, others with eager and interested politeness, to wish M. Chamberlain a happy New-Year. When I came down-stairs the family were marshalled in the dining-room to receive me, according to the custom in every household. Formal greetings were exchanged thus:

"Good-morning, Mr. F. How do you do this year?"

"Good-morning, Mr. C. Thank you, I'm very well thus far; and how are you, this year?"

"Very well, I thank you. Let me wish you a prosperous and happy year, and paradise at the end of your days."

"Thank you, Mr. C., for so comprehensive a wish. May the same fortune attend you!"

When the health of the New-Year had been drunk, we sat down to breakfast, and Adelard read two formal compositions, from himself and Artemise, his sister, expressing their gratitude, and their good wishes for their kind-hearted parents. When the tears had been wiped all around we began breakfast, and the year opened with a cold, clear morning, whose brightness was reflected in the spirits of everybody. During the morning, and indeed the whole day, relatives called on one another, and ate doughnuts and drank a glass of liquor. The houses were decorated with bouquets, crowns, crosses, and hearts made of marguerites, grasses, and mosses, all dyed in the most gorgeous colors. The most noteworthy feature of the day is the good-will toward men that is then cultivated.

When I arrived at the church, everybody was shaking hands and wishing a happy New-Year. Even those who had been unfriendly went about seeking one another, and meeting with at least frank and cordial faces, to begin the year with fair intentions. Those with whom I had even exchanged a few words gave to me also a hospitable greeting. I have never seen elsewhere so public and general a demonstration of forgiveness and good-will. The entire parish ran about with open hand and face and abundant good-humor. Then we went in to mass, and to see the priest receive his people in the church. His sermon was a short, pleasant, and patriarchal instruction. He dwelt upon the causes for thankfulness during the past year, for regrets at lost opportunities, and for hope and resignation. Then, after making his yearly report of the population, number of baptisms, marriages, and deaths on the church register, he took to himself the good wishes which all his parishioners undoubtedly tendered him in their minds. As the children had gathered about their father for his blessing, so his people had that day come to the church for his blessing as the father of the parish. And he then expressed his good wishes, in particulars, for each class and age of his people, according to their respective needs. It was not an empty form, for he, as well as most of his simple-minded listeners, was visibly affected.

STUBBLE AND SLOUGH IN DAKOTA

A DAKOTA CHICKEN-WAGON.

N OW I am conscious that all my life I have seen men who owned shot-guns and setter-dogs, and that these persons were wont at intervals to disappear from their usual haunts with this paraphernalia. Without thinking, I felt that they went to slay little birds, and for them I entertained a good-natured contempt. It came about in this wise that I acquired familiarity with "mark," and "hie-on," and "No. 6 vis No. 4's": By telegram I was invited to make one of a party in Chicago, bound West on a hunting expedition. It being one of my periods of unrest, I promptly packed up my Winchester, boots, saddle, and blankets, wired "All right—next train," and crawled into the "Limited" at Forty-second Street.

"West" is to me a generic term for that country in the United States which lies beyond the high plains, and this will account for my surprise when I walked into the private car at the St. Paul depot in Chicago and met my friends contesting the rights of occupancy with numerous setter-dogs, while all about were shot-gun cases and boxes labelled "Ammunition." After greetings I stepped to the station platform and mingled with the crowd—disgusted, and disposed to desert.

A genial young soldier who appreciated the curves in my character followed me out, and explained, in the full flush of his joyous anticipation, that we were going to North Dakota to shoot ducks and prairie-chicken, and that it would be the jolliest sort of a time; besides, it was a party of good friends. I hesitated, yielded, and enlisted for the enterprise. Feeling now that I was this far it would be good to go on and learn what there was in the form of sport which charmed so many men whose taste I respected in other matters, and once embarked I summoned my enthusiasm, and tried to "step high, wide, and handsome," as the horsemen say.

The happiness of a hunting party is like that of a wedding, so important is it that true love shall rule. The *pièce de résistance* of our car was two old generals, who called each other by an abbreviation of their first names, and interrupted conversations by recalling to each other's memory where some acres of men were slain. "A little more of the roast beef, please—yes, that was where I was shot in this side;" and at night, when quiet reigned and we sought sleep, there would be a waving of the curtains, and a voice, "Oh, say, Blank, do you remember that time my horse was hit with the twelve-pounder?" and it banished dreams. There was a phlebotomist from Pittsburg who had shot all over the earth. He was a thorough sportsman, with a code of rules as complicated as the common law, and he "made up tough" in his canvas shooting-clothes. There was a young and distinguished officer of the regular army who had hunted men, which excused him in the paltry undertaking before him; and, finally, three young men who were adding the accumulated knowledge of Harvard to their natural endowments. For myself, I did not see how jack-boots, spurs, and a Winchester would lend themselves to the stubble and slough of Dakota, but a collection was taken, and by the time we arrived in Valley City, Dakota, I was armed, if not accoutred, in the style affected by double-barrel men. All I now needed was an education, and between the Doctor, who explained, expostulated, and swore, and a great many "clean misses," I wore on to the high-school stage. Like the obliging person who was asked if he played on the violin, I said to myself, "I don't know, but I'll try."

In the early morning three teams drove up where our car was side-tracked, and we embarked in them. The shot-gun man affects buck-colored canvas clothes, with many pockets, and carries his cartridges in his shirt fronts, like a Circassian Cossack. He also takes the shells out of his gun before he climbs into a wagon, or he immediately becomes an object of derision and dread, or, what's worse, suddenly friendless and alone. He also refrains from pointing his gun at any fellow-sportsman, and if he inadvertently does it, he receives a fusillade such as an Irish drill-sergeant throws into a recruit when he does amiss. This day was cool

ON THE EDGE OF A SLOUGH.

and with a wind blowing, and the poor dogs leaped in delirious joy when let out from their boxes, in which they had travelled all the way from Chicago. After running the wire edge off their nerves they were gotten to range inside a township site, and we jogged along. The first thing which interested me was to hear the Doctor indicate to the driver that he did not care to participate in the driver's knowledge of hunting, and that in order to save mental wear he only had to drive the team, and stand fast when we got out, in order that from the one motionless spot on the prairie sea we could "mark down" the birds.

The immensity of the wheat-fields in Dakota is astonishing to a stranger. They begin on the edge of town, and we drive all day and are never out of them, and on either side they stretch away as far as one's eye can travel. The wheat had been cut and "shocked," which left a stubble some eight inches high. The farm-houses are far apart, and, indeed, not often in sight, but as the threshing was in progress, we saw many groups of men and horses, and the great steam-threshers blowing clouds of black smoke, and the flying straw as it was belched from the bowels of the monsters.

During the heat of the day the chickens lie in the cover of the grass at the sides of the fields, or in the rank growth of some slough-hole, but at early morning and evening they feed in the wheat stubble. As we ride along, the dogs range out in front, now leaping gracefully along, now stopping and carrying their noses in the air to detect some scent, and finally— "There's a point! Stop, driver!" and we pile out, breaking our guns and shoving in the cartridges.

"No hurry—no hurry," says the Doctor; "the dog will stay there a month." But, fired with the anticipations, we move briskly up. "You take the right and I'll take the left. Don't fire over the dog," adds the portly sportsman, with an admonishing frown. We go more slowly, and suddenly, with a "whir," up get two chickens and go sailing off. Bang! bang! The Doctor bags his and I miss mine. We load and advance, when up

who had charge of my early education in .45 calibres, which ran, "Take yer time, sonny, and always see your hind sight," and by dint of doing this I soon improved to a satisfactory extent. The walking over the stubble is good exercise, and it becomes fascinating to watch the well-trained Lewellen setters "make game," or stand pointing with their tails wagging violently in the nervous thrill of their excitement, then the shooting, and the marking down of the birds who escape the fire, that we may go to them for another "flush." With care and patience one can bag at last the whole covey.

At noon we met the other wagons in a green swale, and had lunch, and seated in a row under the shadow side of a straw stack, we plucked chickens, while the phlebotomist did the necessary surgery to prepare them for the cook. At three o'clock the soldier, a couple of residents, and myself started together for the evening shooting. We banged away at 1000-yards range at some teal on a big marsh, but later gave it up, and confined ourselves to chicken. In the midst of a covey and a lot of banging I heard the Captain uttering distressful cries. His gun was leaning on a wheat "shock," and he was clawing himself wildly. "Come, help me—I am being eaten alive." Sure enough he was, for in Dakota there is a little insect which is like a winged ant, and they go in swarms, and their bite is sharp and painful. I attempted his rescue, and was attacked in turn, so that we ended by a precipitous retreat, leaving the covey of chickens and their protectors, the ants, on the field.

A CONFERENCE IN THE MUD.

comes the remainder of the covey, and the bewildering plenty of the flying objects rattles me. The Doctor shoots well, and indeed prairie-chickens are not difficult, but I am discouraged. As the great sportsman Mr. Soapy Sponge used to say, "I'm a good shooter, but a bad hitter." It was in this distressful time that I remembered the words of the old hunter

We next pushed a covey of grouse into some standing oats, and were tempted to go in a short way, but some farmers who were thrashing on the neighboring hill blew the engine whistle and made a "sortie," whereat we bolted. At a slough which we were tramping through

"DON'T SHOOT!"

to kick up some birds "marked down," one suddenly got up under our feet and flew directly over the Captain, who yelled "Don't shoot!" as he dropped to the ground. It was a well-considered thing to do, since a flying bird looks bigger than a man to an excited and enthusiastic sportsman. We walked along through the stubble until the red sunset no longer gave sufficient light, and then got into our wagon to do the fourteen miles to our car and supper. Late at night we reached our car, and from it could hear "the sound of revelry." The cook did big Chicago beefsteaks by the half-dozen, for an all day's tramp is a sauce which tells.

After some days at this place we were hauled up to Devil's Lake, on the Great Northern road, which locality is without doubt the best for duck-shooting in Dakota. We were driven some sixteen miles to a spur of the lake, where we found a settler. There were hundreds of teal in the water back of his cabin, and as we took position well up the wind and fired, they got up in clouds, and we had five minutes of shooting which was gluttony. We gave the "bag" to the old settler, and the Doctor admonished him to "fry them," which I have no doubt he did.

It was six miles to a pond said to be the best evening shooting about there, and we drove over. There we met our other two teams and another party of sportsmen. The shallow water was long and deeply fringed with rank marsh grass. Having no wading-boots can make no difference to a sportsman whose soul is great, so I floundered in and got comfortably wet. After shooting two or three

mud-hens, under the impression that they were ducks, the Doctor came along, and with a pained expression he carefully explained what became of people who did not know a teal from a mud-hen, and said further that he would let it pass this time. As the sun sank, the flight of ducks began, and from the far corners of the marsh I saw puffs of smoke and heard the dull slump of a report.

"Mark—left," came a voice from where

"MARK—LEFT."

TROOPING HOMEWARD IN THE AFTER-GLOW.

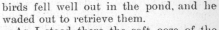

the young Harvard man with the peach complexion and the cream hair had ensconced himself in the grass, and, sure enough, a flight was coming toward my lair. I waited until it was nearly over, when I rose up and missed two fine shots, while the Harvard man scored. The

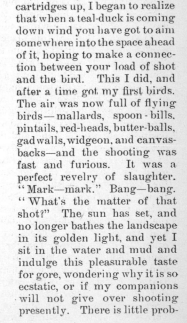

"MARK!"

birds fell well out in the pond, and he waded out to retrieve them.

As I stood there the soft ooze of the marsh gradually swallowed me, and when in answer to the warning "mark" of my fellows I squatted down in the black water to my middle, and only held my gun and cartridges up, I began to realize that when a teal-duck is coming down wind you have got to aim somewhere into the space ahead of it, hoping to make a connection between your load of shot and the bird. This I did, and after a time got my first birds. The air was now full of flying birds—mallards, spoon-bills, pintails, red-heads, butter-balls, gadwalls, widgeon, and canvasbacks—and the shooting was fast and furious. It was a perfect revelry of slaughter. "Mark—mark." Bang—bang. "What's the matter of that shot?" The sun has set, and no longer bathes the landscape in its golden light, and yet I sit in the water and mud and indulge this pleasurable taste for gore, wondering why it is so ecstatic, or if my companions will not give over shooting presently. There is little probability of that, however. Only darkness can end the miseries of the poor little teal coming home to their marsh, and yet with all my sentimental emotions of sympathy I deplore a miss. If slough-shooting has a drawback, it is its lack of action—it is a calm, deliberate shedding of blood, and a wounding of many birds, who die in the marshes, or become easy prey for the hawks, and it's as cold-blooded as sitting in water can make it.

We give over at last, and the fortunates change their wet clothes, while those who have no change sit on the seat knee-deep in dead birds and shiver while we rattle homeward. Our driver gets himself lost, and we bring up against a wire fence. Very late at night we struck the railroad, and counted telegraph poles and travelled east until the lights of the town twinkled through the gloom. Once in the car, we find the creature comfort which reconciles one to life, and we vote the day a red-letter one. The goose-shooting came later than our visit, but the people tell marvellous tales of their numbers. They employ special guns in their pursuit, which are No. 4 gauge, single-barrelled, and very long. They throw buckshot point-blank two hundred yards, and are, indeed, curious-looking arms. The chicken-shooting is not laborious, since one rides in a wagon, and a one-lunged, wooden-legged man is as good as a four-mile athlete at it. He must know setter-dogs, who are nearly as complicated as women in their temper and ways; he must have a nose for cover, and he can be taught to shoot; he can keep statistics if he desires, but his first few experiences behind the dogs will not tempt him to do that unless his modesty is highly developed. If he become a shot-gun enthusiast he will discover a most surprising number of fellows — doctors, lawyers, butchers, farmers, and Indians not taxed—all willing to go with him or to be interested in his tales.

The car was to be attached to an express train bound west that night, to my intense satisfaction, and I crawled into the upper berth to dream of bad-lands elk, soldiers, cowboys, and only in the haze of fleeting consciousness could I distinguish a voice—

"Remington, I hope you are not going to fall out of that upper berth again to-night."

THE RESCUE OF THE WHALERS

THE peculiar species of whale from which whalebone is procured is only to be found in the polar regions amid the eternal ice, and scarcely a year passes without leaving its history of ships crushed and lives lost. In 1871 thirty-two vessels were driven ashore by the ice and crushed, while in 1876 thirteen were caught in the ice near Point Barrow, drifted in to the northward with the strong current, and neither they nor the sixty men left on board have ever been seen or heard of again. It is supposed that this current, which, as Professor Nansen has proved, sweeps through Bering Strait and across the pole, carried them into the polar basin, where they were crushed and sunk, leaving no trace behind.

With the advent of spring large schools of whales make their appearance, forcing their way under the floes and through the leads in the ice, bound to the northward. They follow the ice along the shores of Alaska to Point Barrow, and then turn to the eastward along the northern shore, where it is supposed they find good breeding-grounds. Late in the fall they come back, and go south again along the shores of Siberia.

The fleet of whaling-vessels reach Point Barrow during the first part of August. Arriving there, they follow up the whales to the eastward, as far as and sometimes farther than the mouth of the Mackenzie River. It is along here they make their greatest catch; but they must not remain too long in the season, and the whaling captains generally reckon on leaving that neighborhood by the middle of September, in order to reach Point Barrow again before the last part of that month. From there they work their way over to the westward, pursuing their whaling south along the coast of Siberia, and finally come out through the Bering Strait not later than the middle of October.

The fall of 1897, for some unknown reason, came exceptionally early, and when the fleet reached the vicinity of Point Barrow they found the way blocked, for the northerly winds had blown the pack ice down on the shores, and the new ice had begun to make. Some of the vessels of the fleet, having made a good catch, had started out early and got clear just in time; but eight of them—the steamers *Orca*, *Jessie H. Freeman*, *Belvedere*, *Newport*, *Fearless*, *Jeannie*, and the sailing-vessels *Wanderer* and *Rosario*—were caught. This in itself was bad enough, but as they all had expected to reach San Francisco not later than early in the winter, none of the vessels had supplies enough to last them until spring, the earliest date when help could be expected to reach them, and starvation stared the crews in the face. When those of the fleet that had escaped the fatal grip of the ice reached San Francisco early in November, steps were at once taken to ascertain whether help could not be sent to them. The subject was thoroughly discussed at a cabinet meeting, with the result that the President decided to assign the task of getting help to the imprisoned men to the revenue-cutter service, the officers of which had seen so much of Arctic duty.

It was a novel experiment, starting an expedition into the frozen North during the winter, and as the duty was thought to be dangerous, volunteers were called for, and it was my good fortune to be among those selected for the expedition. The revenue-cutter *Bear* had but just returned from her usual summer cruise in

Arctic waters, and certain repairs were very much needed; but as she was the best and most available vessel for the trip, her commander, Captain Francis Tuttle, was telegraphed on the 10th of November to make all haste to fit her out for the trip north. Repairs that were absolutely necessary were hurried through, all the stores, outfits, and fur clothing taken on board, and she finally sailed from Seattle on the 27th of November, fitted out for a year's absence in the polar regions. It is extremely doubtful if ever an expedition was fitted out for an absence of a year in that part of the globe in such an incredibly short time— only eighteen days. The officers selected for her were as follows: Captain, Francis Tuttle; 1st Lieutenants, D. H. Jarvis and J. H. Brown; 2d Lieutenants, E. P. Bertholf, C. S. Cochran, J. G. Berry, B. H. Camcen, and H. G. Hamlet; Chief Engineer, H. W. Spear; 1st Assistant Engineer, H. N. Wood; 2d Assistant Engineers, H. K. Spencer and J. I. Bryan; and Surgeons, S. J. Call and E. H. Woodruff.

The plan was for the *Bear*, after forcing her way north as far as possible, to land a party, which was to proceed overland as far as Cape Prince of Wales, where they would find several herds of domestic reindeer. These were to be driven up the coast to Point Barrow, to serve as food for the imprisoned whalers. To pack any considerable quantity of provisions was impossible, because, as the domestic deer from Siberia have not yet been introduced into Alaska in sufficient numbers, the usual, and indeed the only, transportation in Alaska in the winter is by means of dog-sleds. A team of from seven to nine dogs can draw a sled loaded with from 500 to 700 pounds, but for any extensive trip where the trail is bad, 300 to 400 pounds is considered a good load, and as the food for these dogs must be carried along also, it will readily be seen that it is quite impracticable to pack provisions for any but yourself and dogs for any great distance. The officers designated for this overland trip to Cape Prince of Wales were Lieutenant Jarvis, Dr. Call, and myself. Jarvis, who was to command the party, had served eight seasons in the Arctic Ocean on the *Bear*, was familiar with the coast, knew the natives well, and was eminently well fitted to carry the plans to a successful finish. Besides the provisions for the ship's com-

pany, the *Bear* had taken on board 12,000 extra rations for the shipwrecked men when she should reach Point Barrow in the spring.

We reached Unalaska, the chief of the Aleutian Islands, on the 8th of December. We left, after coaling, on the 11th, and started north on the really serious part of the undertaking. The weather holding good, we made fair time, so that on the morning of the 13th we passed St. Lawrence Island, and having seen little or no ice, we began to hope to be able to make a landing somewhere on the south side of the Cape Prince of Wales peninsula. In the afternoon, however, we began to strike the mushy water (that is, water on the point of freezing), and considerable drift ice began to make its appearance, so that about five P.M. the captain decided it would be impossible for us to get much farther, and we turned and stood for Cape Vancouver, as the next available landing-place. At the time we were in latitude 63° 30', about twenty-five miles northeast from St. Lawrence Island, and only eighty miles from Sledge Island, which is close to the mainland, and it seemed too bad we could not land there, as it would save about seven hundred miles of travel on land. However, there was no help for it, and we headed for Cape Vancouver.

Here we found that fortune favored us, for the water was clear all the way to the shore, although, as we subsequently learned, the ice had shut that place in up to within a few days previous, when the strong southeasterly gale prevailing had driven it off to the westward and cleared the beach for us. There was a small village here, and as the *Bear* was the second vessel that had landed there in the memory of the oldest inhabitant, our arrival created quite a stir. Lieutenant Jarvis went ashore in one of the ship's boats, and having learned that there were plenty of dogs to be had in the village, preparations were immediately made to land our outfits, and by the time it began to grow dark our provisions, clothing, and camp-gear had been landed safely on the beach, our good-byes to our shipmates had been said, and we stood on the shore watching the boat as it went back to the *Bear*, wondering whether we should ever see our friends again. There was another man with us, F. Koltchoff by name, who was to be employed with the government herd of reindeer near St. Michaels, and was to be taken with the expedition as far as that place. We landed about four miles from the village. The natives came to meet us in their kyaks, and transported our outfit to the village. We footed it, arriving soon after. We found this village, the name of which was Tununak, to consist of a half-breed Russian trader and his native wife and children, together with about a dozen of his wife's relatives. His name was Alexis Kaleny, and as it was he that owned the dogs, and indeed everything else in the village, arrangements were made with him to take our party as far as St. Michaels, where we counted on getting a supply of fresh dogs to continue the journey. As one of the dog teams we were to use had returned only that day from an eight days' trip, and needed rest, Lieutenant Jarvis decided to use the next day for completing our arrangements and packing the sleds, and to make an early start on the 18th.

The Alaskan sleds are built of wood as light as is consistent with strength, and lashed together with hide ropes, so that the whole frame-work will give readily and not be easily broken by the constant

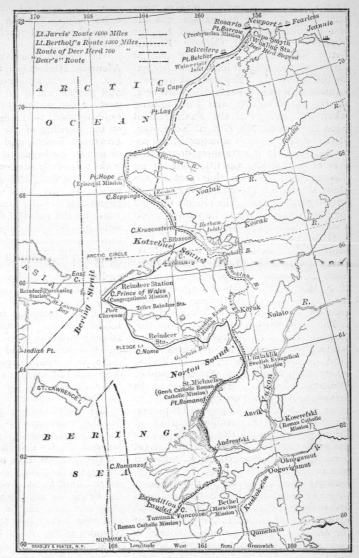

THE ROUTES OF THE MEMBERS OF THE RESCUING EXPEDITION.

rough usage to which they are subjected. The sled is from nine to ten feet long, and eighteen or twenty inches wide, with the runners one foot deep, shod with walrus ivory or strips of bone fashioned out of the jaw-bone of the whale. The rails or sides are about eighteen inches high, and at the rear end of the sled are handles coming up high enough for a man to push and guide it without bending very much. There is a cover made of light drilling which is spread in the bottom of the sled, and large enough so that after the articles have been packed on snugly it hauls up over the load and the ends overlap on top. The load is then lashed the whole length of the sled with hide thongs. By this arrangement your sled will stand considerable shaking up and capsizing without spilling the load.

The morning of the 18th dawned bright and clear, and we were all astir early and ready for our start. We took with us four sleds, each with a team of seven dogs, harnessed in pairs, with the leader in front. Jarvis, Call, Alexis, and myself each had a sled, with an Eskimo to help. About seven o'clock, amidst an almost deafening howling of the dogs, we were off, and were soon initiated into the mysteries of sled travel.

I have seen many pictures of the manner in which the Eskimos travel, and the man is generally seated comfortably on the sled cracking a whip, and the dogs are going at a smart gallop; but we soon found that picture to be a delusion and a snare. Journeying in the Arctic regions consists mostly in pushing behind the sled, for the poor little animals frequently have to be helped over the rough places and in going up hill or any rise in the ground. Where there is no beaten trail—as was the case most of the distance we travelled—the dogs have nothing to guide them, and one man is obliged to run ahead. He generally runs some distance, and then walks until the head team comes up with him, when he runs on again. When the snow is hard and the road level, the dogs, with an average load, will maintain a trot which is too fast for a man to walk, and not so fast as he can run. By alternately running and walking, one does not become greatly fatigued. Natives who travel from village to village are so accustomed to this mode of travel that they can keep it up all day without showing signs of fatigue.

Instead of travelling along the coast from Tununak to St. Michaels, where Alexis told us the road was apt to be very rough, he proposed to guide us across the country, striking the Yukon River at Andreafski, there being native villages scattered along the route at convenient intervals, so that we could hope to reach one every night, and thus get a few fresh dogs in case any of ours gave out. The first day we had to cross a range of mountains apparently some 1500 or 2000 feet in height, and in some places the rise was so steep that it required three or four of us to help the dogs pull each sled up. By the time we reached the summit we began to think how delightful our journey was to be if our trail led us over many such mountains, since we had some 1600 miles to go and this was only the first day. The sight before us was not very encouraging, for we beheld a mountain, higher and steeper than that we had just ascended, with a deep valley between.

We soon forgot our troubles in the excitement of the descent into this valley, for the dogs were turned loose and we prepared to coast down. Trees there were none, and the road looked clear, with only a few patches of brush to keep away from. Each of us straddled his sled, and, with a native behind to do the guiding, started. All the tobogganing I had ever done, even shooting the chutes, was tame compared to this. It had taken about five hours to toil up this mountain, and it took about half an hour to come down. At first we did not go very fast, for the snow was quite deep in places and our sleds heavy, but as soon as we got up a momentum we seemed to fly. Once in the descent I lost my balance, and in a second found myself half buried in the snow and the sled rapidly disappearing. But here was where the experience of the native came in, for he thrust out his foot and in some dexterous manner turned the sled, so that it was overturned in the deep snow.

At the bottom we had to wait awhile for the dogs, for they had been obliged to come down on foot. They hove in sight, coming at a good gait; in fact, they had to come fast, for having got started, they had to keep it up, and one poor little fellow, who could not make his legs go fast enough in the deep snow, was being dragged by his fellows.

The rest we enjoyed sitting on our sleds while coming down, together with the excitement, put us in good spirits again, and we started for the second mountain with a better grace, for now we had the coasting to look forward to.

When we reached the bottom of this second mountain, Alexis showed us the village at which we were to stop; not more than three or four miles away, and a level road before us. Our arrival at this place, which rejoiced in the name of

TRAVELLING WITH DOG-SLEDS.

U-kog-a-mute, created quite a sensation, and Alexis explained to us that, with the exception of one or two of the Jesuit missionaries, white men had not travelled through this section of the country since the days of the Russian occupation of Alaska. As it was late when we arrived, we decided not to pitch our tent, but to spend the night in one of the native huts.

These huts are built in a circular fashion, and are about half underground, with the roof arched over by means of brush and what wood the natives could pick up in the rivers in the spring. The whole is then banked up with earth in the fall before the ground is frozen. The floor is made of rough slabs of wood, and in the centre of it is a small opening large enough to admit a man's body. This leads into a passage large enough to crawl along, and finally emerges into a smaller hut, built like the other one, which in turn opens into the outer air. Over each one of the openings is hung a piece of deer-skin or seal-skin. In the roof of the large hut is an opening, over which is stretched a covering made of the dried intestines of the whale, walrus, or seal, and, being translucent, admits the light during the day. The Eskimos appreci-

ate the fact that hot air rises, for the outlet through the floor, being covered, only admits a small amount of cold air, while the opening at the top, being tightly ceiled, does not allow any of the warm air to escape. They do not have any fires in the hut, as a rule, for wood is scarce, and the heat from the bodies of the dozen or so inmates of each hut is sufficient to make the temperature inside quite comfortable. The cooking, when any is done, is carried on in the outer entrance. While this arrangement of not letting the warm air escape has its advantages, we found that it has its disadvantages as well, for no sooner did we all crawl in through the passage and emerge into the hut than our untutored noses were assailed with an odor that could not be equalled in any part of civilization that we knew of. The combination produced by old and decayed fish, ancient seal blubber and oil, together with the natives themselves, who do not see the necessity of going to all the trouble of melting the snow just to get water to wash their bodies with, has to be encountered to be appreciated; and beating a precipitate retreat, we hastened to pitch our tent.

Our camp-gear consisted of a wall-tent,

A SNOW-HOUSE ENCAMPMENT.

stove and pipe, two frying-pans, two camp kettles, two tea-kettles, an axe, two rifles and one shot-gun, with ammunition, and in addition each man was provided with a knife, fork, spoon, tin plate, and tin cup. The tent was made of light cotton drilling, ten feet long, eight feet wide, and seven feet high, with walls three feet high. The stove was a simple sheet-iron box, twenty-two by fourteen inches, and twelve inches deep. The pipe was fitted in lengths which telescoped into each other, and were short enough to go inside the stove, so as to take up as little room as possible on the sled. Our provisions consisted of tea, sugar, beans, bacon, pork, flour, and hard bread. The beans and pork had been cooked before starting, and only required to be warmed over at meals, and, besides, were thus ready to be eaten in case we were obliged to camp where no wood was to be had. Our clothing was made principally of dog-skin, and besides not being warm, was bulky and heavy, and thus added greatly to the fatigue of travelling. The sleeping-bags were made of goat-skin lined outside with blanket, and provided with two covers, one of canvas and the other of rubber. They weighed thirty pounds each, and besides adding greatly

to the weight to be carried on the sleds, were not very warm. These articles were the best that could be obtained at Seattle, however, and as the weather was not severe until after we had left St. Michaels, at which place we obtained a proper outfit, they answered our purpose very well.

The doctor was our self-appointed cook, and as soon as he had stewed up some pork and beans and made the tea, we all ate a hearty meal, had our smoke, and crawled into our bags, where we were sound asleep in a few minutes, for all hands were pretty well tired out with this first day of unaccustomed travel.

The next morning Alexis made our hearts glad by informing us that, as far as St. Michaels, anyway, we would not be troubled by any more mountains, for our road now led us across the Yukon River delta, which mainly consisted of frozen swamps and small streams. We broke camp, lashed our sleds, and started about seven, as soon as it was light. But what impressed me most was how the guide knew which way he was going. There was no visible trail; we crossed and sometimes followed numbers of small streams, and the guide did not seem to take much account of our small pocket-compasses. There did not seem to be any marks by which to tell the general direction, for the country was level, and there was nothing to be seen in any direction but snow, with a few clumps of brush here and there.

Shortly before sundown we reached the next village, the name of which we discovered, by dint of perseverance, to be Ki-yi-lieug-a-mute. Here Alexis informed us that some of his dogs were too young to stand further travel, and that the dogs he had hoped to replace them with at this village were away, and not expected to return for two days. As this would cause a delay, Lieutenant Jarvis decided to take two of the good teams and go on ahead with Dr. Call and two of the native guides, leaving me to follow with Koltchoff and Alexis as soon as possible. By this arrangement he would lose no time, and could have all necessary arrangements made when we arrived at St. Michaels. So early next morning the provisions and outfits were divided, and Jarvis and Call said good-by.

As there was only one tent, I was reduced to the necessity of sleeping in one of the native huts, and having a whole day before me, I concluded to make a tour of inspection to find out which seemed least odorous. There did not appear to be much choice, and having selected one at random, I broke myself in to my new quarters by going inside for a few minutes at a time. This I kept up during the day, each time remaining a little longer, with such good results that by night I was fairly acclimated, as it were, and after eating the usual evening meal, turned into my sleeping-bag, imagining I was comfortable. When I awoke in the morning I found that the foul air had given

me a raging headache, but when I got out in the open air it soon passed away. That evening the dogs returned to the village, and having bargained for their use, Alexis informed me that we could resume our journey the following day. It is wonderful how soon one can become accustomed to odd conditions, for

THE MEMBERS OF THE OVERLAND PARTY.

I awoke the next morning without any bad effects, and from that on never particularly noticed the odor of the huts.

We were off as soon as there was light enough to see, and from this on until we reached Andreafski the country travelled over did not differ, and the journey was practically without incident. As we approached the Yukon the brush was more plentiful and larger, and we scared up several flocks of ptarmigan, or arctic grouse—the first game I had seen in the country. As I only had a rifle, Jarvis having taken the shot-gun, I was unable to obtain any, for these birds are perfectly white in the winter, and very hard to distinguish against the background of snow. As Jarvis had left me without a thermometer, I had nothing but my feelings to give me any idea of the degree of cold. The day we separated, the mercury registered 23° above zero, and although some days seemed to be colder than others, I attributed the fact to the rising of the wind. Judge of my surprise, then, at finding, when we reached Andreafski, that the thermometer registered 15° below zero. Of course I knew it was colder than when we started, but travelling daily in the open air we had not felt the gradual change. As soon as I saw what the thermometer had to say, I began to feel cold.

Andreafski is one of the trading-stations of the Alaska Commercial Company, and several white men and their families live there. Jarvis had arrived two days

The trail led down the frozen Yukon, and as the road was good, our progress was much faster than in coming across the delta; and it seemed, too, as if we had suddenly struck into a civilized country again, for, whereas before we reached the Yukon we had met but an occasional native and sled, here we frequently came across parties of miners travelling up or down the river, for several of the steamers carrying miners to the gold districts had been frozen in at different places in the river, and the miners were constantly going from one to the other. When we reached the mouth of the river and made our camp at Point Romanof, our guide Alexis was taken very ill, and it transpired he had not been really well when we started, for he had caught a heavy cold which had settled on his lungs, so that he was in great pain, and we had to sit up all night with him. I could do nothing to aid him, for I had no medicines, and, in fact, was not enough of a doctor to know what was the matter with him. The next day he was not able to walk, and had to sit all day on his sled, and as the other native had developed some kind of a sore knee, he also had to ride, in consequence of which Koltchoff and myself had to take turns running ahead of the dogs for the next two days.

THE DEER TRAIN BEFORE LOADING.

before, and had given the people a delightful surprise by bringing letters which they would not have received under usual conditions until the following spring; but Uncle Sam's thoughtful postmaster had sent all the mail destined for that part of the country with the expedition.

Having replenished our larder, we left Andreafski the following day, the 27th.

When we reached St. Michaels, about noon on January 1, I found that Jarvis had reached there two days before, and had left again a few hours before we arrived, leaving me a letter of instructions. From this I learned that the large government herd of reindeer which had been

A SHORT HALT.

maintained at Port Clarence had been transferred to Unalaklik, was now on its way to that place, and had reached the head of Norton Sound. Jarvis accordingly had made his arrangements to travel that far by dog teams, and from there to Cape Prince of Wales by deer-sleds, which was supposed to be much the faster mode of travelling. He was then to start the herds of deer still in the vicinity of the latter place on their way up the coast. As it would require several herders to drive the deer, and there was no chance to get provisions between Cape Prince of Wales and Point Hope, I was to transport 1000 pounds of stores from Unalaklik across what is known as the Portage, to Kotzebue Sound, and meet him and the deer herd at Cape Blossom.

As soon as we reached St. Michaels I requested Dr. Edie, the surgeon attached to the military post at that place, to examine Alexis, whereupon it developed that he had a bad case of double pneumonia, and was a very sick man. So he was put to bed and attendants furnished him, and under the doctor's care he managed to pull through; but it was a hard task, and for three months he was flat on his back, and it is quite certain, but for the excellent care and treatment he received, he would never have gone

back to his home at Tununak. The dogs we had used thus far were badly in need of rest, for their feet were all cut and sore from breaking through the crust on the snow, but as dogs were scarce at St. Michaels, and I had to wait for the return of the two teams Jarvis took with him, I bought the best one of Alexis's teams, as it would probably be in good shape again by the time I would be able to start.

Here I obtained a sleeping-bag, clothing, and boots of deer-skin, and discarded those articles brought from the ship, Jarvis and Call having done the same. The sleeping-bag is made of the winter skins of the deer sewed together with the hair turned in, long enough for a man to lie at full length inside, and fitted with a flap to haul over the head after getting in. The boots are made of the skin from the legs of the deer, the hair outside, while the soles are the hide of the oogrook, or large hair-seal. Inside the boots are worn deer-skin socks, with the hair next the feet, and inside these again are worn one and sometimes two pairs of heavy woollen socks. The shirt, or parkie, is made of the summer skins of the deer, these being lighter, and is double—that is, it is really two parkies in one, so that there is hair next the body, and outside as well. It is fitted with a hood, which is trimmed around the face with wolf-skin, for the hair of that animal being long and coarse, it affords excellent protection from the cold and biting winds. The trousers are generally single, and made of the thick winter skins, with the hair turned out. Deer-skin combines two very essential properties—it is very warm and very light; in fact, the double parkie does not weigh any more than the average double-breasted sack-coat of civilization, and our sleeping-bags weighed only twelve pounds. Over the parkie is worn a snow-shirt made of light cotton drilling, so that the driving snow will not get into the hair of the parkie and wet through to the skin. Our hand-covering

Imagine a road strewn with rocks and bowlders of all sizes, packed close together, and some idea of our trail will be gained. Our progress was necessarily slow, as the sled required constant watching and guiding to keep it from overturning, which, however, it did very frequently, despite our best efforts, and the next three days were very fatiguing; but we finally pulled into Unalaklik on the evening of the 8th, without any serious mishaps. We passed two natives, however, on the way, who were packing their load on their backs, their sled having been broken by the difficult trail.

Unalaklik has a native population of some two hundred, with a Swedish mission school, and a trading-station belonging to the Alaska Commercial Company, managed by a Norwegian named Englestadt. By this time the thermometer was registering during the day from 35° to 40° below zero, but as we were well provided with skin clothing we did not suffer from cold, except when we

ESKIMO CHILDREN.

consisted of deer-skin mittens, with woollen gloves or mittens inside, so that when it became necessary to work around the sled or adjust the dog-harness, the clumsy deer mit could be slipped off, and the hands still be protected by the woollen gloves while working.

On the 6th of January, my dogs' feet having healed properly, I concluded to go on to Unalaklik, and there intercept the other teams returning, in order to save that much time. I took a native boy with me as a guide, and although Unalaklik is but sixty miles from St. Michaels, it took us three days to make the trip, for the road led along the shore, where the ice had shelved and piled up, making an exceedingly rough and hummocky trail.

were obliged to face the wind in travelling. After waiting here at the log house of the trader until the 15th, and the dogs not having yet arrived. I concluded to go on to Koyuk, at the head of Norton Sound, taking what provisions I could with my one team, pick up all the dogs I could on the way, and send them back for the remaining part. On the way, as expected, I fell in with the two teams Jarvis had sent back, but as they seemed to be played out, they were of no use to me.

At Koyuk, which is a native village composed of two huts, on the 19th, I found myself with but one team, for the extra teams I had been led to expect at this place were not visible. So the following day I started for Golofnin Bay, three days'

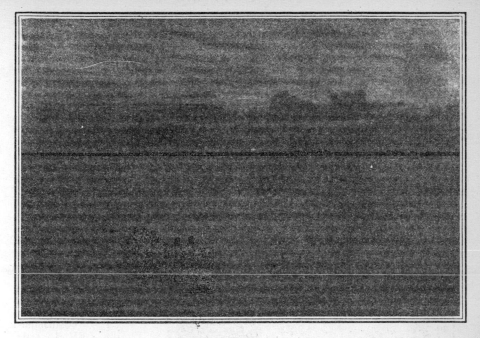

THE MIDNIGHT SUN.

travel to the westward, where there was another trading-post, hoping to be able to get the necessary dogs there. Again I was doomed to disappointment, however, for all the dogs belonging to that station were absent on a trip into the country. A few miles from here was the government herd of reindeer, and there I went next; and after much talking with the Lapp herder in charge (for the superintendent, Mr. Kettleson, had gone up the coast with Jarvis), succeeded in convincing him I was an officer, and obtained some sled-deer and two drivers. With this outfit I returned to Koyuk, reaching that place on the 29th, and there found two more dog teams waiting for me, with the rest of the provisions. In response to an urgent note I had sent to him by a native runner, the trader at Unalaklik had managed to scrape together these two teams, but they were a sorry lot of dogs.

A deer-sled is about half as long as a dog-sled, very much wider, and not so high, so that it cannot be easily overturned by the somewhat erratic movements the deer ofttimes indulges in. The deer-harness consists of a wooden collar and a belly-band. The trace by which he

hauls the sled is made fast to the collar and belly-band, and leads under him and between his hind legs to the sled, being made of hide, and covered with soft fur where it takes against his legs, so as not to chafe through the skin. Around the base of the horns is secured the strip of hide rope which the driver uses as a guiding-line. As a single deer is generally used to each sled, and he soon tires with a load of more than 150 pounds, one man drives a train of several, each deer being secured by his guiding-line to the sled ahead, while at the same time his trace is fastened to the sled he is to draw. The head sled is used for the driver only, who generally sits down, except when he is obliged to trot alongside to keep warm. In this way, if the deer are well trained and follow readily, one man can drive a train of ten or more. The deer we had were not very well trained, however, and one man drove but three, thus leaving but four of the six sleds for freight. The real advantage of the deer lies in the fact that food for them does not have to be carried if one is passing through a country where the moss is plentiful. In travelling we usually halted once during the day to allow

THE STATION AT CAPE SMYTH.

the deer to feed, and again at night, at which times he paws up the snow with his hoofs, using them very skilfully, thus exposing the moss beneath. When the snow is very deep, this causes the deer much labor, so that after dragging a sled all day, and working half the night for his food, he seems to need a day of rest in each four or five, for, after all, the deer is rather a delicate animal. The dogs, on the contrary, are very tough little fellows, and will travel day after day right along if properly fed, unless their feet become badly cut by the crusty snow.

From Koyuk we followed the course of the Koyuk River, making short-cuts occasionally where the stream turned aside from our general direction, until we reached the head of that stream, when we struck across the hills until we came to the source of the Buckland River, which we then followed to its mouth. This brought us to Escholtz Bay, and after that we kept along the coast to the mouth of Hotham Inlet. We passed through a gently rolling country, which was devoid of trees or shrubbery except along the rivers, where we found brush in abundance, together with some scrubby pine-trees.

Each night, when we reached a clump of pines at which the guide had decided to camp, the deer train was driven a mile or so to leeward, so that the dogs would not scent them during the night and cause a stampede. Then one of us would pitch the tent while another chopped a supply of firewood, and still another unharnessed the dogs and unloaded the sleds, for the dogs would devour everything left within reach. Boots or skin clothing left carelessly exposed were always found half chewed in the morning, for the poor little fellows never get a square meal when travelling in winter, and are ravenous. We would then start the fire in the stove, and another outside the tent to help melt the snow or ice, to obtain water for drinking and cooking. The beans, which had been boiled before starting, were always frozen so solid they had to be chopped off with the axe, and indeed everything that had the least moisture in it was frozen solid in a day. Our meals consisted of pork and beans cooked over in the camp kettle, tea, and, when the hard bread gave out, "flap-jacks." We would mix up a batter of flour and water, and make the flap-jacks as large as the frying-pan to save time, using the bacon for grease, and when that was gone seal oil took its place. The Eskimos are experts at this sort of cooking, but as they never wash their hands, I always did my own and let them cook for themselves.

After the meal was finished we would proceed to the very trying task of feeding the dogs. Each man took in his arms one dried fish for each dog, and then tried to get his team all together and away from the others. The poor hungry little fellows would jump up after the fish, and in their eagerness to obtain a mouthful it was a difficult matter to keep from being knocked down and bitten. But finally a fish would be thrown to each one, and then you would have to stand by with a club to drive off any dog that gulped his fish down and then tried to steal from the others. As soon as all the fish intended to be used had been given out and devoured, and the dogs saw no more was coming, they would lie down quietly and go to sleep, and we would then go to our tent, close the flap to keep out as much cold air as possible, and I would enjoy my smoke, and watch the natives puff contentedly at their curious long ivory pipes. And finally, having finished our smoke, we would crawl into our bags and be asleep in a jiffy. Sometimes we were obliged to camp where there was not a sign of wood, and then our supper would be frozen pork and beans and cold water, which latter we always carried with us on the sled in a pail, wrapped tightly in some article of clothing to keep it from freezing solid. In the morning the one that awoke first would arouse the others, and we would have our breakfast and smoke, load the sleds, harness the dogs, and be off again at seven o'clock.

As I have said, our guide led us through a comparatively level country, and had the snow not been very deep and soft, we would have made a quick trip across. As it was, we were obliged to use snow-shoes nearly all the time, and often had to tramp back and forth ahead of the dog teams in order to pack the snow down for the little fellows. We did not reach Cape Blossom until the evening of February 11.

Meanwhile, Jarvis and Call, travelling light, had pushed rapidly along the coast from St. Michaels until they reached the government herd of deer to which I have already referred, whence they sent back their dog teams for my use, and taking deer-sleds, kept on to Point Rodney, at which place was a herd of 138 deer, owned by an Eskimo called Charley (his native name being Artisarlook). The government had contemplated the use of its large herd for an expedition up the Yukon, for the aid of the miners there, and Jarvis had

THE SURVIVORS OF THE DOG TEAM THAT DRAGGED US TWENTY-FOUR HUNDRED MILES.

been instructed not to take from that herd unless compelled to do so. It is difficult to make an Eskimo understand that you can pay back a debt you may wish to contract unless you have the visible means at hand, and had Charley not known Jarvis for several years, and always been treated well by the officers of the *Bear*, it is extremely doubtful if he would have allowed his deer to be taken. It was not without many misgivings, however, that he did finally let them go, for it must be remembered they represented the support of his family and those dependent upon him. He was also afraid there might be delay in obtaining the deer from Siberia in the spring, and then the other natives would laugh at him, and this last is a very serious offence from a native stand-point. But all his scruples were finally overcome, and he not only allowed his deer to be taken, but agreed to leave his family and go along to help drive the herd. Leaving Dr. Call to come with Charley and the herd, Jarvis proceeded along the coast, stopping at Port Clarence to arrange for provisions to be sent to Point Rodney for the use of Charley's family during his absence, and reached Cape Prince of Wales January 24. At this place is a mission in charge of Mr. W. T. Lopp, and in his charge also were 294 deer, mostly belonging to the American Missionary Society, the remainder being owned by natives engaged in herding them. It was of course an easy thing to obtain the deer from Mr. Lopp, provided the Treasury Department would guarantee their return, but the same argument had to be gone through with the natives as with Charley. However, the fact that Charley had let his deer go, together with the additional persuasion of Mr. Lopp, soon induced them also to part with their deer. This would give Jarvis a herd of 443, including a few straggling deer he had bought from outside natives, and this was thought to be sufficient for the people at Point Barrow. Several days were now taken up with the preparations that had to be made, the sleds repaired, and the necessary fur clothing put together, but on February 3, Dr. Call having come up with Charley and his herd, the whole outfit was ready to start on its long journey north. This was no light undertaking, for there were some 700 miles through practically uninhabited country to be travelled, and the herd was to be driven by Alaska natives entirely, while it had always been supposed that none but experienced Laplanders or Siberians could care for or drive a herd of deer properly. The sequel shows that the Eskimos were fully equal to the task, for the herd reached Point Barrow in a very short time, and with a surprisingly small number of casualties among the deer. Mr. Lopp being well acquainted with the native language, and having his herders well in hand, agreed to accompany the expedition to Point Barrow to overlook things generally in the deer-camp, and when the start was made on February 3, besides Jarvis and Call, there were Lopp and six herders in the outfit, necessitating eighteen sleds to carry the provisions, tents, and camp-gear.

The route lay along the northern part of the Cape Prince of Wales peninsula, about fifteen miles from the coast, where the deer-moss was plentiful. The method of driving the deer was quite simple. The herders would go close up to the herd, which would at once start ahead in a walk. Then, with one herder on each flank and a couple in the rear, they would keep the deer moving, the flanking herders preventing any deviation from the general direction to be travelled. The little deer-dogs, of which there were three, were of great service. They would keep behind the herd, and whenever any of the deer would straggle or attempt to get to one side, the dogs would run after them, bark and snap at their heels, and force them back to the herd. These little dogs were of the Lapland breed, about as large as a collie, and seemed to be untiring. Each night the herd was halted at places where the snow was not very deep, so they would be able to feed with as little exertion as possible. During the winter months the deer give very little trouble, for they seldom stray or wander from the main herd, being content to crop their fill of the moss, and then lie down until started ahead in the morning.

The guiding-line of the sled-deer is always left on his horns, so he may be easily caught and harnessed when wanted. The herd was driven on an average from ten to fifteen miles a day, and towards evening, when it was time to go into camp, the deer train would drive ahead, find a spot where the moss was plentiful, pitch the tent, build the fire, and get the evening meal all ready for the weary

HOUSE AT POINT BARROW IN SUMMER.

herders when they came up with the herd. During the day it was usual to halt the deer about noon to feed, at which time the men would fortify themselves for the afternoon with tea and hard bread.

In travelling along the coast-line there is always drift-wood to be picked up for fires, but when the trail leads back from the coast, and the trees are very few, small sticks are gathered during the day, and put on the sleds, in order to have enough to cook with at night and the following morning. Fires are seldom used for warmth alone in travelling, for inside the tent one is screened from the wind, and once you are in the sleeping-bag no fires are needed. The only delay in travelling in winter is caused by the blizzards. At such times the wind picks up the loose dry snow, and drives it with such force and in such quantities that one cannot see ten feet ahead, and it is impossible to face the gale. The only thing to do at such times is to make camp at once and wait for the wind to go down. Often people who have become separated have wandered about until they dropped from exhaustion, and have then frozen.

One day when the snow was driving so that the sled ahead could not be seen,

Jarvis was seated on the rear deer-sled of the train. Suddenly his sled struck a stump in the road, which broke the trace. He shouted as loudly as he could, but all to no avail; no one could hear him, and the man on the sled ahead could not see what had happened. So after waiting some time for some one to come back, Jarvis concluded that they would not notice he was left until the train stopped to camp—which proved to be the case—and crawled into his sleeping-bag, which he fortunately had on the sled with him. Had he tried to run after the train, he would probably have lost the trail and wandered about all night; but deer will follow a trail when a man could not see.

When the herd had travelled to abreast Cape Espenberg, Jarvis decided to go to the coast, procure dogs at some village, and come on ahead to meet me at Cape Blossom, leaving Lopp to follow with the deer as quickly as possible.

I had reached that place on February 11, and he and Call drew up on the evening of the 12th, having crossed on the ice from Espenberg that day. Of course, as we had not seen each other since we parted company December 20, we had lots to say, and sat up far into the night telling each other all about it. On the 15th Jarvis left for Point Hope, leaving me behind with the provisions for Lopp and the herders, and instructions to follow with the herd as soon as it came along.

The weather up to this time had been generally good, very few days having been lost, and although the mercury was now registering between 40° and 50° below, we did not experience any great inconvenience except during a blizzard, and then our tent proved a good refuge. Sometimes. however, the wind was too strong for the tent to stand, and then we were forced to build a snow house. We would find the most convenient drift, dig a hole in it large enough to hold us all, and roof it over with blocks of snow cut

THE "ROSARIO" CRUSHED IN THE ICE.

ing no opening at all. The warmth of our bodies would soon raise the temperature so that the snow would begin to melt on the inside, and here we would remain until the blizzard had passed or blown itself out. The dogs outside were all right, for they would curl up and go to sleep, no matter how hard it blew or how cold it was. When the snow drifted over them they would get up, shake it off, and lie down for another nap.

There was plenty of drift-wood to be picked up at Cape Blossom, but waiting is very tiresome in a country where one sees nothing but an expanse of snow and ice, and I was very glad when Lopp showed up on the 18th. He had crossed on the ice with the deer herd from Cape Espenberg to Cape Krusenstern, reaching the latter place the previous morning. At a native hut there he found a letter from Jarvis, telling him where I was to be found, and had come over to Cape Blossom with dog teams, leaving the deer behind for a rest.

As I had sent back all my dog teams, we loaded the provisions on my deer-sleds and Lopp's dog-sleds, and we returned to Krusenstern, reaching there on the 19th. Here we remained until the 21st, to afford the deer a much-needed rest, and then started along the coast toward Point Hope. Our good fortune as to the weather now left us, and for the next few days we had a succession of blizzards, during which time we scarcely made five miles each day. One morning, after having been obliged to camp the previous afternoon on account of the driving snow, we awoke to find our tent nearly drifted over, only the ridge-pole showing. We were obliged to dig ourselves out, and

with our long knives, leaving a hole to crawl in through, and filling up the cracks, where the blocks joined, with loose snow. Our provisions and sleeping-bags were then put inside, and we would crawl in ourselves and block up the door, leav-

THE OFFICERS OF THE "BEAR" IN UNDRESS UNIFORM.

then spent the whole forenoon digging to recover our sleds and outfit. When we reached the mouth of the Kivalena River, at which Lopp was to strike inland to cut off the long journey around Point Hope, I left him, having procured the necessary dog-sleds, and proceeded to this latter place, where, according to instructions, I was to meet Jarvis again. When I got as far as Cape Seppings, I learned from some natives that he had gone back to the Kivalena to meet Lopp, so I waited until he returned, when we both kept on to Point Hope, reaching there on the 2d of March. There being a considerable store of flour and other provisions at Liebes's whaling-station here, it was decided I should remain at this place to care for any of the shipwrecked men Jarvis might send down from Point Barrow, should he find that measure advisable upon reaching the latter place. On March 4, having replenished their stores, Jarvis and Call set out again, this time for the last stage of their journey, and after a very arduous trip, for the snow was very deep and the road bad, they reached Point Barrow on the 29th.

When the whaling-vessels found themselves hemmed in by the ice the previous fall, three of them—the Orca, Freeman, and Belvedere—had by desperate efforts succeeded in cutting and blasting their way around Point Barrow and as far as the Sea-Horse Islands, about fifty miles farther south. Here the Orca was crushed, and sank soon after, her crew escaping to the Belvedere. Later the same day the Freeman, being nipped and threatened with destruction, was abandoned, her crew also escaping across the ice to the Belvedere, which had managed to get in behind the Sea-Horses, where she was protected from the crushing pressure of the ice pack. A day or two later the Freeman was set fire to by some natives, and was destroyed. Here, then, was a worse state of affairs—these two crews destitute, for of course whatever stores the two ships had remaining were lost. At Cape Smyth, ten miles south from Point Barrow, is a shore whaling-station managed by Mr. Charles D. Brower, who has lived in northern Alaska for nearly fifteen years. Having quite a supply of provisions, he took matters in hand when disaster overtook the vessels, and, but for his care and management, it is certain that many of the men would have perished before the expedition came to their relief. Brower employed some 200 natives, and the stores referred to were principally for their support during the winter. With about 300 whalers to feed in addition, things did not look very cheerful. The situation of the ships was as follows: the *Rosario* close to Point Barrow, the *Newport* and *Fearless* about a mile off shore, fifteen miles to the eastward, and the *Jeannie* some thirty miles farther eastward, and four miles off shore—all, of course, frozen in the ice. The whereabouts of the *Wanderer* was not known at that time, but it was subsequently ascertained that after finding out how the ice was at Point Barrow, she made her way back to Herschel Island, where the whaler *Mary D. Hume* was wintering, with two years' supplies.

Brower held a consultation with the captains, and it was decided that the vessels should keep on board as many as their stores would support, and send the rest of the crews to his station at Cape Smyth. He then called together his natives, explained to them that all his provisions must be saved for the white men, and told them that they, being well supplied with fur clothing and accustomed to the severe cold of the country, must go back to the mountains and make great efforts to kill all the wild deer they could find, and that though he could not give them any flour during the winter, as usual, they would be well rewarded in the spring when the ships arrived from the south. The natives having assented to this, they took their dogs and sleds, travelled back into the mountains some 150 or 200 miles, and so faithfully did they follow the instructions of Mr. Brower that, during the winter, up to the time when Jarvis arrived, they killed and sent into the station over 1000 wild deer. Providence seems to have had a hand in this, because for some unknown reason the wild deer wandered to that part of the country in greater numbers than had been known for twenty years. Brower gave up all his stores to the whalers, and divided them into daily rations, but the amount was so little that many would have starved but for the deer the natives sent in from the hills. Even with these the daily allowance was limited, but it sufficed.

When the expedition arrived with the government herd, the poor fellows enjoyed the first square meal they had seen for many a long day. It was a memorable afternoon, that 29th of March, when

THE "BEAR" CAUGHT IN THE ICE AT CAPE SMYTH.

ICE PILED UP BY THE CRUSH THAT NEARLY STOVE IN THE "BEAR'S" SIDE.

Brower saw two strange sleds approaching from the south; and he could scarcely believe his eyes when these sleds drew up at his house and he was greeted by Lieutenant Jarvis. His first impression was that the *Bear* had been lost somewhere on the coast below, for he had seen that vessel leave in the fall, and could not imagine what would bring any of her officers up to that part of the country in the middle of winter but shipwreck. When the poor half-starved sailors learned that there was a herd of over 400 deer coming up the coast for them, they could scarcely contain themselves for joy.

The following day, the deer herd having reached a place about twenty miles below Cape Smyth, where the moss was abundant, Lopp halted it, and went on ahead to join Jarvis. Having left his wife and family at Cape Prince of Wales, Lopp was very anxious to get back, now that his work was done, so after resting for a few days he started on his return, leaving Charley and one herder behind to look after the deer. As I had, in the mean time, made a trip up the coast from Point Hope as far as the Pitmegea River, and there cached provisions and dog food for the use of whoever might be coming down the coast, Lopp did not have to pack supplies for the entire trip, and thus being able to travel light, he made the trip in ten travelling days, and reached Point Hope April 19. Resting

his dogs there for a few days, he set out again on the 23d, and reached Cape Prince of Wales May 5, thus having, together with his herders, driven a herd of reindeer over bad roads of snow and ice, through a country but little known, dragging all their provisions a distance of about 700 miles, and then returned to his home, in the remarkably short time of three months and two days.

The powers of endurance of the Eskimo dogs are wonderful. The team I bought at St. Michaels, having already brought us that far, took me to Golofnin Bay, back again to the head of Norton Sound, and then across the country to Cape Blossom. From there it took Jarvis to Point Barrow, and finally returned with Lopp to Cape Prince of Wales, thus having travelled over 2400 miles. It had dragged heavy loads, most of the way over difficult trails, and had had only a few days' rest at odd times. Only one dog was lost out of the seven (he having been shot at Cape Smyth); the other six were in excellent condition at the end of the journey. It must be remembered, too, that when travelling through country where villages are few and far between, dog food must be carried along, and most of the time these dogs received but one meal a day, and that meal was a small one.

The day after Jarvis arrived at Cape Smyth he investigated the state of af-

HAULING COAL FROM THE "BEAR" TO THE WHALING-SHIPS.

fairs, and found that though the men had fared better as regards food than could possibly have been expected, they were very badly off in the matter of quarters. In the fall, when Brower had got all the surplus men from the ships to his station, he found the problem of providing quarters for them difficult. There were other buildings besides his own station at Cape Smyth, but though Dr. Marsh, the missionary at that place, had a school-house in which he taught the natives, he did not offer it for the use of the ship-wrecked men. The old government refuge station, which had been built to accommodate 100 men in an emergency, had been sold to the Pacific Steam-Whaling Company, and by it leased to Mr. E. A. McIlhenny, who occupied it at that time, being engaged in scientific pursuits; but he declined to take in any but the officers of the wrecked vessels. There was still another house, an old dilapidated building called "Kelley's old house," and after taking as many as he could into his own house, Mr. Brower, feeling he had no real authority to *force* the men upon anybody, was obliged to quarter the remaining seventy-eight men in this old building, fifty by twenty-five feet. Of course in such cramped quarters it was impossi-

ble to get sufficient ventilation and still keep the house warm enough to live in, and besides, it was very difficult to keep the men and the building clean. When the expedition arrived, Lieutenant Jarvis having authority from the department to assume charge of affairs, immediately made such arrangements that the school-house and refuge station were brought into use, and the men provided with decent quarters. The old house, being in a deplorable condition, was torn down, and used for firewood, which was very scarce, for all the drift-wood for miles along the beach had been burned during the winter. Owing to the scanty allowance the men had lived on, and the bad quarters in which they had been obliged to live, scurvy had begun to make its appearance, two men being down with it and two more being threatened; but Dr. Call soon got the upper hand of the dread disease, and with the men in comfortable quarters, such sanitary regulations were enforced as would prevent its return. The men were obliged to take exercise regularly, and when there was no work to do, they had to play ball. A ball-game with the ground covered with snow and the thermometer away below zero was certainly a novelty.

It could now be said that the overland expedition had finished the difficult part of its task, for the men were comfortably quartered and in good health, the arrival of the deer herd had dispelled any possible fear of starvation, and there was nothing to do now but to keep the men occupied and in good health and spirits, and wait patiently as we might for our ship to arrive in the spring.

After the *Bear* had landed us at Cape Vancouver in December, she steamed back to Unalaska, where she remained during the winter. On the 14th of the following June she again pointed her head toward the north. On the 19th she passed St. Lawrence Island, but was turned back by the heavy ice later in the day, when she tried to reach Indian Point on the Siberian coast. The following day she again ran into heavy drift-ice, but finally managed to work through into St. Laurence Bay, Siberia, reaching there on the 22d. Here she met the steam-whaler *William Bayless*, and having learned from her that Lopp had returned to Cape Prince of Wales, the *Bear* was worked through the ice over to that place, where Captain Tuttle received from Lopp all the news of the expedition up to the time the latter had left Point Barrow. Learning that the wrecked men would be in need of clothing by the time he reached them, Captain Tuttle steamed over to St. Michaels, obtained a supply of under-clothing, and again turned the *Bear* north. She reached Point Hope July 15. I came on board, and after giving all the news I had, was more astonished than I had ever been in my life by receiving the news that our country was at war with Spain, and Admiral Dewey had won the glorious victory at Manila.

On the 16th we left, and succeeded in working through the drift-ice as far as Point Lay, where we anchored on the 18th in response to signals from the shore. Soon after a canoe came alongside, and Captain Sherman of the wrecked *Orca*, together with several natives and members of the wrecked vessels, came on board. They had come down the coast, sometimes hauling their canoe over the ice, and sometimes paddling and sailing, to bring a letter from Jarvis to Captain Tuttle, telling him the situation at Cape Smyth. From Sherman we learned that the ice was very heavy to the northward, and he did not think we would get very far.

Captain Tuttle made the attempt, however; but at Icy Cape the ice turned us back, and we anchored at Point Lay again on the 21st. Another fruitless attempt was made the following day, and on the 23d, Sherman having brought the information that the *Belvedere* was short of flour, Lieutenant Hamlet was sent up the coast with a canoe-load of provisions to that vessel. He reached her all right, but, owing to the heavy ice along the shore, he did not reach Cape Smyth until the day after the *Bear* arrived. On the 25th the ice opened up a little, and we got as far as Wainwright Inlet, but were compelled to stop there on account of the fog. On the 27th the fog lifted, and we managed to push through the leads and get around the shoals off Point Belcher, but were obliged to run off shore and lose the land on account of the heavy drift. We soon got a good opening, however, and headed in again, and about eight o'clock in the morning, July 28, we made fast to the ground-ice at Cape Smyth, opposite the station. This ground-ice is the old ice of the polar seas piled up by the crushing of the floes, until this mass gets so deep in the water that it grounds, and there remains until it is blown off again by a gale. Where we made fast the water was seventeen fathoms, and yet this ice was hard and fast on the bottom.

In a little while we saw the people coming out to us on the ice, and soon Jarvis climbed over the side, and later the doctor. We gave them a hearty welcome, but as soon as they had made their report to the captain and heard the war news, they asked so many questions that we all forgot the shipwrecked sailors in the excitement of discussing the war and the only thing we then knew—the battle of Manila. Later in the day Jarvis went ashore again to send off the men we were to take down, and by the following day most of them had come on board.

By this time a westerly wind had sprung up, and the drift-ice began to get so heavy we were forced to move into a little bight in the ground-ice to escape it. The wind was increasing all the time, and although we could see the pack coming in, we could not get through the heavy drift, and on August 1 the *Bear* was jammed tight up against the ground-ice by the pack, and we were in the same position as the vessels the previous fall, only there was hope for us because it was early in the season and the water was not freezing. The only thing we could do now was to look out for a crush and wait patiently for an easterly wind to carry the pack-ice off shore and open a lead. On August 3, the wind chopped around to the southwest, disturbed the pack, and brought on a pressure, so that our port side was pushed in a few inches. The snapping, cracking, and grinding of the timbers is a frightful sound, and for a few minutes it looked as if the stanch old *Bear*, that had seen so many cruises to the Arctic, was at last to leave her bones there, but fortunately the pressure ceased before any real damage was done. The danger was not over, however, for with the wind blowing on shore a pressure was likely to occur at any time, and it was almost sure that the next time the *Bear* was doomed. Provisions were hastily gotten up and all preparations made to abandon her should it become necessary. For the next few days no one went asleep without expecting to be called at any time, and every morning we gave a sigh of relief to find the good old ship still safe.

Meanwhile the *Belvedere* had freed herself from the ice that had made around her during the winter, and was ready to start south as soon as the drift-ice cleared from the shoals outside her; the *Rosario* had been crushed when the ice broke up early in the spring, her crew taken to the station at Cape Smyth, and were now on board the *Bear;* the *Newport* and *Fearless* had worked their way close to Point Barrow, and the *Jeannie* was expected to put in an appearance at any time. On August 3 she succeeded in working up to Point Barrow, and as a lead had opened inside the ground-ice, all three vessels came down and made fast on the inshore side of the piece we were jammed against. On the 7th we made an attempt to blast a passage through, but powder proved to have very little effect on ice grounded in seventeen fathoms, and we were of course unsuccessful. There was now a long succession of unfavorable winds and calms until the 15th, when the wind came out from the eastward, the pack began moving off shore, and by midnight there was only about fifty yards of ice outside us. The pack had by this time loosened sufficiently to allow the *Bear* to move back and forward a little, so steam was made on all her boilers, and she began to force her way through, but it took all the fore-

noon, backing and filling under a full head of steam, to get clear. About noon on the 16th, after a final rush at the barrier of ice, the *Bear* forced through, and we sent up a rousing cheer as we found ourselves in open water once more. We proceeded down the coast to where the *Newport, Fearless,* and *Jeannie* were waiting for us, and after giving them each sufficient coal and provisions to last until they could reach the nearest port, the *Bear* steamed away southward, having on board ninety-three officers and men of the wrecked vessels. At Port Hope we picked up nine more destitute seamen, the crew of the schooner *Louise J. Kenney,* which had been driven ashore a few days previous. We steamed into Seattle on the 13th of September, 1898, after an absence in the Arctic regions of nine months and a half, and with a consciousness of having performed the task allotted to us.

The sled journey of the overland expedition from Cape Vancouver to the northernmost limits of Alaska, a distance of some 1600 miles, is, I believe, the longest ever made by a single party in one winter. That no lives were lost and there are no stories of fearful suffering to be told is due, I am convinced, to the care and good judgment exercised, rather than to any fortuitous circumstances. Hardships are of course inseparable from Arctic travel; a bath is an unheard-of luxury; one is never quite free from unwelcome little visitors inside the fur clothing so long as there are natives in the party. Many times we crawled into our sleeping-bags hungry, when the weather or lack of fuel rendered cooking impossible; running, walking, and pushing behind a sled through deep snow and over rough and difficult trails of broken ice are very fatiguing and exhausting; the weather is very cold, but though the thermometer registered as much as 50° below zero during our travelling, there were only two cases of frost-bite in the party, and these were slight and the result of carelessness in not paying proper attention to the nose, which member, being very much exposed, is most likely to be the first affected; but in an Arctic expedition properly fitted out, if discretion and judgment are used in travelling and camping, it appears to me to be quite unnecessary for the members to undergo any great amount of real suffering, except in case of an extraordinary succession of adverse circumstances.

THE CITY OF THE STRAIT

ETROIT is one of the oldest cities on this continent. Before Hendrik Hudson set foot on the island of Manhattan, and while Henry IV. still sat on the throne of France, the Hurons pointed out the site whereon it is built to Champlain, the founder of Quebec, as the natural gateway to "the vast seas of sweet water," and then was born in the brain of the great French navigator the dream of a "New France," which should extend from the Atlantic to the Pacific, and have Quebec and Detroit as its eastern and western fortresses.

This dream was inherited by the French monarchs; but it was not till ninety years later that one of them attempted to make it a reality. Then Louis XIV. commissioned the Sieur Antoine de la Mothe Cadillac, who from 1694 to 1699 had been in command at Mackinaw, to found at Detroit a settlement, and erect there a fort to hold the region of the Great Lakes for the French government. This was done; and Detroit, under the successive reigns of Henry IV., Louis XIII., XIV., and XV., was for nearly sixty years a French town—a bit of "sunny France" hidden away in the heart of the western wilderness; and such it might have remained to this day had not Wolfe, one dark night in September, 1759, scaled the heights of Quebec, and on the Plains of Abraham changed the fate of North America. The surrender of Detroit soon followed the conquest of Quebec; and then it became an English town, and the western head-quarters of the British power in America. It so remained—the extreme outpost of Western civilization—until July 11, 1796, when, in pursuance of the peace of 1783, it was quietly transferred to the United States. Thus we see that Detroit has had a unique history. Three times has it changed its nationality, and with each change assumed totally different characteristics. At first it was French, then English, and last of all American, and in the present town may be seen a curious blending of the traits of these various peoples. The old French *habitant* and the courtly English resident have long slumbered in their graves, but the close observer will detect that their spirits still walk abroad, and perambulate its streets arm in arm with the irrepressible Yankee, who in his seven-league boots is now striding across the continent. Brother Jonathan has everywhere the astonishing energy which, in wellnigh a single day, raised Chicago from its ashes; but here he has been held in check by those old worthies, who have now and then whispered in his ear the fable of the hare and the tortoise. This accounts for the fact that Detroit is to-day a curious compound of modern progress and old-time conservatism—a city of vast enterprises, but enterprises based on a broad, substantial, and enduring basis.

It was a sweltering day in July, 1701, when Cadillac, with his little fleet of birch-bark canoes, turned southwest from Lake St. Clair, and entered the broad, clear, beautiful river now known as the Detroit. Had some native of the forest stood then upon its banks, he must have been lost in wonder at the unwonted spectacle of the strange flotilla. Twenty-five birchen boats—some measuring six feet wide and thirty-five feet long—gaudily decorated with Indian symbols, and waving gayly the flags of France, glided gracefully down the stream to the exhilarating sounds of the fife and the drum, and the joyful shout that a long journey was over. The boats were manned by fifty soldiers in "bright blue coats and white facings"; and carried four officers and fifty emigrants, with an abundant store of provisions and all the tools and utensils needed in the building and settling of a new town in the wilderness. Besides, there were on board two Roman Catholic priests, for, like all good Frenchmen, Cadillac had a tender concern for the souls of his people. He intended they should not neglect the mass, or forget their pater-noster. They had come a weary journey of forty-nine days, in those frail boats, over rough waves, the men bearing them on their shoulders on the long portage between the Ottawa River and Lake Huron, and it was but natural they should rejoice at the end of their voyage.

Where the river leaves Lake Huron it is more than half a league in width, and broken by picturesque islands; but as it flows southwestward it contracts into a single channel, and gradually narrows till at about ten miles' distance it has a breadth of only half a mile. This is the strait which was to give its name—Détroit—to both the river and the city to be built upon its northern bank. Here, at a sudden bend in the stream, the canoes were drawn up on the beach, and landing, the voyagers ascended to a level plateau which rose by successive terraces to a height of about fifty feet above the bed of the river. From this elevation they had a view of the whole broad water as it flows southward, shut in at first by steep bluffs, but then broadening out, dotted with beautiful islands, till at the distance of about twenty miles its clear green current is lost in the deep blue waves of Lake Erie. The river here is three miles wide, discharging a greater volume of water than

any other in the world, excepting only the Niagara and St. Lawrence, which receive its flow. Cadillac was a man of broad, forecasting intellect, but it may be questioned if even he would have credited a prediction that within two hundred years that river, frost-bound as it is nearly four months in the year, would give passage to a greater annual tonnage than would enter London—the largest seaport in the world. And yet such is the fact, as shown by the maritime tables for the year 1884.

Cadillac formed a temporary encampment under the great spreading trees, and, within two days, laid the foundation of a church in which to worship God after the manner of his fathers. Then he staked out the ground for a fort and a stockade, and set at work to get the settlers housed before the winter, which he knew from experience to be sometimes severe in this latitude. The stockade is supposed to have included about twenty acres. It was located on the first rise of ground near the river—in what is now the business part of the city—that the guns of the fort might command the strait and the opposite shore; and was made thus roomy to allow each settler space for a dwelling inside the pickets, safety being the thing to be first thought of by the new settlement. The settlers were but a handful, and they knew themselves surrounded by at least forty thousand savages, friendly then, but liable at any moment to become hostile upon occasion of some real or fancied injury. The area within the stockade was laid out into lots and streets, and surrounded by a lane twelve feet in width, to allow the garrison, in the event of attack, free access to every part of the enclosure. Thus Cadillac was soon in command of a walled city, built, it is true, of rough logs, and not in the latest style of European architecture, but reasonably secure, if bravely defended, against attacks from such desultory warriors as the Indians. By means of this fort the French secured control of the Great Lakes and the fur trade of the Northwest; and here the traders and soldiers of that nation congregated, and proclaimed Louis XIV. lord paramount of all the vast region that stretches away to the setting sun.

Cadillac landed on the 24th of July, and by the close of the following month the chapel, the fort, and the dwellings of the settlers were erected, and the settlement had assumed all the order of an established community. Soon after this, Madame Cadillac, who had been left behind at Quebec, plunged into the wide wilderness to rejoin her husband. It was a thousand miles, in a birch-bark canoe, rowed by half-clad Indians or still more savage half-breeds, and the route was through a dense forest and over great seas swept by the September storms; but this brave woman undertook the journey attended by only a single female companion. When subsequently reminded of its hazards and hardships, she simply said, "A woman who loves her husband as she should has no stronger attraction than his company, wherever he may be; everything else should be indifferent to her." Cadillac has been censured for being "often involved in troubles caused by his rashness and prejudices," but whatever may have been his faults, he must have possessed noble traits of character to have inspired the strong devotion of such a woman.

The adventurous Frenchman had now built a capital, and assumed the Governorship of a vast territory. His next step was to people his settlement, and obtain the permanent good-will of the natives of the lake region. To these ends he resorted to the novel expedient of settling the Indians about him, and encouraging his soldiers to marry their young women. In this way he hoped to augment his population, and attach the aborigines to him by ties of kinship. The natives received his overtures kindly, and before long four different tribes had established settlements within cannon-shot of the fort—the Miamis and Pottawatamies within half a mile on its either side, and the Hurons and Ottawas on the opposite side of the river, near the present town of Windsor. His scheme for intermingling the white and red races was equally successful, for the Indian maiden soon learned to prefer Johnny Crapeau for a husband. He did not require her to plant his corn and dig his potatoes while he was away upon the hunt or lounging idly about the wigwam. Too highly civilized for that, he cultivated his own beets and cabbages, and arraying his dusky mate in gaudy gown and gewgaws, set her over his household to entertain his guests and preside as an in-door divinity. The extent to which this intermarrying of the French and Indians was carried may be inferred from the fact that the account-books of Judge John

W. Edmonds, who, in 1837, was appointed by President Jackson to pay the Pottawatamies for their Michigan lands, show that fully one-half of that tribe bore French names, or were distinctly classed as half-breeds. The employés of the Hudson Bay Company followed the fashion thus set by Cadillac, and the result was the numerous people of mixed blood who have so recently been in rebellion against the Canadian government. But the offspring of the Detroit marriages did not become half savages. Many of them, in the second and third generation, were so highly civilized as to hold office, lead in society, and found some of the most influential families in Michigan.

To enable them to raise agricultural products, Cadillac granted the settlers land outside the fort, generally in strips having a few hundred feet of frontage upon the river, and extending back so as to form tracts of from thirty to fifty acres. He conveyed these lands in actual fee, and in some instances they were the source of large fortunes to the old families; but in every grant Cadillac reserved to himself certain rights, which curiously illustrate the sort of feudal system which he attempted to establish.* He sought to reproduce in those uncivilized wilds the system then existing where he was born, in Haute-Garonne, France—to form there a literally new France—and for a time he succeeded. But it was the France of Louis XIV., and if the system had not been annulled by the coming in of the English, it would have been swept away by the progress of the eighteenth century.

The settlement grew, and many came to it during the sixty years of French rule that followed, whose names are still borne by some of the best families of Detroit. They brought their wives with them, and formed about the commandant a select society that gave a tone of cultivation to the better part of the white community. They were a high-principled, order-loving class, and their descendants of to-day comprise the conservative element which is so distinct a feature in Detroit society. But in all these years the town was in a nebulous

* All grain was to be ground at his mill, and he exacted an annual tribute as Grand Seigneur. The curious reader will find his system fully detailed in *The History of Detroit and Michigan*, by Silas Farmer—a work recently published, which is very full and accurate in all that relates to the "past and present" of both the city and State.

GROSSE ISLE LIGHT.

state—the nucleus French, the surrounding element a dusky barbarism. In the nature of things there could be no general and thorough amalgamation of these opposite elements, and consequently the town could not crystallize into a compacted community. But with the coming in of the English a new order of things was inaugurated. The Pontiac war soon followed, and that drove the savages from the suburbs. Then the people became more homogeneous, but the French were still an important element. They still retained their own language and religion, and they never affiliated cordially with the English, though the two nationalities had enough in common to make of each other friends and neighbors. It was no longer an attempt to marry civilization and barbarism, but an endeavor to make two white races not overmuch in love with one another

dwell peaceably together in one household.

The Pontiac war was a crisis in the history of Detroit, and if tradition is to be trusted, the town was then saved from destruction by one of those romantic incidents that enliven the dull record of carnage which forms so large a portion of our Western annals. It was in 1763. Pontiac had formed the extensive coalition by which he hoped to drive the English back to the east of the Alleghanies. Detroit was their western stronghold, and that taken, his purpose would be half accomplished. The fort here was therefore fixed upon for the first attack, and the wily savage sought to capture it by stratagem. He was well acquainted with the works and garrison, for his home was in the neighborhood, and he had a "summer seat" only a few miles away, at

THE RIVER AT NIGHT.

Grosse Isle, now a favorite rural resort for Detroit people.

About three o'clock on the afternoon of May 1, 1763, Pontiac made a visit to the British commandant, Major Henry Gladwin, and proposed to him a council at the fort, to which he should come with some of his principal warriors, to smoke the pipe of peace, and brighten the chain of friendship between his people and the English. Suspecting no treachery, the Englishman assented, and a date was fixed upon for the meeting. Before the appointed day arrived, Gladwin was told that the Indians were borrowing saws and files of his blacksmith, and that some of them had been observed sawing off the ends of their rifle barrels. To this, though it was a singular circumstance, he gave but little thought, until it was explained to him on the day preceding the proposed council. Then a beautiful Ojibway maiden, who is said to have been enamored of Gladwin, came to his quarters, bringing a pair of moccasins she had at his request made from an elk-skin he had furnished. He was much delighted with her beautiful workmanship, praised it highly, and requested her to make him another pair from the remainder of the peltry. She hesitated, but after a time took the skin and departed.

But she did not at once leave the fort. She lingered long about the entrance, as if uncertain whether to go or stay, until her continued hesitation attracted the attention of the sentry on duty. Who knows what struggle was then going on in the bosom of this simple child of nature —what balancing between fidelity to her race and love for the pale-face chief, whose lawful bride could not be an Indian maiden? The question of the soldier, why she was waiting, brought her to a sudden decision. Quickly she turned, and entered again the quarters of Gladwin. Holding out the pelt to him, she said, "I cannot take it; I cannot make you the moccasins."

"Why not?" he asked. "Why refuse me so small a favor?"

"Because I may not be able to bring them to you," she answered; and then, in reply to some further questions, she disclosed Pontiac's meditated treachery. Sixty of his bravest warriors had filed off the barrels of their rifles so they might be hidden under their blankets, and thus armed they would come to the council on the morrow. At a given signal from

Pontiac they were to massacre the commandant, and then fall upon and slaughter the garrison, who, taken unarmed and unawares, would be able to make but fee-

THE DEPOT AT NIGHT.

ble resistance. The knives had been already sharpened to take the scalps of the Englishmen.

Pontiac had fought on the side of the French during the war which ended three years before; but he had since been on terms of close amity with the English; and, moreover, was, to all appearance, too noble a savage to be guilty of deliberate treachery. But the warning of the Indian maiden was explicit, and only a fool stops his ears at the sound of danger. Gladwin had but a slender garrison of one hundred and thirty men, and Pontiac had two thousand warriors within the sound of his rifle. The odds were terrific; but the commandant did not shut his gates upon the savages. He met them, as Pontiac proposed, in friendly council; but was prepared to officiate, in case of treachery, at an extensive Indian funeral.

On the following day—May 9, 1763—Pontiac came to the fort with sixty warriors, each having his blanket about him. Precisely at the hour appointed he entered the north gate—about where the First National Bank of Detroit is now located—and at the head of his warriors moved along a street lined on both sides with glittering ranks of redcoats, while at various points polished brass cannon glowered down upon him. At every corner he saw groups of fur traders, armed to the teeth, and every few seconds heard the measured tap of a drum, betokening warlike preparation. Astonished at the unexpected display, he was at first morose and silent; but after a few moments he turned to Gladwin and said, "Why do I see so many of my father's young men standing in the streets with their guns?" He was told it was a custom of the English at the reception of distinguished guests; and then, stately and silent, he moved on to the council-house.

Here, his warriors seated in a circle about him, he rose, and holding in his hand a belt of wampum that was to have given the fatal signal, he made to Gladwin a fervid harangue, professing great friendship to the English. But he did not give the concerted signal, and he finally sat down amid the silent astonishment of his Indians. Then Gladwin approached him, and lifting the corner of his blanket, under which his rifle was concealed, charged him with his treachery, adding that this one breach of faith would be overlooked, but swift vengeance would follow another act of duplicity or aggression. The council then suddenly broke up, the Indians hastily retired, and the Pontiac war followed.

I am persuaded there is more truth in this tradition than in much that has been written of the "queenly Pocahontas"; and if this were all that is told of the beautiful Ojibway maiden, she might be enshrined in history with Nancy Ward, the prophetess of the Cherokees. But tradition adds that she took to fire-water, and one day, when unduly under its influence, fell into a vat of boiling maple syrup, and so perished ingloriously. Alas, that so much fidelity and loveliness should come to an end in a kettle of hot molasses!

Detroit now underwent a fifteen months' siege, during which Gladwin and his men performed feats of genuine heroism. The most unfortunate event that occurred during its progress was the slaughter of Captain Dalzell, who, with a small force, had imprudently ventured from the fort to attack the Indians. He was ambushed and massacred by Pontiac near a large white-wood-tree, which still stands, not far from the centre of the city—the only remaining memorial of those years of havoc and bloodshed. If that old tree were endowed with the faculty of speech, what a tale it might tell of the heroism of the men who there, on the outer ramparts, gave up their lives for civilization!

Ten years of peace now followed, during which Detroit grew rapidly in population and prosperity. Under British enterprise it became the emporium of a vast trade in furs, and the wealth that gives leisure for cultivation soon brought its best society to a condition of refinement which rivalled that of the seaboard cities. The rough Indian trader was there, scarcely more refined than the untutored savage; but mingling with him was the cultured British officer, and the aristocratic French resident who had become rich by trade and the growth in value of his landed possessions. The extent of the trade in furs, considering that it was conducted over the lakes eastward altogether in birch-bark canoes, was a thing that strikes us with astonishment. When the English took possession, in 1760, they found on storage here furs of the value of half a million dollars; and soon the trade so increased that as many as two hundred thousand beaver-skins were shipped in a single year. Crowds of Indians, in their brightly painted bark canoes, were constantly coming and going upon the river, bringing the peltries of the deer, the otter, and the beaver, and carrying away the numerous articles of civilized production which they received in exchange; for all trade was barter. Often these gaudy craft completely lined the river bank, and the vicinity of the fort soon became the mart of a thriving commerce. The canoes were both shop

ON LAKE ST. CLAIR.

and dwelling-house for the aborigines. In them, turned bottom up, and slightly canted to one side to allow of an easy entrance, whole families lived by day and lodged by night—the copper-colored brave and his dusky mate, with the small pappoose strapped to a board upon her back, and an indefinite number of "little Injun boys" rolling in the sand at her feet, clad only in a raiment of bear's-grease to protect them from the swarms of insects that infested the quarters. Here the head of the house displayed his wares—peltries, baskets, brooms, mats, and moccasins—and exhibited a keenness at bargaining fully equal to that of his more civilized white brother. Lovers of the picturesque, no doubt, enjoyed this traffic, if not overfastidious in the matter of dirt.

The war of the Revolution followed, during which Detroit became the centre of British operations in the West. No one locality in the East was the scene of so great activity, or witnessed so much of the horror and barbarity of war. But into the details of this period we would

not now enter. At this time, when she is harassed by foes without and within, we would speak only kindly and lovingly of our great mother across the water. She planted civilization on this continent, and she is destined to carry it around the globe, whoever and whatever may attempt to stay her progress. An irresistible moral force, her work is the uplifting of the race, and she will do this work unless the world goes backward. This is her "manifest destiny"; and if she did not see it as soon as we, it was not her fault, but that of her king and his ministers. The man the British kept in command at Detroit during the first half of the war, though born on British soil, was no true Englishman. He was a human tiger, delighting in blood, and letting loose upon the defenceless border settlements the savage knife and tomahawk, till the old council-house was piled high with the scalps of his own kindred. But he met his Nemesis in George Rogers Clark, who came upon him on March 5, 1779, when he was intrenched with a much larger force at Vincennes, and forced him to an unconditional surrender. Sent into Virginia, he was put into irons by Thomas Jefferson, and only escaped hanging through the intercession of Washington. He was finally paroled, but never afterward was a factor in the war.

A better specimen of an Englishman was Colonel Arent Schuyler De Peyster, who succeeded Hamilton in command at Detroit. He had a difficult task to perform, for the whole French population sympathized with the revolted colonies:

but he executed it with such tact, discretion, and kindness that he won "golden opinions from all sorts of people." He was constantly harassed by secret foes and open enemies—the most powerful among the latter being the indefatigable George Rogers Clark, the one dream of whose life was the capture of this stronghold. Failing in this, Clark went to a drunkard's grave, and so missed a niche in our history alongside of John Sevier and Isaac Shelby. That he failed was owing altogether to the military skill and untiring vigilance of Colonel De Peyster.

De Peyster was a thorough Englishman, though born in New York, and belonging to an old Huguenot family. He was a man of fine cultivation, and, with his accomplished lady, gave a high tone to the Detroit society of that period. After the close of the war he settled in Scotland, and became the friend of Burns, who in 1796 was a private in his regiment of Dumfries Volunteers. It was to him that Burns addressed his "Poem on Life":

> "My honored colonel, deep I feel
>   Your interest in the poet's weal;
> Ah! now sma' heart hae I to speel
>   The steep Parnassus,
>   Surrounded thus by bolus pill
>   And potion glasses."

De Peyster was himself a poet of some pretensions, having conducted a rhyming correspondence with Burns, and published a volume of poems.

Though a far-inland town, Detroit had, even then, the manners of the seaboard, and its fashions were those of the London and Paris of the period—somewhat late, however, to allow of a ninety days' sail from Europe, and a two months' paddle up the Mohawk and across Lake Erie. The ladies wore dresses with long skirts and short waists and still shorter sleeves, and quite as often veiled their faces as their bosoms; while the gentlemen went in shovel hats and powdered periwigs, with silk hose and knee-breeches, ornamented with broad buckles. On festive occasions, which were numerous even in the midst of the war, there was no end to the display of silk and satin gowns and gold-bespangled shoes, and costly jewels glittered in the slow and stately dance that moved through the richly furnished drawing-rooms with the solemn precision of a funeral. This was among the upper classes. The more democratic citizen went

> "In coat, no dainty cloth of France,
>   Bedizened with extravagance,
> But shaped of blanket, black or blue,
>   Though not unknown the scarlet hue.
> Bound were the cuffs and pocket flap
> With fur sufficient for a cap,
>   And on the collar too enough
> To make his wife a stylish muff,
>   While moccasins of caribou
> Covered his feet instead of shoe.
> Gartered about his knees were seen
> Leggings of baize of lively green;
>   His blanket wrapper 'twas polite
> To mention by the name of white,
> For though through darkening hues it went,
>   'Twas only time or accident;
> His mighty buck or woollen mittens
> Would hold at least a brace of kittens;
>   And when he sought to cut a dash,
> He girt him with a crimson sash,
>   And crowned his long and curling locks
> With spoil of woodchuck, 'coon, or fox,
>   While o'er his shoulders broad the tail
> Streamed like a comet on the gale."*

The town at this time, though a century old, contained only about three hundred houses, one-half of which are supposed to have been within the stockade. A census taken July 20, 1782, shows that it had then a permanent population of 2190, 178 of whom were slaves; but a numbering of the people made in 1796 gave it only 500. This large falling off is to be attributed to the withdrawal of the British garrison and the exodus of English people which occurred with the change of government, many of them then leaving to found Amherstburg, a village lower down the river, in Upper Canada. Some Englishmen remained, but the larger portion of the citizens were now of French descent, speaking the language and clinging to the customs of their forefathers.

Soon afterward a considerable number of French immigrants arrived; but no settlers from the Eastern States came to Detroit till 1805, when a few families fixed their abode here; but they do not seem to have been accorded a very cordial welcome by either the French or English residents. The former had sympathized with the colonists in their struggle with the mother country, but they appear to have liked the Yankees best when they were at a comfortable distance. However, the latter did not thrust themselves upon the frontier settlement, being probably deterred not so much by a natural diffidence of character as by the conviction that the place was forever cut off from the seaboard by the Falls of Niagara, and consequently was no suitable field for

* Judge James V. Campbell, of Detroit.

Yankee enterprise. For "Clinton's Folly"—as the Erie Canal was termed—had not then so much as entered the dreams of its great originator.

Between 1805 and 1825—when the canal was completed—Detroit seems to have taken a Rip Van Winkle nap, during which it actually shrank in vital proportions. A census taken October 1, 1805, shows that it then had 525 heads of families—equivalent to a total population of at least 2000, while one taken as late as 1828 gives it only 1517. However, the case was not exactly one of suspended animation. It was simply a cessation of growth and shrinkage of integument, occasioned by two unfortunate occurrences—a destructive fire, and the infliction upon the town and territory of the most anomalous government ever known in this country.

In the summer of 1825 cannon planted at intervals along the line of the Erie Canal, all the way from Albany to Buffalo, announced that Clinton's great work was completed, and the West married to the East by a bond that is indissoluble.

FORT STREET PRESBYTERIAN CHURCH.

Its gates were no sooner opened than a tide of emigration set through them westward. Soon all over New England and eastern New York whole families, and in some instances whole hamlets, were on the move, and such an exodus followed as never was seen except when the Israelites came up out of Egypt, and the Kalmucks fled across the steppes of Asia. At one time it seemed that rural New England would be depopulated. Its best and youngest blood joined in the exodus; and to this fact may be traced the high character and wonderful enterprise of the West of to-day. The first wave rested for a while in western New York, and then the gathering tide swept gradually westward along the lakes and the Ohio,

and finally, in 1830, it touched the shores of Michigan. Then for the first time Detroit became in reality an American town.

In the beginning of 1830 Detroit numbered 2222 people; that is, it stood precisely where it was in 1805; and this during a quarter of a century when the population of the country generally had increased in a ratio altogether unparalleled in history. But now the old town began to feel the general impetus. It increased fourfold in the next ten years; and thus it has gone on ever since, doubling about every decade, till now it numbers, with its suburbs, fully 200,000 souls.

The acorn bears no sort of resemblance to the oak, and yet its great trunk, broad leaves, and wide-spreading branches are all enclosed in the little bowl which lies

EXAMPLES OF DETROIT ARCHITECTURE.

at our feet, waiting to be fed by the juices of the earth, and invigorated by the sunshine. So in the dead-alive old French-English town we have been considering was enfolded the great city one sees now, from the dome of its City Hall stretching miles away in stately rows of brick and stone, along broad shaded avenues which branch from a central hub like the spokes of some great cart wheel. The slow-paced conservatism of its old-time residents is still seen in the modern city; but it is now so wedded to Yankee enterprise that we meet here an almost ideal community, safe but progressive, not engrossed in mere money-getting, but cultivating as well the social amenities of life, and extracting from existence, as it passes, a healthful and rational enjoyment. In proportion to its size, Detroit has a smaller foreign population than any city in the Union, and as the bulk of its people are of Eastern birth or extraction, it is to-day more truly New England in character than the good town of Boston itself. In no sense is it a Western town. In 1880 the numerical centre of the Union was found to be fifty-eight miles west of Cincinnati. With the speed at which population is now travelling westward, Detroit will soon be the central city of the country.

The great fire of 1805 was a present calamity but a future blessing to Detroit, for it enabled the town to escape from narrow lanes into broad open avenues stretching straight as an arrow in all directions. Those old dead and gone worthies did not, perhaps, forecast the future; but, if they did not, they planned "better than they knew," for they laid out the new town on lines that only needed to be filled up and extended to make a future city of regular yet picturesque beauty. This will strike any one who ascends to the roof of the City Hall and looks down upon the straight, symmetrical streets, crossed every now and then by broad, branching avenues. But what will surprise him most will be the great array of fine dwellings and palatial public edifices he will see in every direction. On none of the latter has so much money been squandered as on the Capitol at Albany;

but in number and uniform elegance they are not equalled by the public buildings of any city of similar size in the Union. The same remark applies generally to the private dwellings. Long vistas of West Fort Street and Jefferson and Woodward avenues are merely rows of private palaces, overhung with great trees, and seated amid beautiful grounds that are parks in miniature. Beauty, too, is blended with use in the business portions of the city. Some of the warehouses are superb structures; and Griswold Street, the financial centre, is as far in advance of State Street in Boston and Wall Street in New York as our time is of the last century. This street, beginning at the High School, and running to the river, where at the dock are moored fleets of vessels, is occupied almost exclusively by lawyers and bankers; and this has led a recent writer to apply to it the rhyme of Horace Smith:

"At the top of the street the attorneys abound,
And down at the bottom the barges are found.
Fly, Honesty, fly to some safer retreat,
For there's craft in the river and craft in the street."

If the observer should climb the two hundred steps that lead to the cupola of the City Hall, he would be nearly as many

GRISWOLD STREET.

feet from the ground, and looking down from this height, he would be lost in wonder at the extent of the view, and the evidences everywhere apparent of wealth and enterprise. Whichever way he might turn, he would encounter a striking prospect. A broad panorama would be spread out below and around him—the wide river, the distant lake of St. Clair, the opposite Dominion of Canada, and the widely expanded city, extending for miles in all directions. At his very feet he would behold a vast hive of human activity—great throngs surging through the spacious streets, hundreds of furnaces belching their thick smoke to the sky, shrieking trains threading their rapid way upon the outskirts, and in the distance countless white-winged craft going and coming on the island-dotted river. Figures, it is said, do not lie; nevertheless they seldom give us as vivid ideas as the sight of the eye. And yet we may form a vague conception of the commerce of Detroit when we are told that 6000 steam and sailing vessels, manned by crews numbering 22,000 men, come and go here in a single year; and we may conceive of the wealth of the town if we understand that the assessed value of its real and personal property in 1884 was $110,721,955—in other words, an amount which, divided equally, would give every man, woman, and child within its limits the snug sum of $728.

From this vast height the men below dwindle into pigmies, and even the stately buildings, which look so imposing when viewed from the ground, assume much less striking proportions. There is nothing like a distant view to strip things of their individual magnitude. It is the prospect of the eagle when he looks down in his lofty flight and thinks upon the insignificance of man and all his puny belongings. But the dome of the Detroit City Hall is not as high up as the eagle soars, and hence the observer there catches none of the lordly bird's impressions of the littleness of human things. On the contrary, he is amazed at the evidences he everywhere sees of the mighty forces that are ever at work in the brain of man, pent up in the little globe which he carries about under his beaver. He sees these forces in the palatial buildings, the thronging avenues, the white sails that everywhere bespangle the broad, gleaming river. The very stone structure on which he stands—ninety feet front, two

hundred deep, and two hundred again to the top of its flag-staff—by the patient might of man has grown up in two hundred years from the rude log citadel where Cadillac housed his men, and Hamilton stored his human scalps, bought at so much per head, till piled so high that a tall man could not reach to their summit. Other evidences of human enterprise and energy lie below, and it may not be amiss to give them a few moments' consideration.

However, the first and most agreeable things that strike the eye are not the work of man, but of nature. These are the numerous small parks that everywhere dot the landscape—oases of green in a wide waste of brick and stone. One of these, and the most beautiful, the Grand Circus, is adorned with two fine fountains, and located in the very heart of the city. Here the tired citizen comes of sultry nights, and in the spray-laden air finds refreshing coolness. This park is semicircular, and divided into two parts by Woodward Avenue, and from it all the principal streets radiate. The avenues often intersect the streets at oblique angles, and wherever they do are smaller parks, triangular in form, and frequently adorned with fountains. The Campus Martius can scarcely be called a park, for it is paved with stone, and in the midst of the ceaseless hum of business. It faces the City Hall, and in its centre is the Soldiers' Monument, designed by Randolph Rogers, and erected at a cost of sixty thousand dollars. The figure of the Indian maiden which surmounts it is intended to symbolize the State, and the inscription it bears tells that it was "Erected by the people of Michigan in honor of the martyrs who fell and the heroes who fought in defence of Liberty and Union." North of this monument, and facing the Campus Martius, is the Opera-house—an elegant stone structure capable of seating two thousand persons. Glancing along Woodward Avenue, one block from the City Hall, is seen, at the north end of Griswold Street, the imposing High School, with, in its rear, the valuable museum of the Scientific Association, which is freely opened to the public four days in the week. Just beyond, on Gratiot Avenue, is the Public Library, a large and substantial building, occupying the centre of a square, and containing upward of forty thousand volumes. Beyond, the United States Cus-

FOUNTAIN IN THE GRAND CIRCUS.

tom-house, a large and fine building on Griswold Street, is the Michigan Central Depot, twelve hundred and fifty feet long and one hundred and two wide, with a self-supporting iron roof covering a space which is but a single room; and near it stands a grain-elevator, with a cupola that resembles the tower of a cathedral. The largest church edifice to be seen is the Roman Catholic cathedral; but there are many fine specimens of church architecture, one of which is shown in our illustration of the Fort Street Presbyterian Church.

No less than fifty miles of street railway diverge from the City Hall, and thread every portion of the city. The longest of these is the Fort Wayne line, which extends to the large fortification which now defends Detroit. The works enclose sixty-five acres, and there are

WALTER HARPER.

NANCY MARTIN.

none more substantial in the country. Near the foot are the water-works, of which a view is given on page 344. Everywhere the observer sees evidence of business enterprise and wealth almost without limit, and as he turns away to descend again to the solid earth, it may be that he will exclaim, "Surely there can here be no poverty." But should he think this, he would be mistaken. There is great wealth here, but it is not divided equally, and here, as elsewhere, are rich and poor. "As towns grow, beggars multiply," and even in Yankee towns there is poverty, and this not for the reason that Yankees are idle and thriftless, but because there are some evils inseparable from our present civilization which naturally entail want and wretchedness. We must go back to barbarism if we would have none

THE HARPER HOSPITAL.

who hunger and thirst, no naked to clothe, no sick or aged to relieve, and no prisoners to visit. In that happy state nakedness is the normal condition, the sick are left to die without the aid of doctors, and the aged are knocked on the head to help them to the hereafter. Detroit has poor, but its people have read the twenty-fifth chapter of Matthew. Last year they relieved 3569 persons, at a total expenditure of $27,429 77. It has also sick and aged and orphaned young, and for these it has provided numerous asylums, a Home for the Friendless, and various other institutions, the most notable among which is the Harper Hospital, which owes its existence to

of the poor should be taught, free of charge, the industrial arts. It does this on a large scale, and its whole working has been most satisfactory.

Within a month from the making of Mr. Harper's magnificent gift the hos-

DISTANT VIEW OF BELLE ISLE PARK.

the munificence of a benevolent but eccentric gentleman, who twenty-five years ago endowed it with his entire worldly possessions, on the curious condition that the city should pay him during his life an annuity of $2000. This, in the course of five years, he voluntarily reduced to $600. The hospital was to be not only a home for the sick, but a school where the youth

pital received a similar endowment, and on similar terms, from a Mrs. Martin, familiarly known as Nancy Martin, who at the time kept a vegetable stand in the market. She gave it all her property—

UNITED STATES SHIP-CANAL ON LAKE ST. CLAIR.

valued at the time at $15,000—with the stipulation that a small house should be built for her at an expense of $450, and she be allowed an annuity of $600. She is said to have been originally a coarse, rough-spoken woman, who, on occasions, had been known to "swear like a trooper," but the sweet influences of charity soon softened her manners. She relinquished her stand in the market, became more mild and womanly, and in 1875 died in the "full odor of sanctity." The property which these two persons thus donated is now valued at over $200,000, and the building erected upon it is probably the finest devoted to similar uses west of the Hudson. In its reception-room hang the portraits of its honored founders, Walter Harper and Nancy Martin.

The most extensive of the city's parks is situated just outside of the corporate limits, in mid-channel of the beautiful river. It comprises seven hundred acres—the whole of

the island of Belle Isle—and is destined to rival the Central Park of New York in rural magnificence. Seven hundred thousand dollars have already been expended upon it, and "the end is not yet." A distant view of it may be obtained from the Detroit shore, but the visitor will most probably take one of the small steamers which are constantly plying up and down the river for a nearer inspection, and in that case he would no doubt prolong his

Entrance to Fort Wayne.

The Water Works.

trip as far as Put-in-Bay, where Perry defeated the British squadron, and paved the way for the recapture of Detroit by Harrison and Isaac Shelby. If the trip should be on a moonlit night, it would be all the more enjoyable. Scattered through the whole course of the stream, at intervals of not more than a mile, are islands ranging in size from one acre to several thousand acres, and altogether the scenery is excelled in beauty by that of no other river, except it may be the St. Lawrence. One of the largest islands is named Grosse Isle, on which is the lighthouse shown in the engraving on page 332. On this island Pontiac had a summer residence, and it is a favorite resort for Detroit people in hot weather.

Probably nothing so truthfully reflects the intelligence and moral character of a city as its public journals. The press is at once the creator and reflex of public opinion, and a newspaper of high moral tone cannot long exist in a degraded community. Judged by its public journals, Detroit must therefore be a city of high moral and intellectual character. Nowhere in the country is there a press of greater ability, or one that treats current issues with more calmness and dignity, or less of acrimony and personality. Some of the journals are strongly partisan; but they conduct their controversies with courtesy—handle polished weapons with the skill and address of gentlemen. The personal relations of the leading editors are also said to be of the most friendly character; and this must be so if an anecdote current in regard to two of the most prominent of the fraternity be at all veracious. One of them, it is said, when jaded with his daily work, sent to his opposition neighbor to help him out with an editorial, saying to his Irish messenger, somewhat figuratively, "Ask him to oblige me with about half a gill of editorial." The servant repeated the message literally, when the opposition editor coolly took from the wall of his sanctum the portrait of a certain long-eared quadruped, and told the man to present it to his master with his compliments.

"But it's not that his honor is axing for, sir," answered the Hibernian. "He is wanting an editorial, and not a pictur of the editor."

The principal journals publish the news of the world at the same hour that it appears in the seaboard cities, and some of them are extensively circulated. One— the *Free Press*—has had the enterprise to open a branch office and issue a weekly edition in London, where it has attained a circulation of 75,000 copies, owing, no doubt, very largely to its general character, but more especially to the articles of C. B. Lewis (better known as "M. Quad"), who is perhaps the most unique and gen-

uine humorist this country has produced, excepting only Artemus Ward and Hosea Biglow.

"M. Quad" is not a humorous "artist"— a boss mechanic who manufactures jokes as a carpenter does packing-boxes, with saw and jack-plane and much exudation

C. B. LEWIS ("M. QUAD").

of perspiration. He is naturally and spontaneously funny. Humor gushes from him like champagne from an uncorked bottle, bubbling and effusive, and drenching us, whether we will or not, with laughter. And there is wisdom with his wit—strong, homely common-sense mixed with a racy, unctuous humor which makes his wisdom as grateful to our taste as whale oil is to the palate of an Esquimau. He is not a "product of the soil," with a local flavor. He is of universal relish, as is witnessed by the wide popularity that the Detroit *Free Press* owes to his contributions.

It is not generally known when or where he was born, nor is it a matter of much consequence, since his career did not begin till he was blown up, some fifteen years ago, on an Ohio River steamboat. He is, perhaps, the only example of a man who has been lifted into fame by being tossed a hundred feet into the

THE SOLDIERS' MONUMENT.

air, and coming down, more dead than alive, to tell the story. He did this. Standing at his printer's case, when he was so far recovered as to limp about, he put into type "How it feels to be blown up," and the whole West burst into laughter. That laugh made "M. Quad" famous. He was then transferred from the composing-room to the editorial department, and ever since short extracts from the *Free Press* have been copied into every journal throughout the country.

About ten years ago he invented—or rather created—"His Honor," and "Bijah," and "Brother Gardner," of the "Lime-kiln Club"—characters totally dissimilar, but each as natural, original, individual, and ludicrous as any in American literature. "His Honor" presides over a police court, and makes sage reflections upon men and things as they come into his field of view. "Brother Gardner" is a shrewd and quaint gentleman of color, who has all the idioms and characteristics of his race, but is not a burlesque of our colored fellow-citizens; he handles his own people gently, but satirizes the foibles, frailties, and weaknesses of the whites inimitably. His say-

ings might be termed explosive wisdom— the reader is sure to imbibe a wise thought, but it is certain to explode within him. "Artemus Ward" created one character; "M. Quad" has given birth to three, and each one has, during a period of ten years, given delight to millions.

The man is precisely what we are led to expect from his writings. He is by turns "His Honor," "Bijah," and "Brother Gardner," with the dry humor and quaint wisdom that is peculiar to each character. "If there is an odder man than he in the country," said a Detroit gentleman to me not long ago, "we would like to have him sent along with the circus." His looks, his manner, even the tones of his voice, are peculiar and eccentric. He talks as he writes, and always without any seeming premeditation. His "den," as he calls his "sanctum," in an upper story of the *Free Press* building, is a curiosity shop filled with odd mementos and knick-knacks. Here is a bit of rope that helped to hang a murderer, and a pair of shackles of the old slave time; there are bullets from Gettysburg, powder-flasks from the *Merrimac*, and swords, sabres, muskets, and shot and shell from a score of battlefields; while around the walls, side by side with portraits of Sheridan and Custer and busts of Grant and Lee, are pictures of a dozen of the most noted criminals. But the oddest thing in the room is a slender man of about forty, with close-cropped gray hair, heavy mustache, keen, intent eyes, and an earnest, somewhat eager expression, who sits at an old-fashioned table, and looks up with a smile of welcome as a stranger enters his apartment. This is "M. Quad," known among his personal acquaintance as C. B. Lewis; and he works away at that table eight hours in a day, writing, at high pressure, short paragraphs or political leaders, and now and then seeking relaxation in a little merriment with "Bijah" and "Brother Gardner," for his best work is done as a relief from the daily drudgery of journalism.

The Revisers have not been able to amend the text, "Woe unto you when all men shall speak well of you," and if it is to be taken literally, "M. Quad" is in a bad way, as all his acquaintance unite in saying that he is temperate, social, domestic, kind-hearted, a lover of his friends, and a hater of nobody. He is also, they say, open-handed, and so given to charity that, though imposed upon seven times in a day by fraudulent mendicancy, he again seven times in a day empties his pockets to the pleadings of distress. He is also said to be modest, and not at all puffed up by the fact that he has a weekly audience of a million, nearly one-half of whom are matter-of-fact Englishmen, who take him with their beefsteak and ale, as a sure help to a healthy digestion. He is spoken of as odd and eccentric, and that he may be, but I incline to the opinion that this peculiarity is due to the fact that Nature produced him in one of her genial moods, when she would do the world a kindly turn by bestowing upon it a gentle soul, who should do us good by spreading for us a wholesome feast of mingled wit and wisdom.

Considering its past progress—growing in fifty years from a town of 2000 people to a city of 200,000—it is not difficult to predict the future greatness of Detroit. It has all the elements of growth and stability—hereditary caution combined with a spirit of enterprise that is constantly pressing it onward and upward; and hence it cannot fail in another fifty years to take a front rank among American cities.

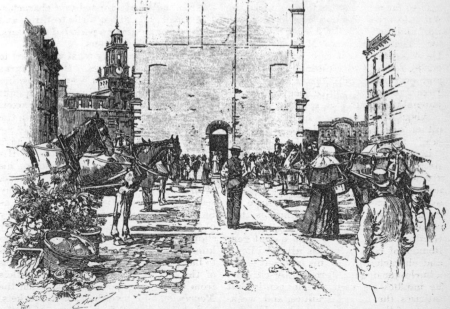

AT THE MARKET.

A DAY'S 'DRIVE' WITH MONTANA COWBOYS

SOFTLY outlined in dark masses, a wall in the east against the clear sky, over which the first faint flush of early morning is slowly stealing, height upon height, rise the mountains. Gray in the shadow of still lingering night, the wide plain stretches at their feet. In the blue dome above, the stars, going to rest after their nocturnal vigil over the slumbering earth, extinguish their shining lanterns one by one, and the moon, veiling her mild face in the fleecy folds of a soft, low-lying white cloud, is slowly sinking below the horizon, as if fleeing in maiden modesty before the ardent gaze of the coming sun-god.

Rosy red, glowing as with a deep warm fire, brighter and brighter grows the sky; darker, yet more clearly in the rich purple of their shadows, loom the mountains, until the sun, shooting long, glittering shafts of yellow light up to the zenith from behind them, sheds the reflection of its approaching glory far over the level surface of the prairie, chasing away the shades of night and rousing sleeping nature from her dreams.

Down in the camp, in the shelter of a grove of low trees hard by the bank of the little stream which cuts through the plain, winding in graceful curves until lost in the mouth of the cañon over there in the mountains, they are already astir, and the smoke of the watch-fire, replenished with an armful of the dry sage-brush and burning brightly, rolls upward in a straight blue column, while the black face of the negro cook, shining like polished ebony in contrast with the huge flapping white felt hat that overshadows

A COW-BOY.

it, is bent over the camp kettle, filled to the brim with steaming coffee for the men's breakfast, some of whom stand, stretching their limbs and yawning, around the fire, while others wander down to the stream to make their hasty toilet, calling to one or two sleepy comrades looking up with slumber-clouded eyes and dishevelled heads from out of the heap of blankets and buffalo-robes spread on the ground. The horses are picketed near by, and are cropping the nutritious "bunch" grass; and scattered on all sides for a mile or more over the plain, some still lying on the soft ground, others standing reposefully in little groups, chewing the cud and sniffing the sweet, cool morning air, are hundreds of sharp-horned, half-savage cattle, their forms relieving dark against the yellowish-brown expanse of prairie.

Up comes the sun over the mountains; brighter and brighter glows the sky. Away off there, loping stealthily along, now stopping for a moment to look back over their shoulders, now trotting on again, a few coyotes are sneaking back, with drooping bushy tails and pointed ears, to the cover of the little "coulees" and mound-shaped buttes at the base of the hills, like coward prowlers of the night seeking their dens at the coming of the light. The discordant, laughing cry of the magpie, flitting from bush to bush by the banks of the little river, mingles with the whistle of the broad-winged curlew, and far, far up in the heavens two black specks in the blue ether, swinging round and round in great circles, an eagle and his mate are soaring.

Rustle now, boys, rustle! for you have a long and hard day's work before you. You must get away in the cool of the morning, for these hundreds of cattle must be driven through the narrow cañon in the mountain to-day, and the evening must find them slaking their thirst in the cool streams and feeding on the rich "bunch" grass on the great plains on the other side of the "divide." Rustle there, you lazy fellows! No time for "monkeying" round now. Roll up your bedding, pack your wagon, get your breakfast, and away!

A picturesque, hardy lot of fellows, these wild "cow-boys," as they sit on the ground by the fire, each man with his can of coffee, his fragrant slice of fried bacon on the point of his knife-blade, or sandwiched in between two great hunks of bread, rapidly disappearing before the onslaughts of appetites made keen by the pure, invigorating breezes of these high plains. See that brawny fellow with the crisp, tight-curling yellow hair growing low down on the nape of his massive neck rising straight and supple from the low collar of his loose flannel shirt, his sun-browned face with the piercing gray eyes looking out from under the broad brim of his hat, his lower limbs clad in the heavy "chaps"—or leather overalls —stained a deep reddish-brown by long use and exposure to wind and weather, his revolver in its holster swinging from the cartridge-filled belt, and his great spurs tinkling at every stride, as, having

drained the last drop of coffee, he puts down the can, and turns from the fire toward the horses, picking up as he goes the huge heavy leather saddle, with its high pommel and streaming thongs of rawhide, that has served him as a pillow during the night. Quickly his "cayuse" is saddled, the great broad hair-rope girths tightly "sinched," the huge bit slipped into the unwilling mouth, and with a bound the active fellow is in the saddle. Paw, pony, paw; turn your eyes till the whites show; lay your pointed ears back; squeal and kick to your heart's content. Oh, *buck* away! you have found your master; for the struggle does not last long. The practiced hand, the heavy spurs, and stinging whip soon repeat the almost daily lesson, and with one last wicked shake of the head the wiry "cayuse" breaks into his easy lope, and away go horse and rider to their appointed station on the flank of the great drove.

The others soon follow, camp is broken, the wagon securely packed ready for the road, and the work of the day commences. The cattle seem to know what is coming. On the edges of their scattered masses the steers lift their heads and gaze, half stupidly, half frightened, at the flying horsemen; as the flanks are turned they begin closing in toward one another, moving up in little groups to a common centre. Now and then a steer or some young bull, more headstrong or more terrified than his comrades, breaks away and canters off clumsily over the prairie. In a moment he is pursued, headed off, turned, and driven in toward the herd again. As they "close in mass"—to use an apt military phrase—"rounded up" on all sides by the swift-riding cow-boys, they are gently urged onward by the drivers in the rear, until the whole herd is slowly moving forward, feeding as they go, in a loose wide column, headed toward the break in the mountains that indicates the mouth of the cañon through which it is to pass.

Gradually the prairie is crossed; quietly and gently the nervous brutes are crowded more closely together; two or three of the men gallop on ahead to the opening of the pass, guarded by two cone-shaped mounds like redoubts thrown out to protect the entrance to the fastnesses of the mountains, in order to head off stragglers and to turn the leaders of the herd into the narrow trail that runs in between the

THROUGH THE CANON.

high, tree-covered, rocky walls of the cañon. So! so-o-o! gently calling, quietly and patiently urging, the drivers bunch the horned multitude together into one almost compact mass. So-o-o! So! gently! gently! push, boys, push in from both sides, curb your horses, keep them quiet. So! so! drive slowly from the rear, press on slowly, yet firmly, until the head of the herd enters the pass.

Patter! patter! patter! the rushing, confused roar of hundreds of hoofs striking the hard road-bed, a queer sound, filling the air with a low yet penetrating noise, like the falling of millions of hailstones on dry leaves, not the heavy and sharp ringing tramp of iron-shod horses, but a shuffling, soft, although distinctly marked muffled rolling, something like that produced by the distant passage of a heavily laden freight-train. Slowly, irresistibly onward through the wild cañon—the frowning walls of sandstone and gigantic pines towering on one side, on the other and below, rushing and foaming over its rough bed, the river—pushing forward like a stream of liquid lava from some vomiting crater, long drawn out in a crowded, dense column on the narrow, winding trail, moves the mighty herd. A thick, smoke-like cloud of yellow dust—through which the sunlight breaking lights up the tangle of horns, swaying and tossing in the distance like foam cresting the angry billows of some dark, storm-lashed torrent—hovers above; a heavy, sweetish odor fills the air; and mingling with the pattering rush of the hoofs and the roar of the stream comes the occasional booming bellow of some frightened steer.

Very slowly and cautiously the herd moves forward; sometimes there is a halt in front; those in the rear crowd up more closely; very gently, and with soothing cries, the experienced cow-boys urge them on again. It is ticklish work, for a momentary panic may drive scores of them down the precipitous sides of the mountain. Already this morning an unfortunate steer, pushed in a sudden, panicky rush of his companions over the edge of the trail, has fallen down into the foaming torrent, and been dashed to death on the jagged rocks a hundred feet below. Riding slowly in the rear, look along the trail and over the backs of the advancing cattle up the cañon ahead. Sometimes the road descends until the stream licks the earth at its side, spreading in little shal-

A REFRACTORY STEER.

low pools across it, sometimes cutting through it, as it curves abruptly around some point of rocks, only to recross it again further on.

And now the cañon widens, and, succeeding the high rock walls and great trees, its sides gradually merge into gently rising, grass-covered slopes; the river too is broader, its surface shining like polished silver, and betraying its onward movement only by an occasional soft ripple and low lap-lap of the water against its overhanging banks, from which, breathing out the sweet fragrance of thousands of newly opened buds, the wild rose bushes hang down their slender branches. Away up the slopes, dancing and nodding their pretty heads in the soft breeze, the gayly colored wild flowers—yellow sunflowers, daisies, blue harebells—mingle their bright hues, melting into one another on the distant round hill-tops, covering them as with a carpet of the softest velvet.

Let the herd move more easily now, drifting slowly along, and opening its ranks a little, so as to enable the hungry brutes to crop at the fresh juicy grass as they go; you have leisure to open your saddle-bags and take a little lunch, *sur le pouce*, and a "swig" of whiskey and water, if you have any. Or you can light your pipe as you let your bridle fall on your cayuse's neck, and lounge in your saddle, folding your arms, and resting your elbows on the flat, round top of the high pommel, keeping, however, a watchful eye on your charges lest some adventurous two-year-old wander away from the drove and lose himself in the deep coulees or ravines that, cutting through the rounded spurs of the hills, run down to the edge of the trail. Although the sun is now high in the heavens, and pours down the full power of his rays, the breeze tempers the heat, and there rises no blinding, choking dust from the soft grass, except a little cloud now and then where some tyrannic bull or surly steer widens the space about him by a short, vicious charge at some encroaching comrades. The afternoon wears slowly away, the herd constantly advancing, except for a short halt now and again at some inviting spot, where the grass grows luxuriantly or the stream crosses. The hills are smaller, there are wide openings between them, and soon a broad plain, rich in the marvellous color of its shifting light and shade, and covered with brown waving grass and great patches of bluish-gray sage-brush, stretches to the far horizon, flat and apparently level as a billiard table, full of promise of rest and refreshment for the hot and tired beasts.

There are plenty of good camping places this evening. Grass there is in abundance; the herd is still following the course of the rivulet, so water in plenty is at hand; and fuel of the best for a camp fire can be had for the trouble of cutting a few armfuls of the sage-brush.

The cattle feel that the hour of rest has come, as, unrestrained by the drivers, they wander at freedom out on the prairie, or stand knee-deep in the water, drinking it in in long draughts, and elevating their dripping muzzles to "moo" forth their contentment. The horses are unsaddled and allowed to browse, and as the sun is sinking in the west and the fires are lighted, all hands busy themselves in preparation of the evening meal.

The long twilight sets in, gradually melting into the shades of night; silence reigns over the prairie, broken only by the far-off yelp of the prowling coyote, or the crackling of a dry twig as some restless steer moves about in the sage-brush. The tired cow-boy, the events of the day briefly discussed with the after-supper pipe by the glowing embers of the fire, spreads his bedding on the ground, rolls his blanket about him, and, his head resting in the seat of his saddle, is soon buried in the dreamless sleep of the hardy frontiersman.

IN A HABITANT VILLAGE

PHILIPPE ST. GELAIS pushed my canoe from the club's float before the sun had struck the tops of the towering spruce along the river banks. All the forenoon I whipped the black, foam-specked pools as we worked up-stream through splashes of sunlight and frothy shallows. At noon we stopped to lunch under the drooping branches of a sweet-smelling balsam farther up-stream than I had ever come before. When we had finished our trout and bacon, I lay down on the soft, white lichen to enjoy the warm sun and listen to the wash of the river and to the voices in the breeze. My guide, picking up a coal from the embers in the fire, flipped it into his pipe-bowl with a dexterous movement of his knotty hand, and the pleasant smoke of *tabac Canadien* drifted by me.

"Is it that the *m'sieur* would be wearied if I speak more about St. Anne?" he asked.

"No, Philippe, you know I always like to hear about your home," I answered. "But can't we go and visit your folks? You say it is not far. Would it be a difficult trip?"

"*Pas, m'sieur,*" he assured me, "it is a voyage of the most easy—of two hours only. But, *m'sieur*"—he moved uneasily —"but it is not good at my house like the club to which *m'sieur* belongs. He might have of disappointment when he arrived at there and the family be tiresome to him. Yet, if he wishes to go, I will guide him so far as there with the most great pleasure."

"*Très-bien,* Philippe, let's go."

Quietly and swiftly, with that grace he

HABITANTS GETTING WATER FOR HOUSEHOLD PURPOSES

had inherited from his *coureurs des bois* ancestors, he cleaned the few camp-dishes and had them back into the canoe before my pipe burned out.

"All is well, *m'sieur*," he said shortly, picking up the paddle and respectfully bowing.

I took my seat in the middle of the canoe and Philippe silently stepped in behind me. The delicate craft glided into the stream, its wake widening out to the banks and twisting the inverted forest into strange moving forms. The wood about us was utter quiet—made stiller by the sense that from its depths a myriad beady eyes watched our passing. Even the wind died away in this canyon of trees, and only the gurgle of the stream and the swish of Philippe's paddle broke the silence. At length the water grew icy cold; the Laurentides rose high about us, and along the narrowing banks the birches leaned over and met above us.

"*Entends!*" Philippe whispered, raising his paddle as he listened. "That is a *coq* at the house of Picard. It is soon now—but soon."

And so it was. A field appeared in the wilderness—and there was the first house we had seen since we left the club that morning.

"Ah, it is the house of Picard," came the voice from behind, "and here is the lane where he gets water."

"From the river?" I asked.

"*Oui,* it is that we get all our water from the *rivière,*" he replied. "Sometimes, though, in the winter, one is not able to get of it, and it is then that one melts of snow, but it is not good like the *rivière.* He is only a small *rivière,* this, and he often makes of anger in the spring-time when he is big, and has even killed a few of us, but we others habitants love him because he is much to us, *m'sieur*—and he brings one home, too," he added, tenderly.

Philippe grounded the canoe below an old mill with its ominous rumble of wooden machinery and the splash of its creaking water-wheel. Then we scrambled up the bank on to the edge of the village. Steep-roofed houses two stories high, all well whitewashed, and sitting at any angle to a winding street, huddled as though for protection about a gray stone church that towered from a clump of Normandy poplars. The sun hit the white houses with dazzling brightness and danced on the shining, tin-covered church roof. Dahlias and sunflowers drooping over the picket fences about the gardens brushed our sleeves as we walked down the board walk that lined but one side of the street. The pleasant drone of busy flax-wheels wafted through open doors. Children peered around corners or flattened their noses against windows as we passed. Old men and old women with white bonnets on were smoking and knitting on their *galeries* in the warm sun; others were talking leisurely in the road to passing neighbors. All the men tipped their hats as they bowed to us. On the steps before the door of an old log-house a man was cutting his son's hair.

"*Bo' jou',* Chagnon," Philippe spoke to him, and then, turning to me, said: "He is the owner of the *moulin* where it is that we left the *canot.* He has *b'en d'argent*—he. His father was the *seigneur.*"

Near each house was a structure of stone and mortar, usually across the road, and built on a platform of logs.

"What is it that they are?" Philippe said, repeating my question in *patois.* "They are *fours,* where one makes the bread to bake. We have not of ovens in the stoves of our houses like the *messieurs* have at the club."

Through the long, clear shadow from the church a thin column of smoke rose from a big-mouthed chimney in the end of a roof that turned up at the eaves—over two *galeries.*

"*C'est b'en* that mother will have the supper soon," Philippe said. "One has much of hunger after he is on the *rivière* all day—is it not?"

As he spoke the church-bell sounded over the peaceful valley. I looked up to the spire and saw the sun's last rays turning the gilded cross on its apex into a brilliant yellow flame against the deep blue of the Canadian sky. Philippe stopped, took off his old frayed hat, and, with his eyes to the ground, muttered a prayer. Down the road was another man saying angelus also, bowed before a tall wooden cross that rose from a tangle of brambles and berry-bushes. When Philippe ended the prayer we went on and were soon at his house.

The kitchen was a spacious low-posted room, with long strips of brightly dyed rag carpet on its uneven floor. A large cross, bound together with caribou thongs, and a print of the bleeding heart hung over a door that opened into the only other room on the ground floor. The air was filled with the smell of frying pork and the high-pitched *patois* of Philippe's mother making profuse apologies for the appearance of the room. The little children hung about her while she was getting the supper-table ready, looking shyly around her flowing homespun skirts at me, until their father spoke to them and they all sat down on a long green bench in the deep shadow under the stairway.

"Now if it is pleasing to the *m'sieur,*" madam said at last, wiping a chair with her white apron for me and lighting a lamp, "we will eat before the *souper* makes itself cold."

There was a clatter of chairs as we gathered around a big bowl of pea porridge steaming in the centre of the table by the lamp. Each ate directly from it with a big iron spoon. Reaching across the red table-cover, I thrust mine in with the others, and finding it very appetizing, praised it to madam.

"*Merci!*" she returned, her bony face smiling gratefully; "but it is easy to make of it. The *m'sieur* will find it in all the homes of us. Since the church laid of taxes on all the things in our gardens, we habitants have raised much of peas, for, *m'sieur* "—she added, smiling—" it named not the pea in the law, and they have much of strength *aussi*. Is it not, Lacomb?"

"*Oui*," came his deep voice through a mouthful of fat pork, but it was far less eloquent than the ponderous shoulders on his sturdy frame or any movement of his body. His muscles forced against his red-striped shirt whenever he passed me the unsalted bread or the maple sugar.

"Ah, one sees with ease that the *m'sieur* eats not with so many of chil-dren," he remarked, his keen eyes glint-ing in the lamplight; "he reaches for things not fast enough."

"There are eighteen to us," his *créa-ture* put in proudly. "Philippe has the most of age. He has twenty years, and little Angela here has three months."

I expressed surprise at the number and asked if the neighboring families were so large.

"*Mais oui, m'sieur*," she replied, quick-ly, "and one cannot have a too large family. *M'sieur le curé* says that well of children pleases the Heaven much. If a *figure* marries herself and has not of them, it is a curse, *certainement*."

"*Oui, c'est vrai*," Lacomb agreed; "but the most great thing that ever to one comes is to have an *avocat* in the family. We feed ourselves with hope that it will be Joseph in this family," he add-ed, placing his gnarled hand on the boy's shock head.

"Is it that the *m'sieur* wishes more of tea?" Philippe's sister Marie asked, reaching across the table with the stone teapot.

"No, thanks," I answered, for I had eaten quite enough. The soup-bowl and the dishes which had been heaped with potatoes and *pem-bina* were empty. The family arose, and Philippe, La-comb, and I went out into the twi-light, while mad-am and the chil-dren washed the dishes in a wood-en sink.

A PARENTAL DUTY

"ONE SEES LITTLE FROM THESE MOUNTAINS"

"The *m'sieur* says that he would have of pleasure to hear you play," Philippe said to his father as we sat down and tilted our chairs against the house. "Will you get the violin?"

The village was wrapped in the soft gray of the long Canadian dusk. The windows of the houses glowed from the warm lights within. The distant mountains deepened in the gathering gloom. The sound of voices and the occasional strains of homely habitant *chansons* drifted through the village as others came out for their evening smoke or strolled down the plank walk to gossip with their neighbors.

"That was Picard, the town-crier," Philippe said, after a full-faced fellow with bristling side-whiskers had stopped to talk with him and gone on again.

"The town-crier," I repeated; "what does he do?"

"*Mon Dieu,* is there not a *crieur public* in the *ville* of the *m'sieur?*" he asked.

I explained as simply as I could that we once had them, but that now we had newspapers containing the news of the whole world delivered to our houses two or three times a day. "How," I asked, "could there be criers in cities a hundred times larger than St. Anne?"

I waited to see what this child of Na-

ture would say, whose whole life had been spent in this remote valley and on those few streams that flowed out of it—into an unbounded world of trees.

"To have a hundred more, *m'sieur,*" came the answer.

Lacomb came out with his fiddle.

"*Excusez moi, m'sieur,* it is that I must put the bull at the church into the barn before I play," he said, and started across the street. "Picard auctions him next Sunday after mass for the Infant Jesus."

"Oh, *oui*—the town-crier!" Philippe exclaimed, remembering I had asked him a question. "He stands on the steps of the church after *masse* and tells what it is that has happened in the week and gives notices of sales of cows and pigs. He has much of memory—Picard."

As Lacomb returned, a tall figure in a black *soutane* and low-crowned black felt hat came with him. It was the *curé.*

"*Bon soir, mes enfants,*" he said, stepping on to the *galeric.* Philippe gave his seat to him, and the *curé,* sitting down, drew a pipe from his pocket.

"The *m'sieur* is a stranger in St. Anne," he said to me, and scratched a match on the plaster of the house, lighting up his kindly old face and glinting the iron-rimmed spectacles on his thin nose. "He

THE PLEASANT DRONE OF BUSY FLAX-WHEELS

fishes with Philippe?—*oui,* it is as I thought. But one comes not often so far up the *rivière*—a stranger is rarely in St. Anne." Then he asked me a score of questions about the world I came from. We talked until the twilight faded into darkness. I told him of the various life in our large cities; of their traffic and of their buildings.

After a long silence he said, "Ah, *oui, oui,* I have heard and also read some little of what it is that the *m'sieur* says, but is it quite true—all?"

I assured him that it was and that it was but a very little of the whole.

"Ah, *excusez moi,*" he replied; "the *m'sieur* sees that the life of us is very different from his, and it is that I have seen but little of what he speaks that I

him a little doubted. I have seen once only the *chemin de fer* or of the others things that the *m'sieur* says are common in his country, and one is able not to make a clear mind about them from reading. The *m'sieur* is the only man to whom I ever talked who came from there. The others habitants are able not to read and know less of it, for one sees little from these mountains but woods and rivers and the spire of St. Henri—*c'est tout.* But it is well, for they are happy," he added, smiling, and, knocking the ashes from his pipe against the wheel of a water-cart that stood by, arose.

"*Bon soir,*" he said, and went off towards the *presbytère,* and the darkness swallowed him up.

After he had gone Lacomb began to

play, and Philippe's voice resounded up the street with:

Je voudrais bien me marier,
Mais j'ai grand' peur de me tromper;
Ils sont si malhonnêttes!
Ma luron, ma lurêtte,—

Neighbors came over and sat along the *galerie* or went into the kitchen—all joining in the familiar *chansons* which Lacomb played. Before long there was a good gathering, both young and old. As it got too cold outside, Lacomb went in, and everybody followed. Marie sat down to the organ and the two began to play. I sat down by Philippe's *grandmère,* who was smoking and knitting by a clock that reached to the ceiling.

"The violin of Lacomb is very old," she told me, pressing the tobacco into her pipe with her forefinger. "She come from Normandie many of years before I was born. She was always in the family —the violin. Lacomb plays on her often before the house, and it is he who is able to play best in the village. The feet of the *garçons* are not still for long when he makes the bow to jump across her—the *m'sieur* will soon see."

Even as she spoke François Chagnon went over to Lacomb. "Make the music to go more fast," I heard him say, "more fast. Is it not that it is too slow?"

Lacomb smiled, but did not speak. His head bent farther over his instrument. His caribou *botte sauvage* struck the *catalan* harder and faster, and his horny fingers skipped more nimbly over the strings.

Philippe and François carried out the stove, while others rolled up the long breadths of carpeting and the little braided rugs. Philippe threw his arm about the miller's daughter and they skipped across the floor. The rest were quick to follow his example, and the room was soon in a whirl of flying couples.

"Ah, it is as I said—the dance begins," said the *grandmère,* her mouth puckering into a satisfied smile. "But *voyez,* it is Marie who wishes to dance with *m'sieur*—see!"

I glanced across the room and saw she was looking at me. I rose and joined the dance with her. Hour after hour we whirled among the flying sashes and homespun skirts. Occasionally a couple would stop to wipe their faces or drain a glass of home-brewed beer from a big stone pitcher on the table, then dance on again as enthusiastic as before; but the music never halted. The old *grandmère* knitted through it all, but her little deep-set eyes followed every movement of the dancers. Those sitting or standing about the room were smoking with her. A thick dust from the floor filled the air. The room became hot and close. At last, wearied and dizzy, I excused myself and went outdoors into the fresh air.

All was still out there. The valley and the village were lit with a strange phosphorescent glow. The long tongues of the aurora borealis were streaming over half of the sky, silhouetting the church spire against its brightness.

"The northern lights are very beautiful to-night," I told the *grandmère* when I came in. "You should see them."

"The *éclairon,*" she gasped, and, jumping up, went out on to the *galerie.* I followed and found her staring blankly at the sky, her hands clasped over her breast. "*Sacré bleu,* it is bad—too bad," she repeated, and went in as abruptly as she came out. I stayed to enjoy the glory. The sky grew much brighter. The vapory shafts of delicate violet and rose now shot far down the southern sky, and the aureola had reached the zenith.

The music ceased inside. The habitants came out, and as they looked heavenward a silence fell on them. It grew profound, then intense. I could hear some one's watch tick.

No one spoke or moved, until the *grandmère,* stretching her withered hand skyward, began a low monotonous chant. It was weird and eerie. My scalp seemed to move. The words were so indistinctly spoken I could not catch their meaning. The others joined her, and the song swelled through the village and reechoed from the distant sombre mountains. One by one the villagers began to leave, and the song gradually died away. Some, however, still sang as they went down the road. The dance was over. As I turned into the house with Philippe I asked him what the song meant.

"The country is very dry, the *m'sieur* knows," he answered, securing the door with a heavy wooden bolt. "We have a drought in the country, and if the *éclairon* is very bright during a drought, it is

that there will be only little of harvest—
v'là! it is too bad. So we prayed to-night
that it may not come true this autumn.
It is a superstition of the oldest. Some
believe it not. I hope that it is not
true, but I don't know," he added, shrug-
ging his shoulders.

The tall clock near the red stairway
struck eleven. The children had clattered
off to bed. Madame led me up the stairway to my chamber. It was a compact
little room, just large enough for a
four-poster and a two-storied stove that
sat in the partition to heat two rooms
at once. Everything in the chamber
was home-made, I think, from the
crazy-quilt on the bed to the clumsy
latch on the door.

"I have of hope that the *m'sieur* will
sleep well," she said, parting the chintz
curtains of the bed and poking the

feathers about. "But before I go I will
make him to be safe through this night.
This is *eau bénite*." She reached down
a green bottle from a peg at the head of
the bed by the crucifix, and, kissing it,
dipped a spruce spray that was tied about
its neck into the bottle and sprinkled the
holy water over the coarse homespun sheets.

After she had gone I threw back the
wall-paper covered sashes of the inner
window and opened a swinging pane in
the outer. The sky still vibrated with
the glory of the waning *éclairon*. Now
and then I heard notes of the song growing fainter and still more faint, until
they died away, and only the lonesome
wind in the leaves by the window and
the distant murmur of the Rivière des
Chutes broke the sombre hush that lay
over the village of Philippe St. Gelais's
home—St. Anne.

YOUR UNITED STATES

WHAT strikes and frightens the backward European almost as much as anything in the United States is the efficiency and fearful universality of the telephone. Just as I think of the big cities as agglomerations pierced everywhere by elevator-shafts full of movement, so I think of them as being threaded, under pavements and over roofs and between floors and ceilings and between walls, by millions upon millions of live filaments that unite all the privacies of the organism—and destroy them in order to make one immense publicity. I do not mean that Europe has failed to adopt the telephone, nor that in Europe there are no hotels with the dreadful curse of an active telephone in every room. But I do mean that the European telephone is a toy, and a somewhat clumsy one, compared with the inexorable seriousness of the American telephone. Many otherwise highly civilized Europeans are as timid in addressing a telephone as they would be in addressing a royal sovereign. The average European middle-class householder still speaks of his telephone, if he has one, in the same falsely-casual tone as the corresponding American is liable to speak of his motor-car. It is naught—a negligible trifle—but somehow it comes into the conversation!

"How odd!" you exclaim. And you are right. It is we Europeans who are wrong, through no particular fault of our own. The American is ruthlessly logical about the telephone. The only occasion on which I was in really serious danger of being taken for a madman in the

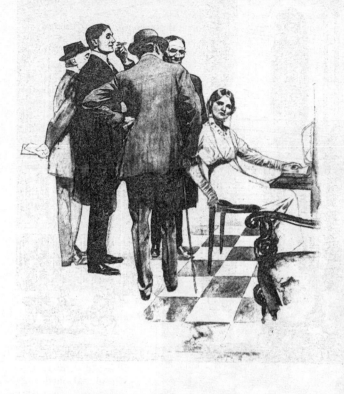

THE OPERATOR'S DESK IS ALWAYS A CENTER OF ACTIVITY

United States was when, in a Chicago hotel, I permanently removed the receiver from the telephone in a room designed (doubtless ironically) for slumber. The whole hotel was appalled. Half Chicago shuddered. In response to the prayer of a deputation from the management I restored the receiver. On the horrified face of the deputation I could read the unspoken query: "Is it conceivable that you have been in this country a month without understanding that the United States is primarily nothing but a vast congeries of telephone-cabins?" Yes, I yielded and admired! And I surmise

that on my next visit I shall find a telephone on every table of every restaurant that respects itself.

It is the efficiency of the telephone that makes it irresistible to a great people whose passion is to "get results"—the instancy with which the communication is given, and the clear loudness of the telephone's voice in reply to yours: phenomena utterly unknown in Europe. Were I to inhabit the United States, I too should become a victim of the telephone habit, as it is practised in its most advanced form in those suburban communities to which I have already incidentally referred. There a woman takes to the telephone as women in more decadent lands take to morphia. You can see her at morn at her bedroom window, pouring confidences into her telephone, thus combining the joy of an innocent vice with the healthy freshness of breeze and sunshine. It has happened to me to sit in a drawing-room, where people gathered round the telephone as Europeans gather round a fire, and to hear immediately after the ejaculation of a number into the telephone a sharp ring from outside through the open window, and then to hear in answer to the question, "What are you going to wear to-night?" two absolutely simultaneous replies, one loudly from the telephone across the room, and the other faintlier from a charming human voice across the garden: "I don't know. What are you?" Such may be the pleasing secondary scientific effect of telephoning to the lady next door on a warm afternoon.

Now it was obvious that behind the apparently simple exterior aspects of any telephone system there must be an intricate and marvelous secret organization. In Europe my curiosity would probably never have been excited by the thought of that organization—at home one accepts everything as of course!—but, in the United States, partly because the telephone is so much more wonderful and terrible there, and partly because in a foreign land one is apt to have strange caprices, I allowed myself to become the prey of a desire to see the arcanum concealed at the other end of all the wires; and thus, one day, under the high protection of a demigod of the electrical world, I paid a visit to a telephone-exchange in New York, and saw therein what nine hundred and ninety-nine out of every thousand of the most ardent telephone-users seldom think about and will never see.

A murmuring sound, as of an infinity of scholars in a prim school conning their lessons, and a long row of young women seated in a dim radiance on a long row of precisely similar stools, before a long apparatus of holes and pegs and pieces of elastic cord, all extremely intent: that was the first b r o a d impression. One saw at once that none of these young women had a single moment to spare; they were all involved in the tremendous machine, part of it, keeping pace with it and in it, and not daring to take their eyes off it for an instant, lest t h e y s h o u l d s i n against it. W h a t they were droning about it was impossible to guess; for if one stationed oneself close to any particular rapt young woman, she seemed to utter no sound, but simply and without ceasing to peg and unpeg holes at random among the thousands of holes before her, apparently in obedience to the signaling of faint, tiny lights that in thousands continually expired and were rekindled. It was so that these tiny lights should be distinguishable that the

A CORNER OF THE FILING SECTION

illumination of the secret and finely appointed chamber was kept dim. Throughout the whole length of the apparatus the colored elastic cords to which the pegs were attached kept crossing one another in fantastic patterns.

We who had entered were ignored. We might have been ghosts, invisible and inaudible. Even the supervisors, less-young women set in authority, did not turn to glance at us as they moved restlessly peering behind the stools. And yet somehow I could hear the delicate shoulders of all the young women saying, without speech: "Here come these tyrants and taskmasters again, who have invented this exercise which nearly but not quite cracks our little brains for us! They know exactly how much they can get out of us, and they get it. They are cleverer than us and more powerful than us; and we have to submit to their discipline. But—" And afar off I could hear: "What are you going to wear to-night?" "Will you dine with me to-night?" "I want two seats." "Very well, thanks, and how is Mrs. . . .?" "When can I see you to-morrow?" "I'll take your offer for those bonds." . . . And I could see the interiors of innumerable offices and drawing-rooms. . . . But of course I could hear and see nothing really except the intent drone and quick gesturing of those completely absorbed young creatures in the dim radiance, on stools precisely similar.

I understood why the telephone service was so efficient. I understood not merely from the demeanor of the long row of young women, but from everything else I had seen in the exact and diabolically ingenious ordering of the whole establishment.

We were silent for a time, as though we had entered a church. We were, perhaps unconsciously, abashed by the in-

A YOUNG WOMAN WAS JUST FINISHING A FLORID SONG

tensity of the absorption of these neat young women. After a while one of the guides, one of the inscrutable beings who had helped to invent and construct the astounding organism, began in a low voice on the forlorn hope of making me comprehend the mechanism of a telephone-call and its response. And I began on the forlorn hope of persuading him by intelligent acting that I did comprehend. We each made a little progress. I could not tell him that, though I genuinely and humbly admired his particular variety of genius, what interested me in the affair was not the mechanics, but the human equation. As a professional reader of faces, I glanced as well as I could sideways at those bent girls' faces to see if they were happy. An absurd inquiry! Do *I* look happy when I'm at work, I wonder! Did they then look reasonably content? Well, I came to the conclusion that they looked like most other faces—neither one thing nor the other. Still, in a great establishment, I would sooner search for sociological in-

as intensely absorbed as these appeared to be. But the illusion was there, and it was effective.)

I learned that even the lowest beginner earned five dollars a week. It was just the sum I was paying for a pair of clean sheets every night at a grand hotel. And that the salary rose to six, seven, eight, eleven, and even fourteen dollars for supervisors, who, however, had to stand on their feet seven and a half hours a day, as shopgirls do for ten hours a day; and that in general the girls had thirty minutes for lunch, and a day off every week, and that the Company supplied them gratuitously with tea, coffee, sugar, couches, newspapers, arm-chairs, and fresh air, of which last fifty fresh cubic feet were pumped in for every operator every minute.

ABSORBED IN THAT WONDROUS SATISFYING HOBBY

"Naturally," I was told, "the discipline is strict. There are test wires. . . . . We can check the 'time elements.' . . . We keep a record of every call. They'll take a dollar a week less in an outside place—for instance, a hotel. . . . Their average stay here is thirty months."

And I was told the number of exchanges there were in New York, exactly like the one I was seeing.

formation in the faces of the employed than in the managerial rules.

"What do they earn?" I asked, when we emerged from the ten‑atmosphere pressure of that intense absorption. (Of course I knew that no young women could possibly for any length of time be

A dollar a week less in a hotel! How feminine! And how masculine! And how wise for one sort of young woman, and how foolish for another! . . . Imagine quitting that convent with its guaranteed fresh air, and its couches and sugar and so on, for the rough hazards and promiscuities of a hotel! On the other hand, imagine not quitting it!

Said the demigod of the electrical world, condescendingly: "All this telephone business is done on a mere few hundred horse-power. Come away, and I'll show you electricity in bulk."

And I went away with him, thoughtful. In spite of the inhuman perfection of its functioning, that exchange was a very human place indeed. It brilliantly solved some problems; it raised others. Excessively difficult to find any fault whatever in it! A marvelous service, achieved under strictly hygienic conditions—and young women must make their way through the world! And yet— Yes, a very human place indeed!

The demigods of the electric world do not condescend to move about in petrol motor-cars. In the exercise of a natural and charming coquetry they insist on electrical traction, and it was in the most modern and soundless electric brougham that we arrived at nightfall under the overhanging cornice-eaves of two gigantic Florentine palaces — just such looming palaces, they appeared in the dark, as may be seen in any central street of Florence, with a cinema-show blazing its signs on the ground floor, and Heaven knows what remnants of Italian aristocracy in the mysterious upper stories. Having entered one of the palaces, simultaneously with a tornado of wind, we passed through long, deserted, narrow galleries, lined with thousands of small, caged compartments containing "transformers," and on each compartment was a label bearing always the same words: "Danger, 6,600 volts." "Danger, 6,600 volts." "Danger, 6,600 volts." A wondrous relief when we had escaped with our lives from the menace of those innumerable volts! And then we stood on a high platform surrounded by handles, switches, signals—apparatus enough to put all New York into darkness, or to annihilate it in an instant by the unloosing of terrible cohorts of volts!—and faced an enormous white hall, sparsely peopled by a few colossal machines that seemed to be revolving and oscillating about their business with the fatalism of conquered and resigned leviathans. Immaculately clean, inconceivably tidy, shimmering with brilliant light under its lofty and beautiful ceiling, shaking and roaring with the terrific thunder of its own vitality, this hall in which no common voice could make itself heard produced nevertheless an effect of magical stillness, silence, and solitude. We were alone in it, save that now and then in the far-distant spaces a figure might flit and disappear between the huge glinting columns of metal. It was a hall enchanted and inexplicable. I understood nothing of it. But I understood that half the electricity of New York was being generated by its engines of a hundred and fifty thousand horse-power, and that if the spell were lifted the elevators of New York would be immediately paralyzed, and the twenty million lights expire beneath the eyes of a startled population. I could have gazed at it to this day, and brooded to this day upon the human imaginations that had perfected it; but I was led off, hypnotized, to see the furnaces and boilers under the earth. And even there we were almost alone, to such an extent had one sort of senseless matter been compelled to take charge of another sort of senseless matter. The odyssey of the coal that was lifted high out of ships on the tide beyond, to fall ultimately into the furnaces within, scarcely touched by the hand-wielded shovel, was by itself epical. Fresh air pouring in at the rate of twenty-four million cubic feet per hour cooled the entire palace, and gave to these stokeholes the uncanny quality of refrigerators. The lowest horror of the steamship had been abolished here.

I was tempted to say: "This alone is fit to be called the heart of New York!"

They took me to the twin palace, and on the windy way thither figures were casually thrown at me. As that a short circuit may cause the machines to surge wildly into the sudden creation of six million horse-power of electricity, necessitating the invention of other machines to control automatically these perilous vagaries! As that in the down-town district the fire-engine was being abolished because, at a signal, these power-houses could in thirty seconds concentrate on any given main a pressure of three hundred pounds to the square inch, lifting jets of water perhaps above the roofs of sky-scrapers! As that the city could fine these power-houses at the rate of five hundred dollars a minute for any interruption of the current longer than three minutes — but the current had never failed for a single second! As that in one year over two million dollars' worth of machinery had been scrapped! . . . And I was aware that it was New York I was in, and not Timbuctoo.

In the other palace it appeared that the great American scrapping process was even yet far from complete. At first sight this other seemed to resemble the former one, but I was soon instructed that the former one was as naught to this one, for here the turbine—the "strong, silent man" among engines — was replacing the racket of cylinder and crank. Statistics are tiresome and futile to stir the imagination. I disdain statistics, even when I assimilate them. And yet when my attention was directed to one trifling block of metal, and I was told that it was the most powerful "unit" in the world, and that it alone would make electricity sufficient for the lighting of a city of a quarter of a million people, I felt that statistics, after all, could knock you a staggering blow. . . . In this other palace, too, was the same solitude of machinery, attending most conscientiously and effectively to itself. A singularly disconcerting spectacle! And I reflected that, according to dreams already coming true, the telephone-exchange also would soon be a solitude of clicking contact-points, functioning in mystic certitude, instead of a convent of girls requiring sugar and couches, and thirsting for love. A singularly disconcerting prospect!

But was it necessary to come to America in order to see and describe telephone-exchanges and electrical power-houses? Do not these wonders exist in all the cities of earth? They do, but not to quite the same degree of wondrousness. Hat-shops, and fine hat-shops, exist in New York, but not to quite the same degree of wondrousness as in Paris. People sing in New York, but not with quite the same natural lyricism as in Naples. The great civilizations all present the same features; but it is just the differences in degree between the same feature in this civilization and in that—it is just these differences which together constitute and illustrate the idiosyncrasy of each. It seems to me that the brains and the imagination of America shone superlatively in the conception and ordering of its vast organizations of human being, and of machinery, and of the two combined. By them I was more profoundly attracted, impressed, and inspired than by any other non-spiritual phenomena whatever in the United States. For me they were the proudest material achievements, and essentially the most poetical achievements, of the United States. And that is why I am dwelling on them.

Further, there are business organizations in America of a species which do not flourish at all in Europe. For example, the "mail-order house," whose secrets were very generously displayed to me in Chicago—a peculiar establishment which sells merely everything (except patent-medicines) — on condition that you order it by post. Go into that house with money in your palm, and ask for a fan or a flail or a fur-coat or a fountain-pen or a fiddle, and you will be requested to return home and write a letter about the proposed purchase, and stamp the letter and drop it into a mail-box, and then to wait till the article arrives at your door. That house is one of the most spectacular and pleasing proofs that the inhabitants of the United States are thinly scattered over an enormous area, in tiny groups, often quite isolated from stores. On the day of my visit sixty thousand letters had been received, and every executable order contained in these was executed before closing time, by the co-ordinated efforts of over four thousand female employees and over three thousand males. The conception would make Europe dizzy. Imagine a merchant in Moscow trying to inaugurate such a scheme! A little machine no bigger than a soup-plate will open hundreds of envelopes at once.

They are all the same, those envelopes; they have even less individuality than sheep being sheared, but when the contents of one—any one at random—are put into your hand, something human and distinctive is put into your hand. I read the caligraphy on a blue sheet of paper, and it was written by a woman in Wyoming, a neat, earnest, harassed, and possibly rather harassing woman, and she wanted all sorts of things and wanted them intensely—I could see that with clearness. This complex purchase was an important event in her year. So far as her imagination went, only one mail-order would reach the Chicago house that morning, and the entire establishment would be strained to meet it.

Then the blue sheet was taken from me and thrust into the system, and therein lost to me. I was taken to a mysteriously rumbling shaft of broad diameter, that pierced all the floors of the house and had trap-doors on each floor. And when one of the trap-doors was opened I saw packages of all descriptions racing after one another down spiral planes within the shaft. There were several of these great shafts—with divisions for mail, express, and freight traffic—and packages were ceaselessly racing down all of them, laden with the objects desired by the woman of Wyoming and her fifty-nine-thousand-odd fellow-customers of the day. At first it seemed to me impossible that that earnest, impatient woman in Wyoming should get precisely what she wanted; it seemed to me impossible that some mistake should not occur in all that noisy fever of rushing activity. But after I had followed an order, and seen it filled and checked, my opinion was that a mistake would be the most miraculous phenomenon in that establishment. I felt quite reassured on behalf of Wyoming.

And then I was suddenly in a room where six hundred billing-machines were being clicked at once by six hundred young women, a fantastic aural nightmare, though none of the young women appeared to be conscious that anything bizarre was going on. . . . And then I was in a printing-shop, where several lightning machines spent their whole time every day in printing the most popular work of reference in the United States, a bulky book full of pictures, with an annual circulation of five and a half million copies—the general catalogue of the firm. For the first time I realized the true meaning of the word "popularity"—and sighed. . . .

And then it was lunch-time for about a couple of thousand employees, and in the boundless restaurant I witnessed the working of the devices which enabled these legions to choose their meals, and pay for them (cost price) in a few moments, and without advanced mathematical calculations. The young head of the restaurant showed me, with pride, a menu of over a hundred dishes—Austrian, German, Hungarian, Italian, Scotch, French, and American; at prices from one cent up as high as ten cents (prime roast-beef)—and at the foot of the menu was his personal appeal: "I desire to extend to you a cordial invitation to inspect," etc. "My constant aim will be," etc. Yet it was not *his* restaurant. It was the firm's restaurant. Here I had a curious illustration of an admirable characteristic of American business methods that was always striking me—namely, the real delegation of responsibility. An American board of direction will put a man in charge of a department, as a viceroy over a province, saying, as it were: "This is yours. Do as you please with it. We will watch the results." A marked contrast this with the centralizing of authority which seems to be ever proceeding in Europe, and which breeds in all classes at all ages—especially in France—a morbid fear and horror of accepting responsibility.

Later, I was on the ground level, in the midst of an enormous apparent confusion—the target for all the packages and baskets, big and little, that shot every instant in a continuous stream from those spiral planes, and slid dangerously at me along the floors. Here were the packers. I saw a packer deal with a collected order, and in this order were a number of tiny cookery utensils, a four-cent curling-iron, a brush, and two incredibly ugly pink china mugs, inscribed in cheap gilt respectively with the words "Father" and "Mother." Throughout my stay in America no moment came to me more dramatically than this moment, and none has remained more vividly in my mind. All the daily domestic life of the small communities in the wilds of the West and the Middle West, and in the wilds of the back streets of the great towns, seemed to be revealed to me by the contents of that basket, as the packer wrapped up and protected one

article after another. I had been compelled to abandon a visitation of the
West and of the small communities
everywhere, and I was sorry. But here
in a microcosm I thought I saw the simple reality of the backbone of all America, a symbol of the millions of the little
plain people, who ultimately make possible the glory of the world-renowned
streets and institutions in dazzling cities.

There was something indescribably
touching in that curling - iron and
those two mugs. I could see the table
on which the mugs would soon proudly stand, and "father" and "mother" and children thereat, and I could
see the hand heating the curling-iron
and applying it. I could see the whole
little home and the whole life of the
little home. . . . And afterward, as I
wandered through the warehouses—pyramids of the same chair, cupboards full
of the same cheap violin, stacks of the
same album of music, acres of the same
carpet and wall-paper, tons of the same
gramophone, hundreds of tons of the
same sewing-machine and lawn-mower—
I felt as if I had been made free of
the secrets of every village in every State
of the Union, and as if I had lived in
every little house and cottage thereof
all my life! Almost no sense of beauty
in those tremendous supplies of merchandise, but a lot of honesty, self-respect,
and ambition fulfilled. I tell you I could
hear the engaged couples discussing
ardently over the pages of the catalogue
what manner of bedroom suite they would
buy, and what design of sideboard. . . .

Finally, I arrived at the firm's private railway station, where a score or
more trucks were being laden with the
multifarious boxes, bales, and parcels, all
to leave that evening for romantic des-
tinations such as Oregon, Texas, and
Wyoming. Yes, the package of the woman of Wyoming's desire would ultimately
be placed somewhere in one of those
trucks! It was going to start off toward
her that very night!

Impressive as this establishment was,
finely as it illustrated the national genius
for organization, it yet lacked necessarily, on account of the nature of its
activity, those outward phenomena of
splendor which charm the stranger's eye

in the great central houses of New York,
and which seem designed to sum up all
that is most characteristic and most dazzling in the business methods of the
United States. These central houses are
not soiled by the touch of actual merchandise. Nothing more squalid than
ink ever enters their gates. They traffic
with symbols only, and the symbols, no
matter what they stand for, are never in
themselves sordid. The men who have
created these houses seem to have realized
that, from their situation and their importance, a special effort toward representative magnificence was their pleasing
duty, and to have made the effort with
a superb prodigality and an astounding
ingenuity.

Take, for a good, glorious example,
the very large insurance company,
conscious that the eyes of the world
are upon it, and that the entire United
States is expecting it to uphold the
national pride. All the splendors of all
the sky-scrapers are united in its building. Its foyer and grand staircase will
sustain comparison with those of the
Paris Opéra. You might think you were
going into a place of entertainment!
And, as a fact, you are! This affair, with
nearly four thousand clerks, is the huge
toy and pastime of a group of millionaires, who have discovered a way of
honestly amusing themselves while gaining applause and advertisement. Within
the foyer and beyond the staircase, notice
the outer rooms, partitioned off by bronze
grilles, looming darkly gorgeous in an eternal windowless twilight studded with the
beautiful glowing green disks of electric-
lamp shades; and under each disk a human head bent over the black-and-red
magic of ledgers! The desired effect is
at once obtained, and it is wonderful.
Then lose yourself in and out of the
ascending and descending elevators, and
among the unending multitudes of clerks,
and along the corridors of marble (total
length exactly measured and recorded).
You will be struck dumb. And immediately you begin to recover your speech
you will be struck dumb again. . . .

Other houses, as has been seen, provide
good meals for their employees at cost
price. This house, then, will provide excellent meals, free of charge! It will
install the most expensive kitchens and

richly spacious restaurants. It will serve the delicate repasts with dignity. "Does all this lessen the wages?" No, not in theory. But in practice, and whether the management wishes or not, it must come out of the wages. "Why do you do it?" you ask the departmental chief, who apparently gets far more fun out of the contemplation of these refectories than out of the contemplation of premiums received and claims paid. "It is better for the employees," he says. "But we do it because it is better for us. It pays us. Good food, physical comfort, agreeable environment, scientific ventilation — all these things pay us. We get results from them." He does not mention horses, but you feel that the comparison is with horses. A horse, or a clerk, or an artisan—it pays equally well to treat all of them well. This is one of the latest discoveries of economic science, a discovery not yet universally understood.

I say you do not mention horses, and you certainly must not hint that the men in authority may have been actuated by motives of humanity. You must believe what you are told—that the sole motive is to get results. The eagerness with which all heads of model establishments would disavow to me any thought of being humane was affecting in its naïveté; it had that touch of ingenuous wistfulness which I remarked everywhere in America—and nowhere more than in the demeanor of many mercantile highnesses. (I hardly expect Americans to understand just what I mean here.) It was as if they would blush at being caught in an act of humanity, like school-boys caught praying. Still, to my mind, the white purity of their desire to get financial results was often muddied by the dark stain of a humane motive. I may be wrong (as people say), but I know I am not (as people think).

The further you advance into the penetralia of this arch-exemplar of American organization and profusion, the more you are amazed by the imaginative perfection of its detail: as well in the system of filing for instant reference fifty million separate documents, as in the planning of a concert-hall for the diversion of the human machines.

As we went into the immense concert-hall a group of girls were giving an informal concert among themselves. When lunch is served on the premises with chronographic exactitude, the thirty-five minutes allowed for the meal give an appreciable margin for music and play. A young woman was just finishing a florid song. The concert was suspended, and the whole party began to move humbly away at this august incursion.

"Sing it again; do, please!" the departmental chief suggested. And the florid song was nervously sung again; we applauded, the artiste bowed as on a stage, and the group fled, the thirty-five minutes being doubtless up. The departmental chief looked at me in silence, content, as much as to say: "This is how we do business in America." And I thought, "Yet another way of getting results!"

But sometimes the creators of the organization, who had provided everything, had been obliged to confess that they had omitted from their designs certain factors of evolution. Hat-cupboards were a feature of the women's offices—delightful specimens of sound cabinetry. And still, millinery was lying about all over the place, giving it an air of feminine occupation that was extremely exciting to a student on his travels. The truth was that none of those hats would go into the cupboards. Fashion had worsted the organization completely. Departmental chiefs had nothing to do but acquiesce in this startling untidiness. Either they must wait till the circumference of hats lessened again, or they must tear down the whole structure and rebuild it with due regard to hats.

Finally, we approached the sacred lair and fastness of the president, whose massive portrait I had already seen on several walls. Spaciousness and magnificence increased. Ceilings rose in height, marble was softened by the thick pile of carpets. Mahogany and gold shone more luxuriously. I was introduced into the vast antechamber of the presidential secretaries, and by the chief of them inducted through polished and gleaming barriers into the presence-chamber itself: a noble apartment, an apartment surpassing dreams and expectations, conceived and executed in a spirit of majestic prodigality. The president had not been afraid. And his costly audacity was splendidly justified of itself. This man had a sense of the romantic, of the dramatic, of the fit. And the qualities in him and his *état major* which had commanded the success of the entire enterprise were well shown in the brilliant symbolism of that room's grandiosity. . . . And there was the president's portrait again, gorgeously framed.

He came in through another door, an old man of superb physique, and after a little while he was relating to me the early struggles of his company. "My wife used to say that for ten years she never saw me," he remarked.

I asked him what his distractions were, now that the strain was over and his ambitions so gloriously achieved. He replied that occasionally he went for a drive in his automobile.

"And what do you do with yourself in the evenings?" I inquired.

He seemed a little disconcerted by this perhaps unaccustomed bluntness.

"Oh," he said, casually, "I read insurance literature."

He had the conscious mien and manners of a reigning prince. His courtesy and affability were impeccable and charming. In the most profound sense this human being had succeeded, for it was impossible to believe that, had he to live his life again, he would live it very differently.

Such a type of man is, of course, to be found in nearly every country; but the type flourishes with a unique profusion and perfection in the United States; and in its more prominent specimens the distinguishing idiosyncrasy of the average American successful man of business is magnified for our easier inspection. The rough, broad difference between the American and the European business man is that the latter is anxious to leave his work, while the former is anxious to get to it. The attitude of the American business man toward his business is preeminently the attitude of an artist. You may say that he loves money. So do we all — artists particularly. No stockbroker's private journal could be more full of dollars than Balzac's intimate correspondence is full of francs. But whereas the ordinary artist loves money chiefly because it represents luxury, the American business man loves it chiefly because it is the sole proof of success in his endeavor. He loves his business. It

is not his toil, but his hobby, passion, vice, monomania—any vituperative epithet you like to bestow on it! He does not look forward to living in the evening; he lives most intensely when he is in the midst of his organization. His instincts are best appeased by the hourly excitements of a good, scrimmaging, commercial day. He needs these excitements as some natures need alcohol. He cannot do without them.

On no other hypothesis can the unrivaled ingenuity and splendor and ruthlessness of American business undertakings be satisfactorily explained. They surpass the European, simply because they are never out of the thoughts of their directors, because they are adored with a fine frenzy. And for the same reason they are decked forth in magnificence. Would a man enrich his office with rare woods and stuffs and marbles if it were not a temple? Would he bestow graces on the environment if while he was in it the one idea at the back of his head was the anticipation of leaving it? Watch American business men together, and if you are a European you will clearly perceive that they are devotees. They are open with one another, as intimates are. Jealousy and secretiveness are much rarer among them than in Europe. They show off their respective organizations with pride and with candor. They admire one another enormously. Hear one of them say enthusiastically of another: "It was a great idea he had—connecting his New York and his Philadelphia places by wireless—a great idea!" They call one another by their Christian names, fondly. They are capable of wonderful friendships in business. They are cemented by one religion—and it is not golf. For them the journey "home" is often not the evening journey, but the morning journey. Call this a hard saying if you choose: it is true. Could a man be happy long away from a hobby so entrancing, a toy so intricate and marvelous, a setting so splendid? Is it strange that, absorbed in that wondrous satisfying hobby, he should make love with the nonchalance of an animal? At which point I seem to have come dangerously near to the topic of the singular position of the American woman, about which everybody is talking. . . .

WINTERING AMONG THE ESKIMO

ETHNOLOGY is as important in history as is archæology. We study races now in their childhood to understand in part the forgotten peoples that were our grandsires. We dig up stone axes and cooking-pots from the caves of Kent and the gravel banks of the Seine, and we know something of the material furnishings of our ancestors' lives. But we are less interested in the steps that lead from the stone pot to the steel cooking-range than we are in the history of some other more idealistic developments.

It happened that the organizers and promoters of the Anglo-American polar expedition were alive to these and other reasons for the study of the "primitive" hyperboreans. Zoologists, botanists, and geologists have long been part of the regular equipment of arctic expeditions, but this was the first which placed the investigation of man on a level with that of the white owl, the first to make a position on its staff for an officer who should have a technical training for the investigation of primitive people similar to that required of the geologist who was to study the various phenomena of earth and ice. It was the fortune of the writer to be selected for this work as ethnologist.

The people to be investigated were the Eskimos east of the Mackenzie River. These are the least known people of the North American continent, for certain groups of them have never seen a white man, while others contain a few adventurous individuals who have made long trips to one of the trading posts of the Hudson Bay Company. Those just east of the mouth of the great river have, it is true, been in intermittent contact with whites for twenty years, but their habits of thought and mode of life have been little changed by extraneous influences.

A slight knowledge of arctic conditions and a glance at the map of North America make it clear that a ship bound for the mouth of the Mackenzie has to pass through a great deal of difficult and dangerous water on its way eastward from Bering Strait along the north coast of Alaska; a second glance at the map also shows that from the railway terminus at Edmonton in mid-western Canada there is a direct down river route to the home of these Eskimos, the easiest, most direct, most romantic of the routes that lead to the heart of the arctic north.

The northward river journey takes one through an unhackneyed land of much fascination. Stranger than anything one sees, however, is the fact that what one sees is so little known. When one floats down a river whose current of three miles an hour sweeps between banks three miles apart, one is tempted to wonder how many New-Yorkers would say at a guess that the Mackenzie was probably about the size of the Hudson, or how many Londoners know that it exists. A steamboat captain on the Yukon smiled at me indulgently when told that the Mackenzie was a trifle the larger stream. This aristocrat among rivers has succeeded admirably in keeping out of the public prints.

But no matter how little known the river or how strange to the outside world the Indians that are the sole dwellers on its banks, a description of them has no place in an account of the life of the Eskimos. Not even as a preface do they have a right to appear, for neither is the Eskimo an Indian nor does the great river play any important part in the lives or known history of these littoral people.

My reason for going overland and down stream to the mouth of the Mackenzie has been suggested above—it was the fear that the ship sailing through Bering Strait from Victoria, British Columbia, might not reach the country to be investigated. She did not, and *Harper's Magazine* has already told of her wreck at Flaxman Island on the north coast of

A FUR-TRADER'S POST ON THE MACKENZIE

Alaska. By the first of September, 1906, I had already waited a month at the mouth of the river for a ship that never was to come. At that time, equipped with one suit of light summer clothing, a rifle and two hundred cartridges, a note-book, pencil, and a camera with all too few films, I ceased being the temporary and became the permanent guest of the Kogmollik Eskimos.

My home for the autumn months was at Shingle Point on the Arctic coast just west of the river delta. The Eskimos here, although of the same blood with those east of the river, have been since 1889 in fairly close contact with the whalers who winter at Herschel Island, some sixty miles to the westward. One of them, my particular host, who has had the name "Roxy" conferred on him by some Nantucketer, has served on board whalers and speaks English fairly well.

At Shingle Point, in the tent home of this half Anglicized Roxy, I had my first introduction to the charming home life of the Eskimo. At that time these house-hold ways, that differed so strangely lit-tle from the best ideals and rarest ex-amples of my own people, were credited in my mind partly to the influence of the Herschel Island missionaries, whose in-timate Roxy had been for years. Later in the winter, however, I learned from his unsophisticated countrymen farther east that courtesy and most of the gentler virtues are deeper in the Eskimo's blood and breeding than they are in ours. But most of these things I understood fully only after many months had made me one of them through a sufficient mastery of their language and mode of thought; they therefore are more properly dealt with in the later pages of my story.

This was a fishing community in which I found myself. Although there were a few deer within a reasonable distance inland, their pursuit was so much less certain than our nets that only the small boys hunted them, and that mostly for the fun of it. From childhood up I had disliked the taste, the smell, and the very name of fish, and now it was only too clear that we were facing a winter of nothing but fish—fish without salt. The process of breaking myself to the diet was a rather difficult one; for a week or so I took only one meal a day, and that in the evening, after getting up an appetite on a thirty-mile tramp over boggy tundra land. By the end of the first month I could eat fish in any of the approved Eskimo styles. We ate them fresh or "high," raw, boiled, or baked, and without knife, fork, or table manners.

SHOOTING THE CASCADE RAPID, ATHABASCA RIVER

Our family (which consisted of nine, men, women, and children) were very solicitous about my eating so little, and prepared the fish in the most tempting way known to them. Towards sundown, when they saw me coming home across the hills, Navalluk, Roxy's fourteen-year-old adopted daughter, would spit a fresh salmon-trout before the fire to have it roasted against my arrival. When it was nicely baked she would lick a plate of Roxy's clean with her tongue (for they knew white men's ways and insisted I should have a plate); she then spread a towel on the ground, placed my dinner upon it, and said she hoped the fish tasted better to-day than it did yesterday, sometimes adding that this was the prettiest fish she had seen among all those caught since morning.

The incident just told is set down with a purpose that the reader may possibly allow to escape him—he may think that the writer is merely joining himself with the many who, from the earliest times, have pointed out that the Eskimo's ideas of cleanliness differ materially from ours of to-day (though their table manners may not vary so much from those of King Arthur's Round Table). The intention is rather to bring out the qualities of mind and heart that are fundamental in the action, although

not so superficially apparent as the difference from our ordinary mode of cleaning plates.

Our camp at Shingle Point is about sixty miles east of Herschel Island and twenty west of the most western mouth of the Mackenzie, and is on the regular route of boat and winter travel from the Eskimo settlement at that island to those in the delta and east of it. Boats were consequently passing us daily coming from the west; most of them were whale-boats, purchased in former years from the whalers for furs or deer meat and occasionally for service aboard the ships. In these boats the Eskimos have become skilful sailors, being no less venturesome and resourceful in stormy weather than the best of the white whalers.

Many from the boats going eastward came ashore to have a meal and chat, while some camped for a day or a few days, so that most of the time we had a village of from ten to fourteen tents. This gave me an opportunity to observe the village life, which on this coast is becoming rarer year by year. Formerly the people used to winter in little towns of three to fifteen houses, but now they live in isolated dwellings usually some twenty miles apart.

Our tent, being the permanent one,

was largely the centre of activity in the tent village. In front of it on clear days the men gathered in a circle, making or mending nets or doing other useful work, for an Eskimo—man or woman—is almost never idle. The women meantime, unless engaged in preparing food or making garments, were off on the tundra with the children picking berries. Some of them would wander off several miles, carrying heavy two or three year old children on their naked backs inside their skin blouses; for that is the way they have of keeping the babies safe and warm. The blouses of women over fourteen are made loose for this purpose; the baby is kept from sliding down by a belt resting against the small of the woman's back behind, and going diagonally up over her breasts in front. Air for the child to breathe is provided by the gown fitting loosely at the back of the mother's neck.

THE ESKIMO CHILD IS CARRIED NAKED AGAINST THE MOTHER'S BACK

When a woman returns to the tent village with an apron or a towel full of berries, these are placed in a large trough, seal oil poured over them, and the mess stirred up with the hand. Then a well understood cry is raised, and all within hearing come running for the feast. We ate by taking fistfuls after the manner of children, and ended by licking our hands clean. Learning to eat this dish was for me somewhat easier than acquiring a taste for the fish.

When a meal of fish was in question the proceeding was in general similar. Some woman who happened to feel like it would boil a huge kettle in her tent, or else prepare a troughful of raw fish by pulling off their skin with her teeth.

Then the familiar cry was raised, and men and women came scurrying from all directions. When there were too many to get within reaching distance of the fish tray, the women and children would gather around a separate one in the next tent. If there were fewer women than men, some of the men would eat with the women. This is one of the many indications of the perfect social equality of the sexes among Eskimos; with most tribes of Indians, having to eat with the women would be an unendurable disgrace. The procedure at meals was occasionally varied by bringing the tray of food to the outdoor working place of the men where they sat chatting and making nets. If the fish was boiled soft, we ate by reaching in and taking a pinch from the side of a fish with thumb and two fingers; when the fish were raw we each took a whole one and ate it as one might corn from the cob, finally throwing away the "insides" of the fish as one would the core of an apple.

A special circumstance, and one that throws some light on Eskimo character, was that one of them—an immigrant who had brought the name of Anderson from Kotzebue Sound, Alaska—had in his tent half a sack of flour and some molasses. Imagining I must be pining for bread, he and his wife occasionally made a few pancakes, to a feast of which I was specially bidden, to the exclusion of the rest of the community—for they were "used to rotten fish," as Anderson put it. The cakes were a treat, though a little gasoline had been spilled on the flour—enough to cause it to be given to an Eskimo by a captain who considered it unfit for food even when his crew had only two weeks' rations ahead of them. I had told Anderson of my dislike for fish, and so he insisted on my sharing the cakes and molasses daily with his five-year-old daughter, whom he pampered with delicacies which he and his wife did not allow themselves. He said he still remembered how bad white men's food tasted to him when he first had to eat it in Kotzebue Sound, and he guessed Eskimo food must taste just as bad to me. He had learned since that white men's food is not in reality bad, but merely tastes so to Eskimos when they are not used to it; his opinion was that I would find the same thing true of Eskimo food. I did.

One day, when it was blowing cold and sleety from the northwest, a schooner came in sight, plunging and indistinct in the mist, although only half a mile offshore. For a moment we thought it might be the exploring schooner *Duchess* come at last with supplies for me. The craft was, however, soon recognized as the Eskimo schooner *Penelope,* a sketch of whose fortunes deserves a paragraph.

Some twenty years ago the *Penelope* was built with towering masts and leaden keel to be a pleasure craft of grace and speed. But she fell on evil days, was sold, refitted as a whaler, and sent to winter in the Beaufort Sea. Her voyage was not successful, and she was sold to four immigrant Eskimos from Alaska for a pile of black and silver fox skins and pelts of mink and marten that were worth a pleasant sum. Since then she has been captained, manned, and navigated by Eskimos, and has, among other things, wandered far up the west coast of Banks Land into waters the navigation of which is considered to have reflected glory on officers of the British navy.

The present occasion was a fateful one for the *Penelope.* She had been rented by a Norwegian sailor named Stein and manned with Eskimos to go to Cape Parry and try to recover whalebone and valuable furs from the steam whaler *Alexander,* which had been wrecked there and abandoned in a storm on the 13th of August. At Shingle Point the *Penelope's* crew decided that winter was too close for going farther, "struck," and all came

ashore, so that Stein could do nothing but drop anchor and follow suit. A few days later a storm from the north drove the schooner ashore. She is now on the beach at Shingle Point, valuable only for the lead on her keel and the cordage of her rigging. She is probably the first and only ship ever owned and operated by Eskimos; in that and in her previous vicissitudes as a pleasure craft and whaler she is not among the least interesting of the wrecks that strew the various arctic shores.

The *Penelope* brought us a temporary accession in population through her dozen Eskimo families, and also a permanent one in Mr. Chris Stein, who now built a house on shore. The place is well adapted for wintering in that it is abundantly supplied with driftwood for fuel, but badly in that fishing operations must cease with the coming of ice in the fall, while in the delta and to the east of it fish are caught by both hook and net all winter.

While the sea is open an Eskimo does his fishing from shore by pushing one end of the net out with a slender pole sixty to eighty feet long, while one end of the net is fast to a stake on shore. Only a few are caught while the nights are light and the fish can see to avoid the nets, but when the season advances and the hours about midnight become dark, great numbers are secured—seatrout, herring, and other varieties. Our household maintained four sixty-foot nets, and we occasionally took in 2000 to 9000 fish a night.

The fish are cleaned by the women as soon as caught, and placed in log-covered ground caches safe from the dogs. As the fish-catching for winter begins early in summer, a few of these caches become rather malodorous towards fall. But just as some people like game and venison a trifle high, and others have a taste for putrid cheeses, so many of the Eskimos prefer tainted fish to fresh, and with as much reason as there ordinarily is for national tastes in food. I have friends who have become fond of sour milk in Asia and locusts in Africa; as for the tainted fish, I grew to prefer it decidedly to fresh fish when raw.

The arctic winter began with the freezing of the bays and ponds the first week

"TRACKING" SCOWS UP THE ATHABASCA

in October. I was gradually being broken in to native ways; by the middle of October I had thrown away my nearly outworn woollen suit and was fur clad from head to heel, an Eskimo to the skin. I never regretted the lack of a single item of such arctic clothing as money can buy in America or Europe, and in this my experiences agreed completely with those of the officers and crew who (unknown to me) were wintering some three hundred miles to the westward. A reasonably healthy body is all the equipment a white man needs for a comfortable winter among the arctic Eskimos.

About the middle of October we were visited by a band of Nunatama, or inland Eskimos, who reported the killing of many deer. Their camp was some hundred miles to the southward in the Rocky Mountains, beyond the divide, and where the waters flow toward the Yukon. It was at once decided that we of Shingle Point should fit out two dog teams and make the trip to this hunting camp, where we were promised as much boneless meat as our team could haul. In overland travel that means about six hundred pounds to the six-dog team. I was, of course, anxious to go on this expedition to break myself to winter travel (which I supposed would be full of hardships) before the weather got too cold.

Many people imagine that travelling with dog teams means sitting on a sled and cracking a long whip while the dogs whirl you across the snow fields at a mad pace. It does mean something like that in parts of Labrador and on the inn-studded trails of the Alaska gold country, but in the far north, and, indeed, wherever wide stretches of uninhabited territory have to be crossed, the process is very different. All you can expect of your team is that they haul the camping outfit and food enough to take themselves and you across the stretch that must be covered. Wherever the snow is unusually soft or the path a little steeper than common the driver must push hard behind his load to assist the team, if he does not have to hitch himself to the sled and haul continuously.

The deer-hunters had come to the coast for their sleds which they had left near Shingle Point the previous spring. There were four of them; we therefore started with six teams loaded so heavily for the trip with fish for ourselves and the dogs that it was at once evident we could hardly hope to bring back a pound of deer meat for every pound of fish we had to take for provisions; the meat would, however, be an agreeable change in our diet. The snow was soft, and all of us had to haul steadily at our sleds, while one man walked ahead of the leading team "breaking trail" by tramping the snow down with his snowshoes. This was all hard work and warm work, for the thermometer seldom indicated more than thirty degrees of frost, or two degrees above zero, Fahrenheit.

Travelling ten hours we made about twelve miles per day, necessarily following the winding course of a river valley, as one must always do in the mountains. Most of the time we were on the ice of this nameless river, but continually had to leave it on account of the surface being flooded. This happens with mountain rivers even in February, with the mercury sixty degrees below zero, for the streams keep damming up by freezing to the bottom, and must then necessarily flood, as they run down a steep grade. This surface water again soon freezes over, but forms dangerous travelling in that one often breaks through and gets his feet wet—a thing that may easily lead to a serious frost-bite.

At the end of eight days we got to the top of the divide. As the land now sloped south, we made the ninth day a good one and reached the hunting camp by night. This was situated on an unnamed branch of the Porcupine, and the houses were built in about the most northerly clump of small trees on this part of the continent.

On the way south we had had thick fogs continuously. We therefore saw no deer, though the tracks of large bands, as well as those of pursuing wolves, crossed every half hour the river course which we were following. At the deer camp the animals were so plentiful that the men did not take the trouble to go after them, but merely maintained a lookout on clear days from a hill behind their camp. If they saw a band suitably near, they would go out, spend half a day in getting it surrounded, and then usually kill off the animals to the last one. Most of these deer-hunting Eskimos were good shots, and their rifles were of the most modern American and European types, using smokeless powder and "soft nose" bullets.

The houses at this camp were dome-shaped ovals, the frame of birch stuffed with moss. The door was a small hole in the side and covered with a heavy mountain-sheep skin fastened by one edge above the opening. Deer-tallow candles were used for lights, and the cooking was done on an open hearth in the centre of the house just under the only window. This window was of thin, oiled skin, moderately transparent, and was removed whenever the fire was to be lit, so that the hole in the roof served both as a window and as a chimney.

After resting at this camp three days and helping to secure a few deer, our two sleds started for the coast with about a thousand pounds of meat, half of which we consumed in the eight days it took us to get home. The days were getting short and the mercury was gradually falling.

About November 20 the sun ceased rising at noon above the coast ranges of the Rocky Mountains to the south of us, and the arctic night of about eleven weeks began. This was a period I had looked forward to with misgivings, for most writers on wintering in the north have given harrowing descriptions of the depressing monotony of the period of twilight and darkness—perhaps because they really felt it, possibly because the reading public is supposed to expect the gruesome and horrible in the midwinter's experiences of the genuine arctic explorer; these horrors seem designed to take the place of the thrilling and hairbreadth adventures he is usually obliging enough to have for his readers' delight as soon as returning spring makes it convenient for him to go out and have them. By adroit questions I tried to find out in advance how the Eskimos passed this dread period, and I did find out. It is then too dark to hunt caribou, they told me, so they would perhaps make a three or four hundred mile trip to visit somebody; perhaps stay at home because they expected visitors. They seemed to dread the "night" about as much as a city man does his summer vacation. This was as disappointing as finding no fire after running seven blocks, but I bolstered up temporarily my waning faith in the chroniclers of arctic adventure, the heroes of the frozen north, by imagining that I should doubtless be privileged to suffer as they did in the darkness, even though my misery might have no company from the Eskimos, whom the processes of evolution had blinded against the real wretchedness of their lives. But in this also I was disappointed, and was finally forced to conclude that my trip was in so far a failure that I should have to return home in one, two, or three years without the halo of conspicuous suffering. "Do in Rome as the Romans do" is a precept that makes for comfort and contentment in places that differ materially from Rome of the Latins, but it is an unfortunate rule to follow if you are seeking picturesque experiences that shall later be of service in the drawing-rooms of the cultured. I followed it with disappointing success; and you, following it, could probably pass a longer arctic night than mine among a more remote group of Eskimos without even realizing it was tedious or wishing you were elsewhere, except as when in Chicago you may wish you were in Boston.

Some subsidiary reasons and two important ones made it undesirable that the whole winter should be spent at Shingle Point—our stores of fish did not seem adequate, and Roxy and his family were too sophisticated for profitable study through their previous intercourse with whalers. East of the Mackenzie delta, on the other hand, few of the people have had anything to do with the whalers, and the habits of most of them are little changed by white influences, while none of them speak English. Therefore, on the morning of the 1st of December, Roxy, Sitjak (a boy of eighteen), and I started with a team of six dogs and a sled loaded with fish to cross the delta of the Mackenzie. It is commonly said that the delta flats of a great river (and the Mackenzie is over a hundred miles wide at the mouth) make more difficult travelling than any similar area in the same latitude. For one thing, it would be almost hopeless for a man who does not know the channels to try crossing, for the irregular shaped islands covered with willow make it imperative for the sled to follow the channels, many of which are "blind" and all of which are tortuous in their windings. My men were both brought up in the delta and had each crossed it many times by sled in winter and canoe in summer, and still, on the morning of the second day, they announced that we were lost. The first day we had had a howling blizzard, a thing that seldom stops an Eskimo on a journey —though the journal of many a white explorer is filled with the familiar entry, "Blizzard to-day; remained in camp." In river deltas, however, the natives often camp for fear of getting lost, but this we had not done, because we had taken only six days' allowance of fish against a six-day trip, for there were already signs of a scarcity at Shingle Point. It took us two days of ploughing our way across willow-clad islands through deep snow to find the right channel again; we had made one-sixth of the distance and eaten half our fish, so we decided that both men and dogs should go on half rations.

This journey was, among other things, my initiation into the mysteries of the snow house. We were travelling in twilight and darkness (for the sun had been below the horizon a week), blizzards blew most days, and the temperature ranged from 25° to 40° below zero. This was not cold, but cold enough when the wind was blowing, and cold enough to make travelling uncomfortable had we used tents. To make clear the difference between a snow and a tent camp one might quote from the record of sufferings of almost any arctic explorer who preceded Peary—a man who differs notably from his forerunners in his willingness to learn from the Eskimo how to live in comfort and travel safely. That willingness is the foundation of his present pre-eminence as a sledge traveller.

The experience of those who tent in the arctic during the colder winter months is to be summarized about as follows:

When the tent has been pitched the temperature within it is some fifteen or twenty degrees higher than outside, or —30° if it is —50° in the open; one is damp and warm from the strenuous exercise of the day, but soon becomes cold, and shivers; one crawls into his sleeping-bag and makes entries in the diary clumsily with one's mittens on (cf. Nansen's account); the heat from one's body forms hoar frost on everything in the tent, and congeals in the sleeping-bag, so that it becomes stiff and heavy with ice during the day's travel when it freezes, and soaking wet when one gets into it at night and thaws it out; this in turn wets one's clothing, and the trousers and coat freeze stiff as sole-leather when one breaks camp in the morning; the twenty-four hours are a round of wretchedness, and the ice-crusted tent and icy sleeping-bags become a heavy load for the sled. Accounts of such sufferings as these are appetizing reading for those who revel in the contemplation of mis-

shaped hut; then, on the principles of architecture that apply to domes, whether made of stone or snow, the beehive house is completed. Two men can in an hour build a house large enough for eight to sleep in. When the house is completed a doorway is cut in its side near the ground, skins are spread over the floor, one brushes himself as clear of snow as possible and crawls inside. The oil

HELPING A DOG TRAIN THROUGH THE SNOW

ery; they are also amusing to those who know how easily most of these difficulties could have been avoided; they may even some time come to take high rank as works of humor, should the reading public ever become intelligently familiar with the facts and conditions of the north.

When one follows Eskimo methods the conditions are markedly different. On any treeless open (unless it be perhaps during the first month of winter) an area of compactly drifted snow is easily found; the snow-knives (of bone or iron, according to circumstances) are brought out and the surface of the drift is divided into blocks of domino shape, say fourteen by thirty inches and four inches thick; these are then placed on edge and end to end in a circle the size of the desired ground area of the dome-

lamps are then lit (in the case of the white man a "primus" stove may take their place), and the house is soon brought to a temperature considerably above the freezing-point; for snow is one of the best known non-conductors of heat, and the intense cold of the outside penetrates the walls only to a very slight degree. But when the house gets warm the inner side of the snow dome begins to thaw, and the water formed is sucked up into the snow, blotter fashion; when this water penetrates far enough into the snow to meet the cold from the outside it freezes, and your snow house is turned into an ice dome so strong that a polar bear can crawl over it without danger of breaking through. (In fact, at Baillie Island, where the dogs sleep in the entrance passages to the snow houses, the first warning of a bear's approach often comes through hearing the animal crawling over one's roof.) The Eskimo is particular about good ventilation, though he prefers the room a little close to having it below the freezing-point. The size of the ventilating flue in the roof, therefore, is gauged pretty closely on the amount of available fuel one has to burn, and ranges (roughly) from an inch to four inches in diameter.

When once inside the house the Eskimos strip naked to the waist and hang their clothes to dry on pegs in the wall. On some journeys we had sheet-iron stoves (procured from whalers in former years), which we installed in the snow houses, and in which we built roaring fires. That we frequently kept the snow house at an uncomfortably high temperature for hours without melting it may seem strange to those unfamiliar with the effects of the interaction of low and high temperatures, but those who have lived in northern New England or Dakota are familiar with the sight of ice half an inch thick persisting for days on the inside of a window in a room that is nevertheless comfortably warm. The same cold that keeps the window frost-covered would keep a snow house from melting away.

One is well placed to take comfort in the ingenuity of man overcoming a harsh environment when, sitting snug, warm, and lightly clad, one listens to an arctic blizzard whining helplessly over the ice vault that two hours before was an oval snow-bank. I longed for a dressing-gown and slippers, but one cannot burden his sled with such luxuries. There was no cold to make the hands numb in writing the diary, no frost to congeal on the bed-clothing and make them wet, none of the night's discomforts and the morrow's forebodings that have been the stock in trade of the makers of arctic books. And when we broke camp in the morning we did not burden the sled with an ice-stiffened hundred-pound tent, but stuck

ESKIMOS BUILDING A SNOW HOUSE

in our belt the ten-ounce snow-knife, our potential roof for the coming night.

The place we were making for was the south end of Richard Island, where Roxy expected to find his cousin Ovayuak at the village site of Kigirktayuk. On the evening of the eighth day, after being on half rations for five days, we reached the place, and found no house nor traces of people. We then ate half our remaining fish, which gave us a quarter of a square meal, and held a consultation. This consultation consisted of Roxy's declaring there was no use in consulting, for there was but one thing to do—leave everything that could possibly be left behind and travel eastward as fast as we could, for there were sure to be people somewhere along the coast. The next day we were moving at 3 A.M. We left behind our rifles and ammunition, part of our bedclothing, my instruments, and all the writing materials except a pocket notebook. Two of the dogs were already played out and walked behind the sled, two of us hauled on shoulder straps to help the remaining four dogs, and one man walked ahead to break trail. By 3 P.M. the dogs had all given up pulling and the men alone were hitched to the sled, but we had covered a good thirty-five miles. The next day we had made about thirty miles, when we came upon recent sled tracks, which indicated by their direction that they must be going towards Imnaluk—a fishing place often inhabited and distant about five miles. The fresh tracks so enlivened our dogs that when we hitched them up we found they would pull the sled along quite readily. Al-though starved, they had been rested by our doing their work for them all day.

To the Eskimo, or to the white man travelling in the wilderness, the experience just related was no adventure, and is set down merely to give an approximately true picture of one phase of arctic travel. True, had we failed for two or three more days to find a house and food, we should have had to eat some of our dogs, and the thing would have become a little more like an adventure. To my Eskimo friends the experience was merely a mild joke, and seemed to have put them in even better spirits than was ordinarily the case.

When we got within half a mile of the house at Imnaluk three or four young men came running to meet us, and when they learned we were hungry one of them hurried ahead to see if the women were getting any food ready. At the house our team was unhitched for us while we were bundled into the warm igloo, where a huge trough of boiled fish heads was waiting for us. This was a dish of which I had previously " steered clear," but which from that time on I recognized as a delicacy indeed. This raised me considerably in their esteem, though I already stood rather high by reason of eating my fish without a fork. I already had several native names, and I here acquired a new one, which means, " The white man who knows that fish heads are good to eat."

With this meal began my life with that branch of the Kogmallik tribe which is still little contaminated by the influence of whalers and missionaries.

A HALT ON THE DELTA FLATS

NORTH POINT.

MILWAUKEE.

TO most persons first impressions of a new locality outweigh quantities of subsequent information. Therefore we who admire this charming city, and desire every one else to do so, recommend you to arrive by water. Milwaukee stands exactly in the centre of the globe: all the world is open to her easterly by lake and ocean; westerly, by land. Approaching on the steamboat from Chicago, or Grand Haven, or the North, one first descries at dawn the bluffs upon which the town is built, and advances toward it with the rising sun.

The water through which you press your way, leaving behind a foaming and rainbow-touched wake, is green in the morning light with that special tint held by crude petroleum, and it is penetrated with beams of slanting light that lend it a brightly fibrous appearance, entirely different from ocean water. Glancing ahead, the eye catches a blue and bluer reflection, until, far away, indigo is the only color. Nearing the coast, you speedily detect a sharp line, three or four miles from shore, where the blue water stops, and a pale verdigris-green tint begins. This shows a sudden shallow, and marks the real old coast-line, upon which the river-mouth has encroached in a deep in-

dentation. A few moments later the steamer has passed the breakwater, which is fringed with fish-poles, like an abatis, has got by the miniature light-house and the pretty life-saving station, has turned the elbow into the river, and is poking its way along the narrow channel, between elevators, warehouses, and railway structures, through swinging bridges and a maze of shipping, up to its wharf in the centre of the city.

There is this disadvantage in this ingress, however, that you see too much of the river at first. It is a narrow, tortuous stream, hemmed in by the unsightly rear ends of street buildings and all sorts of waste places; it is a currentless and yellowish murky stream, with water like oil, and an odor combined of the effluvia of a hundred sewers. Nothing could better illustrate the contaminations of city life than the terrible change its waters undergo in a mile from their sparkling and rural cleanliness, up above, into this vile and noxious compound here among the wharves. Yet it is the very centre of the city's business, and to its presence Milwaukee owes its beginning, and a large part of its present existence. The nasty waters uphold a crowded and ever-busy fleet, and float grain steamers too long to turn around there.

We are informed that the very earliest civilized knowledge of the site of Milwaukee goes back to about the year 1674, and to that indefatigable missionary and keen adventurer, Father Marquette. That he took any special notice of the locality, does not appear. Later, other French missionaries and traders, journeying southward from Green Bay, which they called St. Francis Xavier, and which was the western outpost of the Jesuits during the early half of the last century, went ashore here at long intervals, and visited the Indians, who seem to have made the mouth of the river a permanent abiding-place; but for more than a hundred years after the Abbés Joly and Marquette were there, nobody thought well enough of the place to stay there.

NORTH POINT LIGHT.

I can fancy various features about the locality at that time not altogether inviting. The long line of bluffs which form the western shore of Lake Michigan was broken by a gap of half a dozen miles, where a shallow bay rounded in. The low inner shore of this bay amounted to little else than an immense swamp of wild rice, with a sand-bar and a hill or two to break the surf, and a distant view of forest-clad hills and oak openings beyond, and bluffs to the northward. Finding a devious way through this swamp came a river from the north, a smaller stream from the south, and a little rivulet from the west.

Such geography would scarcely prove attractive to a frontiersman, when so much better land was ready to his choice. But commerce stepped in ahead of æs-

thetics, and dictated the foundation of a city, where presently the æsthetic was quite content to reside—which means that it was a capital place for an Indian to get his living, and that accordingly it became the permanent camp or head-quarters of a community of them. The tribe found in possession by the first traders were the Mishimakinaks, whom the very first mention introduces to us as "those runagates.... a horrid set of refractory Indians." Just in what they proved "refractory," Colonel Peyster fails to tell us.

There is still greater doubt as to the meaning and correct orthography of the name. The first time it occurs is in Lieutenant James Gorrett's journal, September 1, 1761, where he states that a party of Indians came from *Milwacky*. Colonel Peyster writes it *Milwakie*. In 1820

A GLIMPSE FROM NORTH POINT.

Dr. Morse records that *Mil-wah-kie* was settled by the Sacs and Foxes, and that the name was derived from the word *man-awakie*, meaning "good land," which recalls Peyster's assertion that the name of

so well.   It appears that one of Onaugesa's boon companions was an alleged poet named Pashano.   In some *affaire de cœur* the trader offended the poet's sensitive soul, who retaliated by prejudicing the

AT THE FOOT OF GRAND AVENUE.

the river was *Mahn-a-waukie.*   A Chippewa interpreter spelled it with fewer letters, but confirms the rendering, "good" or "beautiful" land.   The French seem to have written it *Milouaqui* in their early dispatches home.

The Indians' town was at the very mouth of the river, and buried its dead on the hill which now forms the abrupt foot of Michigan Street.   Their chief was Onaugesa, a Menomonee, whom Laframboise, the first trader from Mackinac, found to be "a good Indian."   Laframboise retired after a while, and his brother succeeded him, but did not get along

chief against him, the result of which was that the man of business soon abandoned his post.   When Onaugesa realized that he had foolishly cut off his nose to spite his face—to wit, driven away the trader who had regularly supplied him with rum in exchange for his good-will—he reflected upon the source of his misfortunes, and in a day or two the meddlesome laureate went mysteriously to the happy hunting grounds.   This began a vendetta that made the whole region too hot for traders for several years.   Finally, however, a French half-breed named Vieau began coming down every spring from

DOWN THE RIVER FROM GRAND AVENUE BRIDGE.

Green Bay, and going back in the fall. He did so well that after a few years another Frenchman, who had been his clerk, built himself warehouses, married Vieau's daughter, and becoming popular among the Indians, proposed to settle permanently here. This young man was Solomon Juneau, and his block-house stood where now is the intersection of East Water and Wisconsin streets.

This happened only about 1820, yet it reads like a romance of at least five hundred years ago. For several years Juneau was the sole white inhabitant of the region, only occasionally visited by a wandering trader, trapper, or missionary. The nearest post to him was "a miserable settlement called Eschikagon, at the mouth of Skunk River, some ninety miles across dense forests to the south." All supplies came by water from Mackinac, the head-quarters of the American Fur Company, and the settlers lived a far more isolated and truly frontier life than it is possible to do now anywhere in the United States except in Alaska.

Juneau was sharp, and in 1831 secured from the Indians a cession of all the region, claiming for himself a large tract on the east side of the river. Then he began to advertise the advantages of settlement there, and one by one got neighbors.

Among the earliest were two gentlemen whose names are household words in the city—Byron Kilbourn and George H. Walker. They had enterprise and knowledge and money. Kilbourn took up a tract on the west side, and Walker south of the Menomonee, and for many years after, these quarters of the city were known respectively as "Kilbourntown" and "Walker's Point." In 1834, Milwaukee County was set apart from Brown County, which has since been similarly subdivided a score of times, until its former ducal proportions are reduced to a mere hand-breadth at Green Bay. This act showed the enterprise of the pioneers, for there were then not white men enough in the region to fill the offices provided for by the county organization. More kept coming, however, from Detroit and Buffalo and New England, and the wheezy steamboats of that early day in lake navi-

LOADING A GRAIN STEAMER.

gation began to make the struggling village a stopping-place.

Juneau's log warehouse was the headquarters for gossip. "Here were wont to congregate," says the chronicler Wheeler, "pioneers and sailors to hear long-expected tidings which had floundered through mud and forests and over prairies for weeks before they reached the settlement; on the same spot the merchants and multitude generally now read from a bulletin the news of the world, which comes fresh and quivering over the wires from every point of the compass once a day."

Such was the irregular, muddy, prosaic beginning of this great and attractive lake port. One hears a pleasant or a comical incident now and then, of Indian threats which sound thrilling, till you find they never amounted to action, and of adventures that were almost perilous; but really there is little romance about it. A town grew up, partly on a sand-hill, and partly in a mud-hole (one being cut down to fill the other up), because men found they could accumulate wealth there.

Nearly all this money was to be made through commercial channels, and these channels led down the river and up the lakes—as channels are very likely to do. However, they were not deep and broad enough for the great vessels which in imagination (and finally in fact) were to enter the port. The first public effort, therefore, was directed toward harbor improvement, but it was several years before the general government would listen to the call for help. Congress was deaf in its Northwest ear, as Major Domo, a famous character, used to say. Finally it appropriated $30,000, and grandly wasted it in the wrong place. The river runs along parallel with the lake shore for more than a mile, only separated from it by a narrow strip of beach. Common-sense suggested the cutting through of this bar close up to the town, but the engineers preferred to construct a harbor a mile away, down at the mouth. The result was that Chicago scored a big point in its rivalry, and Milwaukee a few years later had to make her "straight-cut" through the beach where she should have done it at first. This gave her what some persons have called the best harbor on the upper lakes, albeit it is only a narrow river and two short breakwaters. Now it is proposed to run out into the bay for several hundreds of yards an immense stone jetty, costing a million or two, and thus form the bay into a harbor of refuge; but this is not begun yet.

All these expensive harbor improvements would never have been undertaken, of course, had not the trading post grown with marvellous speed into a city and shipping port; and this, in turn, would never have come about had not there been a rich agricultural region behind it, and a large influx of farming population. When one remembers that fifty years ago Wisconsin was an utter wilderness, a howling, untutored, worthless stretch of forest and prairie; sees now the universal cultivation of all its southern half; marks how the pine woods are disappearing in the north, and how immigrants are scattering themselves singly and in colonies over all that region—he is amazed that so much could have been done in so short a time. But comprehending this fact, the concomitant—namely, that such populous centres should arise as Chicago, Milwaukee, La Crosse, St. Paul, Minneapolis, and the other large towns of the "Golden Northwest"—causes no wonder at all.

With her harbor built, her ships accumulating, Milwaukee was quick to see that she must adopt the new invention of railways, and began to extend lines inland to bring the crops to her granaries. The railways built their tracks down on the flats, and helped to fill in large areas. They placed their stations, freight dépôts, and shops there, and attracted business, until now the old miles square of marsh has dwindled to a few well-curbed canals and deep slips where vessels lie to be loaded. Chiefly, however, the railways served the interests of Milwaukee in making it not only an easily accessible buying market for the rural districts, but the most available point at which to dispose of crops.

A GRAIN ELEVATOR.

In order to handle these vast crops, which are poured into the city at harvest-time and later, several of those enormous buildings called elevators have been built by the railway companies and by private enterprise. All lake-port and sea-port citizens are very familiar with these structures and their use, which is for the storage and transhipment of grain, but they will perhaps pardon an explanation of them to the more benighted people who live off the "trunk lines."

In order to begin at the beginning—get to the bottom, as it were, of an elevator—one must climb to the very top. The building is perhaps one hundred and fifty feet long by seventy-five feet wide, and, like all of its class, it rises eighty feet or more to the eaves, above which a narrow top part, forty or fifty feet higher, is perched upon the ridge-pole. It is built of wood, sheathed with corrugated iron a lit-

PRIVATE RESIDENCES.

When grain is bought—perhaps a hundred car-loads from the vast fields of Dakota or the wide farms between here and St. Paul—the train is backed right into the elevator, and stands so that opposite each car door is a receiver, which is a kind of vat, or hopper, in the platform. By the help of steam-shovels, operating almost automatically, two men in each car will in ten minutes or less empty the whole train.

As fast as the grain is dumped, the receiver delivers it to iron buckets holding about a peck each, which are attached to endless belts, and travel up a sort of chimney, called a "leg," to this roof chamber. These buckets will hoist 6000 bushels an hour at their ordinary rate of speed. That is equal to one bucket going up 24,000 times, at the rate of 400 times a minute—tolerably lively work!

tle way up, and then slated the rest of the way.

Entering one end, where two railway tracks run into the building, we find a narrow wooden stairway, and begin our ascent. The flights are short ones, but eighteen are stepped over before we emerge into the topmost attic. Alongside of us, as we climbed, has been running the strong belt which carries the power from the great engine on the ground-floor to the gearing in the roof—a belt of rubber canvas four feet wide, and perhaps two hundred and fifty feet long.

To-day up here in the topmost loft there is nothing doing, and we are saved strangulation. The light hardly penetrates through the cobwebbed windows, and the most pulverous of dust lies everywhere half an inch deep, showing the marks of a few boot soles, many foot-prints of rats, and the lace-like tracks of hundreds of spiders and bugs. You step over and under broad horizontal belts as you make your way gingerly from one end of the attic to the other. They run the fans that winnow the grain as it comes up in the buckets, after which it is dropped into the hoppers, ten feet wide, and twice as deep, that open like hatchways every few feet in the centre of the floor. Now all is perfectly quiet; we are so high that even the clamor of the wharves does not reach us. But when the machinery starts in motion, then fearful roars, and clash of cogs, and whipping of slackened belts, assault the garret, until this whole upper region rocks like a ship in a gale, and chaff and dust cloud the eyes and stifle the throat.

Descending one story, we find another garret, with nothing in it but the square bodies of the hoppers. Going down a second flight shows us that the hoppers are suspended not upon pillars, but loosely on iron stirrups, so as to shake a little, and the iron gate which lets on or shuts off the fall of the grain through the tubular orifice at the bottom is operated by steam.

CENTRAL FIRE STATION.

There are twelve of these hoppers. Sticking up through the floor underneath each one gape the flaring mouths of twelve spouts or sluices, all of which point directly at the gate in the hopper, as though earnestly begging its bounty of grain. Every one of these 144 spouts leads into a bin, near or distant, and all are numbered, so that the superintendent knows which spout conducts to any one bin, and can distribute his cargoes accordingly, the result of his choice being recorded in cabalistic abbreviations upon a blackboard close by. A movable conductor is swung into place between the hopper and the spout, the gate pulled open, and down slides the wheat, with a musically rushing noise, into the grateful bin.

To see the bins we descend again, this time reaching the top of the wide part of the building. We walk very circumspectly, in the half-light, amid a maze of beams, stringers, and cross-pieces of wood and iron. The whole interior of the elevator below this level is now seen to consist of a series of rooms, between which there is no communication. They are ceilingless, and the only exit from them is through a spout in the bottom. Peering over the edges from the narrow foot-walks, we can only guess how far the person would fall who should lose his balance, for the eye can not reach the bottom: it is sixty-five feet below, and hidden in darkness. Of these deep bins there are 144, some twice the size of others. Sometimes they are all full at once, and hold eight or nine hundred thousand bushels, weighing fifty millions of pounds, and good for over two hundred thousand barrels of flour.

Yet it was not until the winter of 1840 that the first cargo of grain was ever shipped from this port, and it required the whole winter to accumulate 4000 bushels. Forty years have passed, and there are now in Milwaukee no less than nine elevators, which have a storage capacity varying from 200,000 to 1,000,000 bushels each, the total capacity being 5,330,000 bushels. They can ship over a million bushels a day, but can take in only about half as much, the grain requiring twice the time and trouble to go up as it does to come down. Every available foot of stor-

VIEW ON THE RIVER.

age space, I am told, was required last winter (1879–80) to accommodate the business here, and then there was not room enough.

What is the reason for this large and steady growth against the powerful competition of a great neighbor? It is found in the fact that Milwaukee wheat has from the first been subjected to the most rigorous and honest inspection, and the grade No. 1, or No. 2, or any other grade marked as such, is known in Liverpool or Mark Lane to be precisely what it is stamped. So trustworthy is this brand and reputation that Milwaukee's wheat, derived from just the same fields as Chicago's or Duluth's, will fetch one or two cents more a bushel every time.

These elevators are almost all owned by railway companies, and constitute an important element in their power throughout the Northwest, while at the same time they are a source of great strength to the city in its race with competitors, since railway lines strive to direct all the grain trade to Milwaukee, cutting out Chicago and other rivals.

The greatest of all these railways, whose existence is so vital to the city, is the Chicago, Milwaukee, and St. Paul, which owns enough miles of track to make a road—side tracks and all—from the Atlantic to the Pacific. Its lines ramify through the whole Northwest, and are to be "pro-

duced" (as we say in geometry) all over the Northern plains from the Black Hills to Athabasca Lake. Feeding this artery to supply the Milwaukee elevators are the Northern Pacific, the railway from Manitoba, the lines which enter St. Paul and Minneapolis from Dakota, Nebraska, and Northern Iowa, the various other railways coming eastward through Southern Wisconsin. In addition to this, the great Chicago and Northwestern company send a powerful branch here, and help to make Milwaukee a point intermediate between Eastern and Western traffic. Over the West Wisconsin road come the staples from the Chippewa, Eau Claire, and St. Croix regions. Three routes lead to Green Bay and the northern part of the State. The Wisconsin Central now extends a clear line from Milwaukee to Ashland, Lake Superior, running almost directly through the centre of the State, and opening up a country rich in prospects. At present it is chiefly useful as a lumber road, but settlement upon its abundant lands is proceeding rapidly, and when the proposed connecting link between it and the Northern Pacific at Duluth is made, it will become a second channel through which the wheat of the Upper Missouri prairies can flow into Milwaukee's granaries. Several shorter lines have lately been opened, contributing to the city's prosperity; and a route, no doubt some day to be built, is projected as an air-line road to St. Louis, which shall take in great coal-fields on its way. Such a road might be an important accession to the manufacturing interests, in reducing the cost of fuel, which is now brought from the soft-coal fields of Iowa, and from the anthracite mines in more distant Pennsylvania.

These railways and the steam-ship lines, this export of wheat and lumber and farm produce, and import of rural supplies, have produced a city of solidity and magnificence, which you may go far and not find equalled. Its broad, Nicholson-paved business streets are bounded for block after block with warehouses and offices that would do credit to New York; and there is probably no finer building in the Northwest, devoted to a similar purpose, than the new hall of the Chamber of Commerce. Limestone from home quarries and gray Ohio sandstone are much used in construction, and ornamental iron fronts are common, but the customary building material is a brick which burns yellowish-white instead of red, the clay lacking the iron which by oxidation under heat gives the ferruginous tint. There are only one or two buildings in the lower part of the city constructed of red bricks, but their handsome effect is being copied somewhat by painting. Taking each building separately, one can not altogether admire the taste which seems to have dictated them (and the same may be said of the more ostentatious residences in many cases), yet the general effect is undeniably fine.

As for public buildings, they are not many nor prominent. The County Courthouse is a handsome, dome-crowned structure of Lake Superior brown stone ensconced in trees and shrubbery; the Postoffice is a commodious building, which looks as if it was carved out of cheese, and makes you blink for its whiteness; churches are hidden away among foliage and houses until you can't see any one of them very distinctly, except the two vast towers of the Cathedral on the south side; and the beautiful tower of the water-works remains about the only really ornamental public edifice in a city where

THE COURT-HOUSE.

nothing is disgraceful except its market, and that is being rebuilt.

Milwaukee is certainly handsome, business-like, and healthy. It has about it an air of cleanliness, morally and physically, and an appearance of thrifty activity remarkable in contrast with the slatternly look of many large Eastern and Southern towns. All these things serve to make it a "Cream City," not in general tint alone, but *crème de la crème* among its prosperous sister towns in the Northwest. Yet it is difficult to pick out any one feature, and say of it, *that* is characteristic and peculiar, something whereby a person might know the city if he saw it in a vision, or was mysteriously landed in its midst, apart from all other towns. Boston has its round "swell fronts" and antique streets, Philadelphia its marble steps and solid shutters, and so on; but Milwaukee has little that is peculiar, unless it be the universality of yellowish-white bricks, which is shared by nearly all the towns between Lake Huron and the Upper Mississippi.

SOLDIERS' HOME.

Nor is it strange that it should be diffi-cult to find special peculiarities in so com-posite and so young a town. I have tried again and again in Chicago, Detroit, St. Paul, Burlington, and other Western cities to find a type of face or a style of carriage different from New York or New England, but found it impossible to do so. In a hundred years the case may be differ-ent. *Now*, these men and women are New York and New England transplanted; two-thirds of them were born in the East. They have brought with them the min-gled customs of all the Atlantic centres of civilization, and have fitted them together to suit the new exigencies of the North-west. Even the rural population are not as gawky and rustic as you will find in any back county of the East. They have travelled somewhat, and seen strangers. Their eyes are opened, and their attention alert. As for the long-haired plainsmen, and 'coon-skin-capped hunters, and other mythical characters of the "West," of course you see no more of them, nor as many, as you may find on a bright day in the Bowery. The only bit of "character" I can think of to be found anywhere in the city or surroundings are the few lazy old wood-sawyers who sit astride of their

saw - bucks on the comfortable side of the City Hall, and take long naps or spin yarns while waiting for a job. But even these old fossils are not differ-ent from the work-ing classes all over the country; and the same is true of ev-ery grade of society. You continually see countenances famil-iar to you, feel an impulse to rush for-ward and claim an old acquaintance on every other corner. One house or shop front shows a tradi-tion of Pennsylva-nia, another suggests some Broadway idea, a third adopts a pe-culiar bit of Bos-tonianism, while a fourth imitates a prominent sign-board in New Orleans. How is a chronicler to recognize anything as yet grown out of this composite, cos-mopolitan growth, occurring similarly in a dozen cities, to characterize any one? Possibly in another century the evolution of circumstances will bring out some spe-cialty in each whereby their divergence can be perceived.

Perhaps, nevertheless, in the case of Milwaukee, a distinguishing feature may be found in the large grounds that sur-round nearly all of the private residences in the finer parts of the city. For a town of so large a population this matter of space is accomplished in a way quite sur-prising to an Eastern man. Several of the residences, even in the heart of the town, occupy a whole block, or half a block, and horticulture finds many en-thusiastic votaries. As a consequence, double houses and solid blocks of houses flush with the sidewalk are very few. This is partly because general sentiment is averse to it, but chiefly because a man who can afford to rent in such a block will prefer to find means to build for himself. Milwaukee is a city of *homes;* its people own the houses and lots where they live, to an extraordinary extent; and this is true from highest to lowest—as well down below Wisconsin Street, and "over the Rhine," as up on the bluffs that overlook the azure lake. The architecture of the whole city, also, business and residence portions alike, is pleasantly varied. This gives the streets down town an animated look, and up town lends that village air to the well-shaded avenues which always seems doubly delightful when combined with such evidently urban advantages as good pavements and faucet water, gas and municipal protection. Just what styles of architecture prevail it would be difficult to say. The big Grecian house, with pillars in front from porch to cornice, the square-topped, fortlike brick, the pretentiously cheap Mansard-roof, are all absent, as is also the gambrel-roofed moss-grown home so quaintly attractive in the suburbs of most New England towns, and which, of course, no one would expect to see here.

A half-Dutch, half-English cottage style of house, with no end of peaks, gables, and surprising little points and angles, is the universal thing, and nine out of ten of these houses that succeed one another for miles and miles of prettiness are painted slate-color. But though the houses are not plain, the town owes its beauty not so much to ornamental architecture, which has generally too much of the "gingerbread" look about it to please a severe taste, as to the abundance of shade trees everywhere, and to the care which is taken of the grounds. In many of the streets, also, a wide space of sharply curbed and well-trimmed lawn separates the roadway from the sidewalk, and often you may go block after block without finding a fence between you and the slightly elevated or

FOUNTAIN IN THE PARK.

A PACIFIC CONTEST AT THE SOLDIERS' HOME.

terraced door-yards, whose shaven greensward runs continuously past a dozen houses with no boundary wall to interrupt. Particularly is this true of Grand Avenue—a worthy rival of far-famed Euclid Avenue in Cleveland. This gives one the idea that he is making his way through a park rather than along a public street. Another pleasant custom is that of placing an ornamental gateway and rounding steps at the corner, where a house stands at the intersection of two streets, giving a far more imposing effect than one would imagine.

Until very lately a prejudice has existed—quite unfounded, I think—against living on the bluffs that overlook the northern half of the bay; the city consequently grew southward into the marshes, and westward up the slopes between the Me-

nomonee and Milwaukee rivers, leaving its northern side open. Five years ago, Prospect Street was a grass-grown, muddy lane. Now it is one of the very finest avenues in town, and the backs of all the house lots on its eastern side run to the brow of the lofty bluff, at whose feet the restless lake is always beating. Down toward the foot of this handsome street another branched off at an acute angle, and the property owners about there bought and set apart the triangle inclosed as a little park, which is now very pretty. They constructed a fountain like a pile of rocks there, on condition that the city should always keep it running, wherein they made a good bargain. The peculiarity and excellence of this fountain is that there is plenty of water in it—rushing streams having force and weight dash out with a noise and wetness thoroughly refreshing, whereas in the majority of fountains a few tender trickling drops only keep the iron-work glossy, and distress one with an idea that the affair is just on the point of drying up. This is much the case with that handsome structure, intended as a fountain, that ornaments the park of the Court-house.

The pavement runs out Prospect Street for more than a mile, and continues into a favorite drive for five miles, with a side track kept in order for equestrians; and it was out this road that the Veteran Soldiers camped at their late reunion, and the beer gardens there did then—and yet do—a very thriving business. Five miles from the Post-office brings one to Whitefish Bay, and a magnificent view of Lake Michigan beating upon her cliffs just as the salt ocean worries the headlands of Montauk or Navesink.

This is out of town, though, and one need not go so far to watch the beauty or fury of the capricious lake. At the foot of Prospect Street the bluff has been terraced and sodded for a long distance, and so converted into a sort of boulevard or esplanade, where you may loiter and enjoy the fresh air. From this charming spot the bay is spread before you in a vast semicircle, sweeping from Minnewawa, the north point, to Nojoshing, its southern terminus, five miles distant, and leading the eye in front to a boundless horizon. No ocean picture can be broader or more majestic; it may give the beholder a more impressive feeling of terrible power, but never will it show the varying and delicate touches of beauty that the sparkling light waters and the brilliant sunshine combine to paint upon the surface of Lake Michigan. The swift and shifting changes the clouds work in the dissolving tints of blue and green; the sudden way in which silver and gold and the scarlet or rosy reflections of gaudy clouds are thrown down—all this is beyond

pen or space to describe, higher than pencil or brush can truly depict. The lake, indeed, is the great fact which confronts you everywhere in Milwaukee. Its azure mass rises as a wall to confront the view whenever you turn your face to the eastward, filling with deep blue the arch under the trees at the end of every cross street.

Having this lake always before their eyes, and ever supplying pure and fresh breezes, and having streets so broad and well shaded, with such an abundance of pleasant gardens just across the low fence, wherein your eyes may feast to your heart's content, Milwaukee hardly needs a park. Nevertheless, just out of the city, to the westward, are the handsome grounds of the Soldiers' Home.

This institution is one of the four or five provided by the United States government as asylums for men in distress who have served creditably as volunteer soldiers in the Union army. They could not desire a more comfortable or pleasanter home. It is interesting to saunter through the commodious and orderly building; to see how every office of the household, from

A LAGER-BEER BREWERY.

IN THE BEER VAULT.

and go into that great campaign of the hereafter whither every man marches under sealed orders.

I have said that the lake was the "one great fact" about Milwaukee. The other great fact in Milwaukee is lager-beer. Probably the city is more widely known for this than for anything else. Her breweries ship their delectable product to all parts of the world, and have won compliments for its excellence even in the historic gardens of Bavaria. The beer business is a rapidly growing one, also, as the statistics of the Chamber of Commerce show, for it is less than thirty years since the first shipment was sent to tempt the willing appetites of New-Yorkers. In 1865 only about 65,000 barrels were manufactured in the whole city, and this was regarded as a large amount. Now there are a score of breweries, and for the year 1879 the records of the collector of internal revenue show a total of 548,770 barrels of beer sold by the brewers of Milwaukee, showing an increase within a year of 122,430 barrels. In making this amount of beer the brewers of Milwaukee used 1,234,632 bushels of barley, equivalent to 1,509,017 bushels of malt, and 1,097,540 pounds of hops, and realized for the product, at the wholesale price, the sum of $4,938,930. Still they find it necessary to continue enlarging their facilities, so widespread has become the demand for this favorite beverage. The barley is gathered from the entire Northwest, and even from California.

The beer is made from very carefully selected materials, and by men of the most approved experience in brewing. Extreme care is taken in every detail of the work from beginning to end, and finally, no beer is allowed to leave the cellars until it is at least five months old; whereas many brewers, particularly in the East, sell their product only three or four months after it is made. It has been asserted that there is a difference in the water, or the air, or some other natural

that of night-watchman to that of scullion, is performed by men, and so well that a woman-hater would hug himself for joy. The inmates all wear the army blue, and spend their time wholly in a well-earned *dolce far niente*. It is enjoyable to watch the groups of grizzled veterans, with their pipes and cards, in the smoking-room, or listen to their stories of the old days as they lie at full length under the trees, and gaze across the hazy, purple city to the far sun-lit lake beyond, in delicious and dreamy contrast to their former activities and hardships. As the city extends itself, this charming domain will ultimately be its real park, no doubt, for the Soldiers' Home will find itself utterly without tenants before many more years. The deaths are very rapid now, and every year more and more of these aged and scarred veterans, who are now beginning to feel how the war shortened their lives by drawing too heavily on their youthful energies, strike their tents in this world,

SUMMER NIGHT IN A MILWAUKEE BEER GARDEN.

circumstance, which makes beer west of the Alleghanies superior to that manufactured on the Eastern slope; but Milwaukee men say this is erroneous, and that it is all a question of better knowledge and extraordinary caution in respect to all parts of the brewing process, and the age which the beverage is permitted to attain before it is sold.

No doubt the success of Milwaukee lager is a result of the demand for very good beer which has arisen from the fact that this community contains so many Germans who are both judges and lovers of beer. Out of the 116,000 people in the city, over 60,000 are of that nationality. It is said that in the Second Ward, the northwestern corner of the town, there is not a single American, French, or Irish family. Whether this is so or not, it is certain one sees none but German faces, reads German signs, hears Teutonic speech, and catches all the flavor of the Father-land underneath an unmistakably American crust. Any one can understand what is meant by this last phrase if he goes to the railway station and marks the appearance of the crowds of immigrants that daily pour in there, fresh from the voyage. Then let him take a Walnut Street car, and ride through the west side. The faces are the same; the dress is only slightly different; but there is an entire change, hard to define, in the *sentiment* of all that the late immigrant says and does.

There being so many Germans and so much good beer, those out-door pleasure parks so dear to the German mind are in great number and handsomely appointed. Milwaukee quite emulates Cincinnati in this respect. They are pretty places, being laid out with well-shaded walks, parterres of flowers, rustic colonnades, rock-work, fountains, and all the other accessories of landscape gardening on a miniature scale. There are also bowling-alleys and billiard saloons attached, and in the middle stands a concert hall, where a band discourses music to the crowd. Two of the largest of these gardens are on the high ground over in the Second Ward, but the majority of them are up the river, where a little steamer runs, and plenty of row-boats are handy for pleasuring. When there is a set programme, and good music may be expected, a very respectable crowd of both Germans and Americans will be found gathered at the gardens.

MY EXPLORATIONS IN UNKNOWN LABRADOR

I N undertaking a Labrador expedition
of exploration it was my purpose to
carry to completion the plans which
Leonidas Hubbard, Jr., my husband, had
mapped out for himself in his expedition of 1903.

Mr. Hubbard planned to explore and
map one and perhaps both of the two
large unknown rivers of northeastern
Labrador—the Northwest River, draining
the great interior lake, Michikamau, to
Hamilton Inlet; and the George River,
draining the northern slope of the plateau
to Ungava Bay,—to witness the annual
caribou migration said by the Indians
to take place about the upper waters
of the George River; to visit in their
home camp the Nascaupee Indians, or
" Barren Ground People "; and to secure

to the name, besides the honor of map-
ping the rivers, that of being first after
McLean to cross the six hundred miles
of unexplored wilderness lying between
Hamilton Inlet and Ungava Bay. In
1838 John McLean, a trader of the Hudson Bay Company, had crossed this
part of Labrador, but he left no map,
and his account of the journey is so
incomplete that to this day it is not certain what route he took. Thus the country still remained *terra incognita.*

The tragic ending of Mr. Hubbard's
expedition is well known. The fatal
mistake in the rivers, to which so many
things contributed to lead him, was
made, and he failed to accomplish his
purpose; but that did not prove his expedition a carelessly and ignorantly

OUR STARTING-POINT, NORTHWEST RIVER POST, LAKE MELVILLE

planned undertaking. On the contrary, all the information obtained by his survivors from the Indians at Northwest River Post in December of that year went only to show that had it not been for the mistake in the rivers the expedition would have been entirely successful. I knew, what, strangely, does not appear in the published account of the trip, that the Indians who hunt that country make the journey from Northwest River post to Lake Michikamau by the Nascaupee route in twenty-one days, and that they do not consider it a hard journey, nor one nearly so difficult of achievement as that which Mr. Hubbard actually made.

It seemed to me fit that my husband's name should reap the fruits of service which had cost him so much, and in the summer of 1905 I undertook and in every particular successfully completed the work which Mr. Hubbard had so greatly desired to have the honor of doing.

My expedition demonstrated that geographers were mistaken in supposing the Northwest River, draining Lake Michikamau, and the Nascaupee River, draining Seal Lake, to be two distinct rivers. They are one and the same, the outlet of Lake Michikamau carrying its waters northeast to Seal Lake, and thence southeast to Hamilton Inlet. The head waters of the Nascaupee River I traced northward through Lake Michikamau and the other lakes and streams leading to the height of land—a narrow strip of bog some three hundred yards in width,—and located the head waters of the George River immediately beyond it, following three hundred miles to its mouth the course of the stream, which, at its source a tiny rivulet, is at its discharge into Ungava Bay a great river three miles in width, and securing correct maps of the waters traversed. I witnessed also the annual caribou migration, and visited in their home camps the two bands of Indians inhabiting the northern slope of the plateau—the Montagnais and the Nascaupees,—travelling three hundred and fifty miles of wilderness before seeing any human faces other than those of my crew. On the 27th of August I reached the George River Hudson Bay Company's post at Ungava, first after McLean to cross the country.

The entire journey of six hundred miles was accomplished in a few hours less than sixty-one days, forty-three days of actual travel and eighteen days in camp; for we did not travel on rainy days, and sometimes not on Sunday. We had all we could eat all the time, and at the journey's end there was, including my gifts to the Nascaupee Indians, a surplus of one hundred and fifty pounds of provisions.

With me I had three men of my crew, chief among whom was George Elson, the Scotch Indian who had so loyally served Mr. Hubbard on his expedition of 1903, and whose devotion had culminated in his nobly heroic, though unsuccessful, efforts to save Mr. Hubbard's life. The other two were Joseph Iserhoff, a Russian half-breed, and Job

Chapies, a pure-blood Cree Indian. All three had been born and brought up in the Hudson Bay country, and were expert hunters and canoemen. They had come to me from Missanabie, some eight hundred miles west of Montreal.

Monday morning, June 26, found us at our real starting-point in Labrador, Northwest River Post, Lake Melville, and at work in earnest. There was a really perplexing array of stuff when the outfit was unpacked and spread out in the store. It seemed as if the little canoes could never hold it all. The men looked a little doubtful too. I wondered what I should have to leave behind.

M. Duclos, of the French post, and Mr. Cotter, of the Hudson Bay Company, cheerfully raided their kitchens to supply my lack in utensils, the flour-bags were finished and filled, and before noon Tuesday most of the outfit was packed, and the men tried it in the canoes. There were two of these, canvas-covered, and nineteen feet long, thirteen inches deep, and thirty-four inches wide, and with each three paddles and a sponge. The remainder of the outfit consisted of 2 balloon-silk tents, 1 stove, 5 12″ water-proof canvas bags, 2 9″ water-proof canvas bags, 1 doz. 10-lb. water-proof balloon-silk bags, 392 lbs. of flour, 4 lbs. baking-powder, 15 lbs. of rice, 20 lbs. erbswurst, 20 cans of standard emergency rations, 12 lbs. tea, 60 lbs. sugar, 1 oz. crystalose, 4 cans condensed milk, 12 lbs. chocolate, 4 cans condensed soup, 5 lbs. hard-tack, 200 lbs. bacon, 14 lbs. salt. There were kitchen utensils, 3 small axes, 1 crooked knife, 2 nets, 2 rifles, and 3 tarpaulins. For each of the men there were a 22-cal. 10″ barrel single-shot pistol for partridges and other small game, a bowie-knife, and a pair of light wool blankets. They took also two pairs of "shoe-packs" each.

For myself I had a revolver, a hunting-knife, and some fishing-tackle; one pocket folding-kodak, one pan-oram kodak, a sextant, a barometer, a thermometer. I wore a short skirt over knickerbockers, a short sweater, and a belt, to which were attached a handsome embroidered cartridge-pouch and my revolver and knife. My hat was a rather narrow-brimmed soft felt. I had one pair of heavy leather moccasins reaching almost to my knees, one pair of high sealskin boots, one pair low ones, which M. Duclos had given me, and three pairs of duffel. Of underwear I had four suits and five pairs of stockings—all wool. I took also a rubber automobile-shirt, a long Swedish dogskin coat, one pair leather gloves, one pair woollen gloves, and a shirt-waist—for Sundays. For my tent I had an air mattress, crib size, one pair light, gray camp-blankets, one light wool comfortable weighing three and a half pounds, one little feather pillow, and one hot-water bottle.

Thanks to the courtesy of M. Duclos, Gilbert Blake had been added to my crew. Gilbert was one of the two young lads of the rescue party George Elson

WIND-BOUND ON MICHIKAMAU

had sent back two years before when his desperate efforts to get help had brought him to Donald Blake's house. He was one of the trappers whose paths run to Seal Lake, and he could guide us so far by the trapper's route, should we go that way. Beyond that we should have to hunt the way.

We started at 3.15 in the afternoon of June 27, 1905, with a few days more than I had hoped added to the time we should have to do the work. It was alarmingly short at best. I had been informed at the Hudson Bay Company's post at Rigolett that their ship *Pelican* would be at the George River post at Ungava the last week in August. This ship was my only means of returning to civilization before winter. That left just two months to cross the country, a distance of six hundred miles.

Thirteen miles above Grand Lake we came to where the Red Wine River flows in from the south. Here on the north

bank the first of the portage routes by which the Indians avoid the roughest parts of the river leads out to run through a chain of lakes, entering the river again at Seal Lake. By this route the Indians reach Seal Lake from Northwest River in less than two weeks, taking just twenty-one days to make the journey through to Lake Michikamau.

When at Northwest River I had secured a map of both routes from them. The trappers told us that going by the river it would take us a month to reach Seal Lake. I wished very much to go by the river route, because that is the way Mr. Hubbard would have gone had he not missed the way. Yet our time was short. It was hard to decide which was best to do. George Elson had had experience of what it means to try to find a way through Labrador lakes. The trail was old and might not be easily found. Our map was crude, and we knew that we should not be able to make the trip as quickly as the Indians even at best, and it was quite possible that a good deal of time might have to be spent looking for the trail. Going ashore, the men examined the trail. When they returned to the canoe the decision was reached to keep to the river.

As the river grew more and more difficult, part of the outfit had to be portaged. One day, two miles above camp, about half a load of outfit was put into one of the canoes, and slipping the tracking-line round the bow, George and Gilbert went forward with it, while Job and Joe got into the canoe to pole. Had it not been for my confidence in them I should have been a little anxious, for here the river was very rough, and close to the shore where they would have to go was a big rock, round which the water poured in a way that to me looked impassable. But I only thought, "They will know how to manage that," and picking up my kodaks, I climbed the

TREE AT LAKE MICHIKAMAU, WHERE RECORDS WERE LEFT

banks to avoid the willows. I had just reached the top, when, turning round, I saw the canoe turn bottom side up like a flash, and both men disappeared.

I stood unable to move. Right away Joe came up. He had caught the tracking-line and held to it. Then I saw Job appear. He had not been able to hold to the canoe; the current had swept him off, and was now carrying him down the river. My heart sickened at the sight, and still I could not move. Then an eddy caught him, and he went down. Again he appeared, and this time closer to us, for the eddy had somehow thrown him inshore where the water was not so deep. He was on his back now and swimming a little, but could neither get up nor turn over. I wondered why the men stood there watching him without a move. Then it dawned on me that George was holding the canoe, and I found my voice to shout, "Run, Joe!" Joe's own experience had for the moment dazed him, but now he suddenly came to life. Springing forward, he waded out and caught Job's hand before he was carried into deep water again. As he felt himself caught in Joe's strong grasp, Job asked: "Where is Mrs. Hubbard? Is she all right?"

For more than a week our progress was very slow, for there was much carrying to be done. Twenty-five miles above the first rapid we were obliged to leave the river, which here became impassable. The tributary stream along which our way next led us was too large to be called a brook, and learning from Gilbert that it was a great marten country, I called it Wapustan River. This also we found a swift stream. It dropped from ledge to ledge down rocky hillsides. For much of the seven miles we followed it there was rough portaging to be done, though

SKINNING THE CARIBOU

in places the outfit could be taken up in the canoes.

On Saturday, July 15, we left the Wapustan and began on a nine-mile cross-country trip, working up to the northwest, from which direction a brook flows. A two-mile carry brought us out on Saturday evening to a lake at its head. After dinner Sunday we again went forward. It seemed very fine to have a whole mile of paddling. From the head of the lake a mile of good portaging brought us to waters flowing to Seal Lake.

Our way now led through three exquisitely beautiful little lakes to where their waters drop down over rocky ledges in a noisy stream, on their way to Seal Lake. Here on the left of the outlet we made our camp. On either side rose a high hill only recently burned over—last summer, Gilbert said. George, Gilbert, and I climbed the hill back of our camp in hopes of catching a first glimpse of Seal Lake, but we could not see it.

Slipping down the hill again, I reached camp just as supper was ready, and after the meal George and I crossed to climb the hill on the other side, which rose five hundred and forty feet above our camp. A brisk climb brought us to the top in time to see the sunset and one of the most magnificent views I had ever beheld. George, being taller, caught sight of the lake before I, and said, "There is Seal Lake."

It blew cold on the mountain and a shower passed over from the northeast, but it was soon gone, and the sun set over the hills in a blaze of red and gold. The way down the mountain seemed long. When we reached camp at 9.15 P.M. it was still quite light. Joe had been fishing, and had four brook-trout for my breakfast. Job and Gilbert had been down the valley a couple of miles prospecting, and soon came in with the information that a mile below camp we could put our canoes in the water. Beyond there would be two short portages, and then we should not again have to take them out of the water before reaching Seal Lake. The day following we camped at the head of the lake.

Beyond Seal Lake the river is not so difficult, though at one place we were obliged to leave it for nine miles of its course, where it is crowded between high rocky hills, flowing narrow, swift, and deep—too swift and deep for either poles or paddles. Monday, July 31, we reached the lake country east of Michikamau, and a little before noon Tuesday morning, August 1, we came in the fourth lake, to where the river flows in from the south down three heavy falls and rapids. On the west side of its entrance to the lake we found the old trail. The blazing was weather-worn and old, but the trail was a good one, and had been much used

MRS. LEONIDAS HUBBARD

in the days long ago. The portage was a little more than a quarter of a mile long, and we put our canoes into the water again in a tiny bay above the islands.

We had lunch a little way above the portage, and in the afternoon passed up the short reach of river into another lake, stretching, the men thought, about ten miles to the east and twelve to fifteen miles west. The lake seemed to average about four miles wide. The narrowest part was where we entered it, and on the opposite shore, three miles away, rose a high hill. It seemed as if we should even now be in Michikamau, perhaps shut from the main body of the lake only by the islands. From the top of the hill we should be able to see, we thought, and paddled towards it.

The hill was wooded almost to the top. Above the woods was the barren moss-covered summit. It seemed to me as we climbed that I should strangle with the heat and the flies and the effort, but most of all with the thoughts that were crowding my mind. Instead of being only glad that we were nearing Michikamau, I had been growing more and more to dread the moment when I should first look out over its broad waters. Sometimes it seemed that I could never go to the top, but I did.

The panorama of mountain and lake and island was wonderful. For miles in every direction were the lakes. Countless wooded islands, large and small, dotted their surfaces, and westward beyond the confusion of island and water around us lay the great shining Michikamau. Still we could see no open way to reach it. Lying along its eastern shore a low ridge swept away northward, and east of this again the lakes. We thought this might perhaps be the Indian inland route to George River, which Mr. Low speaks of in his report on the survey of Michikamau. Far away in the north were the mountains with their snow patches, which we had seen from Lookout Mount. Turning to the east, we could trace the course of the Nascaupee to where we had entered it on Sunday. We could see Lookout Mount, and away beyond it the irregular tops of the hills we had come through from a little west of Seal Lake. In the south great rugged hills stood out to the west towards Michikamau. North and south of the hill upon which we stood were big waters. The one to the south we hoped would lead us out to Michikamau. It emptied into the lake we had just crossed in a broad shallow rapid at the foot of our hill, a mile and a half to the west.

George showed me, only a few miles from where we were standing, Mount Hubbard, from which Mr. Hubbard and he had seen Michikamau; Windbound Lake and the lakes through which they hoped to find their way to the great lake; the dip in the hills to the east through which they had passed on their long portage.

As we crossed a long lake the next day, Wednesday, Job remarked that there was some current here. On nearing a point to the west we were startled by a sudden exclamation from him. He had caught sight of a freshly cut chip on the water. We stopped and the chip was picked up. The two canoes drew together. It was examined closely, and an animated discussion in Indian went on. It was fine to watch them, and a revelation to me to see an ordinary little chip create so much excitement. The conclusion finally reached

was that the wind had brought it here in the night from our own camp.

Passing a point, the canoe again stopped some distance beyond it. Another brisk conversation ensued, and then I learned they had discovered a current coming from the south, and we turned to meet it. Following it up one mile south and one mile west, we came to where the river flows in from the south in a rapid. This was really a joke. We had so comfortably settled ourselves in the belief that the rapids had all been passed. Job and Gilbert had taken off their "shoe-packs" with the prospect of a good day's paddling, and here were the rapids again. Our course for four miles above this point was up a tortuous, rapid river. It seemed to flow from all points of the compass and in almost continuous rapids. The rapids were not rough, but the currents were fearfully swift and seemed to move in all directions. They are more dangerous than many of the rougher rapids.

MRS. HUBBARD TALKING WITH INDIAN WOMEN

THE ARRIVAL AT GEORGE RIVER POST AT UNGAVA

About 2 P.M. we came out to a lake. It was not very large and its upper end was crowded with islands. Four miles from the outlet the lake narrowed and the water flowed down round the islands with tremendous swiftness. Again it widened, and a mile west from the rapids we landed to climb a hill. Everybody went, and by the time I was half-way up, the men were already at the top, jumping about and waving their hats and yelling like demons—or men at a polo match. As I came toward them, Gilbert shouted, " Rice pudding for supper to-night, Mrs. Hubbard." It was not hard to guess what all the demonstration meant. We could not see all the channel from our hilltop, there were so many islands; but it could be seen part of the way, and, what was' most important, we could see where it led straight west to Michikamau.

Once more in the canoes, our way still led among the islands up the swift-flowing water. It was not till 5.15 P.M. that we at last reached the point where the Nascaupee first receives the waters of the great lake. Continuing west-ward near the shore of a long island, we landed shortly before 7 P.M. on its outer shore to make our first camp on Lake Michikamau.

It was a beautiful place and had evidently been a favorite with the Indians. There were the remains of many old camps there. Near the shore grew a thick wall of stunted spruce, and back of this an open space some fifty yards wide, sloping gently up to the greenwoods above. On going ashore we caught sight of a flock of ptarmigan just disappearing among the bushes. The men gave chase, but the birds managed to elude them, and they came back empty-handed. Here the flies and mosquitoes were awful. It made me shiver just to feel them creeping over my hands, not to speak of their bites. Nowhere on the whole journey had we found them so thick as they were that night. It was good to escape into the tent.

Next morning I arose early. It was cloudy but calm, and Michikamau was like a pond. How I wondered what fortune would be ours in the voyage on this big water—the canoes seemed so tiny here. I called the men at 6.30 A.M., and at nine we were ready to start. Before our start, Job blazed two trees at the landing, and in one he placed a big flat stone, on which I wrote with a piece of flint Joe brought me:

HUBBARD EXPEDITION
ARRIVED HERE AUG. 2ND, '05.

Underneath it the names of all the party. Then we embarked, and it was " All aboard for George River!" our next objective point.

The way the men managed the canoes in the lake was fine to see. They were as much at home on Michikamau as they had been in the rapids of the Nascaupee. By 10 A.M. of our third day on the lake we could see plainly the long rocky point at the entrance of the bay at its northern extremity. The wind was blowing the waves straight against it, and it looked fearsome to me. Now the sails had to come down, for we were going too much into the wind. Fortunately for us, it calmed a little when we got to within half a mile of the point, and at 10.30 A.M. we passed safely round it into the sheltered bay.

We had not reached our haven too soon. Almost immediately the wind rose again, and by noon was blowing so strong that we could have done nothing in any part of Lake Michikamau, to say nothing of crossing the upper end in a heavy south wind.

Nine miles to northward we made camp on an island in Lake Michikamats, which is some twelve miles long and from two to four miles wide. My tent was pitched in a charming nook among the spruce-trees, and had such a beautiful carpet of boughs, all tipped with fresh green. The moss itself was almost too beautiful to cover, but nothing is quite so nice for carpet as the boughs. Through the night the south wind rose to a gale and showers of rain fell. Sunday morning I was up at 7 A.M., and after a nice, lazy bath luxuriously dressed myself in clean clothes. Just after 9 A.M. I lay down to go to sleep again. I had not realized it before, but I was very tired. My eyes had closed but a moment when a rat-a-tat-tat on the mixing-pan announced breakfast.

There was much speculation as to what we should find at the head of Lake Michikamats. If only we could see the Indians we should be all right. Our caribou meat was nearly gone, and we could do very well with a fresh supply of game now. There would be a chance to put out the nets when we reached the head of the lake, and the scouting had to be done. The nets had not yet touched the water.

It was nearly noon next day when the men, preparing dinner, caught sight of a big stag caribou swimming across to the point south of us. There was a spring for the canoe, and in much less time than it takes to tell it the canoe was in the water, with Job, Gilbert, and George plying their paddles with all strength. As the beautiful creature almost reached the shore, a flying bullet dropped in front of him and he turned back. His efforts were now no match for the swift paddle-strokes that sent the canoe lightly towards him, and soon a shot from George's rifle ended the struggle. He was towed ashore, bled, and brought to camp in the canoe.

The following day we got our first glimpse of the great caribou migration. On the west shore of the lake we found thousands of the beautiful creatures gathered on a plain at the foot of a barren hill. Later we saw them swimming to an island three-quarters of a mile out, making a broad, unbroken bridge from shore to shore. For fifty miles beyond this point the country was alive with them.

Wednesday we passed northward from the head of Lake Michikamats through several small lakes and streams, and at 5 P.M. we arrived at the height of land. A short portage of three hundred yards and we put the canoes into a little lake, which proved to be the source of the Great George River. We camped that night where its waters begin their swift descent to Ungava Bay.

Some fifty miles below the head of the river we came upon the Indians. There were only the women of the tribe there. The men had gone to Davis Inlet on the east coast to trade for their winter supplies, and had not returned. These people we found belonged to the Montagnais tribe. They received us in friendly manner, eagerly urging us to remain longer with them. George Elson spoke to them in their own tongue, and here we learned that we were but two days' journey from the Nascaupee camp, farther down the river. The women speak only their own language, but we learned that some of the men speak English quite easily.

Sunday morning, August 20, I awoke in a state of expectancy. We had slept three times since leaving the Montagnais camp, and unless the Barren Ground People were not now in their accustomed camping-place we ought to see them before night. Many thoughts came of how greatly Mr. Hubbard had wished to see them and what a privilege he would have thought it to be able to visit them.

It seemed this morning as if something unusual must happen. It was as if we were coming into a hidden country.

As we paddled along at pretty brisk rate, suddenly George exclaimed, " There it is."

There it was indeed, a covered wigwam high up on a sandy hill which sloped to the river and formed the point round which it flowed to the lake among the mountains. Very soon a second wigwam came in sight. At first we saw no one at the camp. Then a figure appeared moving about near one of the wigwams. It was evident that they had not yet caught sight of us; but as we paddled slowly along, the figure suddenly stopped, a whole company came running together, and plainly our sudden appearance was causing great excitement. There was a hurried moving to and fro, and after a time came the sound of two rifle-shots. I replied with my revolver. Again they fired, and I replied again. Then more shots from the hill.

As we drew slowly near, the men ran down towards the landing, but halted above a narrow belt of trees growing near the water's edge. There, it was plain, a very animated discussion of the newcomers was going on.

We all shouted: " Bo jou! Bo jou!" (Bon jour!)

A chorus of Bo jous came back from the hill. George called to them in Indian, " We are strangers, and are passing through your country."

The sound of words in their own tongue reassured them, and they ran down to the landing. As we drew near

we could hear them talking. I, of course, could not understand a word of it, but I learned from George later what they were saying.

It was a strangely striking picture they made that quiet Sabbath morning, as they stood there at the shore with the dark-green woods behind them and all about them the great wilderness of rock and river and lake. They had strongly Indian faces, and those of the older men showed plainly the marks of the battle for life they had been fighting. They were tall, lithe, and active-looking, with a certain air of self-possession and dignity which almost all Indians seem to have. They wore dressed deerskin breeches and moccasins, and over the breeches were drawn bright-red cloth leggings, reaching from ankle to well above the knees, and held in place by straps fastened about the waist. The shirts, some of which were of cloth and some of dressed deerskin, were worn outside the breeches, and over these a white coat bound about the edges with blue or red. Their hair they wore long and cut straight round below the ears, and tied about the head was a bright-colored kerchief. The faces were full of interest. Up on the hill where the wigwams were the women and children and old men stood watching, perhaps waiting till it should develop whether the strangers were friendly or hostile.

" Where did you come into the river?" the chief asked.

George explained that we had come the whole length of the river, that we had come into it from Michikamau, which we reached by way of the Nascaupee. He was greatly surprised. He knew the route and had been at Northwest River. Turning to the others, he told them of our long journey. Then they came forward and gathered eagerly about us. We told them we were going down the river to the post at Ungava.

" Oh, you are near now," they said. " You will sleep only five times if you travel fast."

My heart bounded as this was interpreted to me. It meant that we should be at the post before the end of August, for this was only the 20th. There was still a chance that we should be in time for the ship.

We then inquired about the river. All were eager to tell about it, and many expressive gestures were added to their words to tell that the river was rapid all the way. An arm held at an angle showed what we were to expect in the rapids, and a vigorous drop of the hand expressed something about the falls. There would be a few portages, but they were not long, and in some places there would be just a short lift over; but it was nearly all rapid.

"And when you come to a river coming in on the other side in quite a fall you are not far from the post."

There was a tightening in my throat as I thought, "What if I had decided to turn back rather than winter in Labrador!"

Meanwhile the old women had gathered about me, begging eagerly for tobacco. Of course I did not know what it was they wanted, and when the coveted tobacco did not appear they began to complain bitterly. "She is not giving us any tobacco." And again, "See, she does not want to give us any tobacco." George explained to them that I did not smoke and had no tobacco. I succeeded in appeasing them, however, by gifts of flour, tea, pork, and rice, and accompanied them to their camp on the hill for a necessarily short visit, seeing and talking with the younger women and children, and learning a little of what life means to them.

When the word went forth that we were about to leave, all gathered for the parting. I was looking about for something which I might carry away with me as a souvenir of the visit. The chief's daughter stood near, and stepping towards her, I touched the beaded band on her hair, thinking that perhaps they had others they might be willing to let me take. She drew sharply away and said something in tones that had a plainly resentful note in them. It was, "That is mine." I determined not to be discouraged and made another effort. Stretched on a frame to dry was a very pretty deerskin, and I had George ask if I might have that. This seemed to appeal to them as a not unreasonable request, but they suggested that I take one that was dressed. A woman who wanted my sweater went into the wigwam and brought one out. It was very pretty, and beautifully soft and white on the inside. She again pleaded for my sweater. I felt so sorry to have to refuse her, but had to do so. I handed her back the skin, but she bade me keep it. They gave George a piece of deerskin dressed without the hair—"To line a pair of mitts," they said.

When I said "Good-by," they made no move to accompany us to the canoe.

On the evening of August 22 we reached the foot of Indian House Lake, and the day following began the descent of what proved to be one hundred and thirty miles of almost continuous rapid. The river was fearfully steep, there being places where the little canoes were carried down at the rate of a mile in four minutes. We had five days of almost constant rapid running.

Saturday at noon my observation showed us very near our destination, and we camped at night within ten miles of the post. The men smiled a little incredulously when I said we should be at the post before noon Sunday. There was a bit of quiet fun Sunday morning after breakfast over my putting the remainder of the tea into a bottle to keep as a souvenir of the trip. I learned later that it was the opinion of the crew—expressed in Indian, of course—that the tea would probably taste good at lunch. However, inside of two hours we were in sight of what I knew must be the island opposite the post, and before 11 A.M. there was a sudden exclamation from George—"There it is!"

Half an hour later Mr. Ford, agent at the post, followed by a retinue of Eskimos, came over the mud left by the retreating tide to meet us, while Mrs. Ford waited at the foot of the hill, all as eagerly excited at our arrival as I was to reach the post. As my hostess, with shining eyes, took my hand in greeting, she said, "Mrs. Hubbard, yours is the first white woman's face I have seen for two years."

In reply to eager questioning I was told that the ship had not arrived, and would not be there until the middle of September.

INDIAN EDUCATION

LITTLE INDIAN BOYS AT CARLISLE.

THERE are many, no doubt, who will smile at the title of this article, much as if it had read, "Education for Buffa-loes and Wild Turkeys." Such, however, will be likely to read it, as others will from a more sympathetic stand-point. For it is evident that, from one stand-point or another, public interest is excited upon the Indian question now as perhaps never before.

With the opening up of the country, and the disappearance of the game before the settler's axe and locomotive whistle—to say nothing of treaty "reconstruction" and Indian wars—the conditions of the Indian himself have radically altered, and perhaps not in all respects for the worse, since the shrewd Saponi sachem declined William and Mary's classical course for his young braves, because it would not improve them in deer-stalking or scalp-lifting, but, not to be outdone in graciousness, offered instead to bring up the Royal Commissioners' sons in his own wigwam, and "make men of them."

Fat Mandan, on the contrary, seems to think that to make men of them is just what Hampton will do for the boys he is so proud of, and he looks to them to help him to work, not to hunt. It is possible that red and white theories of education and manhood have healthily approximated in fifty or a hundred years.

To a young colonel of the Union army in the late war, as he stood on the wheel-house of a transport, with his black regiment camping down on the deck below

GROUP OF INDIAN YOUNG MEN BEFORE EDUCATION.

him, floating down the Gulf of Mexico through the double glory of sunset sky and wave, there came, like a vision shaped half from dreamy memories of his island home in the Pacific, and half from earnest thought for his country's future, a plan for a practical solution of one of her troubles, and the salvation of the race that was its innocent and long-suffering cause. Four years later the dream which had faded in the stern realities of war was called into life by the exigencies of the new era, and took tangible form as a normal and agricultural school for freedmen at Hampton, Virginia, twenty miles from the port where slaves first landed in America, and on the very shores where they were first made free as "contraband of war."

The growth of this institution under the charge of its originator was described seven years ago in this Magazine, since which time it has attracted the attention of leading thinkers upon education and race problems in this and other countries, and become widely known as an exponent of the value of manual-labor training in education of men and women—certainly as far as the black race is concerned. Twelve years have proved its mission in the South to be no "fool's errand."

As the Hampton school was founded on the theory that "the gospel of work and self-help" is essential to all human development, and therefore as good for negroes as for Sandwich-Islanders, why should it not try the same for the Indian?

Visitors to St. Augustine from '75 to '78 remember as one of the chief attractions of that ancient city the Indian prisoners at Fort Marion, held there by the United States government for their conspicuous part in a revolt of their tribes —Kiowas, Comanches, Cheyennes, and Arrapahoes in Indian Territory. Many brought away from the old fort not only polished sea-beans, bows and arrows, and specimens of primitive painting, but a few new ideas on the Indian question, and a surprised sense of some strange transformation going on in savage natures under the forces of kindness and wisdom.

What this transformation was, and what were its subjects, no words can so well set forth as do two photographs which lie before me as I write; one taken of the prisoners on their arrival at Fort Marion in chains, ignorant of the fate before them, defiant, desperate, plotting mutiny and suicide; the other, a group of the same men, three years later, received into an

Eastern school to continue the education begun at St. Augustine.

It was fortunate not only for these poor prisoners, it may be, but for the whole In-

youngest thus staid, and of these seventeen were received at Hampton Institute, on request of Captain Pratt, for the sake of its industrial training.

GROUP OF INDIAN YOUNG MEN AFTER EDUCATION.

dian question, that the officer under whose charge they were put, and who had assisted in their capture, Captain R. H. Pratt, of the Tenth Cavalry, U.S.A., was a man with room in his nature for the united strength and humanity which are at the bottom of this work, whose results have placed him at the head of the most important single movement ever made in behalf of Indian education.

Delicate womanly hands of both North and South, enlisted by the captain's earnestness, freely joined to help his work when the dark minds were roused to some curiosity as to the mystery of the gay-colored alphabet he had hung on their prison wall. And when, at the end of three years, the United States decided to send the prisoners home, some would not let go their work. The War Department's permission was secured for as many of the prisoners to remain as were willing to go to school, and could be provided for by private benevolence. Twenty-two of the

It was not, therefore, in utter dismay that the inmates of Hampton were roused from their slumbers one April night by a steamboat's war-whoop, heralding the midnight raid of sixty ex-warriors upon their peaceful shores, and hastened out to meet the invaders with hot coffee instead of rifle-balls, to welcome some of them as new students, and bid the rest godspeed to their homes in Indian Territory.

The bearing of the new effort upon the whole question of Indian management was early recognized at Washington. By special act of Congress authorizing the Secretary of War to detail an army officer for special duty with regard to Indian education, Captain Pratt's valuable assistance was secured in inaugurating the work at Hampton. The Indian Commissioner, the Secretaries of War and the Interior, and the President were among the most interested visitors to the Indian class-rooms and workshops, and have given the enterprise all the sympathy and

NEGRO AND INDIAN BOYS AT HAMPTON.

encouragement in their power. The result of their inspection was the decision of government to take an active part in the effort it had sanctioned.

Six months after the St. Augustines were received, there was therefore a second Indian raid on Hampton Institute, consisting of forty-nine young Dakotas, chiefly Sioux, with a few Mandans, Rees, and Gros Ventres, for each of whom the United States stood pledged to appropriate $167, reduced subsequently to $150, yearly, while it should keep them at the school. This appropriation is the extent of United States aid to Hampton, which is not, as some have supposed, a government school, but a private corporation, supported chiefly by Northern benevolence. The school agreed on its part to supply the deficiency of the government appropriation, amounting to from $60 to $70 a year, on an average, for each of the Indian students who are on its hands for the whole year round, and to put up the needed buildings, which it has done, at a cost thus far of $14,000. Nine of the sixty-dollar scholarships are given by the American Missionary Association of New York, and the rest have been made up by friends, of different sects and sections.

The school consented to undertake this large addition to the new mission which had come unsought to its hands, on condition that half of the fifty to be brought should be girls. Indian views of woman's sphere interfered with this condition for the time, however. As Captain Pratt says: "The girls, from six years of age up to marriage, are expected to help their mothers in the work. They are too valuable in the capacity of drudge during the years they should be at school to be spared to go. Another equally important obstacle is the fact that the girls constitute a part of the material wealth of the family, and bring, in open market, after arriving at marriageable age, a certain price in horses or other valuable property. The parents fully realize that education will elevate their girls away from this property consideration." The captain, who collected the party, was able, therefore, to bring only nine girls and forty boys, of ages ranging from nine to nineteen years, with one exception of a mother, who could not trust so far away the pretty little girl she wished to save from a life like her own.

The new arrival was a new departure in Hampton's Indian work. The wild-looking set in motley mixture of Indian and citizens' dress, apparently trying to hide away altogether under their blankets, or shawls, or streaming unkempt locks, made a contrast with the soldierly St. Augustines, evidently obvious enough to the latter, whose faces betrayed some civilized disgust, as well as tribal prejudice, as they looked on in the glory of their fresh school uniforms. It was not long, however, before they were exchanging greetings in the expressive sign-language that all could understand.

A Cheyenne, Sioux, and Ree—representatives of tribes which have often been at war with each other—made up a group for statuesque pose and significant contrasts fit subject for sculptor or poet, as Comes Flying and White Wolf stood wrapped in their blankets, watching, half compliant, half suspicious, the grave and speaking gestures with which Little Chief freely offered what he had so freely received.

"I tell them, Look at me; I will give you the road."

The St. Augustines generally did good service in showing the road to the new recruits. The hospitality of the colored students, somewhat overtaxed by the inroad of nearly double the number of boys expected, before their new quarters were ready for them, revived with the changes wrought by soap and water, and won full victory when, on taking possession of their new "wigwam" a month later, the Dakotas made a spontaneous petition, through their interpreter, for colored room-mates to "help talk English." The volunteers who generously undertook the mission became quite fond of "their boys," and emulous of each other in bringing them forward in such minor arts of civilization as the proper use of beds and hair-brushes.

Thus helped by willing hands, red, white, and black, and joined from time to time by companions, from their own and other tribes, till they now number over seventy, the Indian students have been two years on the new road, and Hampton now has contrasts to show as convincing, if not as dramatic, as those of St. Augustine. It is difficult, indeed, to associate the gaunt young *gamins* that sat about in listless heaps two years ago with the bright, busy groups of boys and girls at study or play, or singing over their work.

The effort has been for a natural, all-round growth rather than a rapid one. Books, of course, are for a long time of no avail, and object-teaching, pictures, and blackboards take their place, with every other device that ingenuity is equal to, often on the spur of the moment, to keep up the interest and attention of the undisciplined minds that, with the best intentions and strong desire to know English, have small patience for preliminary steps. A peripatetic class was thus devised to relieve the tedium of the school-room, and had, to speak literally and figuratively, quite a run. It usually began with leap-frog, and then went gayly on to find its "books in the running brooks, sermons

in stones," etc. Geography is taught with moulding sand and iron raised dissecting maps; arithmetic at first with blocks. The Indians are particularly fond of each, and the advanced class is quite expert in adding up columns of figures as long as a ledger page, and equal to practical problems of every-day trade and simple business accounts.

Nothing, however, can equal the charm of the printed page. It has the old mystery of "the paper that talks." "If I

"LOOK AT ME; I WILL GIVE YOU THE ROAD."

can not read when I go home," said a young brave, "my people will laugh at me." The gratitude of the St. Augustines over their first text-book in geography was touching. Reading, writing, and spelling are taught together by the word method and charts. Later, attractive little primaries have been very useful, and unbound numbers of children's magazines, such as are used in the Quincy schools. Most of the Dakotas can now read at sight as simple English as is found in these, and are beginning to take pleasure in reading or in listening to easy versions of our

GROUP OF INDIAN GIRLS BEFORE EDUCATION.

childhood classics of Robinson Crusoe, and Christopher Columbus, and George Washington with his little hatchet. One of their teachers who tried the hatchet story on them in preparation for the 22d of February says: "Such attentive listeners I never saw before. They were perfectly enraptured. They understood everything, even to the moral. A few days after this I was annoyed by talking in the class. When I asked who did it, every one blamed his neighbor. I said, 'Now, boys, don't tell a lie. Who will be a George Washington?' Two boys at once stood up and said, 'We did it.'"

Another teacher was less successful with her moral, in trying to explain a hymn they had learned to recite:

"Yield not to temptation, for yielding is sin;
Each victory will help you some other to win."

The next day one of the girls came to her, exclaiming, triumphantly, "I victory! I victory! Louisa Bullhead get mad with me. She big temptation. *I fight her*. I victory!"

One can but sympathize with another who was "victory" in a different sort of encounter. A party of excursionists landed on the Normal School grounds in the summer, and hunting up some of the Indian students, surrounded them, and with more regard for their own amusement than for wasting courtesy on "savages," plied them with such questions as, "What is your name? Are you wild? Can you speak English? Do you live in a house at home?" till even Indian patience was

exhausted, and one girl turned upon her inquisitors. When they began, "Are you wild?" she replied, with a look that perhaps confirmed her words, "Yes, very wild; are *you* wild?" "Can you speak English?" "No, I can not speak a word of English."

They understand much of what is said before them, and are sensitive to allusions to their former condition. Three of the little girls at work in their flower garden, as a visitor passed, came running to their teacher with the indignant complaint, "That gentleman said, 'Poor little things!' We are not *very* poor little things, are we?"

Talking naturally comes slower than reading or understanding, but improves with the confidence gained in daily association with English-speaking companions and the drill of the class-room. They are beginning to think in English, for they speak it sometimes to each other, and the little girls are often heard talking English to their dollies, considering white babies, perhaps, or having less fear of their criticism. Phonic exercises are found useful. One evening a week is given to English games, and one to singing, under the instruction of one of the former band of "Hampton Student" singers. He has succeeded in the difficult task of transcribing several of their own wild love songs, words and notes, and in teaching them to sing simple exercises by note in time and tune, though their first efforts were about as harmonious as a Chinese orchestra. They have picked up many of the hymns and plantation melodies sung by their comrades, and are as fond of singing over their work. Monthly records of each one's standing in study, work, and conduct are sent home to their agencies, and on the back of each card a little English letter from each who is able

the care of stock. Both have ample room also in the large brick workshops erected and fitted up by the generosity of Mr. C. P. Huntington, of New York. A sixty-horse-power Corliss engine, given by Mr. G. H. Corliss, supplies the power to these shops, and to a saw-mill, where all the

"WE ARE NOT VERY POOR LITTLE THINGS, ARE WE?"

to frame a few sentences of his own. These cards have had a great effect upon the parents, to whom they are shown by the interpreters, and are a strong incentive to the children.

The mornings only are given to study, and the afternoons to industrial training and exercise, with Saturday as a holiday. The school farm of two hundred acres, and the "Shellbanks" farm of three hundred and thirty, the latter given chiefly in the Indians' interest by a lady friend in Boston, afford abundant opportunity for training both races in farming and

lumber used on the place is sawed. All the bricks used are also made on the place. Some of the Indians work in the saw-mill and engine-room. Besides the farmers, the division of labor for the boys thus far includes blacksmiths, carpenters, wheelwrights, tinsmiths, engineers, shoemakers, harness-makers, tailors, and printers. They are also employed as waiters and janitors. Special effort is made to have each of the agencies from which they come represented by as many different trades as possible. They like to work about as well as most boys, are slow, and

INDIAN COOKING CLASS, HAMPTON.

need watching, but show a special taste and aptness for mechanics. At present most of the shoes worn by the Indian boys are made entirely by Indian hands. Trunks, chairs, and tables, tin pails, cups, and dust-pans, are turned out by the dozens, and most of the repairing needed on the place is done in the various shops. The carpenters, under direction of a builder, have put up a two-story carriage-house twenty-four by fifty feet, weather-boarded and shingled. A Cheyenne (St. Augustine) and a Sioux are each proud of a fine blue farm cart made entirely by their own hands. All the shops report improvement. Their instructor in farming, a practical Northern farmer, says: "They don't like to turn out early in the morning, but otherwise do as well as any class of workmen, and seldom now have to be spoken to for any slackness. It is common to see five or six in a hoeing race, with the end of a beet or corn row for the goal."

A natural, and therefore valuable, stimulus to their energies, and doing much to make men of them, has been the payment of wages. Part of the government ap-propriation is given to them in this form instead of in clothing. They are expected to buy their own clothing out of it, except their school uniform. There is some waste, but more profit, in the lessons thus taught of the relation of labor to capital.

The military organization of the school, thus far under the charge of Captain Henry Romeyn, Fifth Infantry, U.S.A., has been an important aid in their discipline, and general setting up of body and spirit. Sergeant Bear's Heart and Corporal Yellow Bird are as proud of their command, and as careful to maintain the honor of their stripes, as any West-Pointer; and the fleet-footed little "markers" would doubtless fight for their colors, if they would not die for them. Yellow Bird is janitor of the wigwam, and the present teacher in charge reports, "A cleaner school building I never saw." Saturday is general cleaning day. Only the outside of the platter was civilized at first, but the effect of clean halls was soon apparent. They wanted a clean house all through, and the boys went voluntarily down on their knees and scrubbed their own rooms.

During the summer vacation, from the middle of June to the first of October, the boys who remain at the school alternate farm-work with camp life at "Shell-banks," sleeping in tents, living outdoors, cooking for themselves, fishing, hunting, and rowing. For two summers a selected number—this year seventeen boys and eight girls—have been scattered among the farmers of Berkshire County, Massachusetts, working for their board, sharing the home life, and improving in health, English, and general tone. They have won a good report from the families which have taken them, even better this year than last, and have done much to increase public sympathy for their race.

The co-education of the sexes is regarded at Hampton as essential to the development of both these races in which woman has been so long degraded. The Indian girls' improvement has been as marked as the boys'. Their early inuring to labor has its compensation in a better physical condition apparently, and their uplifting may prove the most important factor in the salvation of their race. Besides the class instruction which they share with the boys, the girls are trained in the various household industries—washing, ironing, cooking, the care of their rooms, and to cut and make and mend their own clothes and the boys'. They all have flower gardens, and take great delight in them, and in decorating their rooms. The cooking class, under a teacher who has had charge of the "North End Mission" cooking school in Boston, is a very favorite "branch." Its daily successes are placed triumphantly upon the table of the class they belong to, and no doubt find the regular road to the hearts of the brave.

A *love-letter* picked up on the floor of a school with Hampton's views on co-education need not inevitably shock even pedagogic sensibilities. Written in an unknown tongue, however, with only the names to betray it, a translation by the private interpreter seemed only a proper precaution. If I confide it to the gentle

TWO INDIAN GIRLS AFTER A SUMMER VISIT TO BERKSHIRE.

reader, the Indian lovers will be neither the worse nor the wiser, while some others may find in it valuable suggestions for similar correspondence.

"NORMAL SCHOOL, *February 3*, 1879.

"MISS ——— ———: I said I like you, and I want to give you a letter. Whenever I give you letter, I want you answer to me soon. That's all I want, and I will answer to you soon after. When you give me letter, it raises me up. It makes me heart-glad, *sister-in-law*. When I talk, I am not saying anything foolish. Always my heart very glad. I want you let me know your thought. I always like you and love you. I am honest about what I say, I always keep in mind. I want always we smile at each other when meet. We live happy always. I think that's best way, and you think it is and let me know. And I want to say one thing—don't say anything to Henry. I don't think that's right. And I say again, when I give a letter, keep nicely and not show to any one. If they know it, it not good way. They

take us away, and that is the reason don't show it. Hear me, this all I am going to say. I like you, and I love you. I won't say any more. *My whole heart is shaking hands with you.* I kiss you.   Your lover,
                              "____ ____."

At the last anniversary of Hampton, Secretary Schurz remarked in his speech: "One day, soon, a very interesting sight will be seen here and at Carlisle. It will be the first Indian School-visiting Board. Within a few days twenty-five or thirty Sioux chiefs, among them some warriors whose hands were lifted against the United States but a few days ago, Red Cloud and others, will go to Carlisle and come here to see their children in these schools."

Last May, accordingly, this "Indian School-visiting Board" reached Hampton. The meeting between them and their young relatives would have convinced the most skeptical that the heart of man answers to heart as face to face in water, whatever the skin it beats under.

As the Gros Ventre and Ree chiefs gathered the children of their own tribes around them for a special talk, Son of the Star beckoned one of the older girls to the front, and searching some mysterious depths of his blanket, drew forth a dirty little coil of string about two feet long, unwound it, straightened it carefully, and let it hang from one hand to the floor, with the other outlining some little form about it, bringing quick-flitting smiles to the face of the girl, while the whole ring looked on with evidently intelligent interest, though not a word was spoken. Handing the string over to the girl, he dived into his blanket once more, producing this time a little worn pair of baby shoes. But at this his watcher broke down entirely in a flood of tender tears; for the whole silent pantomime had been a letter from home describing the growth and beauty of the little sister she had left winking in its cradle basket two years before.

Son of the Star was a fine specimen of an old chief of powerful proportions. Poor Wolf, in full Indian costume, and glory of porcupine quills and eagle feathers, had put a finishing touch to his dignity by an incongruous and ludicrously solemn pair of huge gold-bowed spectacles, which made him look like a caricature of Confucius.

The Gros Ventres were particularly anxious to see Ara-hotch-kish, the only son of their second chief, Hard Horn, who had

been prevented by some accident from accompanying the expedition. They found the little fellow in the workshop painting pails, and pressed around him in an admiring group. Ara's dignity was fully equal to the occasion. He worked away with an air of superb indifference, vouchsafing the old chiefs no notice whatever, except to elbow them aside, when his pail was done, to set it up and get down another, only a side glance now and then through his long lashes, and the shadow of a demure smile around his firm-set lips, betraying that he was taking in everything, and enjoying his honors.

All the chiefs were delighted spectators at the merry games of the evening "conversation hour." In an evil moment, however, the 15-14-13 puzzle was explained to Confucius by some of his young Gros Ventres, and he proved his common origin with white humanity by succumbing instantly to its spell. For the rest of the evening his gold-bound goggles bent over the maddening squares as if they were the problem of his race, set, according to its white brethren's favorite arrangement, with thirteen facts, fourteen experiments, and fifteen theories in hopeless reversion.

A visit from Bright Eyes, the eloquent young advocate of the Poncas, was a very powerful stimulus to the girls, as showing them what one of their own race and sex might become. After she left, one of the older girls said to me, with a pretty, timid hesitancy, "Miss Bright Eyes—I wish I like that." Her own soft bright eyes shone with a soul in them as she added: "When I came to here, I feel bad all time; I want go home; I no want stay at Hampton. Now I want stay here. I not want go home. I want learn more, then go home, teacher my people."

A few weeks after, on the visit of the chiefs from Dakota, this girl, at her own urgent request, stood up before the whole conclave and the school, and with flushed cheeks and downcast eyes told her people's rulers what the school was to her, and begged them to send all the children to learn the good road. Her speech, which, in order to reach all the chiefs, had to be translated by two interpreters, passing through English on the way, was listened to with respectful attention.

The most important result of Bright Eyes's visit to the school was to rouse in her own heart the desire to make use of her hold upon public sympathy for the permanent benefit of her Indian sisters. With this desire she offered her services to speak at the East in behalf of a project of some Northern friends of the school to enlarge its work by erecting a building for Indian girls, to cost, complete and furnished, $15,000. A beautiful site adjoining the school premises, and now inclosed in them, was given as a generous send-off by a lady friend. It will give room for the training of at least fifty more Indian girls at Hampton, thus effecting the desired balance of the sexes. The Secretary of the Interior has signified his readiness to send them from the agencies with the same appropriation as for the boys, of $150 per year apiece. There is every assurance of their readiness now to come. It is for the friends of the Indians to decide whether Hampton's work for them shall be thus rounded and established, and the timid prayer be heard, "I wish I like that."

Carlisle, Pennsylvania, like Hampton, Virginia, is classic ground in American history. Under the shade of its unbroken forests Benjamin Franklin met the red men in council. A British military post in the Revolution, and falling into the hands of the Continentals, the Hessian-built guard-house is still shown as once the place of André's confinement, before his greater disaster.

The last and greatest change of fortune, which has filled the empty armories with ploughshares and pruning-hooks, and the soldiers' quarters with a government school for Indian children—as if the spirit of the earliest and sacredest of Indian treaties still lingered in the groves of Penn—was brought about through a bill introduced in the winter of 1879 in the House of Representatives, entitled "A bill to increase educational privileges and establish additional industrial training schools for the benefit of youth belonging to such nomadic Indian tribes as

have educational treaty claims upon the United States." It provided for the utilization for such school purposes of certain vacant military posts and barracks as long as not required for military occupation, and authorized the detail of army officers by the Secretary of War for service in such schools, without extra pay, under direction of the Secretary of the Interior.

The House Committee on Indian Affairs, in favorably reporting upon this

LITTLE INDIAN GIRL IN HER ROOM.

bill, urged that the government had made treaty stipulations specially providing for education with nomadic tribes, including about seventy-one thousand Indians, having over twelve thousand children of school age; that the treaties were made in 1868, and in ten years less than one thousand children had received schooling. It was further urged that "the effort in this direction recently undertaken and in successful progress at the Industrial and Normal Institute of Hampton, Virginia, furnishes a striking proof of the natural aptitude and capacity of the rudest savages of the plains for mechanical, scientific, and industrial education, when removed from parental and tribal surroundings and influences"; and that "the very considerable number of agents, teachers,

HARNESS-MAKING APPRENTICES, CARLISLE.

missionaries, and others engaged in educational work who have visited and witnessed the methods of Hampton, join in commending them as just what the Indian needs, while the intercourse between the youth at Hampton and their parents has produced extraordinary interest and demand for educational help from these tribes."

The importance of this measure was so recognized that even in anticipation of subsequent favorable action upon it by Congress, with a wise cutting of red tape, the War Department turned over Carlisle Barracks to the Interior, and Captain Pratt was detailed to bring children from the Northern agencies before the frosts came, which would have delayed it another year. The transfer of the post was effected on the centennial anniversary of the battle of White Plains, eliciting from Secretary McCreary a felicitous remark upon the coincidence which on such memorial day gave up to Indian education a post for eighty years used as a training school for cavalry officers to make war chiefly upon Indians.

Taking with him Hampton's godspeed, and two of his most advanced Dakota boys for interpreters and "specimens," the captain started for Dakota in September, 1879, returning in a few weeks with eighty-four.

All but two of the St. Augustines from Hampton also accompanied their captain to Carlisle, to form a starting-point of English speech and civilization. One of these young men, a Kiowa, with a companion who had been under instruction at the North, went on alone to Indian Territory in advance of Captain Pratt, and by their own influence they gathered forty-two children and youth from their own agency for Carlisle. These, with some more from other agencies in the Territory, were brought by the captain to the school, and it opened with one hundred and forty-seven children on the 1st of November, 1879.

The President's next Message and the report of the Secretary of the Interior again commended to public attention the importance of the work at Hampton, with the new efforts to which its "promising results" had led at Carlisle and at Forest Grove, Oregon, where arrangements were made for the similar training at a white boarding-school of a number of Indian boys and girls belonging to tribes on the Pacific coast, under charge of Captain Wilkinson, who is making it quite successful under many difficulties.

Additions and changes from time to time have brought the number at Carlisle up to one hundred and ninety-six at the present time, fifty-seven of whom are girls. Besides the Sioux and St. Augustines, there are in lesser numbers other Cheyennes, Arrapahoes, and Kiowas; also Comanches, Wichitas, Seminoles, Pawnees, Keechis, Towaconies, Nez Percés, and Poncas, from Indian Territory; Menomonees from Wisconsin; Iowas, Sacs, and Foxes from Nebraska; Pueblos from New Mexico; Lipans from old Mexico; to which will probably be added fifty Utes from Colorado, the first of the tribe ever in a school. Many of the number are children of chiefs or head-men; among others, of White Eagle, head chief of the Poncas; Black Crow, American Horse, and White Thunder, noted chiefs of the Sioux. The famous old chief Spotted Tail had four boys there and a daughter, with two more distant relatives, but, on his visit to them, took umbrage at finding his half-breed son-in-law no longer needed as interpreter, and went off in a huff, with all his little Spotted Tails be-

A CLASS-ROOM.

hind him.   For this hasty action he was called to account, immediately on his return, by his people, who could not understand why, if Carlisle was a bad place, he should not have brought their children away too, and on hearing the other side of the story from the chiefs who had accompanied him, asked to have him deposed for "double talking."   One of the indignant parents, with the mild name of Milk, in writing upon the subject to Captain Pratt, says, with some lactic acidity, "Spotted Tail has been to the Great Father's house so often that he has learned to tell lies and deceive people."   It is pleasant to add that a judicious letting alone had the due effect, and he has requested the government's permission to send his children back to Carlisle.

Many visitors go to Carlisle to see the Indians.   Some of them, it must be acknowledged, are disappointed.   After alighting at the commandant's office, and being courteously received by Captain Pratt or one of his assistants, the spokesman of the party asks politely if they may "first look about by themselves a little."   Cordial permission given, they set forth, but in the course of half an hour are back again with clouded brows, and the appeal, "We thought we might see some Indians round; can you show us some?"   A smile and a circular wave of the hand emphasize the assurance that a score or two of noble red men are within easy eye-range at the moment. Following the gesture with a glance over the green where the boys and girls are passing, perhaps, to their school-rooms, the shade of unsatisfaction deepens, and

they explain: "Oh, but I mean *real* Indians.   Haven't you some real Indians— all in blankets, you know, and feathers, and long hair?"

A little allowance must be made for sentiment in human nature, and if these easily disappointed visitors stay long enough, they may be gratified with an occasional "real Indian" dance of a gentle type, or without much trouble the well-named maiden Pretty Day might be persuaded to attire herself, as becomes a high-born princess of the plains, in her cherished dress of finest dark blue blanket, embroidered deer-skin leggings, and curiously netted cape adorned with three hundred milk-white elk teeth, each pair of them the price of a pony.

Aboriginal picturesqueness is certainly sacrificed to a great extent in civilization. One who is willing to relinquish the idea, however, of a menagerie of wild creatures kept for exhibition, will not regret to find instead a school of neatly dressed boys and girls, with bright eyes and clean faces, as full of fun and frolic as if they were the descendants of the Puritans.

The barracks stand on a knoll half a mile from the town.   From the upper piazza of the commandant's quarters the eye sweeps over a beautiful landscape.   Spurs

SLATE OF LITTLE SIOUX BOY AFTER SEVEN MONTHS' TRAINING AT CARLISLE.

gers to toes without bending the knees.

Long brick buildings, ranged in a hollow square with double sides, are variously occupied by school-rooms and quarters for students and teachers, offices, dining-room, kitchen, hospital, etc. The large stables of the garrison have been, for the most part, converted into workshops and a gymnasium. A little wooden chapel has been put up for the school, simply a long room, well lighted and furnished with settees, but this has been all the building needed. So many substantial edifices, in tolerable order to start with, have been a great advantage. This is especially noticeable in the school building, two stories high like the rest, the upper half of which affords four school-rooms, each fifty feet by twenty-four, and two recitation-rooms of half the length. All are furnished with comfortable desks, blackboards, and all the conveniences of a well-ordered school. The lower story, containing the same room, allows for doubling the number of students, which is the captain's desire.

A walk through these pleasant class-rooms is of great interest. Each contains from thirty to forty pupils, under the constant care, for the most part, of one teacher, who, as may be imagined, has her hands full to keep all busy and quiet, but who does it, somehow, to a remarkable degree. As at Hampton, the great object is to teach English, and then the rudiments of an English education, and the methods employed are similar.

The results possible can not be more

of the Blue Ridge circle it in front and rear, from five to eight miles away, the old town lies down in the hollow, green fields stretch between, and the little "Tort Creek" winds its very tortuous way round the post grounds and through a grove of old trees. Beyond the flag-staff in front of the house is the parade-ground, where the boys drill and the girls play. A pretty sight it is to see the merry little crowd enjoying a game of ball, or with heads up and toes trying to turn out, taking off the boys' "setting-up drill," with shouts of laughter, finishing all up properly with the difficult achievement of touching fin-

fairly shown than by a slate not gotten up for the occasion, but filled with the day's work of one of the pupils—not the best offered, but chosen because it was the work of a little Sioux boy of twelve or thirteen, who, seven months and a half before, had never had any schooling in any language, and did not know a word of English, nor how to make a letter or a figure. He evidently did know how to make pictures, as most of his race do. The blackboards of an Indian recitation-room are usually rich in works of art illustrative of the day's doings, or memories of home life.

The industries, agricultural and mechanical, are under the charge of master-workmen; a skilled farmer, carpenter, wagon-maker, and blacksmith, harnessmaker, tinner, shoemaker, baker, tailor, and printer. All the boys not learning trades are required to work in turn on the farm. Twelve acres of arable land belong to the post, and twelve more have been rented—two hundred could well be used. The articles manufactured in the shops are taken by government for the agencies. Under this wise encouragement they have already turned out wagons and farm implements, dozens of sets of harness, hundreds of dozens of tinware, and numbers of pairs of shoes, besides doing all the mending, and making all of the girls' clothing and most of the boys' underwear. The amount of students' work on these varies. No waste is allowed; the master-workmen do the cutting out and planning for the most part, but the apprentices are brought forward as fast as possible, and the masters say they are up to any apprentices. Indeed, the enthusiastic master-tinsmith put a challenge into a Carlisle paper, which was not taken up, offering to back Roman Nose, one of the St. Augustines, against any apprentice with no longer practice, for $100 a side. One of the young Sioux shoemakers took his

father's measure when he visited the school, and sent him by mail, after he went home, a pair of boots made entirely by himself.

The two printer apprentices are prac-

TINNER'S APPRENTICES, CARLISLE.

ticed chiefly upon the monthly "organ" of the school, the *Eadle-Keatah-toh* (*Morning Star*), a very interesting little sheet. One of the boys, however, Samuel Townsend, a Pawnee from Indian Territory, prints a tiny paper, the *School News*, of which he is both editor and proprietor, writing his own editorials and correcting his own proof.

The girls' industrial room makes as good showing as the boys'. Many have learned to sew by hand, and some to run the sewing-machine. Virginia, daughter of the Kiowa chief Stumbling Bear, made a linen shirt, with bosom, entirely by herself, washed and ironed it herself, and sent it to her father. Two Sioux girls have made calico shirts for their fathers. Mending is very neatly done. At Carlisle, as at Hampton, the tender maidens sweeten industry with sentiment, and carefully rummage the darning basket for the stockings of the boys they like the best.

The young St. Augustine from Hampton who went to Indian Territory to col-

COOK AND HIS DAUGHTER GRACE.

many — fifteen. I see all my people, my old friends. But I not think about the girls there. But Laura, she think. She tell me she be my wife. I bring her here, Carlisle. She know English before. She study and sew. Now Laura's father dead, since come here. Now I think all the time, I think, who take care of Laura? I think, by-and-by I find place to work near here; I work very hard. *I* take care of Laura."

Besides this frank damsel, who "thinks" to so much purpose, he brought with him a bright little sister of his own, and several brothers and sisters of the other St. Augustines, all of whom are among the most promising of the Carlisle pupils.

lect pupils for Carlisle, took wise advantage of the opportunity to bring back a sweetheart for himself. His naïve account of the affair to the captain makes a good companion piece to the Hampton love-letter.

"Long time ago, in my home, Indian Territory, I hunt and I fight. I not think about the girls. Then you take us St. Augustine. By-and-by I learn to talk English. I try to do right. Everybody very good to me. I try do what you say. But I not think about the girls. Then I go Hampton. There many good girls. I study. I learn to work. But I not think about the girls. Then I come Carlisle. I work hard; try to help you. By-and-by you send me Indian Territory for Indian boys and Indian girls. I go get

Carlisle, like Hampton, has met with much sympathy from its neighbors. It is illustrated, with other points, in an item which appeared in a Carlisle paper during the visit of the Sioux chiefs: "A few mornings since we noticed one of the young Indian men passing in the direction of the post-office, and at his side a comely Indian maiden. The day being warm, the young man carried a huge umbrella to shield them from the sun. Only a short distance in front of them several Indian chiefs were stalking along, wrapped in blankets, and bare-headed. The contrast was so striking that it attracted the attention of many persons on the street. And the conclusion was irresistibly forced upon all who noticed the incident that the Indian school is proving a great success."

The visit of the Sioux chiefs to Carlisle was prolonged to eight or ten days, and, with the exception of Spotted Tail's uncomfortable episode, was pleasant and profitable to all.

Accompanying the party was one Indian named Cook, who, not being a chief, had not been invited to come at government expense, so he came at his own expense, all the way from Dakota, to see his little girl at the Carlisle school. He was greatly pleased with her surroundings and progress, and the day after he arrived went out into the town and bought her a white dress, a pair of slippers, and a gold chain and cross. Arrayed in these gifts, he took his precious "Porcelain Face" out with him to have their photographs taken to carry home.

Both Hampton and Carlisle afford excellent opportunity for study of race character. The chief conclusion will be that Indian children are, on the whole, very much like other children, some bright and some stupid, some good and some perverse, all exceedingly human. The untamed shyness, so much in the way of their progress, seems to be as marked in the half-breeds as in those of full blood, unless they have been brought up among white people. It wears off fastest in the younger ones, in constant meeting with strangers, and association with new companions. A certain self-consciousness and sensitive pride is left which is not a bad point in the character. A quick sense of humor is its correlative, perhaps, and both may result from the trained and inherited keenness of observation which appreciates both the fitting and the incongruous.

The pupils at Carlisle and Hampton are in constant receipt of letters from their parents and friends, written some in picture hieroglyphics, some in Sioux, and some, through their interpreters, in English, but all expressive of earnest desire for their progress in school. About a hundred of these letters were sent to the Indian Department by Captain Pratt, forty of which were referred to the Senate in answer to Senator Teller's resolution against compulsory education for the Cheyennes. Indian sentiments on education expressed by themselves, and the real effect upon Indian parents of sending their children to a white man's school,

no one need question who reads the following specimens of these letters, translated from the Sioux:

"PINE RIDGE AGENCY, DAKOTA, *April* 15, 1880.

"MY DEAR SON,—I send my picture with this. You see that I had my War Jacket on when taken, but I wear white man's clothes, and am trying to live and act like white men. Be a good boy. We are proud of you, and will be more so when you come back. All our people are building houses and opening up little farms all over the reservation. You may expect to see a big change when you get back. Your mother and all send love.

"Your affectionate father,
"CLOUD SHIELD."

"ROSEBUD AGENCY, *January* 4, 1880.

"MY DEAR DAUGHTER,—Ever since you left me I have worked hard, and put up a good house, and am trying to be civilized like the whites, so you will never hear anything bad from me. When Captain Pratt was here he came to my house, and asked me to let you go to school. I want you to be a good girl and study. I have dropped all the Indian ways, and am getting like a white man, and don't do anything but what the agent tells me. I listen to him. I have always loved you, and it makes me very happy to know that you are learning. I get my friend Big Star to write. If you could read and write, I should be very happy. Your father, BRAVE BULL.

"Why do you ask for moccasins? I sent you there to be like a white girl, and wear shoes."

A small Indian girl who wanted to exhibit her knowledge of a good big English word, announced that she had come East to be "cilyized." I hope I have shown sufficiently that it is the effort of Hampton and Carlisle not to *sillyize* the Indian. Let us not, on the other hand, sillyize ourselves. One great lesson of the missionary work of fifty years has been to work with nature and not against nature; the next must be to be content with natural results. We forget that we are ourselves but the saved remnant of a race. I can not do better on this point for both schools than to quote from an address of General Armstrong: "The question is most commonly asked, Can Indians be taught? That is not the question. Indian minds are quick; their bodies are greater care than their minds; their character is the chief concern of their teachers. Education should be first for the heart, then for the health, and last for the mind, reversing the custom of putting the mind before physique and character. This is the Hampton idea of education."

MONTREAL

IDWINTER life in Montreal offers many brilliant and fascinating scenes. What visitor, for example, can forget the toboggan slide on a gala night? The white obscurity of moonlight gives the snowy world a distant, visionary look; and the sky is strange, with a misty luminous atmosphere that puts out the stars and yet allows the moon to peer through shifting veils of ruddy smoke. A galaxy of lights and fires all down the mountainside and over the plain tinges the snow with intense colors, and marks a stream of warm humanity running freely in the arctic night. The stream is of buxom young men and women, delusively lightsome and fluffy in blanket suits, stepping quickly past you on the upward path toward the invisible summit; the sounds of their glad but decorous voices seem to be almost lost in the space and the silence of a winter night—a low babbling brook of confiding sounds. Presently the toboggans come swooping down as on the wing; the rush is breathless; the compact row of figures, the eager crouching steersman, the cloud of snow whirling up in their wake, all flash upon your sight like a magic picture, from the dimness of night into the vividness of a red light or a green, or the shadowy glow of a bonfire. The vision has gone into obscurity ere you saw it; and you follow it downward in wonder by the audible perspective, as it were, of vanishing shouts.

Then, again, you will recall that you seem to gaze into another world in seeing the ice palace. It is an opalescent castle intensely brilliant in the sunshine, with walls of translucent shadows edged with prismatic hues. One expects to meet Kubla Khan at every turn within those walls of light, faint, cool, pearly colors. Even when men come and storm it as an army of snow-shoers, it still remains an unearthly vision; it becomes an ice volcano shooting rockets and candles, and raining fire over winter snows; or a castle all incandescent in red or green lights. The snow-shoers with their torches then wind up the mountain and about its summit, while more pyrotechnics are shot from that height into the sky. The carnival on skates is still more memorable, a unique scene of great beauty. The rink is brilliant, with a floor of ice like a mirror, in the centre an ice fountain with marble statues, all about it rows of people sitting patiently in the cold, the great roof hung with flags, and the whole lighted with electricity. The band strikes up, and calls out two long lines of skilful skaters, youths and maidens, dressed in fancy costumes; they and their reflections in the ice mirror wind about the rink for a time in various figures, and then break up into a general mêlée, going round and round the rink by the hour, and offering a continual kaleidoscopic interchange of colors and costumes. The city is thus full of cheerful life and leisure, sports and gayeties. The bracing air lends a zest to all enjoyments.

GENERAL VIEW OF McGILL COLLEGE.

Montreal is a striking exception to the text that a house divided against itself cannot stand. Its divisions are so fundamental and persistent that they have not diminished one iota in a century, but rather increased. The two irreconcilable elements are Romanism and Protestantism; the armies are of French and English blood. The outlook for peace is well-nigh hopeless, with two systems of education producing fundamental differences of character, and nourishing religious intolerance, race antipathy, social division, political antagonism, and commercial separation.

Nevertheless, this city of disunion flourishes as the green bay-tree, with a steady if not an amazing growth, which is due chiefly to the separate, not the united, efforts of the races.

The English social life of Montreal is in a transition state between the former garrison life and the developments that commercial life will bring. Up to 1872 the city was garrisoned successively by many regiments of distinction, having in command prominent members of the English aristocracy. Society then consisted almost entirely of about two hundred army officers, a few government officials, and the English ladies of the town; a few French Canadian families of the better class who adopted English ways, and a very few civilians, were admitted to this somewhat aristocratic company. Society therefore was formed on the army ideals, habits, etiquette. When the English regiments were withdrawn, society lost its chief features, and the removal of the capital to Toronto, Quebec, and finally to Ottawa took away the bureaucracy. Since then, with a marked increase of wealth, society has acquired new elements; foreign influences also have added somewhat to the disorganization. Hence the polish of society has very naturally declined somewhat, but the conventionalities helped by the persistence of military traditions and a strong general spirit of conservatism still maintain their prominence in social intercourse. On the other hand, hospitable customs, the buoyant health and spirits of the people, and their easy good-fellowship, cultivated by the practice of out-door sports, help to balance these conventional tendencies and to keep them from becoming too weighty a burden on the national character. The colonial relations still give to society its dominant features—English fashions, manners, and customs; but intercourse with the United States introduces some secondary elements from American life, which have increased much since the departure of the English garrison and the growth of trade with the United States.

The population comprises three race divisions—the English-speaking Scotch, English, Irish, and Americans; the French Canadians; and a few mixed families of English and French. Foreigners are almost unknown in Montreal, if the Americans be excepted. The community or society in general has no clearly defined castes. What aristocracy there was disappeared with the garrison; and as English aristocratic manners and customs seem ill adapted to this commercial community, all attempts in this direction have failed. Society thus lacks the order and the power that may be derived from large homogeneous and reasonable divisions; unhappily it suffers, as many other communities do, from the pettiness of small divisions or cliques. The ultra-fashionable set changes *personnel* rather rapidly, with the changes of wealth, but preserves enough leaven of polish from decade to

VICTORIA SQUARE.

Young woman stopping at the Windsor Hotel

decade to raise the material. The national character and many homes well furnished in the English style give to the city a delightful air of comfort, cheerfulness, and solidity. One of the largest and most important social elements of Montreal are the professors of McGill University. The Americans, about one hundred families, are not a prominent element in fashionable life. The Scotch are easily the leading people here, as they are so generally in British colonies. And the Irish fill here their customary industrial and political rôles, generally in peace and order, but now and then with an Orange riot or some outbreak of hatred against the French Canadians.

The social season in Montreal is naturally midwinter, and a charming season it is: gayeties, as they say, come and go with the snow. The chief forms of entertainment are dinners, quite English in style and appointments, American parties, with dancing, balls, and five-o'clock teas. In public amusements the city is somewhat deficient, considering its size and its metropolitan importance in the

Dominion. The clergy of both religions regard the theatre with much disfavor; and the division of the population as to language also makes the development of the drama difficult. But notwithstanding these hinderances two theatres are supported; in one of them the celebrities of the day play short engagements from time to time. The snow-shoe concert deserves mention as a feature of some originality; it is generally a creditable amateur performance of songs, choruses, readings, etc., in the key of high hilarity; and the clubs all seem to have a good number of members who can carry off such affairs in a manly, pleasant way. For a stranger the audience is the chief interest—a lot of well-made athletic men, of whole-

Street arab. French quarter

some color, despite the confinement of their professional or commercial lives. Montreal is said to possess the secret of forming successful clubs—a power naturally developed where society matters are such a prominent element. The English have two social clubs, the St. James and the Metropolitan, besides a number of societies devoted to special pursuits. The Hunt Club, having the oldest pack of hounds and the finest establishment in America, contains much of the *élite* of Montreal society. The climate leads to some features of organization not found in the hunts of England; the club has a house, regular membership to support it, accommodations for visiting members and horses, and it joins to its special amusement the social feature of dances given in its house in winter. The club meets, occurring twice a week from September till

One of the Swells of the Victoria Skating Club.

BONSECOURS MARKET.

snow falls, present one of the most picturesque sights about the city, with fine horses, fine riders, the scarlet coats, and the eager hounds bursting across the country after the wily fox.

Athletics are the chief amusement and the keenest interest of a large part of the well-to-do men and women of Montreal. This life centres, perhaps, about the large gymnasium which is the head-quarters of various branches of the Athletic Association; but physical well-being is secured by many other means—a most enthusiastic yet reasonable practice of many out-of-door pastimes: lacrosse, foot-ball, boating, bicycling, hunting, golf, racket, tennis, racing, skating, tobogganing, curling, snow-shoeing, fishing, shooting, and cricket create in the city an unusual number of successful clubs. And as if these were not enough, the English population, not half of the total of about 175,000, support with good attendance quite a complete volunteer military service. It contains one cavalry regiment, one corps of engineers, one battery of field artillery, one of garrison artillery, two rifle regiments, one of Highlanders, one of Fusileers. The French Canadians furnish only a rifle regiment. As has already been intimated, besides gayeties and athletics, church-going and works of piety are a prominent element in social occupations. The city is remarkably full of churches of both religions, and charitable institutions abound to an unusual extent.

Intellectual interests are not a prominent element of Montreal life. The literary life of the city has but just begun to shine, beyond a very small circle of local writers, into the ranks of society. But that literary interests are awakening in society is shown by an increase of study, if not yet by many notable productions. There are now the usual clubs for the reading of Shakespeare and Browning, and many other societies looking to social improvement through the cultivation of letters. Montreal is said to be the chief book centre of Canada, but the city does not possess a public general library, excepting the Frazer Institute, just struggling into existence; the libraries of individual institutions do not cover well any other topics than theology and civil law, and the six chief libraries together, of both languages, contain only about 100,000 volumes. The press of Montreal is very much hampered by the constant necessity of being politic in a sharply divided community. Music suffers from the disfavor with which the churches regard the drama; for without successful theatres or an opera an orchestra cannot be maintained, and the art thus lacks its chief means of expression. There are, however, some amateur organizations of public use; the Mendelssohn Choir, which treats the public now and then to

part songs and light choral works; the Philharmonic Society, but lately formed, which gives two or three concerts each winter; military bands and a number of lesser companies testify to some interest in the art. But it is generally conceded that the study of music is quite lukewarm, and that music is not an important part of social life; the choirs of the city inevitably reflect the general level of the art. Montreal is but just beginning also to adorn itself with painting and sculpture. The Art Association, incorporated in 1860, is doing much to cultivate the public taste by exhibitions and instruction; and education also includes more or less study of technical art. The pictures in the Roman Catholic churches are insignificant, but a few good canvases are to be seen in two or three wealthy houses. The chief satisfactions in Montreal are not intellectual and artistic gratifications, but gayeties, out-door sports, and a conservative piety. Living costs much less than it does in the chief cities of the United States; social entertainments are not led by rival extravagance; the moderate pace of life al-

CHRIST CHURCH CATHEDRAL.

BONSECOURS CHURCH.

lows men of business to take some leisure without dropping out of the race. The dominant qualities of this English colonial community are comfort, cheerfulness, and solidity.

The French Canadian upper classes are in a singular social condition. They form a society that is mature, being the product of an old and complete system of education, laws, language, customs, and religion. They are gregarious by nature, and given to social enjoyments; they are naturally a capable race; they have always been most closely united in national interests and sympathy, and opposed to internal variations in culture as well as to external influences; and they have, relatively to the cost of their education and their living, always been sufficiently well-to-do to command what education their Church chose to give. It is true that the conquest deprived the national life of most of its seigneurs and leaders of society, and that the old families since then have died out or sunk into the ranks. But these misfortunes merely changed the *personnel* of society from the titled to the professional class, which, if more democratic, is also more numerous and more active. Courtliness of manners undoubtedly declined; but the institutions of learning were in no way disturbed; the religious, moral, and intellectual forces and interests and tendencies were not changed. The race has increased wonderfully in numbers and power and means of culture; and it seems probable that society has grown with the growth of the country to be both larger and more cultivated than it was before the conquest. And as to keeping steadfastly to its characteristics, so faithfully have the French Canadian Roman Catholic manners, customs, traditions, education, language, laws, domestic life, social unity, been preserved that the race is a marvel to all visitors. It seems, then, not unjust to say that French Canadian society is quite mature, sufficiently numerous, and in native capacity able to sustain a social life of varied interests and elevating efforts. The surprise is therefore great to find the society of this largest and most wealthy of French Canadian communities almost without social organization, lacking social leaders, amusements of worth, intellectual, scientific, and artistic centres and activities. Doubtless the lack of large fortunes and some other material circumstances may have contributed somewhat to this result; but it cannot be doubted that the chief cause is the fact that the civilization of the French Canadian people is to such an extent moulded and restricted by its religious guardians.

The chief beauty of Montreal is the vastness of its surroundings. From the mountain you look upon a view of almost limitless expanse, and of singular nobility and simplicity. You stand high above an immense plain; its monuments are a group of isolated mountain cones; you salute in the distance the Green Mountains and the Adirondacks, for these are outposts of our republic. The St. Lawrence, joined by the Ottawa near by, flows straight on through the plain; you feel the might of its rush, and you almost hear the roar of its gleaming and enormous rapids. The vast expanse of sky, the majestic pageantry of clouds, the clear sunlight all about and so far away, the generous wind of this pure Northern air—all of it is broad and full of nobility. Then the city at your feet has but little that bemeans this magnificence. It stretches about five miles along the river, and runs about two miles back, over a series of terraces rising to the mountain; factories, mills, and the homes of workmen are at each end, and the central portion is occupied by the shipping, the public buildings, the business thoroughfares; near the mountain, along wide shady streets, are the houses of the middle and upper classes. Victoria Bridge, markets, elevators, spires, domes, and huge monasteries rise above the common level of roofs. The green plain lies all about it, and the forest runs down the streets and stretches its arms over the homes of men. As you descend for a walk about town you pass many delightful views, nooks, gullies, lanes, and turns of road and path in this Mount Royal park. In architecture the city disappoints any one looking for artistic and picturesque features. An old church or two and a château or two of the French régime awaken your expectations, but lead to no satisfaction. And yet the general impression it gives is decidedly one of beauty and brightness.

Montreal presents a seaport 250 miles inland from salt-water, 1000 miles from the Atlantic. It is also singular as a seaport without the usual forest of masts. Black ocean steam-ships, white compact lake steamers, canal-boats, and river steam-boats are almost the only craft to be seen. There is, however, one sailing vessel, the quaint *pinplat*, square-bowed, square-sterned, flat-bottomed, with one tall mast covered with square sails. Manned by the primitive French Canadian habitants, it comes to town with wood or hay, and forms the most picturesque element of the port. The river-front is fine. The wharves at the water level are provided

BONSECOURS MARKET—MARKET-DAY, JACQUES CARTIER SQUARE.

with a railroad and with removable freight sheds—for the ice sweeps away everything that is perishable—and the Lachine Canal continues the frontage around large basins. Back of all this rises a stone revetement wall supporting the river street, and above this again stands a long line of massive warehouses, the Bonsecours Market and Church, and the Custom-house. In its general plan, solidity, and unity it reminds one of the quais of Paris. But it presents a sight in the spring impossible to that brilliant capital. When the St. Lawrence awakens after his long sleep, the ice collects, *shoves* over the wharves and even over the high wall, and presents a chaos of blocks, a veritable *mer de glace.* The spring freshet is an event of anxiety and very often of loss to the city. The water-side seems to be without the usual seaport slums; its massive business front is clean, sedate, and very proper.

The unfailing attraction of a market scene will draw you to Bonsecours. The old church has fallen a prey to the lack of veneration, so strange and yet so common in this Roman Catholic community —the very champion of tradition. Before recent repairs were done it was picturesque with its line of shops backed up along the foot of its plain high wall. Within the church is a statue of the Virgin which was carried through the streets in religious procession to stop the cholera many years ago; and again in 1885, to destroy the small-pox. The market-place offers a quaint lot of people, generally dull, heavy, material, but kindly. On one side of the walk rise the Hall and the line of little booths, selling the small wares of an economical people; on the other is a line of one-horse carts loaded with small lots of farm and garden produce. The scene is singularly devoid of color or oth-

NOTRE DAME DE LOURDES.

er beauty. The customers are generally of the middle and the lower classes, dressed very plainly, even with a sombre effect, in black or dark stuffs without ornaments. The peasant has abandoned his homespun, but he is still an elementary man. The dealing is done in a quiet way, with low voices and a decorous spirit; no one is hurried. As a rule there is no market price; a vender, either on the market or in the French Canadian retail shops of the city, asks generally at least double what he expects to get; and the buyer always offers about half what is asked. The French Canadian is by nature so litigious and intriguing that a prompt bargain is distasteful to him; he desires the disputation of dickering and

CLOCK AND GATEWAY OF ST. SULPICE.

the excitement. After an endless amount of fencing and changing of prices the habitant will leave the store, and the shopkeeper will complacently call him back; and when the customer gets home and finds that his purchase is dear, he justifies it by saying that he got a lot of dickering thrown in for nothing.

Montreal is divided sharply into two parts, the French and the English, the East and the West ends. In each part the business portion lies near the river, the wealthier homes near the mountain. In the poorer French region the signs, the trades, the domestic life, the houses, are all distinctly French and quite Continental in character. The streets have lines of small houses of one or one and a half stories, with dormer-windows peeping out of steep roofs, and here and there a little niche of a piazza; a lane now and then gives some shadowy and broken forms and quiet nooks. But all unity and effectiveness are lost by the presence of many modern houses utterly plain and ungracious.

The chief business streets of the city—St. James, Notre Dame, McGill—give a good impression by their massive limestone buildings, both public and commercial. Here and there in the town is met a touch of grace and beauty, as in the English cathedral and the Chapel of

Notre Dame de Lourdes. The cut-stone residences along Sherbrooke and other streets at the foot of the mountain embody well the leading tones of the English life here—solidity, comfort, and cheerfulness. But you feel everywhere that Montreal is distinctly a Northern city: the winter predominates; the best life is within, both in character and in architecture.

Naturally enough the most interesting features of the city to an American visitor thus strolling about are those connected with the leading element of the French Canadian life—those of the Roman Catholic religion. Here, among a Roman Catholic population noted chiefly for their lack of wealth, is building a cathedral one-third the size of St. Peter's, and of the same shape, excepting that this one has a pointed roof to shed snow. They have already, besides many other churches, the great Notre Dame, the largest in America excepting the cathedral of Mexico. It seats 10,000 people, and will hold 15,000. The official poster at the door asserts that the great bell in the tower is the largest in the world. It is the eighth bell in size, weighing only 24,780 pounds. In the interior, vast but somewhat harsh and gaudy, you may see an ornate spiral pulpit and a bronze statue of St. Peter, of which the toes are well polished. You can continue visiting churches and chapels all day. None of them contain any art of importance, but they reveal a religious life of the Middle Ages kept up with marvellous force in this nineteenth century. One of the pleasantest scenes of this religious life may be witnessed in the city of the dead. In the cemetery on the mountain, along the streets of tombs, are erected little grottoes, each having in colored alto-rilievo a tableau of the stations of the cross. A priest leads slowly the flock from station to station, and explains to the kneeling people the dogmatic value of the sufferings portrayed. The trees, birds, chants, sunshine, and the murmuring winds all combine to make the ceremony touching. The route ends on a knoll where three huge crosses and figures represent most realistically the final agony. When I visited the place, of a fine June day, a company of convent girls and nuns were holding a merry picnic at this place. After their picnic they knelt for prayer, and then drove away rejoicing. On many of the graves are evidences of tender regard for the departed—little plaster statues of saints, photographs big enough to contain the entire community; and to-day the same ratio holds, for the largest edifices of the city are convents. And as the population of the city is divided as to religion, the place has a duplicate of nearly every kind of charitable institution, besides a great number of churches. Probably the chief obstruction to the city's growth is this ecclesiastic element. I was told that about

THE WAY OF THE CROSS IN THE CEMETERY.

of the deceased, or little altars with candles and crucifixes, set up in glass-covered little boxes or toy chapels. The most noted grave of the place is undoubtedly that of Guibord, buried at the point of English bayonets after years of opposition and even riotous commotion over his interment. His rest was secured by filling his grave with cement strengthened by hoops and scraps of iron, and on top was laid a huge stone block, rough, obdurate, immovable. The inscription, however, was not so enduring. It has been entirely erased.

Montreal seems to be full of gigantic monasteries. Indeed the city was founded by building first of all a monastery twenty per cent. of the property pays no taxes; many religious corporations manufacture various articles and make a ruinous competition with the working classes; and much of the land is locked up in religious orders that will neither sell nor improve it.

Montreal has always been the metropolis of Canada, in being from the earliest days of the colony the central starting-point for the fur-trader, the missionary, and the explorer. Its picturesque epoch is that of the French régime, so admirably described by Mr. Parkman; and it preserved for nearly a century after the conquest at least an after-glow of romance in the Hudson Bay Company's operations at

Lachine. But the railroads and canals have at last banished the bark canoe, the Indian, the voyageur, and the missionary to more remote posts of the interior. Missions and the fur trade proved to be very unproductive elements for the growth of a colony; the city grew with amazing slowness. In 1765, after nearly a century and a quarter of existence, the city had but 5733 souls. The English brought new forces and elements, but still it moved slowly, and did not reach 15,000 till 1819, and 59,000 till 1852. The disadvantages that the St. Lawrence and the climate imposed on trade even as lately as fifty years ago had much to do with this backwardness. Navigation was difficult in summer and impossible in winter. No ocean vessel larger than 300 tons could come up the St. Lawrence above Lake St. Peter, because of the shallowness of the river in that expansion. And the St. Mary current just along the city front is so strong that vessels used to lie below it for days or even weeks awaiting a fair wind, and even the steam-boats of early times had to add many yokes of oxen to their power. Such obstructions naturally enough deprived Montreal of the clipper ships that helped so powerfully to develop American trade; but the city had a fair share of the commerce of the continent, done in smaller vessels. Of course the winter closed the port for five or six long months. Inland navigation was even more difficult, for the St. Lawrence and the Ottawa present at once impassable rapids. The slow growth of Montreal for two centuries was therefore inevitable.

The chief elements of its trade were the importation of goods from Europe, the selling and forwarding of them to western towns, the sending of supplies to the lumbermen of the Ottawa, the exportation of grain, and the fur trade. It was nearly all a carrying trade; and this was precisely what was most difficult in those days. The building of steam-boats and the opening of the Lachine and Ottawa and Rideau canals had improved matters very much by 1830–40. But the active growth of Montreal dates from 1850 to 1860, in answer to the opening of the St. Lawrence system of canals, the completion of the Victoria Bridge, the deepening of Lake St. Peter, the building of the Grand Trunk Railway, and the formation of ocean steam-ship lines. Such a number of great commercial advantages rarely falls upon a city in a period of ten or fifteen years. The canals of the St. Lawrence are the greatest achievements of the kind in the world, considering the small population of the two provinces that built them—about 400,000. They are much larger than those of the United States; indeed some men consider them to be too costly for the best results, since they have not paid the dividends expected. If a part of their cost had been invested in other ways, the country perhaps would have benefited more. Montreal now possesses many advantages, giving it good prospects of an indefinite expansion. At the head of ocean navigation and the beginning of inland navigation, it is naturally the most central port for importation, distribution, and exportation. Thus far it has been this natural key of the great St. Lawrence highway to the centre of the continent. If, however, the canal system of the St. Lawrence should be enlarged to pass ocean vessels directly to the lakes, some elements of her importance will probably wane. The ocean fleet of Montreal consists of five weekly lines of steamers to Liverpool and Glasgow, eight fortnightly lines to London, Bristol, Newcastle-on-Tyne, Hamburg, Antwerp, the lower St. Lawrence, Newfoundland, and Cape Breton; there are also many independent steamers. The inland fleet, while of smaller vessels, aggregates a little more tonnage than the ocean fleet. The business of the port in 1887 reveals these totals: value of exports, $29,391,798; value of imports, $43,100,183; customs duties collected, $8,745,526; number of sea-going vessels, 767; tonnage of sea-going vessels, 870,773. Four lines of railways enter the city—the Grand Trunk, the Canadian Pacific, the Central Vermont, and the Southeastern. The railways take nearly all the westbound traffic, and the water brings nearly all the east-bound, which is composed mainly of grain, lumber, and minerals. A great quantity of American grain passes in bond through the port bound for European markets. Although Montreal is the most important port of Canada, and Canada is the fourth maritime country of the world, yet the imports of the city do not represent by any means the total of the imports of the St. Lawrence bound for upper Canadian towns. Importation in Canada has always been more diffused than it is in the United States, where the

BANK OF MONTREAL AND POST-OFFICE.

seaports do almost all of that business. In Canada many merchants of smaller inland cities import directly a great part of their goods. Although the traffic of Montreal has increased at a more rapid ratio than that of New York, or perhaps that of any other port of this continent, yet this showing is somewhat deceptive as an indication of the general prosperity of the Dominion; for Montreal is the only port for all western Canada, while no city in the United States enjoys such a monopoly. Of the traffic of the continent Montreal has not attracted quite its share of increase, but the growth of its trade is nevertheless very satisfactory.

A great deal of the wealth of Montreal is in bank stock, and it is said that about

$15,000,000 of it goes and comes between Montreal, New York, and Chicago in obedience to the stock market. The state of trade is not a healthy one; long credits prevail, and the attendant evils are common. Manufactures have been added only since about 1875 to the other commercial elements of Montreal, and the city offers some advantages in this line by its cheap fuel brought from England as ballast or from Nova Scotia, by its central position, and by the cheap labor drawn from the contented, docile, unambitious French Canadians. The city is by far the chief manufacturing centre of Canada; it turns out now almost anything from a locomotive to a cigar. And as her markets are extended in the west indefinitely by the commercial traveller and the railway, the city must grow rapidly in this department of civilization. Montreal's relations to the lake States and to New England were formerly much more intimate than they are now. Before the telegraph and railroad brought the farmer's market to his door the commercial traveller was more often a buyer than a seller. Montreal merchants used to travel in the lake States to buy produce more than to sell; but they also sold goods in the lake cities, and did a large share of the carrying trade. The most of the grain they brought went *via* Montreal to Europe, and, on the other hand, some of the Ontario grain crossed the lakes to American mills. In New England Montreal found a considerable market for agricultural products and for lumber if reciprocity existed for anything besides defaulters. Americans were then a prominent element in Montreal. Several Boston hardware firms founded branches there, and did the most of that business; the hotels and inns were all in the hands of Americans; most of the jewelry stores and hat stores also. They were prominent in the movement to make Hochelaga the commercial part of the city, whereby quiet water would have given better facilities to shipping, and level land would have offered space for the commerce of the town. But only two or three names of that colony now remain. The Americans now in Montreal are not at the head of very important branches of trade. They do something in coal and in small manufactures for the Canadian market, and a few have sunk money in lumber and in mines.

The French Canadian merchant does not hold a commanding position commercially. French Canadians themselves prefer to deal with English houses and to work for English employers. In the entire province scarcely a French Canadian has ever organized an important successful enterprise; lumbering, wholesale trade, public works, are almost invariably in other hands.

VIEW FROM THE CUSTOM-HOUSE.

FOUR DAYS IN A MEDICINE LODGE

THE medicine-lodge* of the Blackfeet Indians, who are Sun-worshippers, is the ceremony that among other tribes is called the sun-dance. It is not, as is commonly supposed, a mere festal dance; it is the most important of all religious ceremonies, the occasion when the entire tribe assembles—some to fulfil their vows to the sun, some to fast and pray, and some to find the diversions and social enjoyments which, the world over, are associated with large gatherings of people. During a sojourn of several summers in northwestern Montana, among the Piegan division† of the Blackfeet Indians, I was adopted by one of the chiefs, Mad Wolf, who is especially prominent in the sacred rites of the Blackfeet. I was baptized with an Indian name, and formally initiated as a member of the tribe.

My new relationship gave me every facility for studying the origin and significance of the medicine-lodge. I was fortunate also in securing, by means of a graphophone, many records of their songs. The following Blackfeet legend gives

the tradition of the medicine-lodge: Many years ago the Sun appeared in a dream to a beautiful young girl of the tribe, saying, "You are mine; if you marry him who is pleasing to me, you will live to be old, and will always have good luck." Many of the leading young men of the tribe wished to marry her, but each was in turn refused. Finally there came to her a young man who said: "I am poor; I have no lodge, neither robes nor horses; but I ask you to become my wife." The girl answered him: "The Sun has taken me to be his own; I can marry no one without his permission. If you go to the lodge of the Sun, and he should consent, then I will marry you." Turning his face toward the setting sun, the young man started on his journey. He travelled many days, praying, as he went, to the birds and animals for help. He had crossed prairies and mountains, but every evening the sun disappeared so far ahead of him that he grew discouraged, and thought that his journey would never end. Finally the animals heard his prayers, showing him the trail which led to the Big Water. There the birds also came to his assistance, carrying him to a far-away island, where he found the lodge in which the

Sun lived with his wife, the Moon, and their only son, the Morning Star. The young man was declared to be worthy by the Sun, who started him upon his homeward journey by the Milky Way, or Wolf Road, the trail said to be travelled by the spirits of the Indian dead. When departing he received the Sun's blessing, with the promise that, when any of his people were sick, a vow to build a medicine-lodge, as an offering to the Sun, would be rewarded by the recovery of the sick.

During a recent winter of great severity, it happened that the wife of Mad Wolf was taken sick. None of the remedies of the Indian doctors helped her, and though the medicine-men sang their strongest songs, the evil spirits refused to depart. One morning she struggled to the door of the lodge, and stretching forth her arms to the rising sun, she prayed: "Pity me, O Sun! for you know that I am pure. Give me back my strength, and before all the people I promise to build for you a medicine-lodge!" Before the snow began to melt, the squaw was well; and when, in the spring, the warm winds began to blow, true to her vow, the wife of Mad Wolf began her preparations for the medicine-lodge. The fulfilment of her vow, which I had the good fortune to witness, gave a special interest and a deeper religious significance to the raising of this medicine-lodge.

BULL CHILD BLOWING
MEDICINE-WHISTLE

The service-berries had turned red and the grass had grown long upon the prairie, when the Indians living in the northern section of the reservation assembled near Mad Wolf's lodge, where he was making medicine for the sun-dance. The southern section of the tribe gathered under Running Crane, who was also making medicine. In their separate camps the Indians waited patiently until they could move together to the place where the entire tribe was to assemble and the medicine-lodge was to be raised.

The morning of the last day of June dawned clear and beautiful upon the prairies and mountains. I had been informed of the time and place where the Piegans would meet, and, while awaiting their arrival, had walked to the summit of a high ridge overlooking a wide expanse of rolling prairie, now covered everywhere with green grass, made rich and luxuriant by the frequent rains of early spring. At sunrise I saw a band of Indians approaching from the north, and when they came near enough I saw that they were led by Mad Wolf, and that his followers included White Grass, Chief Elk, Morning Plume, Middle Calf, Double Rider, and Bear Child. The warriors were in the van, followed by the little cayuses, or ponies, drawing the travois laden with supplies. Then came a long line of heavy wagons, in which were strange-looking medicine outfits, and lodges. The rear-guard was composed of the older men, squaws, and young girls. Each family was followed by a lot of mongrel dogs, all as gaunt and hungry-looking as a pack of prairie-wolves. The site of the encampment, which had been deserted and silent since the breaking up of the last Piegan camp, twelve moons before, became a scene of bustle and confusion. A white village of Indian lodges, springing up as if by magic, immediately spread itself over a large tract of prairie.

In the afternoon Running Crane came in from the south. With him were many leading men—Little Dog, Little Plume, Curly Bear, Medicine Bull, and Mountain Chief. In this outfit were three medicine-women, so weakened by fasting that, unable to stand without assistance, they reclined upon the ground, while a tepee was erected over them. During the medicine-lodge, which lasts four days and four nights,* these consecrated women

* "Four" seems to be the sacred number of the Blackfeet. The rites of the medicine-lodge continue through four days and four nights. Four "sweat-houses" are constructed prior to the raising of the medicine-lodge. Four "coups" are counted in the ceremony of cutting the hide into thongs. Four lines of warriors move toward the centre while

INDIAN HORSE-RACE

fast, and are continually praying to the
Sun for their people. They may only
leave the lodge during the hours between

chanting the song, "The Raising of the Pole."
A similar use of the four cardinal points, and
the ceremonial value of four and multiples of four,
throughout the sacred rites of the Hopi snake-
dance of the Pueblo Indians of northeastern Ari-
zona (*vide* article by George Wharton James in
June *Outing*, 1900), seemed to indicate that their
religious rites have had a common origin, probably
in the sun-worship of the ancient Aztecs.

sundown and sunrise, and may only partake of a little water for their sustenance.
Their faces, hair, and blankets are covered with the sacred red paint. The medicine-women are held in high honor by
the Indians, for they must have led perfectly pure lives before the entire tribe,
and must have been kindly disposed toward all its members. It yields great re-
nown to a tribe to give a sun-dance, for
all of the Indians throughout the West

hear of it, and some come hundreds of miles to be present. The medicine-man who is to lead the ceremonies is a great man, and it is believed that he will live long. At the medicine-lodge I saw representatives from many of the leading tribes of the Northwest—Crees and Bloods from the north; Assiniboines, Pondres, Gros Ventres, and Sioux from the east; Kootenais and Flatheads from the west.

During the day about fifteen hundred Indians had gathered, and there were upwards of two hundred lodges. The camp was in the form of a circle, the circumference of which was about two miles. The natural surroundings were inexpressibly beautiful. A few miles to the west were the Rocky Mountains, over which hung a bank of heavy wind-clouds. The sun, which was sinking behind Mount Red Chief, lighted up the sombre cloud masses with a splendid coloring, while its bright rays, streaming to either side, formed a magnificent "sunburst," with the mountain-peak for its centre. A dark blue haze, resembling smoke, was rapidly mounting the eastern sky —the forerunner of the coming night. Upon the surrounding ridges herds of horses were quietly feeding, while here and there could be seen a solitary Indian who had wandered off for meditation or solitude.

The days before the great ceremony of the medicine-lodge I spent in studying the varied life of the camp with its mingling of amusements and religious rites. In the evenings the lodges were lighted up by firelight, and the shadows of the Indian families were projected in enlarged outlines upon their canvas coverings. For the most part, the Indians were comfortably seated around their fires, talking over the incidents of the day. While passing a small and tattered lodge, I heard the wailing and sobbing of an Indian, whose child had recently departed to dwell in the ghostly Sand Hills far to the east, where the spirits of the Blackfeet reside after death. From another lodge came the sound of the monotonous drumming and singing of an Indian doctor while endeavoring to drive away the evil spirits who held possession of the sick; and farther on I heard angry cries, followed by a series of yelps. The door-flap suddenly opened, and out rushed an offending dog, which quickly disappeared in the darkness, followed by the imprecations of an angry squaw. The life of a nomadic Indian camp has most of the contrasts in human experience that we find in compact cities. Though the most striking extremes of wealth and poverty are absent, the lights and shadows of domestic joy and sorrow, of health and sickness, of pathos and humor, of the grave and the gay, of love and hate, of the old man's wisdom and thoughtfulness and the young man's folly and reck-

WHITE CALF

A PRAYER TO THE SUN

lessness—all of these are present, with even sharper contrasts because of the closeness of their contiguity.

I lay down upon my blankets, with the sky for my roof. The full moon had risen from the prairie, flooding the camp with its light. Many of the white lodges, with their crowns of tapering poles, stood out in sharp relief against the burnished eastern sky. To the west were the dim outlines of the rugged Rockies, behind which the evening star was slowly sinking. The young men on picket duty were making their rounds upon horseback, singing at intervals an Indian "night song," a custom handed down from the forefathers. In the centre of the camp several dogs started up a mournful howl. Suddenly, as if in response to a prearranged signal, hundreds of dogs, in all parts of the camp, joined in what the Indians call a "moon howl," which closely resembles the dis-

mal howling of an enormous pack of wolves. Gradually their chorus died away. When everything was quiet again two young warriors passed near me on horseback, singing a beautiful "wolf song" in perfect time with the slow trot of their horses. They passed so close to my blankets that I saw them very clearly, their strongly colored Indian clothes showing distinctly in the undimmed moonlight. Their song ended in the perfect imitation of the howl of the wolf.

On the following day I witnessed several exciting horse-races. The course, which was along the south side of the camp, was very picturesque, facing the west, with snowy peaks for a background. The Indians of the prairies go wild over racing, and are superb horsemen, riding bareback the most vicious of unbroken broncos. The chief race of the day was between the horses representing the Indians and the cowboys. At the finish a crowd of Indians gathered who had staked many of their possessions upon the result, and who cheered wildly as their horse won by a narrow margin.

About noon Mad Wolf rode through the camp, announcing in his powerful voice that there was to be a dance. "Let all the young men go to their lodges and dress themselves in their most beautiful clothes, and let every one come." When the young men assembled, coming in twos and threes from different parts of the camp, they were dressed in their gayest and most elaborate Indian clothes, the picturesque effect being heightened by the tinkling sleigh-bells strapped about their legs. The dancers sat down in a semicircle, and when forty or fifty had arrived the singers began, accompanied by drums.

First came the dance of the warriors, in which every one who took part had been in battle. This was followed by the dance of those who had been wounded. One fine-looking old fellow, whose arm had been shot off by an enemy, entered into the dance with great energy, carrying the feather-decorated bone of the missing arm. One dancer— "Jack-behind-the-Ears"— continually aimed his rifle as if in the act of shooting. He had received his name from an exploit in which he had shot his enemy behind the

JACK-BEHIND-THE-EARS
DANCING

ear, and was now going through the motions which recalled the deed. Another man, who had been a noted stealer of horses from the enemy, carried a horse carved from wood. Others had tomahawks, arrows, costly shields, and war-bonnets. Every movement of the dance and the distinguishing marks of the dancers had a significance, which it would have been impossible for an outsider to understand. At one time two lines of dancers, singing a war-song, slowly advanced toward each other. Here and there a warrior dropped as if shot, then others rushed in and went through the motions of scalping them. The moral

effect of the scalping was evidently displeasing to White Calf, the head chief, for, suddenly stepping into the circle, he motioned to the dancers to stop.

The leader of the dances was Black Weasel, a large and handsome Indian, whose seat in the surrounding circle was marked by a sword driven into the ground. When it was time to commence a figure he moved about the circle, stick in hand, hustling out the dancers and giving sharp cuts to those who lagged behind. He was as considerate, however, as he was energetic, and devoted part of his attention to seeing that the women and children were comfortably seated and were supplied with water. The most interested of the large circle of spectators seemed to be Short Robe's little daughter, who was seated with her family. Her bright black eyes, beaming with filial admiration, followed every movement of her father as he took part in the dance. Her copper complexion and long hair hanging over her shoulders were in striking contrast with the brilliant scarlet of her costume. Her dress, which was like that of a squaw, was beautifully decorated with beads, and her leggings were also beaded. Around her waist was a miniature squaw belt closely studded with shining brass-headed tacks. As she watched the dance her body swayed to and fro, and her small moccasined feet kept time to the beating of the drums.

Late in the afternoon the dancers rested for a short interval to join in the feast of a puppy, which was placed in the centre of the circle by squaws. While they were feasting, Running Crane, an old chief, addressed the people, saying: "I am now glad in my heart to see you gathered together. The young men are all dressed in their most beautiful clothes, and they dance well. It is not often that we have fun,—only once a year. The shooting has all been stopped, and we have ceased to count 'coups,'* but we are

* A "coup" is primarily the striking of an enemy in battle. "Counting coups" is the narration of deeds of bravery in battle.

SHORT ROBE AND DAUGHTER IN FULL DRESS

all happy here. I hope that the Great Father at Washington will not stop our coming together, for it does not last long. Let the old people keep the boys quiet, that we may break camp and return to our homes without having any disturbance. I am now through. My name is Running Crane." Mountain Chief then arose. He told of the old days and how he used to dance, and he advised his people to give many horses to the Sioux, who had come from the far east to visit. He held a small stick, which represented a good white horse, and, when he had finished speaking, stepped across the circle and handed the stick to a Sioux Indian. From the crowd of spectators there came the voice of another old chief, who exclaimed, "Good boy, giving away your horse so

INDIAN DANCERS

generously!" After the feast, the dance was continued until sundown.

That evening I heard the notes of a love-song, sung by a young man passing near to the lodge of his sweetheart. It is probable that the girl alone knew for whom the song was intended. Mad Wolf's lodge was surrounded by green boughs — a sign that a sacred service was being held: and as I approached I heard the Indians chanting as they "made medicine." I stood awhile, listening to the chanting. At intervals the low monotone of the men was joined by the shrill voices of the women. Gradually the song died away and there was silence, broken by Mad Wolf's voice, who directed a squaw to throw more wood on the fire. A brighter flame lighted up the lodge, and though I was far from sure that my presence would be welcome, I decided this was my opportune moment. I lifted the flap of the tent and stepped in. By the uncertain firelight I could distinguish Mad Wolf seated in the place of honor at the back of the lodge. He smiled, and motioned to me to be seated. On Mad Wolf's left, and taking a prominent part in the service, was Curly Bear. There were also White Grass, Three Bears, and Eagle Head. Three Bears was unusually large and burly. When I was seated, he extended toward me an enormous hand, giving me a hearty shake. To the right of Mad Wolf were the sacred medicine-women of Mad Wolf's band, their heads bent as if in prayer. Weakened by long fasting, they seemed scarcely able to sit erect, and at times were supported and ministered to by other squaws. Between Mad Wolf and the fire, in the centre, was a small altar covered with ground-cedar. Alongside of it were the red medicine-sticks, pipes, and several medicine-bags, which were to be used in the religious service. While lying in the lodge and watching by the firelight my Indian brothers earnestly engaged in the sacred rites, I too, for the time being, imagined myself an Indian, and joined in the low, measured chant.

SWEAT-HOUSE COVERED WITH BLANKETS

Before long my attention was aroused by sounds from outside, which told me that the young bucks had come forth from their lodges and were roaming about, ready for any excitement or adventure. I left Mad Wolf and his companions so deeply engaged in their solemn service that they seemed not to notice the sounds without or my withdrawal. When I stepped out from the dimly lighted lodge into the bright moonlight I met a group of dancers, dressed in their gay trappings, who were passing through the camp, singing in unison a night song of unusual sweetness. At every step the bells fastened about their legs jingled. A horse passed, ridden by two young bucks, who were singing snatches of a dance-song while making the rounds of the camp. As I followed them I was suddenly startled by a succession of piercing war-whoops. A crowd of Indians rushed out with clubs from behind a lodge, and closing around the singers, beat their horse. The horse plunged and bucked, but the riders held their seats. Finally, amid laughter and shouting, they distanced their pursuers, galloping off over the prairie.

The sound of drums came from a large lodge around which a crowd of Indians had gathered. Inside were a number of warriors singing and dancing about the fire. Crawling underneath the side of the lodge, I found myself among the squaws, who were so occupied with watching the dance that they did not seem to notice my entrance. I discovered that I was in the lodge of Cream Antelope, a leader of the society of Crazy Dogs, who were now celebrating a dance which it had been their custom to give in the old days, when about to go upon the war-path. The dancers had thrown off their blankets, and their naked, painted bodies looked wild and grotesque in the firelight. In the circle were Half Body and Medicine Owl, with horned bonnets and necklaces of grizzlies' claws; also Big Beaver, Mountain Chief, and Big Crow, each dancer representing a wild animal. They sang a war-song as they danced; the shrill war-whoop being given with startling effect at frequent intervals.

The dancers were suddenly startled by the explosion of fire-crackers thrown upon the top of the lodge. The Crazy Dogs sat down, both surprised and indignant at the interruption. When they began again there came the clatter of a horse's hoofs, followed by several more loud explosions. One of the dancers arose in wrath, and seizing his war-club, rushed madly after the intruder, who fortunate-

RAISING THE CENTRE POLE

ly escaped. The Crazy Dogs then held a council, and decided that the shooting was in violation of their medicine-laws, and that the dance must therefore be discontinued.

As a preliminary to building the medicine-lodge, four sweat-houses were built by leading men of the tribe. A framework in the form of an ellipse is made of intertwined willow branches, about four feet in height, which are firmly set in the ground. This frame-work is covered over with hides and blankets, while the skull of a buffalo, decorated with red and black paint, surmounts the top. By means of red-hot stones, the temperature in the sweat-house is raised to a high degree. Strange visions frequently appear to the medicine-men as they lie within, praying and chanting. Mad Wolf entered the fourth and last sweat-house, by the side of which the medicine-lodge was to be built. Dried sweet-grass was burning upon the heated rocks, and placing his hands in the smoke and rubbing them over his body, he chanted and prayed to the Sun, saying, "May our lives become as strong as the stones we have placed here." Then, taking water into his mouth, he sprinkled it upon the hot stones. As the steam arose he prayed again, "May our lives be as pure as the water, that we may live to be old, and always have water to drink."

For the centre pole of the medicine-lodge the young men selected a cottonwood of considerable size, with a forked top, felled it, and dragged it from the river-bottom to the site of the lodge, with yelling and shooting of guns. They were followed by others bearing smaller poles and leafy branches. The cutting of the thongs that were to bind together the framing poles of the lodge was made an important ceremony. The warrior who was privileged to cut the hide was selected by a young woman who had been appointed for the purpose by the medicine-women. The man to whom the honor fell stood before the assembled people, holding a knife, the blade of which was covered with the sacred red paint. As he cut he counted "coups," saying, "Behold, I made an expedition against the Sioux, a number of whom I killed."

WITHIN THE MEDICINE-LODGE

He then cut two strips from the hide. Again he spoke: "At another time I went against the Crows, and stole four horses, all of which I brought home." In this manner four "coups" were counted, thongs being cut after each. From the crowd there arose the shrill voice of a squaw, singing, "Good boy! Brave man! Well done!" His relatives then arose and danced, because their brother had thus gone through many dangers and had returned to his people safe and happy.

During the afternoon the people brought offerings to the Sun, many of which were afterwards distributed among the old women of the tribe who were poor and helpless. Blankets, robes, food, and clothing were thrown together, until the pile assumed large proportions. Many horses were also given, and these were distributed by the warrior who had been chosen to cut the hide. According to the custom, those who give horses receive an equal number in the following year; while those who are presented with horses are expected to give in return the same number at the next medicine-lodge. After a feast of dried tongues and service-berry soup, the men dispersed to their lodges.

When they reappeared they were in paint and war-clothes, and they held aloft long poles lashed together near the top so as to form a cross, like a pair of shears, for lifting the poles in place. They formed in four lines toward the north, south, east, and west. Gradually the four lines advanced, converging with slow step toward the centre of the camp, while hundreds of Indian voices sang in unison the ceremonial hymn, "The Raising of the Pole," which is in marching time. The solemn notes of this great song floated out upon the still evening air, and the sunset light fell upon the strong and earnest faces of the medicine-men and the picturesque bonnets and trappings of the warriors.

At the setting of the sun, Medicine Bull, the leading medicine-man present, shouted, "Hurry! raise the pole quickly, that the medicine-women may eat and drink, for they are famished!" The crowd also shouted "Hurry!" and the centre pole was raised by means of ropes. The girder poles were next carefully lifted into place by means of the shearlike poles, and branches with foliage were placed against the sides of the lodge. The door of the medicine-lodge faced toward the east. Inside, and opposite to the entrance, a small booth of boughs interwoven with ground-cedar was built for the exclusive use of the medicine-men. During the four days' ceremony they do not leave this booth for either eating or drinking.

When the people had returned to their lodges, Medicine Bull entered the booth to pray and make medicine. Although the night was cold, he was stripped to his breech-cloth, his body being decorated with paint, the sacred red representing the Sun, and the black the Moon.

On the following morning the people surrounded and crowded into the medicine-lodge in such numbers that it was almost impossible for others to enter, or for those that were within to withdraw. A space, however, was kept open in the centre for the warriors, who danced, dressed in their war costumes and with faces hideously painted. In former years it was the custom for those who had made vows to the Sun for deliverance from sickness or battle to fulfil those vows at this time with remarkable feats of self-torture. Slits were cut in their breasts, and rawhide ropes were inserted beneath the muscles, tied securely, and fastened to the centre pole, around which they danced until they tore themselves loose in their frenzy. This barbarous and revolting custom has, however, entirely ceased, under the firm hand of the United States government.

The medicine-men are believed to have power over the weather, and at the time of the medicine-lodge are expected to drive away all storms, and to make favorable weather while it lasts. An incident that happened during this medicine-lodge illustrates the manner in which the medicine-men acquire and sustain their standing with the tribe. In the early afternoon a dark storm-cloud, with its eastern side extending far out over the prairie, was seen slowly advancing along the main range of the Rockies, directly toward the encampment. The Indians anxiously watched the medicine-men, who were quick to realize that the event was big with the possibilities of success or failure for their office. Medicine Bull and Bull Child, standing in front of their people, entered into a sort of competition in prophecy, but with much better success than the competing prophets of Baal. Bull Child, blowing his whistle and facing the black cloud, spoke in a loud voice. "See," he said, "a storm comes from the mountains over the prairie, and you people would get wet; but I am powerful and my medicine is strong. That cloud will now separate, and there will be no shower." All the people watched the cloud intently. A sudden change in the wind averted its course, and it divided as Bull Child predicted. Medicine Bull, jealous of the success of his rival, said, "Bull Child, you are wrong; that cloud is separated, but my medicine is stronger. It will again unite and return, and will wet all the people." Again the eyes of the Indians eagerly watched the divided storm-clouds, which came together, and continuing to spread, at length passed over the encampment with a heavy rain.

Men, women, and children came before the medicine-men, who, having their faces painted with the sacred red paint, gave them their blessing of "Long life and good luck." The squaws carried their pappooses to Medicine Bull, who, taking them in his arms and gazing intently at the bright sun, prayed, holding at the same time in one hand a bunch of eagle feathers, and in the other a buffalo tail. During each of the four days of ceremony there was frequent dancing in the medicine-lodge, when the warriors counted "coups" and narrated their deeds of bravery.

Upon the last day of the sun-dance, when all the tribe were assembled, Mad Wolf, the great orator of the Piegans, stepped into the circle. With his left hand he held his blanket around him, while with his right he made a gesture signifying that he wished to be heard. When there was silence, he began in a strong, full voice: "Men and women, there is nothing bad that I have now to tell you, and I speak to you with a good heart. Send your children to school, for if they can learn the talk of the white man, they will be a great help to us. The buffalo have gone, the antelope and the rest of the game also, and we now have nothing more to depend upon. Try your best to make a living upon your ranches, and look well after your cattle, for if you raise and care for them, you can make a good living. Let every one

DESERTED FRAME-WORK OF SWEAT-HOUSE, WITH BUFFALO SKULL ON IT

leave whiskey alone, for it is bad to have anything to do with whiskey. That is all for this part. The only one whom we now have to depend upon is the Great Father at Washington, who helps us in every way. All you people should obey his laws and give heed to his advice. I now wish you may feel the sunshine of joy in your hearts, that you may have a happy day and night, and that you may have no trouble. This is all."

In the morning of the fifth day after the building of the medicine-lodge, Running Crane with his band departed for the south. On the following day Mad Wolf left, followed by the remainder of the tribe. I sat alone in the midst of the recent camp, watching them as they moved across the prairie toward the north. When they had disappeared in the distance, I turned for a last look upon the medicine-lodge, which was now the one conspicuous object upon the bare and desolate prairie, surrounded on every side by the smoking embers of the many lodge fires, whose owners had disappeared. In a few years the ancient customs and ceremonies of the Indians will have disappeared as completely.

WOLF SONG

Transposed from Graphophone Record by Arthur Nevin.

THE PASSING OF THE FUR-SEAL

WHATEVER may be the outcome of the effort of the United States to prevent the extinction of the fur-seal, it will always be a significant fact in the history of international and colonial politics that the Dominion of Canada for nearly eight years has been able to oppose successfully the interests of the United States, Great Britain, and Russia in the seal herds. The United States and Great Britain appeared to be reaching an agreement dictated by both commercial and humane considerations in 1888, but the Dominion government interfered in behalf of a few pelagic sealers, and negotiations were suspended. At that time Russia was desirous of obtaining for her herd the same protection it was hoped would be granted to the American herd. Here are three of the most powerful nations of the world restrained by a colony of one of the powers from doing not only what prudence suggests, but what humanity and good faith demand. There was never a finer example of the wrongs that may be perpetrated by an irresponsible community possessing national powers, but not having international obligations. Two powers, the United States and Russia, owning the islands on which the seals of the two herds breed, and where alone they can be hunted and killed with a proper regard for the preservation of the species, have leased the right to kill to private citizens, and they are in honor bound to protect the rights which they have granted. All the skins obtained either by pelagic or island fishing are dressed and dyed in London, so that the interests of citizens of England are identical with those of the United States and Russia.*

Opposed to the citizens of the United States and Russia who are regularly engaged in the business of seal-hunting under proper restrictions imposed by their governments, and who pay for the privilege, which they have the right to enjoy, are a few Canadian vessel-owners, with their masters and crews. In 1894 the British North American sealing fleet consisted of fifty-nine vessels; in 1895 it consisted of sixty-five vessels. It is unfortunate that citizens of the United States engage in pelagic sealing, but they have as an excuse the fact that the United States have agreed to an open season during which the seals may be slaughtered in Bering Sea and North Pacific Ocean. There are about half as many vessels in the sealing fleet of the United States as in the Canadian fleet. The commercial importance of pelagic sealing, and the injury that is inflicted by means of it on the lessees of the governments of the United States and Russia, may be judged from the fact that in 1894 142,000 skins were taken by the pelagic sealers, and only 15,033 on the Pribyloff Islands.

It is the intention of this paper to make clear the interests involved in the Bering Sea controversy, the inadequacy and injustice of the Paris award, the powerlessness under it of the executive branch of our government to guard the seals, and the manner in which Great Britain has shifted from one ground to another, until now

* Of 142,723 skins taken by pelagic sealers in 1894, 138,323 were dressed and dyed in London.

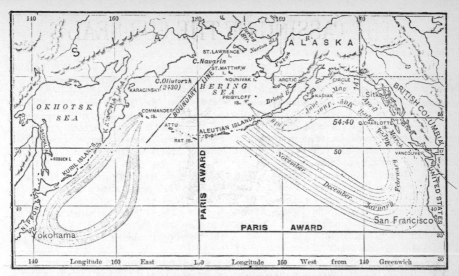

MAP SHOWING THE LOCATION OF THE AMERICAN HERD DURING EVERY MONTH IN THE YEAR.

her statesmen seem not only to have surrendered to the demands of the little fleet of British North American sealers, but to have determined, by inaction at least, to permit the destruction of the seals, thus ridding themselves of a controversy, and retaining for the empire the affectionate loyalty of such British subjects as are engaged in the ownership and navigation of some threescore schooners.

It was in 1887 that Mr. Bayard, then Secretary of State, wrote to the ministers of Great Britain, Russia, Japan, Germany, and Sweden and Norway, inviting their governments to enter into such an arrangement with the United States "as will prevent the citizens of either of these countries from killing seals in Bering Sea .... by such methods as at present are pursued, and which threaten the speedy extermination of those animals, and consequent serious loss to mankind." Lord Salisbury promptly acquiesced in the humane suggestion that the United States and Great Britain should adopt a code of regulations "for the preservation of the seals in Bering Sea." He thus admitted that the seals were in danger of destruction, and that rules and regulations, to be adopted and enforced by the two governments, were essential to their preservation. In February, 1888, Mr. Phelps, then our minister to Great Britain, informed Mr. Bayard that Lord Salisbury consented to a close season in Bering Sea for fur-

seals, to extend from April 15th to November 1st. The Russian ambassador asked that whatever regulations might be agreed upon for Bering Sea should be extended to that part of it in which the Commander Islands are situated, and also to the Sea of Okhotsk, in which Robben Island is situated. These islands, it should be explained, are the breeding-grounds for the Russian herd, as the Pribyloff Islands are the breeding-grounds for the American herd.

The two herds of seals have substantially the same habits. At the conclusion of the breeding season they set out on what is called their "long swim." The Pribyloff Islands are a little north of 55° latitude, near the coast of Alaska, and the Commander Islands are in about 54° 40′ latitude, near the coast of Kamchatka. The seals start south in October, the American herd swimming through the passes of the Aleutian Islands, southeastwardly, until they reach the latitude of 35° in the neighborhood of San Francisco. Then they turn eastward and then northward, and follow the trend of the coast until they reach the passes of the Aleutian Islands again, through which they swim to their breeding-ground. The Russian herd swim southerly to a point south of latitude 35°, turn in towards the Japanese coast in the vicinity of Yokohama, and then swim north along the coast of Nippon, past Yezo and the Kuril Islands, to the Commander Islands and Robben Island. The accompanying map shows the course of the two herds, and the position of the American herd during each month of its journey. While the two herds have been considered to be distinct, there is now reason to suppose that the slaughter of the seals on the eastern side of Bering Sea has driven American seals to the western side. The absolutely close season maintained in American waters during the existence of the *modus vivendi* led to the inauguration of pelagic sealing on the Russian and Japanese coasts. The Russian government's desire that its herd should receive whatever measure of protection might be accorded to the American herd will be understood from this explanation of seal habits.

It was agreed then, in the spring of 1888, by the statesmen who had taken part in the negotiations, that the close season ought to extend over all of Bering Sea, and over that part of the Okhotsk Sea in which is Robben Island, from April 15th to November 1st. It is true that the agreement was not official or formal, but it is clear that the minds of the correspondents had met. So interested was M. de Staël, the Russian ambassador at London, that he suggested that the powers should prohibit the importation into the protected area of "alcoholic drinks, fire-arms, gunpowder, and dynamite." The shooting of seals had begun to be general, and this method of destroying the animals has always been frowned upon, not merely because of the fact that the use of shot-guns facilitates pelagic sealing, but because many seals, especially those heavy with young, sink after they are shot, and thus the destruction of the species is greatly hastened. The position taken by M. de Staël in 1888 is especially interesting in view of the recent attitude of his government in the controversy.

In April, 1888, Lord Salisbury suggested that the close season should terminate on the 1st of October instead of the 1st of November, and Mr. Bayard suggested, in turn, the 15th of October as the date of termination, adding, however, "although, as I am now advised, the 1st of November would be safer."

Matters stood thus when, in June, 1888, Mr. White, our Secretary of Legation in London, informed Mr. Bayard that Lord Salisbury had received "a communication from the Canadian government stating that a memorandum on the subject would shortly be forwarded to London, and expressing the hope that, pending the arrival of that document, no further steps would be taken in the matter by her Majesty's government."

Negotiations were not resumed until 1890, when Mr. Blaine was Secretary of State. It is unnecessary for the purposes of the present article to follow the correspondence that took place between Secretary Blaine and Assistant-Secretary Wharton, on one side, and Sir Julian Pauncefote, speaking for Lord Salisbury, on the other side. Notwithstanding the devices that were attempted by each side, with a view of gaining a diplomatic advantage over the other, it was clear that the question in the minds of all who participated in the controversy, except of course the Dominion authorities, was one of humanity and good faith. It is probable that Lord Salisbury wished to go as far as he could for the protection of the seals from destruction without disappointing the pelagic sealers of Canada. The Dominion government had taken up the cause of these sealers, and was pushing it with energy. Its agents were in London, and they had the ear of the Premier. At any rate, in June, 1890, he denied that he had ever given to Mr. Phelps the assurance that he would agree to a close season lasting from the 15th of April to the 1st of November, and he was literally right. There was carried on at the same time a correspondence concerning the seizure of British sealers by the United States. The result of these negotiations was the establishment of the *modus vivendi*, which lasted for two years (1892 and 1893), and this was followed by the agreement between the two governments that the questions between them should be submitted to arbitration.

The result of the arbitration was the award made by the Paris Tribunal, August 15, 1893. The findings of the Tribunal on questions of right were adverse to the United States. Coming to the ethical question, as to the duty of the two governments to prevent the citizens of both from exterminating the seal, the Tribunal decided that the "concurrence of Great Britain is necessary to the establishment of regulations for the proper protection and preservation of the fur-seal in or habitually resorting to the Bering Sea." Nine articles were then adopted, embodying regulations, so far as rules could be prescribed by the Tribunal. These regulations were not self-operative. Operative regulations could be adopted only by the governments of the two countries concerned. The articles adopted by the Tribunal embodied the ends that were to be attained through the joint regulations to be agreed upon by the two countries. The means for protecting the seals were not adequate, and the British government did not exert itself in 1894 to make even those means effective.* During the season of 1895 it even declined to join in regulations similar to those agreed upon in 1894 for the proper enforcement of the regulations enacted by the Tribunal. The Tribunal settled nothing that had not been recognized as just by both parties, but when it was determined that the British Empire had discretion in the matter as to framing regulations to carry out the scope and intent of the award—regulations which had been enacted into law by both countries—the imperial government was at the mercy of the Dominion, and declined to exercise that discretion in the manner plainly demanded by the spirit of the award.

The articles forbade the killing of seals within sixty miles of the Pribyloff Islands, or in the American part of the North Pacific Ocean and Bering Sea north of the thirty-fifth degree, during the months of May, June, and July. From the 1st of August until the 1st of May licensed sealers might catch seals under the award of the Tribunal under certain conditions. Sailing-vessels alone were to be employed in the business; each vessel was to be provided with a special license, and was to fly a distinguishing flag; the number and character of the catch were to be noted in his log-book by the captain of each sealer, and the entries were to be communicated by each of the governments to the other at the end of each fishing season; the use of nets, fire-arms, and explosives was forbidden.

The main objection to these articles is that the closed season is not long enough, and that the prohibition of sealing within a zone of sixty miles is of very little value. In his first proposition, which was conveyed to Mr. Bayard February 25, 1888, Lord Salis-

bury suggested that the close season should extend from April 15th to November 1st. This was in answer to a proposition made by Mr. Bayard that there should be a close season extending from April 1st to November 1st. Subsequently Lord Salisbury suggested that October 1st would be late enough for the termination of the season, and Mr. Bayard expressed his willingness to accept October 15th as the date. It does not seem to have occurred to any one connected with the negotiations on either side during Mr. Cleveland's first administration that a close season extending from the 1st of May to the 1st of August would sufficiently "protect and preserve" the fur-seal of the North Pacific Ocean and Bering Sea. The Canadians, indeed, in 1890, persuaded Lord Salisbury to suggest a close season in May and June, and another in October, November, and December; but, as was long since discovered, the Canadians are more desirous to kill than to preserve the seal. As a matter of fact, under the award of the Tribunal, the pelagic sealers are able to follow the seals on their way home nearly to the passes of the Aleutian Islands, and to slaughter them in great numbers during August, September, and October, and especially when they are crowded into the passes on their way south. In this slaughter they use spears, which, experts say, are even more fatal in skilled hands than shot-guns.

The prohibited zone of sixty miles affords the seals very little protection. The Tribunal seems to have supposed that when the seals reach the breeding-grounds they remain on the islands or in the immediate vicinity until the time comes for the departure on their "long swim." This is far from being the truth. The seals leave the islands during the breeding season for rest and food, and they are often found sleeping or feeding at long distances from the islands, sometimes travelling two hundred miles from the breeding-grounds. It is during the breeding season and far outside of the zone of sixty miles that much of the slaughter goes on. It is true that Mr. Blaine, in a letter to Sir Julian Pauncefote, dated December 17, 1890, said, "The President will ask the government of Great Britain to agree to a distance of twenty marine leagues" (sixty miles); but that distance was suggested by Mr. Blaine on the theory that the close season should extend from the

* Only one British cruiser, H.M.S. *Pheasant*, patrolled Bering Sea in 1894. In 1895 the same vessel was the only one in Bering Sea.

15th of May to the 15th of October. In 1888 Mr. Bayard notified Mr. Phelps that "to prevent killing within a marine belt of forty or fifty miles from the islands" during a period extending from April 1st to November 1st "would be ineffectual as a preservative measure."

During the negotiations which were carried on by Mr. Blaine and Mr. Wharton from 1890 until the conclusion of the treaty of arbitration on May 7, 1892, Russia was silent. It will be recollected that in 1888 the Russian ambassador to Great Britain was so much interested in the subject and so much concerned as to the welfare of the Russian herd that he not only asked for a close season for his side of Bering Sea and for a part of the Okhotsk Sea, to correspond with that which might be agreed upon for the eastern side of Bering Sea, but he suggested that the regulations should forbid the importation of fire-arms within the protected area. At that time every commercial interest in the seal fisheries received the friendly countenance of its government. It was not until the predatory sealers of the Dominion interfered that the imperial government began to show signs of an indisposition to do anything for the preservation of the seals. It was then, too, that Russia became strangely silent.

Mr. Blaine did not underestimate the importance of an alliance between the two countries whose interests are common, because they own the breeding-grounds of the two herds. The representative of the Russian government then in charge of its legation at Washington was Baron Rosen. He supposed that Russia was of the mind that was expressed by her ambassador at London in 1888; and it was natural, in any event, that he should assume that the two countries would be glad to co-operate. The necessity of such co-operation was made more pressing because it was clear from the time that Mr. Bayard's efforts were checked by the interference of the Dominion that the imperial government did not propose to risk its influence with this important British colony by interfering with the Canadian pelagic sealers and poachers. In view of all this it is not strange that Baron Rosen should have assumed that a treaty of alliance would be gratifying to his government. He therefore entered into a negotiation with Mr. Blaine that resulted in an agreement between the two, which was formulated in a protocol. The agreement was that the two countries would act together for the protection of seal life, and to that end would prohibit any pelagic sealing in Bering Sea. The protocol was sent to St. Petersburg, but Baron Rosen never heard from it officially, and it was a long time before any word concerning it was received from Russia. Then our minister to Russia, on inquiring at the Russian Foreign Office as to the fate of the protocol, was told that the Czar's government would not think of becoming a party to any arrangement concerning the seal herds in Bering Sea without previous consultation with the British government. If this protocol had been followed by a treaty engaging the two powers to protect the seals by preventing all pelagic sealing in the waters of the Bering and Okhotsk seas, the question that has so long vexed the diplomatic representatives of the United States and Great Britain would now be settled, for it cannot be supposed that the British Empire would undertake to maintain what the two powers forbade. But a great change had come over Russia, for events had been happening in her diplomatic relations with Great Britain which made the maintenance of friendly relations with that power of the gravest importance. Russia's desire was cleverly taken advantage of by the British minister at St. Petersburg to effect a settlement of the seal-fisheries question on the west side of Bering Sea that has enured to British interests in negotiations with the United States; and for some years to come it is not likely that Russia can be induced to thwart England's purposes in Bering Sea. At first it was the situation in Central Asia and the question of the establishment of a buffer state between India and the Russian advance that caused the silent indifference of Russia to the peril of her seals and of the rights of her lessees. Now it is the situation in the far East and the doubt as to what relations shall be established between herself and Great Britain as a result of the defeat of China by Japan. Again it is the resurrection of the Eastern question as a consequence of the massacres in Armenia, and the possible interference with the Sultan's government by the Berlin treaty powers, or, if not by them, by England in union with Russia and France. The complications in Asia have deprived the United States of an alliance that is natural, and that was once supposed to be almost realized. Not only that, but, for the purpose of aiding the Dominion's case against this country, Great Britain has made apparent concessions to Russia in Bering Sea that are not concessions at all, while Russia has apparently been willing to throw at least her passive influence, not only against the United States, but against those who pay her for the privilege of hunting seals on the Commander Islands.

These negotiations between Great Britain and Russia were pending and were concluded while the Paris Tribunal was in session. The British government conceded to Russia a protected zone of ten miles along Russian shores and of thirty miles around the Commander and Robben islands. It was not a generous concession; indeed, it was far from adequate; but its willing acceptance by Russia greatly weakened the American case before the Paris Tribunal. If Russia accepted a protected zone of thirty miles around her rookeries, why should not the United States be content with a protected zone of sixty miles?

The answer to the question is that Russia's herd had been only recently invaded by pelagic sealers, that her seals had never been protected beyond the three-mile limit, partly because they had not been attacked, and that therefore the concession was a real gain. Above all, however, Russia felt but little interest in her fisheries, and was willing to accept any price that Great Britain offered to keep her in good-humor. As to Great Britain, the vessels of her Canadian subjects had been seized by Russian officials off the Commander Islands, and something had to be done not only to limit but to define their rights. By fixing this inadequate zone she obtained for the Canadians the right to kill Russian seals on the high seas. Moreover, she also gained a strong argument against the contention of the United States that a protected zone of sixty miles around the Pribyloff Islands would not be sufficient. How eager the home government was in this matter is shown by the fact that its representatives at St. Petersburg neglected, in their first arrangement with the Russian Foreign Office, to induce the latter to persuade the United States to become a party to the arrangement concerning the western waters of the Bering Sea. The consequence of this oversight was that American sealers had the right to hunt on the Russian side to the three-mile limit, while the Canadians were obliged to keep outside of the thirty-mile limit. While this did not make much difference to the Russians, owing to the comparatively small number of American sealers, the Canadian government protested in the following year, and when the arrangement was renewed the Czar's government agreed to procure the assent of the United States to the exclusion of American sealers from the thirty-mile zone.

In the mean time the award regulations of the Paris Tribunal were enacted into law, and further regulations were made by the United States and Great Britain for carrying out the articles of the award. By this time the United States stood alone. The indifference or defection of Russia had greatly aided the Canadians, and although the British government continued to profess a desire to do all in its power for the preservation of seal life, the influence of the Dominion sealers was dominant. It is clear that the enforcement of the inadequate rules laid down by the Tribunal depends entirely on the good faith and earnestness of the two governments upon which rests the duty of making the laws and rules for realizing the objects of the award.

If both nations had desired, regulations might have been adopted that would have rendered any evasion of the provisions of the award at least difficult, but such regulations, although agreed to in 1894, were refused by Great Britain for the season of 1895. This was not the fault of the officers of the United States who were charged with the duty of helping to frame the regulations. The award forbade merely the use of fire-arms. It did not forbid the possession of them, nor did it make such possession by a vessel navigating the treaty waters presumptive evidence of intended illegal use. Such a presumption is necessary for the enforcement of the law against the use of fire-arms, and it has always been recognized as an essential provision of protective acts. Such a presumption was promptly enacted into law by Congress, but this law applies only to American citizens. The British act of 1891 for the enforcement of the *modus vivendi* provided as follows:

"If a British ship is found within Bering Sea having on board thereof fishing or shooting implements, or seal-skins, or bodies of seals, it shall lie on the owner or master of such ship to prove that the ship was not used or employed in contravention of this act."

The British act of 1894 for the enforcement of the Paris award omitted this provision, although the necessity of such a rule of evidence was recognized in the British act of 1893, which was passed for the enforcement of the agreement with Russia, and in which the provision of the act of 1891 was incorporated. This act repealed the act of 1891, and was made to apply to the American as well as to the Russian side of the Bering Sea. This rule of evidence was in existence, therefore, when the Tribunal made its award, and it must be presumed that when the arbitrators laid down the rule that nets, firearms, and explosives should not be employed, they did so with the understanding that the existing laws prescribing this rule of evidence would remain in force, for it was known then as well as it is known now that the use of fire-arms for killing the seals cannot be prevented if sealers are permitted to carry such weapons. The language of the award, however, enabled the British government to insist on changing the rule of evidence, while the President and his advisers were powerless. The effective power which the United States possessed over Canadian sealers was that which was obtained through the agreement with the British government in the form of joint regulations, and if the British government declined to prevent the use of fire-arms by making their possession *prima facie* evidence of illegal intent, the United States, in loyalty to the arbitration to which it had submitted, was obliged to yield. But the British government was not earnestly desirous of preventing pelagic sealing, or of attaining the objects which the Paris Tribunal declared to be desirable. This was shown by its eagerness to avail itself of the language of the award to change a rule of evidence, which it had itself declared to be essential by embodying it in two acts of Parliament. Since this refusal, by an act passed June 26, 1895, Great Britain has also changed the rule as it affects the arrangement with Russia. For more than a year the possession of fire-arms by a Canadian sealer in the Russian zone was presumptive evidence of an intention to shoot seal, while on the American side there was no such presumption, although there was no such agreement between Russia and Great Britain as to the shooting of seals as there was and is between the United States and Great Britain. During the season of 1895 there was no such presumption as to sealers navigating either side of Bering Sea, except American sealers. The Congress of the United States, intent on making the regulations of the Paris Tribunal effective, and determined to carry out the objects of the award, prescribed the rule of evidence in the act of April 6, 1894, which is the American act for the enforcement of the award. Therefore, before the Paris Tribunal made its rules for the purpose of preserving the fur-seal, the same rule of evidence applied to both American and British vessels. The possession of forbidden weapons was presumed to indicate an intent to use them.

Since the award was made this presumption has applied to American sealers only. The British government insisted that Canadian sealers should not be put to the necessity of proving that their possession of arms was innocent in the view of the law and of the spirit of the award. This meant that Canadian vessels were to be permitted to use fire-arms within the protected area; for it is almost impossible, in the absence of the presumption, to convict a sealer of the actual use of his arms for killing seal. Under the American rule the sealer must prove that he did not kill seal with the fire-arms on board his vessel; under the British law the sealer cannot be convicted unless the government can prove that the fire-arms were used to kill the seals. There could be no better evidence than this deliberate change of the rule of evidence that the British government's intention was to secure for the Canadian sealers the right to use fire-arms for the killing of seal, and to that extent to violate the spirit and purpose of the Paris award. In further support of this conclusion we have the case of the British schooner *Wanderer*, which was seized on the charge of shooting seals. Under the regulations of 1894 her arms had been sealed by an officer of the United States. When she was subsequently searched by the captain of one of the American patrol fleet, an unsealed shot-gun and other evidences of shooting were discovered. She was taken and turned over to an officer of the British navy. She and her captain should have been tried by a court of admiralty, but she was released without any trial whatever by the British Admiral Stephenson. A similar course was taken by the British naval authorities with reference to the sealer *Favorite*. It has been clear from the first that the British government has changed its mind since Lord Salisbury assented to the proposition made by Mr. Bayard in 1887, and that, the award of the Paris Tribunal to the contrary notwithstanding, nothing will be done by the imperial power to prevent the pelagic sealers of the colony from murdering the seals on the high seas at their pleasure.

The device of sealing prohibited arms was a principal feature of the regulations of 1894. It applied both to licensed sealers and unlicensed vessels. It was intended to facilitate the enforcement of the regulations, and to protect the captains of vessels navigating the North Pacific and Bering Sea from undue detention. It was agreed that when a vessel was in the prohibited zone, or in the other parts of the sea during the prohibited season, or if the vessel were not a licensed sealer, but was navigating these waters, the arms whose use was forbidden might be officially sealed. If the seals were broken, the presumption that the arms had been used illegally was strengthened. If they were not broken, the vessel was not unduly detained. This provision was of great importance both to innocent vessel-masters and to the officers of the navy and of the revenue marine who were charged with the task of protecting the seal herds from unlawful invasion and attack. The British government declines to continue this regulation.

In order to enforce the regulations of 1894, the British government sent only one vessel, the *Pheasant*, to Bering Sea for patrol duty, although the majority of the vessels employed in pelagic sealing were Canadian. The President of the United States sent a fleet of twelve vessels. Could anything more clearly indicate British indifference to the enforcement of the Paris award?

Another bit of evidence that the imperial government has no intention of aiding the government of the United States to prevent pelagic sealing and to preserve the fur-seal is its refusal to accept the recommendatory declaration signed in Paris by Baron Courcel, Justice Harlan, and Senator Morgan. The declaration was as follows:

"In view of the critical condition to which it appears certain that the race of fur-seals is now reduced, in consequence of circumstances not fully known, the arbitrators think fit to recommend both governments to come to an understanding in order to prohibit any killing of fur seals, either on land or at sea, for a period of two or three years, or at least one year, subject to such exceptions as the two governments may think proper to admit of. Such a measure might be recurred to at occasional intervals if found beneficial."

The evils of the situation have been called to the attention of the British government, and they are as well understood at London as they are at Washington. It has been shown that the change in the rule of evidence as to the inference to be drawn from the possession of forbidden arms during the close season, or in prohibited waters, nullifies the agreement that fire-arms shall not be used, but the British government not only refuses to restore the presumption that was once established by its laws, but in June, 1895, it changed the rule also as to sealers in Russian and Japanese waters.

Our government is not represented before the tribunals which try the British sealers that are seized by American cruisers for violation of the law. Therefore there is no one to watch and defend American rights in what we now know to be, so far as this question is concerned, an unfriendly jurisdiction.

All the regulations requested by the United States are essential for the proper carrying out of the Paris award, and the fact that the British government has failed or refused to meet our own government must be accepted as evidence that the Canadian pelagic sealers have succeeded in forcing it to abandon the attempt to prevent the destruction of the fur-seal by Dominion sealers. With American sealers it is different, and it is reported that during the season of 1895 the British cruiser devoted all its energies to preventing violations of the act of Congress by vessels from this country, notwithstanding the fact that the Canadian sealers outnumbered our own at least two to one.

Not only have the suggestions looking

to the extension of the award and to the cure of its demonstrated inadequacies been negatived by the British government, but in May, 1895, after the season had begun, this government was notified that even the insufficient regulations of 1894 would not be renewed. This refusal was based on the ground that the award did not prohibit the possession of fire-arms by sealers, and therefore the British government declined to enter into an arrangement which would make it well for Canadian vessels to secure the sealing of their arms. This decision by the home government was received with great joy in the Dominion, for it enormously facilitated the use of fire-arms in the killing of seals.

The result of the Paris award has been disastrous to the seals and to the sealing industry. Before the refusal of the British government to renew the regulations of 1894 the subject had been considered in Congress. In answer to a resolution introduced into the House of Representatives by Mr. Dingley of Maine, Secretary Carlisle stated that from the statistics of the pelagic catch of 1894 "it becomes evident that during the present season there has been an unprecedented increase over preceding years in the number of seals killed by pelagic sealers, both in American and Asiatic waters. This increase has caused an alarming decrease in the number of seals on the islands, as hereinafter explained.... The alarming increase in the number of seals killed by pelagic sealers.... emphasizes the conclusion expressed in my annual report to Congress that long before the expiration of the five years, when the regulations enacted by the Tribunal of Arbitration are to be submitted to the respective governments for re-examination, the fur-seal will have been practically exterminated."

Bills were introduced in both Houses of Congress contemplating the destruction of all seals by the government, and thereby a determination of the question. On one of these bills, that introduced by Hon. William L. Wilson, the Ways and Means Committee made an interesting report. This bill provided that the President should invite the appointment of a joint commission by the United States, Great Britain, Russia, and Japan, and an arrangement for a *modus vivendi* pending the proposed investigation. In the event of a refusal by Great Britain

to agree to the *modus vivendi*, and to make proper regulations to carry it out, the Secretary of the Treasury was to be authorized to arrange for the killing of the seals as they visited the Pribyloff Islands. The bill was passed by the House of Representatives, and if it had been permitted to become a law, it might have compelled the Dominion to consent that Great Britain should change her course; for if the section directing the killing of the seals as they visited the islands had been executed, the quarry of the Canadians would have been destroyed, and the United States would have reaped the advantage. Rather than that, Canada would have preferred the enforcement of the Paris award. But when the bill reached the Senate its passage was prevented by the objection of Senator Morgan, who had been one of the arbitrators. This conduct on his part was especially strange, because he had devoted his time and his energies to insisting that the administration was not doing all that it might do to enforce the award, although the administration was really doing all that was possible in view of the regulations which had been made by the Tribunal.

So much for the effort of Congress to come to the aid of the executive department of the government. In its report on the Wilson bill the Ways and Means Committee presented tables showing the effect of pelagic sealing on the catch.

It appears from these tables that the annual pelagic catch on both sides of the Pacific Ocean increased since 1890 from 51,814 to 142,000 in 1894, and that the Pribyloff Islands catch decreased from 104,521 in 1886 to 15,033 in 1894. It also appears that the destruction of the Russian seals now exceeds that of the American seals, and that the pelagic catch in Asian waters has increased from 5847 in 1891 to 58,621 in 1894. In the season of 1895 the catch fell off. This was because of perceptible diminution in the herds. It is evident that the seals have already begun to disappear. The legitimate catch on the Commander Islands for 1895 was 17,700, as against 27,300 in 1894. The catch on the Pribyloff Islands was about 15,000.

The pelagic catch was as follows:

Japanese coast	35,000
American northwest coast, about	12,000
Bering Sea	50,000
Total	97,000

In 1894 the pelagic catch was 142,000.

The commercial interests are succumbing to the pelagic sealer, and it is apparent that the seal is doomed unless Great Britain and Russia can be persuaded to defend the interests of their citizens against the determination of Canadians to kill off the seals as rapidly as possible. The interests of this country cannot be protected under the Paris award unless Great Britain not only co-operates, but agrees that the findings shall be extended, and the regulations made more effective than they can be if the language of the award is strictly adhered to. At present, however, Great Britain is yielding to the malign influence of the Dominion, and, so yielding, has practically defeated the conclusions of the arbitration which she proposed and to which she submitted. Eight years ago Lord Salisbury was inclined to agree to effective regulations before the arbitration and before any law had been enacted by the respective governments, while now the British government is opposed to regulations under the law passed to enforce the award, absolutely necessary to prevent Canadians from exterminating the seals. Russia has also in the mean time become indifferent to her herd or to the interests of her lessees, because the Czar has larger questions to settle with her Majesty's government. All sealing ought to be stopped for at least three years, and after that the close season ought to be extended, but this cannot be accomplished under the Paris award. Now, as formerly, Great Britain or Russia is a necessary ally of the United States if the seals are to be preserved; but Great Britain refuses to carry out the findings of the Tribunal, while Russia is preoccupied with her Eastern questions.

THE THREE TETONS

"IT is perfectly absurd for you to keep going to Europe in this way, summer after summer," remarked the Maiden, with the emphasis and exaggeration peculiar to younger sisters.

"We have only been twice," murmured the married sister, apologetically.

"But once is enough. That is, if you haven't seen Colorado, and the Yellowstone, and Tacoma, and Alaska, and Yosemite. Of course one wants to go once—"

"I should think so," murmured Mrs. Thayer.

"And of course, if you want art, or history, or architecture, or associations, you must go to Europe for them. If you were going for the winter, or to study anything, I could understand it. But you are not. You are going only for the summer and for scenery. And you will go straight to that miserable little Tyrol"—

"Miserable little Tyrol!" exclaimed Mrs. Thayer, in dismay.

—"When you might go to the Yellowstone."

"Do you really mean, Mabel, that if you were I"—Mrs. Thayer here grasped faintly for the married dignity which was her only hope in the struggle—"you would give up the Tyrol for the Yellowstone?"

"Listen," said the Maiden. Opening her latest guide-book, she read something to the effect that the best of the Rhine, the Hudson, and the Saguenay, the whole of Switzerland, the Pyramids of Egypt, Lake Maggiore, and the Royal Gorge of the Arkansas combined would not begin to compare with the glories of the National Park on the Yellowstone.

"You can't believe that everything in a guide-book is true."

"But if only a third of it is true, it is enough, as Mercutio would say." The Maiden closed her book, and left the room with dignity.

Mrs. Thayer continued her packing; continued it, indeed, with an increased energy, which seemed to imply that nothing should ever induce her to desert the Tyrol. Still, it was disconcerting. Part of the pleasure of going to Europe is in being looked upon as a privileged creature by one's envying friends; and to be actually looked down upon because one was going to the Tyrol was really quite unendurable. So it was with a little pat of added fierceness that the lady put more and more "things" into her trunk, and if the luggage were to have been labelled at all, she would certainly have fastened a tag to it marked very conspicuously, "Tyrol."

Nevertheless, in the seclusion of her own chamber that night, she might have been heard to say to her husband, with decision, "Henry, I think it is very foolish for you to insist on going to Europe in this way, summer after summer."

"We have only been twice," murmured Henry, in some astonishment.

"But once is enough. That is, until we have seen something of our own country. Of course one wants to go once—"

"I have noticed that one did," murmured the Imperturbable.

"And of course, if you want art, or history, or associations, or architecture, you must go to Europe for them. Or if you want to study something. But we are only going for the summer, and to see scenery, and I don't suppose any scenery in Europe can compare with what there is in the Northwest. The guidebooks say—"

"My dear, you surely don't believe all the guide-books say to be true."

"If only an eighth of it is true, we ought to see it," said Mrs. Thayer, with great decision.

So it happened that at the breakfast table Mrs. Thayer, known henceforth in these pages as the Convert, announced that as Henry was so anxious to go to the Yellowstone, she had consented to give up the Tyrol, Mr. Thayer having merely stipulated that, for sacrificing his ocean voyage, he would be allowed to take the party as far as St. Paul by way of the Great Lakes.

At St. Paul they would meet the Ruthvens, who should come up from their ranch to join the party—Anna and Donald Ruthven, better known to their immediate friends as the Romantic and the Man of Sense. It had been harder to persuade the Man of Sense to give up his ranch than to induce the Imperturbable to sacrifice his trip to Europe; but the Romantic had, of course, carried the day at last, and the afternoon of the 9th of August found them all dining merrily in the dining car of the Northern Pacific, as the long train swept slowly out of St. Paul.

"Oh, Mabel, look at the wind on that field of grain! It is perfectly lovely!" exclaimed the Convert.

"I know it," said the Maiden, without, however, lifting her eyes from her omelet and hot rolls. "But don't call my attention to it. Papa said if I wrote anything more in my letters about the 'waving wheat fields of Dakota,' or that fish that people are always catching in a cold river at the Yellowstone and cooking in a hot one without taking it off the hook, or the egg that they are forever boiling in a geyser, he should stop corresponding with me; and papa's letters, you know, are valuable. He said I was only to mention it in case I found that we could catch and boil the fish in the same river."

At four o'clock that afternoon they entered the Bad Lands of the Little Missouri. Whist and magazines were discarded, and for two or three hours no other amusement was necessary than to look from the car windows. Almost in a few minutes, as it seemed, they had passed from broad level tracts like the Kansas prairies to plains dotted so thickly with the little low round hills known as buttes that the comparison of a checker-board covered with checkers was the first to suggest itself. Sometimes the buttes rose higher in fantastic pinnacles and grotesque turrets, but as a rule they were little and low and round, owing their impressiveness not to what they were, but to the testimony that they bore to the tremendous agencies which had made them what they were. For these were no soft grass-grown hills, neither were they splendid masses of great rock. Their hardness and roughness were more terrible than those of rock, as a human face wrinkled and scarred with wounds is more terrible than one cut out

MINERVA TERRACE.

of stone. For these had been mounds of beautiful soft gray or blue clay, with streaks of innocent lignite, till terrific pressure or centuries of consuming heat had made them what they are—masses of conglomerate hard as rock, but many, colored as a painted wall, wearing still the sign of their constant martyrdom in rings of pale blue fire showing half-way up at the surface, the sure signal that the pale blue clay that is still pale shall yield at last, though it take ten thousand years, to the silent force that is eating its heart out, and has left its sides worn and wrinkled with the slow agony.

As they left the cars at Livingston the heat in the valley was intense. Only three hours more, and they would be in the marvellous precincts of the Park.

Patience! The Maiden kept repeating it softly to herself, for her heart was heavy with unspoken dread. She knew her guide-book; she knew that this approach to the Park from Livingston was counted one of the wonders of the trip. She knew that they were passing through the "Gate to the Mountains," and that this was the lower cañon of the Yellowstone. But she had been through Colorado, and refused to accept this for a cañon. Fortunately the Convert had never been to Colorado. The Maiden noticed, with a sense of relief, that her sister was really quite delighted with the scene, and was

convinced that this was a cañon. She saw her listening with awe to the familiar fact that mountains which looked in the translucent atmosphere as if you could reach them in a few minutes were really ten or twelve miles away. It was much to be thankful for that the Convert had nothing but the Tyrol with which to compare this first cañon of the Yellowstone; but for her, who had seen Colorado, ah! what should she do if the Yellowstone were not so fine, after all, as the Royal Gorge and Mosquito Pass and Clear Creek Cañon and the tiny Green Lake at Georgetown?

"Are you a coupon, sir?" asked a quiet voice as they stepped from the cars at Cinnabar.

"No."

"Would you like my team, then?"

"Yes."

It was one of those inspirations which sometimes do not deceive the impulsive traveller. Concord coaches with inviting outside seats stood about, and the Convert was gazing at them rather longingly, with the reminiscences they suggested of jolly times in her youth at the White Mountains. But the Man of Sense knew a man when he saw one. Any one so unlike a New York hackman as this quiet fellow with a team not intended to interfere with the "coupons" was a person to be cultivated. Into his three-seated vehicle they stepped at once.

The road was not yet reassuring. It was dull, dusty, glaring, and disappointing. It brightened a little as they entered the Park; there began to be pretty streams tumbling gracefully over rather fine rocks, with occasionally a nice little view or picturesque wall of stone. But the heart of the Maiden confessed to itself that they need not have come two or three thousand miles to see that; it was quite as pretty up at the dear little White Hills in New Hampshire, and a thousand times lovelier in Colorado!

On they crept; up the steep, narrow road, through cold, dull woods of uninteresting dead trees. Really it was almost horrid!

Then suddenly, without an instant's warning, they swept into a magnificent natural plaza. Mountains hemmed it in, rising one above another, and giving glimpses through the rifts between them of those rare and glorious views which are not frequent in the Park, but which do exist, though the traveller, bewildered with greater and finer wonders, reaches a point when he takes a mere "view" as a matter of course, hardly noticed, and passed over in his diary without comment. Mountains to right of them, mountains in front of them, mountains behind them, though the plaza was itself so high and so open that there was no stifling sense of being shut in by mountains, as there is at the Profile House in New Hampshire, for instance; and to the left of them—what?

Apparently a sheeted mountain, ready for burial. Between the dark hills rising like sentinels around it a plateau of many acres, with great terraces leading up to it, lay covered, not with snow, but with something white as snow, thrown alike over plateau and terrace; cold, spectral, weirdly silent in the faint dusk just lit by a young moon. It was not dead; Vesuvius itself were hardly more alive; for this was the mountain of the Mammoth Hot Springs, with a fiery and living torture at its heart and in all its veins.

"You mean," said the Man of Sense, when the Romantic had reached this stage of explanation, "that what looks like ice, a frozen Niagara, is really rock, built up of a deposit chiefly calcareous, taken up in solution by the hot water forcing its way to the surface through cretaceous strata, and then solidified by evaporation."

"Yes," said the Romantic, meekly, "that is what I meant."

"And you were quite right, my dear. That is exactly what it is."

In another moment they were at the steps of the hotel, gazing curiously at the long and wide veranda, eloquent of at least one place left in the United States where it is still possible to "rough it." Complete emancipation from Worth spoke in the flannel dresses of the ladies, the booted, belted, and spurred appearance of the gentlemen, the broad sombreros of the waiting guides. Piazza chairs there were in abundance, but nobody seemed to be occupying them. No one wanted to rest. This was no weary waiting-place for tired chaperons watching for the young people to come back from their "good times." The chaperons themselves were having the "good times." Pacing the piazza, leaning over the railing to gaze at the newcomers, chatting in eager groups full of excitement over to-day's excursion or to-morrow's plans, all was gay alertness, the cheerful restlessness of people whose veins are alive with keen vitality.

Nor was the charm lost when they stepped within. The immense cool spaces of the corridors, the walls thickly studded with horns of the elk and deer and with heads of the buffalo and mountain sheep, the hard floors on which lynx, wild-cat, and bear, stuffed, but singularly life-like, seemed to be running about at ease—all spoke of strange and new experience.

"Oh, Anna," exclaimed the Maiden, in a burst of relief from her overcharged heart, "the uniqueness has begun!"

"I notice," said the Man of Sense, "a pleasing absence of band, and of halls for dancing. It argues well for a place where people are having too good a time in other ways to care to dance."

Pleasant little parlors there were, but the great corridors upstairs, fitted up with fireplaces and easy-chairs and tables, were evidently the favorite lounging-places, if indeed at the Yellowstone any one ever wanted to lounge.

"I always supposed it was the Hot Springs that were mammoth—didn't you?—but it seems it's the bed-rooms," said the Convert, as she was ushered into a corner chamber with four immense windows, and a ceiling so high that, as the Man of Sense remarked, any angels watching over their slumbers would be too far away for practical assistance in case of burglars.

"You are right, my dear, as you always are," said the Man of Sense, later, as they descended to the supper-room. "It is evidently the bed-rooms that are mammoth, not the chops." He looked ruefully at the morsel of mutton which was supposed to raise canned peaches and very thin cake to the dignity of "supper."

They would stay here another day, for they knew that the great springs and the terraces, known at the hotel as the "Formation," were well worth being more than gazed at from the piazza. The gentlemen after supper sauntered to the office to study into the best

THE "FORMATION."

methods of travelling through the Park when they should be ready to leave the springs, and the ladies lingered in the halls, and wandered out on the piazzas, amused beyond measure at what the Maiden had well described as the "uniqueness" of the Mammoth Hot Springs as a summer hotel.

The gentlemen soon returned, but with puzzled brows. It seemed that with all their much study-ing of guide-books they had come quite unprepared for the genuine emergency.

"Did you know that the upper geyser basin is *fifty-six miles* from here, and that the lake is over seventy and the falls and the cañon nearly seventy miles?"

"Mercy, no!" exclaimed the ladies.

"And that if we go by the stage route we shall be expected to make the whole of that fifty-six miles to the upper geysers in one day? To think that we gave up going out of the Park by way of Beaver Cañon, because they said it would be a hundred miles' staging that we should have to do in two days, only to get here and find that fifty miles' staging a day is the average expected of us all through the Park!"

"Fortunately, though, we are not what Phillips calls 'coupons,'" added the Man of Sense. "Their tickets allow them five days in the Park, which sounds beautifully when you are in New York. But the trip in the cars from Livingston to Cinnabar is counted as one of the days; they get here at the springs about seven o'clock of that day, when it is too dark to do anything but look at the Formation from the piazza, and they leave after a half-past-six breakfast the next morning for that awful fifty-six miles by stage to the upper geysers. They get there about seven o'clock at night, and leave again right after breakfast the next morning for the forty-mile trip to the falls. They can't go to the lake at all, for there is no accommodation there for the night, and it is too long a jaunt for one day even to these inveterate stages. So they have a little longer respite than usual at the falls; but they leave at eleven o'clock to spend the whole of their last two precious days in getting back where they started from, over precisely the same road!"

"The life of a 'coupon' cannot be worth living," murmured the Imperturbable, with solemnity.

"Under these circumstances," announced the Man of Resources, "we think of hiring our own private team to go as we please."

"Of course," exclaimed the ladies.

"But even then there are difficulties. There are only four hotels in the Park after we leave here, and one of these we shall have to reach every night at all hazards. By paying our four dollars a day at these hotels we shall be better off than the unfortunate 'coupons' in being able to stay at each place as long as we please; but we can't go to the lake any better than they can."

"So with this combination of circumstances," continued the Man of Resources, "what do you say to providing ourselves with a complete outfit, and camping out?"

"Perfectly lovely!" exclaimed the ladies.

It can do no possible harm to tell the whole truth about the Yellowstone, and to acknowledge that while the great Park contains certainly the seven wonders of the world in natural magnificence, the great spaces between these different wonders are immense distances of utterly uninteresting scenery, which one traverses over roads covered with a white blinding dust which is very nearly intolerable. It is true that the hot springs, and the geysers, and the Paint Pots, and the falls, and the cañon, and the lake, and the many-colored pools, are worth any amount of trouble in getting to them; but it is also true that they are worth taking any amount of trouble to lessen the trouble; and since it could all be removed by so simple a thing as a few rails and a locomotive, it is certainly a pity that a state of things should be left existing which prevents the very young, the very old, the very fastidious, or the very weak, from enjoying the real wonders of such a journey.

In the mean time, however, there is no railway, and our friends, as the next best thing, would hire special teams and camp out. The Man of Sense at once hurried back to the office, and could be heard giving royal orders for a princely retinue of teams, saddle-horses, guides, cooks, tents, and supplies, till he was arrested by a fiery glance from the Parsimonious.

"I have been talking with Phillips," she announced. "He has an outfit, and will let us have two four-horse teams and two saddle-horses, a cook, two wall tents, with mattresses and all utensils, for twenty-five dollars a day."

"Bravo, Romantic!"

"You know how much we liked him when he drove us up from Cinnabar. I am inclined to trust him because he said, frankly, when we asked him how he thought we should like camping out, that the ladies of the last party didn't like it at all. And he thinks we could lay in enough supplies to last us ten days for seventy-five dollars. That would be three hundred and twenty-five dollars in all for ten days, or six dollars and fifty cents per day apiece."

"Most noble lady!"

"If we went as the 'coupons' do, it would cost us nine dollars per day apiece

A PACK TRAIN.

—five for staging, and four for hotels. Only," she confessed, with a sigh, "we shall have to stay more days going our way."

"But we shall have ten days in the Park, and ever so much more fun, for only twenty dollars apiece more than we should have to pay for five days and precious little fun on the regular routes."

"It is done," said the Man of Sense.

"And the seventy-five dollars for supplies," added the Maiden, "will include beer and a dog."

"So that if we are lost on any of the alpine solitudes which you insist exist in the Park, we can eat dog?"

That night they slept the sleep of the just, waking to a cloudless morning for their tramp over the Formation.

Phillips being busy with preparations for camping, Joseph was pressed into service as guide. It was very cool in the corridors of the hotel, but a single step from the piazza proved their light satteen travelling dresses more comfortable than the blue flannel gowns still waiting for the reputed frost of the Yellowstone. Colored glasses were necessary to shield the eyes from the intense glare in the sunlight of the snowy terraces, dropping one after another for two miles from the dark pine woods above and around them, like a series of beautiful frozen cascades.

"I notice there is only one man who has the courage for figures," said the Man of Sense, referring to his guide-books as they crossed the white plateau at the base of the extinct springs, and paused at the foot of Old Liberty Cap, the cone of an extinct geyser, towering fifty feet into the air. "He seems to know all about it, and declares that it took just fifty-four centuries to build up this thing."

"I can tell you who *he* is," said the knowing Joseph, with a laugh. "He's the man that tells you the Boiling River puts fifty thousand barrels of hot water into the Gardiner every twenty-four hours. I've often told him he'd oughter have let us know when he was going to measure it."

"'Any estimate of the age of the lower terrace would be purely conjectural,'" read the Man of Sense from another guide-book. "Still, I suppose there is no doubt about its being a matter of centuries. In that case, how soon do they expect to finish repairing the Devil's Thumb?"

For they had walked over to the smaller column, which was not only extinct, but crumbling with age and decrepitude. Art was endeavoring to assist nature, and repair the waste by bringing water from the hot springs just above in wooden troughs, letting it trickle down the sides of the cone and evaporate, to leave its snowy deposit to repair the ravages of time.

"Well, that feller that knows so much about the figgers," explained Joseph, "says the Orange Geyser builds a foot in a century. And he says the hot springs will deposit a sixteenth of an inch in four days. All I know about it is that I can put a beer bottle under some of the falling water, and turn it round once or twice, and have it beautifully coated over, with a white crust that won't crumble, in a day or two."

"Question: if you can coat a beer bottle in a day or two, how long will it take to build a geyser cone? Come, Mabel, you were last at your books."

"Fifty-four centuries," answered the Maiden, promptly.

"Correct. You may go up to the head;" and the Imperturbable pointed to the upper terrace towering above them.

It was not at all a steep climb, but they had to be wary about stepping into the little rills of hot water trickling down from the upper springs.

"What is that dust?" exclaimed the Convert, suddenly. "I never saw dust rising from ice before."

"Well, marm," said the smiling Joseph, "in the first place, 'tain't dust; and in the next place, 'tain't ice. The dust is steam, and the ice is formation."

"Of course," said the Convert. "I ought to have known. But I can't divest myself of the idea that all this white rock is arctic snow."

"Well, I don't know," said the Imperturbable; "this isn't exactly what I should call arctic."

He had been, with the Maiden, the first to reach the top, and was gazing into the depths of the first of the Mammoth Hot Springs. The wind had blown toward him a sudden whiff of the hot sulphurous steam, and he had stepped back quickly, only to find that he had stumbled into one of the innocent-looking rills, that was decidedly warm even through his boot.

But what a magnificent sight it was! The whole snowy mass that had looked cold and silent under the pale moon the night before was now glowing, gleaming,

pulsating with life under the morning sun. For perhaps a hundred acres the white surface was studded with brilliant pools, set like jewels, clear as diamonds, lovelier in color than opals, in rims of fretted frost delicate as lace and firm as marble. Over these coralline edges trickles softly the gentle overflow of the lovely lakes, falling, falling, tremulously and without a sound, over the fluted reed-like columns of the terraces below, only to leave them harder than they were before.

"Isn't it incredible," said the Man of Sense, "that water so particularly clear should hold anything in solution so particularly hard?"

"I don't know," murmured the Imperturbable, dreamily. "It's like the careless remark of a woman who has packed her trunks for Europe that *some time* she would like to go to the Yellowstone; it sounds remarkably simple, but you will find before long that there is an adamantine purpose at the bottom of it."

They had reached by this time the curious little lake with hot springs bubbling up on one side of it, so that by choosing your spot you could have a bath at any temperature you pleased.

"Them as likes their bath hot goes in on the left," explained the intelligent Joseph, "and them as likes it cold goes in on the right, and them as likes it middlin' goes in in the middle."

They looked patiently at all the curiosities which Joseph insisted upon their seeing in the woods, but were glad to emerge at another part of the terraces, where the view seemed even finer than before. Nothing but the warm bright air about them served to remind them that it was not winter. Even the exquisite coloring of the water, a lovely robin's-egg blue, and the almost gorgeous coloring of the terraces where part of the deposit had formed in columns or streaks of the richest orange and red, or of the daintiest pink or creamy yellow, failed to detract from the general effect of acres upon acres of snow and ice.

It seemed almost as if in this vast area every square inch was worth bending down to examine. They took a last lingering look at Cleopatra's Bowl, and then began the easy descent. How softly and slowly these noiseless little rills, not in the least like restless, turbulent cascades, slip over the rim of their beautiful basins and down the fluted walls of the terraces, may be judged from the fact that Joseph told them they could only go down the way they were descending, because the wind that day was blowing the overflow toward the other side.

"Ah!" said the Maiden, with a happy sigh; "it has been like going to Pompeii and Venice and the Alps and the Milan Cathedral and the arctic regions all in one morning."

Half past nine the next morning! The unfortunate "coupons" had breakfasted three hours before, and had whirled away on their mad career through the Park to reach the upper geysers before dark, without having seen anything more of the Formation than is visible from the hotel piazza. But the Man of Sense had decided that his party should camp for the night where the "coupons" merely dined; so there was no hurry for them about starting, and they had indulged in a leisurely and quiet breakfast.

"Leisurely and quiet are good adjectives," comments the Imperturbable, looking over my shoulder. "They seem to express a good deal, and yet they don't tell anything. It was leisurely, because even the hard-hearted waiter took pity on my piece of steak this morning, and offered to get me another, for which I had to wait; and it was quiet, because I had discovered that nothing was gained by making a row."

Immediately afterward they were summoned to the piazza. The caravan was ready, and Phillips wished the comments of his patrons before starting the team with supplies ahead, that luncheon might be ready for the party wherever they might decide to take their "nooning."

The Romantic and the Maiden were in ecstasies. It is true the noble steeds were not exactly champing their bits with impatience to be off, nor was there anything princely in the general appearance of the retinue. There was, indeed, a somewhat striking likeness to a prairie schooner about each of the teams, and the saddlehorses presented every guarantee that they would be "safe." But it was all redolent of fun and freedom, and "good times." It was very complete. Straps and buckles and little bags and boxes were fastened to the wagons for every conceivable necessity. The camera was slung neatly to the canvas roof, the lantern hung bewitchingly over the canvas for the tents, beer peeped from under the driver's seat, and Bob was wagging his tail in his eagerness to start.

"All right, Phillips," was the final verdict, and with a wave of his hand, and the royal edict to the cook, "Lunch on the Gardiner; we'll be there by one o'clock," Phillips dismissed the vehicle of tents and supplies, while the ladies went in to finish packing the trunks to be left behind, and the travelling bags to be taken with them.

In another hour they too were ready to start. Nothing daunted their enthusiasm, for they had confidence in Phillips.

The start was certainly a great success. The day was heavenly; the roads for a few miles are exceedingly good, especially as you sweep through the grand and impressive "Golden Gate," and the fine white dust and glare had not as yet become intolerable.

So they were still unwearied and enthusiastic when at one o'clock they looked down from the brow of a little hill to see a camp fire burning brightly on the edge of a pine wood, grass studded with blue gentians spread for a carpet at their feet, the Gardiner River flowing cheerily within easy reach, and mountains with light snow on them beautiful in the distance.

And it was their own, their very own, camp fire! A hot luncheon was ready for them, and the delicious odor in the air was coffee. When the Romantic produced napkins, their happiness was complete.

An hour or two after luncheon, however, the long drive began to grow tedious.

"When does the scenery begin?" inquired the Convert, wearily.

"Well, there isn't much scenery," acknowledged Phillips, "till you get to the Morris Basin, where we camp to-night. Then you'll have scenery enough."

"But there are the Obsidian Cliffs," said the Maiden, anxiously.

"Obsidian Cliffs?" ejaculated Phillips. "Why, you ain't expecting much from them, are you?"

"Yes, I was," murmured the Maiden, a little sadly.

"Why, they're nothing in the world but glass."

"But I don't see a mountain of glass every day; and the guide-books say that the cliffs 'glisten in the sun like burnished silver.'"

GIANT GEYSER IN ACTION.

Phillips had the cruelty to laugh. "How can they glisten like burnished silver when they're black as ink?"

"Black as ink!"

"Yes, black as ink."

"But, Phillips," said the Man of Sense, taking pity on the absolute dismay in the Maiden's face, "they're volcanic and basaltic, and all that sort of thing, don't you know. And another of the guide-books says they are probably unequalled in the world."

"May be unequalled obsidian," replied Phillips, dryly; "but they ain't unequalled cliffs, by a long shot. Now are they?"

They were at a loss to understand this abrupt question till they noticed that he had stopped the team suddenly.

It was impossible not to laugh. In his

eagerness to have them judge for themselves, independent of guide-book influence, Phillips had driven them almost past the cliffs without their noticing that there were any cliffs. Of course they are something one wants to see, and it is interesting to know that the road ingeniously built by Colonel Norris over the blocks of obsidian that had fallen where the road must go is probably the only piece of glass road in the world. Not to be turned back by a massive barrier that could not be hewn nor drilled nor blasted, Colonel Norris built great fires on the blocks, expanding the glass, and then had his men deluge the fires with cold water from Beaver Lake, cooling the brittle glass so suddenly that great masses of it were broken up. The road was then built for half a mile with this novel material.

Nevertheless the cliffs are hardly a "value" in the scenic effect. Far from "glistening like burnished silver," they are merely a big mass of black rock streaked with gray, though small bits of the obsidian picked up from the road have the cold black glitter of jet in the sunshine.

It was five o'clock when they entered the Norris Geyser Basin.

"I hope we're in time for you to see the Monarch to-night," said Phillips.

"Never mind if we're not," said the Man of Sense, cheerfully. "If we're too late, we can run over and see him to-morrow morning before breakfast."

"No, you can't," said Phillips. "The Monarch Geyser *is* a monarch up here in the Park. You can't go to see him when *you* get ready; you've got to go when *he's* ready."

They laughed at this reminder that nature here was the despot, and that sightseeing in Wyoming was something different from hunting up a cathedral or a water-fall.

"He goes off about six," announced Phillips.

"All right; we'll take a look at him. Where is he?" asked the Imperturbable, gazing about as if so lordly a creature ought to be visible from any stand-point.

"He's half a mile up the road there. If you like the walk, dinner'll be ready when you get back."

They were thankful for the walk; they were tired, but only tired of driving.

Half a mile up the road they did indeed come upon their first geysers, not as yet any great or famous ones, but a whole field of innumerable little ones, bubbling, burning, boiling away, and sending up their columns of white steam—a curious sight certainly to the *blasé* sight-seer weary of cathedrals.

"But they're exactly like the pictures of them," said the Romantic, in a tone of disappointment.

"What would you have, my dear? I am lost in speculation when I attempt to conceive what your verdict would have been if they had not looked like the pictures of them."

"And the coloring!" exclaimed the Convert. "Look at those pools! One is turquoise blue, and one is a splendid orange, and one is rose-color, and one is the richest crimson."

"But don't stop," said the Maiden, piteously. "I know the Monarch will go off before we get there."

"No hurry," said the Man of Sense, as they turned back to the road. "Nothing ever goes off till the Romantic gets there."

A few minutes later they saw where the Monarch must be, though there were as yet no signs of him, from a group of people waiting patiently upon the rocks.

"How do you dare to sit so near the crater?" asked the Convert, noticing that the group were hardly twenty feet from a chasm that was expected momently to send up eighty feet of boiling water.

"Oh, the water never splashes on the rocks," was the confident reply. "It just goes up and comes right down."

"And how long have you been waiting?"

"An hour," was the reply, with a sigh.

"Never mind," said the Man of Sense; "it's all right now. Announce to his Majesty," turning gravely to the Maiden, "that the Romantic is waiting."

In ludicrous answer to his jest, just as he finished speaking there was a rumble and a roar, and behold! his Majesty was there.

In five minutes he had gone again, but it was a magnificent sight.

No hour could be so enchanting for these geysers as one just before twilight, when a wintry sunset lingers in the sky, and the whole expanse of white formation, dotted with columns of white curling steam and glowing pools of water that seem to hold "the light that never was on sea or land," has all the effect of one of Landseer's lovely, lonely landscapes, lit with a coloring of its own, and truly neither of the sea nor land.

Oh, why would it grow dark? Nothing but the gathering darkness would ever have sent them home. Yes, *home;* for the little camp that had been pitched for the night, with its glowing fire and its waiting dinner, lent a "value" of unmistakable cozy comfort to the grandeur of the Yellowstone Park.

It was a pretty scene where the camp had been pitched. Close by gleamed the dozen white tents that formed the hotel where the "coupons" dine, while the green expanse of pretty meadow, shut in by pines glowing with the rich red light of sunset, was dotted with the tents of travellers camping out. Brightly flowed the river past the tents; brightly gleamed the camp fires through the trees; brightly glowed the faces round the tempting dinner on the grass.

At nine o'clock the Maiden disappeared in the ladies' tent. Only, however, to emerge looking prettier than ever. She had completely changed her costume, and was a lovely "value" in the landscape as she stood holding back the white canvas of the tent door, while the fire-light played on her skirt of heavy crimson flannel, her little tight-fitting jacket of dark blue edged with Astrakhan, and the tiny cap of Astrakhan and blue set jauntily on her golden curls.

"Well, Mabel?"

"We dress for the night at the Yellowstone instead of undressing," explained the Maiden, with dignity. "It is warm now, but there will be a frost before morning. Phillips says so."

"But, Mabel, if the thing is to be cold at the Yellowstone, you want to be cold. You never can go home properly and tell people that you were half frozen in August, if you wear all that furry armor."

"Yes, I can. That is the point of it. You must be cold with all your winter things on. Anybody could be cold with only a summer overcoat."

It seemed incredible that they could need all the blankets Phillips had provided.

"But then, when you think of it," said the Man of Sense, "we're a thousand feet higher above the sea than the top of Mount Washington. Why shouldn't we be cold?"

And they were cold before morning. That is, they didn't suffer, for there were wraps in abundance, and the delicious invigorating air playing around them was something quite unlike the deathly chill of a cold chamber.

"Hot water, fresh from the spring!" was the novel cry outside the tent of the ladies. "You can't have cream in your coffee, for the milk froze in the pail; but the hot pool didn't freeze, by a good deal. Come out and see the frost."

But quickly as the ladies dressed, spurred to activity by the splendid air, the desire to get out, and the tempting sputtering of bacon evidently turning crisp over a fire just outside their tent, the frost was almost gone before they came out to look at it. As soon as the sun goes down at the Yellowstone it is singularly cold, but as soon as the sun comes up it is singularly warm.

"I wonder what makes it seem so heavenly?" said the Romantic. "It is just like a June morning, in spite of the cold and the absence of roses."

"I know what it is, Anna," said the Maiden, slyly. "It's the beautiful stillness. You pretend that you like those horrid Kansas winds at the ranch, but you don't. There isn't any wind; that's what makes it so lovely."

Undoubtedly it was. The slightest breeze of the clear cold air might have destroyed the charm of the out-of-doors breakfast, in spite of the camp fire. But there was not a zephyr moving. The delicious crisp freshness simply existed all around you, ready for the breathing, but not fluttering so much as the hem of your garment.

And now to break camp and away; that is, they would leave Johnson and Sam to break camp, and they would "away." As they were to stop at the Gibbon Paint Pots, there would be time for Johnson and the camping "outfit" to pass them later on the road, and have luncheon ready for them at the head of the Gibbon Cañon.

All was stir and excitement. Twenty or more different encampments were breaking up; horsemen galloped away toward the Firehole or toward the springs; patient wagons took their heavy loads of camp equipage and toiled after the eager horsemen. Nothing was left of the little settlement that had been so full of life the night before but the quiet tents of the hotel, where even now dinner was being prepared for the next "coupons."

The Man of Sense and the Maiden would ride that morning. The day before it had been too hot, and the saddle-horses had been allowed to plod along by the wagons. In the afternoon it would be again too

"I don't see why they associate everything around here with Satan, just because it is hot," said the Romantic. "Those little white puffs are pretty enough to make it seem as if it were here that they

hot, perhaps; but at eight o'clock nothing could be more tempting than a ride as far as the Paint Pots.

The road led them by the field of geysers, looking strangely different in the bright morning air. More than a hundred of them seemed to be "up and at it," sending up their light curling wreaths of steam with a zeal that never flags, even with the thermometer about them at 40° below zero.

were manufactured for the sky. Nature never thought we should come up here to catch her at it; but she is blowing soap-bubbles that float up into the blue, and stay there like innocent little white clouds that have never touched the earth."

"Very pretty — very pretty indeed," said the Man of Sense. "But they look more to me like the smoke of the future locomotive that I hope is to put us through this park some time."

"And to me," said the Man of Sense, whose favorite resource was his Kansas ranch, "they look more like the smoke from the chimneys of my future tenants, when I build up a big town at Carneiro."

"Well, the guide-book hits it about right this time; it calls it 'an infernal little dell'; and as it has over two thousand active volcanic vents, I think we had better turn the whole thing over to Satan, after all."

Two hours later they entered the curious grove, about a mile from the main road, where the Paint Pots are.

There are more than five hundred of them, and they are admirably named. The little pools are like nothing so much as great paint pots, and the bubbling, boiling, gurgling mass seething within them is like nothing so much as paint. It is soft, smooth, and satiny to the touch, though it turns hard later in lovely coral-work around the basins, only to crumble away if you try to preserve it.

But the wonder of these hot paint pots is the coloring. Because I have been quite frank, and acknowledged that the Yellowstone is not a "pretty place" through its whole three thousand square miles, I shall expect you to trust me when I tell you where it is pretty, and to believe me when I say that these colored paint pots are alone worth a journey of many miles to see. It had been curious to see pools of so many different colors far apart from each other at the Norris Basin; but here, within two or three feet of each other, were pools some of which were blood red, some sulphur orange, some delicate rose-color, and some looking as if filled with hot cream.

Here, too, is the one great joke of the Park. It is a great pool apparently full of white paint. The effort of this thick white paint to be a geyser, resulting in a sputter, sputter, sputter—gurgle, gurgle, gurgle—blob, blob, blob—and then for a moment silence, is something so ludicrous that no one can stand beside it and not laugh aloud in sympathy. It is not the seething of the hot spring, nor the bubbling of the boiling pool, nor the hiss of steam rushing from subterranean caverns, nor the roar of the geyser; it is sputter, sputter, sputter—gurgle, gurgle, gurgle—blob, blob, blob—till the spectator is convulsed with merriment.

The scenery that afternoon was the most interesting they had had on the road.

The Gibbon Cañon is finely picturesque, and they had been repaid by the beautiful Gibbon Falls, lovelier even than the lovely Minnehaha, for the scramble down the hill-side from the road.

Nevertheless, they were strangely tired, almost too tired to enjoy the really noble view, when Phillips suddenly drew up his horses where they could look down into the valley of the Firehole River, and across to the great Divide, sending the head-waters of the Columbia down one side to the Pacific, and the springs of the Missouri down the other to the Gulf of Mexico.

"Now," said Phillips, in a tone of intense satisfaction, "if you'll get out the field-glasses, I shouldn't wonder if we could see the Three Tetons."

"What in the world are the Three Tetons?"

"They're mountains."

"But we can certainly see mountains enough. I don't believe it is worth while to dig out the glasses."

"But they're two hundred miles away."

"Oh, we've seen lots of mountains as far off as that," announced the Man of Sense, "in the San Juan country, from the Marshall Pass. Isn't that the valley down there where the weary cease from jolting and the horses are to rest?"

"Yes, sir; that's where we camp for to-night—eight miles farther on."

"Eight miles!" sighed the Romantic. "Then don't let's wait to hunt up any Tetons."

So they hurried down into the valley, leaving the Tetons, as it were, behind them.

They camped for the night in a grove of pines, just at the entrance to the picturesque road that leads out of the Park through Beaver Cañon to the Union Pacific Railway. It was a pretty spot, with a spring of clear water tinkling close beside their tents, their mattresses laid on fragrant boughs of pine, the river flowing within sight, and Marshall's comfortable hotel within reach.

Not that they wanted a hotel, except that one of the hot sulphur baths would be grateful after the dust and heat of the drive.

The next morning they explored the Devil's Half-Acre, and it was worth exploring. Though only a repetition in kind of what they had seen before, it was all on a much larger scale. Instead of tiny pools

FALLS OF THE YELLOWSTONE.

there is here a great lake, with its basin rimmed with so many and such rich colors, and its water of such deep and heavenly tints, that the very vapor from it is tinged by reflection with hues of pale blue or delicate pink. From this lake runs a phenomenal little brook. The water in the lake is of limpid turquoise blue; for a few yards the water of the brook is thick and white, like rich cream; for a few more yards it

CRATER OF "OLD FAITHFUL."

runs over a bed distinctly and brightly crimson; then for a few yards more its course is marked by a perfectly defined band of brilliant yellow. There's a definite break in each color; they do not run into each other. The same water drops in its course entirely different deposits.

Here, too, is the horrible crater of the greatest geyser in the world, the Excelsior, whose eruptions are fortunately few, when it sends 300 feet into the air water enough to wash away bridges over small streams below, rumbling with a roar to be heard for miles, and scattering over acres rocks a hundred pounds in weight. The crater is dreadful enough when not in action; but into this seething, burning, frightful abyss of boiling horror a little rill of clear, perfectly cold water, fed from the snowy uplands in the distance, drops gently, unceasingly, unafraid.

Nothing further diversified the scene until about noon. Phillips halted suddenly and asked, "What do you think of that?"

They looked up for a geyser, and off for a mountain, and around for a forest, but could see nothing extraordinary.

"Try looking down."

Then they cried out with wonder.

They were on the brink of the Morning-glory Pool, the most beautiful of all the pools, lovely enough to tempt one from New York if nothing else were to be seen at the Yellowstone Park. It is exquisitely named; for it is precisely like a morning-glory flower. Its long and slender throat, like the tube of the blossom, reaching from unknown depths below, branches out in ever-widening snowy walls, forming at last a perfectly symmetrical and exquisite chalice, which is filled with water of the loveliest, clearest, robin's-egg blue. The rim of the chalice is delicately and regularly scalloped, like the flower, and is edged with a tiny line of hard coral from the deposit.

Ten minutes later they drove into the upper geyser basin, which the "coupons" reached at nightfall of their first day out. It is a cleared space of three or four miles, in which there are said to be nearly five hundred springs and geysers, twenty-six of them being unequalled elsewhere on the surface of the globe for size, splendor, and the tremendous flood of water they send forth. But our party had been so steeped in wonders that they hardly cared now to look at each geyser cone, though perhaps every one is worth separate examination, especially that of the Grotto, with its fantastic arches crusted with opals and lined with mother-of-pearl.

They drove directly to the head of the basin, where Old Faithful stands picturesquely, setting a noble example to his followers in beauty, sublimity, and punctuality. He saluted as they approached, sending a splendid fountain for a hundred and fifty feet into the air, and they went into camp in pine woods just across the way, where the warm spray from his hourly greeting would perhaps blow into their faces.

It was the first time they had gone into camp at noon, and they enjoyed a leisurely lunch, with the prospect of a whole afternoon not to be wasted in the wagons.

"Quarter past two," said the Man of Sense, looking at his watch as Old Faithful again rose into the air while they were lingering over their coffee and cigars. "He's on time. It's the fashion, you know, to have a tall old-fashioned clock in your dining-room, and Faithful is about the tallest one I ever saw. I judge, too, from the figures they give about here, that he is old enough to suit the very latest style."

"Do you know," said the Maiden,

thoughtfully, "I think it's even funnier to see him go down than to see him come up. If the geysers were great hot fountains, playing all the time, they would be wonderful enough ; but to see them come up and go down, like a jack-in-the-box, without your having even to touch the spring—"

"A hot spring too," murmured the Imperturbable.

And now for the rest of the afternoon they separated. The Maiden and the Man of Sense took the saddle-horses and rode off through the woods to see the Lone-star Geyser. The Convert and the Imperturbable wandered off for a tour of inspection on foot. The Romantic announced that she should stay where she was and write letters.

"A geyser is a geyser," she announced, with undeniable accuracy. "When you have seen one, you have seen all. Of course they're remarkable and splendid and magnificent and all that; but they are not half as lovely or as interesting as the pools. One Morning-glory Spring is worth a dozen Faithfuls. I have come to the point when I don't even look round at him if he happens to go off when my back is turned."

But even she was moved when she heard of the Laundry : the set tub of solid rock, just the shape and size of a genuine wash-tub, filled with natural soapsuds. Here all the washing of the hotel is done, a picturesque Chinaman bringing over the clothes in his nicely balanced buckets to throw them into the bubbling, frothy pool, fish them out again when they had been tossed about enough, and run them through a wringer in the tent conveniently near.

The next day they retraced their track of the day before for eleven miles. Then at the Fire-

"IF YOU MUST HAVE A WATER-FALL."

hole they turned off to pastures new, in the direction of the falls and cañon.

Three or four miles before you come to the falls the country takes on a distinctly New England charm, and is really extremely pretty, with the rushing river, the pleasant woods, the lovely wild flowers, and the picturesque rocks. They went into camp close by the river, lunched, and then went over to the hotel for more saddle-horses with which to ride down the cañon.

The hotel here is also in tents, but it has the most picturesque location of any, in a thick grove of pines. The falls are hardly more than half a mile away.

"Yes," said the Man of Sense, as they dismounted and scrambled down the rocky slope to look up at the falls. "If you must have a water-fall, that is as good a water-fall as you could have."

A hundred feet higher than Niagara, it is far more beautiful than Niagara, in spite of the loss of breadth, because of its magnificent setting in the noblest mountain scenery. It adds to the impressiveness, too, that you can see hardly anything of the river before it makes the plunge. It makes an abrupt turn just before its leap, so that what you see is not a long, prosaic stream dropping suddenly over a rock, but only what looks like a small and quiet pool sending this splendid messenger to the river below.

They did not linger, beautiful as the scene was; they were impatient for the cañon.

The falls are usually considered to be the main object of this part of the trip, but the cañon is very fine even from that point. The guide-books do, indeed, "advise" the tourist, "if he has time," to go on a mile farther to Point Lookout; but in point of fact there should be a stringent law that no one should be allowed to enter Yellowstone Park who will not promise to ride eight miles down the cañon, as a mental and moral stimulus to the noblest impressions of his life, and also in justice to the Park. I say "down the cañon," because you follow the river on its downward course; but you do not go through the cañon as you do through those in Colorado; you walk through lovely woods above the cañon, and look down over the edge of these magnificent cliffs at the gorgeous scene before you. The milk-white walls drop suddenly from the very edge of the dark pine forests, down, down,

down, down, carved into most splendid grottoes, holding perhaps snow in their deep recesses, rising again in slender pinnacles, on which the eagles build their nests, and may be seen fluttering around them, looking like sparrows in the distance; down, down, to the river, clasped, but not held, in this splendid embrace, not lying, as the guide-books say, "like a green ribbon" or "a silver thread" at their base, but writhing, gleaming, hurrying from these strong arms like a great, glittering, splendid serpent, alive, determined, terrible, but too far away to be dangerous, its emerald scales glorious in the sunlight.

Yet it is not the height of the cliffs alone, nor their wonderful sculpture, that makes the Yellowstone cañon what it is. The cliffs in Colorado are often higher and steeper, and quite as beautifully carved. As one of the guides put it, "There's cañons 'most anywhere; but they ain't painted." Here, if anywhere, is the place to recall Sir Thomas Brown's definition of nature, as "the art of God." The splendor of color at the Yellowstone—the gorgeous streaks of crimson, orange, violet, and green—are even more wonderful than the snowy walls themselves. It is less the color than the purity of the color that makes the scene such a wealth of glowing loveliness. These are not merely alternate layers of dull red and pale yellow, curious but faint, like those which are thought so remarkable at Gay Head; nor does "snowy" mean here, as it is apt to do when applied to nature, merely a soiled and grimy gray. What is snowy is milk white; what is red is blood red; what is pink is the loveliest rose-color.

Should they go to the lake? It would be a twenty-mile drive, and a light haze that promised rain almost persuaded them to give it up. However, they kept on—the soul of the Man of Sense torn within him as he saw wild-duck, geese, and snipe hovering by the hundred over the river, and even a herd of antelope in the distance.

A light shower came up, but it was so interesting to discover what all the little belts and buckles and bags were for—to keep the team water-proof—that they decided it was rather cozier to have it rain. But if it had rained cats and dogs, they would have forgotten it all as they approached the loveliest sheet of water they had ever seen.

If it were merely a vast expanse of wa-

GRAND CAÑON OF THE YELLOWSTONE.

ter, its mere size, though it covers 150 square miles, would not be worth the effort to get to it; for although it is a curious fact that so large a body of water is to be found so far above the level of the sea that if Mount Washington were to be sunk in it to the sea-level, the surface of the lake would still be half a mile above the top of the mountain, there is nothing, of course, to make you realize this when you stand beside it. All its statistics are interesting—its immense area, its great height, its depth of nearly 300 feet not far from shore—but, so far as the facts are concerned, you might as well stay at home and learn them from the geographies. Its surpassing loveliness is due to the fact that it is not one great prairie of water, stretched out before you so that you see the whole of it at once; it curves and bends and narrows and widens into beautiful rivers and noble bays; over it, across it, and through it float myriads of white swans, ducks, geese, pelicans, and sea-gulls; at times it stretches out in a long line of sounding surf, breaking white upon a pebbly beach; it is dotted with lovely islands, and it is all held in place by mountains 10,000 or 12,000 feet high, clad all the year round with snow.

"In short," said the Man of Sense, "if you take Mount Desert—minus, of course, Rodick's and the hauled mealers—multiply it by ten, put some snow on the mountains, throw in a little of the Bay of Rio and the Palisades of the Hudson, add the whole of the Lake of Como and a few of the Thousand Isles of the St. Lawrence, you will have something approaching the loveliness of Yellowstone Lake."

They pitched the tents in pine woods close to the shore. Trout leaped almost onto their luncheon table; little squirrels peeped, and ran for the crumbs; wild flowers blossomed all about them in reckless profusion; lonely sea-gulls watched them curiously from the lake. The sun came out, and the Man of Sense and the Imperturbable took the saddle-horses and went in search of the Natural Bridge, not, however, till they had banked the ladies' tent, in case of a harder rain, with heavy sods so full of blossoming flowers that they formed a beautiful little parterre of brilliant flower beds.

And the heavier rain came indeed. It was a thunder-shower glorious to see as it came up over the lake in great purple clouds that soon spent themselves in heavy hail. Still more glorious was it to see it disappear, when at last the ladies, who had been perfectly secure in their warm tent, dared to push aside their canvas door and look at the big hailstones nestled among the pink and blue blossoms of their flower bed, and then across to the mountains, white with a heavier fall of snow, and with exquisite little clouds, tinged with a rosy sunset, drifting in and out of the ravines.

"Supper is ready," said the Maiden, confronting the gentlemen as they rode into camp. "But you said we were not to take in any hauled mealers."

"But you would let two moistened wanderers dry themselves by your fire, wouldn't you," said the Man of Sense, with an insinuating smile, "if they promised to tell you all about the Natural Bridge?"

In spite of the lovely scene, as the moon rose over the lake, it was a sorrowful conclave that gathered about the camp fire that night. They had seen the Park; that is, they had seen the seven wonders, and had done all they could that summer. It remained for them now to get back to the railroad, seventy-eight miles away, and then home again. And, after all, they had not seen the Three Tetons.

A CANADIAN PILGRIMAGE

"MIRACLES.—The French papers of Saturday evening relate that creditable persons who made the pilgrimage with the Association of the Sacred Heart recently were witnesses to two miracles at La Bonne St. Anne. A young girl named Marie Levesque, who had only walked with difficulty, during the last two years, with the aid of crutches, was radically cured. The second case was that of a young Irish lad. It is stated that on leaving the church this lad, with some friends, returned to the boat which was to bring him back to Quebec. He was only a few minutes on board when, suddenly throwing his crutch under a bench, he exclaimed to one of his companions, 'Oh, I forgot to leave my crutch in the church.' 'But you want it,' replied his friends. 'No, not at all; I have no longer any use for it;' and with that he began to walk about the deck, his infirmity having entirely disappeared."

The foregoing paragraph met my eye as I glanced over one of the Quebec dailies one evening while awaiting a few purchases by my companion in a small stationery store of the Lower Town.

"Do people believe that these miracles are genuine?" I asked this of the girl behind the counter, pointing to the item.

"Why, of course," said she; "and I'm afraid you are a person of very little faith indeed." I was conscious of a very reproachful look from her dark eyes as she continued, "I see that you have never visited the Church of Our Lady the good St. Anne."

I mentally resolved that this, at any rate, should not longer be numbered among my sins of omission, and so, after tea, bargained for a team, good for sixty miles, to start upon the following morning.

Le Moine, the contemporary local chronicler, gives his readers some account of the origin of the Church of St. Anne de Beaupré, and the guide-books, with which every tourist down the St. Lawrence has his pockets stuffed, call attention to it as one of the standard attractions of the voyage. To the faithful it is the shrine of Lourdes, the Paray-le-Monial of the Western World, the most highly venerated spot in America, and is regarded with the same superstitious awe that Mexicans entertain toward Guadalupe and its divinely pictured blanket.

June 26, the anniversary festival of St. Anne, witnesses a great visitation into the little hamlet, overflowing its hotels and miraculous shrine, while upon every other day of the year a smaller crowd of devotees are here to be found. Advertisements of "pilgrimages" are frequently to be seen in the Canadian papers, and these, which are usually excursions promoted for the benefit of "Young Men's Institutes," or the parish church, together with the large number of visitors drawn hither through curiosity, or invalids in hope of relief, make up a current of travel highly profitable, and supporting a daily steamboat line from Quebec. The annual number of pilgrims is about 25,000.

St. Anne was the mother of the Blessed Virgin. After death her body reposed in the cathedral at Jerusalem until it was sent thence by St. James to St. Lazare, the first Bishop of Marseilles. This prelate afterward dispatched it to St. Auspice, the Bishop of Apt, who concealed his precious charge in a subterranean chapel. Goths and Vandals swept the church from existence, and for seven hundred years St. Anne rested forgotten. During brilliant ceremonials in the cathedral of the town, upon the occasion of the advent of Charlemagne, several miraculous incidents led to the recovery of the remains from the grotto, effulgent with divine radiance, and fragrant with heavenly odors. So read the chronicles of the Church.

Certain colonists in the Canadas were commanded by an apparition to erect a church in honor of St. Anne upon its present site, which was done in 1658, and ten years later this new shrine was enriched by a relic, which was nothing less than a bone of the hand of St. Anne. This is still retained and carefully preserved, its exposition being a favor but rarely vouchsafed even the faithful.

It was long the custom of all ships returning from voyages to anchor here and honor St. Anne by a broadside. Old writers also speak of large villages of Indian proselytes which were located in the vicinity.

The name of St. Anne has always been a favorite in Canada, where, indeed, nearly every hamlet and railway station is canonized. There are said to be thirteen parishes in the Dominion bearing her name.

Our pilgrimage to St. Anne's began directly after an early breakfast. Visitors to Quebec are familiar with the first six miles of the road, as it leads to the Falls of Montmorency. Passing the walls near the Hôtel Dieu, we drove down through the Lower Town, across the St. Charles drawbridge, and into the open fields. Here the road has the character of an English lane, environed by small latticed inns and country homes. Then the turnpike surmounts a hill, giving a superb retrospect of Quebec and the river, with the ruins of Montcalm's home in the foreground.

From every little hamlet twin church spires, sheathed with glistening tin, point above the foliage, and great black crosses mark the resting-places of the village dead. The farms stretch from the road to the river, half a mile away, narrow and attenuated, giving every holder a frontage upon both.

The houses are a study. Their heavy stone walls are scrupulously white, and pierced by small windows fitted with an inside sash to better guard against the winter blasts. The roofs are steep, and end in a peculiar and graceful upward curve at the eaves. These, too, are usually whitewashed, and the huge chimneys are incased in wood.

Everything and everybody is French, and the tricolor flaps in big flags and little ones where the union-jack is seldom seen. Little girls of undeniably Gallic origin ran beside our carriage, holding up bouquets of sweet-pea and marigold.

The amiable Frenchwoman who presides over the little hotel at the Falls stared after us in wonder at the unaccustomed sight of two travellers passing her famous cataract without so much as stopping for a moment's look.

The object of our trip was, however, of

A FRENCH CANADIAN VILLAGE ON THE ST. LAWRENCE.

the supernatural rather than picturesque order; still we could not forbear noticing the brown and buxom Ruths who followed the clumsy two-wheeled hay-carts through the stubble, or the dark-eyed Maud Mullers, in woollen caps and jerseys, turning the hay through the short Canadian reaping-time. Even the family mastiff is made to earn his share, the little boys driving him in harness to the fields with the mid-day lunch, and back with miniature loads of hay.

Bird-cages swing in nearly every porch. Ranks of aged Lombardy poplars mingle their dark and compact shafts in the light and shadow of road-side scenes that have changed but little in two hundred years.

At intervals along the road small chapels were seen, which are used but once annually, when the shrines inclosed are exposed to receive the votive offerings of processionists winding with stately chant along the dusty highway upon some festival day. Wooden crosses, sombre and time-stained, stand half buried in tangled verdure. I recall one, decorated with models of tools and implements, symbolizing a life of toil at the bench and in the field, closing in the full faith of the Church.

Our objective point, the Church of St.

Anne de Beaupré, stands at the base of a steep hill crowned with farms, behind which the land again rises, forming Mont St. Anne, the most elevated point upon the river, being 2687 feet in altitude.

Seen from the deck of a passing steamer, the hamlet appears to straggle aimlessly along the road, at a distance of a quarter of a mile across marshy flats.

Four years ago a new church was built —a handsome and classic structure, yet lacking a spire—and the patron saint graciously deserted the old church upon the hill-side, where she had so long succored weak humanity, and took up her abode in the new quarters provided.

In front of the handsome and classic edifice is set a large circular fountain, about which stood a number of pilgrims engaged in the obviously unusual work of washing their hands and faces, which were duly wiped upon handkerchiefs or coat tails. Close at hand the proprietors of a small booth drove a good trade in the sale of beads, amulets, relics, and lithographs of the Virgin.

Passing the poverty-smitten, diseased, and tattered groups upon the steps of the edifice, we entered. The interior failed to bear out exterior promise, for the walls were rough-cast, the beams unpainted,

THE NEW CHURCH OF ST. ANNE DE BEAUPRÉ.

and seats of the most primitive fashion. Near the door a boy was held up on the shoulders of men while he chipped away with a knife at a heavy cross, tossing the slivers to an eager crowd of devotees, to be carried home as relics.

Along the walls were hung a number of very ancient paintings. One of these, a portrait of the patron saint, is said to be from the hand of Le Brun, the French artist, and was presented by the Marquis of Tracy. Others were painted by Lefrançois, a Franciscan monk who died in 1685. One is a representation of St. Anne hovering over a ship in distress.

Upon a post the following notice was conspicuously tacked:

"As the number of masses asked in honor of St. Anne exceeds those that can be celebrated in this church, the faithful are informed that as many as possible will be said here, and the balance at other churches of this parish within the space of about a month from their reception.

"————,
"Priest of the Parish of St. Anne de Beaupré."

By far the most conspicuous feature of the place was a towering trophy of crutches and canes, raised within the rail dividing the altar from the auditorium. These were of all sizes and shapes. Two fresh additions rested against the rail, where they had evidently just been deposited by the newly recovered owners.

Down the aisle toward us hobbled an old man with the help of two assistants. His crutches were discarded, but his features revealed a pain which gave the lie to his feeble praises of the saint at his res-

toration. At the rail a mother knelt, holding close a pigmy babe; and when she passed out her face was raised with new hope, but I saw in the face of the child only the seal of dissolution.

The priests in attendance moved about with a listless, mechanical air, bowing at stated places and intervals, one of them presenting a glazed medallion portrait of the saint to the lips of kneeling suppliants. The air of every-day occupation seemed impressed upon the whole drowsy scene, unrelieved by music or the usual pageantry of the picturesque Romish service.

As we walked up the single village street we passed the old man, who still dragged his weak frame bravely along,

THE OLD CHURCH OF ST. ANNE DE BEAUPRÉ.

the two attendants upholding him. The agony in his every lineament would have won the admiration and roused the artistic enthusiasm of Parrhasius himself.

In one favorable particular the village of La Bonne St. Anne will ever remain green in memory. Our horses were well groomed and fed, and we sat down to a palatable dinner of spring chicken flanked by varied adjuncts, preceded by soup and followed by a plethoric pie, all served by a laughing French maid, who utterly declined to comprehend our efforts in her language. Our bill entire amounted to sixty cents. Inquiry developed the fact that regular board was rated at about thirty cents per diem, whereupon we seriously considered the desirability of this region as a place of summer resort for parents with large families.

SOME AMERICANS FROM OVERSEAS

ALTHOUGH all the inhabitants of the United States, Indians excepted, are either of foreign birth or the direct descendants of those native to other lands, though the unwavering policy of our government from its inception has been to encourage immigration, and though we owe most of our material development to the tireless industry of toilers from abroad, it is, and always has been, the habit of native-born Americans to assume airs of superiority toward their fellow-citizens from oversea, and to express for them a contemptuous dislike. In this, however, we do not stand alone, for to all peoples of the earth the stranger within their gates is one to be pitied, disliked, or hated. To the home-abiding European an American is of an inferior race, and pitied for his crude ideas of civilization. In what we are pleased to term the "Dark Continent" the black-skinned sons of Ham despise the progeny of Japhet because they are white; while to the Mongols of Asia people of the western world are "foreign devils," to be hated always, and killed if opportunity offers.

We of America do not seek to kill the immigrants whom we have invited to assist in the upbuilding of our great republic, but we nevertheless despise them, and rarely hesitate to express this feeling with a brutal frankness. While this ever-present animosity is general and applies to all foreigners, it has epochs of especial virulence against especial classes. Irish, Germans, and Scandinavians have been denounced in turn; but to-day the first outrank us all in the learned professions, the second are our merchants and manufacturers, while the third have become the agriculturists upon whose efforts are based the very foundations of our national prosperity. Bereft of these three, we should resemble a man partially paralyzed in brain, functional organs, and limbs. We have had paroxysms of fear concerning the Italians, Poles, Hungarians, and Bohemians, who have built and are building the railroads of the East, as well as over the Chinamen, who have performed a similar service in the West; but these have been alleviated. More recently our energies in the line of denunciation have been directed against a class of immigrants from Slavonic countries, who are settling certain regions of the Northwest that American farmers have deemed worthless for purposes of agriculture.

Much has been written and said against the "filthy Russians," the "ignorant Finns," the "grovelling Polanders," and even the thrifty Icelanders, who have established themselves in that portion of Uncle Sam's domain. They are charged with crowding out the native-born American, stealing from him his birthright of free land, clinging to their own language and customs, refusing to become Americanized, lowering the standard of citizenship, reducing the price of labor, and in many other ways demoralizing the community at large. So clamorous were these charges that this Magazine became interested in the subject, and decided to send into the Northwest a representative who should visit the Russian in his lair, the "Finn" in his cave, and the Icelander in his den. Having been chosen for this service, I started early last summer for the State of North Dakota, where, as I was informed, the Slavonic hordes had made their principal invasion.

The Russians, being the newest comers, and also the most bitterly denounced by that class of Americans who glory in the title of "Know Nothings," claimed my chief attention, and at St. Paul I learned that they were to be found in greatest numbers somewhere along the line of the Northern Pacific Railroad, west of the Missouri River. At Bismarck I was so fortunate as to meet a young Americanized Russian who has been instrumental in bringing more of his people to this country than any other person. He had been a medical student in Russia, became connected with a nihilist plot, was suspected, arrested, and sentenced to Siberia, but made his escape, and came to this country five years ago. He at once took steps to become naturalized, and now, as Dr. C. C. Young, is an American citizen, intensely proud of his adopted country, enthusiastic concerning its institutions, particularly its liberty of speech, and is able to converse in excellent English wholly acquired since coming here.

"A nihilist," said Dr. Young, "is not an anarchist, nor even a socialist. He is merely one who desires with all his heart, and above everything else in this world, the liberty of speech and action that is the birthright of every living soul, and which is guaranteed to every American by the Constitution of the United States. Oh, you Americans should be the very happiest people on earth, for you have everything that the rest of the world is striving to gain."

The doctor surprised me by stating that "his Russians," as he termed those settled in the Dakotas, were of Teutonic stock, and not Slavs at all, save as they had adopted Slavonic customs and modes of life during a residence of several generations in Russia. According to him, Peter the Great, by liberal promises, induced several colonies of German farmers to settle in his dominions, where they were to teach his people their methods of agriculture. Each family of these colonists was given a house and land, on which all taxes were remitted, the men were exempted from military service, they were allowed to retain their own religious forms, and were free to return to their own land whenever they pleased. Under these favorable conditions the colonists flourished and multiplied for two hundred years, becoming in that time Russianized in everything save their language, religion, and independence of thought and speech. In Germany some of them had been Lutherans, while others had remained Catholics, and to this day their descendants have retained these forms of belief through all vicissitudes of fortune.

At length these semi-independent and liberty-loving people became so numerous, and on account of the extraordinary privileges granted them excited so much discontent in the down-trodden communities in which they dwelt, that the Russian authorities became alarmed, and decided upon their repression. So, by imperial ukase, Czar Alexander III. arbitrarily revoked all concessions made to them by his famous ancestor. Thus by a stroke of the pen the Germano-Russians were reduced to the servile condition of their Slavonic neighbors, and saw naught before them save a future of hopeless misery. Rather than accept this, vast numbers of them attempted to leave the country. Many were intercepted and forced to return. Some were imprisoned, transported to Siberia, condemned to death, or otherwise punished for striving to gain other liberty than that allowed by the Czar; but thousands made good their

THE HOUSE OF RUSSIAN SETTLERS IN MERCER COUNTY, NORTH DAKOTA.

Showing the first and second stages—the original sod house on the left, the more recent adobe house on the right.

escape. Of these fortunate ones, some settled in Germany, others went to the Argentine, and so great a number came to this country that ten thousand of them are estimated to be settled in the Dakotas.

In North Dakota I found their farms scattered along the sluggish prairie waterways from the Missouri River west to the Bad Lands of the Montana border, and met them in all the little railroad towns from Mandan to Medora, which they use as shipping and trading points. Thus in New Salem, Kurtz, Hebron, Dickinson, Richardton, and Glen Ullin were seen the wagons of Russian farmers, drawn by teams of big strong horses, and heavily laden with wheat in sacks, or more lightly freighted with recently purchased goods. Always, too, there were passengers— broad-shouldered, stolid-looking men, wide-hipped, squarely built women, and innumerable children, sturdy and brighteyed.

The men have already discarded their Russian costume, and appear in the conventional slouch hat, flannel shirt, short sack-coat, and jean trousers tucked into boot-legs of the American frontier; but the women retain the characteristic dress in which they came from oversea. It is invariably of gray or dark blue homespun, with scant skirts barely reaching to the ankles, heavy cowhide shoes, coarse yarn stockings, and a triangular kerchief knotted beneath the chin, covering their smooth black hair. Everything is severely plain and serviceable, without an attempt at ornament, except that the younger women generally display some point of

color, such as a red ribbon or brightly bordered kerchief. The children are miniature counterparts of their elders, with the exception that the skirts of the little girls are so long as to hide their feet.

I followed several of these families to their homes, distant from ten to fifty miles from the railroad, and was always made shyly welcome as a friend of Dr. Young, whose influence over them is unbounded. Having been told that they lived like pigs in mud hovels, I was prepared for some very unpleasant experiences during my stay with them, especially at night; but in every case I found the anticipation much worse than the reality. To be sure, all the houses that I visited, with one exception, were constructed of mud; but so is every brick building in the land, and these Russian dwellings were far from being hovels. All had board floors, and contained at least two rooms. While those of the more recent arrivals were built of sod, in every case where the proprietor had been two or more years in the country his house was a long, low, but neatly finished and very substantial structure of sun-dried brick, made of mud mixed with straw, and differing in no way that I could see from the adobes of Mexico. The framing was of unhewn cottonwood timbers hauled from the nearest riverbottom, and in many cases the interiors were ceiled with boards. The roofs were of closely laid poles or rough boards covered six inches deep with adobe, while every house had wide chimneys and glass windows. Many of them, as picturesquely foreign in appearance as though transplanted bodily from Russian steppes, were neatly whitewashed both inside and out, while often both doors and window-casings were painted a bright blue.

As the sod houses of the new-comers are not storm-proof for more than two years, they are considered as only temporary makeshifts until time can be taken to mould adobe brick and erect more permanent dwellings. Thus the adobe house, which is often given a stone foundation, marks the abode of him who has been in the country three or four years, and but few Russians have dwelt in Dakota for a longer time. Most of them had, however, made previous and unprofitable attempts at farming in the northwest territories of Canada, to which they were attracted by specious promises and low rates of transportation.

The third stage of the Dakota settler's progress is marked by a shingled roof projecting with wide eaves over the low walls of his adobe house; while the fourth, which I saw reached by but one man, and he had been in this country seven years, is the frame-house stage. The old-timer who has gained this height of prosperity lives in Mercer County, which is almost wholly settled by Russians, and his neat dwelling, containing six rooms, all on the ground-floor, stands on a crest of the water-shed between the Missouri and Big Knife rivers, commanding a glorious view of twenty miles in every direction. This man owns six hundred and forty acres of land, all of which is upland prairie, such as American farmers, having in mind the rich valleys of the Red, James, and other wheat-region rivers, had deemed unfit for cultivation. Nor could it be profitably cultivated with their extravagant methods; but its Russian owner, in 1897, put one hundred and sixty acres into wheat that yielded him eighteen bushels to the acre, forty more into flax and potatoes, and enclosed the remainder with a wire fence as a pasture for his two hundred head of cattle. On the open range he herded a flock of sheep, and from the free prairie meadows he cut one hundred tons of hay, which he hauled home and stacked for winter use.

His stables and out-buildings, low but thick-walled and warm, form two sides of a square that opens to the south, while his dwelling and its adjacent granaries form the third side. Besides owning several teams of fine horses, a herd of cattle, and a flock of sheep, he raises pigs, chickens, turkeys, and ducks; sends eggs and butter to market every week, is not in debt to any man, has $1000 in bank, and is estimated to be worth $10,000 more. Seven years ago, when he located where he still lives, he had less than $500 with which to make his new start in life, and he was fifty miles from a railroad. But he had pluck, energy, and thrift, besides a family of sons and daughters who had been educated to hard work.

Now, though the old man still hauls his wheat fifty miles to the railroad, he can count twenty-three homesteads from his own house; and though most of his sons and daughters have left him, he is proud of the fact that they are raising families of bright young Americans who will honor his name and bless him for their heritage of freedom.

This first settler can speak but a few words of English, and his children use it with difficulty; but his grandchildren talk the language of their adopted country as fluently as they do the Russo-German of their parents. They attend schools where only English is taught, and in which the law of North Dakota compels them to gain a rudimentary education. They ride the unbroken cow-ponies of the range with the fearlessness of young Indians, and celebrate the Fourth of July as though to the manner born; but the acme of their Americanization was reached in a thirteen-year-old lad whom I met in the valley of the Knife River. Alone on the prairie, miles remote from a house, and with no sign of human presence in a wide range of vision, he was herding sheep on a bicycle. He was a cheerful little chap, and claimed that a wheel gave much less trouble than a pony, because it did not have to be watered, and never ran away. It was also very good to chase coyotes with when they came sneaking around his sheep, and he believed that if he could only induce one to stick to the road, he could run it down.

Yes, he was a Russian, that is, he was born in Russia, but he did not remember much about the place he came from, and was forgetting what he did remember as fast as he could.

The wildness of the region in which this solitary young wheelman was herding his sheep was shown in a few minutes after I left him by a small bunch of antelope that dashed out from a "draw," and ran for nearly a mile parallel to the trail along which I was driving. Of course I had no gun, and they knew it.

That night I spent with a Russian family whose chief pride in life was their flower-garden, a tiny enclosure filled with poppies, marigolds, sweet-pease, mignonette, and pansies, which they tended

reluctantly departed, taking with them the only lamp in the house. Upon this I slipped out from those beastly feather beds, softly closed the door, and began hurriedly to undress.

Inside of a minute the door was flung wide open, revealing my host, followed by his wife and others. As he smilingly inquired after my comfort, and if there was anything I wanted, or at least I thought

THE THIRD STAGE OF THE RUSSIAN SETTLER'S FARM-HOUSE.
The adobe house, granaries, and stables forming three sides of a hollow square.

with assiduous care. It was the only out-of-door flower-garden that I saw among them, though in nearly every house a few potted plants brightened the windows.

These Russians had been accused of being filthy in their habits. I did not find them more so than are many native-born Americans of my acquaintance, though, to be sure, certain of their customs were not such as a fastidious person would approve; while others would at least strike him as peculiar. It was, for instance, somewhat embarrassing when I was ready to go to bed to have the entire family gather curiously about, with the evident intention of witnessing the performance. In vain did I try to out-sit them, but they declined to leave, and remained, laughing with each other in high enjoyment of the situation. I was dead tired, and finally, in despair, crawled fully dressed between the two feather beds prepared for my resting-place, where I quickly feigned to be asleep. Upon this the spectators

he did so, I replied that I only wanted to be left alone. With this they all cheerfully sat down, prepared to keep me company so long as I should remain awake, and I again retired to my feathers. This time I really fell asleep, and when I next awoke it was with a lively sense of suffocation. The house was hermetically sealed against the admission of air, the outer doors were locked, not the smallest chink pierced the two-foot-thick walls, and not a window could be opened, as I proved by strenuous effort. At length, in desperation, I picked up a stool and drove it through the window nearest my bed. The entire sash went out with a prodigious clatter, that brought the affrighted family to my room. As I could not satisfactorily explain my action, they evidently believed me to be crazy, and watched me apprehensively until daylight. Before leaving that oppressively hospitable house I was allowed to pay for the broken window, but my host refused any recompense for board or lodging.

Another custom brought from the old country was that of greeting new arrivals or speeding departing guests with kisses from the men and simple hand-shakes on the part of the women. Even a minister who visited one house in which I was staying heartily kissed all the men on both cheeks, and merely shook hands with the women. At home also the women and girls went barefooted, while the men and even the small boys wore boots.

It did not seem wholly nice to have to wash in the same tin basin and use the same towel with which the entire family had performed their ablutions; but I remembered the historic towel of the mining-camp hotel used by thousands of men without complaint, and held my peace. I did hate, however, to see the radishes

Bread, cheese, milk, and radishes formed the bill of fare for breakfast and supper in every Russian house that I visited; but for dinner there was an addition of greens and coffee, with an occasional frying of bacon. The bread, made of unbolted wheat flour and baked in mud ovens, was as light and sweet as any that I ever tasted, and when on one occasion I drew a long black hair from a slice that I was eating, my hostess remarked, nonchalantly:

"Ach! Dot mak nottings."

It is, however, unfortunate to have been educated to fastidiousness if you must live among Russians of the peasant class.

The prime causes of success among these foreign-born farmers with lands that Americans had declared only fit for grazing are thrift and frugality. They

THE BAD LANDS TO THE WEST OF THE RUSSIAN SETTLEMENT.

that were to be served for breakfast cleaned in the same useful basin; nor was it pleasant to have one of the children capture my tooth-brush and closely imitate my recent use of it.

My hostess skimmed the cream from a pan of milk with her hand; but as I had seen the same thing done by an Irish woman in Mexico, I could not credit the custom with being peculiarly Russian.

protect from the weather their expensive farm machinery, while the native-born nearly always leaves his in the fields where it has been used, from one season to another. The American wheat-farmer exhausts his rich lands by planting them to the same crop year after year, burning his straw, and restoring nothing to the soil that he has taken from it. The Russian varies his crops, or allows his land to

A WHEAT VILLAGE IN THE RED RIVER VALLEY.
Showing four grain-elevators and the general nature of the surrounding country.

lie fallow in alternate years, and ploughs in his straw.

It costs the American about thirty-five cents to raise a bushel of wheat and deliver it to an elevator within a mile of his field. The Russian can raise wheat on poorer soil, haul it fifty miles, and place it on board the cars for several cents per bushel less money. When the latter goes to town he carries provisions with him and sleeps in his wagon; the American puts up at a hotel. The Russian rarely eats fresh meat, but his more civilized neighbor must have it three times a day.

The American engages in stock-raising on a large scale, allows his cattle to pick up their own living on the open range the year round, and loses half of them during a hard winter. His competitor from oversea only raises such stock as he can feed and care for, with the result that even in the severest winters he saves it all. He is narrow-minded and conservative, and his methods are those of the Old World, where of necessity his sphere of operations was limited. The American, especially in the West, brought up with large ideas, scorns a small economy as he does a petty meanness. He despises the small but sure profits with which the foreigner is satisfied, and prefers to assume great risks with the hope of large returns.

A fusion of the two races should yield most desirable results; but at present they will not come together. The native-born regards the naturalized citizen with dislike and contempt; while the new-comer has to overcome both fear and mistrust of those whose ways are so different from his own. Throughout the West the young American who marries a foreigner is considered to have lost caste and disgraced his family; while the foreign-born are said to be equally prejudiced against such inter-racial alliances. These antagonistic feelings cannot be eradicated in minds that have held them for a lifetime, but it is probable that in another generation they will largely if not wholly disappear.

The birth-rate among Russo-Americans shows a phenomenal increase over that of the old country, and the substantial "mud houses" of the Dakota prairies swarm with children. I was disappointed at not seeing these future citizens in school, but at the time of my visit no school was in session. I did, however, see several district school-houses in communities wholly Russian, and found plans in progress for the building and support of others. On every hand were evidences that North Dakota, with her fifty per cent. of foreign-born citizens, is fully alive to the value of education, and is providing it to the full extent of her resources. The little wooden school-houses dotting her wind-swept prairies, the substantial brick academies to be seen in every town, the well-equipped agricultural college at Fargo, and the promising State university at Grand Forks—all prove her earnestness of effort and her realizing sense that nothing else will so readily amalgamate the diverse elements of her population.

The land of which the Russian immigrants have taken possession presents a limitless succession of long easy slopes, softly rounded uplands, and broad valleys holding occasional streams or glinting chains of water-pools at which the range cattle quench their thirst. Contrary to the generally preconceived ideas of the great Western plains, there is nothing flat nor monotonous about the country; while its very bareness of trees adds a charm to the superb sweep of landscape over which the eye may roam. In hazy distances conical buttes are uplifted, or sharply outlined cliffs mark the erratic course of the turbid Missouri. Nearer at hand the monotone of neutral-tinted prairie grasses is occasionally relieved by serpentine lines of dark green, indicating the timber fringe of water-courses.

Both heat and cold can be borne with comparative ease in the atmosphere of this region; for it is as invigorating as a tonic, and so dry that the word humidity is unknown to the vocabulary of those privileged to breathe it. Potable water exists everywhere within twenty feet of the surface, and the whole country is so uniformly underlaid with beds of lignite that every farmer may if he chooses open a coal-mine on his own property.

The wonderfully picturesque Bad Lands bounding the Russian holdings on the west were formed by the burning out of enormous coal-measures, and the consequent falling in of the superimposed crust. This chaotic rearrangement of the landscape has left a vast region of pinnacled butte and frowning mesa, precipice and cliff, stately architecture, exquisite sculpture, and savagely distorted forms— all burned to vivid colors by the fierce heat that created them, and chiselled into shape by the cunning hands of wind, rain, or frost. Nestled among these are valleys and gorges covered with rich grasses or pungent sage, in which animal

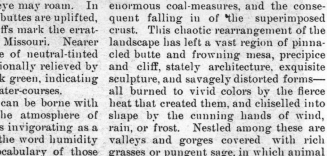

life from the adjacent plains finds shelter from winter blizzards and deadly snow drifts. Thus the Bad Lands form a notable game-preserve and a desirable cattle-range. Here are located the world-famous ranches of the late Marquis de Mores and of the Hon. Theodore Roosevelt, the hospitable Custer Trail Ranch, owned by the Eaton Brothers of Pittsburg, and many others equally interesting though not so well known. Here an

AMERICAN CHILDREN OF ICELANDIC PARENTAGE AT THE GARDAR DISTRICT SCHOOL.

THE SOD HOUSE OF AN ICELANDIC NEW-COMER.

occasional Russian, quick to recognize natural advantages in his line of business, has appeared with a flock or herd. The cowboys of the Bad Lands hate the Russians, dread their encroachments, and would fain exclude them from this favorite range; while the latter, stolid but tenacious, are equally determined to share it. This state of affairs cannot fail to create a fierce competition in ways, means, and methods that in the end must result favorably to all concerned.

Having spent ten days among the Russians of North Dakota, and learned to entertain a decided respect for this most recently arrived class of our immigrant farmers, I set forth in search of another colony from oversea, who, coming from the most poverty-stricken of all European countries, could now show the results of a twenty-year residence in the New World. It is a community of Icelanders, driven from their beloved island home by the rigors of its climate and unproductiveness of its soil, and now settled along the line of the Great Northern Railway in Pembina, the northeastern county of North Dakota. Here, in the land formerly governed by Joe Rolette, and occupied by the half-breed descendants of French voyageurs, Scotch engages of the Hudson Bay Company, and American fur-traders, families of Icelanders now form a large proportion of the population. Although I had at the outset no idea of where to find these people, a study of the map was sufficient to locate them; for who but Icelanders would name their post-offices Walhalla, Gardar, Akra, Hallson, Eyford, Maida, and Hensel?

My way to these led first to the extreme eastern border of the State, and then down the broad Red River Valley, the most glorious wheat-garden of the world, due north to the Canadian border. A railway ride of two hundred miles over this country, which is as level as a floor, through an almost unbroken wheat-field of thirty bushels to the acre, and extending to the horizon on either side, is at once an object-lesson and a delight. At that season the wonderful valley was a sea of undulating green, dimly bordered on the west, near its northern confines, by the distant blue of the Pembina Mountains, bisected by the dark timber belt of its river, and dotted at short intervals with tiny islandlike hamlets clustering about groups of tall grain-elevators, or the protecting groves planted around substantial farm-houses. Against the intense blue of the sky smoke clouds from other and far-away trains suggested passing steamers, while at night the electric

THE FIRST HOUSE OF AN ICELANDIC SETTLER.

lights of the larger towns simulated the warning beacons of a coast.

Forty years ago this vast wheat-field was a buffalo-pasture, through which wound the dusty trail traversed by long trains of creaking two-wheeled Red River carts, each drawn by a single ox, and laden with robes or furs from Pembina for the St. Paul market. Now all is changed—the whole face of the land, the people, their industry, and their methods of transportation. The home-made carts creeping at a snail's pace gave way to river boats, and those in turn to the railroad. The rich freights of furs have been supplanted by a still richer freighting of wheat, while the light-hearted but improvident half-breed with his French-Indian patois has disappeared before the sturdy advance of an English-speaking race of husbandmen; and who shall say that the change is not for the better?

Not all the farmers of the Red River Valley were English-speaking when they first settled its fertile acres. Men of diverse nationalities were attracted by the fabulous richness of its soil, until its tongues were as those of Babel; but in due time the language taught in its public schools prevailed over all others.

Most interesting of the many comers from oversea who have here found new homes are the Northmen from Iceland, who, like their Russian followers, first settled in Canada, on the low lands surrounding Lake Winnipeg. There drowned out by floods, they were compelled to a second migration, this time to the United States, where they located in Pembina. Warned by their recent experience, they sought lands from which no flood could drive them, and finally selected a plateau known as the "Sand Ridge," which, though well-timbered, contains the poorest soil in that entire region. Fortunately the Sand Ridge is of such small area that later comers were forced to take the much richer and treeless lands on either side.

In this locality the Icelandic colony has grown and thriven, until to-day, twenty years from the date of its foundation, it is a thoroughly Americanized community, numbering several thousand intelligent and prosperous people. It is well represented in the State Legislature, and has furnished to Pembina County many of its leading ministers, lawyers, and doctors—all of whom were born in Iceland, and only came to America when in their teens. In spite of their foreign origin, these men retain no trace of it in speech or thought, save in a broader liberality than is common to native-born Americans, and an intimate acquaintance with the Northland classics, of which most Americans are profoundly ignorant.

In the Gardar district school I found fifty bright youngsters of Icelandic parentage gathered beneath the same flag that floats above the school-houses of New England, and studying the very text-books used by the descendants of the Puritans. At recess the boys played baseball preparatory to a match game with a neighboring school, and were as keenly alive to its niceties as though they belonged to some Eastern interscholastic league. They were intensely interested in the photograph that I took of them, and were vastly proud of the fact that it was intended for publication in a great magazine.

These young Icelanders were as well-behaved a lot of children as I ever met, trained to politeness and a respect for their elders, eager to understand without being inquisitive, and, above all, courteous to each other. All of them can speak Icelandic as fluently as English, and every one can read in the vernacular the grand sagas of the far northern isle that their fathers still hold in fond remembrance.

Like all other poverty-stricken immigrants in this country, the Icelanders made their start in rude little houses of logs or sod, and holding but one or two rooms. After a lapse of twenty years these have so completely disappeared that it was difficult to discover one of them in all the county. With the advent of prosperity their places have been taken by roomy and well-built frame structures, neatly painted, and flanked by great barns. Although there is little to distinguish the dwellers in these comfortable houses from any other Americans of their class, a few old-country customs still remain with them, such as the caring for birds, and the piling of their firewood in conical stacks that may not be buried by drifting snows. In one house I found a very quaint, very clumsy, and very ancient cradle, in which many generations of Iceland babies had been rocked; while in another sat a bright-eyed old woman spinning wool with a wheel of most primitive pattern. In their churches all illuminated texts, as well as the service-books, are printed in Icelandic; but the minis-

AFTER TWENTY YEARS.

The present dwelling of the Icelandic settler whose first house is shown on the opposite page.

ter of the Gardar church, who, though born in Iceland, had been educated in an Ohio college, was one of the best read and most interesting men whom I met in North Dakota.

That these Icelanders, who but a score of years ago were poverty-stricken foreigners, ignorant of the customs, language, and institutions of this country, are to-day so thoroughly Americanized that it is difficult to detect a trace of their foreign birth, is cheering evidence of the possibilities latent in all immigrants from oversea. They have accomplished nothing that the despised Russians do not bid fair to equal, and even to excel, in an equal length of time, since facilities for learning and succeeding are many times greater in the North Dakota of to-day than they were twenty years ago.

Across the Red River in Minnesota, with its 2,000,000 of population, of whom one-fourth are Scandinavians, 134,000 are Germans, 11,000 are Bohemians, 9000 are Poles, 8000 are Finns, 6500 are Russians, and 108,000 are foreigners of other nationalities, the process of amalgamation was found to be fully as rapid as in North Dakota, and in most cases even far-

the outset. Eliminating these, leaves for consideration only Finns, Poles, Bohemians, and Russians.

Flying visits to communities of each of these located along the lines of the Northern Pacific and Great Northern railways disclosed them to have attained a degree of Americanization intermediate between those of the Russians and the Icelanders of North Dakota. In every case I found them to be frugal, thrifty, and industrious, largely guided in their temporal as well as in their spiritual affairs by their ministers or priests. Wherever I met these men they appeared to be conscientious, liberal-minded, and well educated. The Minnesota school laws compel the education in English of every youth in the State, and in every foreign-born community that I visited it was quickly evident that the children are being thus taught. They always spoke fluent English, generally without an accent, and above every school-house floated the American flag that they are thus taught to love and respect above all other national emblems.

As the result of a month's experience among the oversea Americans of two great agricultural States, I am convinced that there is nothing to be feared but everything to be hoped from such immigrants, no matter what their previous condition, as are willing to till the soil and people the wide vacant spaces of our vast territory. So long as the existing school laws are enforced, their children, even in the first generation, will become as truly Americanized as are the descendants of those earlier immigrants who settled the Atlantic coast. Whatever dangers exist in unrestricted or in par-

RESIDENCE OF THE ICELANDIC PASTOR OF THE GARDAR CHURCH.

ther advanced towards a thorough Americanization. Of course the Germans and Scandinavians have so thoroughly identified themselves with this country that they can no longer be considered as foreigners, while the 50,000 natives of the British Isles settled in Minnesota have hardly been regarded as foreigners from

tially restricted immigration must then be sought, not on our Western prairies, but in our cities, where the very atmosphere of the congested tenements is moral poison; and here, too, the most effective preventive of anarchy and crime lies in an enforced *primary* education of the children.

MOOSE-HUNTING WITH THE TRO-CHU-TIN

T HE Tro-chu-tin are better known as "Klondike Indians." Their village, numbering sixty or seventy souls, was located at the mouth of the Klondike River until white men discovered gold on Bonanza Creek and crowded them away to its present site on the Yukon, two miles below the town of Dawson. One morning early in January three Indians sought an interview with Captain Hansen, agent of the Alaska Commercial Company—"Isaac," the chief; "Silas," a "smart" young man; and "John," a former chief and medicine-doctor, or *shuman*. Silas, having been interpreter for the traders, spoke middling English; Isaac, worse; the old man, none at all. On this occasion Isaac was spokesman. Said he:

"First time, Jack McQuesten all same Injun papa; Yukon Injun all same her children. Just nup, McQuesten he gone; A. C. Company all same Injun papa; her children hungry." The meaning of this was that the Alaska Commercial Company, from the time when it received the lease of the Seal Islands and came into a practical monopoly of the fur trade of Alaska, had

exercised through its various agents, one of whom had been Jack McQuesten, a paternal care over the native tribes, by directing their hunts and feeding them when fish, moose, or caribou were scarce or difficult to obtain. As the Indians had been accustomed during the quarter of a century before the discovery of the Klondike to appeal for aid in time of hunger to McQuesten, it now seemed proper to lay before the visible representative of the company at Dawson the fact that they were on the verge of starvation. This condition was not exceptional. The salmon in the Yukon are abundant; the moose nowhere on the North-American Continent are so large as on the rivers entering the Yukon, or more plentiful; and the Barren Ground caribou, or wild-reindeer, run in bands often numbering thousands; but nowhere does an Indian exert himself until the last pound of "grub" is gone.

Captain Hansen told them in reply that it was true that the "A. C." Company now was "all same Jack McQuesten," but times had changed. It was no longer necessary that they should consider how much fur there was on the beaver's back, but how much *meat* on the moose's bones. He had no food for them, nor for the white men (it is still fresh in mind that starvation stared us all in the face that winter). They must hunt the moose and bring the meat to the white men, and then, but not until then, could he give them food from the store.

Several days after the above conversation a friend introduced me, in the street at Dawson, to a tall, rather angular individual, dressed in a black fur cap of peculiar design, a coat of gorgeous "upholstery"-pattern ed Mackinaw blanket, "store" trousers further encased in leggings of the same fancy material as the coat, moose-hide moccasins with pointed toes and bright scarlet tops. A pair of large caribou-skin mittens hung from his neck by a thick

plaited green and white worsted cord, and he was further protected from the dry arctic cold by a knit yarn scarf wrapped once around his neck, the ends being tied behind his back out of the way. In features he was a North-American Indian,

though of the Northern interior "Woods" Indian type; light brown in color, with prominent cheek-bones, a strong chin, aquiline nose, a large mouth with a stringy black mustache that drooped at the ends, and a flashing eye, that gave the impression both of mastery and shrewdness. Although he carried himself with conscious self-respect, Isaac, as I saw him that first time and during our subsequent "partnership," would have presented a droll appearance anywhere save in the busy street of a Northern mining-camp, where every other man wore a shirtlike "parka," and other articles of native dress appropriate to the place and season.

After an effusive greeting and vigorous hand-shaking, Isaac readily assented to my proposition to accompany the village on the hunt; first, however, warily inquiring whether I could snowshoe, and then saying that I should bring along two sacks of flour, five pounds of tea, I do not know how much sugar—in fact, a quarter of a year's outfit, including a tent and the usual miner's sheet-iron stove! Isaac's handling of English was atrocious and unique, while of course my knowledge of his own language was nil; but by much repetition, aided by gestures, I gathered that the hunt would last until the sun rose high above the horizon—three months later ; that he expected me to "grub-stake" him with provisions, which he would repay out of the first moose he killed; that the hind quarters belonged to the hunter who shot the moose, the rest to the village; that he and I were "pudnas" (partners), and would give each other a fore shoulder; and when the smoke inside the "skin house" made his eyes "too much sick," he would come into my tent. The time, however, being more than I could spare for such an adventure, I cut down the grub-list, and further resolved that if I could not live in the "skin houses" exactly like one of them, not to go at all.

On the 13th of January the sleepy miners' camp was startled by a wild, screaming, howling cavalcade of Indians—men, women, boys, girls, and babies—and dogs of all degrees of leanness, the dogs hauling birch toboggans, on which were piled smoke-browned house-poles, skins, and blankets, with

babies and pups, the women driving the dogs, and nearly every man hauling
a Yukon miner's sled (Isaac had explained that nearly all the dogs had been
sold to the miners).   The procession, a quarter of a mile long, numbering
forty or fifty people and as many dogs, turned up a smooth trail on the frozen
surface of the Klondike, the dogs, poor things, howling dismally as the
women with shrill voices and long sticks urged them on.   Two miles from
the Yukon, above the mouth of the Bonanza Creek, the head of the caravan stopped, and Isaac marked the place for the camp at the edge of the
river, alongside a dense grove of spruce-trees.   As we turned off the smooth
miners' trail every person old enough to walk slipped into snow-shoes, as
the snow was about two feet deep.   The women took long-handled wooden
shovels and removed the snow off the ground an elliptical space eighteen
feet long by twelve feet wide, banking it all around two feet high.   While
some covered the exposed river gravel with green spruce boughs and kindled
a fire in the centre, others cut sticks three to five feet long and set them
upright a foot apart in the bank of snow, the long way of the intended
house, leaving an opening at one side two feet wide for the door.   The
house-poles, an inch thick and ten or twelve feet long, whittled out of
spruce and previously bent and seasoned into the form of a curve, were then
set up in the snow at the ends of the camp to the number of sixteen or
twenty, their upper ends pointing toward the middle in the form of a dome
ten feet high.   These were strengthened by two arched cross-poles underneath, the ends of which were lashed to the side-stakes with withes of willow
twigs thawed out and made pliant over the fire.   Over this comparatively
stiff frame-work next was drawn a covering of caribou-skin, tanned with
the hair on, made in two sections, and shaped and sewed together to fit the
dome.   The two sections, comprising forty skins, completely covered the
house, except in the middle, where a large hole was left for the smoke to escape, and at the doorway, over which was hung
a piece of blanket.   The toboggans with the balance of the loads were hoisted upon pole scaffolds

each side of the house, out of reach of the dogs, who looked and acted as if ready to devour anything from a moccasin to a rawhide toboggan-lashing. Not until the house was done and enough wood stacked before the door to last until morning did any one stop for a moment. In a climate where the temperature remains not higher than thirty degrees below zero, and occasionally drops to fifty or sixty below, it is dangerous to dally, as white men are prone to do under the same conditions.

In our little village there were seven lodges. In the chief's house were nine persons and eleven dogs, divided into two households, each having a side of the fire to itself. On ours were Isaac, his wife, Eliza, with a nursing boy less than a year old, myself, and three native dogs—Chicken (child), Gagul (broken-leg), and John; also a tawny "white man's dog," Beaber, taken to board, a small black native pup, and an extremely miserable short-haired white man's pup, wrapped in a blanket to keep from freezing, and weighing just fourteen pounds by Isaac's spring scales. On the other side were a middle-aged, stockily built man known as "Billy," or "the missionary's man," and his wife, with two girls respectively about eight and ten years of age, and a boy of the same uncertain age, four large native dogs, and two pups. The human occupants kneeled or reclined before the fire, which was ingeniously built to throw the heat in two directions and to draw well, notwithstanding which latter, I soon discovered that it was often necessary to lie close to the ground, and when the smoke became too thick, to lift the lower edge of the skin covering. We cooked a loaf of baking-powder bread in a frying-pan. A scrap of bacon and a cup of tea completed our meal. The Indians were really near starvation. Isaac himself had the only sack of flour in the village. Each family had its own cooking outfit,

consisting of a frying-pan, a tin milk-pan, a tin dish-pan, several tin cups and plates, and a small tin pail for boiling tea, and a larger one, holding two or three gallons, for making soup and boiling meat and washing the children's under-garments.

The following morning before daybreak word was given, "All go." Toboggans were rattled off of caches, and houses taken down and loaded as swiftly as they had been set up. We made ten miles, part way on a miners' trail, the rest on snow-shoes, and camped exactly as before. It was still dark when all hands were awakened, the stars were shining brightly, the white aurora flashed feebly in the northern sky, the black domes of the village were dimly outlined against the snow and the black wall of spruce, and a few sparks and thin smoke were rising from the early fires. Isaac went outside and began to declaim in a loud voice. He spoke not in the smooth, melodious tongue of the Eastern Indian, but slowly and deliberately, in short, crisp, incisive monosyllables. When he was done, he informed me in broken English that we were to hunt on the left-hand side of the river. He buckled on his belt full of "forty-five-seventy" cartridges, and went outside.

Some time afterwards a young man who was warming himself by our fire asked me if I "go hunt moose." Ducking out of the narrow door, and seizing rifle and snow-shoes off the cache, I fell into a trail along with two shadowy figures, with rifles over their shoulders. In half an hour it was light enough to see that my companions were a boy of about twelve, with a large repeating-rifle, and the old *shuman*, John, dressed in a coat of bright orange blanket and nether garments of caribou-skin. He carried a single-barrelled shot-gun in a caribou-leather case handsomely embroidered with beads and red cloth, and a sort of pouch made of black cloth, richly beaded, for holding bullets and caps, hung on his breast, while a leather-covered powder-horn hung at his side. After we had walked seven miles, the river valley, in increasing light, was seen to be several miles across, the white frozen stream winding between low flat banks covered with a growth of scrubby spruce, beyond which rose evenly sloping mountains covered sparsely with small spruce, birch, and cottonwoods. The trail made by several snow-shoes ahead of us turned abruptly to the left. The boy and I turned into the spruce. The old man kept on alone, and we saw no more of him.

We reached the hill and were quite on the crest of the first ridge when the toe of one of my snow-shoes broke off. Motioning Indian fashion for the boy to go ahead, he disappeared among the snow-laden trees, leaving me to limp slowly on. It was just twelve o'clock by the watch when I heard a rifle-shot, followed quickly by another. The next thing I was in a moose's feeding-ground, and saw snow-shoe tracks running hither and thither among the bowed-down birches, in evident pursuit. Plunging on the moose's trail, down the back side of a little hill, I had not gone two hundred yards before I saw smoke among the evergreens, and the familiar

figure of Isaac and several others around a long fire, and two others near by skinning a large moose which lay in the snow. It was a gory sight— the white snow splashed with the blood, the Indians in variegated red, yellow, and green blanket coats, holding portions of the moose's vitals in the flames on sticks, and greedily licking up the fat that dripped into the snow. They were all smiling and happy. They had made the fire without axes, simply breaking off dead limbs with their hands. The two Indians soon had the moose skinned, and proceeded to separate part from part, using only their hunting-knives. After cutting off a chunk of ten to fifteen pounds of meat for each person present, the rest of the meat was covered with snow, and the smaller pieces were wrapped in spruce boughs and made into a pack, a braided rawhide cord, which each carried, being used as a sling. At just one o'clock each of us shouldered a pack, and we started back single file, reaching camp at dark, having travelled about eighteen miles. On the way we passed another moose, which an Indian was skinning. That accounted for the second shot. That night the old *shuman* and Billy, who had gone off separately, returned, each with a piece of moose, making thus *four* moose for the first day's hunt.

No wonder every one was happy! Even the dogs, who had been having nothing but a thin soup of boiled salmon-heads, took a new lease of existence. Our moose was a fat cow. The moose are still too plentiful for the Indians to stop to consider the ultimate consequence of killing cows at this season, when they are heavy with young. Indeed, they much prefer the cow to the bull. "Mull [bull] moose," said Isaac, "too much tup [tough]; cow moose plenty fat; *he* all right." He would eat the cow moose himself, and sell the bull moose to the miners.

The following day we moved camp seven miles, and the morning after that a man went ahead with an axe and cleared a trail for the women and toboggans, who hauled the meat into camp, where it was taken into the several houses and laid over poles at the side of the house, so as to be guarded from the dogs. The hides were brought in-doors, and women at once set to work dressing them. The hair was shaved off; then the skin was turned over, and all the sinew and meat adhering was removed by means of a sort of chisel made of a moose's shin-bone; and finally scraped, a work requiring a whole day of incessant and tiresome labor. The skin was now washed in a pan of hot water, and then wrung dry with the help of a stick as a tourniquet. After which the edges were incised for subsequent lacing into a frame, and then hung out-doors over a pole. The tanning, with a "soup" of liver and brains, is done the next summer. After which the skin is smoked, and made into moccasins, gold-sacks, etc. The various portions of the moose were divided among the village. One family got a head, another a slab of ribs, another the fore shoulders. The shin-bones were roasted and cracked for

the marrow; the ears, although nothing but cartilage, were roasted and chewed up; the rubberlike "muffle," or nose, and every particle of flesh, fat, or gristle that could be scraped from head or hoofs, were disposed of. Even the stomach was emptied of its contents and boiled and eaten; but the very choicest delicacy was the unborn moose, which was suspended by a string around the neck and toasted over the fire. With plenty of meat, the village was in no hurry to move. There were no regular meals now. Whenever one wanted anything to eat, he cut off a piece of meat and threw it into a frying-pan. In our house some one was cooking about all the time. No one cared for salt: it is a civilized habit they have not yet acquired. Moose-meat answers all requirements of nature, and one can live on it alone.

The killing of a fat cow moose is celebrated by a feast. Our first was prepared by Isaac. Two or three of the largest tin pails were brought into the house, and an Indian selected by the chief as cook filled them with water from an ice-hole in the river, and hung them over the fire, with all sorts of odds and ends of meat and bone. While the meat was cooking, the hunters gathered inside to the number of twenty-three, lying on their backs with their feet to the fire, completely filling the little room. They laughed, talked, smoked, until about noon, when the cook brought out a large wooden spoon, and skimming the pure grease off the top of the kettles, passed it around the circle. Each took a sip at the fiery-hot, saltless tallow, apparently regardless of considerable moose-hair and wood-ashes. When the meat was done, a number of milk-pans and plates were partly filled, each one's share being apportioned according to the size of his family.

Considerable merriment was caused by Isaac, ever fond of a joke, who inquired how much of my allowance I was going to give to a certain fat, greasy, very muscular, dusky young lady in another lodge, whom they seemed

to have had picked out for me as a "partner," in case I remained in the country. Isaac hastened to explain, however: "Injun no fool; just laugh." A cup or kettle of tea was set before each person, and all hands sat up and pitched in with hunting-knives and fingers. Now I learned the way to eat meat: people who eat nothing but meat surely ought to know the way. You grasp the bone, or roll of fat, tightly in the left hand, and seize the other end firmly in the teeth. Then with the hunting-knife, dagger fashion, in the other hand, keeping both elbows well out, and lifting the lips away so that no accident may happen by a slip of the knife, you bring the keen edge squarely downward, severing as much as you wish for a mouthful. Never have I seen so much energy thrown into eating. Whatever was left in the pans was handed out to the women and children, and eaten in their respective houses. Then we lay back for more smoking and talking until another batch of meat was ready. At 3 P.M. pans and plates were again filled, and again disposed of, to the accompaniment of the same fierce arm and elbow movements. Thus ended a day of feasting, which, come when it may, is really the "Sunday" of a hunting people. Several sleds took meat to town, where it readily sold to the miners for $1 25 to $1 50 per pound. When all the meat had been cared for, the hides were hoisted on poles into trees out of reach of wolverenes, to be picked up at the end of the hunt. We journeyed leisurely on, making six or seven miles each day, and hunting both sides of the river. By the time we reached the Forks of Klondike, forty miles from Dawson, nearly four weeks had elapsed; just thirty-two moose had been killed, and eaten, sold, or "cached" until the final homeward trip.

The broad valley and mountainous banks of the Klondike are an admirable feeding-ground for the moose. The temperature in winter is exceedingly cold and crisp, but the snowfall is light, and by reason of the intense cold the snow does not settle or pack. There is so little wind, especially during the early part of the winter, that the snow accumulates on the trees in strange and often fantastic masses, giving the landscape, especially on the mountain-tops, the appearance of having been chiselled out of pure white marble. On

account of its lightness, the snow is no impediment to the long-legged, gaunt moose, which is not obliged to "yard," as in southern deep-snow regions, but wanders at will from valley to mountaintop in search of the tender twigs of willow, white birch, and cottonwood. The Indians surround the moose in its feeding-ground, and as it runs, one or more of them is tolerably sure of a quick shot.

Their skill with the modern repeating-rifle is remarkable, especially in view of the fact that comparatively few years ago they had no guns at all, but stalked and killed the moose with bow and arrow alone. The "old-time" way of hunting the caribou was for a band of Indians, number of sometimes fifty and more, to surround the unsuspecting herd and run in upon them at a given signal. The frightened animals were easily shot down, and sometimes out of a herd of several hundred not a single one escaped. Billy, who asserted that he himself had killed moose with a bow and arrow, preferred to leave the round-up and hunt alone. Three of the moose that fell to his rifle he shot through the head as they lay in their beds in the snow.

Not many years ago the Tro-chu-tin dressed entirely in the skins of animals. The sable, mink, otter, and beaver of the Yukon are of great fineness and value, the sable especially being considered second only to the Russian sable. In exchange for furs, they received from the traders guns, ammunition, tea, tobacco, sugar, flour; also extremely thick blankets, which often weigh twelve pounds, and are made expressly for the Northern trade. Out of these, as well as of fancy cottons and bright flannels, they made garments that have now to some extent supplanted the old. The younger men affect a bright Mackinaw coat that vies with the spectrum in brilliancy and variety of color. One fellow was the proud possessor of a coat striped in brown, pink, yellow, blue, and green; and another of a coat checked in large squares of pink, green, blue, yellow, and lilac. With these are worn blanket trousers stuffed into the tops of moccasins. The old men, who cling tenaciously to old customs, wear a garment, comprising trousers and moccasins in one, made of caribou-skin, with the hair inside. These are worn next the skin. One old man wore, in addition, a "parka," or shirt, made of white rabbit-skins cut into strips and plaited, leaving openings through which one could thrust the fingers; and yet in the coldest weather he wore positively nothing else, except a blanket hood and mittens of rabbit-skin. The mittens are generally made of caribou-skin, with the hair inside, and are very warm. The women, when in-doors, wear a dress of light cloth fashioned on civilized lines, but when travelling they don either a blanket coat over a shortish skirt of the same, or a voluminous over-dress of caribou-skin, having a hood, which upon occasion may be hauled over the head, but in which commonly reposes the baby. The women's head-gear is invariably a large fancy silk or cotton kerchief knotted under the chin. The skin dress reaches half-

"Gagul"

way from the knees to the ground, deer-skin legging-moccasins protecting the lower extremities. The little girls wear garments similar to their mothers, while the boys wear a shirt of caribou-skin, with fur outside, made with a hood for pulling over the head. Their legs are encased in diminutive skin trousers with feet, while the mittens of the very smallest children are sewed fast to their sleeves. When a small boy gets ready to go out-doors, he lies on his back and sticks his legs into the air, while the mother draws on his "pants."

The children, dressed in their warm thick furs, have as happy a time as children anywhere. Most of their play is out-of-doors, where they make play-houses in imitation of the large ones, and roll about in the snow like little polar bears. Sometimes they take papa's snow-shoes and slide down some little bank, but they did not use the toboggans for that purpose. A favorite game was "kli-so-kot," or "throwing-the-stick." A row of five or six small stakes is set up in the hard-packed snow of the village street, and another row thirty or forty feet distant. Each contestant provides himself with two clubs, and taking turns, they throw these at first one, then the other, of the group of upright stakes, the one who knocks down the greatest number of stakes being the winner. Although these Indian children are so tough, they are great cry-babies. One of the things the women particularly wanted to know was whether white babies cried very much. Isaac's "hope of posterity" was a fearful nuisance. He was crying about a third of the time. Not a regular cry, but a nasal, monotonous drone, punctuated at intervals by three or four inward catches of the breath. He would keep this up for perhaps half an hour without the slightest diminution, until humored or petted. Often Billy's boy would imitate him, with the result only of increasing and prolonging the distressful performance. I rarely saw a child punished, and never one whipped.

The grown people in their own amusements were as simple-minded as the children. They had learned what a camera was, but they had never seen any one make pictures "by hand." I drew everything I saw, and it amused them to recognize the various members of the village and the different dogs. They never tired looking at the sheets and passing them around the circle, screaming with laughter as they recognized some person or dog. I was given the name "picture-man." Some of the old men and women objected to having their pictures made, but it was more from fear of ridicule than superstition. Isaac himself had objections to "hand pictures" of himself, as he called them. He asked me privately, as a favor, not to make any. "Machine picture, *he* all right." He evidently thought it did not befit the dignity of chief to become an object of even harmless merriment.

The dogs are a feature of every Northwest Indian village. Ours were a ragged, wolfish, scrawny, poor, miserable lot, the best, with few exceptions, having been sold to the miners for twenty times what they were worth a few years ago. That dogs could be treated so and live, or not fly in des-peration at the throats of their human, or inhuman, owners, was a constant wonder to me. Like wolves, they are able to go for days at a time with next to nothing to eat. Even when we were revelling in moose-meat the dogs received only what no one could eat, namely, bones, gristle, the scrapings of the moose-hides, and whatever else they could pick up. A "Siwash" dog, under such conditions, grows up a natural thief. He is proud of it. I have watched one sit blinking before the fire, apparently oblivious of everything but the warmth, but when a morsel of food fell to the ground, like a flash he would cut it out, and if it proved sizable,

"Four-Bits."

he would spring for the door, yelling to the sound of a stream of whacks of the poker-stick. One time he failed to locate the coveted morsel, which had, been thrown to a puppy. As the woman laid the stout stick soundly over his back the dog yelled as if he was being murdered, but he would not run, and between the yelps I saw him, with an agonized expression that was ludicrous in spite of the cruelty, trying with his eye to find the meat. At length he found it and made for the door. I have seen a little pup, by nature kind and playful as a kitten, beaten with the fire-poker by a child a year old.

Another time I undertook to deliver, with a toboggan and one dog, a shoulder of meat Isaac had sold to a miner on Hunker Creek. I asked Isaac's wife what I should take to feed the dog. She replied, nonchalantly, "Nawthin'." "But," I replied, "I may be gone two days. What shall I take?" "Nawthin'." Sometimes they go to the other extreme. "Patsy" could not stand "Siwash" dog-fare, and grew steadily thinner. Isaac had set great store by the pup, for which he had paid, I believe, two dollars, and was expecting in the course of a year to get two hundred dollars for him from some miner. The dog was now so weak he could barely stand. In the distribution of shreds from a moose-hide, Patsy's leanness attracted the notice of an Indian woman. She tried to see how much he could hold, so she filled him up. He grew as big around as a stove-pipe, and the hair, not being very thick anyhow, his sides had much the same shiny appearance. He still looked up for more, and finally got so full he could not lift himself, which amused us all.

Soon after the first day's hunt Isaac had conveyed word to me that one or two of the Indians were nervous about my hunting with them in the bunch, lest when the moose ran I should shoot an Indian instead of the moose. He stated that although he himself did not share that fear, he thought it best I should hunt alone in future, as they now had few Indians, and could not afford to lose any. It was a rather hard compliment, but as the camp life of the people themselves was so interesting, it really mattered little whether I hunted at all. At the Forks we remained upwards of a week, the Indians securing in that time twelve more moose. Here I made long excursions, in some cases ten miles from camp, hunting alone on the sides and tops of the high mountains. But in the first place I had misjudged the ease with which a moose could be picked up; in the next place I was not acquainted with the country, nor was I able to learn from the Indians' well-meant directions just what ground they were hunting over. So that at the end of a week of the hardest and most persistent hunting of which I was capable I found myself without a moose to call my own.

One day after an unusually long tramp, wherein I had resolved to get beyond the snow-shoe tracks of the Indians, I had remained overnight at a new miner's cabin, returning to camp next day. Being unable to dry the perspiration and frost from my clothes thoroughly as by the direct blaze of the skin house, a cold set in that took a sudden and serious turn. I followed the Indians another stage up the "North Fork," but realizing the danger, I started back, and leaving the sled behind, succeeded in reaching a miner's cabin, where for six days I lay unable to eat or sleep. Isaac and his people had cared for me as one of themselves, but now their solicitude, expressed in language I could not understand, but in looks that left no doubt, could be of no assistance. Isaac reported in Dawson: "Picture-man too much sick. Mebbe two days he all right, mebbe two days he dead." My partner came after me with a basket-sleigh and four stout dogs. Meanwhile I was up and on my way home, and passed him in a bend of the Klondike River. The Indians killed in all about eighty moose and sixty-five caribou, much of which they sold to the miners in Dawson, as Captain Dansen advised them, and invested the proceeds in finery and repeating-rifles.

AMERICA'S UNCONQUERED MOUNTAIN

MOUNT McKINLEY, thought to be the highest peak of North America, has to the present remained unexplored. The mountain was known to the Indians and to the Russians for a great many years, but it was not known to be of extraordinary height until after the present name was attached to it by W. A. Dickey, who, while prospecting at the head of Cook Inlet in 1897, saw from a small mountain a part of the Alaskan Range, one hundred miles away, and made a rough sketch of it. The gold stampede of 1898 brought to this part of Alaska several government expeditions, and the combined effort of these exploring enterprises, but more especially the work of the party under Alfred H. Brooks, has given us considerable knowledge of this Alaskan Range. From a mountaineering standpoint, however, all of the great peaks of this range are unknown.

The Alaskan Range takes a northeasterly course through central Alaska from Cook Inlet, thus dividing the drainage systems of the three greatest Alaskan rivers, the Kuskokwim, the Sushitna, and the Yukon. Our work was limited to the central portion of this range, which we will call the McKinley group. This group extends from the head waters of the Yentna River, one hundred and forty miles, to the Cantwell River. There are in this group four very remarkable peaks, named in the order of their altitude, and from northeast to southwest—Mount Mc-Kinley, 20,300 feet; Mount Foraker, 17,100 feet; Mount Russell, 11,350 feet; and Mount Dall, 9000 feet. With my companions we assumed as our task for last summer an effort to climb Mount McKinley, and to explore as much of the neighboring range as the season would permit. Everything in Alaska is difficult, but the trials of mountaineering there are the troubles of the highest Alpine peaks multiplied many times.

In organizing this expedition I was fortunate in finding men well fitted for the arduous duties in hand. The party included Robert Dunn and Ralph Shainwald, of New York, Fred Printz and Walter Miller, of Seattle, and John Carroll and two Indians, of Alaska. For some time I hesitated in making a decision about the route to the mountain. The eastern slope was entirely unknown, but the distance to it was only one hundred and fifty miles up glacial rivers. The western slope had been partially examined by Messrs. Brooks and Rearburn of the Geological Survey, but the route to it was five hundred miles long. Both sides could not be attacked in one season, and on the recommendation of Mr. Brooks, I chose the western slope for the first assault.

With little knowledge of the mountain, but with a fair knowledge of the main difficulties *en route,* I equipped our expedition accordingly.

Accompanied by Mrs. Cook, I left New York on May 26, stopping at the Yackima Indian Reservation, east of the Cascades. We picked out fifteen excellent pack-horses; these were taken to Seattle. The mountain equipment was brought from New York. At Seattle we purchased our general outfit, and all were placed on the steamer *Santa Anna,* and promptly transported to Cook Inlet through the kindness of the Pacific Packing and Navigation Company.

The entire party left Seattle early in the morning of the 10th of June,

WESTERN SLOPE OF MOUNT McKINLEY
From 8000 to 15,000 feet altitude.   Peters Glacier in foreground

fully equipped for our summer work. After an interesting voyage along the Alaskan coast the *Santa Anna* dropped her anchor in Cook Inlet, a half-mile from the shore at Tyonek, about midnight on the 23d of June. A strong tide carried the water past the ship like the current of a rapid river. The night was clear and crisp, with sufficient light to see distinctly the pearly slopes of the volcanoes Iliamna and Redoubt, under a purple haze, far to the south. At three o'clock the first horse was placed in slings and thrown overboard, to swim ashore as best he could. The other horses, with good reason, objected to this kind of treatment, and their resistance was so great that we were compelled to devise another method of getting them into the water. The animals were led into the usual horse-box, which was then hoisted out of the hold and lowered to the water. There with a great deal of caution the horses were urged to plunge into the icy waters of Cook Inlet, and men in boats either led or followed them ashore. In a few hours our horses and

outfit were safely landed, the *Santa Anna* steamed seaward, and we were left to work out the problem of getting to Mount McKinley.

Tyonek is a small trading post, with perhaps twenty Indian families, five or six white men, and one woman; and we found there deserted United States army barracks, which we occupied as our headquarters. Two days were spent in breaking in horses which did not take kindly to packs. This was both exciting and profitable work, the men obtaining a good knowledge of horse-taming, under the excellent tutorage of Mr. Printz, and the horses so thoroughly trained to our purposes that we had little trouble later.

In Cook Inlet all journeys by land or water are regulated by the tides. All boats, large or small, leave with the tides, for the tidal current carries them eight miles per hour. Alongshore it is only possible to travel at low tide. Even fishing, hunting, and certain kinds of mining are possible only at certain stages of the tides. Indeed, in Cook Inlet, as in the bays of Biscay and Fundy, life

FORDING A GLACIAL STREAM NEAR MOUNT MCKINLEY

CUTTING STEPS IN THE ICE

moves with the tides. It is always the first topic of conversation, and when we started, on the morning of June 25, we were compelled to wait for low tide.

Our horses were packed with one hundred and fifty pounds each, then guided to the beach to follow the lead-horse. In four hours we travelled ten miles, camping about two miles south of the Beluga River, on a flat where wood, grass, and fresh water—the three necessities of a good camping-ground—were easy of access. On the following morning our course was through a thick jungle to the Beluga River, which we reached early in the afternoon. In the river we soon saw large numbers of white whales (belugas), after which the river takes its name, and on the opposite side we observed a large grizzly-bear, apparently getting a meal of fish.

The Beluga River is a deep, rapid stream, about two hundred and fifty yards wide, which takes its origin among the glaciers of the Tordrillo Range. To ferry men and equipment across this and other large streams farther north we hired a boat at Tyonek; and it was placed in charge of Miller, who, with the assistance of Shainwald, reached our camp on the Beluga late in the evening. The packs were ferried across the same evening, and on the following morning the lead-horse was urged into the river and towed by the boat, while the other horses were thrown into the stream from the bank. They followed a short distance, and then went down the stream with the current in a bunch, snorting and swimming as if crossing swift streams had been their main occupation. Arriving on the north shore the mosquitoes and flies tormented them immediately.

The animals were quickly packed, and, under the direction of Dunn, the pack-train was started across country, partly over an old Indian trail, for the Skwentna River. We anticipated considerable difficulty in getting the boat up the swift streams northward in time to ferry the party across, and at the last moment I decided to join Miller on his mission. In

RESTING, ON SOUTHWESTERN RIDGE OF MOUNT McKINLEY

were the curious mountains, of equal height, characteristic of the Kenai Peninsula. To the north, Mount Sushitna, dull, black, and gloomy, wrapped in storm-clouds, apparently but a stone's-throw, though fifteen miles away, and to the eastward of it is the great broad delta of the Sushitna River, covered by a dense green verdure, almost tropical in luxuriance. It was a scene which changed in color and interest very rapidly as the long twilight of the arctic midsummer night advanced. In the morning the tide came and lifted us as easily as it had left us, and then we pulled for the left fork of the Sushitna River. We soon found that the current of the river was too strong for rowing, so we tried towing. At noon we came to a small Indian settlement, where we got an Indian by the name of Stephen to assist us. On the morning of July 2, after nearly four days of the hardest kind of river boating, we reached Sushitna Station, a small trading post twenty miles up the river. The weather had been uniformly bad, but it did not prevent the gnats and mosquitoes from doing their worst. These persistent pests followed us over the waters in clouds, with a buzz that drove us to the verge of insanity. Our hands and faces were so badly bitten that we developed serious forms of inflammation, followed by pain, fever, and torture indescribable. All of this in spite of great care in protecting ourselves by veils, gloves, and a mosquito-proof silk tent. I have seen mosquitoes and allied pests in all parts of the world, but the Sushitna denizens are certainly, in my experience, by far the most desperate in their attack upon men and beasts.

our small dory we drifted down the Beluga, out through a great delta into Cook Inlet, and thence the tide carried us swiftly towards the mouth of the Sushitna River. While we were eagerly looking for the stream, the tide suddenly went out, and left us high on a vast mud flat a mile from shore and three miles from the water at low tide. This was exactly what we had tried to avoid, for we knew that the rising tide was likely to come with a swell and swamp our boat.

The ensuing night caused us a great deal of anxiety, but the scene about us was impressive. The sun sank under the rugged snowy peaks of the Tordrillo Range, leaving a warm, rosy afterglow over everything. Even the mud, ordinarily black and repulsive, which covered our surroundings, glittered with reflected colors. Redoubt volcano, eighty-five miles south, in a cloak of violet snow, belched huge tongues of fire and clouds of vapor. One hundred and twenty miles south, still plainly visible, was Mount Iliamna, clear-cut, a cone of snow-bright purple standing against a sky of dark purple-blue. Then as the eye ran across the great expanse of rushing waters of Cook Inlet it rested upon a sea of fascinating blues and purples and violets, flooded by the rose and gold of the parting sun. Far off to the west, under a haze of blue,

At the station we secured Evan, an Indian friend of Stephen, to assist us, and also obtained a better river-boat. We were to meet the pack-train at a point fifteen miles up the Skwentna River in a week after leaving the Beluga. We had spent five days in working twenty miles, and now there were sixty miles of worse waters ahead of us before we could join our party, and our Indians told us that it would take twenty days to meet the horses.

Soon after leaving the station we pulled up the Yentna River, which, like the Sushitna River, is a great glacial stream three-quarters of a mile wide, taking its origin mostly from the regions about Mount Dall. By poling and towing, rowing, pushing, and all kinds of devices, we averaged twelve miles daily. The fifteen miles up the Skwentna River to the canyon, which we were told could not be made in less than a week, we covered in but little over a day. On the morning of the 8th of July we pitched camp on a small island in the Skwentna River, two miles below the canyon, the appointed place. Nothing was seen of our companions, though we had expected the pack-train to have been in waiting several days. By noon of the same day we heard a voice, and soon we observed the pack-train moving along the southern side of the river. The Skwentna is here about five hundred yards wide, and plunges over a gravel bed at the rate of eight miles per hour. The men and outfit were quickly ferried over, but we had considerable trouble in swimming the horses. One horse was carried downstream five miles, and was only secured by the great skill and diligence of Printz; but the animal was so nearly exhausted that it never recovered its normal strength, although it followed us to Mount McKinley.

The course of the pack-train from the Skwentna River was almost due north, twenty miles to the Keechatna River, and to this point it was also necessary to take the boat. The horses marched over swampy, low country; the boat descended the Skwentna, and ascended the Yentna River to the Keechatna River. Before leaving the Yentna River we ascended Mount Yenlo—or "Tahlietah," as the Indians call it.

We did not have time to ascend the highest spur of Mount Yenlo, but we reached an altitude of 4200 feet, and from there we got an excellent view of the McKinley group, and also of the great, broad valleys of the Sushitna and Yentna rivers. In the Yentna River we discovered several large uncharted islands.

We ascended the Keechatna River late at night, July 13—so late that it proved too dark to find a camping-place. It was a welcome sound when at eleven o'clock we heard voices and saw the camp-fire of our companions on the south bank of the river, in a swamp among spruce-trees. On the following morning we crossed the stream, and found a better camping-ground. Dunn reported much difficulty in crossing the low, wet country. The horses were frequently mired, and both men and horses showed signs of a hard time. After a day's rest the horses were started with light packs upstream along the soft ground of the banks and over many slews to the first high ground. The boat, with an increased load, followed. Our camp on the evening of the 15th was on a foot-hill about ten miles from the mouth of the river. From here our Indians were sent back. They were good, faithful helpers, and we would gladly have taken them farther, but they were eager to return to their fishing-grounds, and we could not have carried food enough for them had they continued with us.

Our route now lay westerly along the Keechatna River, and this in many respects proved to be our most difficult trail. Continued rains, thick underbrush, rapid streams, and difficult slopes, as well as horse-flies and mosquitoes, all combined to retard our progress. Our horses soon failed in strength, and were so sick that we could march them only three hours every second day. Their legs were very much bruised and lacerated by the brush, their skins so thoroughly bitten by horse-flies and mosquitoes that they developed cellulitis and a kind of blood-poisoning. Our packer called the disease distemper, but I am inclined to ascribe the entire trouble to direct poisoning through open wounds. A somewhat similar affection is commonly known among the Indians and prospectors who are much bitten.

GUIDING A HORSE ASHORE, COOK INLET

We left the Keechatna River late in July, and ascended into a broad glacier-worn valley. The absence of trees and shrubs made good travelling here. Blueberries were very abundant, and so were signs of bears. We saw one as we got well into the mountains, and we quickly had vision of bear steaks; but the bear also saw us, and betook himself out of range. We rediscovered Simpson Pass, and through it, at an altitude of 4500 feet, we crossed the Alaskan Range, and quickly descended into the Tateno River, a tributary of the Kuskokwim River. During almost all of July we had wet weather, but this, with the mosquitoes, was now left behind as we passed along the western slope of the range. Horse-feed, however, failed us in the Kuskok-wim, and our horses, though steadily improving for a time, again began to fail.

The scenery up the Keechatna was usually hidden from us by the dense forests through which we were compelled to travel. Occasionally we got a glimpse of rounded mountains three thousand to four thousand feet high. To the south we observed frequently high, picturesque peaks in unexplored areas. We should have liked to investigate this region, but our main object compelled us to press onward. As we rose out of the Keechatna River we got a glimpse of the first remarkable mountain scenery at close range — to the north, a great brown tongue of ice, Caldwell Glacier, nearly three miles wide, with arms reaching to unknown heights between steep, snowy slopes. The water which comes over, under, and through this glacier with a mad rush gives origin to the Keechatna River. Before us was the broad, green depression, with black, cloud-crested, slaty peaks six thousand feet high, to both sides. This valley leads to several passes through the Alaskan Range—one to the south, which Brooks discovered; another, westerly, named by Lieutenant Heron, Simpson Pass; and there is probably still another between the two. Before entering Simpson Pass, we crossed a milky stream, which came from a cavern leading to Fleischmann Glacier. This glacier in size and surrounding is similar to Caldwell, and its drainage joins the same river. Simpson Pass is a deep gorge leading rapidly to a broad glacial stream, called, by Heron, Tateno River. Here game was abundant, but grass for our horses very scarce. On the steep slopes of the mountain north of Tateno River we saw hundreds of mountain-sheep. In the low country, fool-hens, ptarmigan, rabbits, and squirrels were abundant.

Two days' march brought us into the Kuskokwim River, among mountains six thousand feet high, appropriately named, because of their color, Terra Cotta Mountains. Here again our lot was unfortunate. The horses again failed because of the scarcity of grass, and, worse still, John Carroll, who had been ailing for some time, found that he could no longer keep up with the pack-train, and returned, taking with him one horse to carry his provisions. Our party now consisted of five men and thirteen horses; the horses each carrying about one hundred pounds. Just ahead of us at this time was Egypt Mountain, a pyramid of red sandstone; a little farther north, Farewell Mountain; and beyond the great green expanse the spruce-covered valley of the Kuskokwim. Soon after passing Egypt, we bid farewell to the Kuskokwim, and set a course northeasterly along the northern slope of the Alaskan Range above the tree-line. Here the grass improved; blueberries and game were abundant. Horses and men were well fed, and made good progress.

We now entered a region which promised much game, and while we did not see the large number of caribou reported by Brooks, we nevertheless encountered large game almost every day while on the western side of the range. In the valleys of the glacial streams we saw moose. In one or two places we crossed moose-paths that had been depressed three or four feet below the usual surface of the ground by the great number of fresh moose-tracks. In the region where blueberries were abundant we saw large brown grizzly or glacier bears. On the more level grassy plains we encountered hundreds of caribou. Far up the sides of the steep mountains we observed great herds of mountain-sheep. By way of small life, there were about us usually fool-hens, ptarmigan, ground-rats, and squirrels, and there probably were other forms of small life which escaped observation because of the rapidity with which we were compelled to march through the country. Although we tried bear and moose meat, we found that the caribou meat of large fat animals was usually very satisfactory, and so easy to get that we did not attempt to kill other game. There probably is no other area in North America which offers such an abundance of large game.

The country between the Kuskokwim and the Tonzona River was very rough and irregular; we were constantly ascending and descending rounded foot-hills and ridges, from a few hundred feet to two thousand feet in altitude, which were usually separated by glacial streams. While we were not delayed by swamps or forests here, nevertheless these irregularities impeded our progress considerably. Now and again we obtained a glimpse of the McKinley group, but we could barely see the peaks and almost nothing of the lesser mountains in the immediate vicinity. To the eastward within a few miles we could nearly always see the precipitous slopes of the rocky, ice-crested foot-hills of the main range.

On August 8, as we rose over the dome-shaped mountain, nearly five thousand feet high, we saw the broad gravel bed of the Tonzona River, and, beyond, the extensive glacial benches, apparently almost level. On these benches there were a large number of white boulders, and from our position they made the opposite shores of the Tonzona appear like the site of a big city.

Six days' travel took us over the flat country at the base of Mount McKinley. Here our camp was on the Tatlathno River, at an elevation of two thousand six hundred feet, in the uppermost limit of willows. We were now fourteen miles northwest of the great peak, and our position seemed particularly favorable for the first attack. Men and horses were somewhat fatigued from the continuous forced marches. The animals now had a chance to rest while we were to attack the mountain

But to place the men in the best trim possible, I decided to give them a rest of two days.

In forty-eight days we had marched a tortuous course of five hundred miles through swamps and forests, over glacial streams, up and down mountain-sides, and always across a trackless country. We did not ride, but walked, to get to this point, where our work, that of ascending Mount McKinley, was to begin. In this march we had hoped to get to the mountain by the first of August, but the illness of our horses during the early part of the trip delayed us a great deal. Still, with all this delay we marched faster than our predecessors, and gained fifteen days over a similar route by the Geological Survey party. The season was now advancing rapidly; storms were beginning to pour down from Mount McKinley with a great deal of rain. The temperature ranged from 45° to 60° F. The glacial streams were much swollen. Still, our position seemed so favorable and the mountain appeared so easy from our point of observation that we felt certain of reaching the summit within a few days. Our days of rest were spent in making final preparations for the alpine work. We had carried with us a sufficient quantity of hard biscuits for the mountain ascent, but these biscuits had been so much in water, and were so often crushed by accidents to the pack-horses, that we soon decided to use them. But now we were compelled to devise some kind of bread for the high altitude, because there bread could not be baked. It occurred to me that we might bake our bread in the usual way with a reflector, and then toast and dry it, after the manner of the German zwieback. For this purpose I detailed Dunn and Miller to go down the river a few miles where they could procure spruce wood, and within twenty-four hours they successfully baked sufficient bread, toasted and dried it thoroughly for mountain work. This, I think, is a new thing in mountaineering, and it certainly proved excellent for our purposes.

Our mountaineering equipment was very simple and extremely light. As food for each man—pemmican, 1¼ pounds per day; zwieback, 4 oz. per day; sweetened condensed milk, 4 oz. per day; tea. We had also a small quantity of cheese and some erbswurst; both of these, however, proved unsatisfactory. Pemmican, bread, tea, and condensed milk seemed to satisfy all our wants. For fuel we had wood alcohol, to be burned in aluminum stoves, and also petroleum, to be burned in a primus stove. The latter proved by far the more successful. We carried no dishes, except a spoon and a few cups, pocket-knives, and one kettle, in which we melted snow to get water for our tea.

There was nothing unusual about our clothes, except a large eider-down robe (the down attached to the skin of the birds). The robe was so arranged that it could be made into a sleeping-bag and an overcoat. Our tent was made of silk, after a special pattern which I devised for polar work. It was large enough for four men, and weighed less than three pounds. Each man carried a regular alpine axe, and in his ruchsack he was to carry his sleeping-bag, glacier rope made of horsehair, provisions, and a general outfit for a ten days' stay in the mountains. This weighed forty pounds.

Mount McKinley presented a formidable face from our camp. The upper ten thousand feet were, during the day, usually wrapped in dark clouds. The best view was obtained when the sun was lowest, and by far the most impressive view was during the long hours of the blue twilight. In a bright light the mountain seemed dwarfed. The foot-hills, the glacial depressions, and the striking irregularities were then run together into a great heap of mingled snow and rock, but the feebler play of light at dawn and sunset brought out all of the sharp edges, the great cliffs, the depressions, the lesser peaks, and the difficult slopes. To the northeast there was a long ridge with a gradual slope, but this ridge was impossible as a route to the summit because of several lesser peaks, which absolutely barred the way. To the southwest there was a more promising ridge, also interrupted by a spur, but which we hoped to get around. The western face of the great peak between these ridges, above twelve thousand feet, was an almost uninterrupted cliff of pink granite, so steep that snow would not rest upon it. Hence the only way to the summit from the west was along the southwesterly ridge.

Aiming for this ridge, we moved our entire camp with the horses along the southern bank of the river to a point on the main stream where it came from a huge moraine. Crossing here, we ascended into a narrow valley of four thousand two hundred feet, and there pitched our base camp. Here grass was abundant, and the outlook for an easy ascent was good, but it rained incessantly. On the following day, with five horses, the entire party pushed over a series of moraines to a glacier which took its origin in an amphitheatre. The glacier travelling was quite difficult for the horses; deep snow and numerous crevasses made the task tedious and very dangerous. We pitched our camp at an altitude of seven thousand three hundred feet on the glacier near a part of the wall of the amphitheatre to the southwest, the only place where the slope was possible for an ascent. During the night a great deal of snow fell, and on the following morning we left our horses, and in a snowstorm ascended this slope to eight thousand three hundred feet, only to find that farther progress was absolutely cut off by a precipitous descent, which we afterwards learned led down two thousand feet into the bed of Peters Glacier. We remained on the glacier another night, and explored the area for a route out of the glacier basin; but the only outlet was toward Mount Foraker. We now decided to descend and try to get into Peters Glacier by some other route. This glacier sweeps the whole western side of the mountain from the southwest to the northeast. To the east of it McKinley rises in an alternate series of precipitous granite cliffs and overhanging glaciers. To the westward are three rows of foot-hills, the inner mountains rising to an altitude of from seven thousand feet northward to eleven thousand feet southward. We followed the glacier for eighteen miles, rising on it nearly five thousand feet, and then pitched camp near the southwestern ridge, behind which the glacier takes its origin. From a point near our camp we heard avalanche after avalanche thunder down the great slopes, and we felt the glacier under us shake as if moved by an earthquake. This noise of rock and snow slides and the quiver of the earth are characteristic

of McKinley. We heard or felt them everywhere near the mountain, and the dangers from this source are very great.

On August 29 we made our first assault on the slope of the main peak, selecting again the southwestern ridge, which from every observation of the mountain offered the only chance to gain the summit. In Peters Glacier our altitude was eight thousand feet. We began the ascent in the track of a harmless avalanche of soft snow. This gave us a good slope for a few hundred feet, and then we were forced to cut steps up a slope ranging from forty to seventy degrees. Our greatest difficulty was not the work of chopping steps in the ice, but the effort of removing fourteen inches of soft snow before we found trustworthy ice upon which a safe footing could be made. Slowly but steadily we advanced against a freezing wind charged with drift-snow, until the setting sun forced us to seek a camping-place. We found nowhere a level place large enough for our tent, so we were compelled to dig away snow and cut down the ice for a tent flooring. This camp was at nine thousand eight hundred feet. The day following the slopes were steeper and the difficulty of cutting steps greater, but we rose to eleven thousand feet, where we were again compelled to cut a camping-floor to keep from rolling down three thousand feet.

At this camping-place we were confronted by a wall of solid granite, which rose almost perpendicularly four thousand feet above us. Accompanied by Printz, I ascended three hundred feet more to examine a possible route around the spur, but this we could not find, and no other route to the summit from here. If we could only have found some snow or ice slope we felt that progress could be made, but this cliff could not be surmounted by us. With a feeling of keen disappointment we descended, and knowing that there was from the west no other chance to do better, we made our plans to cross the range and examine the eastern slope. In doing this we crossed a blank in our charts of one hundred miles, and made several discoveries which to us proved more interesting than mountaineering. These discoveries will be described in a future article.

AS we descended from our second attempt to climb Mount McKinley, we were made to realize by frozen grass and increasing snow-storms that the season for mountaineering had closed; furthermore, the north wind convinced us that if we wished to get out of the country before the long winter and the night stilled the subarctic world about us, we must quickly reach the head waters of some big stream. We did not care to go to the Yukon, because in doing so we would cover explored territory. We could not return as we had come, because horse-feed along the western slope of the range was already frozen. We were not yet ready to leave Mount McKinley, provided we could only linger at some point where our retreat would not, as was likely in our present position, be suddenly cut off. Altogether, our purposes would seem best served if we could cross the range and get into the Sushitna Valley; but the possibility of such an effort seemed doubtful, in the time at our disposal, unless we were fortunate enough to find a pass within a few days' travelling. Accordingly, we resolved to make a desperate attempt to cross to the eastern slope of this great range, and, in the event of failure in this, our alternative was to make the deep waters of the Toklat, and travel thence by raft to the Tanana River.

Though thwarted by an insurmountable wall, we had ascended Mount McKinley far enough to get a good view of its entire western slope. The walls of the main mountain rise out of Peters Glacier, which sweeps the entire western slope. Avalanche after avalanche rushes down the steep cliffs and deposits its downpour of ice, rock, and snow on the glacier. Beyond Peters Glacier is a remarkable ridge of lesser mountains, extending about sixteen miles parallel to the great mountain. Its altitude is 7500 feet at the north, and it gradually rises to 11,900 feet at the south. The ridge is weighted down with all the ice it can possibly carry. Many glaciers grind down the gorges on both sides, and along the western slope every cliff is heavily corniced with ice. The altitude of the lower clouds here ranges from 6000 to 10,000 feet, and when looking at Mount McKinley from the west, during the greater part of our sojourn, we could see only this great ridge, the main mountain usually being obscured under heavy clouds. For this unique geographical feature I shall suggest the name Roosevelt Ridge. West of Roosevelt Ridge is a series of snow-free foot-hills, mostly pyramidal in shape, for which I shall suggest the name Hanna Foot-hills. We descended a dome-shaped mountain six miles south of this ridge, from which place we made our final attack. The mountain referred to is entirely covered with ice, and its summit reaches an altitude of 14,000 feet. This will appear on our map as Mount Hunter, in honor of Miss A. F. Hunter, of Newport. In the eastern end of Roosevelt Ridge there is a huge amphitheatre, in which rises a glacier about two miles wide and six miles long; this glacier, in honor of one of our companions, will receive the name of Shainwald Glacier. Over Shainwald Glacier we made our first ascent to an elevation of 8300 feet.

As we were about ready to start on our uncertain effort to cross the range we found ourselves deserted by six of our horses. In their eagerness to get grass the animals had wandered downstream toward the main valley of the Kuskokwim. The seven remaining horses were easily able to carry our reduced packs, so we allowed the wayward horses to seek their fortunes in lowlands among the caribou and moose.

On the morning of September 4 we started on our long, weary march along the western slope of the foot-hills above the tree-line. The slopes were long and difficult; and the travelling, after our mountain experience, proved very tiresome. Every sudden descent from the high altitudes produced a feeling of languor, with difficult heart action. This after-effect of mountain-work was to us much worse than any effect of ascending altitudes. So much was the fatigue felt that as we ate lunch on a prominent hill, we picked out our evening camp only a few miles away. The lunch was eaten with some relish because we were hungry and had worked hard. It was the usual meal of boiled caribou ribs, cold and without salt; also without bread or anything else except glacial water. While we were picking the bones, our horses were searching little depressions for a few sprigs of grass which had not been frozen, and as we rounded up our horses we saw several caribou. Printz with a rifle, and Shainwald with a revolver, crept stealthily around a hill into a ravine, and soon we heard a volley of shots. We

THE SOUTHWEST RIDGE
Steps were cut for 3000 feet up this steep wall

A DIFFICULT DESCENT

followed with the horses and took the choice bits of a fat bull. Then, within an hour, we were headed for the willows of a small creek, and here the Nimrods spied and secured a moose, which was very good excuse for shortening our day's march. So we camped in moose haunts in a swamp, where we built a huge camp-fire and ate an incredible amount of moose-steaks, while our horses climbed the neighboring hills for the vanishing grass.

Packing our horses, on the following morning, with an abundance of fresh meat, we then took a course for Muldrow Glacier, beyond which we hoped to find a pass. In two days, marching seven hours daily over tundra, we reached the terminal moraine of this great glacier, and then we marched southeasterly to examine the mountains. Our course hitherto had been close to that of Brooks and Reaburn, and their map, though quickly made, was found to be remarkably correct. But now we were to traverse absolutely unknown territory, and the task thus became doubly inter-

esting, though much more difficult. In our course we first discovered a glacial stream pouring through a canyon only a few hundred feet north of Muldrow Glacier. We followed this stream into a broad valley, and there learned that the river was the output of a system of glaciers among a cluster of sharp peaks seven miles east of the Muldrow Glacier.

As we left the lateral moraine of the big glaciers, travelling on the gravel bars of the newly discovered river, we moved through a great broad valley, which we later discovered extended nearly fifty miles northeasterly. To the east were the high snow-capped mountains, from 7000 to 10,000 feet high, while to the west were brown weather-worn mountains of from 5000 to 7000 feet altitude. The valley had a general width of seven miles, and an average elevation of four thousand feet; and I named it, in honor of one of our companions, Dunn Valley. On September 8 we camped in the canyon of a small stream at the base of a rounded black mountain,

THE WALL THAT STOPPED US

Granite mass, 4000 feet high, which proved an impregnable obstacle to the ascent of Mount McKinley

spreads out into numerous channels over a great bed of glacial silt about a mile wide. This river takes a course almost due north across Dunn Valley, and then it enters a canyon, after which it probably takes an easterly course to the Toklat River.

Nearing the centre of Harvey Glacier, we met the pack-train, carefully guided by Dunn, Printz, and Miller, between two great pillars of granite, which mark the gates of the divide. From here the task of getting the horses over and around wide crevasses became extremely difficult. And as we ascended higher, the horses frequently slipped into wide gaps, deceptively bridged by snow. Our horses, however, were now pretty well used to all kinds of hardships, and though they were thoroughly frightened by frequent falls into dangerous caverns, they carried their packs nobly and safely over the divide.

The most difficult task for the horses, among their long series of hard adventures, was the descent from this gla-cial pass. In less than two hours they came down three thousand feet at an angle sometimes too steep for the men. It was a route over sharp stones, ice, and frozen ground; but the animals, with their feet and legs cut and bruised—leaving bloody stains everywhere in their trail,—followed us without urging towards the green fields of the lower valley. We were lucky enough to cross a green slope of long young grass just as we were aiming to strike camp. From here the famished animals refused to be urged on, and we quickly removed their packs that they might eat to their utmost capacity. It was their first feed of grass which had not been frozen, for more than two weeks.

We now took a course nearly due south over a marshy country towards the main Chulitna River. Our next camp was on a bluff to the main tributary of the Chulitna, which came from the unknown glaciers only ten miles west of the place where we crossed the range. The underbrush here was so thick and the canyons

ROOSEVELT RIDGE AND HANNA FOOT-HILLS
Along western side of Mount McKinley

places, we saw long lines of snowy dots zigzag on the sunny rocks; these were mountain-sheep in great numbers, but our larder was too well stocked and our time too precious to seek them. Around us and toward the unnamed brown mountains northward we saw innumerable ptarmigan.

After plotting our course for the following day, we descended to our camp among scrub-willows. Here we found coal in the stream's bed and, near by, signs of petroleum. On the day following we moved our pack-train to the river we had seen from the Black Head, but, much to our disappointment, the southerly outlook here did not promise a pass. Beyond, the main valley widened, the glacial streams became more numerous, willows were larger, and signs of game more abundant. Our camp on the 9th was near a salt-lick, where many animals had congregated to eat the salty soil. The drainage all along Dunn Valley was northward into the Toklat River— the valley itself probably had been carved out by some vanished glacier. To the eastward the valley ended in a series of hills, and there we felt that we were certain to find a pass. On the 10th we camped on a large stream at the end of our newly discovered valley, and from here, looking southward, we discovered a wide cut through the ridge. Through this opening, over a glacier, came the moist, cutting easterly winds. The horses were desperately hungry and were bent on deserting us. To guard against this we set up a watch through the night, but in the dense blackness of midnight they escaped and back-trailed. On the morning of the 11th, while Dunn and Printz searched for the horses, Shainwald and I explored the prospective pass. In an hour we had ascended the face of the new glacier and walked over ice very much crevassed. Ahead were two possible routes to cross the range—to the north and to the south of a nunatak which projected above the glacier. We gradually rose to an elevation of 6100 feet, crossing hundreds of crevasses in a thick snow-storm, and as we came to the end of the easterly arm of the glacier the snow-cloud vanished, the weather cleared, and with a good deal of pleasure we looked down into the green valley of the Chulitna, the main tributary of the Sushitna River. The descent, however, seemed very difficult for our horses, though possible in an emergency like ours.

We next sought a course through deep soft snow around the nunatak to the westerly arm. A cloud of snow swept the glacier, and so thoroughly blotted out the huge mountains to each side that we were compelled to travel by compass. For nearly two hours we marched up this arm, keeping our glacial rope tight, almost expecting to drop into crevasses every moment. Suddenly we broke through the cloud, and just beyond Shainwald's toes was the brink of a precipice with a perpendicular drop of three thousand feet. We quickly stepped back, and then beheld the most desolate mountain wilderness which it has ever been my lot to behold. Here were the easterly foot-hills of the McKinley group, black, ragged peaks, dotted by spots of fresh snow. We were at an altitude of seven

thousand feet, and these mountains were a little higher. The most remarkable feature was their apparently uniform height of about 7500 feet. Over this expanse of jagged peaks there drifted heavy silver-edged clouds. Sometimes we could see over them, at other times under them, but at nearly all times through them. This remarkable cloud effect also induced a mirage, which drew up some mountains to such heights that we could see huge needles of rock so far above us that we believed ourselves discoverers of several peaks that rivalled Mount McKinley.

As we returned, the clouds were now, for a time, swept out of the divide by a strong northerly wind, giving us a good view of the glacier over which we had advanced in a snow-storm. It is about eight miles long and somewhat less than two miles wide. The highest mountains on each side are 8000 feet, and from these several small tributaries pour down their frozen output. This new glacier I have named Harvey Glacier, in honor of Mr. George Harvey.

The drainage from Harvey Glacier

FIDÈLE GLACIER, THE LARGEST OF INTERIOR ALASKA

THE WALL THAT STOPPED US
Granite mass, 4000 feet high, which proved an impregnable obstacle to the ascent of Mount McKinley

spreads out into numerous channels over a great bed of glacial silt about a mile wide. This river takes a course almost due north across Dunn Valley, and then it enters a canyon, after which it probably takes an easterly course to the Toklat River.

Nearing the centre of Harvey Glacier, we met the pack-train, carefully guided by Dunn, Printz, and Miller, between two great pillars of granite, which mark the gates of the divide. From here the task of getting the horses over and around wide crevasses became extremely difficult. And as we ascended higher, the horses frequently slipped into wide gaps, deceptively bridged by snow. Our horses, however, were now pretty well used to all kinds of hardships, and though they were thoroughly frightened by frequent falls into dangerous caverns, they carried their packs nobly and safely over the divide.

The most difficult task for the horses, among their long series of hard adventures, was the descent from this gla-cial pass. In less than two hours they came down three thousand feet at an angle sometimes too steep for the men. It was a route over sharp stones, ice, and frozen ground; but the animals, with their feet and legs cut and bruised— leaving bloody stains everywhere in their trail,—followed us without urging towards the green fields of the lower valley. We were lucky enough to cross a green slope of long young grass just as we were aiming to strike camp. From here the famished animals refused to be urged on, and we quickly removed their packs that they might eat to their utmost capacity. It was their first feed of grass which had not been frozen, for more than two weeks.

We now took a course nearly due south over a marshy country towards the main Chulitna River. Our next camp was on a bluff to the main tributary of the Chulitna, which came from the unknown glaciers only ten miles west of the place where we crossed the range. The underbrush here was so thick and the canyons so numerous that with our horses we were forced to take to the stream-bed for our route. Getting into this glacial stream, we found excellent travelling, but the slews soon narrowed, and led us into a canyon with walls three hundred feet high. The rushing, milky waters among richly tinted cliffs, crowned by trees in beautiful foliage, made a picture sublimely fascinating; but just at this time we were not so much interested in landscapes as we were in making rapid progress.

We had used our last bread. The supply of tea and sugar was exhausted; and the horses, in an unguarded moment, had deprived us of all our salt. Of meat and beans we still had an ample supply, but everything else except a reserve of pemmican had either been eaten or spoiled by water. We were still anxious to examine Mount McKinley from the east, and all our energies were bent on getting to the mountain as quickly as possible. The winter, however, was advancing with an alarming pace. Even the low mountains about us were blanketed by newly fallen snow, and the temperature was falling to the freezing-point every night. We desired to get out of this canyon and cut a trail, but we dared not lose the time. Fully knowing the danger of following an unknown stream through a canyon, we still had no alternative.

We marched down-stream, crossing from bank to bank as the river turned, to find footing for our horses. At first these crossings were not difficult, but the stream gathered force very rapidly. On the second day's march down-stream the horses were compelled to swim at almost every crossing, and it was necessary to cross the river thirty to forty times daily. The men tried to ride the horses, behind the packs, but in swift streams they were frequently thrown off. For three days we swam and forded this icy stream, and then we were aroused to the dangers of the task through an accident by which a man and a horse were carried down-stream and thrown against a cliff. A similar accident was likely to occur at any time. The horses could not be taken much farther. For the safety of ourselves and our outfit we now sought to build a raft.

The Chulitna proper is formed by the union of the glacial stream down which we came and a clear-water stream of somewhat less volume, the latter draining the extensive low country towards the head waters of the Cantwell River. About two miles below this fork the canyon was considerably broken down, and here we found small flats covered with tall cottonwood-trees. In the absence of better wood we camped here and built a raft. The cottonwood-trees were fifteen inches thick, about eighty feet high, remarkably straight, and free of limbs. We cut logs thirteen feet long and carried them to a convenient launching-place, where we fastened them with cross-bars lashed by ropes, making two tiers about eight feet wide. After the raft was finished, we learned to our sorrow that it would barely carry two men. The wood was evidently too heavy for raft-building.

Printz and Miller floated the raft, while the others followed with the horses. The stream got larger, more rapid, and even more dangerous to swim. After having gone only two miles we saw dry spruce-trees a short distance westward up a large creek of clear water. Here we camped and built two good rafts, and then came the sad task of leaving our horses. Good, faithful animals that they had been, it seemed heartless to leave them to meet an almost certain death, either as a result of deep snow or from the onslaught of wolves. Each man had among the animals one or two pets, and nobody had the boldness to deliberately kill any of the noble creatures. The grass was good here, and we argued that when the deep winter snow came they might possibly dig under it and find a bare subsistence. On this clear stream, then, about eighteen miles north of the big glacier, we left seven of the finest and most faithful horses that ever traversed the wilds of Alaska.

Taking to the rafts, we quickly descended the Chulitna through a series of small canyons divided by cross-canyons. Early in the afternoon of September 19 we camped on a bar about eight miles southeast of the moraine of a great glacier. The lower end of this glacier had been partly charted by government parties, but nothing was known of its

HARVEY GLACIER

upper reaches. We now set for ourselves the task of exploring the glacier, and over it the eastern slopes of Mount McKinley, which had not yet been seen by us. With our outfit and supplies for three days packed in our rucksacks, we ascended the terminal moraine on the following morning, and then climbed for eight miles over the most wonderful accumulation of glacial débris that I had ever seen. At the first bend we left the glacier, and ascended the steep slopes of a series of mountains, from which we hoped to see the course of the glacier and the great peak.

We climbed to an elevation of 6000 feet, but then our progress was barred by cliffs. From here, however, we were able to map the glacier and a large mountainous area. The glacier starts from the northeast side of Mount McKinley and flows almost due east for fifteen miles, where it receives a large arm from the north. Five miles southeast of this another arm swells the bulk of the

great icy stream, and then it takes a circular course, swinging toward the Chulitna. The lower edge is seven and one-half miles wide, its length is about forty miles, and the lower ten miles are so thoroughly weighted down by broken stone—the product of landslides—that no ice is visible. It is thus the largest interior glacier of Alaska, and it probably carries more moraine material than any other glacier in the world.

Somewhat later we discovered a smaller but similar glacier which drains the southeastern side of Mount McKinley. These two glaciers I have named in honor of my wife and daughter—the larger, Fidèle Glacier; and the smaller, Ruth Glacier.

Mount McKinley from the east gives a much clearer impression of great altitude. We could not see the lower ten thousand feet, but the upper slopes, though difficult and perhaps impossible of ascent, are more nearly accessible than those of the west. The upper ten thousand feet are rounded like a beehive, and three spurs offer resting-places for glacier ice, over which a route to the summit may, perhaps, be found.

The season had now so far advanced that if we cared to avoid being detained for the winter, we saw that we must take to our rafts quickly and descend the Chulitna River. We had still to raft sixty miles of an unknown stream. Our supply of provisions was nearly exhausted and our clothing was torn into rags. Hatless and almost shoeless, we pushed our raft over bars, wading icy streams several hours daily, until we reached the deep waters of the Sushitna River. We arrived at Tyonek on September 26, just four months after our start. In that time we had walked over seven hundred miles, and by boat and raft we had travelled three hundred miles. We had explored a good deal of new territory. We had ascended Mount McKinley 11,400 feet, encircled the McKinley group, and made a fair geological and botanical collection. Altogether, we had done all that determined human effort could in the short time of an Alaskan summer.

As to the future efforts to climb Mount McKinley, it is not likely that the highest peak in North America will be abandoned as impossible of ascent until the great mountain has been thoroughly explored for a route from every side. I hope to be able to make an attempt from the east. In the mean time other mountaineers will consider the project. Any attempt to reach the summit is sure to prove a more prodigious task than Alpine enthusiasts are likely to realize. The area of the mountain is far inland, making the transportation of supplies and men a very arduous task. It is surely the steepest of all the great mountains, and arctic conditions begin at the very base. Unlike Mount St. Elias, the glaciation is not extensive enough to offer an all-ice route. The prospective conqueror of this immense uplift must pick his path over broken stones, icy slopes, sharp cliffs, and an average slope of forty-five degrees for at least fourteen thousand feet. It is an effort which, for insurmountable difficulties and hard disappointments, is comparable with the task of expeditions to reach the north pole.

THE LOWER ST. LAWRENCE

IN the Isle d'Orleans, Province of Quebec, I found the manners of the people those of well-to-do habitants living about twenty miles from the capital and going often to town. Moreover, the pretty island draws many people from the city, particularly during the summer season, either to live or to drive along its shores, diversified with unpretentious cottages, the usual church spires, the piers ending with a light-house tower, the boat-builders' yards, and the clean shingle beaches under overhanging trees; and these citizens naturally shed about them more or less of the city's shrewdness. As the parish had been founded in 1679, it had attained to a ripe age. The community had evidently enjoyed more advantages than those of newer and more remote localities.

While conversing with the people I was in the habit of taking notes, as I had done elsewhere in my travels. But here this custom appeared to excite suspicion, so that often I was received with coldness and constraint. After mass on Sunday I knocked at the open door of a benignant old man whom I had met the day before. There were other old men in a row, seated in severe and comical reserve; no one spoke at first in reply to my knock, but at last the woman of the house in a questionable way bade me come in. For half an hour I used all the persuasiveness at my command, even when helped by curiosity and inward amusement; but all my efforts to thaw them were vain; even the genial old man was now as dry as the others; only the woman, true to the superiority of her sex here in education, intelligence, and perception, became a little softened, and looked upon me as one of the human kind. But my advent among them had aroused in some way the national suspicion, and conscious that even if I labored for a month I could not remove their mistrust, I withdrew and returned to my canoe. The explanation was subsequently given me, partly by acquaintances who knew the people, and partly by knowledge of the people's history, traditions, and superstitions. In early times officers of the government went about the parishes and took the names of those liable for military duty, who were afterward often called out; and even to this day the ignorant habitants have a great unwillingness to give their names; even the census officer is often much annoyed unless the curé tells his flock to give him information; moreover, many of them believe that any man who has their names or their portraits can command their persons through occult forces. Seeing me write often had thus given them very grave apprehensions. Then they generally believe in witchcraft, and one of the means for warding off spells is to place the thumb of each hand in the palm and close the fingers over it three times. My habit of coddling my thumbs may have been taken as a sign of uncanny relations.

When I resumed my cruise on the broad St. Lawrence the ocean itself reached in to me one of its mightiest arms, in one of the greatest valleys of the earth, among mountains crowned with clouds and primeval forest. The South Shore rises in wide fertile slopes to wooded hills, and cherishes a narrow strip of humanity along the water's edge; indeed, the road is like the string of a rosary, with French Canadian farm-houses for beads, and a spire every six or eight miles bearing a cross. In running eastward you pass the wide tidal meadows of St. Thomas; the cliffs of St. Roch, capped with Quixotic windmills on the barns; the sugar-loaf hills of Ste. Anne; the wide mud flats of Rivière Ouelle, with a pound to catch white whales, and eel weirs almost as frequent as teeth on a comb; the French watering-place Kamouraska, safe within the Cap au Diable; other resorts at Rivière du Loup and Cacouna; the picturesque harbor of Bic; and then past bolder shores at Les Murailles, and the mountains of Ste. Anne, to the great headlands of Gaspé. But this South Shore, with its strip of fertility and its rosary civilization, affords but a contrast to the general character of the St. Lawrence. The North Shore restores to the eye the dominant ruggedness of the region in raising from the very gates of Quebec to Labrador the mountain wall of the Laurentides. Here and there a hill-top is bared for a parish church and its attendant village and fields; clefts in the wall shelter a fertile nook at La Baie St. Paul, La Malbaie, and another cleft gives entrance to the Saguenay. But these bits of cultivation are but spots of light and human life in a wilderness. The great valley is a worthy setting for this mighty arm of

"THERE WERE OTHER OLD MEN IN A ROW."

RETURN FROM DUCK-SHOOTING.

the sea; and so are its storms, which seem as if they must fill the entire universe. If the seamen of the St. Lawrence are exceptionally superstitious even in this superstitious class, they have some justification in the exceptional dangers and eccentricities of these waters. The river just below the Isle d'Orleans is eight miles wide—merely the beginning of the lower St. Lawrence; in the next 150 miles it gradually attains a width of thirty-five miles at Metis; in another hundred it becomes about sixty miles at La Baie des Sept Isles. The Canadian in his pride refrains from drawing a line to separate the river from the gulf. As a matter of fact the lower St. Lawrence is an estuary rather than a river. I presume that the gulf may be safely recognized at La Baie des Sept Isles. It

AT LOW TIDE.

is a triangular sea, about 500 miles long from northeast to southwest, and about 350 miles wide from Newfoundland to this bay. The region of the St. Lawrence has such remarkable natural fea-

tures that even the matter-of-fact reports of the Admiralty are not without interest. The navigation of these waters presents exceptional difficulties: the existence of numerous islands, reefs, bars, and rocks

ON THE RUSH MEADOWS.

in the channels; the irregularity of the tides and currents; the severity of the climate, especially toward the close of the navigable season; and, above all, the frequent fogs: these are difficulties that may well cause much anxiety, and call for the exercise of all the seaman's vigilance, prudence, and ability. Besides the recorded variations and deviations of the compass, the magnetic attractions of the shores are said to complicate the cap-

tain's problems. Ice is often a dangerous element here: in the spring—May in this latitude and often June also—the entrance and the eastern parts of the gulf are frequently covered with drift ice that besets vessels for many days; icebergs are common there during the summer, and navigation is closed by ice, as a rule, from November 25th to May 1st.

Such is the nature of the river that ships often spend more time in sailing up the St. Lawrence than in crossing the Atlantic; generally they require eight or nine days to beat up to Quebec from Bic, 140 miles; they can sail only during the flood, five hours, and then must anchor, unless the wind changes. The clumsy coasting schooners, requiring always a are frequented during six months of the year by several lines of transatlantic steam-ships, a fleet of Norwegian barks for timber, and a limited number of coasting steamers and schooners.

On leaving the Isle d'Orleans I had kept in the middle of the river, where its

GATHERING AND LOADING SALT HAY.

fair wind, sometimes spend a month in going sixty or eighty miles.

With so many dangers as I have set forth, the reader might think that the St. Lawrence is not navigable; but thanks to an efficient system of lighting and piloting, these waters are one of the great commercial arteries of the continent; they vastness bears in upon you with full force. But the course has not the monotony of unbroken waters; it leads through a little archipelago of wooded islands and bare rocks, where you go happily onward with a light wind on a summer day—that is, happily onward until you enter the mournful souvenirs of Grosse Isle. This quarantine station for the St. Lawrence was established in 1832, when the cholera raged in Europe. It was administered by an army surgeon aided by a military detachment; but since 1862 a resident physician superintends it, helped by a corp of civilians. It is a rocky island with pretty woods and a few fields, sheds for the sick, two churches and parsonages, wharves, and quarters. The chief event in its gloomy history is recorded on a little marble monument in a field: "In this secluded spot lie the mortal remains of 5424 persons, who, flying from pestilence and famine in Ireland in the year 1847, found in America but a grave."

The strength and vitality of the sea pervades the air of this vast region of the lower St. Lawrence; it is full of the snap and vigor of the fall, tempered by the comfort and luxuriousness of the summer. After clearing from Quarantine, Youth seemed again to perch on the bow as a westerly breeze bore me along among the pretty scenes of the archipelago. Perhaps the islands are the more attractive for being such welcome shelter in the great waters. Some of them, however, are beautiful in themselves, as well as for their striking surroundings. I remember particularly the western end of the Isle aux Grues; a beach of clean slate shingle skirts along many knolls and dells, and past picturesque cliffs overhung with cedars and maples; and within the woods are little glades where clusters of juniper and of waving ferns stand on natural grass-plats running about the irregular avenues of the wood. Looking seaward in any direction from these sheltered nooks, at the islets of rock near by, the wide expanses of turbulent currents, and the far-distant shores overtopped by mountains, you feel afresh the exceptional grandeur of the St. Lawrence. At the eastern end of the island, beyond the farms, broad salt-meadows connect the Isle aux Grues with its twin the Isle aux Oies; at low tide cattle were feeding on rushes about the schooners left high and dry by the ebb. These meadows are celebrated shooting-grounds. The habitant now and then harnesses a dog to a small cart containing a shovel, tamed geese of the wild species to act as decoys. Arrived at the edge of the meadows, he hides the cart in the grass, goes down the wide beach to about half-tide mark, and digs a pit about four feet deep, in which he can

sit on a bunch of grass without showing his head above the level of the mud; he puts out the decoys, and hides with his dog in the pit, to shoot until the rising tide drives him away. Two old men of the parish—one of them not less than eighty-two years of age—formed a striking group one fall day returning from their cold and cramping sport. They strutted down the street proudly by their dog-cart loaded with decoys and game, tattered, tottering, muddy from head to foot, but jolly and loquacious to those who came and complimented them. The St. Lawrence was once very prolific in fish and game, and although it is no longer very profitable in this regard, yet by the sheer force of tradition many of these unambitious people are still drawn to its beaches more than to their lands and industries. Men live to a good old age by its healthful shores. In the hamlet of the island I saw upon his door-step a cheery old man who had worked for the present owner of the manor, for his father, for his grandfather, and for his great-grandfather; square-built, broad-browed, he was still able to commend to our notice the pig he was fattening about the door; and when we left him he said, with quietude and courtesy, "Bon jour, ces messieurs." This old-time address in the third person, full of feudal deference, went well with the simplicity and quaintness of the ancient man.

I now left the islands to cross over to the North Shore. It is a long passage, that will not interest the reader—unless he happens to be caught on it by a blow. Perhaps he will do as well to visit some of the scenes I have met with on other cruises in this region.

The cutting of rushes for hay at St. Thomas, L'Islette, Beaupré, and other places is a characteristic scene. If you paddle along these muddy shores at low-water, dodging bowlders, and running around the ends of basket-work fences for fisheries, and if you happen there near the full-moon of September, you will find the flats alive with mowers cutting rushes. These natural meadows, covered at high tide, are often many miles in length, and even as much as a mile in width; back of them rise the bluffs of the river, and then the fields and fences leading away up the long slopes to the forest-covered hills. Each farm extends its narrow frontage—generally about 200 yards

THE CONFESSIONAL IN CABIN OF STEAMER.

wide—down across these meadows to low-water mark; the hay and the fish are often the most valuable products of these small St. Lawrence farms. In fact these meadows in the earliest days of the col-ony were the attractions that first drew settlers to found the oldest parishes. At Rivière Ouelle, for example, the mouth of the valley and the tidal meadow along the shore were divided into converging

EEL-FISHING.

strips, like the leaves of a fan, that each settler might have a portion of salt hay, and this part of the parish is still called L'Éventail. But to return to the present hay-makers. The groups of bare-legged men mow eagerly down to the water's edge until the tide comes in; then they stretch a rope across the lower end of their swaths, and twist some rushes loosely about it to float it and make it thick enough to catch and hold the grass. Some men now pull at one end of the rope, a man riding on a cart, often driven by a woman, holds the other end, and behind the rope two or three pitch escaped locks of grass over the line into its enclosing curve; thus the swaths are gathered into one mass that grows in size and advances inland as the tide rises, and at last it reaches the foot of the bank as

WINTER FERRY ON THE ST. LAWRENCE.

quite an island of floating verdure. Here it is held by the rope until the tide has fallen somewhat and left it accessible to carts. Then groups may be seen all along the foot of the bluffs—women with broad hats and bare ankles, men bare-legged and muddy, little one-horse carts standing by mounds of grass; and all work fast, pitching the dripping rushes, raking, hauling loads up the bank, and spreading the grass in fields to cure. It is to me one of the prettiest scenes in Canada. The golden haze of Indian-summer often covers the meadows, the calm pearly river with its ships and islands, and the far-off blue mountains; there is, too, a measure of tender interest going out to these folk at their muddy toil, and leading your eye and your fancy all down the line to the dimmest and farthest group. Often the pressure of work and the hours of the tide bring out the people to work in the moonlit nights.

Among the characteristic scenes often met on the steam-boats of the St. Lawrence is a pilgrimage to St. Anne de Beaupré. One of these trips was organized while I was sojourning once with an habitant near St. Jean Port Joli. Such expeditions are generally got up by the priest and one of the chief merchants of his parish. They either charter a steamboat or get special rates from a railroad, and then take all who wish to go, at a certain price, giving a fair remuneration for the negotiations and management. My host told me that the pilgrimage of the previous year netted two hundred dollars. The project is often announced from the pulpits of several contiguous parishes; it draws thus a large company, with one or more priests to keep good order. Although the boat was not to start until 5 o'clock A.M., and my host lived something less than three miles from the landing, yet we were called at one o'clock, given some breakfast, and started on our way through a dark rainy night. We arrived in good season. The merchant saw no incongruity in selling me a passage for myself and the *Allegro*, although the expedition was announced as strictly a pilgrimage, and we were scarcely pilgrims. At the appointed hour several hundred habitants with lunch baskets and bundles straggled down the pier and embarked. The company, as far as I could judge, contained only three or four men above the peasant class; it was composed chiefly of farmers' wives and daughters. Rows of women sat on the benches and told their beads or their bits of gossip; very many of them kept an eye open for passing acquaintances, and took in a friend now and then, as it were, in parenthesis; here and there a man knelt before his wife to have his cravat arranged; a

few were silent and meditative; chants from time to time sounded from the lower or the upper deck. I had taken shelter with others in the cabin, but three priests soon came in and waved us all out in a most superior manner, and then put on their white surplices; many people flocked in again at once; each priest took his seat in an open portable confessional, divided into two parts by a partition, and to aid the secrecy that envelops the confession partly covered his face with the wide sleeve of his surplice; he then crouched down and put his ear to the grated opening. One woman after another knelt on the other side of the partition and confessed, while some stood about the cabin and awaited their turn. Thus the pilgrims passed the hours of the passage across the St. Lawrence, mingling social intercourse, prayers, meditations, trivialities, hopes of heaven, fears of hell, and anticipations of miracles. But the scene had, on the whole, an atmosphere of dulness and contentment. The pilgrims of a wealthy parish often have their steam-boat decorated with evergreens and flags; I have often heard over the waters their strange medley of sounds—a brass band playing a gay march, the austere plain chants, the babble of talk, and the mutterings of a multitude at prayer.

The lonely spirit of the "Grand Nord" met me face to face when I reached at last the North Shore at the foot of Cap Tourment. The Laurentides dominate even this arm of the sea by their lofty and gloomy grandeur; marching eastward, their forest-covered heads, and farther on their rocky crowns, overlook one another's shoulders with increasing savageness down to the stormy gulf. And their savageness is but seldom broken by a touch of human life, which serves rather to enhance their austerity. The shores east of Cap Tourment are uninhabitable, for the mountains rise right up from a beach of rocks. That barren coast yields about 50,000 eels each autumn, and the South Shore, at Rivière Ouelle, St. Denis, and elsewhere, yields still more. The fishery is often a picturesque sight with its long fence of wicker-work and frames ballasted with stones, the whole sharply relieved with lights and shadows; wings put off here and there to turn the eels into enclosures, and thence into bottle-shaped receptacles, and from there into very strong

RETURN FROM FISHING.

boxes staked down on the mud. I was told that in one of the large fisheries at Rivière Ouelle 3000 eels, averaging two pounds, have been taken in one tide; they packed themselves all straight in the boxes, and so tightly that all were smothered, and in some cases they have been known to burst open these very strong boxes.

The St. Lawrence in winter drew me out for a snow-shoe tramp along the shores at Rivière Ouelle. The only signs of life were here and there the roof of a fisherman's empty hut and fence posts sticking up above the snow-drifts. Beyond the waters and ice stood the mountains of the North Shore. The river in winter is utterly deserted; all the craft are laid up and dismantled, and the sailors stay at home and smoke. The winter ferries of the St. Lawrence are small open boats capable of running on either water or ice. The postman of the Isle aux Coudre uses a little skiff light enough to be handled by one man; by waiting for good weather, the proper hour of the tide, and watching for clear openings between the floes, he has managed to come and go safely these many years between the island and the main-land. But sudden changes of the weather often come over these mountains, the currents run strong, the sea gets up, the water flying into the boat freezes at once and cannot be bailed out, and a snow-squall may prevent one at a critical moment from seeing openings in the ice; he has been caught by these hinderances more than once, and barely escaped with his life. The ferries at more populous places are crossed in a twenty-foot canoe with a crowd of seven men. This ice-canoe is a shapely boat with a very broad flat keel shod with iron to run easily over the ice. The passengers sit wrapped up in furs, and endure the cold as well as they can, while the men paddle swiftly along open passages between shining walls, or haul the canoe over floes diversified with angles, blocks, and fissures in the iridescent ice. It is often an exciting passage, with sufficient exposure and hardship to satisfy those who are curious about arctic travel.

ANTOINE'S MOOSE-YARD

IT was the night of a great dinner at the club. Whenever the door of the banqueting hall was opened, a burst of laughter or of applause disturbed the quiet talk of a few men who had gathered in the reading - room — men of the sort that extract the best enjoyment from a club by escaping its functions, or attending them only to draw to one side its choicest spirits for never-to-be-forgotten talks before an open fire, and over wine and cigars used sparingly.

"I'm tired," an artist was saying — "so tired that I have a horror of my studio. My wife understands my condition, and bids me go away and rest."

"That is astonishing," said I; "for, as a rule, neither women nor men can comprehend the fatigue that seizes an artist or writer. At most of our homes there comes to be a reluctant recognition of the fact that we say we are tired, and that we persist in the assumption by knocking off work. But human fatigue is measured by the mile of walking, or the cords of firewood that have been cut, and the world will always hold that if we have not hewn wood or tramped all day, it is absurd for us to talk of feeling tired. We cannot alter this; we are too few."

"Yes," said another of the little party. "The world shares the feeling of the Irishman who saw a very large, stout man at work at reporting in a court-room. 'Faith!' said he, 'will ye look at the size of that man—to be airning his living wid a little pincil?' The world would acknowledge our right to feel tired if we used crow-bars to write or draw with; but pencils! pshaw! a hundred weigh less than a pound."

"Well," said I, "all the same, I am so tired that my head feels like cork; so tired that for two days I have not been able to summon an idea or turn a sentence neatly. I have been sitting at my desk writing wretched stuff and tearing it up, or staring blankly out of the window."

"Glorious!" said the artist, startling us all with his vehemence and inapt exclamation. "Why, it is providential that I came here to-night. If that's the way you feel, we are a pair, and you will go with me and rest. Do you hunt? Are you fond of it?"

"I know all about it," said I, "but I have not definitely determined whether I am fond of it or not. I have been hunting only once. It was years ago, when I was a mere boy. I went after deer with a poet, an editor, and a railroad conductor. We journeyed to a lovely valley in Mifflin County, Pennsylvania, and put ourselves in the hands of a man seven feet high, who had a flintlock musket a foot taller than himself, and a wife who gave us saleratus bread and a bowl of pork fat for supper and breakfast. We were not there at dinner. The man stationed us a mile apart on what he said were the paths, or "runways," the deer would take. Then he went to stir the game up with his dogs. There he left us from sunrise till supper, or would have left us had we not with great difficulty found one another, and enjoyed the exquisite woodland quiet and light and shade together, mainly flat on our backs, with the white sails of the sky floating in an azure sea above the reaching fingers of the tree-tops. The editor marred the occasion with an unworthy suspicion that our hunter was at the village tavern picturing to his cronies what simple donkeys we were, standing a mile apart in the forsaken woods. But the poet said something so pregnant with philosophy that it always comes back to me with the mention of hunting. 'Where is your gun?' he was asked, when we came upon him, pacing the forest path, hands in pockets, and no weapon in sight. 'Oh, my gun?' he repeated. 'I don't know. Somewhere in among those trees. I covered it with leaves so as not to see it. After this, if I go hunting again, I shall not take a gun. It is very cold and heavy, and more or less dangerous in the bargain. You never use it, you know. I go hunting every few years, but I never yet have had to fire my gun, and I begin to see that it is only brought along in deference to a tradition descending from an era when men got something more than fresh air and scenery on a hunting trip.'"

The others laughed at my story, but the artist regarded me with an expression of pity. He is a famous hunter—a genuine, devoted hunter—and one might almost as safely speak a light word of his relations as of his favorite mode of recreation.

"Fresh air!" said he; "scenery! Humph! Your poet would not know which end of a gun to aim with. I see that you know nothing at all about hunting, but I will pay you the high compliment of saying that I can make a hunter of you. I have always insisted heretofore that a hunter must begin in boyhood; but never mind, I'll make a hunter of you at thirty-six. We will start to-morrow morning for Montreal, and in twenty-four hours you shall be in the greatest sporting region in America, incomparably the greatest hunting district. It is great because Americans do not know of it, and because it has all of British America to keep it supplied with game. Think of it! In twenty-four hours we shall be tracking moose near Hudson Bay, for Hudson Bay is not much farther from New York than Chicago— another fact that few persons are aware of."

Environment is a positive force. We could feel that we were disturbing what the artist would call "the local tone," by rushing through the city's streets next morning with our guns slung upon our backs. It was just at the hour when the factory hands and the shop-girls were out in force, and the juxtaposition of those elements of society with two portly men bearing guns created a positive sensation. In the cars the artist held forth upon the terrors of the life upon which I was about to venture. He left upon my mind a blurred impression of sleeping out-of-doors, like human cocoons, done up in blankets, while the savage mercury lurked in unknown depths below the zero mark. He said the camp fire would have to be fed every two hours of each night, and he added, without contradiction from me, that he supposed he would have to perform this duty as he was accustomed to it. Lest his forecast should raise my anticipation of pleasure extravagantly, he added that those hunters were fortunate who had fires to feed; for his part he had once walked around a tree stump a whole night to keep from freezing. He supposed that we would perform our main journeying on snow-shoes, but how we should enjoy that he could not say, as his knowledge of snow-shoeing was limited.

At this point the inevitable offspring of fate, who is always at a traveller's elbow with a fund of alarming information, cleared his throat as he sat opposite us, and inquired whether he had overheard that we did not know much about snow-shoes. An interesting fact concerning them, he said, was that they seemed easy to walk with at first, but if the learner fell down with them on, it usually needed a considerable portion of a tribe of Indians to put him back on his feet. Beginners only fell down, however, in attempting to cross a log or stump, but the forest where we were going was literally floored with such obstructions. The first day's effort to navigate with snow-shoes, he remarked, is usually accompanied by a terrible malady called *mal de raquette*, in which the cords of one's legs become knotted in great and excruciatingly painful bunches. The cure for this is to "walk it off" the next day, when the agony is yet more intense than at first." As the stranger had reached his destination, he had little more than time to remark that the moose is an exceedingly vicious animal, invariably attacking all hunters who fail to kill him with the first shot. As the stranger stepped upon the car platform he let fall a simple but touching eulogy upon a dear friend who had recently lost his life by being literally cut in two, lengthwise, by a moose that struck him on the chest with its rigidly stiffened forelegs. The artist protested

THE HOTEL—LAST SIGN OF CIVILIZATION.

that the stranger was a sensationalist, unsupported by either the camp-fire gossip or the literature of hunters. Yet one man that night found his slumber tangled with what the garrulous alarmist had been saying.

In Montreal one may buy clothing not to be had in the United States: woollens thick as boards, hosiery that wards off the cold as armor resists missiles, gloves as heavy as shoes, yet soft as kid, fur caps and coats at prices and in a variety that interest poor and rich alike, blanket suits that are more picturesque than any other masculine garment worn north of the city of Mexico, tuques, and moccasins, and, indeed, so many sorts of clothing we Yankees know very little of (though many of us need them) that at a glance we say the Montrealers are foreigners. Montreal is the gayest city on this continent, and I have often thought that the clothing there is largely responsible for that condition.

A New-Yorker disembarking in Montreal in midwinter finds the place inhospitably cold, and wonders how, as well as why, any one lives there. I well remember standing years ago beside a toboggan slide, with my teeth chattering and my very marrow slowly congealing, when my attention was called to the fact that a dozen ruddy-cheeked, bright-eyed, laughing girls were grouped in snow that reached their knees. I asked a Canadian lady how that could be possible, and she answered with a list of the principal garments those girls were wearing. They

had two pairs of stockings under their shoes, and a pair of stockings over their shoes, with moccasins over them. They had so many woollen skirts that an American girl would not believe me if I gave the number. They wore heavy dresses and buckskin jackets, and blanket suits over all this. They had mittens over their gloves, and fur caps over their knitted hoods. It no longer seemed wonderful that they should not heed the cold; indeed it occurred to me that their bravery amid the terrors of tobogganing was no bravery at all, since a girl buried deep in the heart of such a mass of woollens could scarcely expect damage if she fell from a steeple. When next I appeared out-of-doors I too was swathed in flannel, like a jewel in a box of plush, and from that time out Montreal seemed, what it really is, the merriest of American capitals. And there I had come again, and was filling my trunk with this wonderful armor of civilization, while the artist sought advice as to which point to enter the wilderness in order to secure the biggest game most quickly.

Mr. W. C. Van Horne, the President of the Canadian Pacific Railroad, proved a friend in need. He dictated a few telegrams that agitated the people of a vast section of country between Ottawa and the great lakes. And in the afternoon the answers came flying back. These were from various points where Hudson Bay posts are situated. At one or two the Indian trappers and hunters were all away on their winter expeditions; from another a famous white hunter had just departed with a party of gentlemen. At Mattawa, in Ontario, moose were close at hand and plentiful, and two skilled Indian hunters were just in from a trapping expedition; but the post factor, Mr. Rankin, was sick in bed, and the Indians were on a spree. To Mattawa we decided to go. It is a twelve-hour journey from New York to Montreal, and an eleven-hour journey from Montreal to the heart of this hunters' paradise; so that, had we known at just which point to enter the forest, we could have taken the trail in twenty-four hours from the metropolis, as the artist had predicted.

Our first taste of the frontier, at Peter O'Farrall's Ottawa Hotel, in Mattawa, was delicious in the extreme. O'Farrall used to be game-keeper to the Marquis of Waterford, and thus got "a taste of the quality" that prompted him to assume the position he has chosen as the most lordly hotel-keeper in Canada. We do not know what sort of men own our great New York and Chicago and San Francisco hotels, but certainly they cannot lead more leisurely, complacent lives than Mr. O'Farrall. He has a bar-tender to look after the male visitors and the bar, and a matronly relative to see to the women and the kitchen, so that the landlord arises when he likes to enjoy each succeeding day of ease and prosperity. He has been known to exert himself, as when he chased a man who spoke slightingly of his liquor. And he was momentarily ruffled at the trying conduct of the artist on this hunting trip. The artist could not find his overcoat, and had the temerity to refer the matter to Mr. O'Farrall.

"Sir," said the artist, "what do you suppose has become of my overcoat? I cannot find it anywhere."

"I don't know anything about your botheration overcoat," said Mr. O'Farrall. "Sure, I've throuble enough kaping thrack of me own."

The reader may be sure that O'Farrall's was rightly recommended to us, and that it is a well-managed and popular place, with good beds and excellent fare, and with no extra charge for the delightful addition of the host himself, who is very tall and dignified and humorous, and who is the oddest and yet most picturesque-looking public character in the Dominion. Such an oddity is certain to attract queer characters to his side, and

Mr. O'Farrall is no exception to the rule. One of the waiter-girls in the dining-room was found never by any chance to know anything that she was asked about. For instance, she had never heard of Mr. Rankin, the chief man of the place. To every question she made answer, "Sure, there does be a great dale goin' on here and I know nothin' of it." Of her the artist ventured the theory that "she could not know everything on a waiter-girl's salary." John, the bar-tender, was a delightful study. No matter what a visitor laid down in the smoking-room, John picked it up and carried it behind the bar. Every one was continually losing something and searching for it, always to observe that John was able to produce it with a smile and the wise remark that he had taken the lost article and put it away "for fear some one would pick it up." Finally, there was Mr. O'Farrall's dog. A ragged, time-worn, petulant terrier, no bigger than a pint-pot. Mr. O'Farrall nevertheless called him "Fairy," and said he kept him "to protect the village children against wild bears."

I shall never be able to think of Mattawa as it is—a plain little lumbering town on the Ottawa River, with the wreck and ruin of once grand scenery hemming it in on all sides, in the form of ragged mountains literally ravaged by fire and the axe. Hints of it come back to me in dismembered bits that prove it to have been interesting: vignettes of little schoolboys in blanket suits and moccasins, of great spirited horses forever racing ahead of fur-laden sleighs, and of troops of olive-skinned French-Canadian girls, bundled up from their feet to those mischievous features which shot roguish glances at the artist—the biggest man, the people said, who had ever been seen in Mattawa. But the place will ever yield back to my mind the impression I got of the wonderful preparations that were made for our adventure—preparations that seemed to busy or to interest nearly every one in the village. Our Indians had come in from the Indian village three miles away, and had said they had had enough drink. Mr. John DeSousa, accountant at the post, took charge of them and of us, and the work of loading a great portage sleigh went on apace. The men of sporting tastes came out and lounged in front of the post, and gave helpful advice; the Indians and clerks went to and from the sleigh laden with bags of necessaries, the harness-maker made for us belts such as the lumbermen use to preclude the possibility of incurable strains in the rough life in the wilderness. The help at O'Farrall's assisted in repacking what we needed, so

shoe made of heavy blanketing and worn outside one's stockings, to give added warmth to the feet.

"You see, this is no casual rabbit hunt," said the artist. The remark will live in Mattawa many a year.

"GIVE ME A LIGHT."

that our trunks and town clothing could be stored. Mr. De Sousa sent messengers hither and thither for essentials not in stock at the post. Some women, even, were set at work to make "neaps" for us, a neap being a sort of slipper or unlaced

The Hudson Bay Company's posts differ. In the wilderness they are forts surrounded by stockades, but within the boundaries of civilization they are stores. That at old Fort Garry, now called Winnipeg, is a splendid emporium, rather

ANTOINE, FROM LIFE.

more like the establishment of Whiteley, "the universal provider" of London, than anything in the United States. That at Mattawa is like a village store in the United States, except that the top story is laden with guns, traps, snow-shoes, and the skins of wild beasts; while an out-building in the rear is the repository of scores of birch-bark canoes—the carriages of British America. Mr. Rankin, the factor there, lay in a bed of suffering and could not see us. Yet it seemed difficult to believe that we could be made the recipients of greater or more kindly attentions than were lavished upon us by his accountant, Mr. De Sousa. He ordered our tobacco ground for us ready for our pipes; selected the finest from among those extraordinary blankets that have been made exclusively for this company for hundreds of years; picked out the largest snow-shoes in his stock; bade us lay aside the gloves we had brought, and take mittens such as he produced, and for which we thanked him in our hearts many times afterward; planned our outfit of food with the wisdom of an old campaigner; bethought himself to send for baker's bread; ordered high legs sewed on our moccasins—in a word, he made it possible for us to say afterward that absolutely nothing had been overlooked or slighted in fitting out our expedition.

As I sat in the sleigh, tucked in under heavy skins and leaning at royal ease against other furs that covered a bale of hay, it seemed to me that I had become part of one of such pictures as we all have seen, portraying historic expeditions in Russia or Siberia. We carried fifteen hundred pounds of traps and provisions for camping, stabling, and food for men and beasts. We were five in all—two hunters, two Indians, and a teamster. We set out with the two huge mettlesome horses ahead, the driver on a high seat formed of a second bale of hay, ourselves lolling back under our furs, and the two Indians striding along over the resonant cold snow behind us. It was beginning to be evident that a great deal of effort and machinery was needed to "make a hunter" of a city man, and that it was going to be done thoroughly—two thoughts of a highly flattering nature.

We were now clad for arctic weather, and perhaps nothing except a mummy was ever "so dressed up" as we were. We each wore two pairs of the heaviest woollen stockings I ever saw, and over them ribbed bicycle stockings that came to our knees. Over these in turn were our "neaps," and then our moccasins, laced tightly around our ankles. We had on two suits of flannels of extra thickness, flannel shirts, reefing jackets, and "capeaux," as they call their long hooded blanket coats, longer than snow-shoe coats. On our heads we had knitted tuques, and on our hands mittens and gloves. We were bound for Antoine's moose-yard, near Crooked Lake.

The explanation of the term "moose-yard" made moose-hunting appear a simple operation (once we were started), for a moose yard is the feeding-ground of a herd of moose, and our head Indian, Alexandre Antoine, knew where there was one. Each herd or family of these great wild cattle has two such feeding-grounds, and they are said to go alternately from one to the other, never herding in one place two years in succession. In this region of Canada they weigh between 600 and 1200 pounds, and the reader will help his comprehension of those figures by recalling the fact that a 1200-pound horse is a very large one. Whether they desert a yard for twelve months because of the damage they do it in feeding upon the branches and foliage of soft-wood trees and shrubs, or whether it is instinctive caution that directs their movements, no one can more than conjecture.

Their yards are always where soft wood is plentiful and water is near, and during a winter they will feed over a region from half a mile to a mile square. The prospect of going directly to the fixed home of a herd of moose almost robbed the trip of that speculative element that gives the greatest zest to hunting. But we knew not what the future held for us. Not even the artist, with all his experience, conjectured what was in store for us. And what was to come began coming almost immediately.

The journey began upon a good highway, over which we slid along as comfortably as any ladies in their carriages, and with the sleigh-bells flinging their cheery music out over a desolate valley, with a leaden river at the bottom, and with small

made by merely felling trees through a forest in a path wide enough for a team and wagon. All the tree stumps were left in their places, and every here and there were rocks; some no larger than a bale of cotton, and some as small as a bushel basket. To add to the other alluring qualities of the road, there were tree trunks now and then directly across it, and, as a farther inducement to traffic,

THE PORTAGE SLEIGH ON A LUMBER ROAD.

the highway was frequently interrupted by "pitch holes." Some of these would be called pitch holes anywhere. They were at points where a rill crossed the road, or the road crossed the corner of a marsh. But there were other pitch holes that any intelligent New-Yorker would call ravines or gullies. These were at points where

mountains rolling all about. The timber was cut off them, except here and there a few red or white pines that reared their green, brush-like tops against the general blanket of snow. The dull sky hung sullenly above, and now and then a raven flew by, croaking hoarse disapproval of our intrusion. To warn us of what we were to expect, Antoine had made a shy Indian joke, one of the few I ever heard. "In small little while," said he, " we come to all sorts of a road. Me call it that 'cause you get every sort riding, then you sure be suited."

At five miles out we came to this remarkable highway. It can no more be adequately described here than could the experiences of a man who goes over Niagara Falls in a barrel. The reader must try to imagine the most primitive sort of a highway conceivable; one that has been

one hill ran down to the water-level and another immediately rose precipitately, there being a watercourse between the two. In all such places there was deep black mud and broken ice. However, these were mere features of the character of this road—a character too profound for me to hope to portray it. When the road was not inclined either straight down or straight up, it coursed along the slanting side of a steep hill, so that a vehicle could keep to it only by falling against the forest at the under side and carroming along from tree to tree.

Such was the road. The manner of travelling it was quite as astounding. For nothing short of what Alphonse, the teamster, did would I destroy a man's character, but Alphonse was the next thing to an idiot. He made that dreadful journey at a gallop! The first time he upset the sleigh and threw me with one leg thigh-deep between a stone and a tree trunk, besides sending the artist flying over my head like a shot from a sling, he reseated himself and remarked: "That makes tree time I upset in dat place. Hi, there! Get up!" It never occurred to him to stop because a giant tree had fallen across the trail. "Look out! Hold tight!" he would call out, and then he would take the obstruction at a jump. The horses were mammoth beasts, in the best fettle, and the sleigh was of the solidest, strongest pattern. There were places where even Alphonse was anxious to drive with caution. Such were the ravines and unbridged waterways. But one of the horses had cut himself badly in such a place a year before, and both now made it a rule to take all such places flying. Fancy the result! The leap in air, and then the crash of the sled as it landed, the snap of the harness chains, the snorts of the winded beasts, the yells of the driver, the anxiety and nervousness of the passengers!

At one point we had an exciting adventure of a far different sort. There was a moderately good stretch of road ahead, and we invited the Indians to jump in and ride awhile. We noticed that they took occasional draughts from a bottle. They finished a full pint, and presently Alexandre produced another and larger vial. Every one knows what a drunken Indian is, and so did we. We ordered the sleigh stopped and all hands out for "a talk." Firmly, but with both power and reason on our side, we demanded a promise that not another drink should be taken, or that the horses be turned toward Mattawa at once. The promise was freely given.

"But what is that stuff? Let me see it," one of the hunters asked.

"It is de 'igh wine," said Alexandre.

"High wine? Alcohol?" exclaimed the hunter, and, impulse being quicker than reason sometimes, flung the bottle high in air into the bush. It was an injudicious action, but both of us at once prepared to defend and re-enforce it, of course. As it happened, the Indians saw that no unkindness or unfairness was intended, and neither sulked nor made trouble afterward.

We were now deep in the bush. Occasionally we passed "a brulè," or tract denuded of trees, and littered with trunks and tops of trunks rejected by the lumbermen. But every mile took us nearer to the undisturbed primeval forest, where the trees shoot up forty feet before the branches begin. There were no houses, teams, or men. In a week in the bush we saw no other sign of civilization than what we brought or made. All around us rose the motionless regiments of the forest, with the snow beneath them, and their branches and twigs printing lacework on the sky. The signs of game were numerous, and varied to an extent that I never heard of before. There were few spaces of the length of twenty-five feet in which the track of some wild beast or bird did not cross the road. The Indians read this writing in the snow, so that the forest was to them as a book would be to us. "What is that?" "And that?" "And that?" I kept inquiring. The answers told more eloquently than any man can describe it the story of the abundance of game in that easily accessible wilderness. "Dat red deer," Antoine replied. "Him fox." "Dat bear track; dat squirrel; dat rabbit." "Dat moose track; pass las' week." "Dat pa'tridge; dat wolf." Or perhaps it was the trail of a marten, or a beaver, or a weasel, or a fisher, mink, lynx, or otter that he pointed out, for all these "signs" were there, and nearly all were repeated again and again. Of the birds that are plentiful there the principal kinds are partridge, woodcock, crane, geese, duck, gull, loon, and owl.

When the sun set we prepared to camp, selecting a spot near a tiny rill. The horses were tethered to a tree, with their harness still on, and blankets thrown over them. We cleared a little space by the road-side, using our snow-shoes for shovels. The Indians, with their axes, turned up the moss and leaves, and levelled the small shoots and brushwood. Then one went off to cut balsam boughs for bedding, while the other set up two crotched sticks, with a pole upon them resting in the crotches, and throwing the canvas of an "A" tent over the frame, he looped the bottom of the tent to small pegs, and banked snow lightly all around it. The little aromatic branches of balsam were laid evenly upon the ground, a fur robe was thrown upon the leaves, our enormous blankets were spread half open side

PIERRE, FROM LIFE.

by side, and two coats were rolled up and thrown down for pillows. Pierre, the second Indian, made tiny slivers of some soft wood, and tried to start a fire. He failed. Then Alexandre Antoine brought two handfuls of bark, and lighting a small piece with a match, proceeded to build a fire in the most painstaking manner, and with an ingenuity that was most interesting. First he made a fire that could have been started in a teacup. Then he built above and around it a skeleton tent of bits of soft wood, six to nine inches in length. This gave him a fire of the dimensions of a high hat. Next, he threw down two great bits of timber, one on either side of the fire, and a still larger back-log, and upon these he heaped split soft wood. While this was being done, Pierre assailed one great tree after another, and brought them crashing down with noises that startled the forest quiet. Alphonse had opened the provision bags, and presently two tin pails filled with water swung from saplings over the fire, and a pan of fat salt pork was frizzling upon the blazing wood. The darkness grew dead black, and the dancing flames peopled the near forest with dodging shadows. Almost in the time it has taken me to write it, we were squatting on our heels

around the fire, each with a massive cutting of bread, a slice of fried pork in a tin plate, and half a pint of tea, precisely as hot as molten lead, in a tin cup. Supper was a necessity, not a luxury, and was hurried out of the way accordingly. Then the men built their camp beside ours in front of the fire, and followed that by felling three or more monarchs of the bush. Nothing surprised me so much as the amount of wood consumed in these open-air fires. In five days at our permanent camp we made a great hole in the forest.

But that first night in the open air, abed with nature, with British America for a bedroom! Only I can tell of it, for the others slept. The stillness was intense. There was no wind, and not an animal or bird uttered a cry. The logs cracked and sputtered and popped, the horses shook their chains, the men all snored—white and red alike. The horses pounded the hollow earth; the logs broke and fell upon the cinders; one of the men talked in his sleep. But over and through it all, the stillness grew. Then the fire sank low, the cold became intense, the light was lost, and the darkness swallowed everything. Some one got up awkwardly, with muttering, and flung wood upon the red ashes, and presently all that had passed was re-experienced.

The ride next day was more exciting than the first stage. It was like the journey of a gun-carriage across country in a hot retreat. The sled was actually upset only once, but to prevent that happening fifty times the Indians kept springing at the uppermost side of the flying vehicle, and hanging to the side poles to pull the toppling construction down upon both runners. Often we were advised to leap out for safety's sake; at other times we wished we had leaped out. For seven hours we were flung about like cotton spools that are being polished in a revolving cylinder. And yet we were obliged to run long distances after the hurtling sleigh—long enough to tire us. The artist, who had spent years in rude scenes among rough men, said nothing at the time. What was the use? But afterward, in New York, he remarked that this was the roughest travelling he had ever experienced.

The signs of game increased. Deer and bear and wolf and fox and moose were evidently numerous around us. Once we stopped, and the Indians became excited. What they had taken for old moose tracks were the week-old footprints of a man. It seems strange, but they felt obliged to know what a man had gone into the bush for a week ago. They followed the signs, With a glance they read that two teams had passed during the night, going toward our camp. When we returned to camp the teams had been there, and our teamster had talked with the drivers. Therefore that load was lifted from the

ANTOINE'S CABIN.

and came back smiling. He had gone in to cut hemlock boughs; we would find traces of a camp near by. We did. In a country where men are so few, they busy themselves about one another. Four or five days later, while we were hunting, these Indians came to the road and stopped suddenly, as horses do when lassoed. minds of our Indians. But their knowledge of the bush was marvellous. One point in the woods was precisely like another to us, yet the Indians would leap off the sleigh now and then and dive into the forest, to return with a trap hidden there months before, or to find a great iron kettle.

THE CAMP AT NIGHT.

"Do you never get lost?" I asked Alexandre.

"Me get los'? No, no get los'."

"But how do you find your way?"

"Me fin' way easy. Me know way me come, or me follow my tracks, or me know by de sun. If no sun, me look at trees. Trees grow more branches on side toward sun, and got rough bark on north side. At night me know by see de stars."

We camped in a log hut Alexandre had built for a hunting camp. It was very picturesque and substantial, built of huge logs, and caulked with moss. It had a great earthen bank in the middle for a fireplace, with an equally large opening in the roof, boarded several feet high at the sides to form a chimney. At one corner of the fire bank was an ingenious crane, capable of being raised and lowered, and projecting from a pivoted post, so that the long arm could be swung over or away from the fire. At one end of the single apartment were two roomy bunks built against the wall. With extraordinary skill and quickness the Indians whittled a spade out of a board, performing the task with an axe, an implement they can use as white men use a penknife, an implement they value more highly than a gun. They made a broom of balsam boughs, and dug and swept the dirt off the floor and walls, speedily making the cabin neat and clean. Two new bunks were put up for us, and bedded with balsam boughs and skins. Shelves were already up, and spread with pails and bottles, tin cups and plates, knives and forks, canned goods, etc. On them and on the floor were our stores.

We had a week's outfit, and we needed it, because for five days we could not hunt on account of the crust on the snow, which made such a noise when a human foot broke through it that we could not have approached any wild animal within half a mile. On the third day it rained, but without melting the crust. On the fourth day it snowed furiously, burying the crust under two inches of snow. On the fifth day we got our moose.

In the mean time the log cabin was our home. Alexandre and Pierre cut down trees every day for the fire, and Pierre disappeared for hours every now and then to look after traps set for otter, beaver, and marten. Alphonse attended his horses and served as cook. He could produce hotter tea than any other man in the world. I took mine for a walk in the arctic cold three times a day, the artist learned to pour his from one cup to another with amazing dexterity, and the Indians (who drank a quart each of green tea at each meal because it was stronger than our black tea) lifted their pans and threw the liquid fire down throats that had been inured to high wines. Whenever the fire was low, the cold was intense. Whenever it was heaped with logs, all the heat flew directly through the roof, and spiral blasts of cold air were sucked through every crack between logs in the cabin walls. Whenever the door opened, the cabin filled with smoke. Smoke clung to all we ate or wore. At night the fire kept burning out, and we arose with chattering teeth to build it anew. The Indians were then to be seen with their blankets pushed down to their knees, asleep in their shirts and trousers. At meal-times we had bacon or pork, speckled or lake trout, bread and butter, stewed tomatoes, and tea. There were two stools for the five men, but they only complicated the discomfort of those who got them; for it was found that if we put our tin plates on our knees, they fell off; if we held them in one hand, we could not cut the pork and hold the bread with the other hand; while if we put the plates on the floor beside the tea, we could not reach them. In a month we might have solved the problem. Life in that log shanty was precisely the life of the early settlers of this country. It was bound to produce great characters or early death. There could be no middle course with such an existence.

Partridge fed in the brush impudently before us. Rabbits bobbed about in the clearing before the door. Squirrels sat upon the logs near by and gormandized and chattered. Great saucy birds, like mouse-colored robins, and called mid-birds, stole our provender if we left it out-of-doors half an hour, and one day we saw a red deer jump in the bush a hundred yards away. Yet we got no game, because we knew there was a moose-yard within two miles on one side and within three miles on the other, and we dared not shoot our rifles lest we frighten the moose. Moose was all we were after. There was a lake near by, and the trout in those lakes up there attain remarkable size and numbers. We heard of 35-pound speckled trout, of lake trout twice as large, and of enormous muskallonge. The most reliable persons told of lakes farther in the wilderness where the trout are thick as salmon in the British Columbia streams, so thick as to seem to fill the water. We were near a lake that was supposed to have been fished out by lumbermen a year before, yet it was no sport at all to fish there. With a short stick and two yards of line and a bass hook baited with pork, we brought up four-pound and five-pound beauties faster than we wanted them for food. Truly we were in a splendid hunting country, like the Adirondacks eighty

ON THE MOOSE TRAIL.

years ago, but thousands of times as extensive.

Finally we started for moose. Our Indians asked if they might take their guns. We gave the permission. Alexandre, a thin wiry man of forty years, carried an old Henry rifle in a woollen case open at one end like a stocking. He wore a short blanket coat and tuque, and trousers tied tight below the knee, and let into his moccasin-tops. He and his brother François are famous Hudson Bay Company trappers, and are two-thirds Algonquin and one-third French. He has a typical swarthy angular Indian face and a French mustache and goatee. Naturally, if not by rank, a leader among his men, his manner is commanding and his appearance grave. He talks bad French fluently, and makes wretched headway in English. Pierre is a short, thickset, walnut-stained man of thirty-five, almost pure Indian, and almost a perfect specimen of physical development. He seldom spoke while on this trip, but he impressed us with his strength, endurance, quickness, and knowledge of woodcraft. Poor fellow! he had only a shot-gun, which he loaded with buckshot. It had no case, and both men carried their pieces grasped by the barrels and shouldered, with the butts behind them.

We set out in Indian-file, plunging at once into the bush. Never was forest scenery more exquisitely beautiful than on that morning as the day broke, for we breakfasted at four o'clock, and started immediately afterward. Everywhere the view was fairy-like. There was not snow enough for snow-shoeing. But the fresh fall of snow was immaculately white, and flecked the scene apparently from earth to sky, for there was not a branch or twig or limb or spray of evergreen, or wart or fungous growth upon any tree, that did not bear its separate burden of snow. It was a bridal dress, not a winding-sheet, that Dame Nature was trying on that morning. And in the bright fresh green of the firs and pines we saw her complexion peeping out above her spotless gown, as one sees the rosy cheeks or black eyes of a girl wrapped in ermine.

Mile after mile we walked, up mountain and down dale, slapped in the faces by twigs, knocking snow down the backs of our necks, slipping knee-deep in bog mud, tumbling over loose stones, climbing across interlaced logs, dropping to the height of one thigh between tree trunks, sliding, falling, tight-rope walking on branches over thin ice, but forever following the cat-like tread of Alexandre, with his seven-league stride and long-winded persistence. Suddenly we came to a queer sort of clearing dotted with protuberances like the bubbles on molasses beginning to boil. It was a beaver meadow. The bumps in the snow covered stumps of trees the beavers had gnawed down. The Indians were looking at some trough-like tracks in the snow, like the trail of a tired man who had dragged his heels. "Moose; going this way," said Alexandre; and we turned and walked in the tracks. Across the meadow and across a lake and up another mountain they led us. Then we came upon fresher prints. At each new track the Indians stooped, and making a scoop of one hand, brushed the new-fallen snow lightly out of the indentations. Thus they read the time at which the print was made. "Las' week," "Day 'fore yesterday," they whispered. Presently they bent over again, the light snow flew, and one whispered, "This morning."

Stealthily Alexandre swept ahead; very carefully we followed. We dared not break a twig, or speak, or slip, or stumble. As it was, the breaking of the crust was still far too audible. We followed a little stream, and approached a thick growth of tamarack. We had no means of knowing that a herd of moose was lying in that thicket, resting after feeding. We knew it afterward. Alexandre motioned to us to get our guns ready. We each threw a cartridge from the cylinder into the barrel, making a "click, click" that was abominably loud. Alexandre forged ahead. In five minutes we heard him call aloud: "Moose gone. We los' him." We hastened to his side. He pointed at some tracks in which the prints were closer together than any we had seen.

"See! he trot," Alexandre explained.

In another five minutes we had all but completed a circle, and were on the other side of the tamarack thicket. And there were the prints of the bodies of the great beasts. We could see even the imprint of the hair of their coats. All around were broken twigs and balsam needles. The moose had left the branches ragged, and on every hand the young bark was chewed or rubbed raw. Loading our rifles had lost us a herd of moose.

Back once again at the beaver dam, Alexandre and Pierre studied the moose-tramped snow and talked earnestly. They agreed that a desperate battle had been fought there between two bull moose a week before, and that those bulls were not in the "yard" where we had blundered. They examined the tracks over an acre or more, and then strode off at an obtuse angle from our former trail. Pierre, apparently not quite satisfied, kept dropping behind or disappearing in the bush at one side of us. So magnificent was his skill at his work that I missed him at times, and at other times found him putting his feet down where mine were lifted up without ever hearing a sound of his step or of his contact with the undergrowth. Alexandre presently motioned us with a warning gesture. He slowed his pace to short steps, with long pauses between. He saw everything that moved, heard every sound; only a deer could throw more and keener faculties into play than this born hunter. He heard a twig snap. We heard nothing. Pierre was away on a side search. Alexandre motioned us to be ready. We crept close together, and I scarcely breathed. We moved cautiously, a step at a time, like chessmen. It was impossible to get an unobstructed view a hundred feet ahead, so thick was the soft-wood growth. It seemed out of the question to try to shoot

that distance. We were descending a hill-side into marshy ground. We crossed a corner of a grove of young alders, and saw before us a gentle slope thickly grown with evergreen—tamarack, the artist called it. Suddenly Alexandre bent forward and raised his gun. Two steps forward gave us his view. Five moose were fifty yards away, alarmed and ready to run. A big bull in the front of the group had already thrown back his antlers. By impulse rather than through reason I took aim at a second bull. He was half a height lower down the slope, and to be seen through a web of thin foliage. Alexandre and the artist fired as with a single pull at one trigger. The foremost bull staggered and fell forward, as if his knees had been broken. He was hit twice—in the heart and in the neck. The second bull and two cows and a calf plunged into the bush and disappeared. Pierre found that bull a mile away, shot through the lungs.

It had taken us a week to kill our moose in a country where they were common game. That was "hunter's luck" with a vengeance. But at another season such a delay could scarcely occur. The time to visit that district is in the autumn, before snow falls. Then in a week one ought to be able to bag a moose, and move into the region, farther west and north of the great lakes, where caribou are plenty.

SUCCESS.

THE UPPER PENINSULA OF MICHIGAN

INDIAN PACKER.

MINING regions are proverbially barren and rocky, and the upper peninsula of Michigan—at least that portion of it which is so productive of iron and copper—forms no exception to this rule. It is old—older than most of our hills, for it was the first land that was attached to the original Laurentian nucleus about which our continent has been formed. It has, in consequence, always been a favorite field for geological study, and its novel industrial features make it no less interesting to the ordinary traveller.

The face of the country is rugged and seamed and worn. Were it not for its mineral wealth it would remain permanently a wilderness. Lumber companies would invade it here and there, and retire after having robbed the forest of the pine which is found in a few scattered patches. It would be an eddy where the stream of Western migration had left a few Indians and woodsmen to subsist by the methods of primitive life. The land is generally valueless from the farmer's point of view, for the soil is a light drift—too light for wheat—and the climate a winter modified by a season of summer weather too short for Indian corn to ripen. Hay, oats, and potatoes yield the farmer a fair return, but the climate is so rigorous that the securing of shelter and fuel calls for so large an amount of energy that little is left to devote to cultivation. It is a proof of this that a very inconsiderable fraction of the population attempts to subsist by farming, although the freight from Chicago is added to the price of all the staple articles of production—hay, for instance, being from twenty to twenty-five dollars a ton, and milk ten cents a quart. Curiously enough, strawberries and currants reach a perfection unknown in more hospitable latitudes, a Marquette strawberry resembling in size a Seckel pear, and in flavor a wild strawberry. This is owing, no doubt, to the fact that in northern latitudes—Marquette is about as far north as Quebec—the few summer days have from eighteen to twenty hours of sunlight and after-glow, and vegetable growth is virtually uninterrupted by darkness. Light, the botanists tell us, bears the same relation to aroma that heat does to sweetness. Such strawberries as these must be seen to be appreciated, and must be visited to be seen, for they are too large and too delicate to bear travel themselves.

I have spoken of the climate as a winter modified by a short summer. The July and August weather I can vouch for as delightful. Even when the sun is hottest you feel instinctively that there is no prostrating power in it, and the nights are invariably cool. In July the mean daily range was 19°, and the monthly range 50°, the lowest recorded temperature being 38°. Near the lake the presence of so large a body of water which at Marquette never falls below 52°, and on the extreme

northern end of the pe-
ninsula never below 48°,
acts as an equalizer, and
restricts the range with-
in comparatively nar-
row limits. This low
temperature of the lake
water, which is higher
than that of any of the
streams entering it, pre-
cludes the idea of bath-
ing. As a consequence
few of the lake sailors
can swim, and it would
be of little avail to them
as a means of preserv-
ing life if they could,
for the most robust man
if he falls into Lake Su-
perior chills and dies in
a few moments. The
numerous trout streams
in the woods are of an
icy coldness. The snow,
which falls to a depth of
six or seven feet, melts
and sinks into the sandy
ground, to re-appear

MARQUETTE FROM RIDGE STREET BLUFF.

from deep-seated springs with a temperature of 39°, which is exactly equal to the
average annual temperature of the place.
The thick forests prevent the sun from
warming the ground or the water. And
finally the lake is so deep—its bed reaching
several hundred feet below the level of the
sea—that the summer air has little effect
on it before it is again covered with ice
There is no other place on the globe where
so large a body of cold fresh water lies at an
elevation of six hundred feet above the sea.
The air in contact with this deep chilly
water seems to acquire a peculiar vivify-
ing and refreshing quality, quite impossible to describe, but very easy to appreciate. Here must be the great summer
sanitarium or cooling-off place for Chicago
and Milwaukee.

In point of woodland scenery the Michigan wilderness can not compare with the
White Mountains or the Adirondacks.
The great effective feature of height is
wanting, as the elevation is rarely more
than six hundred feet above the lake, and
the general contour is broken and rolling.
The northern shore is much bolder. The
forest southwest of Portage Lake is more
than one hundred miles long, and has escaped devastation by forest fires. It extends into Wisconsin, and as far as I went

—about fifty miles—consists principally of
hard maple. It is capable of supplying
the continent with sugar. Until some
discoveries of copper are made in it, it will
probably remain one of the finest bodies
of woodland in the country. There are
many lovely little lakes and streams
abounding with trout scattered through it.
The eastern portion contains many impenetrable swamps overgrown with tamarack and cedar. The western portion of
this great forest has less of the savage
and forbidding aspect peculiar to Northern woods, and is comparatively open.
The road to Ontonagon passes through it
in one direction, and is barely practicable
for uncovered wagons. It is worth enduring a long railroad journey to be able
to drive forty miles through trees with the
consciousness that you are leaving human
habitations farther behind you at every
step. The forest is singularly devoid of
animal life. Mile after mile is uncheered
by a solitary bird. Possibly you may
chance on the fresh track of a bear or a
deer. If indeed you have the endurance
to watch for six hours without moving, it
may be granted you to see a beaver working on his dam.

There is one short period of the June
day when a Northern forest loses its wild,

ASCENDING THE SLOPE, REPUBLIC IRON MINE.

stern character. It is when the long twilight of the summer evenings passes through the beautiful modifications of the after-glow. The setting of the sun is followed by the usual grayish light, but instead of fading gradually into darkness, the western sky for a space of ninety degrees on the horizon, and to a height of fifteen degrees or more, becomes filled with a soft yellow radiance. This lasts till ten o'clock or later. At half past nine one can read easily. The light is evenly diffused, and there are no shadows. It is as mystic as moonlight, but warmer, more kindly sympathetic. The cheerfulness of day is mingled with the serenity and solemnity of night. Nature speaks of the gentle and the loving in a way that draws the heart to her insensibly, and one perceives how it comes that the inhabitants of high latitudes are so strongly attached to their homes.

The few Indians who are left on the northern peninsula are a peaceful, harmless folk. They live by hunting and fishing, acting as guides for exploring parties, and a few work in a desultory way in the pineries. Many of them own sail-boats, and live in framed houses, and have adopted the white man's clothes. But some still retain the blanket and the wigwam, and can speak only their own language. The father in charge of the Catholic mission at L'Anse, whose knowledge of them is perhaps as accurate as that of any other person, puts their number at two thousand, nearly all of whom can speak English imperfectly. Their tribal relation is slowly decaying—in fact, exists only as a tradition. The name of the tribe he writes

"Otchipwes." He says that they can not
resist the fatal effects of the vices of the
lower classes of whites with whom they
come in contact, and that the numbers of
the full-bloods are gradually shrinking.
The inherited habits of generations are so
built into the constitution of the race that
regular food and shelter have a pauperizing
effect on them. In a few years the only
trace left of them will be the melodious
names of the islands and bays and rivers
where they fished and hunted, unless perhaps a token of their ancestry remain in

Ontonagon, Menominee, and Michigamme,
the last a beautiful word, pronounced as
it is with the broad *a*. It is the name of
a river, a canoe trip down which has all
the charm of wood life without its discomfort. Pewabic is the Indian name of a
low range of hills, and has been changed
by a printer's error into "Penokee," which
is now legally adopted. With what a
manuscript must that printer have con-
tended! So this fine word, signifying
"iron," is lost, except as the name of a
mine, which we trust may immortalize it.

ORE-SHIPPING PIERS AT MARQUETTE.

the darker cheek or hair of some American
citizen of obscure pedigree; for the half
and quarter breeds, though a mongrel
race, seem to have, in contradiction to the
general rule, greater powers of resistance
than the pure-bloods.

It is fortunate that the Jesuits and *voyageurs* came into this country before the
Americans, so that the Indian and French
local names were firmly fastened before
our people took possession; and instead of
the eternal Jackson and Madison and
Adams, and North this and New that, we
have Escanaba, Negaunee, Marquette, Isle
Royale, Grand Portage, Allouez, Pewabic,

The material development of this country, which supports a population of twenty thousand people, depends upon two
distinct industries, the mining of iron ore
and of copper; for the cutting of lumber
is carried on at a few points only, and is
of necessity temporary. The production
of iron ore, which began about twenty-five
years ago, and reached one hundred thousand tons in 1862, has grown steadily till it
touched one and one-half millions of tons
in 1879, and will exceed two millions of
tons in 1882. Most of this immense product is taken to Cleveland, whence it is
distributed by rail to meet the coal of Ohio

DRIVING A HOLE.

water-power, in a huge iron pipe nearly a mile long. It is rather uncanny to see the engine wheels revolving, and the great pumps slowly reciprocating, with no smoke or sound of escaping steam. The pipes and cylinders are cold; snow forms around the exhaust passages; there is no apparent cause for motion. It is a dead machine, working as if alive. But it performs its work efficiently, and the car-loads of ore are raised quickly to the surface. The ore lies in an irregular vertical bed from fifty to one hundred and fifty feet wide, which has been excavated in an "open cut" to a depth of two hundred feet. The walls

and Western Pennsylvania. A comparatively small portion is smelted on the spot in furnaces using charcoal, making a superior but high-priced iron for the better qualities of boiler plates and sheets. There is no better pig-iron in the world than that produced in Lake Superior charcoal furnaces. But vegetable fuel can never compete with mineral fuel in price, though its superiority is as marked in the forge as on the domestic hearth. The great bulk of the ore is shipped from the three ports of L'Anse, Marquette, and Escanaba, where are huge elevated docks, on which the trains of ore cars are run, and their contents discharged into bins underneath, from which it is loaded into lake schooners by opening a trap-door. During the navigation season the thunder of the ore, as it runs from the "pockets" into the holds of the vessels below, is almost continuous.

The Republic is rather the show iron mine of the district, as it is one of the largest and most picturesquely situated. It is remarkable, too, for a very bold and novel piece of mechanical engineering. All the power for pumping and hoisting is supplied, not by steam, but by compressed air, which is conveyed to the mine, from the spot where it is generated by

of this chasm are of deep red jasper and gray quartzite, and from the bridge which spans it give a magnificent effect. At the bottom is a black floor of iron ore, on which men and horses look like atomies. Drilling and blasting between these overhanging massive cliffs look very dangerous, and indeed can hardly fail to be so. The deeper "workings" are far beneath this, and in them a roof of ore is left for protection, which serves at least to hide the danger. Going down into these, we find suites of immense murky rooms, whose floors and roofs and walls are black lustrous magnetic ore. Around the sides the power drills are at work, striking six hundred blows a minute, driven by the compressed air, which is carried in a rubber hose to every part of the mine. They are as rapid as a sewing-machine, and not much larger, but energetic as a steam-hammer, of which, indeed, they are diminutive copies. But two yellow-haired young Danes, who are "driving" a hole by the old-fashioned method of striking alternately with sledge-hammers on a steel bar held in position by their comrade, are much better worth looking at than the busy little machines. They are in a very constrained position, but every movement is full of the grace which comes from a perfect muscular development. They swing their hammers at arm's-length, as their forefathers used the two-handled mace. This is the famous "Bessemer ore," and in a month it will be at the great mills at Cambria, or Joliet, or Harrisburg, and in three weeks more it will be transformed into a steel rail, and in another month it will be in a railroad in Kansas or Dakota, and wheat cars will be rolling on it toward the Atlantic. On its hard, smooth face a bushel of wheat can be freighted a thousand miles for twenty cents less than on a soft iron rail.

Every one in this part of the peninsula is covered with red ore dust and talking about iron. In the hotels, on the streets, in the stations, one hears the words "hematite," "specular," "magnetic," "output of the Norway," on every side. The very clocks are set to "mining time," half an hour faster than the old-fashioned sun time. More than one thousand men are in the woods "prospecting." The large land-owners have adopted the policy of granting "options"; that is, signing an agreement that if any person shall uncover a bed of ore on his land, the finder shall be entitled to a certain interest, generally one-third. Those who obtain these options frequently hire woodmen, for their outfit and a small fraction of the prospective interest, to explore for them. The ore lies in a certain geological formation, called, in the nomenclature of the country, a "mineral range," generally in irregular lens-shaped masses, or, as a mining captain expressed it, "like seeds in a pumpkin" —seeds from four to eight hundred feet long. The strata are so wrinkled and tilted and twisted by the contraction of the earth's surface that it is almost impossible to distinguish their bedding. If the surface were smoothed out again, the upper peninsula would be large enough to make a good-sized Western State. It has been ground down by the great continental glacier, and left covered with sand and gravel and bowlders, on all but the highest parts,

to a depth of from ten to one hundred feet. The prospectors sink a well, which they call a "test pit," through this drift, and if they do not happen to hit the edge of a pumpkin-seed, move a little farther off, and try again. If they strike a bed of "lean ore," or any of the rocks that usually inclose a valuable deposit, they deduce from the inspection of a fragment the most favorable position for a new trial. They possess an acuteness and an amount of rough-and-ready geological knowledge, ac-

UNDER-GROUND IRON MINE.

quired in the mining school of experience, which almost reach the dignity of an instinct. The older companies use the diamond drill for exploring, which bores to any depth and in any direction required, and brings out a core or rod of stone from the hole, giving a consecutive sample of all the material penetrated. Every year new discoveries, new experience, and new mechanical inventions render Lake Superior iron-mining less problematical, and strengthen its position as one of the great permanent industries of the country.

The northern part of the upper peninsula juts out into Lake Superior like a gigantic thumb. This is Keweenaw Point, and through it runs an inclined system of rocks known to geologists as the "copper-bearing series," and to miners as the copper "mineral range." This supplementary peninsula, which is not more than fifteen miles wide, is cleft from one side to the other near its base, and below the level of the lake, by a valley in which lies a long, ir-

easily obtained, are able to earn regular dividends, we can form some idea of the princely income of this magnificent property. At the mine is a village of eight

ENTRANCE TO LOCK, SAULT SAINTE MARIE CANAL, CONNECTING LAKES SUPERIOR AND HURON.

regular sheet of water called Portage Lake, through which large boats pass freely. On the sides of this inlet are the great stamping-mills of the copper mines, and a few miles north of it is the great Calumet and Hecla Mine, which, whether viewed commercially, socially, or industrially, is one of the notable establishments of the world. A slice of conglomerate rock varying from ten to fifteen feet in thickness, and reaching to an unknown depth into the earth, is streaked and veined through more than a mile of its length with copper—not copper ore, which must go through an expensive process of concentration and smelting, but metallic copper, good enough to hammer into pennies and receive the mint mark. One-twentieth or more of the whole mass is copper; and when we reflect that copper is worth three hundred and eighty dollars a ton, that the regular monthly product of the mine is fourteen hundred tons, that other mines whose rock contains one fifth as much copper, and is less

thousand inhabitants, all living on land and in houses owned by the company, and on wages paid by the company. As a straightforward manly development of American civilization this village of Calumet is without a peer. There is no lawyer, and the only justice of the peace is obliged to act as superintendent of the railroad for occupation. There is, indeed, a lawyer in the adjoining and subsidiary village of Red Jacket, but one lawyer is of necessity as harmless as half a pair of shears. No one has ever been sent to State-prison during the ten years of the town's life. During a stay of a fortnight I saw no one under the influence of liquor—a state of things so unnatural in a mining town as to make one feel uneasy. Two "Molly Maguires" from the coal regions would make more noise than the two thousand employés of Calumet. The moral tone is as bracing as the fresh cool air. The miner, instead of eying a stranger sulkily, and as if hesitating which stone he should throw at him, gives him good-day cheerily and heartily, as used the old-time rural population of New England. Here are Swedes, Norwegians, Danes, Finns, Scotch, Cornishmen, Canadians, Russians, Bohemians, Spaniards, Italians, and Germans quietly and harmoniously developing into self-respecting American citizens. Thirteen languages are spoken on the reservation. Mining companies usually prefer this mixture of nationalities, as a security against strikes; for confusion of tongues has been a preventive against unlawful combinations of labor since the

scribe exactly the amount the miners do, making last year a free gift of nine thousand dollars. But it is not so much gratitude for this liberality as the absolute certainty felt by the miner that the company are governed by stern principles of rectitude which gives tone to the Calumet community, and makes it the most efficient body of working-men in the world. It gives the strongest testimony to the immense silent power of character, in this age when we refer everything to the balance of material forces and the action of physical laws. When Fisk had control

A LAKE SUPERIOR COPPER MINE—WASHING THE TAILINGS.

building of the Tower of Babel. The tie which binds wage-earning men together is readily unloosed by race jealousies. A miners' union in thirteen languages is impossible. But the Calumet Company have no reason to fear strikes among any portion of their force. No man is discharged without cause, or forced to lose time. Pay-day is as punctual as the moon. The company employ four physicians, and have built a school-house with ample room for twenty-two teachers and eighteen hundred children, and equipped it with all the most approved aids to teaching. To the miners' aid fund the company sub-

of the Erie Railway, the uncivilized bandit began to crop out in every conductor and brakeman; and if his spirit could enter the Calumet and Hecla direction, its debasing influence would filter through the organization, and make Calumet among mines what the Erie was among railroads.

A great property like this is a trust in more senses than one. With their unexampled facilities for producing copper, the company have the power of crushing competition. They might run the price of the metal up and down as one tosses a ball in the air, until all the companies who are working on a narrow margin were forced to succumb. Their efforts, however, are directed toward securing a uniform price, toward preventing the wide fluctuations which, if promoted, might leave them without competitors. Their overshadowing power has, however, a tendency to check systematic exploration. While it can hardly be expected that another so valuable deposit will be found, it can not be denied that the copper region is as yet imperfectly developed. Capitalists naturally hesitate to enter a business where there is one producer of such preponderating influence.

All the equipments of this mine are of the highest order of mechanical excellence. A depth of twenty-three hundred feet, measuring on the slope of forty degrees, has been reached; and the new compound engine of three thousand horsepower, strong enough to turn the two Corliss engines of the Centennial Exposition backward and to do their work in addition, is capable of supplying power till a depth of four thousand feet is reached. Com-

pressed air at a pressure of sixty pounds is carried to every working point. The mine itself resembles a section of a rectangular city. Eight parallel main avenues, each with its railroad, reach half a mile into the earth. Twenty-three horizontal streets nearly a mile long intersect them. The work goes on day and night three hundred and ten days in the year. Going down into this mine and seeing the perfection of the machinery, the tremendous effects of the nitro-glycerine explosions, the splendid physique and discipline of the force, all material obstacles seem to vanish, and one says involuntarily, "Why not keep on till we touch the centre of the earth?"

The income of this mine ascends to the apex of the social pyramid—if there be in America a social pyramid and it have an apex. The results of the great mining fortunes in our country are for the most part so paltry—a mansion on Fifth Avenue, a villa in Newport, a stable full of nimble horses, a family *fruges consumere*

COPPER ORE CARS.

nati, at best a gallery of chance-selected pictures, are so frequently the highest outcome — that the country is to be congratulated that these yearly millions go into worthy hands and attain worthy objects. It seems an exaggeration to say of an industrial establishment, but it is not too much to say it of Calumet and Hecla, that it adds an honor to a great scientific name.

The Lake Superior mines have the advantage of producing metal free from any alloy of antimony or nickel or arsenic. In many of the mines great masses of native metal are found so large that they must be cut in place with chisels.

All the more important mines are situated on the ancient

workings of a prehistoric race. They seem to have been ignorant of the fact that copper could be melted, for they left behind them the fragments too small to use and the masses too heavy to lift. Every day they subjected it to a temperature nearly high enough, without making a discovery which would have lifted them out of the Stone Age into the Bronze Age, and perhaps have enabled them to survive the struggle in which they perished. They must have been very numerous, and have reached the point of development where they were capable of organizing industry.

In Isle Royale, near the Minong Mine, their pits, excavated to a depth of from ten to twenty feet in the solid rock, cover an area of from three to four hundred feet wide and more than a mile and a half in length. The labor expended here can not have been much short of that involved in building a Pyramid. Isle Royale is ten miles from the nearest land, and is incapable of producing food, so that all supplies except fish must have been brought from some distant point. Their excavations could of course never go below the point at which water would accumulate. Their hammers, frequently to the number of several thousand, are found in heaps where they were evidently placed at the end of the season. As no graves or evidences of habitations are found, we can hardly doubt that the ancient miners lived south of the great lakes, and made yearly journeyings with fleets of canoes to the copper mines. The aggregate amount of the metal which they carried off must have been very great, and it has, I believe, been generally thought that the copper implements of the ancient Mexicans came from this source. M. Charnay in a recent number of the *North American* seems to think that the Mexicans reduced copper from its ores. A chemical analysis of their hatchets would solve the question, for Lake Superior copper is so free from alloys as to be unmistakable.

The superintendent of the old Caledonia

LAKE SUPERIOR COPPER MINES—HOISTING ORE TO THE HEAD HOUSE.

Mine in Ontonagon County kindly took me to the top of a cliff where three Cornish "tributers"—miners working not for wages but for a share of the product—had cleared out one of the ancient pits in the outcrop of the vein. They had brought out a quantity of copper, and had just uncovered a large mass which would weigh certainly not less than seven tons. Many battered stone hammers lay around the mouth of the pit. The active little Englishmen, belonging to a race of hereditary miners perhaps as old as the Mound-builders themselves, had come around the world from the east to finish the work of the departed Asiatic race who reached here from the west at a time to which no date can be assigned. Not far away another party had cut down a dead cedar to make props for their tunnel. As they were putting the log in position, from its centre dropped a small but perfectly formed stone hammer which had never been used. It was made from a stone found, I believe, only on the north shore of the lake. This tree was not far from two hundred and fifty years old; but as cedar is almost indestructible in this climate, it may have been dead several hundred years. The axeman said that he had found several hammers in the centre of cedars. It would seem barely possible that this hammer had been placed in a cleft of the tree, when it was a sapling, that the wood might grow around the groove and serve as a handle. At all events, this one, which I have, was certainly placed where it was—about thirty inches from the ground—by human hands, undoubtedly by the ancient miner himself, when the tree was a twig.

MONTANA

TWO anecdotes told in Montana as characteristic home-made jokes illustrate the spirit of its people. The first one is about ex-Governor Hauser. It is said that, like many another true Montanian, he begins to feel a new and strange regard for small change once he gets east of the Mississippi, a consideration unknown to any man in the Treasure State. It happened, therefore, that when on one occasion he handed two bits—which is to say, a silver quarter—to a Chicago newsboy, and when the boy gave him a newspaper and moved away without making any change, the Montanian called out: "I say, stop! Give me my change." At that the boy looked wonderingly at him. "Oh no," he replied; "you don't want no change; you're a Montana man." The other story is to the effect that a party of well-known Butte and Helena millionaires were enjoying a quiet and friendly game at poker, when a commercial traveller—a stranger to all in the party—manifested a considerable interest in the game, as an outsider. The gentlemen were "chipping in" white chips to admit them to the betting on each hand of cards, and then they were stacking up red and blue chips in great profusion to attest their faith in what cards they held. The drummer found the game irresistible, and taking out a one-hundred-dollar bill, he flung it on the table and said: "Gentlemen, I would like to join you. There's the money for some chips." At that one of the millionaires looked over at the banker and said, "Sam, take the gentleman's money, and give him a white chip."

These are characteristic Montana stories, and they reflect the spirit of the dominant handful of leaders in the State. If these men are not all too used to the making of big fortunes, they are at least bent upon making them, and very familiar with seeing them made. Years and years ago there was just such a condition of affairs in California; now it is peculiar to Montana.

Think of it! Montana, speaking very roughly, is so large a State and with so small a population that it may be said to contain one inhabitant for each square mile of its surface, and yet it has been the boast of those people that no similar band of human beings in the world has approached them in the amount of wealth *per capita* that they have produced. As long ago as 1889 Montana contained less than 150,000 souls, and produced $60,000,000—that is to say that, exclusive of what was consumed at home, the ore, cattle, horses, and sheep sent out of the State brought a sum of money equal to $400 for every man, woman, and child it supported.

It is mainly a mining and a stock-raising State, and these industries have so amply rewarded those who are engaged in them that agricultural and manufacturing development have been unduly retarded. This cannot long continue. So great a State cannot be long given over to grazing herds of cattle, and dotted here and there with mining camps, and when we come to understand what rich farming lands the State contains, and of what vast extent are these parks and valleys, it takes no uncommonly prophetic eye to see the State in the near future checkered with the green and yellow of well-worked farms to a greater extent than it is now ribbed with mountains. The frequent and often easy making of great fortunes has had its natural consequence in causing the postponement of the cultivation of the soil. It has been left for Chinamen to make the valleys laugh with the bloom and verdure of small fruits and vegetables, and the fact that Chinamen were thus employed has tended to make such labor seem so much the less worthy of the white inhabitant. But now the white man has begun to take note of the wonderful results which have followed even this petty farming, and his eyes have been opened to the wide and varied capabilities of the soil, and to the fortunes that lie in it awaiting the great agriculturists who are to come—who, indeed, are beginning work. They earned a million and a half from wheat last year, and nearly two millions of dollars from oats.

But the conditions that have caused mining and stock-raising to monopolize the energy of the original people there have resulted in making Montana a very forward State, a very progressive and interesting fraction of the nation. It will not do for the reader to jump to the conclusion that because mining camps and cattle ranges have been the chief fields of industry, that the population is one of cowboys and shovel-men. On the contrary, Helena, the capital, is one of the most attractive cities in America, and is perhaps the wealthiest one of its size in the world. And scattered all over the State are other fine towns, in which will be found a very cultivated and cosmopolitan people, fond of and accustomed to travel, holding memberships in the clubs of New York and London, living splendidly at home, well informed, polite, fashionable, and intimately related, socially or in business, with the leading circles in the financial centres of the country. It was not long ago in point of actual time that our children were taught to regard the region of the Missouri as peopled by redskins and enlivened by the presence of the buffalo. But it will seem to the tourist of to-morrow that such a characterization of the country cannot have been true in the time of men now alive, so utterly are all traces of the old condition obliterated. As far as such a traveller will be able to judge by what he sees, the Indian will appear to have gone with the buffalo. As a matter of fact, the savage is there still, but he is corralled on reservations as deer are in our parks.

The tourist in Montana will find along his route a chain of thoroughly modern cities, appointed with fine and showy storehouses, the most modern means of street travel, excellent newspapers, luxuriously appointed clubs, good hotels, and all the conveniences of latter-day life. In Helena he will meet something more nearly approaching a leisure class than I saw anywhere else in the Northwest—a circle made up of men who have retired upon their incomes, or who thrive by the shrewd use of capital obtained from industries that do not monopolize their attention. In this respect little Helena is more forward even than great Chicago.

But over and through all of this progress and accomplishment there shines the mysterious and romantic light of a rude era that was so recent as to have involved even the middle-aged men of to-day. It was of the type of that of '49 in California. It was an era of new mining camps, of swarming tides of men thirsty for nuggets, of pistol-bristling sheriffs, of vigilantes, road-agents, Indian fights, stage-coaches, and all the motley characters that gave Bret Harte his inspiration. You may meet some of the men who helped to rid the State of outlaws by the holding of what they gayly spoke of as "necktie parties," and the application of hemp. They are apt to lounge into the clubs on any night, and with them you may see the best Indian "sign-talker" who ever lived, or that quick-handed, "scientific" ex-constable who proudly asserts that in the worst days he arrested hundreds of desperadoes bare-handed, without pulling his gun more than once or twice in his whole constabulary career. They represent the days of the founding of Montana. And yet in the same city where I met such men I encountered others from London, New York, Sitka, San Francisco, and many other capitals; for, as I have said, the new Montana is in close contact with all the world.

Montana is the largest of the newly admitted States; in fact, it is as large as Washington and North Dakota combined. It is one-sixth larger than the United Kingdom of Great Britain and Ireland. It is the third State in the sisterhood, ranking next after Texas and California. It contains 143,776 square miles, and is therefore the size of the States of New York, New Jersey, Pennsylvania, Maryland, Virginia, and West Virginia all rolled together. It is about 540 miles in length, and half as wide. As it is approached from the east, it seems to be a continuation of the bunch-grass plains land which makes up all of North Dakota. But almost all at once upon entering Montana the monotony of the great plateau is relieved by its disturbance into hills, which grow more and more numerous, and take on greater and greater bulk and height, until, when one-third of the State has been passed, the earth is all distorted with mountains and mountain spurs. These are the forerunners of the Rockies, which, speaking roughly, make up the final or western third of this grand and imperial new State. A glance at the map will call to the attention the apparently contradictory fact that the principal seats of population in the State are directly in the Rocky Mountain region. This is difficult for the majority of readers to account for. They think of the Rocky Mountains as great bastions of bare stone—and such, indeed, the main range is; but the spurs and lesser or side ranges are grass-clad or wooded elevations, and even amid the veritable Rockies themselves are innumerable valleys coated with the richest, most nutritious pasturage to be found anywhere in the world. In or beside such valleys are the cities of which I speak, built there to be close to the mines that are being worked in the mountains.

Helena's history shows how such conditions came about. In 1864, after the discovery of placer gold in Alder Gulch had caused a stampede of fortune-seekers to Montana, the second scene of mining activity was Last Chance Gulch. That gulch is now the main street of Helena. The miners began washing the dirt at the foot of the gulch, and the saloon-keepers, gamblers, and traders built their places of business close to where the miners were at work. When the whole surface of the gold-bearing runways had been

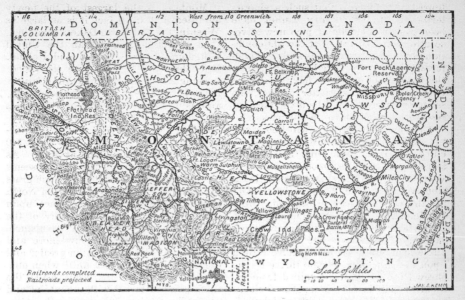

MAP OF MONTANA.

passed through the pans, and $25,000,000 had been taken out in nuggets and dust, the mining ceased, but the town remained. It did not shrivel and languish like Virginia City, the town that had grown up in Alder Gulch, but being at the crossing of all the old Indian trails of the Northwest, and a natural centre of the region, it waxed big, and began a new lease of life as a trading, political, and money capital.

Let me begin a detailed description of Montana by saying that its future as an agricultural State will be dependent upon the extent and number of irrigation ditches that shall be cut in it. The average rainfall upon the eastern end of the State is only about nine inches a year; in the central part, still east of the mountains, it is nowhere more than fourteen inches, I believe. West of the mountains there is a very different country, one that is locally described as "green"; that is to say, the verdure has its natural term of life, and the rainfall is greater there. But that is a small part of the State by comparison with the rest. Yet all over the State, on the great eastern plateau as well as in the valleys among the mountains, the soil is of extraordinary fertility, and it is said that at least three-fifths of it can be laid under the ditch. A glance at the map will show the reader the great lines of the Missouri and Yellowstone rivers, and the fine lines of their branches and feeders, which literally vein the chart. It is, of course, by means of the supply in these waterways that it is hoped the future farms of Montana will be founded and maintained.

Governor Toole, in his last annual message, says that "there was a time when it seemed not improbable that the general government would take hold of this proposition, and under its supervision control and manage the water supply to the advantage of all. It is perfectly apparent, however, at this time (January, 1891) that influences are co-operating which will eventuate in destroying whatever hope we may have had in that direction. Eastern communities, which have set this opposition in motion, appear to be mindful only of local interests, and not of the prosperity of the whole country. Their protest is based upon the claim that the reclamation of these arid lands would subject the settler in the Eastern and Middle States to undue competition, retarding relief from agricultural depression.... The homes which we propose to make," he continues, "are not for us alone, but for every citizen of the United States who has the courage to come and take one. If we are to receive any substantial or speedy benefits from our arid lands, I believe the State must first acquire a title to them, and then undertake by appropriate legislation to reclaim and dispose of them. The government should select, survey, and convey these lands to the State upon such conditions as would secure their occupation and reclamation."

Independent of any such Federal action as is suggested by the Governor, individual enterprise has made itself greatly felt in the provision of irrigation canals, reservoirs, and ditches. If it were not that I fear being credited with a desire to criticise, I would say that the rush and mania for water rights in Montana closely resemble in their impetuosity and greed the scramble for rich lands wherever they are newly opened in the far West, and the not altogether patriotic desire to build new cities in the State of Washington. In Montana irrigation schemes are expected to pay even better than mining; hence the scramble. I ventured to speak of this to a man who was planning to control certain valleys, which he described as being of the size of dukedoms, by "corralling" the waterways in them, by which alone they could be made fit for farming.

"Well," he replied, "we who are on the ground are going to get whatever there is lying round. You don't suppose we are going to let a parcel of strangers preempt the water rights so that we must pay taxes to them? No; we prefer to let them pay the taxes to us."

That was eminently logical, and thoroughly human as well. But it still seems to me that either the State or the general government should own and control the water rather than that a few corporations should seize it, and thereby tax how they please that vast and general industry which will be the chief dependence of and source of wealth to the State. I am old-fashioned in this, since I but borrow the ideas of those central Asian kingdoms whose irrigating systems belonged to the governments, and yet I fancy this repugnance to a monopoly of water will prove a new and controlling fashion when the monopolists begin to fatten on their rents.

As it is, water rights can be taken only by those individuals who mean to and do utilize them for the public. Such a person, or such persons, can file a claim for a water right at the district United States Land-office, but must improve such rights within a reasonable time. These rights are given in perpetuity to the owners, their heirs, assigns, etc., forever. They tap a stream of any part or all of its water if they want to, and run their ditch through what land they please, having the right to go through the land of a non-purchaser to reach that of a purchaser. Then they sell the water at so much per acre per year. The rentals vary between 50 cents and $1 50 an acre. Each farmer taps the ditch with lateral canals, gates being put in to divert the water into the side ditches. A farmer may also lay pipe from the ditch and carry water to his house and farm buildings, arranging an adequate and townlike system of water-works for domestic and stable uses; thus, at what should be a trifling expense, the farmers on irrigated lands may obtain this modern convenience. An important recent decision of the courts is that a man cannot buy water and allow it to run to waste in order to deprive a neighbor of it.

A company preempting a water right takes it on a mountain slope, tapping the stream high above the land to be irrigated. As a rule, the water is not brought to a reservoir. In most instances on the east slope of the Rockies this cannot be done, but the ditches start above the basin land, not only to get a "head" or impetus for the water, but because in Montana the streams are apt to run in the bottoms of deep-water channels. It is a tempting business, because, since the rights are eternal, a company can afford to start even where the first outlay is large; indeed, the more extensive the system and the larger the ditches, the better the profits. The country is certain to grow to meet such improvements, and to pay a handsome revenue as the years go on; and in the mean time the ditches constantly cement themselves and diminish their waste.

The result has been that when a call was issued for data concerning irrigation in Montana, preliminary to a convention for the study of the subject at the opening of this year, it was found that there were already somewhere near 3500 irrigating ditches, the property of 500 owners. Some of these schemes are gigantic. In some instances the project has been to secure not only the water, but the land it is to irrigate, and the water lords expect to reap fancy prices for the land from settlers, in addition to rents which their great-great-great-grandchildren may fatten upon. In other cases, only the water is got by the men or companies, and they are content to confine themselves to the taxes they will impose on the land as fast as it is taken up. The cattle-men of Montana decry these schemes, and beg the officials and editors of the State not to discuss irrigation and small farming, as, they say, settlers may be induced to come in and spoil the stock or grazing business; yet I am told that one company of cattle-men has secured miles of land and the adjacent water rights along the Missouri against the inevitable day when— But the cattle business shall have another chapter.

The largest irrigation scheme that is reported is that engineered by Zachary Taylor Burton, a notable figure in Montana. It is in Choteau County, and taps the Teton River. The main ditch is forty miles long, fourteen feet wide at the bottom, and eighteen feet at the top. The ditch connects and fills two dead lake basins, which now serve as reservoirs, and are fully restored to their ancient condition, not only beautifying a now blooming country, but having their surfaces blackened with flocks of wild swan, geese, ducks, gulls, and other fowl in the season when those birds reach that country. Drives are to be laid around the lakes, and their neighborhoods are likely either to become pleasure resorts or the seats of well-to-do communities. This scheme looks forward to putting 30,000 acres under the ditch. Thus far the cost of preparing the land for cultivation has been five dollars an acre, and the charge for maintenance of the ditches will be about fifty cents an acre a year.

A very peculiar and interesting scheme is that of the Dearborn Company, in the valley of the same name. Here is a valley containing half a million acres, a sixth part of which may be cultivated. The rest is hilly, and will always be grazing land. The valley is between Great Falls and Helena, alongside the main divide of the Rockies. Here are a number of little watercourses — the Dry, Simms, Auchard, and Flat creeks—in themselves incompetent to water their little valleys. These are all to be utilized as ditches. By tapping the Dearborn River with a six-foot-deep canal, thirty-eight feet wide, and only four and a half miles long, this natural system of watercourses is connected with a supply of water fed by eternal springs and frequent mountain snowfalls. The scheme embraces a hundred miles of main waterways and hundreds of miles of laterals. The greater part of the land benefited is obtainable by homesteaders.

I have spoken of the rush for water and land. Let me explain it with an illustration. One of the most lofty and ambitious grabbers in the State was not long ago observed to be engaging in a most mysterious business. He was taking women out into the wilderness, a stage-load or two at a time. They were very reputable women — school-teachers, type-writers, married women, and their friends. They were taken to a large and pleasantly situated house, upon the pretext that they were to attend a ball and a dinner, and get a hundred dollars as a present. It all proved true. Excursion party after excursion party went out in this way, and when the ladies returned to the town that had thus been pillaged of its beauty, they reported that they had fared upon venison and wild-fowl, with the very best of "fixings," and that at the ball a number of stalwart and dashing cowboys had become their partners, tripping their light fantastic measures with an enthusiasm which made up for any lack of grace that may have been noticed. The reader may fancy what a lark it was to the women, and how very much enjoyment the more mischievous wedded ones among them got by pretending that they were maidens, heart-whole and free of fancy! But while those women were in the thick of this pleasure, they each signed a formal claim to a homesteader's rights in the lands thereabout. And as they "prove up" those claims in the fulness of time, each will get her one hundred dollars. The titles to the land will then be made over to the ingenious inventors and backers of the scheme, and the land will be theirs. "Thus," in the language of a picturesque son of Montana, "a fellow can get a dukedom if he wants it." This is an absolutely true account of the conquest of a valley in Montana, and the future historian of our country will find much else that is akin to it, and that will make an interesting chapter in his records.

Governor Toole, in his message for 1891, abandons all hope of Federal supervision of this potentiality of wealth, and concludes his remarks with the statement that he assumes it to be the province of the Legislature to provide "against excessive and extortionate charges by individuals and companies engaged in the sale, rental, or distribution of water, and to prevent unjust discrimination in the disposal of the same to the public." He thinks the right of the State to regulate this matter should be asserted and maintained. He does not discuss the project of having the State develop and maintain the ditches, nor does he touch upon the next best alternative—of insisting that the farmers who own the land shall inherit the water plants after a fixed term of years.

But in considering Montana as it is, the main point is that there are thousands of ditches laid, and to-day a bird's-eye view of the State reveals valley after valley lying ready for the settler, like so many well-ordered parlors awaiting their guests. These parklike grassy bowls needed only the utilization of the water that is in or close to each one. There they lie, under sunny skies, carpeted with grass, bordered by rounding hills, rid of Indians, and all but empty of dangerous animals, waiting for the hodgepodge of new Americanism, to be made up of Swedes and Hollanders, Germans, Englishmen, and whoever else may happen along. What the State particularly needs is men of the Teutonic races, whose blood will not be stirred by the El Dorado-like traditions of vast and sudden wealth made in mining. It wants communities that will not be swept off the farm lands as by a cyclone at the first news that a new "lead" of gold or a new deposit of sapphires has been found in the mountains. Of such inflammable material, sent there in search of gold, and prone not to surrender the hope of finding more of it, has the State thus far been made up. The change is under way; the new people of a new and greater Pennsylvania are coming in, as we shall see. Five years from this, the politicians of Montana will be kowtowing to the farmer vote.

The northeastern corner of Montana is all Dawson County—a tract as big as Maryland, Vermont, and Connecticut. It is all high rolling plains land, now in use for stock-raising. It is well watered by tributaries of the Missouri, and abounds with little valleys, which will yet be very profitably farmed. Custer County, which takes up the remainder of the eastern end of Montana, is the same sort of land, and is a stock-raising country, but is yielding to the inroads of the farming element. It surprised the people of the State by the exhibit sent from there to the State fair last August. Wheat, oats, tomatoes, cabbages, potatoes, pumpkins, and squashes were in the yield, which was wellnigh complete, and of a high quality and size. All the lands that are watered are taken up, and this is true of the greater part of the State. The bench lands form the bulk of what remains. It has been demonstrated that they are very productive if water can be got to them, and since the streams are tapped on the mountain slopes, it is certain that they will, to a large extent, be irrigated.

Choteau County, in the north, and the next one west of Dawson, is a little empire in itself. It is slightly larger than Massachusetts, Connecticut, and New Hampshire. It is 100 miles wide and 225 miles long, and, to borrow a Western expression, the entire population of the Northwest could be "turned loose in it." It is like Dawson County in character—a high rolling plateau given over to cattle, sheep, and the growing of the hardier grains. Rich "finds" of magnetic and hematite iron are reported from there. Park County is a very mountainous, crumpled-up, and rocky area, and is the northern extension and neighbor of the Yellowstone National Park. Sheep and cattle raising and mining are its principal industries, and, on account of the wonderful mining "finds" that have recently been made there, the little county is knocking at the doors of Congress for a favor. Cook City, down on the southern edge of the county, is the beginning of a wonderful mining camp—that is to say, it is wonderful in the amount of ore there that could be profitably worked if coke and coal and transportation facilities could be had at reasonable cost. But, apparently, the only practicable route to the camp is through a corner of the National Park, and the miners are asking Congress to allow the rails to be laid there. They have had a discouraging experience thus far. The mines are principally in the hands of the discoverers, and since a prospector is usually the poorest man in the world, they cannot afford to spend much to make their needs known to the public. The prospector, the reader should understand, is the indefatigable Wandering Jew of the mountains, who prowls about amid every sort of danger, hammer in hand, and dining on hope more often than food, and who, after discovering a "lead," gives an interest in it to capital, and then is very fortunate if he is not frozen out. The metals that have been found in Park County are silver and lead. There is very little gold, but coal has long been very profitably mined at several points in the county.

Gallatin County, next to the westward of Park, is a mountainous and mineral region also, but it contains the Gallatin Valley, which, to the agriculturist, is just now one of the most interesting districts in the United States. This great valley has more snowfall than any county in the State—at least the snow lies there longer than anywhere else. The result of the moisture, in conjunction with the character of the soil, is that the valley is one of the richest grain-producing regions in the State. For years barley has been raised there for the use of the brewers of Montana. When some samples of this Gallatin Valley barley reached New York, the brewers there refused to believe that any such barley was or could be grown anywhere in the world. They thought that what was shown to them was a lot of carefully selected samples. They deputized a committee to visit the valley, and found that the barley which had so astonished them was the common barley of the country. The grain is very clear, almost to the point of being translucent, and is in color a golden yellow. The brewers declare that no better grain for their use is grown in the world. They have organized a company, taken the water right, bought various tracts of land, amounting to 10,000 acres, and are going to try to make the valley the great malting centre of the continent, if not of the world. They have put up malting-houses at two points, have established some twenty miles of irrigating ditches already, and by furnishing the seed and buying the yields are encouraging the farmers of the valley to grow barley. They cultivated 2500 bushels in 1890, and raised sixty bushels to the acre. Last year they had 10,000 acres under cultivation. They

expect in a few years to be selling barley to all the brewers of the country who value what the New-Yorkers think is the best grain obtainable. This is the nearest approach to what is called bonanza or big-scale farming in the State of Montana.

All that central district of the State, including Meagher and Fergus counties, and more besides, has been slow in the development of its mining resources. Mines have been held for years since they were discovered, because it has been hard to make capitalists and railroad men see what was in the country. It is almost always the case in such a wealthy mining region as Montana that news of rich finds is published every day, and capitalists hear the tales of prospectors with fatigued and half-closed ears. But now two routes have been surveyed into Meagher County by the Northern Pacific Company, and the Great Northern and Burlington and Missouri roads are expected to go in. All will head for Castle, the great mining camp of the country, where two smelteries are already turning out lead and silver, and freighting bullion 150 miles to the nearest railway.

Thus we reach the county of which Great Falls is the seat of government and of many interesting industries and operations. This is Cascade County. It is here that the noted and majestic falls of the Missouri occur in a succession of splendid cascades. Here a company, controlled by wealthy men of New York, Helena, and Great Falls, have taken up something like twelve miles on either side of the river at these falls, and have thus possessed themselves of what is undoubtedly the finest and greatest water-power in the West, comprising in all at least 250,000 horse-power, and more easily handled than that of Niagara. An auxiliary company owns a large town site there, and a very promising and considerable town has already grown up to handle the wheat and wool and beef of the region, and to be already the site of smelting-works, factories, and other establishments which have been attracted by the cheap and abundant water-power. In the shrewdness and reasonableness of the management of Great Falls lie much of the hope for its future. The town has never been "boomed." It is planned with broad avenues and streets, and even now contains several blocks of really notable stone and brick buildings along its main street. It has a fine opera-house, club, hotel, and strong banks. Its population is above 7000.

This Cascade County is a very new part of Montana. A small proportion of the land is all that is yet taken, but experiments with this have led the people there to believe that there is no richer land in the State. Thus far the settlers are chiefly Americans. It has been and is yet a grazing country, but it is seen that as civilization pushes into it, the cattle business is being hurt. The difficulty in obtaining cowboy assistance is noticeable wherever farms and well-governed towns spring up, and this difficulty is increasing in this region. The cowboy and civilization are neighbors, but not friends. But it is a good grass country, and the grass is vastly better than that in Dakota, which becomes frozen and loses its nutriment. Here the Chinook winds from the Pacific come in at all times in the winter, never failing to blow upon all except twenty or twenty-five days in each winter. They clear off the snow like magic. Twelve thousand cattle were shipped from Great Falls during 1891. But the wool business exceeded that. From the same point last year nearly three millions of pounds of wool — more than were sent from any other point in the United States — were shipped from the backs of the sheep. Because of the rich soil and good grass, very little sand blows about to load down and damage the fibre of the wool. That is the case everywhere within 150 to 200 miles of the east slope of the Rockies. Sheep in this country have none of the destructive diseases which assail them elsewhere. The sheep and wool industries are going to be enormous in Montana on that account, whether the herding be upon the ranges, as at present, or in small herds managed by farmers, and raised upon the benches and side-hills that will not be brought under the ditch.

But in view of the future of the State, the experiments in agriculture are even more interesting than the harnessing of the cascades of the Missouri to the wheels of manufacture. The sugar-beet grows finely, in answer to the generally discussed project in most of these new States to render that form of sugar-making a leading industry when the lands are well settled. Fine, luscious strawberries grow right out on the plains wherever they have been planted, and one man on Belt

Creek sold $170 worth of currants, raspberries, and strawberries from one acre of ground last year. Barley thrives in the soil, and has no dews or rains to bleach or "must" it when it is ripening. Wheat that is graded "No. 1 Northern" in Minneapolis grows thirty to fifty bushels to the acre. There is an orchard there already, producing fine apples; and here we get the first news of the astonishing potatoes of Montana — "the terrapin of the State," as they have been wittily called.

There are no such potatoes in the world as are grown in Montana. They attain prodigious size, and often weigh three, four, or five pounds apiece. Eighteen such potatoes make a bushel. To the taste they are like a new vegetable. The larger ones are mealy, but the smaller ones are like sacks of meal; when the skin is broken the meat falls out like flour. It must very soon become the pride of every steward in the first-grade hotels, restaurants, and clubs of the cities here—and even in Europe—to prepare these most delicious vegetables for those who enjoy good living. As these potatoes of the choicest quality can be cultivated in all the valleys east of the Rocky Mountains, there will soon be no lack of them. To-day the only ones that have left the State have been the few bushels sent to gourmets in New York, Washington, and San Francisco.

All this country east of the mountains must be irrigated to insure good crops. An early and general development of the farm lands is relied upon, because the great mining camps of the State will consume nearly all the products of the farms as fast as the farms increase in number. There is no danger that the mining camps will not grow and multiply to keep the demand strong. The miners are the best people in the world to farm for, because they produce money and they pay cash. The southern end of Lewis and Clarke County is a succession of fine valleys. Here is Helena, the capital of the State. Six miles away a cluster of gold mines is being reopened, after having produced millions. In this county the largest mine is the Drum Lummon, an English property that has paid dividends for many years. And here are the famous ruby and sapphire fields, on the bed-rock of former benches or bottoms of the Missouri. Strawberries of a large and luscious variety will yield 10,000 baskets to the acre, and have sold in the past at a fixed rate of twenty cents a basket for home consumption. Apples, plums, crab-apples, grapes, currants, and all berries grow in wonderful abundance, and find an eager and high-priced market close at hand. Oats weigh forty and fifty pounds a bushel, as against thirty-two pounds in the East, and a yield of sixty bushels to the acre can be obtained. All wheat that is brought out here for seeding produces a soft grain. It has been sent to Minneapolis to be ground into flour for pastry and cracker bakers. The Cracker Trust is building a big bakery in Helena, to be near this product. It is not a bread-making grain. But a new population is needed to reap the wealth that is offered from small fruits. The Chinamen are harvesting this money now, but they do not meet the home demand. It is a rich country, and will some day dry and can large crops of fruits and berries. The side-hills will graze small bands of cattle. If the bunch-grass sod is ploughed up, there follows a growth of blue-joint grass that is like timothy, and that is very high, heavy, and nutritious. The same result follows irrigation wherever it is permitted.

Jefferson, Madison, Silver Bow, Beaver Head, and Deer Lodge counties, in the mountains, are all very nearly like what has just been described. Mining is the principal source of revenue, and wheat, oats, potatoes, and stock are the other products.

West of the Rockies is quite a different country. It is all practically in Missoula County. The mountains are full of minerals; the valleys will produce anything, apparently, that grows in the temperate zone — even corn. Irrigation is not so absolutely necessary, and is not necessary at all in a great part of it. The land is lower; the rains are heavier; the winds from the Japan current blow there with frequency and strength, and are almost uninterrupted. Verdure remains green there all summer, and the abundance of timber, the many streams, and the verdant hills render the scenery more like what the Eastern man is accustomed to than that which he sees east of the Rockies in Montana. The southern part of Missoula County has been settled many years, largely by thrifty French Canadians, and it contains as fine farms as

will be seen almost anywhere. Here are orchards, and small fruits grow in abundance for shipment to the Cœur d'Alene mining camps in Idaho. Here is a milling company that produced seventy-five millions of feet of lumber last year. In the north is a new country wrested from the Flathead reservation. The Flathead Valley is forty miles long and one-half as wide, possessing a deep soil and a clay subsoil. It is farmed without irrigation. Several tributary valleys of the same quality open out of the main valley. Large crops of grain, hay, vegetables, and fruit have been harvested there, but the farmers have heretofore been without a market, and have subsisted by raising horses and cattle, and driving them abroad for purchasers. The entrance of the Great Northern Railroad, now accomplished, will open up this rich territory, and will develop the timber resources as well as the deposits of coal, oil, and natural gas, which seem to be very extensive there. The mountains are practically unprospected, and have only just been mapped by Lieutenant Ahern, U.S.A., who has philanthropically devoted his summers to that arduous and dangerous work. Indications of quartz are seen on every hand in the mountains. Taking the county as a whole, two years ago not a mining prospect was continuously worked, while now four mines are shipping and paying profits of $40,000 a month. The "leads" in the county are continuations of those in the Cœur d'Alene country in Idaho. Coal as good as the Lethbridge product of Canada is found there in vast quantities. It is a fine sporting region. The Flathead Lake, which has 318 square miles of surface, is cold and clear, and so deep that it has been sounded to a depth of 1000 feet. It is full of landlocked salmon and big trout, and harbors millions of ducks and geese in their season, while deer and winged game are plenty in the country around it. The Flathead Indians, south of the lake, have nice farms, and raise cattle besides. They are self-sustaining, and at least a dozen can be named who have accumulated between $20,000 and $50,000. They are a fine, stalwart people. They are not in reality Flatheads; they have no knowledge that the tribe ever followed the practice of compressing the heads of the children, as was done by the tribes at the mouth of the Columbia River.

It is in this county that Marcus Daly, the mining millionaire, has invested a million dollars in horses and land, and maintains a horse farm that ranks next to Senator Stanford's Palo Alto farm in California. Here also Daniel E. Bandmann, the actor, has 1000 acres of land, and is raising imported Percheron horses and Holstein cattle. Other farmers are in the same business. It is an enormous county, and is so well populated that its people cast 4000 votes at elections. With its ore, timber, horses, cattle, coal, petroleum, grain, and diversified small crops, it is unquestionably the finest county in the State. It would be the richest were it not for Silver Bow, with its one industry of mining.

There is plenty of coal in Montana. It crops out in all the northern counties and in several of the southern ones. It is most profitably worked when the owner is interested in the railroad which carries it from the mines. In all probability, the best coal is found in the Sand Coulee fields, in Cascade County. The Rocky Fork mines, in Custer County, are part of a vast deposit which has all been secured by Eastern capitalists. One hundred coke ovens near Livingston, in Park County, provide coke for use in the smelteries at Butte. Also in Park County are the Timber Line and Horr mines. The coal of the State is semi-bituminous. Only a mere speck of what the State contains is being mined.

We have seen that cattle-raising is a conspicuous industry—if industry it can be called—and is carried on in, I think, every county of the State. Large cattle herds are already things of the past in the western end of the State, and it is evident that farming and settlement will soon drive them out of Gallatin and Cascade counties. It is cause for jubilation that this is the case. It seems strange that cruelty should distinguish this branch of food-raising wherever it is seen and in whatever branch one studies it. From the bloody fields of Texas, where the ingenious fiends in the cattle business snip off the horns of the animals below the quick, to the stock-yards in Chicago, where men are found who will prod the beeves into pens, there to crush their skulls with hammers, it is everywhere the same—everywhere the cattle business has its concomitants of cruelty and savagery.

The reader would not suppose there was cruelty in the mere feeding of cattle on the plains, but let him go to Montana, and talk with the people there, and he will shudder at what he hears. The cattle-owners, or cow-men, are in Wall Street and the south of France, or in Florida, in the winter, but their cattle are on the wintry fields, where every now and then, say once in four years, half of them, or eighty per cent., or one in three (as it happens) starve to death because of their inability to get at the grass under the snow. A horse or a mule can dig down to the grass. Those animals have a joint in their legs which the horned cattle do not possess, and which enables those animals which possess it to "paw." Sheep are taken to especial winter grounds and watched over. But the cow-men do business on the principle that the gains in good years far more than offset the losses in bad years, and so when the bad years come, the poor beasts die by the thousands—totter along until they fall down, the living always trying to reach the body of a dead one to fall upon, and then they freeze to death, a fate that never befalls a steer or cow when it can get food.

Already, on some of the ranges, the "cow-men" (cattle-owners) are growing tired of relying upon Providence to superintend their business, and they are sending men to look after the herds once a month, and to pick out the calves and weaker cattle and drive them to where hay is stored. By spring-time one in every fifteen or twenty in large herds will have been cared for in this way. In far eastern Montana range-feeding in large herds will long continue, but in at least five-sevenths of the State, irrigation and the cultivation of the soil will soon end it. The hills and upper benches, all covered with self-curing bunch grass, will still remain, and will forever be used for the maintenance of small herds of cows and sheep, properly attended and provided with corrals and hay, against the times when the beasts must be fed. The farmers will undoubtedly go into cattle-raising, and dairy-farming is certain to be a great item in the State's resources, since the hills are beside every future farm, and the most provision that will be needed will be that of a little hay for stocking the winter corrals. Last year the cattle business in Montana was worth ten millions of dollars to the owners of the herds. "Providence was on deck," as the cowboys would say.

But the sheep there brought twelve millions of pounds of wool on their backs in the same year. They are banded in herds of about 2000 head, and each band is in charge of one solitary, lonely, forsaken herder, who will surprise his employers if he remains a sane man any great length of time. In the summer these herders sleep in tents, and the ranch foremen start out with fresh provisions at infrequent intervals, and hunt up their men as they follow the herds. In the winter the grazing is done in sheltered places especially chosen. On the winter grounds a corral is built, and thirty to forty tons of hay are stored there for emergencies when the snow lies thick on the ground. It is a prime country for sheep. They get heavy coats, and are subject to no epidemic diseases. The grass is rich and plenty, and the warm Pacific winds soon melt what snows occasionally cover the ground. The wool ranks next to that from Australia. The tendency of the sheep-herders to become insane is the most unpleasant accompaniment of the business, except the various forms of mutilation of the sheep for business reasons. The constant bleating of the sheep and the herder's loneliness, spending weeks and months without any companionship except that of a dog and the herd, are the causes that are commonly accepted to account for the fact that so many herders go insane. Since I found insanity terribly common among the pioneers on the plains in Canada, where no sheep were raised, I prefer to leave the incessant bleating of the sheep out of the calculation, and to call it loneliness—and yet, in my opinion, that is not the sole reason.

The horse market has been very poor for some time, and mules are being raised for the market with better results. The substitution of electric for horse power on street railways has lessened the demand for horses, and so has the use of steam farming implements. There has been an over-supply of horses as well. But the Montana men find horses a good investment. It costs nothing to raise them, and all breeds seem to improve there. They get great lung development, and acquire no diseases. When they cannot be sold for from $50 to $100 apiece, the owners keep them until they do fetch those prices.

The great wealth of the State is in its mines. Butte, in Silver Bow County, is the greatest mining centre not only in Montana, but, with the possible and doubtful exception of one town in Australia, in all the world. The Butte output is of lead, silver, and copper. The total dividends paid by all the mines in the United States which make public their affairs was $16,024,842, and of that sum Montana's mines paid one-quarter, or $4,059,700. That amount was paid in 1891, up to the end of November. Yet the richest mines are owned by private corporations which do not make known their profits. The Granite Mountain mine, in Deer Lodge County, yielding silver, lead, and some little gold, paid its owners, who are mainly in St. Louis, $1,300,000 in the same eleven months, and has sent to St. Louis about ten millions in dividends since it began to pay. Eight years ago the stock in that mine was held at 25 cents a share, and men played pool for it in Helena and Butte.

Butte first attracted the miners in 1864. They did nothing except wash dirt for five years, but they washed out eight millions of dollars. Then they found the quartz, and went down on it, only to find a great deal more silver than gold. As they went down further, they came upon the copper, and started a "boom" that shows no sign of diminution at this date. Butte has added to the world's wealth $140,000,000 in gold, silver, copper, and lead. The largest producers are the Anaconda, Boston and Montana, Colorado and Montana, Butte and Boston, Parrott, Lexington, Alice, Butte Reduction Works, Moulton, and Blue Bird. Those companies operate forty mines, and all have their own works for the reduction of ores. They are all high-grade ores, but some are high-grade in copper and some in silver. The Anaconda people, for instance, get enough silver and gold to render their vast output of copper all profit. As their capacity in copper is the greatest in the world, and as it does not cost them a cent a ton, they control the copper market of the earth. The principal owners of this property are the estate of Senator Hearst, J. B. Haggin, and Marcus Daly. Marcus Daly, who is known in the East as the foremost patron of the turf, came to Montana first on his feet, and worked at washing with a pan. That was less than twenty years ago, and now he is called "The White Czar" in

Montana. He is an influential and shrewd politician, the owner of the second largest horse - breeding farm in the world, the greatest employer of labor in Montana, maintains a metropolitan hotel in a little town in the mountains, disregarding the loss it incurs in order that he may have a place in which to entertain his friends, and finally he maintains a first-class newspaper in the same town or village of Anaconda—a newspaper as good as is published in any city of the second class. The town of Anaconda is where the company reduces its ores. The profits of the company are never made public.

The camp next in importance after Butte is Castle, in Meagher County, sixty miles from a railroad. Barker and Neihart are camps in the same county. The mining is for silver and lead. The biggest mine in the Castle district is the Cumberland, which is known to be a heavy shipper of bullion, but is a close corporation. The mines in the district and in the county need railroads to open them up. Jefferson County is next to Silver Bow in richness, but though it has more paying mines than any other county in the State, the mining is all on a small scale. The Holder Mine, owned in England, is in this county. It paid $400,000 in 1891. There are about thirty districts in Lewis and Clarke County, as against seventy in Jefferson. The richest of the thirty is Unionville, five miles from Helena. The ore is free milling gold. The Whitlatch Union Company has produced $20,000,000 there.

As I have said elsewhere, Deer Lodge, Madison, Beaver Head, and Missoula counties are rich in mine "prospects," but the need of railroads in all except Missoula County hinders work there. The future in mining is not yet in sight in Montana. The mineral veins have been but scratched. For every developed mining district in the State there are ten that are not developed, and that promise as well as any that are now being operated. Moreover, vast reaches of the mountain country have not even been explored. Of copper Montana produced 50,000 tons in 1890; of gold, $3,500,000; of silver, $19,350,000.

A few of the many stories that are told of miners' luck will enable the reader to understand how and why the heads of whole communities may be turned in mining regions. Jim Whitlatch, the dis-

coverer of the Whitlatch-Union mine, near Helena, led a typical Western miner's life. The mine in question is now owned in England, and has produced $20,000,000 in gold. After Jim Whitlatch had sold the property for $1,500,000 he went to New York "to make as much money as Vanderbilt." He was a rare treat to Wall Street, which fattened on him, and in one year let him go with only the clothes on his back. He returned to Montana, began "prospecting" again, and discovered a mine for which he got $250,000. He went to Chicago to rival Mr. Potter Palmer in wealth, and returned just as he did from New York—"flat-strapped," as he would have expressed it. He made still another fortune, and went to San Francisco, where he died a poor man. Another Lewis and Clarke County mine—the Drum Lummon—provides another such story. It was discovered by an Irish immigrant named Thomas Cruse. Although he owned it, he could not get a sack of flour on credit. He sold it to an English syndicate for $1,500,000. But he remains one of the wealthy men of Helena.

There is an ex-State Senator in Beaver Head County who owns a very rich mine, the ore yielding $700 to the ton net. He is a California "Forty-niner," who came as a prospector to Montana, and since discovering his mine has lived upon it in a peculiar way. He has no faith in banks. He says his money is safest in the ground. When he has spent what money he has, he takes out a wagon-load of ore, ships it to Omaha, sells it, and lives on the return until he needs another wagon-load.

There is a queer story concerning the Spotted Horse Mine, in Fergus County. It was found by P. A. McAdow, who sold it to Governor Hauser and A. M. Holder for $500,000 three year ago. They paid a large sum down in cash, and the other payments were to come out of the ground. The ore was in pockets, each of which was easily exhausted. Whatever was taken out went to McAdow, who got about $100,000. Then the purchasers abandoned it, on the advice of experts, and Mr. McAdow took hold of it. He found the vein, over which rails had been laid for a mining car. He has taken out $500,000, and it is still a good mine. One of these children of luck came to Helena with money, picked out a wife, who was then a poor seamstress, hired a hotel, and invited the town to the wedding. The amount of champagne that flowed at that wedding was fabulous, and it is said that the whole town reeled to bed that night.

Butte is the principal seat of the mining work. It is what they call in Montana "a wide-open town," and he who thinks he knows the United States because he can name the buildings which face the City Hall Park in New York would open his eyes and confess his astonishment were he to visit Butte. The old California mining spirit, the savor of the flush times of '49, was transplanted to the Treasure State during the war of the rebellion, and it still leaves strong traces everywhere in Montana. The smallest coin in circulation there is the nickel, or five-cent piece, but the shilling or "bit" is the unit of calculation. Shoeblacks and barbers charge two bits for their work; a drink at a bar costs a bit, and drinks go in pairs at two bits. Whoever wants a postage-stamp will either get no change out of a ten-cent piece, or will have the stamp given to him. Domestic servants are paid no less than $25 a month; waiter-boys in the hotels get $10 a week and their keep; the lowest wages paid to labor are paid to street-sweepers, and they receive $2 50 a day. This is all an inheritance from California and the precedents set in Virginia City, Nevada, long ago. The little one story and two-story square cottages that dot the suburbs of each city are of a type otherwise peculiar to the Pacific coast—a type that is seen at its best in San Francisco, San José, and Oakland.

The disproportionate size of the vicious quarters in each Montana city, and the fashions in these quarters, are inheritances from the era of the California gold fever. The outcast women, who were originally the only women in each camp, have a ward or district to themselves, and there the variety theatre (which is descended from the original Bella Union) and the "hurdy-gurdy houses," or dance halls, and the gambling hells are all clustered. The women have streets to themselves in Butte, Helena, Great Falls—and, for that matter, in Seattle also—just as they do in San Francisco. And, as is the case in California, each house in such a quarter is a one-room or two-room shanty, harboring one occupant. For the true women and the children of each city that end of town is *taboo*.

Butte has more than 30,000 inhabitants, and 5000 of its men work in the mines to produce a mineral output which is within five millions of dollars of the value of the total yield of Colorado. The laborers who repair the streets get $3 50 a day, and the miners earn from $4 to $7. When the shifts or gangs of men change at night — for the work never ceases — the main street of Butte is as crowded as Broadway at Fulton Street at noon. At two or three o'clock in the morning the city is still lively. There is no pretence about the town. It has few notable or expensive buildings, and it is without a good hotel. Deadwood and Butte are the only considerable towns I saw out West of which that could be said. It gives the reader a hint of the "beginnings" of Butte to be told that the site of the best brick and granite building on the main street was won by a man who happened to hold only two "Jacks" at the time he was "called." There are sixteen licensed gambling hells in Butte, and the largest ones are almost side by side on the principal street. They are as busy as so many exchanges. They are large, bare rooms, with lay-outs for faro, craps, stud poker, and other games on tables at every few feet along the walls, each table faced by a knot of men, and backed by a "dealer" and "watcher." The gambling hells keep open all the time except from Saturday midnight to Sunday midnight. In summer the doors stand open, and the gambling may be seen from the pavement. The liquor stores never close, neither do the barber shops, nor—I fancy—the concert halls.

Montana has a saloon to every eighty inhabitants. It has more saloons than Alabama, Georgia, Kansas, and Indian Territory, Maine, Mississippi, South Carolina, West Virginia, Vermont, or the District of Columbia. "One thing I have noticed," said a liquor-dealer of Butte, "is that if a man quits drinking here, he will be dead in a month." This peculiarly businesslike observation veiled a reference to the sulphur fumes, which are the consequence of the presence of many smelteries. The city is at the bottom of a well, the walls of which are tall mountains. High up above the town, around one side of the well, are these smelteries, whose pipes emit smoke and sulphur. In addition to this, they were "heap-roasting" the ore in the open air when I was there, and the sulphur weighted and jaundiced the atmosphere. The people rose in anger and stopped the nuisance.

There are fine schools there, attended by 5000 children. The Catholic parish includes 10,000 souls, and is the largest west of the Mississippi. Butte is the only Montana town that maintains a club of university graduates. Its other club, the Silver Bow, is one of whose club-house appointments and membership any city might be proud. The people there maintain such elevating societies and chapters as those of the Epworth League, the Women's Christian Temperance Union, the King's Daughters, and the Society of Christian Endeavor. There is a cricket club there, and a rod-and-gun club, and a strong Turnverein, or German athletic society. They have some notable displays in those stores which are the head depots of great trading companies that operate far and wide. Whatever is best in London, Paris, or New York can be duplicated in Butte, and it is said that when strawberries are a dollar a basket in New York, this strange city is one of the purchasers of them. Butte has six banks, with a capital of a million dollars, and a million of dollars are paid out there in wages every month.

It is impossible to make room for that which should be told of the cities of Montana generally. It is my opinion that Butte will grow steadily as long as the present mines pay and new ones continue to be developed. It will be a large city, judging from present appearances. Great Falls should, in the logic of its merits, become an important city. Miles City cannot be threatened by any changes in its vicinage except such as will cause it to grow. Missoula will in all likelihood be the capital of a great and rich farming district, and perhaps of a mining section as well. The Great Northern Railway, now completing its highway through the northern counties, must develop at least one sizable town on either side of the Rockies, but the names of those towns are not in my ken. There are going to be many more inhabitants in the State than there are in Pennsylvania—possibly twice as many—and they will build cities.

Though Helena is the capital, it must still fight to retain that honor, the permanent seat of government not yet having been chosen. But it seems almost a foregone conclusion that Helena will remain as it is, for as Butte is the industrial centre, so Helena is the social and financial headquarters. It has most of the concomitants of a chief city—all, in fact, except a first-class theatre. It is commonly credited with being the wealthiest city of its size in the world, and it does boast more than a dozen citizens each worth more than a million of dollars. But it gains that reputation most creditably as the backer of the principal enterprises in the State. In its best residence quarters are many fine and costly houses, and the people in them know the luxuries and refinements of cultivation and wisely managed wealth. Helena has three daily newspapers, which receive the despatches of the chief news associations of the country. A very commendable spirit in Montana finds expression in a State historical society, whose already imposing collections are housed in one of the public buildings in Helena. President Stuart and Secretary Wheeler, in gathering the early newspapers, diaries, photographs, and biographies of the pioneers, are performing a work which will swell in value faster than compound interest enhances the value of money.

All the principal religious bodies are well represented in Helena in church buildings and membership; the schools and other public buildings are the subjects of popular pride; the stores are fine and well stocked. The Montana Club, now building a palatial stone club-house, is very much more like an Eastern than a Western club in all that makes a club attractive. There are other clubs—Scotch, German, literary, musical, mercantile, and athletic; there are military organizations and the lodges of half a dozen secret fraternities, and there is a State Fair Association which maintains a fine race-track. Helena has many manufactures, and eight banks, with a joint capital of two and one-third millions of dollars. Already three transcontinental railways meet there—the Northern Pacific, Union Pacific, and the Great Northern. Among its hotels, the Helena is a most cozy and metropolitan house, and in summer the Hotel Broadwater, in the suburbs, gives to Montana the finest hotel and watering-place in the Northwest. It is the property and venture of Colonel C. A. Broadwater, a pioneer and millionaire, and comprises a park, a hotel of the most modern and elegant character, and the largest natatorium in the world—a bath 300 feet long and 100 feet wide, of natural hot water, medicated and curative, yet as clear as crystal, and without offence to taste or smell. The beautiful Moorish bath-house, with its daily concourse of health and pleasure seekers, its band of music and atmosphere of indolence, is the pleasantest holiday spot in the new States. But, in my opinion, still stronger attractions to Helena are its surroundings and its climate, its 300 bright, sunny, golden days in every year, its crisp, clear, healthful atmosphere, and its picturesque belt of soft, rolling mountain breasts encircling it.

Speaking from the stand-point of physical human pleasure, none of the new States has a climate to compare with that of Montana. There the air is always tonic, even magnetic. It rains on 65 days in the year, but the sun manages to shine more or less even on those days—which come in April, May, and June. The valleys are 4000 to 6000 feet above sea-level. Upon them the soft warm winds of the Pacific slope blow after they have emptied their moisture upon the mountain ranges of Washington. These winds temper the climate of Montana so that it seems not to belong in the cold belt of our most northerly States. It is nothing like so cold as the Dakotas; indeed, there are only a few cold days at a time, mainly in January, with little skating or sleighing, and an assurance that the Chinook breezes are always close at hand. Montana is a sanitarium. No account can be given of the attractions of the State without putting the climate high in the list. It has a magic power to breed enthusiastic love in the hearts of all who live there, even if their stay is of but a few months' duration. The inhabitants all went there to make money, and now they remain to praise the country. A spell, a mania, seizes all alike, and each vies with the other in overestimating the vast number of ox teams that would be required to pull him back whence he came.

Close to Helena, on ledges which mark two former levels of the Missouri River, are the world-famous sapphire and ruby beds, 8000 acres of which, with 2000 other acres under water, have recently been acquired by an English company of noblemen, bankers, jewellers, and others for $2,000,000, the mere value of the gold which it is thought will be taken from the dirt. That sapphires and rubies were there has been known for twenty years or more, some miners having kept the finer specimens, and others having thrown them out of their pans into the river by the hundredweight as pebbles of no value. The truth, as I get it from experts, is that these stones are true rubies and sapphires, and the only opportunity they afford for criticism lies in the fact that very nearly all of them are much lighter in color than the Asiatic gems of the same sort. In other words, pigeon's-blood rubies and sapphire-blue sapphires are found there, but not often. And yet these stones of the lighter shades are of far greater brilliancy than the Asiatic gems that fashion has approved; indeed, they are often like diamonds, and as their hardness is next to that of the diamond, their lustre must prove enduring. The gems are found on the bed rock under eight or ten feet of soil, along with crystals, nuggets of gold, gold-dust, garnets, and pebbles. The land was bought by two Michigan lumbermen, brothers, who now treasure a million in cash and a million in shares of the new English company—rewards for their foresight.

One of the English experts who examined the gem fields announced it to be his opinion that the diamond must sooner or later be found in Montana. All the conditions warrant its existence there. What a State Montana is! Gold, silver, copper, lead, asbestos, tin, iron, oil, gas, rubies, sapphires, and a possibility of diamonds—all locked up in her ribs and pockets!

I see a vision of Montana in the future, yet in the lifetime of the young men of to-day. I see half a dozen such mining centres as Butte, and they are all noble cities, set with grand buildings, boulevards, and parks. I see at least two great manufacturing towns besides. I see scores of great valleys, and other scores of little ones, all gay with the blossoms of fruits and grain, supporting a great army of prosperous farmers. I see tens of thousands of rills of water embroidering the green valleys, and I dream that the men who need that water to make the earth give up its other treasures are not obliged to pay more than the conduits cost, merely to enrich a set of water lords who seized the streams when no one was there to protest. I see the brown hills and mountain-sides of the eastern part of Montana dotted with cattle and sheep in small herds.   The woollen industry has become a great source of wealth, and Montana has robbed New England of some of her factories.   I see in western Montana great saw-mills and mines that were not dreamt of in 1892.   I see car-loads of fruit and vegetables and barley malt rolling into the cities, and out to other States.   I see no Indians except those who work or who serve in the army, and where there were reservations I see the soil laughing with verdure or tracked with cattle.   I see statisticians calculating the value of the annual product of the State; the figures are too stupendous for repetition here. Montana is fulfilling her destiny.   She is one of the most populous and opulent members of our sisterhood of States.

ON SNOW-SHOES TO BARREN GROUNDS

FAR to the northwest, beginning ten days' journey beyond Great Slave Lake and running down to the Arctic Ocean, with Hudson Bay as its eastern and Great Bear Lake and the Coppermine River as its western boundaries, lies the most complete and extended desolation on earth. That is the Barren Grounds, the land whose approximate 200,000 square miles (for its exact area is unknown) is the dwelling-place of no man, and its storms and sterility in its most northerly part are withstood the year round by no living creature save the musk-ox. There is the timberless waste where ice-laden blasts blow with hurricane and ceaseless fury that bid your blood stand still and your breath come and go in painful stinging gasps; where rock and lichen and moss replace soil and trees and herbage; and where death by starvation or freezing dogs the footsteps of the explorer.

There are two seasons and only two methods of penetrating this great lone land of the North—by canoe, when the watercourses are free of ice, and on snow-shoes during the frozen period, which occupies nearly nine of the year's twelve months. The deadly cold of winter, and greater risk of starvation, make the canoe trip the more usual one with the few Indians that hunt the musk-ox. But, because of the many portages, you cannot travel so rapidly by canoe as on snow-shoes, nor go so far north for the best of the musk-

ox hunting, nor see the Barren Grounds at their best, or worst, as you care to consider it. That is why I chose to make the attempt on snow-shoes.

And why did I turn my face towards a country which seemed to hold naught for the traveller but hardship? Well—certainly to hunt musk-ox, the most inaccessible game in the world, and to look upon his habitat at the period of its uttermost desolation; certainly also to study the several tribes of Indians through which I must pass on my way to the Barren Grounds; and *en route* to hunt wood-bison, undoubtedly now become the rarest game in the world. Possibly, too, I went that I might for a time escape the hum and routine sordidness of the city, and breathe air which was not surcharged with convention and civilization.

Arthur Heming, the artist, and I found ourselves, December 27, 1894, at Edmonton, the end of the railroad. We had travelled on the Canadian Pacific *via* Winnipeg and Calgary, and through the land of the Crees, Blackfeet, and Sarcee Indians, without seeing anything so picturesque in the way of costuming as the Winnipeg dragoon and a Sarcee young woman resplendent in beads and glittering tinsel. I really ought to include the mounted policeman, for he too has a uniform which, with scarlet jacket and yellow-striped breeches, is deserving of greater attention. But the mounted po-

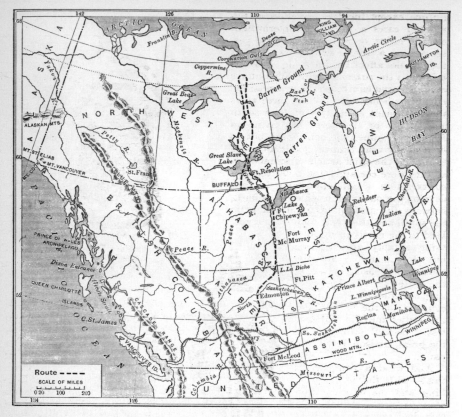

NORTHWESTERN BRITISH AMERICA, SHOWING BARREN GROUNDS AND MR. WHITNEY'S ROUTE.

liceman has that which is far worthier of comment than uniform. He has the reputation of being the most effective arm of the Canadian Interior Department. And he lives up to it. These "Riders of the Plains," as they are called, patrol a country so large that the entire force may lose itself within its domains and still be miles upon miles apart. Yet this comparative handful maintains order among the lawless white men and stays discontentment among the restless red men in a manner so satisfactorily and so unostentatiously as to make some of our United States experiences read like those of a tyro.

The success of the Northwest Mounted Police may be accredited to its system of distribution throughout the guarded territory. Unlike our army, it does not mass its force in forts adjacent to Indian reservations. Posts it has, where recruiting and drilling are constantly going forward, but the main body of men is scattered in twos and threes over the country, riding hither and thither—a watch that goes on relief after relief. This is the secret of their success, and a system it would well repay our own government to adopt. The police are ever on the spot to advise or to arrest. They do not wait for action until an outbreak has occurred; they are always in action. They constitute a most valuable peace-assuring corps, and I wish we had one like it.

Although Edmonton has but a few hundred population, it is doubly honored —by an electric-light plant which illuminates the town when not otherwise engaged, and by a patience-trying railway company that sends two trains a week to Calgary and gives them twelve hours in which to make two hundred miles. But no one, except luckless travellers, at Edmonton cares a rap about intermittent electric lights, or railroads that run passengers on a freight schedule, so long as they do not affect the fur trade. Fur was originally the *raison d'être* of Edmonton's existence, and continues the principal excuse of its being. In the last three years the settlement of a strip of land south and of one to the north has created a farming or ranching contingent, but to date of my visit canned goods appeared to remain the chief article of sustenance, as furs were certainly the main topic of conversation. Edmonton may in time develop the oasis upon which it is built, between the arid plains immediately to the south and the great lone land to the north, into something notably agricultural; but for many years the town will be, as it is to-day, the gateway of the well-nigh boundless fur-producing country to the north, and the outlet for the numberless "packs" gathered by the great Hudson Bay Company.

And what a company is this!—with the power of a king and the consideration of a partner. A monopoly that does not monopolize, it stands alone a unique figure

SARCEE BELLE.

WINNIPEG DRAGOON.

WAPITI-HUNTER.

in the commercial history of the world. Given its charter by the impecunious Charles II. in 1670, the pioneers of this "Governor and Company of Adventurers of England Trading into Hudson's Bay" sailed for the southern shores of St. James Bay, where they set up their first post and took possession of the new country in the name of Prince Rupert. Here they found a rival French company, with a previous charter granted by Louis XIII., and an equally keen sense of Indian barter, so that for many years there was more fighting than trading. When Wolfe, on the Heights of Abraham, crushed the power of France in Canada, the French company entered upon a decline that finally ended in dissolution. But in their stead came numbers of Englishmen, pushing their way westward, eager to trade for the furs of which they had heard so much and seen so little. Thus many trading-posts came into being, and eventually (about 1780) combined to form the Northwest Fur Company, the longest-lived and most determined rival that ever disputed trade with the Hudson Bay Company. It is not my purpose to fill space with historical research, but a brief sketch of this company, and how it came in the land, is necessary to a proper understanding of the country into which I hope to carry the reader.

The Hudson Bay Company had not reached out to a very great extent, being content with the fur gathered by their half-dozen "factories," of which York Factory and Churchill were the earliest and most important. But the Northwest Company brought a new spirit into the country; they pressed for trade with such avidity and determination as to carry

SARCEE AND SQUAW "AT HOME."

them into parts hitherto entirely unknown, and cause bloodshed whenever they met the agents of the rival company. It was the greed for trade, indeed, that quickened the steps of the first adventurers into the silent, frozen land of the North. Samuel Hearne, the first white man to pass beyond Great Slave Lake, made his trip in 1769 by order of the Hudson Bay Company, and in search of copper-mines. It was in pursuance of trade for the Northwest Company that Alexander Mackenzie (1789) penetrated to the Arctic Ocean

down the river which bears his name. I have never been able to see the justice in the command that gave Mackenzie a knighthood and ignored Hearne. The latter's trip was really a most remarkable one—overland a great part, and always the more difficult. Mackenzie's trip, as compared with it, reads like a summer day's pleasuring.

For forty years these two companies traded with the Indians, and fought one another at every opportunity, meanwhile pushing their posts farther and farther into the interior; but in 1821 a compromise was effected, an amalgamation resulted, and the Hudson Bay Company reigned supreme. And so it has continued to reign ever since; for though it retired from the government of Ruperts Land in 1870, and handed it over to the Dominion of Canada for £300,000 sterling, yet, so far as the country is concerned of which Edmonton is the distributing point, the Hudson Bay Company is as much the ruler in fact as ever it was in law. But this particular section, extensive as it is, is only one of the many in which, from end to end of British North America, this company counts altogether something like two hundred trading-posts. Nor are furs its sole commodity; from Montreal to Victoria along the Canadian Pacific Railroad, and at the centres of the Indian countries in which they trade, may be seen the "stores" of the Hudson Bay Company. Its £2,000,000 sterling capital stock is owned in London, but the business of the vast corporation is operated from Winnipeg, with "Commissioner" C. C. Chipman as its executive head.

One surprise at least awaited me at Edmonton. I had expected—I will be more honest, and say I had hoped—Edmonton would prove to be a bit untamed and picturesque. The realization of be-

BREAKING A TRAIL FOR THE DOGS.

ing on this Canadian frontier raised memories of other frontier days across the line, when Colorado and New Mexico were wild and woolly, and the atmosphere was continuously punctured by cowboy whoops and leaden pellets. Edmonton, however, never passed through such a period of real exhilaration. It had its days of waywardness, but its diversions were exceedingly commonplace. A few years ago it was almost surrounded by the battling-ground of the Crees and Blackfeet, and, as a matter of course, harbored red as well as white renegades; there was little law,

and that little was not respected; Indians out in the country killed off their foes from ambush, and in town renegades revealed their coward's blood and lack of originality by stabbing their enemies in the back. There were none of those blood-stirring nights in town such as we used to have on our own frontier; no duels on the main thoroughfare between two prominent citizens, with the remaining population standing by to see fair play; no cowboys to ride into saloons and shoot out the lights; no marksmen so expert as to knock the neck off the whiskey-bottle

AN ENCAMPMENT NEAR CALGARY.

A MEDICINE-MAN'S LODGE.

wrestling with himself after a bout with "40 proof."

Indeed, when I set out, the morning after my arrival, to get all in readiness in the one day that we might make the start for Lac La Biche on the second, I doubted if the citizens had ever heard of the word "hustle." I had been delayed in leaving New York, delayed in having to stop over at Winnipeg to get letters of credit from the Hudson Bay Company, and now I had finally reached the frontier, I was determined to be delayed no longer if effort of mine would provide against it. First of all, the shops did not

in the bartender's hands, and no bartenders who under such conditions did not turn a hair. There was murdering in plenty in and around Edmonton in the old days, but no man maintained a private burying-ground. This is not a distinction without a difference, as those with frontier experience will bear me out. I found Edmonton settled into a steady-going business community, with many hotels and few saloons, and the most exciting sight I beheld during my two nights and a day stop was a freighter

open until nine o'clock, and I, forgetful of being in a latitude where the sun in winter does not show himself before that hour, found myself chasing about the streets in the dawn that, before coming out of doors, I fancied due to a clouded sky. At last the shops and the sun opened for the day, and I succeeded in getting every one on the move. Still, we should not have been able to get away next day, I am sure, but for the consideration of the Hudson Bay Company factor, Mr. Livock, and his chief aid, Mr. Kennard, who were

GOING FOR AN AFTERNOON DRIVE AT EDMONTON.

kind enough to neglect their business to attend to mine. The one happy stroke we had made was in choosing the Queen's for our hotel; it was quite haphazard, but very lucky. Here I found the best board to which I had ever sat down in a frontier town, and host and hostess that did more for me during my sojourn than the bill showed or I could repay.

If such signs were trustworthy, I should have been much elated over the auspicious weather that ruled on the day of our departure for La Biche. Truly it was a beautiful morning, with the temperature some twenty degrees below zero, and a

not for a picnic. I knew perfectly well that I could not carry in a sufficient supply to last until I had covered the 900 miles that lay between me and Great Slave Lake, because of the impossibility of securing enough dogs and sledges to freight it, and I knew that even if I could eat as a civilized man until I reached that point, I should be obliged, when I began my journey into the Barren Grounds, to abandon all hope of eating well, or even plentifully, and live or starve as do the Indians on their annual hunt in that region. Besides, the greatest essential to the success of my trip was speed. I had

OFF FOR LAC LA BICHE.

glorious sun, which touched the ice-covered bushes and trees with sparkling brilliancy; and when we started on our 175-mile drive, all Queen's Hotel, and, I judged, half the town, turned out to bid us God-speed. We had two good horses and a strong box-sleigh, and our load was not heavy, so that I expected to make good time. I had taken only enough provisions from Edmonton to last us to La Biche. There was much that I could have taken, of course, in the way of canned vegetables, meats, etc., and which might have saved me from many a meal of the oftentimes unpalatable stuff which I secured from post to post. But I was going into the country for a purpose, and

set out to make my bison-hunt, to get into the Barren Grounds for the musk-ox, and get back again to Great Slave Lake on snow-shoes — an undertaking that had never before been attempted, and which every one assured me I could not carry out. It meant snow-shoeing nearly 1900 miles, and left no time for leisurely travelling; but I was determined to accomplish what I had planned if it lay within human possibilities; and thus it was that we took no unnecessary freight from Edmonton, for civilized food is so considered in that great North land. Tobacco was the only article of which I took a greater supply; but tobacco is not considered freight up there; it is always a solace, and becomes on occasion a stimulant when there is no meat, and an irresistible lure to facilitate intercourse with the Indians.

It was well we had a stout sleigh, for, much to my astonishment, the snow seemed not more than a foot deep anywhere, while in the road it had been worn down by much travel, and the rocks were numerous and aggressive. We made twenty-two miles by noon of the first day, and took our dinner at Fort Saskatchewan, the most northerly post of the Northwest Mounted Police. Up to this point of the day's journey the road had been plain, and the country not unpleasant to the eye. In fact, in some parts it is rather pretty, of a general rolling character, fringed with small timber, mostly of the poplar variety, though pine is fairly abundant. It looks like, and is, in truth, a grazing country more especially, though the horses and cattle I saw *en route* were rather poor—a condition to be probably expected in a land where everything is new and the settlers lead a hand-to-mouth existence, as all settlers do. An Edmonton enthusiast—I think he must have had property for sale —assured me with great gusto that the land around that town would yield from 35 to 75 bushels of wheat to the acre, and from 100 to 200 bushels of oats, the latter weighing 42 pounds to the bushel; the timber, however, he acknowledged " wasn't much to brag on."

ONE OF THE FIRST STEEL KNIVES TRADED TO INDIANS.

The one well-defined road we had been following all day broadened out towards sunset into a valley, showing in turn several depressions in the snow—here much deeper—which we assumed to be roads. No one at Saskatchewan was able to direct us intelligently, and not a soul had been seen since leaving there from whom we could ask our way. Grierson, who was driving us, and who is one of the Queen's Hotel proprietors, had never before been over the road, but his bump of direction was well placed and abnormally developed. People in this country do not seem to consider knowledge of the roads necessary to reaching their destination. They just start off on the one main and almost only trail, which they follow to its end, when they continue on in the direction

of their objective point. Roads are few and far between in this section, and disappear altogether when you get one hundred miles north of Edmonton. The alleged road to La Biche, which bears to the east of north, is the longest, and the end; beyond, all travel is by dogs in winter and canoe in summer. Grierson knew that Beaver Lake Creek was the point we were booked to reach that night in order to make La Biche in three days' travel from Edmonton, and he was sure it lay to the northeast. So we pegged on, until finally, after chasing several lights that turned out to be the wrong ones, and once nothing less lofty than a planet, which in this far North hung near the horizon, we found the log cabin of Beaver Lake Creek's most distinguished settler. I say distinguished, because his was the only cabin in those parts which boasted of two rooms and a second story—an extravagance, he informed us, he had indulged in with the idea of one day, when the section in which he had located became more populous, putting a stock of merchandise into the " other room," and utilizing the top story as a dormitory for travellers. I concluded he was a host of discernment, with a delicate humor for inciting reform in his guests without offending their previously conceived sense of propriety, for, having refreshed myself in about one and a half inches of ice-water, I was confronted by this black-lettered legend on the cabin door: "Bad luck attend the man that wipes his nose on the towel."

We left the pioneer of Beaver Tail Creek's " 400 " next morning before the sun was up, and by one o'clock had gone thirty-eight miles to Victoria, on the Saskatchewan River. It is the site of a Hudson Bay Company trading-post, and the end of the telegraph line. Once past here, the most rapid means of communication is the " express," as the Indian runner is called. To me, as sportsman, the most interesting feature of Victoria was the fact of its being about the northern limit of wapiti in this particular part of the continent. Formerly, in the days of the bison, wapiti were numerous, particularly near the Battle River, but, although they have not entirely disappeared, they are not now plentiful, and are to be had only by the most skilful hunters. Because of this the Indians living near Victoria resort to every manner of device for a shot, but with indifferent success.

This was our longest day's drive, for we had made very close to eighty miles by eleven o'clock at night, when we camped, and the road, or rather the multiplicity of roads, of the afternoon proved even more perplexing than on the day previous. Our direction lay along the border of a Cree Indian reservation, and was cross-sectioned at times with trails, or at least what in the snow had the appearance of trails, running to the four points of the compass. We knew we had but one point of the compass to follow—of that much, at least, we were sure, and proportionately thankful — but that point seemed to be such a broad one we were constantly at a loss for our bearings. I should be very much relieved to know positively if there was indeed any trail taking a northeasterly course that escaped us, and shall always regret I did not return by that route in the spring on my way back to the railroad, and when the snow had disappeared, just to satisfy my curiosity on that score. We were making for the White-Fish Lake Indian reservation, where we had been told we could find feed and a covering for the horses, and a schoolmaster who would give us a place to throw down our blankets, and the best of his larder. We were not concerned for ourselves, for we carried enough to provide a substantial meal, and, I think, all three of us would have preferred sleeping in the open to the average cabin. But the mercury had fallen a great many degrees since leaving Edmonton, a cutting wind was blowing, and our horses were pretty well worn, with still forty-five miles to go the next day before reaching La Biche. This was why we pushed on, hoping every turn would show the light in the distance that meant rest for us and an extra feed for our team. We finally reached some straggling cabins of the reservation, but should have been searching for that light yet if we had not roused an Indian from his slumbers, whom Grierson, by some startling Cree vocalization, the like of which I never heard before nor since, at length made understand what we were after. Then this drowsy child of nature led the

THE COPPER KETTLE IN WHICH WE BREWED TEA FOR TWENTY-SIX HUNDRED MILES.

way to a schoolmaster, but not to the schoolmaster we had been seeking, whose house was a few miles farther on, we subsequently learned.

The schoolmaster we found was a study in filth. He lived like a dog in a wretched kennel, and talked like a cockney Englishman; indeed, he confided to me, the following morning, that he had come from London, and was living there chiefly to learn the Cree language, that he might later preach "Jesus to the wayward heathen." Meanwhile he was educating him. This cockney's one idea of education seemed summed up in the single word coercion. If the Indians gathered for the dances of their tribe, he scattered them; if they played the games of their childhood, he stopped them; if they asked for reasons, he told them it was the devil in them that they exploited and which he wished to cast out. A logical way, forsooth, of educating the ignorant! And this is why we find the broken-spirited Indian, who realizes he is the creature of an all-powerful master whose ways he cannot understand, so often "converted," but only in individual cases educated and civilized. He is "converted" because it requires only outward acquiescence, and he finds his material life made pleasanter thereby. He is willing to change his "Great Spirit" for the white man's "Great Spirit" when a few beads or an extra ration make the trade inviting. But he cannot be educated without being first civilized, and he cannot be civilized because in most cases the white man does not know how, or does not find it to his interest, to make the attempt in a rational way. At present he distrusts, and sees only that he is being "civilized" off the face of the earth, and remembers the white man in his successive rôles of welcomed guest, greedy hunter, settler, and exterminator. I am not dealing in heroics, and every one knows that the savage must disappear before the civilized man; but if we are to attempt the civilization of those that remain let us first endeavor to gain their confidence, and then follow it up by methods which they can grasp. It is not to be done in one season, nor in two; the civilized red man cannot be brought forth full-fledged, as from a patent incubator; he can be evolved only after long periods of gradual and natural development; yet we expect by mere word of mouth to make him forsake the sentiments of a lifetime, of generations of lifetimes. At the same time he should realize there is a law in the land which punishes and protects him as thoroughly as it does the white man. He should not be allowed to escape with no severer penalty for furtive war-path festivals than that of being merely herded back to his reservation, when white men equally guilty would be hanged or shot. The surest way of civilizing the Indian is through his children, and possibly their children in turn will cease to remember that once their ancestors roamed over the country hunting, and learning the lessons of their common mother Nature, instead of living fenced in on a reservation, ploughing, and studying the precepts of the white man.

BLANKET CLOTHING OF THE EARLY WINTER, BEFORE EXCESSIVE COLD DEMANDS FURS.

We left the Indian reformer early the next morning, after a broken night's rest on a dirtier floor than, I think, I ever saw in an Indian lodge. We must have proved a blessing to that fellow, for we put money in his purse, and such a meal in his stomach as I fancy he had not had for many a long day. The weather had grown colder, and one of our horses gone lame, but our big fur coats to keep out the one, and mustang liniment to relieve the other, put us in travelling shape. We had broken our sleigh, and patched it up again before we camped for our noon-day meal in a squall of snow, but we had covered by that time a good half of the distance which the previous night separated us from our destination. As we neared La Biche we renewed our troubles over diverging roads, but this time our direction was so accurate that the delay was inconsiderable. Moreover, there were others abroad; for the morrow was New-Year's, and Indians and half-breeds were making their way to the company post to partake of the feast which is provided for them annually. They came from either side, and fell into the now well-beaten track we were all travelling; men and women, old and young, some walking, but the majority riding in a sort of box set upon runners, locally known as a "jumper," and drawn by a nondescript kind of beast which we discovered upon close scrutiny to be an undersized, underfed horse, but that more nearly resembled an overgrown jack-rabbit. And thus with the dying sun of the last day of 1894 we made our *entrée* into Lac La Biche with the gathering of the clans.

I do not believe I had ever been in a more advanced state of exhilaration than on first viewing the unsightly cabins of the La Biche post. Farther along on my trip I felt a deeper thankfulness, when hope had almost fled, and mind and body were too jaded to rejoice, but now I was as a boy given an unexpected holiday, who wanted to shout and throw his cap into the air; for here at last I beheld the actual frontier, and the real starting-point of my journey. It was not that the trip from Edmonton had been so long or so hard, for, as a matter of fact, it was pleasant and easy, but it was the realization of being on the scene of action, so to say. When one has planned an adventure, and discussed ways and means and dangers, there is a satisfaction in reaching the base of operations; and when one's friends have tried to dissuade and natives to intimidate you, there is added to satisfaction that other feeling, which puts you on edge, fires your blood, and makes you keen to toe the mark and be off. It was a blessing I arrived in such a humor, for it was sorely tried at La Biche during the three vexing days we were compelled to spend there. I had a premonition we were going to run against a snag when I saw Gairdner, the Hudson Bay Company officer in charge, saunter out of his cabin to greet us; and when he asked if we were not ahead of time, in a tone that implied he would have been better pleased had we been overdue, I felt convinced we were going to be delayed. We were a day in advance of our schedule, having taken but three instead of four days from Edmonton, but as an "express" had been sent Gairdner two weeks before to warn him of our arrival, and as the preparations were only the making of two pairs of snow-shoes, and the engaging of two trains of dogs and drivers, I could not see that our coming was ill-timed.

I think, nevertheless, he was glad to see us (especially Grierson, who had brought along a flask), and he certainly shared the best of his house with us. He told us we had come at the best time of the year to see the Indians; that they were always given a feast and a dance on New-Year's, and that some of them, hearing of our arrival, would probably drop in that night to dance a little for us. Well, they did "drop in," and they as certainly danced, though not a "little." Heavens! how those creatures danced, and what an atmosphere and a racket they created in that house! They began to arrive shortly after we had finished supper, shaking hands with us solemnly on entrance, and eying us stealthily after seating themselves in rows against the walls. Then one of them produced a fiddle, and from the time the first measure was sounded, I think there was no cessation until about two o'clock the following morning.

For a while the exhibition was rath-

HALF-BREED DOG-DRIVER.

er interesting, though never very novel. The common dancing of Indians appears to be about the same all over; there is but one type, though it may assume different expressions, according to prejudice or locality. Either they shuffle around in a circle, or they hop from one foot to the other in lines or separately, or they do all three, with more or less vigor and with or without costuming. At La Biche the dancing is not of the Indian type, it is of the kind one sees in the half-breed camps of Canada, and consists of a species of jigs and reels gone through at a pace that makes you dizzy only to watch. They have their dances where several couples perform, but the most popular seemed that in which separate couples engaged, as many as the floor would accommodate. These face one another, and the man enters upon a vigorous exploitation of the double-shuffle, which he varies with "pigeon wings," and Heaven knows what not, always making the greatest noise of which he is capable. Noise and endurance, I was given to understand, are the two requisites to good dancing; but men and women of course wear moccasins, and only on occasion have board floors to dance on. It was my luck to happen along at one of those "occasions," and to be further tortured by a half-breed company servant, whose great pride was a

AN EDMONTON FREIGHTER.

heavy pair of white man's boots, which he never wore except when threading the giddy maze.

Half-breeds—French and Cree—constitute the larger share of population at La Biche, if I may class as its population those scattered over the immediately surrounding country, and where the settlement consists of just three cabins besides the Hudson Bay Company's. But, after all, the French blood reveals itself chiefly in a few Christian names and in the more fanciful coloring and use of some articles of wear, for there is little French spoken, the children of mixed parentage almost invariably adopting the mother-tongue, Cree. There are not more than one hundred Crees who come into La Biche, which is the most northerly post where treaty money is given, and they are not thriving to any very great extent, nor increasing. The annuity of about five dollars a head is not sufficient to support and just enough to interrupt keen hunting; they plant a few potatoes, which grow here fairly well, but are making no progress towards self-support, as are those of the same nation more to the south.

After what I had seen the night before of the preliminaries to the annual feast-day, I did not expect on New-Year's to be able to make any preparations for our further progress. Long before we had turned out of our blankets the house was literally packed with Indians, and by noon-time the fiddle was going and the dancers had entire possession of the floor. I doubt if I ever saw, outside of some of the Chinese dens in San Francisco, so many crowded into the same space. I lacked the heart to talk business with Gairdner, who, I divined from some of his remarks, had not accomplished, in the way of making ready our dog brigade, all I had expected of him. I simply pitied him for the unpleasant and malodorous fulness of his home, and I pitied his half-breed wife and her daughters, who were kept cooking for and feeding half-starved Indians from early morn until late into the night. Heming took his pencil and scratch pad and I my camera, and we went out to see the New-Year's-day arrivals and the dogs and the Indians.

In front of the fort's stockade were gossiping groups that grew with each fresh arrival, while scattered all about the enclosure, just where their drivers had left them, were the dog trains of the Indians who had come to fill Gairdner's house and eat the Hudson Bay Company's meat. There was no stabling nor feasting for these dogs; in a 24° below zero atmosphere they stretched out in the snow and waited, without covering, and in many cases without food. The Indians with their blanket coats or ca-

ONE "MADE BEAVER" TOKEN, FORMERLY ISSUED BY THE HUDSON BAY COMPANY.

potes, and the dogs and sledges and "jump-ers," made a picturesque whole against the unbroken background of snow, but, like all Indian pictures, its attractiveness faded away on the close inspection that discovered the dirt of the man, and the scraggy, half-starved condition of the beast. These people had never before seen a camera, and many of my plates show them scurrying away or turning their backs. It was only after the most elaborate descriptions to Gairdner, who instructed the interpreter, who explained to the Indians, that we induced one or two "types" to sit in our presence while Heming sketched them. They thought we were making "medicine" against them, but were won over by Heming drawing the moose and caribou, while they watched the animals they knew so well develop under his pencil.

When we returned to the house the dance was still on; it was always "on" during the first thirty-six hours of our stay at La Biche. Formerly the Hudson Bay Company officers merely "received" on New-Year's day; but as the Indians have a custom between sexes of kissing on meeting, and as it did not become an impartial officer to distinguish in this respect between old women and young, unattractive and attractive, the feast was substituted; so now the women are fed and danced instead of being kissed.

I hope that New-Year's night will not be recorded against me. Those Indians danced until four o'clock in the morning, and they danced to my utter demoralization. We sat around and watched the "gymnastics" and pretended we enjoyed them until about one o'clock; then we retired. We all three slept in Gairdner's office, a tiny apartment separated from the main room by a thin board partition, of which a good quarter section in the centre was removed to admit of the two rooms sharing a single stove. There was a piece of loosened sheet-iron tacked to the partition to protect it from the heat, and my head was against that partition, and our blankets on the same floor upon which those Indians sprinted and jumped and shuffled!

New-Year's past and the fiddle hung up, I entered upon the business of our getting under way for Fort McMurray,

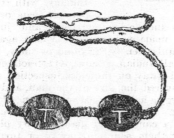

NATIVE "SNOW-GLASSES."

the next Hudson Bay post to the north, and then indeed did the trouble begin. First of all, Gairdner earnestly assured me that I could not make the trip I contemplated, that I could not get into the Barren Grounds, and would risk my life if I did, and could not get Indians to accompany me if I would. Then, after finding me undismayed by the lugubrious prospect, he informed me that he 'had not been able to get matters ready, nor could he say how soon we could start. He had first engaged two men, but both backed out, one because he could not get four dogs together, and the other because he had no house to put his wife in during his absence. Finally he had secured the services of a half-breed called "Shot," who, he said, was the best man in the country, trustworthy and a good traveller, and had spoken to another half-breed, who was just then struggling to make up his mind. Added to this pleasing intelligence, the snow-shoes were being made by an Indian who lived fifteen miles

away, and from whom nothing had been heard. I thought we were at least sure of "Shot"; but the next day he came to us with a large story of his worth, the sacrifices he would make by going with us, and wound up by refusing to budge unless we doubled the wages which he and Gairdner had agreed upon.

For the remainder of this and the next day life was a burden to me. Gairdner was absolutely of no use, as he could have been by standing between us and the Indians in our business. I was obliged to take matters into my own hands, and deal with the wrangling Indians through an interpreter. I finally secured "Shot" on a compromise, intending to take no other man, but drive the second train of dogs ourselves. Then I had a time getting another four dogs and sledge. First the owners would not hire a train without their own engagement (this after I had spent two days trying to induce them to go with me!), then no one man who had a complete train could be found. At last I got two dogs from one Indian and one dog each from two different Indians. Meanwhile I was waiting for "Shot," who was to come prepared for the start as soon as the snow-shoes were finished, and being worried thin by the dog-owners' repeated visits and their clamors for a new deal; having hired the dogs and sledge, they wanted me to pay an additional fee for harness and wrapper, or, if not, to give them a little tea or tobacco or moccasins. I was in constant dread lest their fickleness would eventually deprive me of a train, and I cursed "Shot" roundly for his delay. Meanwhile, too, Heming and I were conditioning ourselves by some running every afternoon, and had settled to the conviction that the hardest part of our trip appeared to be the getting started.

At last on Friday, January 4th, the impatiently awaited "Shot" arrived, with his dogs and sledge in good condition, but the sledge of the second train broken so badly as to necessitate its repair before starting. "Shot" had also brought with him a young Cree Indian called John, whom he recommended as a good runner, and advised me to engage; and afterwards, when Heming fell ill, and John and I pushed on into the country alone, I forgave "Shot" much of what I had harbored against him because of his bringing me that Cree. It was noon before the sledge

"IN A 24° BELOW ZERO ATMOSPHERE THEY WAITED."

had been mended and we were ready to begin packing up for the start. Our personal luggage consisted of a change of shirts and heavy underwear, three silk pocket-handkerchiefs, an extra pair of Irish frieze trousers, a heavy woollen sweater, stout gloves to wear inside the native-made mittens, two pairs of Hudson Bay Company four-point blankets, a rabbit-skin robe (of native manufacture, and very warm), blanket leggings, a caribou-skin capote lined with blanket, a knitted hood, a worsted tuque, "duffel" socks (native-made of a sort of blanket stuff, two to three pairs being worn at a time inside the moccasins), snow-glasses, several pairs of moccasins, hunting-knife, strong clasp-knife, a 45.90 Winchester, half-magazine, and 150 cartridges, pills, and mustang liniment; I had, besides, a compass, my camera (in a strong zinc box), note-books, and some iodoform, antiseptic lozenges, and sterilized gauze bandages, in case amputation because of freezing became necessary. Our provisions included bacon, tea, flour, and a few pounds of potatoes Mrs. Gairdner was kind enough to boil and mash and freeze into a pan for us; our one luxury—or rather mine, for Heming does not smoke—was tobacco. In all we had just 357 pounds, which I was careful to determine, for I was sure "Shot" would be grumbling about the load, and swear we had 600 pounds on each sledge, and I wanted to be prepared to meet him, as I had said we should go light purposely to make good time. We took only one night's fish for the dogs (dogs being fed fish in this country in place of meat), because Gairdner told us we should find plenty at Hart Lake, which we would reach the next night. Finally by three o'clock the sledges were packed, "Shot" and John had bade tender farewells to every man, woman, and child about the post, Gairdner and Grierson had wished us the best of luck, and we began our journey.

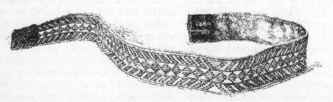

A WOMAN'S PORCUPINE-QUILL BELT.

ON SNOW SHOES TO THE BARREN GROUNDS
BY CASPAR W. WHITNEY

II.—FROM LA BICHE TO FORT CHIPEWYAN.

WITH several Indians running before to escort us beyond the post in approved style, we left La Biche at a pretty brisk gait, and maintained for a good hour a pace which must have carried us six miles. But Heming and I were so delighted at being finally and really under way that no speed those Indians could have set would have been too stiff for us. As we ran we now and again delivered ourselves of congratulations that were expressive if brief, and somewhat disconnected in delivery. We had been delayed three days and a half at La Biche, fussing with Indians that had more time than energy, more promise than execution, and who broke contracts as rapidly as they made them. Gairdner had annoyed me a great deal, and no doubt we had worried him not a little, breaking in upon the even and lethargic tenor of his monotonous life with our "outside" (as the great world is called by the denizens of this lone land) hustling ways. But now that it is all past, and the trip successfully made, we are willing to forgive and be forgiven.

We did not expect to go far that night; our chief desire was to get started; and besides, we knew we should pass several Indian houses, where we must stop, that "Shot" and John might live up to the usual demands of the country courtesy, and shake hands with the occupants, and gossip about the white men they were guiding over the first stage of their long journey. Shaking hands always includes the further ceremony of filling up the pipes and a drink of tea, should the host happen to have any of that luxury, and so when we had left the last Indian lodge, and crossed the northeast end of the lake and got well into the woods, it was sunset,

and time to camp. The going down of the sun is the invariable signal for camping, for the twilight is of short duration, and the Indians will not run the risk of accident by chopping wood after dark. And they are quite right. A cut foot or leg in civilization is ordinarily little more than inconvenient, but in this trackless wilderness any wound that interrupts a man's travelling may lead to his death. And so as the sun begins to disappear below the horizon you grow watchful for a place that is most sheltered and best wooded and nearest the road you are following.

By the time we had gathered firewood it began to snow, and we ate our first meal in the open, with backs arched to windward, and capote hoods pulled up over our heads to keep "the beautiful" from going down our necks. That first night out was an interesting one to me; with recollections of bivouacs in the Rockies, I thought the fire insignificant and the timber small, but the dogs sitting on their haunches watching the thawing of the frozen fish that were to furnish them with supper, and the sledges drawn on the banked-up snow at the head of our blankets, made a novel and picturesque scene.

Every one was sleeping the sleep of the weary, if not of the just, and the dogs had eaten and curled themselves up in the snow for the night, when I finally threw off my meditative mood and rolled up in my blankets.

It snowed all night, and when we broke camp the next morning at six it was still snowing, and there was a cold head-wind that made us move lively to keep comfortable. The trail wound through brush and small timber, and now and again across a small lake, but its greatest length lay over what is called "muskeg," which is Cree for swamp, and the most tiring, patience-testing travelling I ever encountered.

Imagine a landlocked lake swept by furious cross-winds, and its entire surface churned into choppy waves; suppose it suddenly congealed at its angriest moment; further, suppose a deep layer of miry earth covered by thick heavy moss moulded upon it, and stuck full of close-growing stout brush. That is the muskeg. Now fancy walking over a succession of uneven hummocks with brush constantly catching your snow-shoe and slapping your face, and you will have a vague idea of the difficulties of muskeg travel. Level footing is exceedingly scarce, the wind blows the snow "whither it listeth," and you cannot know whether you are about to step on top of one of those innumerable mounds or into one of the many gutters that cross-section the swamp. You know after you have taken the step. Nine times out of ten you land on the slanting side of the mound, and slip and trip and turn your ankle and use yourself up generally. It is exceedingly difficult going, and Heming and I, who relieved one another breaking trail for the dogs, found it very fatiguing.

It was storming hard and getting colder, and I was ahead setting the pace, when, about three o'clock that afternoon, I came upon a log hut, and two trails that bore away in different directions. I wish I could have photographed the scene which slowly materialized from out of the darkness as I stood on the earthen floor within the cabin while my eyes grew accustomed to the changed conditions. On entering I could distinguish only the fire in one end, before which squatted a couple of Indians and a squaw, but gradually the shadows lifted, and I found myself for a few moments busily engaged shaking hands with Indians as fast as the new light revealed them. It was a very small cabin, barely ten feet square, I should say, with a parchment-covered hole in the wall for window, and a door which demanded a bowed head of every visitor. I do not know how many Indians were in that hut, but I recall wondering how they arranged for sleeping, as there seemed hardly space for them to sit, much less lie down. They were about to eat, and several rabbits, suspended full length from a deer thong, and minus only their skins, were twirling and roasting before

THE INDIAN'S STOREHOUSE AND LARDER.

the fire, while others were being prepared for the cooking. I was not partial to rabbit, nor especially happy in the cabin's atmosphere, so when I had warmed a bit I went outside to wait for the dog brigade to come up.

Heming and John hove in sight shortly, but quite half an hour had passed when "Shot" and his dogs loomed up in the storm, that seemed increasing every minute. Then "Shot" and I had our first battle royal. He fancied the smell of the roasting rabbit and the warm cabin; he did not like the sleet driving in our faces, and he wanted to camp. I was annoyed at the interruptions to our progress, disgusted with "Shot" for his vainglorious mouthing at La Biche and his halting gait since leaving there, and determined that night to reach Hart Lake, which was only seven or eight miles farther on, and where we expected to get fish (of which we then had none) for our dogs. In language both pointed and picturesque I reminded "Shot" of my being the commander-in-chief of our little expedition, and made him understand we were out neither for pleasure nor for our health, that we had an objective point, and intended to get there without loss of time, and without camping in every cabin we discovered or being headed off by every severe storm we encountered. "Shot" spluttered a great deal at first, and then looked as if it would give him pleasure to bury his hunting-knife in my flesh; but he sulked instead, and we moved away from the crowded little house and the roasting rabbits.

NATIVE-MADE GARTER.
From an old and lost design.

There had been a broken trail from this point to Hart Lake, but the same storm that was making our walking so arduous had almost obliterated it, and it was long after dark, and the thermometer 30° below zero, when we reached the cabin of the Indian who Gairdner had said would sell us fish enough to last to the McMurray fishery. But, like all the things Gairdner told us, we found realization quite different from promise. The Indian was willing enough to sell, but his cache was fifteen miles away; he had just heard it had been broken into and all his fish stolen, so that he could not say whether or no he really had any; and, at all events, he could not make the journey in one day, and would not start the next (Sunday), because it was the occasion of the priest's yearly visit to this district. I was sorry to jeopard his soul by depriving it of the annual shriving, but I believed my dogs in more urgent need of fish than he of salvation, and I was sure three days' delay at Hart Lake would blight definitely whatever hopes of a future reward I might previously have enjoyed. Therefore I set about to wreck that Indian's peace of mind. Four skins — *i. e.*, two dollars — quieted spiritual alarms, a silk handkerchief to the wife secured a promise to make the trip to the cache and back in one day, and the *coup d'état* was executed by enlisting "Shot's" sympathies through my assuring him that, fish or no fish, I should start Monday morning, and, if necessary, feed our bacon to the dogs, and complete the journey on tea and potatoes, of which latter, I believe, we had a few meals left. Thus it was that I got the Indian started off early Sunday morning for his cache, and saved two souls and eight dogs.

The beneficence of the La Biche priest extended farther that Sunday than he knew. Heming and I blessed his coming without stint, for it emptied of its usual occupants the filthy cabin in which we were obliged to spend the day and another night, and gave us an opportunity to sweep the floor and renew intimate relations with water.

When we took up our journey again Monday morning, with the insufficient supply of fish got from the Indian's despoiled cache, the mercury had dropped to 54° below zero, and there was no longer a broken trail. Our first ten miles lay across a lake, and both Heming and I, who were breaking road, and sinking up to our knees in the snow, were frequently startled by a rumbling as of distant thunder as the ice cracked under us. It was a curious sensation too, to have these explosions occurring at our feet, and vibrating towards the shores in successive and receding detonations, like the rings which widen and follow upon one another when you have thrown a stone into a pond. On one occasion water followed the cracking, and we were obliged to run hard, until we stopped for dinner, to keep our feet from freezing.

The going was exceedingly difficult all day long, in deep snow, across lakes, through bunches of stunted spruce, and over the redoubtable muskeg, where the sledges required constant handling, and never by any chance remained right side up for more than a few moments at a time. Still, the weather remained clear, and when we camped, at six o'clock, the stars were shining brightly, and we had left Hart Lake thirty-eight miles behind us, Heming and I running the last nine miles in one hour and forty minutes.

I had been very much worried over Heming's condition the last two days; on the night we arrived at Hart Lake he seemed considerably worn, and the only consolation I had in the day's delay there was the hope it furnished that the rest would brace him up. But on this night he was completely used up, and I was very seriously alarmed by discovering symptoms of deranged kidneys. I did not then know the cause, and attributed it to strain brought on by hard running. In fact, Heming did not tell me, until I stopped off at Hamilton to see him on my way back to New York, that on the day's run to Hart Lake he had fallen over a log and struck on the small of his back. I only knew at that time that any weakness of the kidneys was not to be trifled with, and I felt it would be extremely hazardous to take him on; so I lay down that night to think rather than to sleep.

It was fearfully cold the following morning, with the going growing harder every hour, and I fell behind Heming to watch how he stood up under the effort. I could plainly see he was laboring with great difficulty, and concluded it would be suicidal for him to continue, getting farther from civilization and physicians every mile, so at ten o'clock I called a halt, and expressed my determination to send him home. Heming was loath to turn back, but appreciated his unfitness for the onward journey, and acquiesced in a decision which must have brought him keenest disappointment.

We had stepped aside for our confer-

ence, and I have little doubt "Shot" fancied us planning something for his discomfort, and was much relieved on learning he was to return. I decided on "Shot" instead of John, because he understood English enough to administer to Heming's wants in case of his collapse. Then, through "Shot's" interpretation, I had to win John's consent to go on with me, and I experienced a very disquieting half-hour indeed while John underwent the elaborate process of making up his mind. First he refused; then he demurred because he had never been in that part

"JOHN."

of the country before, and was as dependent on "Shot" for guidance as we were ourselves; and again he objected because he could not speak nor understand a word of English, and I was as deficient in Cree. However, finally he consented if I would give him a few presents, the nature of which I have now forgotten; and after we had eaten, the two Indians set to work dividing the supplies and repacking the sledges. It was not a very elaborate task, and did not take long. We had eaten the last of the potatoes, and so when the bacon and the tea and the flour had been divided, the blankets separated, and Heming and I had indicated which was which of the two seamless sacks that contained our personal luggage, the sledges were packed and the dogs headed in opposite directions.

Then we went our separate ways, and I took up my journey to the great lone land, over a strange country, and without even the poor satisfaction of talking my mother-tongue.

My regret over Heming's falling ill may be better imagined than described. Foremost, of course, I deplored the loss of a companion on a trip which was to extend over 2600 miles; and of less but still considerable concern was the sudden deprivation of a helpmate, upon whose hardihood and experience I had confidently counted. Heming had had abundant snow-shoeing and some dog-sledging, and I set much value on a knowledge that would, to some extent at least, facilitate our venturesome undertaking. And now here I was, just four days out from La Biche, never having had a web snow-shoe on my foot, nor even seen a dog-sledge, with six days of travel over an unknown country between me and Fort McMurray, the next nearest trading-post. However, unpleasant as the prospect was, I had thought it all over the night before as I lay in my blankets after our hard day's run, and realized the situation as completely as I had settled upon my course. But it was not a happy afternoon, that 8th of January, 1895, which saw me, after the separation, trudging onward in cold and in silence.

If I lamented Heming, most assuredly I did not mourn "Shot," notwithstanding his being the only man in the outfit who knew the country across which we were to journey. He had been a sore trial to me from the day of our departure—nay, even from the very hour of our introduction at La Biche—and I confess to honest relief in ridding myself of him, though I was at the time like a ship cast adrift without rudder. Before starting he had deliberately broken his contract, and followed it up by repeated attempts to squeeze more money out of me when he recognized my helplessness and saw my anxiety to get under way. He exasperated me to such a degree that, knowing an indulgence to my feelings would result in his refusing to go at all, I remember confiding to Heming the great hope that my legs would prove as stout as they had at other times, and enable me to set such a pace as should make "Shot's" tongue hang out before we reached McMurray.

Whether the pace was too hot or he too lazy I cannot say, but certainly when we were once started he kept me busy urging him to faster gait; his train was invariably so far behind as to delay us ten to fifteen minutes at every "spell" (rest), which meant a loss of from six to eight miles in a day's travel. It must have been laziness, because he is a half-breed of massive bone and great strength and over six feet in height. He evidently thought he had got hold of a "moonyass," as a "tenderfoot" is called in this country, with whom he could play any game he chose; and when he discovered his mistake he grew sulky, developed a lame knee, subsequently a sore back, and delayed the

morning start by his reluctance to turn out when called and the length of time he consumed in packing the sledges. The only day of the four he was with me on which I got him to set off promptly and travel smartly was the last one, when the prospect of reaching a deserted cabin for the night's camp carried him on. I could have forgiven him the lagging behind, for the going was hard, and he had none of the incentive that added nervous to my physical energy, but his avariciousness at La Biche and his sullenness on the road hardened my heart, and I cut out his work on a scale that, I fancy, made the parting between us one for mutual congratulation.

And so John and I set out on our journey, neither of us knowing where the morrow might find us, and I with a Cree vocabulary limited to "no," "yes," "hurry," and "how far is it?" I do not know how many miles we covered in the afternoon Heming turned homeward, for I was too thoroughly absorbed in thoughts of what was coming to note the passing, but the camp of that night was, luckily, the best we made on the trip. It was sheltered from the howling wind, wood was plentiful, and with blankets, moccasins, and leggings hung on poles to dry before the blazing logs, might even have been called picturesque, unless that quality may be said to disappear when the mercury registers 40° below zero ten feet from the fire. We were not likely to find so favored a spot another night, and I made John know he should take advantage of the good fire and prepare "bannocks" to last us a few days.

The bannock is simply flour and water and grease thoroughly kneaded and well baked: the usual method of cooking is to shape the dough an inch deep to the inside of a frying-pan, and stand the latter before the camp-fire. The bannock is not beautiful to the eye nor tempting to the fastidious palate; moreover, it never rises superior to that "sadness" which is the characteristic of underdone bread the world over. But the bannock is much better suited to the needs of the tripper or *voyageur*, as the snow-shoe traveller is called, than the light yeast bread of the *grand pays*. The bread of civilization is filling, but lacks substance; the bannock has both filling and substance; and when one has nothing to eat but bread and tea and bacon, and is running five miles an hour from sunrise to sunset day after day, substance is a desirable quality. While John made the bannocks, I attended to thawing fish for the dogs; and when we had both finished and lighted our pipes I undertook to hold my first conversation with him in the language of signs.

The warning most impressed upon me, by all those claiming any knowledge of the country into which I was going, had been against the unreliability of the Indians. I had been told of their tendency to desert under trying conditions, and the little there was to read on the subject emphasized the need of vigilance. That John would grow discouraged, and quietly steal away from camp some night, was a thought which possessed and worried me considerably. I was prepared to see his dismay as we plodded on in the hard going, and to hear his grumbling, even though I could not understand, but I did not propose, if I could prevent it, awakening one morning to find him and the dogs gone. So I engaged John's attention on this our first night together, and in my best pantomime I tried to make him understand that if he staid with me to McMurray and was a "good" Indian, I should be "good" to him, but if he deserted me he had better cut my throat before he left camp, as otherwise I should follow his trail and kill him. John looked very wise and serious during my dramatic

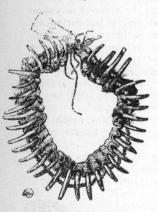

GRIZZLY-CLAW NECKLACE.

recital, and I guess he understood me. Whether he did or not, certainly his discouragement in the trying days we had subsequently never reached a mutinous point, and I fully believe he needed no intimidation to be a "good Indian." I wondered that night, and as the scene has come up before me many times since I have wondered again, what that Cree must have thought of this white man who was pushing into his country at a time when he himself usually remained in-

doors, had pressed him into a service for which he had no liking, and threatened to take his life if he forsook it.

Despite our sheltered position and the big fire, I put in an uncomfortable night in this picturesque camp. It was, in fact, the first of many uncomfortable nights before I adjusted my blankets and robes properly. I had ample bedding, and of course could have got warm quickly enough had I used it all, but that was precisely what I did not want to do. I wished to use the smallest amount of covering possible, and yet be not too uncomfortable to preclude sleep. I did not lose sight of the fact that the cold I was then experiencing was as summer compared with that which I should be obliged to sustain in the Barren Grounds, whither I was going. And as I had trained before leaving New York for extreme physical exertion, so now I began fitting myself for excessive cold. Indeed, I am entirely convinced it was my very careful and thorough previous conditioning that enabled me to withstand the starving and freezing to which I was subjected on this trip, and yet come out of it in sound physical condition and without having had a day's sickness. My camping-out experience had been rather extensive, and was now valuable in suggesting ways of making most out of little. An old campaigner will, simply by his method of wrapping it about him, get as much if not more warmth out of a single blanket than the tyro will out of two. Nevertheless, with all my experience, for the first week I shivered and shook in the bedding I permitted myself, and the temptation to add one more blanket was almost irresistible.

Not that the atmosphere was colder than I had before experienced, for 40° below is by no means uncommon in the Rocky Mountains, where I have camped, but the wind made me so miserable. It blew more than half the time, and nothing could resist its searchings. It went straight through capotes, leggings, and blankets, and made sleep impossible for me several nights on the way to McMurray. The dogs, however, seemed unmindful of either wind or cold. At night, after they had eaten their fish, they would go a few yards from the fire, scratch away a little of the top snow, and then curl up, back to windward. In the morning when they were dragged to harness they left the outline of their body in the snow, and a well-defined depression, which sometimes even showed the ground. Nothing but fur can insure warmth or even comfort in this chilling North. Farther along, and before making my bison or musk-ox hunt, I secured a caribou-skin capote with the fur on, but until I got one I was a shivering victim of the wind. The capote I had fetch-

POLE LODGE IN WHICH MOOSE AND CARIBOU SKINS ARE SMOKED.

ed from Hamilton, Canada, was useless; having been made of unsmoked leather, the first snow-storm soaked and the fire shrunk it; then it was too heavy to run in, and the blanket lining was greatly inferior to fur for warmth. No garment can excel the caribou capotes made by the Indians for exposure in the excessive cold and piercing winds of this North country. They are very light, and do not therefore add to the burden of the *voyageur*, while being literally impervious to all winds, save those deadly blasts of the Barren Grounds.

The Indian tripper in winter first secures stout moccasins and new "duffel," and next looks to his caribou-skin capote. Anything may answer for trousers or head-covering, the former, indeed, being moose or caribou skin, blanket, or "store pants" got at the Hudson Bay Company post in trade, while the conventional hat is supplied by a colored handkerchief wound about the head, just above the forehead and ears, to keep the long hair in place. Formerly it was, and still is in the more remote sections, a moose or caribou thong bound by sinew and decorated with porcupine quill. But the foot-covering must be of the best. Moccasins are made of smoked moose-skin, because of its thickness (though the thinner caribou-skin is equally durable), and are really the pride of the Indian wardrobe. They are the most, and very frequently the

only, decorated piece of his apparel; in presentation they are the vehicle of regard from one Indian to another; they carry the first tidings of a more tender sentiment from the maiden to the young hunter, and are the surest indication not only of the degree of the woman's handicraft, but, if she be married, of the degree of her regard for the husband. An Indian's moccasins are a walking advertisement of his standing at home. Blessed is the civilized world insomuch as its wives are not its boot-makers!

I was not long in reading aright the signs of the moccasins, and ever after, when I required any made at the posts, first sought acquaintance with the husband before ordering. No doubt many a pair of shoes I scanned did not represent the best work of the poor devil's wife, but I found them at least accurate in determining his importance within his own tepee. Moccasin decoration, in fact, practically all Northland Indian ornamentation, is done in beads, in porcupine quill, or in silk embroidery. Silk-work is of somewhat recent introduction, confined entirely to half-breeds, and although rather well executed, is the least effective. The French

MOCCASINS.

half-breeds are largely responsible for the bead embroidery, which is the vogue all over the northern part of this country. One sees moccasins, mittens, leggings, all in the beaded flower patterns, taken from nature, and therefore somewhat noteworthy, but not nearly so striking as the pure Indian designs of the more southerly tribes. The porcupine-quill work is truly Indian, and, at its best, exceedingly pretty,

ANCIENT KNIFE
WITH BEAVER-
TOOTH BLADE.

both in design and coloring, though only the most skilful can do it acceptably, for each tiny quill is woven in separately, and the weaver's ingenuity or lack of it is revealed in the design. The best specimens of this work are seen in the women's belts, though it is put on moccasins, shirts, skirts, gun-coats, as well as on the birch-bark baskets called rogans, and used for every purpose. "Duffel" is a thick blanket stuff, which, together with "strouds," a similar though more closely spun material, the Hudson Bay Company introduced and christened. Duffel is used for socks, and strouds for leggings, and both are manufactured expressly for the trade in this country. The Indian gets his duffel by the yard, and when he has cut it into strips about six inches wide by eighteen inches long his socks are completed. Their adjustment is equally simple, for it is only to begin at the toes and wind the piece throughout its length about the foot. The half-breed takes his duffel home, where it is shaped and sewed into crude socks, and if his wife thinks well of him, and is clever, she will vary them in size (as two or three pairs are worn at a time inside the moccasin), and fancy-stitch them in colored yarn. I tried both styles of sock, and prefer the Indian's simpler kind; it is more quickly thawed out and dried at night; if one end wears or burns, you can rearrange it so that a good part covers the toes and heel—the most important to keep from freezing; and you can fit it more snugly, which is, I think, its greatest advantage, because, if you do not happen to have a wife to direct, or, having one, do not stand high in her estimation, your socks will be of the same size, and all too large. Consequently your feet will slip

about, which is most tiresome in long and hard walking, and the socks will freeze into wrinkles and knots that will cut your toes and instep, and very likely eventually cripple you when your snowshoe strings have also become frozen.

The denial I practised in the matter of blankets proved doubly advantageous. It conditioned me so that very soon I slept soundly and comfortably, and it proved a blessing to John, to whom I gave of my surplus. He was very glad to get the additional blanket, and I never encountered an Indian throughout my trip who was not thankful for any extra covering, even a coat, that I let him have. This is apropos of the declaration made to the venturer into this country that the Indians scorn more than one blanket. I heard it on all sides. "What, two pairs of blankets? Why, the Indians," etc., etc. When these Indians sleep under one blanket it is because they have no second, nor do they keep warm "in the coldest nights." The contrary is all miserable boasting. My experience was that they could not stand any greater cold than I; when it was merely discomforting they were more indifferent to it than a white man would be, for the very good reason that while the white man has always been well clothed and fed and protected, the red man has been half clothed and fed and never protected. Naturally the latter does not mind exposures that must seem somewhat trying on first experience to the former. For instance, in sitting about camp, the Indians, as a rule, wore the same coat in which they had been running, whereas I found a heavier one more comfortable. It was not that the Indians were warm, but they were used to discomfort. I wrapped up less than they when snowshoeing, but more than they in camp. When it came to withstanding the fearful cold and withering storms of the Barren Grounds, my endurance was as great, and my suffering, judging from appearances, not so much as theirs. This is because this particular Indian has no heart, no nervous energy, no reserve force. Confronted by the unexpected or inexplicable, he gives no urgency to his efforts, he seeks no solution; he simply gives up. He has none of that do-or-die sentiment; he prefers to die. Dump an Indian and a bound white man into a snow bank, and the latter would probably freeze to death first, but in a struggle for existence under any conditions the white man would go farther and keep going longer than the red man.

As to the bedding question, when I was on my homeward journey in May I noted Indians sleeping under the same number of blankets they had used while I was making my way towards Great Slave Lake in January. What did surprise me at first, however, was the toughness of their feet. I marvelled how they could sleep with them sticking out from under the blankets, with no other protection from the cold than that furnished by the moccasin. I ceased to wonder once I had viewed the quarter-inch layer of epidermis on the heels and soles.

There is some comfort in the reflection that John and I had a good camp that first night we were alone, for there was bitterness enough in store for us in the next four days. To begin with, it was impossible for me to wear snow-shoes in breaking trail for the dogs, although the snow was nearly knee-deep and the going heavy, because I had never used a web snow-shoe before, and consequently was not sufficiently expert to feel the McMurray trail under the foot and a half of snow —and to follow this trail by feeling it was our only means of guidance. Then our bacon was about out, and we had but one meal of fish for the dogs. Therefore I was not hilarious when we started off at four in the morning in a blinding snowstorm. "Shot" had told me something of the nature of the country over which the trail led, but the country was all alike to us in that storm. I know we went through woods, for several times I fell heavily against a tree, but nothing was visible except on closest inspection. My senses were all concentrated on feeling

DOG-WHIP.

that trail, and my energies directed to weathering the storm, whose fury was beginning to be the more perceptible by the dawning of day, when suddenly I dropped through space—I thought at the time about twenty feet, but I guess it was not more than ten—and the dogs and the sledge and John fell on top of me. When we had disentangled ourselves, I had a more puzzling situation to unravel in determining where we were "at."

I felt sure I had not lost the trail, but corroboration was out of the question, because the road made by our dogs and sledge rendered feeling the underlying old one that had guided me impossible. Going ahead a little distance, I found we were on a lake, but could discover no trail, and the storm made travelling by landmarks impossible even had I known any, which of course I did not. John's search for a trail proved no happier than mine, and then he wanted to camp; but I exhausted two-thirds of my Cree vocabulary in "no" and "hurry" upon him, and we made a wider circuit with no better success. This time he was determined to camp; and the sleet was cutting our faces and the dogs were howling and it was miserable. But we didn't camp. Again I made a cast, and this time for a find. I was sure of a piece of trail, but whence it came and whither it went I could not determine. The snow was either blown away or packed so hard it was simply impossible to follow a trail for any distance. We would travel a little way only to lose it and begin our searching anew; another find, followed closely by a check and yet another heart-breaking cast. And thus, how many miles I know not, we worked our way across that Jack Fish Lake in the teeth of a storm that whirled around us unceasingly, and it was one o'clock when we crawled up the bank and discovered a cabin which I knew must be the one where "Shot" had said I could get fish.

We got our dogs on the leeward side, and then staggered into the cabin, covered from head to foot by ice and numb with cold. The house was full of Indians, but there was no exclamation of surprise upon our appearance. Half-frozen men are of too common occurrence in this Northland to create comment. They made way for us at the fire, of which we did not immediately avail ourselves—for we both had frozen ears and noses—and they pushed the teakettle nearer the glowing coals; but no one uttered a sound, though they eyed me with ill-concealed curiosity. By-and-by, when we had thawed out, John and I drank tea and ate a slice of bacon from our scanty stock, and then I signed him to get fish for the dogs; but much talking was followed only by sullen silence, and no fish were forthcoming. Fish we must have; and as I sat pondering over the situation, I discovered a fiddle hanging against the wall, and thought an excellent opportunity offered of trying the power of music to soothe the savage breast, so I handed the instrument to John, whom I had heard play at La Biche, and what with his fiddling and my distribution of tobacco, it was not very long before we had the Indians jabbering again, and two days' fish for the dogs.

The wind was still howling and the snow falling when we started on an hour later, against the protestations of the Indians, who wanted us and our tea and tobacco to remain overnight; but our supplies were too low to warrant their consumption in idleness, and we had put another eight or nine miles behind us before we made a wretched camp in the muskeg, with scarcely wood enough to make a fire, and not a level spot to throw down our blankets. It cleared up during the night, and when we broke camp the next morning at four the moon shone as serenely as though it had not yielded to a greater and fiercer power the night before. Before daybreak the trail ran into some rather open woods, through which the moon's soft light played with wondrously fantastic effect, and when the first streaks of yellow in the northeast heralded the rising of the sun, we had left the shadow of the trees and were travelling in the muskeg. I shall always remember that morning as giving me the most beautiful picture I ever beheld in nature's album: the sun coming up on my right, the moon going down on my left—one bursting forth in all his golden splendor, while the other slowly withdrew her silvery light. And between and far below the two heavenly rivals plodded John and the dogs and I, footsore and hungry, but appreciative.

I was destined to be brought to earth very suddenly and somewhat ingloriously, for the sun had but just dispelled the gray gloom of early morning, and I was clipping along at a merry gait across the deadly muskeg, with a large lake in sight, and John and the dogs not far behind, when down I tumbled in a heap, with a sprained ankle. Sitting in the snow chafing my ankle was not going to bring us food nor get me to the Barren Grounds, so I wound moose-skin tightly about the injured part, and took my place again before the dogs. At first I could not stand without the aid of a stout stick, and we made headway so slowly that after a few miles I threw away my crutch, and in a determination to try the power of mind over matter, limped on.

I should not advise Christian scientists to put their faith to such a test; no convert was ever more open to conviction than I—spirit willing, mind receptive, but the flesh so mortally weak that every time I put down my left foot it gave way to the knee. And so, faith failing, I gritted my teeth and vowed to get on some way. After a while the pain grew duller, and my leg giving under me, I

DRYING FISH—THE STAPLE FOOD OF MAN AND DOG.

discovered the tight binding and the cold had frozen the flesh; as I could not navigate without the support of the mooseskin binding, and a frozen ankle, though less painful, held me up not so well as a twisted one, I was thereafter occupied quite as much in keeping that ankle alive in all its painful sensitiveness as I was in keeping it going at all. We held our way, however, and the lake I had sighted proved to be Big White Fish, where I traded some tobacco for fish for the dogs, but could get none to eke out the little bacon now left us.

Here I had my first view of the manner in which these fish are hung upon stagings — first to dry, subsequently to freeze, and ever to be beyond the reach of the always half-starved dogs. There are other stagings, combining larder and storehouse for the Indian, and more necessary than his lodge, where he puts his meat, fresh pelts, snow-shoes, and sledges. Snow-shoes and sledges do not sound palatable, but the caribou-skin lacings of the former and moose wrapper and lines of the latter make quite a succulent dish, as meals go in this land of feast or famine. Every Indian cabin or lodge has its staging, and all things eatable are hung upon it for safety. And it is here the dogs do congregate to voice their hunger in mournful howling, and vent their frenzied disappointment in furious fighting. Indian dogs spend most of their time fighting; when it is not one another, it is against death by starvation.

MOCCASINS.

If I failed of increasing our supplies at this settlement, I did get a map, which at least aimed to show me the way to plenty. It was a puzzling creation, that map, which one of the Indians drew in my note-book to give us some idea of the direction of the trail across the six lakes that lay between us and the next Indian camp on White Fish Lake. Once at White Fish Lake, and we had but fifteen miles to John MacDonald's, on Big Jack Fish Lake, the McMurray fishery, and home of one of the best known and hardiest *voyageurs* in the country. But Big

Jack Fish Lake was two days' travel away, and meanwhile my ankle made life intolerable, and the map proved more maddening than the fifteen puzzle. We made only seven miles the afternoon of the day I sprained my ankle; we had covered twenty up to noon; but after my rest I could barely move along, and besides, we were continually falling foul of trails, which appeared coming from everywhere, and went nowhere. All this and the following day we travelled over muskeg, particularly severe on me now, with an ankle so tender, and really only one foot with which to feel the road. But, after all, the muskeg was kinder to us than the lakes, for when we reached these we invariably lost the trail, to find and as speedily lose it again, while it was absolutely impossible to judge from its direction where it eventually left the lake. Indians never by any chance travel straight. Throughout the (about) 900 miles of trail I followed from Edmonton to Fort Resolution, on Great Slave Lake, there is but the single exception of the Slave Lake portage; for the rest, it looks as though the original traveller had sat up all night at Edmonton with a sick friend and a barrel, and then started to walk home. At best its windings are hard to follow, but when one may advance only by feeling, its difficulties become tenfold, and yet it is remarkable how skilled one becomes in this method of procedure. I grew sufficiently expert after a time, and where there was good bottom to the trail, to follow it running, about a five-mile-per-hour gait, though there was literally no indication on the snow's surface of a trail beneath.

Added to the misery of bodily ailment, the map distracted me by its deceptions. The lengths of lines drawn by the Indian to represent the portages between the lakes gave no indication of the comparative distances. The first "line" was short, and we covered it in a couple of hours; the next one was about the same length, but we were half a day crossing the country between the two lakes it joined; the third line was fully four times as long as the longer of the other two, yet we were only half an hour going from end to end of it.

And every little while, when a lost or blind trail dismayed us, and we cast about to find our true course, we looked at each other, John and I, and pitied one another

"SOUR GRAPES."

for living. We could not exchange ideas; we could not have the poor comfort of debating the situation; we could only make a few imperfect signs, which expressed little to the point, and seemed frivolous in the face of a situation so desperate. Once our leading dog, who is always called a foregoer, found the trail on the lake, and showed remarkable sagacity, which, by-the-way, we trusted to our sorrow later. This time, however, he came to our rescue when we were utterly lost; he ceased following the imaginary trail I was hobbling along, and after a few casts, settled to a steady gait in another direction. John also thought he had a trail, which he endeavored to persuade the dogs into following, but the foregoer held his way, and when we investigated we found he had really the only trail of the three. The snow was deeper on this part of our route, which made the walking yet harder; but by one way or another we finally crossed the six lakes shown on the Indian's map, and came to White Fish Lake. Here we managed to get just a meal of

fish for the dogs, but none for ourselves, to which, however, we had become accustomed. We rested two hours, while I bathed my feet, much to the wonderment of the natives, to whom it seemed an unaccountable waste of energy, and rubbed my ankle with some of the mustang liniment I had fetched along from La Biche. There were but fourteen miles between us and John MacDonald's cabin, on Big Jack Fish Lake, when we set out again at two o'clock; and the prospect of talking again, and having a roof over my head, nerved me to faster pace. I was destined to see neither MacDonald nor his house that night. Some Indians had recently travelled between the two lakes, so there was a faint trail, which we followed at so good a gait it was not dark when we came to where the road led out on to Big Jack Fish Lake. But by this time a fierce storm had set in, with snow which completely shut off our view twenty feet distant, and wind that swept away the last semblance of a trail. I tried to feel out the road, then John tried, and then we gave the foregoer his head; and, sure enough, he went off at a rate which convinced us he must have found something. And so he had; but we were not seeking the road he found. We travelled about ten miles to get that knowledge.

There is a point which makes out from the north shore of the lake and divides it into two large bays. MacDonald's cabin is on the western bay. I supposed John knew it was. We had held an animated though not entirely successful conversation at White Fish, which I intended should express my wish that he learn the distance, etc. The Cree for "How far is it?" is "Wah-he-ó-che"; for "It is far," you drop only the "che," and say "Wah-he-ó." But I was not then so learned. So I had asked John, "Wah-he-ó-che—Mac-Donald's?" and John had replied—after some discussion with the other Indians "Wah-he-ó." I supposed him correcting me, and as this particular Cree query was my *pièce de résistance*, "Wah-he-o-ché" —with an accent on the "ché"—again pierced the chilly air, and again he retorted, "Wah-he-ó." Then we wah-he-o-ché'd and wah-he-ó'd until each subsided in silence and disgust at the other's stupidity.

And so we travelled down the eastern bay of Big Jack Fish Lake. It got dark by the time we were well out on the lake; we could not have seen our way in broad daylight, because the snow was thickly falling and the wind savagely blowing as we blindly followed the tail of our sledge. By-and-by I decided we must be going wrong, for I thought the cabin could not be so far off as we had come, and I got John and the dogs turned about to go back and into the western bay. The storm was now squarely in our teeth, and the dogs would not face it. They kept turning and entangling themselves in the harness, while we were faint with hunger and benumbed with cold, and my ankle seemed bursting with pain.

I made the nearest approach I could in the storm to a bee-line for the point, and then followed it around. I had not the remotest idea where MacDonald's house was, but I knew I should have to find it in the morning to get my bearings; so after we had gone about as far down the western bay as we had into the eastern, we camped under a pine-tree, where wood was plentiful, and ate a piece of bacon each and drank a cup of tea, after

a hard day's tramp—which my pedometer registered as forty-four miles. Our dogs ate the last of their fish, John and I were on half-allowance of the poor rations we had, we were lost, and it did not seem as if my ankle would permit me to walk another step. The world was not very bright when we camped that night.

As we sat silently drinking our tea we heard something approaching, and instantly alert, with that protective and hunter's instinct which comes to the traveller of the wilds, listened intently, until we discovered the swishing, grating of a snow-shoe heel. It was Kipling, a famous Soto Indian runner, who had come to invite me to MacDonald's cabin, where, but a mile beyond, they had seen our camp-fire. James Spencer, the Hudson Bay Company's officer in charge of McMurray, had brought thus far on its journey the one winter packet that reaches the railroad from this isolated wilderness, and was returning the next morning early. Here was good news indeed, and good luck—the first of my trip. But John had stuck by me, and I was not going to leave him on the conclusion of so hard a day; therefore I sent my grateful thanks to Spencer, saying I would be on hand the following morning. And so the clouds rolled away, and the worry within and the storm without ceased as I lay down to sleep that night.

It was a very lively scene at MacDonald's next morning, and a most interesting one to me; for the packet was starting on its last stage, and as to carry the packet is one of the few honors in the country, the dogs were handsomer and more gayly harnessed than any I had seen. It was only seventy miles to McMurray, but the two days we consumed in getting there were most trying, and I shall never forget the ten-mile crossing of Swan Lake the first morning. We camped for dinner midway, on an island, but it seemed as though I should never reach it; and a mirage added confusion by placing it now near by and then far away, and all the time the hard ice made running particularly torturing to my ankle. The tea was made by the time I finally put my foot on that island. It was exceedingly hard going for men and dogs all the way to McMurray, for the trail led down Clear Water River, on which the supplies in early days were brought into the country, and the snow was deep. We were all worn, and I was thankful indeed when the light of Spencer's cabin pierced the darkness and I knew I had put 240 miles of my long journey behind me.

How I relished a good wash and a satisfying meal I shall not attempt to say; few of my readers have gone without either or both, and could not appreciate my feelings. Nor could I adequately express my gratitude to Spencer and his wife for their unceasing kindness. I spent one day at McMurray, which is located at the junction of the Clear Water and Athabasca rivers, doctoring my ankle and awaiting fresh dogs and guides; for here John and his dogs, after a rest, turned back. If Spencer had been of Gairdner's sort I should have been delayed again, for none of the Indians took kindly to the trip on to Chipewyan, the next post. Those that had promised backed out, and finally Spencer turned over to me the train which had brought the packet from Chipewyan to McMurray. There were four good strong dogs; François, French half-breed, one of the best dog-drivers and runners in the land; and "Old" Jacob, a Soto Indian, to break trail, who as young Jacob was famous for strength and speed, and who even now could beat all but the very best on snow-shoes. Both could talk and understand enough

English to make some sort of conversation possible, and both knew the road, so that the clouds revealed only their silver lining as we started out from McMurray. I was not seeking trouble, but it came just the same. I had never worn moccasins until I left La Biche. I had never used the web snow-shoe until I left McMurray, and therefore the second day out my feet were so blistered and lacerated by the lacings that blood dyed my duffel, and walking was agony. Hitherto I had been counting my progress by days; now I reckoned by the fires, of which we made three daily, when we drank tea and my misery enjoyed a brief respite. It was cold, bitterly cold, and the wind swept up the Athabasca River, down which we travelled, apparently coming directly from the north pole. But neither wind nor painful travelling nor hunger, which we experienced the last two days, delayed us, and when we finally reached the shores of Lake Athabasca, and viewed the Hudson Bay Company's fortlike post four miles away, it was like a sight of the promised land. I had been twenty days on the road, and come about 580 miles from the railroad, so that, what with lacerated feet, twisted ankle, and fatigue, I was pretty well used up when I passed through the gateway of Fort Chipewyan.

FORT CHIPEWYAN.

DAKOTA

ABOUT half-way between the Atlantic and Pacific oceans, on the northern boundary of the republic, is situated a Territory greater in area than either the kingdoms of Norway, Great Britain, or Italy, and more extensive than the combined surfaces of Maine, New Hampshire, New Jersey, Vermont, Rhode Island, New York, Maryland, two Massachusetts, three Delawares, three Connecticuts, and a half-dozen Districts of Columbia, all united in one. This is Dakota, whose Indian name, signifying leagued, aptly describes her population, drawn from every State of the Union, from all nationalities of the globe, and banded together with the one purpose of founding a home and enjoying the comforts and independence that word implies.

Attempts at settlement for agricultural purposes date from 1856, but the handful of pioneers, confined to the most southerly counties, were constantly harassed and frequently driven from their homes by hostile Indians, so that the increase of population was not noticeable until after the close of the civil war.

Congress created the Territory of Dakota in 1861, and President Lincoln, in the same year, appointed Hon. William Jayne, of Illinois, the first Governor. Eleven years after this date the building of two lines of railway across the eastern boundary—one coming from Minnesota and the other from Iowa, and the discovery of gold in the Black Hills by the expedition under General Custer in 1874, led to a decided activity in the settlement of the Red River Valley, in the north, the counties of the extreme southeast, and the rich mineral district of the west—a growth which, spreading with each succeeding year, marks one of the most marvellous epochs in the history of the population of the West.

The national census of 1860 gave Dakota a population of less than 5000; that of 1870, 14,000; of 1880, 135,000; and five years later this number had increased, as shown by a federal census, to 415,610. Governor Church, in his annual report to the Secretary of the Interior (June 30, 1888), says that the present population of the Territory is 640,823.

Illinois, Kansas, or Minnesota may boast of prairie-land, but nowhere else in America is there a plain so even, broad, and gently undulating as the vast surface of Dakota, an expanse equivalent in length to the distance separating New York city and Cleveland, Ohio, and as far across in breadth as from Philadelphia, Pennsylvania, to Raleigh, North Carolina. An occasional mound or collection of buttes, the low hills of the Plateau du Coteau du Missouri, and the broken borders of the larger streams and lakes, give a slight and pleasing irregularity to such an ocean of level land. The Black Hills, covering nearly four counties, in the southwest, are the only considerable elevations within the Territory. Harney's Peak is 8200 feet high. The surface in general is free from rocky

ARTESIAN-WELL, YANKTON.

of finding strong underground veins at an ordinary depth.

The artesian-wells of Dakota are probably the most remarkable for pressure, and the immense quantity of water supplied, of any ever opened. More than a hundred of such wells, from 500 to 1600 feet deep, are to-day in successful operation, distributed throughout twenty-nine counties, from Yankton, in the extreme south, to Pembina, in the extreme north, giving forth a constant, never-varying stream, which is in no wise affected by the increased number of wells, and showing a gauge pressure in some instances as high as 160, 170, 175, and 187 pounds to the square inch. This tremendous power is utilized, in the more important towns, for water supply, fire protection, and the driving of machinery, at a wonderful saving on the original cost of plant and maintenance, when compared with steam. In the city of Yankton a forty-horse power turbine-wheel, operating a tow-mill by day and an electric-light plant by night, is driven by the force of water flowing from an artesian-well, the cost of obtaining which was no greater than would have been the cost of a steam-engine developing the same power, not counting the continual outlay necessary (had steam been employed) for fuel, repairs, and the salaries of engineer and fireman. What has been accomplished through the aid of natural gas and cheap fuel in building up manufactories elsewhere, may some day be rivalled on the prairies of Dakota by tapping the inexhaustible power stored in nature's reservoirs beneath the surface.

The soil is a rich black alluvial loam from two to four feet in depth, underlying which is a brown clay subsoil of several feet.

The beautiful carpet of natural grasses, buffalo, gramma, and blue-stem, stretching away in a vista confined only by the cloudless horizon, variegated by the coloring of greenest hue of growing grain, and by the bloom of the many flowers peculiar to the prairies, is a sight in the spring-time which fills the mind with that admiration of the grandeur of nature one experiences when upon the ocean or in the presence of mighty mountains. These rich, nutritious grasses are a source of wealth to the farmer and stock-grower

deposit or heavy forests, and the ploughman may turn his furrow for miles with never a deflection because of stump or stone.

The Missouri River, flowing from northwest to southeast, bisects the Territory, and furnishes, within her borders, upward of a thousand miles of navigable waters. The Red River of the North is navigable for steamers of two or three hundred tons burden nearly its entire course.

Smaller streams and lakes of pure water abound in every section, and these are fringed usually with a growth, somewhat sparse, of native trees—the varieties oftener met with including the cottonwood, ash, box-elder, oak, aspen, and willow. Norway pine grows abundantly in the Black Hills, and of suitable size for lumber.

Where the surface supply of water is lacking, wells, sunk or driven, seldom fail

equalling that from the cultivated varieties of the East, and whether fed as hay or grazed from the already cured fields of the prairies, stock eat it greedily, and are fattened at literally no expense.

The notoriety of the Territory abroad has been established mainly, it would appear, on the fame of her wheat crop, and as being the birthplace of the "blizzard." Dakota is satisfied with, and feels that she has fairly won, the title of the grain field of America; but the testimony of her inhabitants and the proof of weather observations (as recorded by the United States Signal Service Bureau, army surgeons, and voluntary observers, covering in all a period of fifteen years) completely refute the standard Eastern idea of Dakota's climate.

The mean annual temperature of the entire stretch of country extending north from the northern boundary line of Nebraska — more than 400 miles — to the southern boundary of Canada is 41.5°, an average higher than that of either the State of Minnesota or New Hampshire. In the section of the Territory situated south of a line extended westward through Huron, on the James River, north of Fort Sully, on the Missouri River, and thence to Deadwood, in the Black Hills, the mean annual temperature is 45°, or about that of Nebraska, Iowa, northern Illinois, southern Michigan, Pennsylvania, and New York. The coldest month of the year is January, the thermometer indicating in that month an average temperature covering the whole area of this vast country of 7° above zero. The mean temperature for July, the warmest month, is 72°. The average temperature of the three winter months is 11.8°; of the spring, 41.1°; and of the summer, 69.1°. The average temperature of the fall (September, October, and November) is 44.1°, or three degrees higher than during the three months of spring. There are really but two seasons in Dakota, summer and winter; the transition from snow to rain, from the cold of winter to the heat of summer, occurring with remarkable suddenness, generally in March, though sometimes as early as February. During the month of January the thermometer frequently registers a very low temperature, occasionally going 40° or more below zero; and yet, contrary to general opinion, these days of extreme cold are

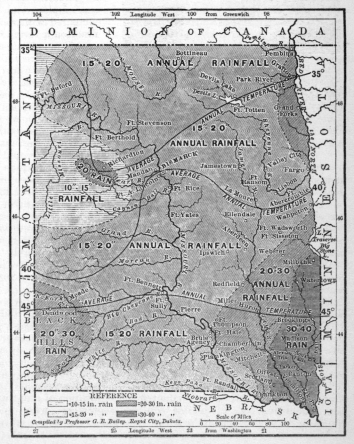

DAKOTA WEATHER MAP.

not the most trying. When it is the coldest the sky is cloudless and the sun shines with a midsummer splendor, the atmosphere is at perfect rest, and the crackling of the frost, the crunching of the trodden snow, together with the intoxicating effect of each breath of dry, frozen air, create an exhilaration almost indescribable. An actual inspection of the thermometer is necessary to convince one that it is really so cold. The atmosphere, almost absolutely devoid of humidity, never penetrates and chills with that cold one feels in the damp, saturated air of the seaboard States. The most disagreeable storms of the winter occur when the temperature is but a few degrees below zero, and are accompanied by strong winds, blowing almost a hurricane, generally from the northwest, which swirl the dry powdered snow in whirlpools through the air, bewildering stock and blinding the traveller. On such occasions traffic is impeded, trains are halted, the farmer makes no attempt to feed his flocks, the wayfarer remains housed, or, if unfortunately caught out upon the prairie (and he is wise), he protects himself as well as possible, but stirs not a step until the storm has passed. Neither man nor beast can long withstand the facing of the keen, penetrating blasts or of the blinding particles of snow. All ideas of distance or of direction are lost in the confusion of the winds and the obscured atmosphere, and without these to guide him the traveller on the prairies is as a ship without a compass.

Fortunately storms of such severity are neither of long duration nor of frequent occurrence. The most disastrous one on record was the storm which swept over the Territory on the 12th of January, 1888, and the one concerning which the most woful exaggerations and distortions were circulated abroad.

The depth of snow upon the ground is light, when compared with the snowfall of the New England States, of New York, of Michigan, or Minnesota; and even though the season may be one of extraordinary severity, the total snowfall of a winter is less than four feet. Travel, overland or by rail, is maintained during the winter months, with but an occasional interruption from drifts of snow deposited by high winds in the depressions of the road.

The summer days are warm, made excessively so at times by the "Chinook wind"—that remnant of the Japan current which, blowing through the mountain passes of Montana, and distributed by the great valley of the Missouri over the plains of Dakota, so materially reduces the cold of winter and adds to the heat of July. But whatever the unusual heat of the day, the temperature invariably falls at night to a degree insuring rest and refreshing slumber.

From the report of the Chief Signal Officer for 1886 (the only report available) it is learned that in Dakota three hundred and two days of the year were classed as either fair or clear, leaving sixty-three days, or an average of only five cloudy or stormy days to a month.

The warmth of summer lingers through the months of September and October, and it is not until late in December usually that winter assumes the mastery.

For pulmonary or bronchial troubles the rare, dry, and pure air is especially beneficial. No breath of miasma taints the atmosphere, and fearful scourges or depopulating epidemics are unknown.

The average annual precipitation (rainfall and melted snow) in the Territory, covering a period of sixteen years, is 22.35 inches. In April the average rainfall is 2.50 inches; May, 3.20; June, 3.64; July, 3.10; and in August, 2.65 inches.

The pulverizing of the naturally impervious sod, the prevention of prairie fires, the planting of trees, the building of cities, railways, and the other changes following on settlement, are bringing about the same gradual but certain increase of rainfall, in Dakota which came with the reclaiming of those sections of the West and Northwest now contained within the boundaries of well-known and prosperous States. The rainfall during the period from 1880 to 1887 exceeded that of the period from 1872 to 1879 by a yearly average of 0.39 of an inch.

The known mineral deposits of the Territory, other than the extensive granite beds of the southeast and the coal fields of the northwest, are confined to the Black Hills region, comprised in the five counties of Butte, Lawrence, Pennington, Custer, and Fall River, on the boundary line separating Wyoming and Dakota.

No other section of equal area on the face of the globe presents the varied resources of this favored spot. Here are valleys of excellent farming land, hills clothed with nutritious pasturage, and

HOMESTAKE MINING WORKS, LEAD CITY.

furnishing natural shelter for stock, and mountains containing many of the minerals most valuable to commerce, science, and art, including deposits of gold, silver, copper, tin, lead, iron, coal, petroleum, salt, mica, marble, and porphyry.

At Lead City, near Deadwood, Lawrence County, are located the largest gold mines and mills in the world, the "Homestake." The ore bodies mined by this company show a working face from two hundred to four hundred feet wide, sinking to an inexhaustible depth. Six hundred stamps, crushing 20,000 cubic feet of rock every twenty-four hours, drop incessantly, day and night, in the several mills, without an intermission even for the Sabbath. During the ten years in which the mines of the Homestake combination have been operated they have produced about $25,000,000 in bullion, and paid over $6,000,000 in dividends to stockholders.

Eight miles south of Deadwood, in the Galena district, silver ore is found in paying quantities, and is successfully reduced by the smelting process.

The Black Hills are seamed with veins of ore-bearing rock, which will return from $25 to $200 in gold to the ton of ore crushed. But unfortunately much of the ore is refractory, and cannot be treated by the ordinary process of amalgamation. Only recently the fact has been established that by the method known as lixiviation the precious metals could be cheaply separated from the stubborn rock, and following this discovery the immediate construction at Deadwood of leaching-works of one hundred tons capacity, at a cost of $120,000, has been undertaken.

Mine owners have been waiting for years the solving of the vexing problem of how to treat the peculiar ores of Ruby, Bald Mountain, and other districts cheaply. The wealth and development which are certain to result to the Black Hills from this discovery can scarcely be estimated.

But of far greater importance to the Territory, and indeed to all America, exceeding in prospective value any mines of the precious metals, are the rich and extensive deposits of tinstone. The United States imports annually tin-plates exceeding $17,000,000 in value—a contribution to English trade which has existed from the foundation of the government, and promised (before the discovery of tin in Dakota was made) to grow with added years. So far as discovered the tinstone is confined within two separate districts—the northern section west of Deadwood, Lawrence County, and the southern or Harney's Peak section between Rapid City, Pennington County, and Custer, in the county of the same name. The tin-

stone is found in granitic veins, sometimes hundreds of feet in width, and yields from two to four per cent. By comparison with foreign tin mines it will be seen that this percentage is unusually heavy. The mines of Saxony return a yield of from one-half to one per cent., while in Cornwall the average is less than two per cent.

English capital is largely interested in the ownership and development of the Harney's Peak deposits, and American tin will soon be quoted in the markets of the world.

Professor Frank R. Carpenter, dean of the Dakota School of Mines, Rapid City, has demonstrated by recent tests that the tin can be separated from the encompassing rock by the very simple process of "jigging," the machinery to accomplish which costing but a comparatively small sum. As a result we may look for the development of tin mines and the erection of separating plants where, before, the large amount of capital required to establish the plant was an insurmountable barrier.

Mica is found abundantly, and is mined for commercial uses. Beds of gypsum and deposits of fire and potters' clay furnish a supply of these materials exceeding any possible demand. Bricks of excellent quality are made in every section of the Territory.

Lignite, or brown coal, underlies all that country west of a line drawn from the Turtle Mountains in the north, to the Black Hills in the southwest,

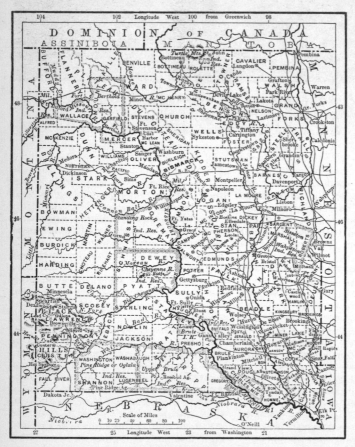

MAP OF DAKOTA.

OPEN CUT OF THE ETTA TIN MINE, BLACK HILLS.

and outcrops frequently in veins varying from five to twenty-five feet in thickness. It is an inferior quality of coal, but burns readily and furnishes a good heat. Mines are operated in Morton, Stark, Billings, and Ward counties, on the lines of the St. Paul, Minneapolis, and Manitoba, and the Northern Pacific railways.

In the vicinity of the mines the coal sells very low, from fifty cents to one dollar per ton, but excessive transportation charges have prevented thus far any general use of this native fuel. The ease with which it can be mined and the great area of the coal fields insure to the inhabitants of the Territory, when the extension of railway systems shall have brought about a reasonable tariff for carriage, a good fuel at one-third the present cost of imported coal.

Natural gas has been discovered in several localities, notably in Sully, Stutsman, Cass, and Spink counties. The discovery in each instance was more the result of accident than of any systematic investigation, and no effort has been made to utilize the flow, with the one exception of the hotel at Ashton, Spink County, where the kitchen fires are fed by this fuel.

In Minnehaha County, in the vicinity of Sioux Falls and Dell Rapids, there is an outcropping of quartzite, with an exposed facing of some sixty or eighty feet. The stone has a pleasing flesh-colored tint, is exceedingly hard, and takes a beautiful polish, equalling the finest granite quarried in Scotland. An army of men finds employment in quarrying, dressing, and polishing the granite used for building and ornamental purposes, and in shaping it into paving blocks, which are shipped to Chicago, Kansas City, Omaha, and other Western cities.

Farming is the chief industry of the Territory, and the growing of wheat is the leading occupation of the farmer. With cheap lands and a rich soil easy of cultivation, requiring no preparation other than the turning of the sod, wheat is grown at a minimum cost for production, which varies from twenty-four cents per bushel, on the bonanza farms of the Red River Valley (where the large area tilled and the employment of special machinery result in more than the usual economy), to thirty-six cents per bushel, the general average of cost on farms of ordinary size. The settler begins his operations on a very small capital, generally no more than four or five hundred dollars, and indeed the sole capital of many who now are prosperous and own valuable farms consisted of muscle and a determination to succeed. From such small beginnings have sprung the present magnificent grain fields of the Territory.

In 1860 less than a thousand bushels of wheat were raised in the Territory; in 1870 the crop amounted to 170,662 bushels; 2,830,289 bushels in 1880; 38,166,413 bushels in 1885; and in 1887, by the estimate of the statistician of the national Department of Agriculture, 52,406,000 bushels, or rather, if the evidences in the hands of the Territorial statistician are to be relied upon, 62,553,499 bushels.

The wheat grown is all of the spring variety, is planted during the months of March and April (sometimes as early as February), and harvested in July and August. Threshing immediately follows, generally directly from the shock, and within about four months from the time of seeding the new crop is on its way to the elevators of Minneapolis, Duluth, and Chicago. The commercial value of Dakota-grown wheat is based on its peculiar hardness, dryness, and richness in albuminoids. These qualities give it a special grade — "No. 1, hard" — and bring the highest market price in the great milling and wheat centres of the world.

Oats, rye, barley, buckwheat, flax, sorghum-cane, potatoes, and all kind of vegetables are grown extensively, and return a large yield. In 1860 the crop of oats amounted to 2540 bushels; in 1887 this had increased to 43,267,478 bushels. The yield of flax in 1887 was 3,910,944 bushels; of barley, 6,400,568 bushels; rye, 316,586 bushels; and buckwheat, 97,230 bushels.

There is a growing tendency among the farmers occupying the well-tilled sections of the Territory toward mixed farming and the diversifying of farm products. Each year sees an increased area sown to corn, oats, root crops, and other fodder for stock.

A few years ago it was said that corn would not mature in this climate. To-day it is the leading crop of the southern counties, and the area planted in central Dakota, the Black Hills, and along the Missouri River Valley is rapidly approaching the acreage devoted to wheat. The yield of corn in 1885 was 7,800,593 bushels; two years later, in 1887, the yield had increased more than 200 per cent., and, as reported to the Territorial statistician, amounted to 24,511,726 bushels.

In 1887 the value of live-stock reached the sum of $43,195,229, a sum fifty per cent. greater than the value of the three principal farm products—wheat, corn, and oats—of the same year. Seven years previous—in 1880—the total value of Dakota's live-stock amounted to $6,463,274, showing an average annual increase, during the period between 1880 and 1887, of about $5,000,000. In 1886 there were owned by the farmers and stock-growers of the Territory 710,934 head of cattle and 199,480 milch cows, valued at $21,445,302; 227,027 horses, valued at $17,618,192; 11,964 mules, valued at $1,194,622; 427,176 hogs, valued at $2,314,013; and 256,209 sheep, valued at $623,100.

Cows, horses, sheep, and other cattle are fed throughout the year almost solely on the native grasses, and do remarkably well, coming out in the spring, if properly cared for, strong and in good flesh. These wild grasses cure to hay upon the ground, and are quite as rich and nutritious grazed in the winter season as in the summer. They cover every acre of prairie, of coteau, of valley land, a generous gift, which is all but wasted in that probably less than one acre of a thousand is utilized.

The climate is comparatively dry, and entirely free from prolonged rainy seasons of spring and fall—an advantage which attracts stock-men, because it insures security from many of those scourges which sometimes carry off entire flocks in the damp, moist climate of other localities. Sheep-raising is a specially successful venture, the diseases commonly so fatal to sheep being unknown within the Territory.

At least half a hundred creameries and no less than a dozen cheese factories are established in the more important localities—a conclusive proof of the growing interest in dairying and mixed farming.

The rapid expansion of the area planted to corn has carried with it a corresponding increase of investment in hog-raising—this increase in 1887 amounting to as much as twenty-five per cent.

Hogs contribute largely to the revenue of the farmer in all that district south of the seventh standard parallel; and packing-houses in many towns not only supply the local demand, but find a market beyond the boundaries of the Territory.

One who has been a resident of this section of the Northwest the past five years cannot fail to observe the rapid improvement in the quality of the stock grown by the farmer. Through the encroachment of settlements and the heavy losses of cattle on the plains during the severe winter of 1886-7 the business of growing stock on ranges, without feed or shelter, has suffered immeasurably. Stock-growers of the Northwest have learned by costly experience that at least a little of that care and expense attending successful ventures in cattle-raising elsewhere is necessary in a country even so favored in the matter of rich grazing lands and equable climate as Dakota, and that, when it comes to feeding and sheltering, it is more profitable to grow an animal of good strain than a common one. As a result we find at the head of the herd on the farm, and exhibited at the county stock shows and Territorial fairs (of which two are held annually—one in North Dakota, one in South Dakota), Short-horn, Hereford, Polled Angus, Holstein, Jersey, and other high-grade cattle, imported draught-horses, and sheep and swine of the best standard breeds.

The Farmers' Alliance of Dakota, an organized movement on the part of those engaged in agriculture to protect and advance their interests, has been in existence four years, and developed great following and strength. The Alliance conducts (for the benefit of its members) a fire-insurance company, having a paid-up capital of $100,000; a hail-insurance company on the mutual plan; a purchasing department, capital $200,000; and an elevator company, with a capital stock of $2,000,000. President H. L. Loucks, the able and efficient head of the organization, estimates the present membership of the Dakota Alliance at 17,000 farmers.

It should be remembered that this position in agricultural development has been attained with only a small fraction of her tillable lands under cultivation, with 27,000,000 acres (or an area greater than that of the State of Ohio) bound up in Indian reservations, not a foot of which, while so reserved, is subject to entry or development, and with 24,000,000 acres of the public domain outside of these reservations (a stretch of country nearly as large as the State of New York) unoccupied.

In 1860 the total value of improved lands in the Territory was rated at $96,445; in 1880, at $22,401,084; and in 1885, at $156,767,918. In 1860 but 26,448 acres were farmed, which in 1880 had increased to 3,800,656 acres, and in 1885 to 16,842,412 acres.

The total assessed valuation of taxable property in 1880 (exclusive of railroads) amounted to $20,321,530, in 1887 to $157,084,365. The average assessed valuation of lands per acre in 1887 was $3 67, and the average tax levy for Territorial purposes, $2\frac{9}{10}$ mills on the dollar. The net annual income of the Territory from taxation amounts to nearly $400,000, and the disbursements to about $325,000.

The total bonded indebtedness approximates the sum of one million dollars, or only three-fifths of one per cent. of the present assessed valuation. Of these bonds $409,100, bearing interest at four and one-half per cent. per annum, sold in May, 1887, for a premium of one-half of one per cent.—a pretty strong endorsement by capitalists of the financial condition of the Territory.

Out of the funds derived from the sale of her bonds Dakota has established and maintains twelve public institutions, with an actual cash investment in the buildings and permanent improvements of each as follows:

Agricultural College, Brookings, Brookings County....	$100,140 00
University of North Dakota, Grand Forks, Grand Forks County	88,241 80
University of Dakota, Vermilion, Clay County	88,500 00
Normal School, Madison, Lake County..........	35,800 00
Normal School, Spearfish, Lawrence County	30,000 00
School of Mines, Rapid City, Pennington County ..	35,820 00
School for Deaf-Mutes, Sioux Falls, Minnehaha County ..	53,512 00
Dakota Penitentiary, Sioux Falls, Minnehaha County ..	101,475 00
Bismarck Penitentiary, Bismarck, Burleigh County......	95,281 20
North Dakota Hospital for the Insane, Jamestown, Stutsman County....	276,200 00
Dakota Hospital for the Insane, Yankton, Yankton County	239,960 00
Dakota Reform School, Plankinton, Aurora County......	30,000 00
Making in all.........$1,174,930 00	

THE CAPITOL, BISMARCK.

These buildings are commodious, tasty structures of brick and stone, surrounded by ample grounds, and supplied in nearly every instance with all modern improvements, such as water-works, drainage systems, electric-light plants, steam-heating apparatus, etc.

Under the terms of the removal of the capital from Yankton in 1883, the city of Bismarck, its new location, donated to the Territory the present Capitol building, together with 320 acres of land—a gift of the value of $200,000.

The total county indebtedness of the Territory, bonded and floating, deducting cash on hand and in sinking-funds, makes a sum less than $3,000,000, or about two per cent. of the assessed valuation of Dakota in 1887.

Ten years ago the commercial interests of the Territory were cared for by the eleven banking institutions then existing, whose united capital amounted to $70,000. The banking and loan business of this year is transacted by two hundred and thirty-seven private banks, sixty-two national banks, and fifty-one mortgage and loan companies, with a total capital thus engaged of $11,293,000.

Seventeen years ago the first mile of railway was constructed across the boundaries of the Territory; to-day there are 4333 miles of completed track within her borders, or a railway mileage greater than that of either California, Kentucky, Massachusetts, or any one of more than one-half of the States of the Union. The construction of newly graded roads during the year 1887 amounted to 1017 miles, of which 716 miles were completed and in operation when the building season closed.

Two companies, the Chicago, Milwaukee, and St. Paul, and the St. Paul, Minneapolis, and Manitoba, each alone own and operate more than a thousand miles of railway in Dakota. The Northern Pacific lines cover 830 miles in the Territory, and those of the Chicago and Northwestern 761. These four great railway corporations of the Northwest, with their main and branch roads, reach not only every important city, town, and village, but far out upon the broad prairies, ahead of settlement or surveys, in an emulous

LEWIS McLOUTH.

strife for the possession of valuable territory.

The principal eastern connections and
markets of North Dakota are Minneapolis, St. Paul, and Duluth; and of South
Dakota, Chicago.

The aggressive, pushing policy of Northwestern railways in extending lines in advance of settlement is the secret of Dakota's rapid development and population.
The first settlers of Kansas, of Minnesota,
of Iowa, sought the West by slow and difficult wagon journeys, and awaited thereafter for years the approach of the steam-
engine, which in those days came only
when the pioneer had sufficiently developed the country to
insure to railroads
a paying traffic.
Now the immigrant
is carried quickly
and comfortably by
palace-car trains to
his new home, be it
on the prairies of
Dakota, the moun-
tain slopes of Mon-
tana, or the ocean
shores of Washing-
ton Territory.

Notwithstanding
this abnormal
growth in popula-
tion and of devel-
opment, the cause
of education has
kept abreast of
progress in other
directions. More

than four thousand public-school buildings are scattered over the length and
breadth of the Territory, serving the double purpose of finger-boards pointing the
youth to knowledge, and guide-posts directing the traveller from one township
to another.

Every single dollar expended in the
construction and maintenance of these
4065 schools has been raised by a direct
tax upon the people, an expenditure which
in 1887 amounted to $1,633,561, or a larger
sum than was devoted to the same purpose by any one of twenty-four States.

The reserved school lands, estimated to
exceed 5,000,000 acres (available when the
Territory attains Statehood), even at present values insure a future school fund
sufficient to cover the most liberal expen-
ditures of the commonwealth.

Seven institutions established and fostered by the Territory provide for higher education and instruction in special
branches. These are the Agricultural College, Brookings; University of North Dakota, Grand Forks; the University of Dakota, Vermilion; the State Normal School,
Madison; the Normal School, Spearfish;
the School of Mines, Rapid City; and the
Dakota School for Deaf-Mutes, Sioux
Falls. All are provided with suitable
buildings, and managed by faculties of
able instructors.

In addition to the public institutions
there are fourteen colleges, universities,
and denominational academies.

HIGH-SCHOOL BUILDING, BISMARCK.

THE UNIVERSITY OF DAKOTA, VERMILION.

Of the denominational institutions having substantial structures and a widespread patronage there are the Yankton College, at Yankton (Congregational); Pierre University, at Pierre (Presbyterian); Sioux Falls University, at Sioux Falls (Baptist); All-Saints' School, at Sioux Falls (Episcopalian); Jamestown College, at Jamestown.

The interest displayed in educational matters is always an index of the religious and moral culture of a community. This holds true of Dakota, where the ratio of schools and colleges to the population is borne out in the number of churches established and pastors supported by the Territory. Towering church spires on the prairie, like signal-lights of the harbor, point out each city, town, or modest village. No matter how recent the settlement, how ambitious the strife for worldly possessions, the church and school are there, the site and foundations for which occupy the first cares of every new community. A recent official publication estimates the entire value of all church property as exceeding the sum of $3,000,000, the number of church edifices at 600, and the number of church societies at 1000, supporting 800 pastors, or an average of one church organization to each post-office in the Territory.

Quite a noticeable feature connected with the settlement of Dakota is the number of young men between the ages of twenty-one and thirty-five making up her population. They predominate, whether on the farm, in the trades, professions, and business undertakings, or in political and official management of Territorial and local affairs, and give to every enterprise that push and ambitious effort which has made a national reputation for the people.

The proportion of foreign-born to the entire population is about one in three, or at least that was the ratio in 1885, as shown by the federal census, and there is no reason to suppose it has changed in the three years since. A majority of the settlers of foreign nativity are Scandinavians, next come the Germans, Canadians, Irish, and Russians, in the order mentioned. One can scarcely name a foreign country which is unrepresented among the inhabitants of the Territory. Colonies of Jews from Poland, Mennonites from Russia, Turks from Roumelia, natives of Iceland, and representatives of nearly every clime, color, and religious sect upon the globe, are here engaged side by side in that struggle for home and independence which marks the better civilization of the world.

With the maturer growth of cities and communities there is observed the birth of literary and scientific organizations, the foundation of public libraries, and an expansion of social amenities.

The largest city of Dakota contains less than 12,000 inhabitants, while the pushing, energetic towns with from 1000 to 5000 population, that confidently look forward to a future akin to that of Chicago or St. Louis, are innumerable. One may judge of the great number of towns and villages dotting the prairies when it is stated that more post-offices are maintained in Dakota by the general government than in Massachusetts.

Bismarck, in North Dakota, the Burleigh county-seat, and the capital of the Territory, is situated on a plateau sloping gently from the low encircling hills to a frontage on the Missouri River—a site apparently designed by nature for the building up of a beautiful and prosperous city. The town was platted in 1872, and named in honor of Prince Otto von Bismarck, as a compliment to the German interests connected with the construction of the Northern Pacific Railroad. The city has a population of 4500, three school buildings, valued at $30,000, six church edifices, United States land-office, City Hall, court-house, brewery, flour-mill, and other manufacturing enterprises, water-works system, electric-light plant, etc. The Capitol building and North Dakota Penitentiary are located on commanding sites near the outskirts of the city. The vast extent of excellent farming lands, the proximity of coal fields, and the advantages of a river commerce are the foundations of the city's growth and prosperity.

Ten years ago the population of Sioux Falls, the Minnehaha county-seat, in the southeastern part of the Territory, was 697. It has now a population of 11,000, and is the largest city of Dakota. Five railroad systems, the Chicago and Northwestern, the Chicago, Milwaukee, and St. Paul, the Chicago, Rock Island, and Pacific, the Illinois Central, and the St. Paul, Minneapolis, and Manitoba, give to Sioux Falls unusual transportation facilities. The Big Sioux River furnishes, at this point, a splendid power in a series of falls, with a total descent of ninety feet. The quarrying, shaping, and polishing of the granite which underlies the city forms one of the chief industries of the place. Sioux Falls is provided with street-car lines, water-works system, gas, electric-light plant, free postal delivery, public library, seven banks, fifteen houses of public worship, five brick

and stone school buildings, and twenty manufacturing establishments, employing more than $1,000,000 in capital. Two Territorial institutions, the South Dakota Penitentiary and the School for Deaf-Mutes, and four colleges, under the management of the Episcopal, Baptist, Catholic, and Norwegian Lutheran denominations, are located in the city.

Fargo, at the head of navigation on the Red River of the North, has grown from the small village of 1874 to its present population, about 10,000. Seven passenger trains leave the city daily for St. Paul and the East, via the Northern Pacific, the St. Paul, Minneapolis, and Manitoba, and the Chicago, Milwaukee, and St. Paul railway systems, whose main lines or branches connect Fargo with every section of the Territory and the two oceans. The city is the financial and commercial centre of North Dakota, having six banks, three incorporated loaning agencies, a flour-mill (one of the largest in the Territory), and several other manufacturing establishments. Six public-school buildings, valued at $125,000, and the Congregational College of North Dakota, furnish excellent educational facilities. Of churches there are eleven edifices, representing various denominations. The county buildings, including a court-house, sheriff's residence, and jail, were erected at a cost of $160,000. In 1887 the assessed valuation of real and personal property in the city amounted to $3,600,000, and in the county to $13,000,000.

One of the prettiest cities of the Territory, as well as the oldest, is Yankton, the first capital of Dakota, situated on the southern boundary line, near the point where the James River empties into the Missouri. The present population of the city is about 5000, with five banks, seven churches, five school buildings, seven newspapers, United States land-office, a fine flouring-mill, two founderies, creamery, woollen factory, linseed-oil mill, two breweries, packing-house, comb factory, marble-works, pressed-brick works, soap factory, and two railroads—the Chicago, Milwaukee, and St. Paul, and the Chicago and Northwestern. Yankton College and the Academy of the Sacred Heart are institutions of higher education, well attended and ably managed.

Situated at the junction of the deep, narrow gorges of two mountain streams, in the very heart of the Black Hills, is

FALLS OF THE BIG SIOUX RIVER.

the city of Deadwood, the centre of a rich mining district, the county-seat of Lawrence County. Incorporated in 1881, the city now has a population of 5000, and supports three national banks (with a paid-up capital of $500,000), two daily and two weekly newspapers, water-works system, electric-light plant, eight hotels, three machine-shops, four planing-mills, two founderies, a 200-barrel flouring-mill, United States land-office, three ward schools and one high-school building, and four imposing church edifices. A telephone exchange, employing 136 men and using 400 miles of wire, connects Deadwood with every important town or settlement of the hills. The business transactions of the city for the year ending April 30, 1888, aggregated $13,000,000, and real estate transfers for the same period exceeded $250,000. The assessed valuation of real and personal property, as returned for the year, amounts to $2,500,000.

Rapid City, another Black Hills town, and the county-seat of Pennington County, has its location on a beautiful and swift stream, where the rugged moun-

tains and broken hills are seen only in the background. The city was located in 1876, and in twelve years has grown into a place of 5000 inhabitants, with four handsome and commodious church edifices, two national banks, street railway, water-works system, electric-lights, telephones, and a great number of substantial brick and stone buildings, including a $52,000 hotel, a $15,000 public-school building, and a fine court-house. The Dakota School of Mines occupies a handsome college building and a well-equipped laboratory, erected by the Territory. One railway, the Fremont, Elkhorn, and Missouri Valley, gives the city eastern connection by the way of Sioux City (Iowa) and Omaha (Nebraska). The opening to settlement of that portion of the Great Sioux Indian Reservation lying between Rapid City and the Missouri River to the east, and the development of the tin interests contiguous on the west, will determine the future greatness of the city.

The city of Grand Forks, the county-seat of one of the richest counties of the Red River Valley, has a population of 7500, with two public-school buildings (heated by steam), seven churches, water-works system, gas-works, electric-lights, three national banks (having a united capital of $500,000), a number of private banks, eight good hotels, two daily news-papers, three weekly, and two monthly, two railway systems, and river naviga-tion. The leading industries of Grand Forks are the handling of wheat and the manufacture of flour and lumber. Three flour-mills, one feed-mill, a brewery (turn-ing out 10,000 barrels of beer annually), two saw-mills (with the capacity of 200,000 feet of sawed lumber per day), two plan-ing-mills, one boiler-works, one foundery, and a number of smaller enterprises give one an idea of the manufacturing inter-ests of Grand Forks. The city has a court-house and jail, a City Hall, fire depart-ment houses, and an opera-house.

The railway and commercial metropolis of central Dakota is the city of Aberdeen, the shire town of the great wheat-grow-ing county of Brown. The Chicago and Northwestern, the Chicago, Milwaukee, and St. Paul, and the St. Paul, Minneapo-lis, and Manitoba railway systems operate lines radiating from the city in seven dif-ferent directions, thus supplying excep-tional advantages in the way of building up jobbing enterprises, advantages which her merchants have diligently improved. The first settlement in the vicinity of Aberdeen was made in the fall of 1880. Now the city has a population of 6000, two fine school buildings, six church edi-fices, water-works system supplied by the pressure from an artesian-well, electric-lights, three daily newspapers, two na-tional and one private bank, opera-house, good hotels, a city hospital, and public and school libraries.

Mitchell, the county-seat of Davison County, was located in 1879, but her sub-stantial and continuous growth dates from the entry of the first railroad, in 1880. In eight years the city has become a place of 5000 inhabitants, with lines of railways reaching north, south, east, west, and southeast. Mitchell has six churches, one private and two national banks, United States land-office, Holly system of water-works, one daily and two weekly news-papers, two public-school buildings, two opera-houses, foundery and machine-shop, a 250-barrel flour-mill, packing-house, and a variety of manufacturing establishments.

The chief city of Codington County,

Watertown, has a favorable location in the fertile valley of the Big Sioux River, at a point three miles distant from the beautiful Lake Kampeska. Six railway outlets give the business interests of the city access to a large and prosperous ag-ricultural district. Although only nine years of age, Watertown has a population of 5000, six churches, three public-school buildings, three national and three pri-vate banks, water-works system, electric-lights, telephones, United States land-of-fice, and one daily, one monthly, and three weekly newspapers. A 300-barrel flour-mill, foundery, and machine-shop, sash and door factory, and paint-works, represent the leading manufacturing in-terests. The city is proud of her many fine buildings, which include a $75,000 bank, a $40,000 hotel, a $30,000 court-house, and an opera-house costing $25,000. The assessed valuation of Watertown's property, real and personal, foots up near-ly $1,000,000.

Huron, on the James River, the central city of that portion of the Territory south of the seventh standard parallel and east of the Missouri River, is located at the junction of two main trunk lines of the Chicago and Northwestern Railroad, and is the division head-quarters and pivotal point of that company's Dakota system. Twenty-two trains, carrying passengers, arrive and depart daily. June 1, 1880, the population of Huron was 300. Her present population exceeds 4000. In this period the city has added the following improvements: two brick school build-ings, valued at $30,000; seven church edifices; artesian system of water-works; sewerage system; electric-light plant; street railway; opera-house; four nation-al banks; two daily and four weekly newspapers; one semi-monthly and three monthly periodicals; free postal delivery; and a United States land-office. The manufacturing establishments include cornice-works; artificial stone works; two flouring-mills; brick-yards; packing-house, and railroad machine-shops, em-ploying 300 workmen.

By the terms of an act of Congress, ap-proved April 30, 1888, about 11,000,000 acres of excellent farming and grazing lands, now contained within the bounda-ries of the Great Sioux Indian Reserva-tion, are to be opened to settlement as soon as the necessary Indian consent shall have been obtained. The lands which the Indians are asked to cede include nearly all of the reservation lying between the Cheyenne and White Rivers, bounded on the west by the Black Hills, and by the Missouri River on the east; all that portion of the reservation which is situated west of the 102d degree of longitude (Greenwich) and north of the main branch of the Cheyenne River; and a part of the Winnebago and Crow Creek Reservation on the east bank of the Missouri. For years the citizens of the Territory, more particularly those residing near the outer barriers of this great stretch of reserved lands, have labored to obtain a passageway connecting the mineral district of the Black Hills with the agricultural area east of the Missouri River — efforts which are soon to be crowned with success. The extinguishment of the Indian title to the tract as designated will be the harbinger of another era of progress and development of the Territory such as was witnessed during the years of 1883-4, and the two Mis-

LOUIS K. CHURCH.

souri River cities and railway termini, Pierre, Hughes County, and Chamberlain, Brule County, occupying strategic points, will assume the position, so confidently expected by their founders, of the most

DEADWOOD, IN THE BLACK HILLS (SOUTH VIEW).

BARTLETT TRIPP.

OSCAR S. GIFFORD.

important commercial marts and railway centres of South Dakota. Each city has excellent schools, fine churches, a splendid water-works system, and the various public buildings and business enterprises of a metropolis.

The present Governor of Dakota, Louis K. Church, was born in Brooklyn, New York, December 11, 1846, and is a lawyer by profession. He was, in 1885, appointed Associate Justice of the Supreme Court of Dakota, and immediately removed to the Territory, where he fulfilled the duties of Judge of the Fifth Judicial District in a manner highly satisfactory to the people.

Before the expiration of his term on the bench, Judge Church received the appointment of Governor of Dakota.

Hon. Oscar S. Gifford, Dakota's Delegate in Congress, also a native of New York, has resided in the Territory seventeen years. He is now serving his second term in Congress.

Hon. Bartlett Tripp, one of the most able lawyers in the Northwest, and Chief-Justice of the Supreme Court of Dakota, is a native of the State of Maine. He removed to Yankton, Dakota (his present residence), in 1869. In November, 1885, he was appointed Chief-Justice.

HENRY GLADWIN, AND THE SIEGE OF PONTIAC

The following article is the result of an attempt to find out something about the man who defeated Pontiac. Applying in person to Mr. Parkman, he told me that he knew nothing whatever about Gladwin, but gave me permission to go through his manuscripts in the rooms of the Massachusetts Historical Society. This I did, but found absolutely nothing. After considerable labor, however, I obtained trace of Gladwin's descendants, and from one of them obtained about one hundred pages of manuscript written in Detroit in 1763. The MS. contained records of courts martial, reports, letters, etc. These are to appear shortly in the Michigan Historical Society publications. I also obtained photographs of

portraits of Gladwin and his wife. The gentleman to whom I am indebted for this courtesy is the Rev. Gladwyn Jebb, of Firbeck Hall, Rotherham, England. The photographs are the only ones ever sent to this country. Also I secured, through Ambassador Bayard, copies of all the references to Gladwin in the British War Office. On these as a basis I have written the Pontiac story from the standpoint of Gladwin, the conqueror.

THE conquest of Canada by the English brought about several readjustments within the territory now included in the State of Michigan. The only settlements were at Detroit, at Mackinac

(Michilimackinac), at Sault Ste. Marie, and at Fort St. Joseph; and of these only the ones at Detroit and Mackinac were of any importance. The seat of government was transferred from Quebec to New York, whence General Jeffrey Amherst exercised military control over the border posts. Under him Colonel Bouquet at Fort Pitt (Pittsburg) ranked the commandant at Detroit; but the latter held a general supervision over the upper-lake posts, and reported directly to General Amherst. Indian affairs were in charge of Sir William Johnson, whose headquarters at Johnson Hall swarmed with Indian retainers and dependents, as well as with his own half-breed children. Under Sir William was his deputy, George Croghan, who was constantly engaged in going from tribe to tribe in his efforts to keep the peace.

Along the Atlantic coast an American population of English and Dutch descent peopled the country. Nominally British colonists, these people practically formed a group of independent states, awaiting only the coming of events already foreshadowed to coalesce into a new nation. From this sturdy civilization the lake region was completely cut off by the Alleghanies. As under the French, so under the English, the lake region continued to be held by garrisons maintained in an Indian country for the protection of the fur trade. The difficulties of the situation arose from the fact that the Indians disputed the right of the French to dispose of the lands to the English; while on their part the English, having no longer to fear the French power, took less and less pains to conciliate the Indians.

Captain Donald Campbell, as he settled down for a long winter at Detroit (1760), was not ill pleased with his situation. The fort was large and in good repair, with two bastions towards the river, and a large, strong bastion towards the Isle au Cochons (Belle Isle); two three-pounders and three mortars made up the battery. Within the high palisades some seventy or eighty houses lined the narrow streets. The fertile country along both banks of the river was cut into narrow farms, fronting on the stream and extending back into the endless forest. The Indians living in the vicinity of the fort as well as the settlers looked to the commandant for both justice and supplies. The British soldiers were contented—a fact

which the captain ascribed to the absence of rum; and the Indians were seemingly friendly, although the supplies issued to them were meagre in the extreme. The social life at Detroit especially pleased the gray-haired bachelor commandant. The French women surpassed his expectations; and the men, although very independent, were ever ready for pleasure. The Sunday card parties at the commandant's quarters, attended by both sexes, gave to life a zest not known at Fort Pitt; and at a ball given in honor of the King's birthday the array of ladies was so fine as to call forth Captain Campbell's hearty commendation in one of his numerous gossipy letters to Colonel Bouquet.* Moreover, both the French and the Indians were as fond of the pleasure-loving captain as their fickle natures would allow.

During the summer, however, emissaries from the Six Nations came to Detroit with large belts, for the purpose of stirring up a general warfare against the English. Matters became so serious that Sir Jeffrey Amherst thought best to send Sir William Johnson to make a treaty at Detroit, and to despatch Major Gladwin with three hundred light infantry to strengthen the western posts. On his arrival, in September, Sir William stated his conviction that the conspiracy against the English was universal; but this opinion was not shared by General Amherst. The latter thought the Indians incapable of doing serious harm; but he ordered, by way of precaution, that they be kept short of powder.

The visit of Sir William Johnson was the greatest social event the people of Detroit had ever known. Captain Campbell was in his element. On Sunday evening he gave a ball, to which he invited about twenty of the French maidens of the settlement. The dance began at eight o'clock in the evening, and lasted until five next morning. It was opened by Sir William and the daughter of the principal French trader, Mlle. Cuillerie, whose black eyes made such a lasting impression on the gallant Indian agent that the exchange of compliments between them appears in the correspondence for several years, the last mention being

* This correspondence forms a part of the Bouquet Papers, calendared in the Canadian archives, and printed at length in vol. xix. of the Michigan Pioneer Collection.

found in a letter from James Sterling, who, on behalf of his wife, returns hearty thanks for Sir William's civilities to her, four years previous. Before leaving Detroit, Sir William also gave a ball, and on this occasion the dancing continued for eleven hours. There was also a round of dinners and calls, at which wines and cordials were served without stint; presents were showered upon the Indians by Sir William, and after the final council the principal inhabitants dined with the diplomat of the forest. In all these festivities Major Gladwin had no part. Lying in a little house within hearing of the lively fiddle and the laughter of the dancers, the fever of the country racked his bones, and made him long for his Derbyshire home. At evening Sir William would visit him to talk over the events of the day and to plan for the future; and it was not until the middle of October that Gladwin was able to leave for Fort William Augustus, on his way to England.

In July, 1762, the Indians learned with satisfaction that England was at war with Spain, and soon the report spread far and wide that the French and Spanish were to retake Quebec and all Canada. Here at last was the chance for which the savages had been waiting. With the help of the French they could drive out the English, and once more receive the solicitous attention of both nations. At this juncture Major Gladwin again appeared at Detroit, this time with orders to establish posts on Lake Superior and to exercise general supervision over the northwestern establishments. Captain Campbell, although somewhat wearied by the sameness of garrison pleasures, remained as second in command; and the favor in which he was held by both the French and the Indians was a decided help to the abrupt and businesslike Gladwin. For company, the officers had Sir Robert Davers, an Englishman of education and adventurous disposition, who had been exploring the Lake Superior country.

As spring came and the February thaws and March rains loosened the ice bonds that for three long months had locked Detroit from the world, Gladwin at evening must often have stood on the platform within the palisades to look out on the tumultuous river, where the great ice cakes from Lake St. Clair, tumbling over each other like marine monsters at play, were hurrying down to the warmer waters of Lake Erie. By day the details of administration kept him busy. The French merchants within the fort grumbled at the increased taxes imposed for the support of a garrison much larger than their own king had maintained;* the outlying posts were continually sending for supplies; General Amherst was cautioning against gifts of ammunition and rum to the Indians; and the savages, having bartered their furs for liquor at Niagara, had no means to purchase the necessaries of life from the traders at Detroit. Some of the French and Indians complained bitterly that Gladwin called them dogs and drove them from his house; and the subsequent career of those who made the charges shows that the commander was an excellent judge of human nature.†

Confident of the power of England to hold all she had gained from France, Gladwin had no suspicion that the Indians would foolishly rush to their own destruction by an attack on the British posts. Living behind palisades, and surrounded by a cordon of discontented and intriguing French, he could have no accurate knowledge of the mischief that for months had been plotted by the Ottawa chief Pontiac, who had established himself, with his wives, on the narrow Isle a Peche (Peach Island), scarcely rising above the waters of Lake St. Clair, and concealed from the view of the fort by the thickly wooded Isle au Cochons. There is no reason to believe that Pontiac had impressed himself upon Gladwin as being in any way distinguished above the other chiefs, and doubtless many of the reports, like those given by Major Robert Rogers,‡ that have come down to us of the Ottawa chief's striking personality are too highly colored. He was of medium stature, was well built, and was possessed of great strength. Absolute and peremptory in manner, he had obtained great influence among the tribes, and was respected by the French. During the fifty years of his life he had absorbed from his contact with white men much that was valuable in the conduct of protracted warfare; and, according to his own account, he had saved the French at Detroit from massacre in 1746, when the great chief Mickinac (the Turtle) came with his northern bands " to carry off the head of

* E. K. Roberts's *Sketches of Detroit*.
† Gladwin MS.   ‡ Rogers's Journal.

the French commander and eat his heart and drink his blood." Doubtless, too, he had led the Ottawas at Fort Duquesne (Fort Pitt) eight years before, when Gladwin for the first time heard the Indian war-whoop. At a great council (1763), held on the banks of the river Ecorse, below Detroit, Pontiac had related to the superstitious Indians a dream wherein the Great Spirit sent his message that they were to cast aside the weapons, the manufactures, and the rum of the white men, and, with help from above, drive the dogs in red from every post in their country. The credulous Indians heard with awe the voice from on high, and left the council prepared to obey the summons.

Detroit being the chief point of attack, Pontiac took it upon himself to surprise and massacre the garrison. On May 1, 1763, forty Ottawas danced the calumet dance before Gladwin's house, the visit being made for the purpose of spying out the land. Four days later M. Gouin, a substantial French settler, brought word that his wife, while visiting the Ottawa camp to buy venison, had seen the Indians filing off the ends of their gun-barrels, evidently preparing for some deed of treachery; and on the evening of the 6th, Gladwin received private information that the next day had been set for the destruction of his garrison. The exact source of this private information is still a matter of more or less doubt.

Carver, who visited Detroit five years after the events to be described, and who published three editions of his *Travels through North America* while Gladwin was still living, relates, without contemporary contradiction, a story that Cass accepted with little hesitation, and that Parkman clings to in spite of the gravest doubts thrown upon it by investigations made subsequent to the first edition of his *Conspiracy of Pontiac*. John R. Williams told Parkman that the plot was disclosed by the daughter of Labutte the interpreter; but Mr. Askin opined that a Pawnee slave gave the information.*

The evening of May 7, according to Carver, an Indian girl who had been employed by Major Gladwin to make a pair of moccasins out of curious elk-skin, brought her work home. The major was so pleased with the moccasins that, intending them as a present for a friend, he ordered her to take back the remain-

der of the skin and make a pair for him. Having been paid and dismissed, the woman loitered at the door, and Gladwin was quick enough to see that something was amiss. Being urged to tell her trouble, she said, after much hesitation, that as he had always been good to her, she was unwilling to take away the remainder of the skin, because he put so great a value upon it, and she should never be able to bring it back. His curiosity being now excited, he insisted that she disclose the secret that seemed to be struggling in her bosom for utterance. At last, on receiving a promise that the intelligence she was about to give should not turn to her prejudice, and that if it appeared to be beneficial she should be rewarded for it, she informed him that at the council to be held with the Indians the following day Pontiac and his chiefs intended to murder Gladwin and his officers, and having massacred the garrison and inhabitants, to plunder the town. Having gained from the woman every necessary particular relative to the plot, Gladwin dismissed her, with injunctions to secrecy and a promise of reward.

A story at once so romantic and so widely accepted deserves tender treatment; but in the Parkman manuscripts this same tale is found in the mouth of one of Rogers's rangers, who, as Cass proves, could not have known the facts. The truth probably has been related by the unknown author of the Pontiac Diary, who says that an Ottawa Indian, called Mahigan, having entered but reluctantly into the conspiracy, and feeling displeased with the steps his people were taking, came on Friday night, without the knowledge of the other Indians, to the gate of the fort, and asked to be admitted to the presence of the commander, saying that he had something of importance to tell him. The gates having been opened, he was conducted to Captain Campbell, second in command, and Gladwin was summoned. They wished to call in the interpreter Labutte, but the Indian objected, saying that he could make himself understood in French. Thereupon he unfolded the conspiracy of the Indians, telling how they would come the very next day to fall on the English. Having obtained a pledge of secrecy, and having refused presents lest the Indians should discover his treachery and kill him, he left the fort secretly. The writer adds

* Parkman's MS. Diary

that Gladwin made a promise not to disclose the source of his information, and that he kept it.*

The crisis had come in the life of the young commandant of his Majesty's forces at Detroit. Although Gladwin could not then have known the extent of the widespread conspiracy which Pontiac had planned, yet he did know that his own steadfastness and his knowledge of Indian warfare were about to be put to the test. He was a soldier by choice and by training, and the seven years he had spent in England's service on the frontiers of America had not been without its hard lessons. In 1755 he had landed on the banks of the Potomac as an ensign in the ill-fated Braddock expedition. He had made one of that band of glittering officers whom the provincial soldier George Washington had envied as they congregated in the old Braddock House at Alexandria, whose now bare but stately staircase and broad halls seem to be peopled by the ghosts of fair ladies and dashing soldier gallants of a century and a quarter ago. In the ambush at Little Meadows he had learned from the brave yet cautious young Virginian that the military science of the Old World was out of place in battling with the denizens of the American forests, and in the campaigns against Ticonderoga and Niagara this new knowledge had stood him in good stead. Scarcely more than a year previous he had given a hostage to fortune by leading to the altar of the little Wingerwort church in Derbyshire a beautiful girl of nineteen, from whose side military duties in America too quickly recalled him. As the prospective head of an old and honorable county family, yet with little besides his profession of arms to give him support and reputation, Henry Gladwin, at the age of thirty-three, must have realized that the peril which now faced his king's supremacy in the wilderness was for him the door to success or to failure in life, according as he should succeed or fail in holding the post of Detroit against the savages whose hostility and crafty treachery now threatened it. And yet perhaps the warning of

* The Pontiac Diary was written in French, probably by a priest of St. Anne's. It was found in the roof of a Canadian house that was being torn down. Three translations exist—one in the Parkman MSS. in the library of the Massachusetts Historical Society; another in Schoolcraft's second volume; and a third in the Michigan Pioneer Collections.

danger to come might be without foundation, as so many other warnings had been. Perhaps the prudent but fickle Indians were bent merely on extorting more presents and still larger portions of rum. Perhaps the broad river, mirroring the placid May stars, was a pathway of peace and not of war, and the stillness of the trackless forest was not destined to be broken by the war-whoop and the death-cry. The morrow would tell the story. If it was to be war, at least he would be found neither unprepared nor wanting in the determination that marks the soldier.

About ten o'clock the next morning, as Carver relates, Pontiac and his chiefs arrived, and were conducted to the council-chamber, where Gladwin and his principal officers awaited their coming. As the Indians passed on, they could not help observing a greater number of troops than usual drawn up on the parade. No sooner had the Indians entered the council-chamber, and seated themselves on the skins prepared for them, than Pontiac asked the commandant why his young men, meaning the soldiers, were thus drawn up and parading the streets. "To keep them perfect in their exercise," was the answer. Then Pontiac began to protest his friendship and good-will towards the English; and when he came to deliver the belt of wampum, which, according to the warning, was to be the signal for his chiefs to fire, the governor and all his attendants drew their swords half-way from their scabbards, and the soldiers at the same instant made a clattering with their arms before the doors, which had been purposely left open. Even Pontiac trembled; and instead of giving the belt in the manner proposed, he delivered it according to the usual way. His stolid chiefs, who had expected the signal, continued quiet, awaiting the result.

Gladwin in his turn made a speech. Instead of thanking Pontiac for the professions of friendship just uttered, he accused him of being a traitor. He said that the English, who knew everything, were convinced of Pontiac's treachery and villanous designs. Then reaching down to the Indian chief seated nearest him, he drew aside his blanket, discovering the shortened firelock. This entirely disconcerted the Indians. Inasmuch as he had given his word, at the time they desired an audience, that their persons should be safe, Gladwin said he would hold his promise inviolable, though they so little deserved it. However, he advised them to make the best of their way out of the fort, lest his young men, on being acquainted with their treacherous purposes, should cut every one of them to pieces. Pontiac endeavored to contradict the accusation, and to make excuses for his suspicious conduct; but Gladwin refused to listen, and the Indians sullenly left the fort.

Late that afternoon six warriors returned, bringing with them an old squaw, saying that she had given false information. Gladwin declared that she had never given any kind of advice.* When they insisted that he name the author of what he had heard in regard to a plot, he simply replied it was one of themselves, whose name he promised never to reveal. Whereupon they went off, and carried the old woman with them. When they arrived in camp, Pontiac seized the prisoner and gave her three strokes with a stick on the head, which laid her flat on the ground, and the whole nation, crowding around, called, Kill her! kill her!

The next day was Sunday, and late in the afternoon Pontiac and several of his chiefs paddled across the placid river to smoke the pipe of peace with the officers at the fort. Gladwin, suspicious of so much protestation, refused to go near them; but Captain Campbell, unwilling to lose a chance to pacify the Indians, smoked the peace-pipe with them outside the fort, and took back to Gladwin the message that on Monday all the nation would come to council, where everything would be settled to the satisfaction of the English, after which the Indians would immediately disperse, so as to remove all suspicion.

At ten o'clock next morning the anxious watchers behind the palisades saw coming around the point of the low island a fleet of canoes; and as the swift-darting boats, hurried by paddle and current, covered the three miles of water, the soldiers counted fifty-six of these barks, each carrying seven or eight Indians. The bows of the canoes rested lightly on the sand of the sloping bank, and the warriors hurried to the fort, only to find the gates fast barred against them. Instead of the cordial welcome they expected, an inter-

* Rogers's Journal. Doubtless this is the origin of the romance of the Indian girl.

preter met them with the message that not above sixty chiefs might enter. Whereupon Pontiac, enraged at seeing the futility of all his stratagems, and yet confident of ultimate success, in his most peremptory manner bade the interpreter say to Gladwin that if all the Indians had not free access to the fort, none of them would enter it. "Tell him," said the angry chief, "that he may stay in his fort, and that I will keep the country." So saying, Pontiac strode to his canoe and paddled for the Ottawa village; and his followers, knowing that the fight was on, ran like fiends to the house of an English woman and her two sons, whom they tomahawked and scalped. Another party paddled swiftly to Isle au Cochons, where they first killed twenty-four of King George's bullocks, and then put to death an old English sergeant. Afterwards the Canadians buried the mutilated corpse; but on returning to the spot, so tradition relates, they were surprised to see an arm protruding from the grave. Thrice the dirt was heaped above the body, and thrice the arm raised itself above the ground, until the mound was sprinkled with holy water. Then the perturbed spirit left the body in peace never since disturbed. Having put to death all the English outside the fort, the Indians sent to Gladwin a Frenchman to report the killing of the woman and her children, and also the murder of Sir Robert Davers, Captain Robertson, and a boat's crew of six persons who had been sent to the St. Clair Flats to discover a passage for one of the schooners bound to Michilimackinac—information that removed all lingering doubts that the Indians were determined to wipe out the English at Detroit.

Pontiac, on his return to the Ottawa village, ordered the squaws to change the camp to the western bank, above the fort. Then, as the night mists gathered upon the tireless river, dropping a curtain between the great chief and his enemies, Pontiac himself, hideous in war-paint, leaped into the centre of the ring of braves, and flourishing his tomahawk, began to chant the record of his valorous deeds. One by one the listening braves, catching the contagion from their mighty chief, were drawn into the ring, until at last every savage was wildly dancing the war-dance. There was no sleep for the garrison that night. Gladwin, as he paced the wide street that encircled the buildings of the fort just within the pickets, took council with himself as to how he might withstand his crafty enemies. Burning arrows, silent messengers of destruction, might easily set fire to the one hundred or more wooden buildings within the enclosure; and the church, standing near the palisades, was particularly exposed, unless, indeed, the superstitious Indians should hearken to their only less superstitious French allies, who had threatened the savages with the vengeance of the Great Spirit if they should attempt to destroy the house of God. The two sixpounders, the one three-pounder, and the two mortars that now composed the battery of the fort were of little avail against an enemy that fought singly and from behind trees or whatever protection the opportunity might afford; but, on the other hand, an English head above the pickets or an English body at a port-hole was the

A LIGHT-INFANTRY SOLDIER OF THE PERIOD.

sure lodgement for an Indian bullet. The garrison was made up of one hundred and twenty-two soldiers and eight officers, together with about forty fur-traders and their assistants. These traders would fight to save their lives, but were inclined to the French rather than to the English. Between this little garrison and the thousand savages was a single row of palisades, made by planting logs close together so that they would stand twenty-five feet above-ground. Block-houses at the angles and at the gates afforded additional protection; and, best of all, the brimming river, whose little waves lapped the sandy shore near the south line of palisades, gave an abundant water-supply. A schooner and a sloop, both armed, might be relied on to keep open the line of communication with Niagara, whence Major Walters would send supplies. Promotion was certain to be the reward of success; and almost as surely the torture-stake would be the penalty of failure.

The chill that comes before dawn was in the air when Gladwin joined the anxious watchers in the block-house. Gradually the black outlines of low farm-houses and the encircling woods melted into gray; and then beyond the wooded island a disk of molten gold, pushing itself higher and higher, made of the deep waters a broad pathway of shimmering light. On the low bluff far up the river Gladwin's anxious eye discovered the lodges of Pontiac's Ottawas, who, under cover of the night, had paddled around the head of the island and noiselessly established themselves above the line of French farm-houses. This meant a siege; and as the commandant was still gazing at the preparations for war, a pattering of bullets against the block-house announced the beginning of hostilities.

During the morning a party of Wyandottes, summoned by Pontiac to a council, stopped at the fort on their way. Fortified by English rum, they went off to the meeting-place, under promise to Gladwin that they would do all they could to appease the Ottawas and dissuade them from further hostilities. Next came a number of the French settlers, bringing with them chiefs of the Ottawas, Wyandottes, Chippewas, and Pottawatomies, who told Gladwin that almost all the French had gathered at the house of the trader Cuillerie, where the Indians were to hold their council. They assured Gladwin that if he would allow Captain Campbell* and another officer to go to the council it would not be hard to persuade the Indians to make peace. At any rate, it

* Cooley and other historians confuse Captain Campbell with Major Campbell, who came later.

"ANOTHER PARTY PADDLED SWIFTLY TO ISLE AU COCHONS."

could do no harm to try; for both the French and the Indians promised to see that the popular old captain and his companion returned in safety that very night. Gladwin, having little hope of turning Pontiac from his purposes, was reluctant to intrust Captain Campbell to their hands; but the captain, relying on the friendship that had existed between him and the savages, no less than on the promises of the French, urged to be allowed to go to the council. The deciding influence that won Gladwin's consent was the absolute necessity * of getting into the fort a supply of corn, flour, and bear's grease; for the garrison had in store not more than enough for three weeks. So, while Captain Campbell and Lieutenant

* The *Pennsylvania Gazette*, August 18, 1763, quotes a trader just arrived from Detroit as saying that the French promised that they would answer, life for life, body for body, for the two ambassadors, and that Gladwin did not like the scheme, but allowed them to go, though he would not order them to.

McDougall went off with high hopes, the prudent commandant, under cover of the darkness, set about gathering provisions from the French settlers across the river.

Scarcely had the embassy of peace crossed the cleared space about the fort when they were met by M. Gouin, who first urged and then begged them not to trust their lives to the now excited Indians. The appeal was vain. Yet even while the party were making their way along the bank of the river they were set upon by a crowd of Indians, at whose hands they would have fared ill indeed had not Pontiac himself come to their rescue. On reaching the council-place they found the largest room filled with French and Indians; and in the centre of the group sat M. Cuillerie, arrayed in a hat and coat adorned with gold lace. He kept his seat when the two officers entered, and remained covered during the conference. When bread was passed he ate one piece, to show the Indians, as he said, that it was not poisoned.* Pontiac, addressing himself to M. Cuillerie, craftily said that he looked upon the Frenchman as his father come to life, and as the commandant at Detroit until the arrival of M. Bellestre. M. Cuillerie appeared greatly pleased. Then Pontiac, turning to the British officers, told them plainly that to secure peace the English must leave the country, under escort and without arms or baggage, as the French had done three years previous. Thereupon M. Cuillerie warmly shook Lieutenant McDougall's hand, saying : "My friend, this is my work; rejoice that I have obtained such good terms for you. I thought Pontiac would be much harder." Hoping against hope for the garrison, but apprehensive of no present danger to himself and his brother officer, Captain Campbell made a short but earnest plea for peace. Then he and Lieutenant McDougall waited anxiously for the usual grunt of approval. The moments dragged, and still the Indians sat impassive. For the space of an hour there was unbroken silence. Captain Campbell, dejected by evident failure, arose to retrace his steps to the fort. "My father," said Pontiac, quietly, "will sleep to-night in the lodges of his red children."

The unusual intelligence that had raised Pontiac above every other Indian chief had led the English to rely on his sense of honor—a quality rare indeed among savages. What civilized races call treachery is to the Indian legitimate warfare. It never occurs to a savage to expose himself to harm in order to accomplish an end that he can attain safely by deception. In spite of all promises, therefore, the two Englishmen were sent, under strong guard, to the house of M. Meloche. That they were not immediately put to death was due solely to the fact that Gladwin had several Pottawatomie prisoners; and, shrewdly enough, Pontiac feared that if the commandant should retaliate on his hostages, that tribe would vanish into the forest, leaving the leader without the support he so much needed.

Captain Campbell and Lieutenant McDougall trusted to the promises of the French more than to those of the Indians. It has been assumed that the French at Detroit were victims of the Pontiac conspiracy only to a less degree than were the English. It is true that there were a few prudent French farmers who gave

* Gladwin MS.

Gladwin what assistance they could give without drawing down on themselves the enmity of the Indians; but it was generally believed among the French that the English would soon be driven out of New France, and that the French king would again be their monarch. For two centuries the warfare between French and English over the fur trade had been as barbarous as war was in Europe during the same time. On both sides of the Atlantic human life was not considered worth a king's serious consideration, and the soldier of that day in every nation was a freebooter, so that it is not surprising that the French traders and woodrangers at Detroit should have seized upon Pontiac's war to despoil their ancient enemies and their conquerors of less than three years' standing. The only cause for surprise is that the French did not from the start openly make common cause with Pontiac. That they secretly gave aid and encouragement to the Indians was repeatedly charged by Gladwin, who regarded the French as the source of all his troubles; and the convincing proof of his assertions is to be found in the official reports of inquiries he caused to be held at Detroit during the siege. The problem for Gladwin was to hold out at Detroit until both the French and Indians could be convinced that the French government would not assist them, and that the peace with England was definite and lasting. The terms proposed to Captain Campbell were offered next day to Gladwin, and the French urged him to escape while he might; but the young Englishman absolutely refused to make any terms with savages. His soldiers caught his spirit, so that he was able to write confidently to General Amherst that he would hold out until succor should come. The schooner *Gladwin*, which bore the despatch, succeeded in eluding Pontiac's canoes; and when the chief reported his failure to M. Cuillerie, the Frenchman jeered at him because five canoes withdrew when but a single Pottawatomie was killed.

At this juncture a long series of disasters came to show the English how serious was the task before them. As one by one the results of Pontiac's cunning planning came to light, everything seemed to give way before the exulting savages. On May 22 news came of the capture of Fort Sandusky. At the inquiry Ensign Paully testified that on May 17 his sentry called him to speak with some Indians at the gate; and on finding some of his own Indians in the party he allowed the seven to enter the fort, and gave them tobacco. Soon one of the seven raised his head as a signal, whereupon the two sitting next the officer seized and bound him, and hurried him from the room. He passed his sentry dead in the gateway, and saw the corpses of his little garrison lying about; his sergeant was killed in the garden, where he had been planting; the merchants were killed and their stores were plundered. The Indians spared Paully, however, and took him to their camp at Detroit, where he was adopted as the husband of a widowed squaw, from whose toils he finally escaped to his friends in the fort.

On May 18 Ensign Holmes, who commanded the garrison at The Miamis (St. Joseph), was told by a Frenchman that Detroit had been attacked, whereupon the ensign called in his men and set them at work making cartridges. Three days later Holmes's Indian servant besought him to bleed one of her friends who lay ill in a cabin outside the stockade. On his errand of mercy he was shot dead; and the terrified garrison of nine were only too glad to surrender at the command of two Frenchmen, Pontiac's messengers, who were on their way to the Illinois to get a commander for Detroit. On May 25, at Fort St. Joseph, seventeen Pottawatomies came into Lieutenant Schlosser's room on the pretence of holding a council. A Frenchman, who had heard that treachery was planned, rushed in to give the alarm, whereupon Lieutenant Schlosser was seized, ten of the garrison were killed, and the other three, with the commandant, were taken prisoners. They were afterwards brought to Detroit and exchanged.

On the 29th the long-expected bateaux from Niagara were seen coming up the Detroit River. With joyful hearts the garrison looked forward to the end of their tedious siege. But as the boats came nearer, the English saw with dismay that Indians were masters of each craft. When the foremost bateau came opposite the schooner, two of the soldiers in her made the motion to change rowing-places. Quickly they seized the Indians and threw them overboard. One Indian carried his assailant with him, and in the

struggle both found death. Another soldier struck the remaining Indian over the head with an oar and killed him. Under the fire of sixty savages on shore, the three plucky Englishmen escaped to the vessel with their prize, which contained eight barrels of most acceptable pork and flour. Of the ten bateaux that had set out from Niagara under Lieutenant Cuyler, eight had been captured, and the force had been completely routed by an Indian surprise and night attack.

Following the capture of the bateaux came the darkest days of the siege. Often during a whole day the Indians, drunken on the rum from the captured stores, did not fire a shot; but in their fiendish glee they gave notice of their presence by sending the mangled bodies of their English captives to float past the palisades in sight of the sentries. To add to these tales of disaster came Father De Jaunay, the Jesuit missionary at Michilimackinac, to tell the bloodiest story of all. On June 2 the Chippewas living near the fort assembled for their usual game of ball. They played from morning till noon, and Captain George Etherington and Lieutenant Leslie stood by to watch the sport. Suddenly the ball was struck over the palisades. A dozen Indians rushed through the gate to get it. Before the dazed sentry could recover, the captain and lieutenant were seized and hurried off. The Indians within the fort had received from the waiting squaws hatchets hidden under their blankets; in an instant Lieutenant Jamet, fifteen soldiers, and a trader named Tracy were put to death; five others were reserved for a like fate, and the remainder of the garrison were made prisoners. Had it not been for the powerful influence of Charles Langlade and his friends the Ottawas, all the English must have perished; as it was, Captain Etherington, Lieutenant Leslie, with fourteen men, were held till July 18, and were then taken to Montreal by the Ottawas.

On Sunday, the 26th of June, Pontiac, for mingled purposes of religion and business, paddled across the green river to attend mass in the little French chapel at Sandwich. When the services were over, the chief selected three of the chairs in which the thrifty French had been carried to church, and making the owners his chairmen, he and his guard set off on a search for provisions. He imitated the credit certificates issued by Gladwin by giving; in payment for cattle, billets signed by his mark—the picture of a 'coon. The provisions were transported to Pontiac's camp near Parent's Creek, and in due time the billets were redeemed in furs.* The next day Pontiac sent another summons to surrender, saying that nine hundred Indians were on their way from Michilimackinac, and that if Gladwin waited till those Indians came, he would not be answerable for the consequences. Gladwin replied that until Captain Campbell and Lieutenant McDougall were returned, Pontiac might save himself the trouble of sending messages to the fort. To this the wily Pontiac made answer that he had too much regard for his distinguished captives to send them back; because the kettle was on the fire for the entire garrison, and if the captives returned he should have to boil them with the others.

On the 30th of June the *Gladwin*, returning from Niagara, ploughed her way up the white-capped river, and landed a force of fifty men, together with provisions and some much-needed ammunition. For two months Gladwin had guarded Detroit against surprise, and had sustained a siege conducted by Pontiac in person, while fort after fort had fallen before the savages. As the Indians returned from their successes elsewhere, they were more and more eager for the overthrow of the one fort that hitherto had baffled all their efforts; and in his extremity Pontiac now turned on the French and threatened to force them to take up arms against the

English. During the siege, however, copies of the definitive treaty between France and England had reached Detroit, and on July 4 Gladwin assembled the French, read to them the articles of peace, and sent a copy across the river to the priest. Thereupon forty Frenchmen, choosing James Sterling as their leader, took service under Gladwin. On this same day a party from the fort made a sortie for the purpose of bringing in some

MRS. HENRY GLADWIN.
From a painting attributed to Romney.

powder and lead from the house of M. Baby, who had taken refuge in the fort. Lieutenant Hay, an old Indian-fighter, commanded the party, and in his exultation over driving off an attacking party he tore the scalp from the head of a wounded Indian, and shook his trophy in the face of his enemies. It happened that one of the savages killed was the son of a Chippewa chief; and the tribe, on hearing of their disaster, went to Pontiac to reproach him for being the cause of

* Rogers cites this issue of Pontiac credit currency as a remarkable instance of that chief's intelligence; and so it would have been but for the fact that it was an imitation. The redemption of it thus becomes the striking portion of the tale.

GENERAL HENRY GLADWIN.
From a photograph of a painting by John Holland.

At midnight on July 10 the sentries in the fort saw floating down the black river a great mass of fire. The flames, feeding on fagots and birch bark, leaped high in the air, lighting up the forest-covered island in the background, and bringing into high relief the whitewashed cottages of the habitans. Hurried by the swift current, a great fire-raft, built by the French and Indians,* made for the two vessels anchored in the stream; but the alert crews had anticipated their danger and were prepared for it. The vessels were anchored by two cables, and as the flaming pile approached, they slipped one cable, and easily swung out of the way of their enemy; nor were subsequent attempts to fire the vessels any more successful.

The hot days succeeded one another all too slowly. On the 29th of July the guards heard firing down the river, and half an hour later the surprised sentries saw the broad surface of the river dotted with bateaux, the regular dip of whose oars was borne a long way on the still morning air. A detachment of 260 men, under the command of Captain Dalyell,†

their ills, saying that he was very brave in taking a loaf of bread or a beef from a Frenchman who made no resistance, but it was the Chippewas who had all the men killed and wounded every day. Therefore, they said, they intended to take from him what he had been saving. Lieutenant McDougall had already made his escape to the fort,* but they went to Meloche's house, where Captain Campbell was still confined. They stripped him, carried him to their camp, killed him, took out his heart and ate it, cut off his head, and divided his body into small pieces. Such was the end of a brave soldier, esteemed, loved, and sincerely mourned in the army, from General Amherst and Colonel Bouquet down to the privates who served under him.†

1763: "No man ever had more reason to expect safety in the hands of these barbarians than this officer had, whose constant attention and goodness to them whilst he commanded at Detroit called at least for security to his person."—Parkman MSS.

Amherst offered a reward of £100 New York currency to the slayer of Pontiac, and a like amount for the death of the chief who killed Captain Campbell.—Parkman MSS.

* Gladwin MS.

† Spelled also Dalzell. In Canadian archives the name is uniformly spelled Dalyell. There is little uniformity in spelling proper names in the records. The only exception seems to be the name of Gladwin, which only Parkman and those who follow him implicitly, spell Gladwyn. In the *Gentleman's Magazine* Gladwin's name appears in 1781 and repeatedly thereafter, and is always spelled with an "i." The spelling "Pontiac" represents the Ottawa pro-

* During his captivity Lieutenant McDougall fell in love with Marie Francoise Navarre, the daughter of Robert Navarre, and after the siege they were married. In consideration of his services the king granted him Isle au Cochons, which he retained until his death in 1780.

† Amherst to Egremmont, New York, August 13,

one of General Amherst's aides-de-camp, and of Major Robert Rogers, had come to put an end to the siege. Captain Dalyell was an officer of undoubted bravery, and the tales of slaughter he had heard at Presque Isle and Sandusky on his way to Detroit doubtless made him anxious to crush Pontiac by one bold stroke. Gladwin, whom months of close acquaintance with the wary Indian chief had taught discretion, gave consent to Dalyell's plan of a night attack only on the threat of the latter to leave Detroit unless such a blow should be struck.* As Gladwin feared would be the case, the treacherous French, learning the details of the plan, immediately put Pontiac on his guard. In the earliest hours of the 31st of July, Dalyell marched a force of 250 men along the sandy bank of the swift-flowing river, past the well-enclosed cottages of the French, and on towards a little stream that fell into the Detroit about a mile and a half above the fort. The twenty-five men in advance had just stepped on the rude bridge across the run when from the ridges that formed the further side of the gully came a volley of musketry that hurled the little band in confusion back on the main body. In the pitchy darkness the soldiers, cheered by Dalyell's steady words of command, swept the ridges, only to find themselves chasing those deadly will-o'-the-wisps, the flashes of an enemy's guns. To fall back was absolutely necessary; but here again the soldiers were met by the rapid firing of the Indians, who had occupied the houses and orchards between the English and the fort, and were fighting behind the strong defences formed by the picket fences. Every charge of the soldiers only enveloped the pursuers in a maze of buildings and trees, while the Indians beat a nimble retreat, firing from behind any shelter that they could find. From an open cellar the concealed savages poured

a deadly fire into the retreating ranks, but still Dalyell was undismayed. Where commands were of no effect he beat the men with the flat of his sword. Major Rogers, trained in Indian warfare, burst open the door of a cottage filled with Indians, and with his New Hampshire rangers put the ambushed savages to flight. Captain Gray fell mortally wounded in a charge. Dalyell, himself twice wounded, went to the succor of a helpless sergeant, when he too fell dead, and the Indians smeared their faces with his heart's blood. Major Rogers,* who succeeded to the command, took possession of the well-built Campau house, where his soldiers, fortified without by solid logs and bales of fur, and strengthened within by copious draughts from a keg of whiskey, held the enemy at bay until two bateaux armed with swivels came from the fort to the rescue. Of the 250 who went out, 159 were killed or wounded, while the Indian loss did not exceed twenty.

This victory of Bloody Run — as the creek has ever since been called — restored the waning fortunes of Pontiac, and every day brought accessions to his forces. Yet never since the siege began was Major Gladwin more hopeful of ultimate success. So the heats of August passed with an occasional skirmish, and September began. The Indians, powerless against the palisades, again turned their attention to the vessels that kept open the food communication with the settlers across the river, and made occasional trips to Fort Niagara for supplies and ammunition. From one of these latter voyages the schooner *Gladwin* was returning on the night of September 4, when, the wind falling, she anchored nine miles below the fort, having on board her command-

---

nunciation; Pondiac—as it is often spelled—is the Chippewa form.

*Gladwin and McDougall agree that the night attack was strenuously opposed by the former. There is a tradition (Fred Carlisle relates it as a fact, in his report of the Wayne County Historical Society for 1890) that Dalyell and Gladwin both sought the hand of Madeleine de Tonnancour, and that when she favored the aide-de-camp, Gladwin willingly sent him to his death. Inasmuch as Gladwin was happily married during the previous year, this story is simply another illustration of the fables that have gained currency in connection with the Pontiac conspiracy.

*After the Pontiac war Robert Rogers became commandant at Michilimackinac, reaching his post in August, 1766. There he speculated rashly, ran heavily into debt, and plotted with the French. Sent in irons to Montreal in September, 1768, he was tried for high treason, but was acquitted, and sailed for England, where he was received at court and fêted by the nobility. In 1775 he returned as a British major on half-pay. He was arrested by the Pennsylvania Committee of Safety in September, 1775, but was paroled. Later Washington refused him an audience; he was proscribed by the New Hampshire Legislature, November 19, 1778; and at Mamaroneck, New York, his British force was defeated, October 21, 1776. He died in England about 1800. His wife, a daughter of Rev. Arthur Brown, of Portsmouth, New Hampshire, was divorced from him in 1779 on the ground of his desertion and infidelity.

er Horst, her mate Jacobs, and a crew of ten men. Six Iroquois, supposed to be friendly to the English, had been landed that morning, and to their brethren was probably due the night attack made by a large force of Indians, whose light canoes dropped so silently down the dark river that a single cannon-shot and one volley of musketry was all the welcome that could be given them. Horst fell in the first onslaught; and Jacobs, seeing that hope was gone, gave the command to blow up the vessel. At that word some Wyandottes, who knew the meaning of the command, gave warning to their companions, and all made a dash overboard, swimming for dear life to be clear of the dreaded destruction. Jacobs, no less astonished than gratified at the effect of his words, had no further trouble that night, and the next morning he sailed away to the fort. Six of the sailors escaped unhurt, to wear the medals presented to them for bravery.*

From the beginning of the siege Pontiac had relied on help from the French in the Illinois country, to whom he had sent an appeal for aid. "Since Father Bellestre departed," he said, "the Indians had no news, nor did any letters come to the French, but the English alone received letters. The English say incessantly that since the French and Spaniards have been overthrown, they own all the country. When our father, M. Bellestre, was going off from hence, he told us, 'My children, the English to-day overthrow your father; as long as they have the upper hand ye will not have what ye stand in need of; but this will not last.' We pray our father at the Illinois to take pity on us and say, 'These poor children are willing to raise me up.' Why do we that which we are doing to-day? It is because we are unwilling that the English should possess these lands; this is what causeth thy children to rise up and strike everywhere."†

This message was indorsed by the Chippewas and by the French inhabitants at Detroit, the latter complaining that they were obliged to submit to Indian exactions. M. Neyons, the French commandant in the Illinois country, acting under pressure from General Amherst (who had learned from Gladwin how essential to Pontiac's success was the expected help

from the French), replied to the appeal that "the great day had come at last wherein it had pleased the Master of Life to command the great King of France and him of England to make peace between them, sorry to see the blood of men spilled so long." So these kings had ordered all their chiefs and warriors to bury the hatchet. M. Neyons promised that when this was done the Indians would see the road free, the lakes and rivers unstopped; ammunition and merchandise would abound in their villages; their women and children would be cloaked; they would go to dances and festivals not cumbered with heavy clothes, but with skirts, blankets, and ribbons. "Forget, then, my dear children," he commanded, "all evil talks. Leave off from spilling the blood of your brethren the English. Our hearts are now but one; you cannot at present strike the one without having the other for an enemy also."

This message had the desired effect. Dated September 27, its contents so dashed Pontiac's hopes that on October 12 he sued most submissively for peace. Being in need of flour, Gladwin granted a truce, but made no promises, saying that General Amherst alone had power to grant pardon. To Amherst the commandant wrote that it would be good policy to leave matters open until the spring, when the Indians would be so reduced for want of powder there would be no danger that they would break out again, "provided some examples are made of our good friends the French, who set them on." Gladwin then adds: "No advantages can be gained by prosecuting the war, owing to the difficulty of catching them [the Indians]. Add to this the expense of such a war, which, if continued, the ruin of our entire peltry trade must follow, and the loss of a prodigious consumption of our merchandise. It will be the means of their retiring, which will re-enforce other nations on the Mississippi, whom they will push against us, and make them our enemies forever. Consequently it will render it extremely difficult to pass that country, and especially as the French have promised to supply them with everything they want."

Then follows the passage often quoted to show Gladwin's cynical brutality: "They have lost between eighty and ninety of their best warriors; but if your

* Chapman Abraham's testimony, Gladwin's MS.
† Gladwin's MS.

excellency still intends to punish them for their barbarities, it may be easier done, without any expense to the crown, by permitting a free sale of rum, which will destroy them more effectually than fire and sword." Parkman closes the quotation at this point; but a very different turn is given to the matter in the next sentence, which is taken from the draught of the letter in Gladwin's own handwriting, as follows: "But, on the contrary, if you intend to accommodate matters in spring, which I hope you will for the above reasons, it may be necessary to send up Sir William Johnson." This is the letter of a warrior who is also somewhat of a statesman.

Pontiac's conspiracy ended in failure. For five months the little garrison at Detroit had been surrounded by a thousand or more savages, and nothing but the untiring watchfulness and the intrepid coolness of the resourceful commandant saved the post from annihilation and prevented the Indian occupation of the lake country.* General Amherst was so well pleased with Gladwin's course during the first four months of the siege that on September 17 he wrote to the Secretary at War, Ellis: "As there have been two deputy adjutant-generals serving here, I have taken the liberty to show a mark of my entire satisfaction of Major Gladwin's good conduct and commendable behavior in appointing him a deputy adjutant-general, but to remain with the troops at Detroit in the same manner as has been ordered. This is no more than a name, but should it be your gracious pleasure to approve it, and honor Major Gladwin with the rank of lieutenant-colonel, I am firmly of the opinion that the promotion of so deserving an officer must at any time be a benefit to his Majesty's service, and this is the sole view I have in mentioning it to you." General Amherst's recommendations were followed, and Gladwin held the rank of lieutenant-colonel until he was made a colonel in 1777; five years later he became a major-general.

It fell to the lot of Colonel Bradstreet,

the hero of Fort Frontenac, to lead the great force that was to confirm the British power in the lake country. The vainglory of that officer led him to make so disgraceful a peace with the Indians that General Gates, who had succeeded Amherst, was compelled to repudiate it. Bradstreet's expedition got no further than Sandusky, but a detachment reached Detroit late in the August of 1764, and on the last day of that month Colonel Gladwin turned over his command and sailed for Niagara, on his way to New York. He was heartily tired of fighting Indians, and preferred to resign rather than to undertake another campaign of that kind. Returning to England, we find him in 1774 living the contented life of a country gentleman. June 22, 1791, while on a visit to London, as he writes to General Gates,* he was presented to George III., who asked him how long he had been in town. "Three weeks," replied the soldier, to the consternation of George Wert, who whispered to him to say he had just arrived. "But as I went to court only on that occasion," says this most unsophisticated of courtiers, "and thought it probable that I should never go there again, I thought there was no harm in speaking the truth."

In April, 1769, Pontiac went to St. Louis. One day he arrayed himself in the uniform of a French officer, given to him years before by the Marquis of Montcalm. After visiting his old friends, he repaired to the village of Cahokia, across the Mississippi, where he joined in a feast given by the Illinois. In the early morning he left the town for the forest, singing as he went. An English trader, Wilkinson by name, thinking to rid his country of a dangerous enemy, promised an Illinois Indian a barrel of rum to murder the famous chief. This treachery on the part of one of their number cost the Illinois dear, for Pontiac's friends did not cease in their vengeance until they had practically wiped out the Illinois nation. The body of the chief was buried with military honors near the fort at St. Louis. "Neither mound nor tablet," says Parkman, "marked the burial-place of Pontiac. For a mausoleum a city has risen above the forest hero; and the race whom he hated with such burning rancor trample with unceasing footsteps over his forgotten grave."

* Amherst to Gladwin, New York, August 10, 1763: "I cannot express to you the satisfaction I feel in considering the behavior of your garrison, which I am very well convinced was in a great degree due to your steadiness and good conduct; and the measures you have since taken in baffling all their schemes fully prove what can be done by British soldiers when handled by a resolute and prudent officer."—Parkman MSS.

* MS. letter; Gladwin's original draught.

THE MONTAGNAIS

AS I walk through an Indian village I am startled by seeing my aboriginal self. We rarely meet our prehistoric ancestors, but here I sit down on the earth with my disconnected forefathers; I talk with men and women who still are absolutely a part of nature. Although a man has no measure of his future progress, yet he learns where he started when he meets a savage. Here I see how far we have come since my family left the woods. These untrodden wilds of human nature have a wonderful interest. They lead you on, by the fascination of discovery, from swamp to glades, through rugged gorges up to commanding summits, and they keep you meanwhile under the enchantment of nature's mysteries. I met yesterday on the beach an Indian coming from a seclusion of two years in the heart of the continent. He had lived without any of what we call the necessities of civilization, and yet he was quite like other men in flesh and limb. The shyness and quietness of nature were upon him so strongly that I would not break into his reserve, nor dissipate the awe I felt in his presence. He had a very different feeling for me; he knew a hundred men, even a whole tribe, far more skilful at

getting a living out of the wilderness, so he had no wonder to waste on an inferior. His wife and family disembarked, and they set up their lodge on the sands with lordly independence.

Betshiamits is the chief mission for these Montagnais Indians, about eighty miles east of the Saguenay. The chapel, parsonage, Father Arnaud's interesting museum of natural history and Indian antiquities, Hudson Bay Co.'s store, and about thirty small square houses are scattered along the bank rising above the sand beach. Across the mouth of the Betshiamits River is a lumber-mill and its attendant shanties. The forest comes down to the village and its fields, and the Gulf of St. Lawrence rolls in upon it, raising all about the mouth of the river a gleaming wall of breakers out on the bars. Their roar is in keeping with the wildness and solitude of the Labrador coast. The whitewashed houses, with crude furniture, seem out of place in an Indian village. The Indians had them built many years ago; they find them convenient for hiding away the goods and chattels not taken to the woods, and for sleeping in if they arrive here too late in the day to put up their wigwams.

A MONTAGNAIS BELLE.

It is a common thing to see the family camping in the yard while the house stands empty. Indeed, they seem far more at home out-of-doors, with the canoe turned up near the wigwam, a few stones for a fire-place, and the unfenced world for their door-yard. The domestic economy is in full view. The acme of a husband's devotion is as rarely seen here as elsewhere; it is only a genius in affection that cuts wood and draws water for his squaw. When the sunset glows through the spruces you see a group of dark, toiling figures against the golden sky, each with her axe bends and plods along under a back-load of wood suspended by a tump-line across the forehead. At the lodge she drops her load, and without remark cuts it up to cook supper. She may take a boy with her in the canoe, and paddle away toward the horizon; hours afterward she returns with a load —wood, the net she has been seining with in some retired cove, and perhaps some fish. She carries her many armfuls across the beach, and gets another squaw to help her bring up the canoe. When a seal is brought in, the squaws and dogs do the butchering. The women often throw a shawl or blanket over some poles, and compose a picturesque group in the shade, sewing, splitting spruce roots for canoe-making, and chatting away as glibly as if they knew English. Their wash-day is

the most ameliorated I have seen. The girl kneels or squats by the tub on the ground, while her beaux lounge close by, and contend for the smiles and the suds, and often her straight black hair hangs down her back, while a younger sister combs it. The door-yard would seem empty without the children playing Indian house-keeping: they stand up poles, cover them with bark, and collect stones for a fireplace; the range of their fancy covers sleeping and eating.

The Indian's home, properly speaking, does not exist; he is not half so domestic as the beaver, which builds a house and raises its family in a given locality. He owns land, yet moves about more than a bird which nests in a tree. Even the bear is a better tenant, and the wood-chuck is an older settler in his neighborhood. These Indians by their mode of living seem to be the shyest and most nomadic and isolated of creatures; but in fact they surprise me with their strong social qualities. We shall see farther on that his material circumstances as well as his instincts mould the life and character of this wild natural man as much as they decide the features of our civilization. Betshiamits is the Indian's Newport, his summer resort by the sea-side, where he lives in comparative luxury, and enjoys a taste of civilization. The wigwam is still his favorite cottage, and certainly this primitive and picturesque shelter is the best suited to his life and character. It has a natural form, like the mound of a mole—an elliptical dome about seven feet high and eighteen feet long. It is made of bent poles sustaining long strips of birch bark; the windows are an irregular opening at each end covered with cotton, and the little door is closed with a curtain. As I stooped to look inside of a lodge, Louis, the Indian host, politely bid me come in. No one, however, arose to give me a chair—there were no chairs; but I crouched along under the roof and found a seat on a chest. The place was full of people, squatting, sitting, and lying about the floor in many different attitudes. The men wear the ordinary costumes of to-day with a red sash about the waist. The women have but one note-worthy article of dress, the Montagnais cap, with its alternate black and red pieces meeting at the top, and its band of bright silk embroidery; they wear a red kerchief or a shawl over the shoulders. Their hair is bound up in a queer little club covering each ear. While the men lounged and smoked, the women chewed gum with remarkable energy. These sat on a piece of matting near the windows and embroidered their caps and moccasins. The children and dogs kept up a moderate activity in coming and going over the crouching figures. The lodge was furnished with a stove, guns, chests of personal effects, cooking utensils,

although it is fragile and portable, yet it is essentially the same house that sheltered the men of this continent unknown ages ago. I inferred that the four families living there—thirteen people and nine dogs—had each a certain part of the lodge, but no boundaries appeared to be established. At night they assembled on their respective plots of floor, I suppose, and drew their blankets over their respective families.

SQUAWS BRINGING WOOD INTO CAMP.

clothes hanging over poles on each side, and heaps of blankets and pillows pushed up against the wall; and there were bags, boots, and bottles enough to fill up the nooks. As there were no beds, shelves, table, etc., the poles of the roof held a great part of these domestic articles; shoes, stockings, and a pail of water were about my head; further on were a branch of tamarack blest for religious uses, vials of holy-water, chaplets, and pictures of the Pope. Even the baby was hung up on the wall in a rude hammock. The community comb is kept in a sheath attached to a piece of porcupine's tail armed with fine sharp quills; this device for cleaning is so efficient as to be rather suggestive. The low arched roof of white poles and rich bark was dimly lighted by the cotton windows near the ground; the walls were shaded by masses of dark clothes, relieved here and there by strong reds and yellows; and the full light fell upon the squaws at the window with bright silks on their laps. It had a domestic, cheerful aspect on that sunny day; but it was an odd little place as a home of ancient date. For

The inmates of this Indian home were the strangest part of the scene. The tidy women were squatting on the floor, some cross-legged like Turks, others sitting on one foot as a cushion, or on their toes turned inward under them, or on their knees and heels. They were quite erect, yet easy, in these attitudes, as comfortable as we are upon luxurious furniture. One of them changed her dress by detachments at my elbow. The men were waiting for dinner; one slept curled up in a heap near the wall; another sat flat on the floor by his wife; and the other two lay stretched across the opposite end of the lodge. The children showed a remarkable capacity for stowing themselves away in grotesque shapes in nooks and corners, whence they stared at me with black bead-like eyes as expressionless as those of animals. Meanwhile the people kept up a general conversation in their own tongue; their voices were low, even in laughter, and expressive of a kind and considerate nature. You notice a good deal of abruptness in their talk; but this is due to their language, in which you

PAUL ST. OUGE.

hear many inarticulate grunts, short, brusque inflections, and long, disjointed, unmelodious words. But when they talk French, which the most of them understand, their speech is quite agreeable. I tried in many ways to engage the squaws in conversation in this tongue, but they turned to me a deaf ear, or else their husband's. It seems that the missionaries advise the tribe to have but little intercourse with whites; they will often pretend not to understand you, or will grant your request without replying to your speech.

In addressing an Indian I realize that I am talking to nature; I feel a complex sentiment—doubt as to making myself understood, curiosity, sympathy, and awe at intruding upon his reserve. Louis was one of those heavy-faced Indians that seem alive, yet as unapproachable as a beaver. For a while his answers seemed to come as if by chance, as the breeze eddies about a rock, or as if sent by some other inward being; a certain courtesy pervaded his reserved manner, but expressed no reverence for a superior; he was simply shy, and refused to come out of his burrow. At last, however, he lost his restraint and became passively sociable.

"How was the hunting, Louis, last winter? Did you get a good lot of fur?"

"The hunting, sir, was very poor. The woods seem to be dead. Ptarmigan, hares, beavers, fish, everything, is so scarce that we can hardly live. We go sometimes three or four days without anything to eat. It's a hard life sometimes."

"What does it cost you to live in the woods?"

"It costs you a good deal. Every year we buy about five barrels of flour, forty pounds of tea, eighty pounds of sugar, seventy pounds of lard, and eighty pounds of pork, that much for each family, four to six persons. We eat almost all of that here on the coast and on the way up to the hunting-grounds; for we take with us only enough provisions to last till we reach the woods, it is such hard work to make the portages. Our supplies, traps, clothes, etc., cost us about $250 or $300 per year. Some families spend more and some less. There in the woods we live on game and fish—no bread or pork, but we have tea there. We need about 3000 hares, 100 beavers, a great many fish. It costs the Indian a great deal to live. And if he gets short of food up in the woods, he can starve to death. There are some trading posts inland, but they sell flour at eight and a half cents a pound, and pork at thirty cents."

"How much do you make out of your hunts?"

"That depends on the season. Sometimes the best hunters get $400 worth of furs; one of our men has sold $22,000 worth of fur to this post; the most of us get from $100 to $200."

I may add that from the earliest times the Indian has always been so improvident as to exhaust all his resources each year; he gets his supplies on credit, with the understanding that he is to pay for them the next summer with his winter furs. This system worked well enough when the Hudson Bay Company was the only accessible trader. The Indians were both disposed and obliged to be faithful to their obligations, so much so as to have made that corporation one of the wealthiest in the world. But since the advent of unscrupulous traders the Indians have learned dishonest tricks, and many of them now sell their furs to other parties than the ones they owe.

The dinner meanwhile had been prepared by one of the squaws. She set out a number of plates on the floor, and Louis invited me to eat of their stewed ducks. I accordingly settled from the chest where I sat to the floor. Only the men came to the meal; for it is a custom among them to serve the men first; the women, having less exposure and travel to endure in winter, consider their needs as secondary; they will absolutely fast when provisions are scarce. And yet, notwithstanding their extra nourishment, in times of starvation the men always succumb first. We helped ourselves from the kettle; and when we had finished, two of the men rolled up into heaps and went to sleep. The women, children, and dogs then gathered about the dishes. Each one had an attendant dog at her elbow, ready for any emergency. The meal was social and pleasant, with good-natured talking, and manners quite deferential. But the dogs were an aggressive element. They were eager and unscrupulous; if a hand remained too long away from the plate, a dog captured the contents. Now and then a yelp, or a crescendo of ire on the word "ahwis," broke the calmness of the conversation. The dog of the prettiest maiden kept advancing his nose toward her plate, and she kept pounding his head with her spoon till he concluded to retreat. Another cur sat very quietly for some time beside a child; but at last he rose in open rebellion. I rushed to the plate. The child screamed, spoons flourished in the air, and screams resounded; and finally the dog settled back on his haunches with a revengeful snarl. When the women had finished their meal they sat still and let the dogs struggle over their laps, and take possession of the entire culinary department. After setting things to rights the women resumed their sewing on the floor, and I left them chatting away the afternoon, more happily than many of our careworn house-keepers in their palaces of taste and educated discontent.

The bark canoe is the Indian's *chef-d'œuvre*. It seems to me not only a beautiful object, but a suggestive emblem of his life. It is the most natural boat in the world: to make it he peels the bark from a birch, splits a cedar for timbers and planks, binds it together with roots,

and closes the seams with pitch from the pine. His tools are an axe, a crooked knife, and an awl made of a deer's bone. No compass and square cover his weakness, for every piece tells the exact truth of his hand and eye; not even a bench removes him from the earth, nor a roof covers him from the sky; he kneels at his work. And the women embody their attachment in the pitch they press into the cracks. It

Fig. 1.

Fig. 2.

CANOE-MAKING.

is nature's model, made by the wild man in the woods. The life of the bark canoe is equally poetic; it floats through mountain lakes with the beaver, and runs rapids with the otter; indeed, all of its companions are creatures of the forest; it is faithful to nature to the very last, when it retires to the shore of some lonely pond to mould under its mound of feathery moss. I never meet this most poetic of wrecks without recalling its romantic human interests. It was the home of a family; it was the scene of the whole tragedy of life, from the beginning to the end, strange with untamed characters, and intense with real storms, real misery, joy, or love, passing in the isolation of the wilderness.

Canoe-building is the chief industrial event of the Indian's life. As the craft lasts in hunting only two or three years, about one-third of the tribe build canoes here every summer. This important work is intrusted only to men of experience. And although they have here some civilized tools, yet the whole operation is full of the Indian's originality; you see men at work sitting on the ground, holding a stick, perhaps, between their feet, to shave it, or on their knees, to plane it, and they depend mostly upon the eye, without measures, in shaping their symmetrical, beautiful craft. I often loitered about the canoe built by Paul St. Ouge, the patriarch of the tribe. Although he is one hundred and five years old, yet he is quite erect, sprightly, and still skilful with his axe and crooked knife.

"Paul, how many canoes have you built?"

"I don't know; about 175; but I sha'n't build many more—the Lord will soon give me another job. I am waiting for Him every day." And straightening up to his full height, he looked off to the horizon with a very expectant and practical expression.

"You must have travelled a good ways in these light craft in a hundred and five years?"

"Yes," said he, turning over his stick on his narrow bench, "I've been everywhere—all over," swinging his long arm toward every point of the compass. Then, as he went on shaving and shaping his sticks, I kept him telling me how he makes a canoe. The birch-bark canoe might be called a cedar or spruce canoe, for two-thirds of its material—the timbers and planks—are of wood. The timbers, or knees, are split out of green stuff, and shaved down to a thickness of a quarter of an inch, and a width of two and a half to three inches. In the woods this is done with a knife, but here a rude bench and a drawing-knife facilitate the work. The timbers, after soaking a week or two, are bent in pairs over the knee, and bound in bundles to season, in the sizes and shapes required at various parts of the canoe. The gunwales also are bent to the desired sheer, and seasoned in shape on the ground by the help of props and weights. After seasoning, the crossbars are morticed into them. The planks or

battens are long strips from an eighth of an inch thick to a quarter along the bottom, and three to four inches wide. The choice of a bark is made with care, to secure one that is tough and free from knot-holes. A canoe generally requires three pieces of bark, the main one covering the bottom and bow and stern, and a smaller one sewed on to the main one on each side to reach the gunwales. After they are peeled from the trees they are tied up in rolls for transportation; and if they have been peeled some weeks before use, they are soaked several days to make them pliable. The loose layers on the outside are stripped away to leave only the tight layers; and the rough grain on the inside is scraped off to make it smooth. The bark is then set up in the general shape of a canoe, to be cut and sewed in the following manner: The main bark is laid on a smooth level ground, the inside surface downward, and a flat frame—shaped like the gunwales, but without any sheer—is laid on the middle of it and weighted with stones to keep everything in place. The bark is bent up along each side of this frame, and stakes are driven in to hold it; the gunwales are set up inside the stakes, and supported by props under the crossbars, and weighted to keep them in position; strips inside and outside the bark keep it flat along the sides. Each edge of the bark is then cut off to receive the additional pieces put on to reach the gunwale; the fulness of the bark along each side is taken out by cutting gores; the additional pieces are cut and pinned in place. Then the squaws come with their split spruce roots, thongs of deer's hide, and awls, to sew up the seams, excepting those at the bow and stern. The long seam of each additional piece has a half-round spruce root laid along the outside, under the stitches, to prevent the rawhide from splitting the edge of the bark; the edges of the gores —not lapping but meeting—are held by a stitch here and there. The edge of the bark is then trimmed off all around, bent over the gunwale, and sewed fast to it with roots. After the canoe is otherwise finished, a lighter gunwale or strip is nailed or wrapped on top of the main gunwale, to cover this wrapping and the edge of the bark, and the crossbars are lashed to the gunwales by roots rove through holes near their ends. When the seams have been sewed and the gunwales finished, the stem and stern seams are sewed up, thus: A pair of light cedar strips a quarter by half an inch are bent to the desired curve of each end of the canoe; a strip is laid on each side of the bow as a kind of welt; the rawhide thongs, passing through the bark and over these strips, draw the two barks closely and firmly together. The bark is then trimmed off along these curves.

The weights and the bottom frame are now removed, and the inside of the canoe is covered with a coat of pitch—resin and grease—and this, again, is covered with some thin pieces of bark. The bark has now been cut to the general shape of a canoe, and secured to the gunwales, and the seams have been sewed up; it is ready to receive the planks and timbers that are to hold it in the desired form. Beginning at the bow, the long thin planks or battens are nicely fitted into the canoe, forming a lining running fore and aft. The peculiarly shaped stem-post is slipped into place. The gunwales had been bevelled on the under and outer corner, to form a groove between them and the bark, to receive the ends of the timbers. Beginning at the bow again, the first timber is cut of the proper length, the ends are slipped under the gunwale at their proper place, and the timber is driven, at its centre, forward over the lining till it stands plumb. It thus stretches the bark taut, and keeps its place. Thus the timbers are successively fitted in, working from the bow and the stern toward midships; they are the moulds that decide the shape of the canoe. And as they are a series of inverted arches springing from the gunwales across the bottom, and standing about half an inch apart, they form the strongest lining of the canoe. The craft is now capsized, the seams are packed full of warm pitch mixed with a dry red pigment, and those of the bow and stern are, moreover, covered with a strip of muslin. The bark canoe is a remarkable invention for beauty, lightness, and strength; I doubt that even the most learned inventor could make anything better adapted to its uses.

The Canadian Indians have a remarkably complete history, dating from the advent of the Jesuits, who first tried to civilize them, and plausible speculation leads us still further back. I have always felt proud of a scalp and a bark

canoe as the most original productions of America. But "one has only to read the narratives of Martin Sauer, Aberne-thy, and Santini in order to see that birch-bark canoes, houses, and baskets, skin dresses and lodges, snow-shoes and calumets, quill-work and moccasins, were, and are probably still, in use among the Tungus, who must have invented them ages before they appeared in the Western Continent; so also scalping, a practice unknown among Malays or any Old World people of the present day, was an accomplishment of the ancestors of Asiatic Koriaks and American Iroquois in the far-off days of Herodotus." If we lose our scalps, there is indeed nothing new for us under the sun. Columbus, after all, may have to surrender the palm to one of our brother canoeists from Asia. "There is no difficulty," says Dr. Pritch-ard, "in supposing them to have passed the strait which divides the two continents. The habitations of the nearest Americans are only thirty or forty leagues distant from the dwellings of the Tchuk-tchis. These people carry on a trade of barter with the Americans. They employ six days in passing the strait, directing their course from island to island, the distances between which are so short that they are able to pass every night on shore. Such was the information obtained by persons sent into the country of the Tchuk-tchis by the Russian government in 1760. In winter the two continents are joined by ice, and the people pass over in one day with their reindeer." If the Asiatics peopled the northern part of our continent, they left very inadequate traces and legends by which we can follow their movements and divisions into the tribes of North American Indians. The two principal Canadian races, the Iroquois and the Algonquins, were found to be generally at war by Cartier in 1535, first one and then the other getting possession of the St. Lawrence. Champlain in 1609 accompanied the Algonquins to Lake Champlain, and with one discharge of his blunderbuss put their enemies to rout. The Iroquois thus became the sworn enemies of the Canadians, and as they inhabited the Mohawk Valley, they naturally became more or less the allies of the Dutch and English colonists. The contrast between the United States and Canada is very striking in the treatment of the Indians. From the very first we kept them at a distance, sent them to fight our neighbors, and all the while pursued our policy of extermination. We may grant the political wisdom of refusing an alliance with an uncivilized and unreliable race, and it is plausible to explain that our tribes were warlike, aggressive, that they did not diminish as fast as immigrants in-

their relations with civilization have been comparatively intimate in four powerful elements, the government, the commerce in furs, the social life by marriage, and the religious influence of the missionaries. The government found its Indian question very much simplified by the Iroquois, who exterminated the Hurons and

SPEARING SALMON.

creased, and that they occupied lands needed by the growing nation; but all this and much more will never excuse our injustice to the Indians.

The Canadians merit but few national reproaches from their Indians. While the English came to America for their own salvation, the French came largely for the salvation of the Indians. Champlain therefore inaugurated at once the veritable and permanent policy of the French Canadian government in making them his allies, and that fostering spirit has always prevailed in the Dominion. The Canadian Indians therefore have been taken into the body of the national life far more than our outcast tribes;

Algonquins, and thus settled their titles to the soil. The other tribes diminished faster than immigrants arrived, and, moreover, they occupied lands not very desirable for agriculture. The slow-growing nation, having room enough to stretch itself, has never found it necessary to turn anybody out—excepting the Huguenots in early days. The Hudson Bay Company controlled the commercial relations of the Indians. It saved them from much of the demoralizing influence of border life; it carefully excluded settlers from encroaching on their hunting-grounds; it dealt with them in a uniform and reliable manner, though at an outrageous profit, and it kept them in their wild natural life, sometimes helping them in distress, yet making them earn their own living. It was, on the whole, a powerful conservative of the Indians by its patriarchal management. Intermarriage and immoral intimacy with European races was quite an element in their lives. It is not very clear that this has been prejudicial to their physical existence, for their means and habits of living have not been changed, and certainly their social life has been improved by civilization. Their chief defects in contact with the whites are immorality, which has decreased, drunkenness, which is not general enough to be injurious, and dishonesty in trading, which we white men can scarcely admit to be fatal. It is a significant fact that although even the faintest trace of Indian's blood predominates over that of the more effeminate yet conquering blood of Europeans, yet the pureblooded Indians have almost disappeared, while the half-breeds now compose the Canadian tribes. The disappearance of the Indians must be due to some hidden psychological influence rather than to any adverse material conditions. Even here, under the best attainable relations with civilization and the least possible change of habits, they are diminishing about as fast as our abused tribes. Scrofula and small-pox are their most common diseases, and they injure their health by unnecessary exposure, overloading on the carries, inordinate feasting and fasting, and excessive labor in running down the reindeer and moose; and their losses are not made up by their small families. Sickness is much dreaded, and if one or two die in a place, any one else who is indisposed thinks he also is to die, and the others gather about and express the same opinion. Those writers err who assert that insanity and deformity are unknown among them; they have a superstition that an evil spirit is taking possession of such persons, to change them into a supernatural creature that will wander about the woods and devour men. They therefore strangle the demented and many of the ill-formed.

The Catholic missionaries are the most interesting and influential element in the Indians' life. Their courage in following the savages into the wilderness, their heroism in dreadful martyrdoms, and their persistent zeal are vividly set forth by Mr. Francis Parkman in his work *The Jesu-*

its in North America. The detested, devoted, and disciplined order of Jesuits never followed a more unselfish aim than in christianizing the American Indian. And these striking figures of Canadian history displayed unsurpassable zeal and courage in their discouraging labors, their dangerous journeys, their disgusting experiences, and their awful martyrdoms. And perhaps no effort requiring so much intelligence and self-sacrifice ever produced such temporary results. They established themselves at Quebec as early as 1625, and built a college even in 1637, where they formed their small army with their renowned perfection of organization. As soon as they had learnt the intricate Indian tongues, they went into the vast wilderness with the savages, and founded missions among these Montagnais, the Algonquins, the Hurons, the tribes of the Great West, and extended the field of their labors from Labrador to Louisiana. They were successful in getting the Indian to transfer his zealous devotion from his manitous and jugglery to the rites of the Catholic Church. The fathers testify to his faithfulness in religious observances, and thank God for the abundance

PARSONAGE.

of their spiritual harvest. It is very likely that they improved somewhat his social existence, but I have met with no statement of the inward results of this conversion on his national or private character.

It seems evident that this conversion produced but a superficial impression, and

THE DEPARTURE FOR THE HUNT.

demanded but an external compliance with forms, for it lacked the vitality of a growing influence. After the abolition of the Jesuits by Pope Clement XIV., in 1773, the Montagnais Indians lost their last missionary .by the death of Father La Brosse in 1782. Secular priests met them here and there—often enough, one would think, to preserve the vital spark; but they no longer had the helpful companionship of the devoted Jesuit, who made himself one of them. When the Oblat Fathers, the present missionaries, resumed the effort to civilize them, in 1844, they found that the Montagnais had lost all traces of Christianity, excepting a tradition of the Jesuits as men, and that they had returned to barbarism in a single lifetime. They number now about 5000, of which one half are converted. The other half still live as heathens, having, however, lost the fur clothes, the war-paint, and the bows and arrows. They are still under the guidance of jugglers; they live in painful fear of one another; for they believe that the lack of game, and consequently starvation, comes from the evil charm cast by some acquaintance, whom they kill on the first opportunity. They often flee from a region when they see a stranger's track. They abandon even their children that are unable to keep up on the march. When a member of a family dies, some of them bury the corpse, while the others move the lodge to a new site; and as fast as death comes they flee from its field, until the last escapes alone from the lodge to die in the forest. When

the Oblat Fathers resumed the missionary labors they had to begin with such people, and meet again the general experiences of the Jesuits in travelling inland among these tribes. They soon made some converts, who brought others to the missions; and now the Fathers meet the Indians at various posts on the confines of civilization. My observation of these Catholic missions was made here at Betshiamits, at Seven Islands, at Moisie, and at Lake St. John, the head waters of the Saguenay.

The modern Montagnais seem to have degenerated. They are generally strong, and enduring as animals, but very homely and ungainly. Some of them seem but half-formed lumps of flesh, bowlegged, in-toed, and as awkward as a goose on land. Their extreme ungracefulness comes from their constant confinement in wigwams, in canoes, or their hampered gait on snow-shoes. A few, however, are erect, elastic figures, with shapely faces and delicate hands. The children are generally as grotesque and chunky as cubs. The wildness of their life shows itself in their actions; they lounge about their tents in attitudes quite beyond the average civilized body. They often get into the most abject positions, heads and limbs together, or the face stuck into the floor of boughs; you might fancy the tribe suffers with *cholera-morbus.* And they have a dog's facility in dropping on to the ground anywhere, at any time, and in any position.

In strolling about this mission I get many glimpses into their nature, but some of their most characteristic traits can be seen only in the freedom and seclusion of the forest. The Indian excels us all in wooing Nature, but he has not the art to write her love-letters. Even a bear does not sit down on the sand with more confidence.

I have reverently practised his grotesque attitudes, and done some loafing in my day, but I cannot reach an Indian's peace of mind. When my family left the woods we gave our birthright of freedom for a mess of duties.

Their contentment seems at times almost supernatural; they sit as still as a corpse, in some uncomfortable position, until you long for a resurrection. The impression is still stronger from the absence of any reverie on their dark faces; they never dream, but always watch. Their happy, careless disposition seems incompatible with their grave appearance; you hear laughter and low but merry conversation in a lodge; you look in at those taciturn faces and wonder who was moved to such levity. On a winter's night, in the heart of a polar wilderness, if you could look into their solitary lodge when the last morsel of food is being devoured, you would find them perfectly contented and joyful, provided that meal was a full one. Their only comment would be that they must turn out early the next morning. They have given up scoffing, joking, and slandering to a considerable extent, for I am told that they are now extremely sensitive to ridicule. This Newport of the Indians has quite as much social life in its way as our resorts. They are constantly visiting, either at their lodges or about the grounds. They evidently make the most of their short season; the youths play ball, the maids frolic, the men smoke and chat in groups about the checker-board, the card-playing on the floor, or the canoe-making, and the women are not silent over their sewing, washing, and butchering. Their nature is really sociable, but their mode of living, by hunting and fishing, isolates them in the forest, and produces many strange animal tendencies. One after-

FINDING A BIRCH-BARK LETTER IN THE WOODS.

noon, while walking on the beach, I saw five canoes coming into port. As they passed the statue of the Virgin each fired a salute. Here and there an Indian of the village looked over the edge of the bluff to see who was coming, and then resumed his lounging. When the canoes were beached, twenty-two people of various ages and ten dogs came out on the sand. While the men carried up some of the luggage, and then the canoes, their families stood together in a picturesque group, rather tired, forlorn, and dirty. They also seemed indifferent to the village and the event of their arrival. At last they got their broad, awkward figures under way, and waddled across the beach, with the paddles in their hands, and mounted the bank to the street. They set up their cabins near the rest, but no one came to welcome them, nor did they expect any salutation. And yet they were regular members of the community, who had not met their friends since the parting of last summer. In a day or two I noticed them quite at home among the rest of the tribe into which they had strayed, as animals browsing about mingle with a herd without any recognition.

The departure for the woods gives another view of their customs. The families that were to "leave town" were on foot early in the morning, packing up for their long and solitary voyage. As I had discovered no leave-taking on the previous day, I was on the watch for it during the loading of the canoes at the water's edge. The cotton sheeting or the tent was spread on the bottom amidships, to protect the bags of flour, rolls of blankets, guns, kettles, traps; there were also rolls of birch bark for roofing the cabin, a roll of baby, packed in moss for swathing-cloths and laced up in its straight envelop, and from three to five dogs in each canoe. The only people on the beach besides the travellers were half a dozen girls, who squatted on the sand, and surveyed the preparations with considerable indifference.

"Aboard!" said the man. His wife struck her paddle against the side of the canoe, and dipped her moccasined feet in the water to get rid of the sand, and then climbed over the luggage to her place in the bow. The dogs were thrown in for the fourth time, the children settled among the packs, and he shoved off. They paddled away in silence, the wife

kneeling in the bow, the heads of children and dogs showing above the gunwale, and the man sitting up on the bar at the stern. Their families and their fortunes were all intrusted to a frail little craft; their separate routes lay through a wilderness, following the tracks of wild animals; and their last stage may be a fruitless hunt, starvation, and death in a polar night. And yet there was not a wave of the hand from a single soul, nor even a last look at a friendly face. I had never before realized how exclusively sympathy is an exquisite flower of civilization.

These converted Indians have been raised above their ancient barbarisms and conjurations; they have come again to observe with fidelity the rites of the Catholic Church, even when alone in the heart of the forest. Their domestic life is improved in regard to cleanliness and decency; but improvidence still goes hand-in-hand with starvation. Immorality has diminished somewhat; but unfortunate girls still have the benefit of a tradition that sterility is a greater blemish than impurity. They are now, as of old, respectful and considerate of one another; their differences are always settled by a quiet conference, or by the judgment of the chief or the missionary, and their domestic life is peaceable and contented. One of the strangest anomalies in their character is an extraordinary sense of freedom and self-appreciation, joined with abject humility of manner; they have a shrinking way of getting out of your path, avoiding your eye, or failing to answer you; their dumbness is partly due to the desire of the missionary that they shall have no intercourse with whites. But notwithstanding this excessive shyness they consider themselves equal to the highest dignitaries of the world.

The missionary who turns a race from a barbarous to a brotherly existence must feel his humility sorely tried with satisfaction. He has, however, a corrective in the loneliness, the mental famine of his isolation. Father Arnaud, Father Babel, and the others have but little diversion; their only social recreation is their season of seclusion once a year in their Oblat Monastery at Quebec. Father Arnaud came to this wide and wild field of duty thirty-two years ago, with the enthusiasm of a young Provencial. He was a lover of Nature and of her dark

BLIND INDIAN AND DAUGHTER SETTING TRAPS.

children of the forest. His travels, canoeing along the Labrador coast to Baffin's
Strait and Hudson's Bay, and through the
inland waters between these regions and
the Ottawa, and wintering in the lodges
of various tribes, have given him many
pleasures in scenery and in opportunities to collect his museum of natural history. Such a life, after all, presents
many charms to an intelligent man, in
the grandeur and the infinite beauty of
nature. Moreover, work and duty enliven the dullest route. He is a robust
man of medium height, with a full, benevolent face, and observant gray eyes.
He has kept through these years of exceptional experience a cheerful and contented spirit; but now and then I saw an
expression of loneliness on his face that
tells of weariness he never mentions.
The hardest of his work is done, his Indians now come to him here, and he lives
in a comfortable parsonage; in the garden, the only oasis I met on the Labrador
coast, he cherishes a few amenities of civilization; there were some vegetables, a
few hardy flowers, some struggling, adventurous apple-trees, a peacock, still

courtly and gorgeous in its exile to a desert, and at the foot of a high black cross grew a cluster of fleur-de-lis. As we walked at sunset into this retreat he passed his arm through mine with a deferential yet sympathetic manner. "This fleur-de-lis, you know, is the royal flower of France, and it recalls my native land; and besides, I am a monarchist; not wishing, however, any harm to your grand republic," he added, with apologetic courtesy.

"You must have found it very lonely in those long journeys and winters with the Indians."

"Well, no; some of my happiest days have been passed among them; they are pleasant companions, and I like the life of the woods."

"Was it not very difficult to give them Christian principles? How did you begin?"

"It was all very simple; it had to be simple, for an Indian of eighteen is not above a white child of six years. It was hard work for them to learn to read their own tongue; but a few learned to read and sing from manuscript books written in the characters of our printed alphabet. As they are exceedingly fond of music, and liked our melodies far better than their own dull chants, they at once took to copying these hymns. Music led them on, till, finally, nearly all have learned to read their hymns and catechism now printed for them. They write a good many letters for me to carry from post to post. And in the woods they frequently give news and make appointments in the hunting-grounds by writing on birch bark, which they put into a split stick erected on some frequented route. This primitive postal service is quite reliable, and brings me news often from even the most remote families; and you would be surprised at the delicacy and strength of sentiment in some of those letters. Their earliest literature, so to speak, is geography, very accurate maps of their country drawn on birch bark to guide the first traders and missionaries; some of them are still preserved by the Hudson Bay Company, at Montreal. But to return to their conversion, their progress was comparatively easy after they became interested in the hymns."

"What do you try to teach them?"

"Simply to read the hymns and catechism. Then our preaching is upon the most elemental duties and morality of Christians. They need nothing beyond this in their simple existence; in fact, they are with us so little, and have such slow minds, that it would be impracticable to do more. They cannot count even beyond ten, excepting by additions to ten, as ten-one, ten-two, etc."

"Do you find any difficulty in governing them?"

"None whatever, if they keep away from the whites. They are very obedient, and they worship the missionary as veritably the representative of God. And we have to be doctor and magistrate as well as teacher and preacher to them. They take very easily the leading ideas of Christianity, and follow them pretty well; and they are very regular in their religious duties, even in the woods."

"But why don't you give them more of the material advantages of civilization, and extend their education more?"

"That is scarcely practicable. They will not change their mode of life. The only way to help the Indian is to give him the simplest code of moral and religious conduct, make him feel the constant criticism of God even in his isolation, and then let him continue his natural life in the woods. They must be kept firmly under control, but only through kind and sympathetic relations, and through the influence of religious duties. I think that your Indians and every wild race could be governed peaceably by such means, instead of by armies and industrial civilization that they will not accept."

The winter life of these Montagnais is essentially the same as that of their heathen forefathers. They all start for the woods in August in their canoes, loaded down with provisions, etc. They travel slowly up the various rivers of the coast in companies to the far interior; there each family leaves its companions as it reaches its hunting-ground, and sets up its lodge on its ancestral domain. They spend a month or more preparing snow-shoes, toboggans, etc., for winter; then, as navigation closes, they put up their canoe and begin the winter's hunt. The game is too small and scarce to allow more than a family or two to live in a given locality; so the arctic winter passes in dreary isolation. But they are happy, contented, and busy. The men breakfast by starlight, and hunt every day excepting Sunday; they follow their line of traps—a two days'

THE DANCE.

march around the camp—and sleep in a trench in the snow without any covering. One likes to fancy them comfortable in warm furs, even while trees burst with the intense cold; but, in fact, fashion rules these wild men as well as our delicate belles; they consider otter and beaver too common for a stylish Indian, wear store clothes, and the same suit of ordinary warmth the year round. The women are busy with camp work, cooking, sewing, dressing furs, and cutting their 200 to 300 cords of wood. The children also help, and set traps near home for rabbits.

When the game is exhausted they shoulder their packs, load their toboggans, break camp, and move off on their snow-shoes to another part of their hunting-ground or to another region. If they are so fortunate as to have a superfluous amount of game or food, they make a *cache* to keep it from animals: the top of a tree is cut off about fifteen feet from the ground, a platform is built thereon, and the goods put upon it are covered with bark. A notice is often stuck up on the bank of the river or lake to invite needy travellers to help themselves; and those who may thus take food, or trespass on a neighbor's hunting-ground, leave a word of acknowledgment and make amends. When game is plenty they make their living easily; but they often fast, and sometimes starve to death. One of the most pathetic objects I have ever seen is a blind Indian here; for life is hard enough to those who have all their keen senses in perfection. This man has

thus far managed to keep his family alive every winter by the help of his oldest girl; she leads him about the forest, tells the signs she sees, helps set the traps, and thus far has led him back to camp. But how often death must have been at their heels!

Indians are still very much guided by dreams. At midnight a hunter may sit up on his blanket, and begin humming and drumming. As his imagination warms, his voice rises with a few words, while he sways back and forth, crouching low over his knees. Other men soon awake, and if the song records a promising vision, they get up and dance until the genius of the dream is won to favor their hunt. It is a unique scene—the figurative language, the dimness of night about the dying fire of the wigwam, and the men jumping wildly to those strange and melancholy measures.

The Indians at Betshiamits and at Moisie honored me with an exhibition of their national dances. The ballroom was a bare log house, dimly lighted by a lamp on a high shelf. A great shadow covered the tawny faces just under the beams of the ceiling, and fell aslant the circle of men, squaws, and children squatting on the floor in front of those standing about the walls. An aged couple and some dogs occupied a bed in one corner, along with a number of babies done up in rolls and corded against the wall. The old woman gave the dogs and her husband to drink from a saucepan, and the old man often lay back on the pillows with one leg across the other to finger his toes. Now and then a squaw picked her way among the crouching figures on the floor to the bed, hauled out her roll of baby, and gave it to suck. The women wore their national caps of black and red, but the men presented more variety, wearing felt hats, or red handkerchiefs that floated about the shoulders, or letting their long, black, straight, greasy hair whip up and down on their cheeks. The band consisted of a drum like a common sieve, hung from the ceiling by a string in front of the drummer-singer. His score was very simple, and yet the low notes of the voice, at a fifth and a fourth below the drum, were quite effective with a sombre color suited to the shadowy, fantastic scene.

The first set was like all the rest in general form: a number of men came out of the crowd, and began following one another around the stove near the centre of the room. Their steps consisted in advancing one foot, ducking, by bending the knees, then sliding back the advanced foot nearly to the other one. Their chief motion was, therefore, ducking, as if the entire company in unison had trodden upon one another's corns; and although they took three steps forward on each foot, yet by drawing this back, they advanced but an inch or two in each measure, and their legs, like those of a dancing-jack, seemed to be jointed only at the knees. The keeping of time was in the ducking, for there was no stamping. After a number of rounds thus in single file about the stove they retired, and some of the squaws came reluctantly out to perform. They danced as the men did, ducking, however, still more suddenly, and advancing still less at each step. They were extremely funny, notwithstanding their great decorum, their rather heavy figures, erect and rigid as statues, with downcast eyes and a shy turn of the head, bobbed up and down with overpowering solemnity. They soon gave place to the men again. A young Huron Indian now took the drum, and sang a more spirited and varied air to enliven the dance. The men closed up the file, forming a continuous circle of ducking figures. Their steps were longer and freer, and they began moving their arms about, and grunting, "Hé! hé! hé!" As the drumming quickened, they increased their grotesque contortions and their shouting; here and there a man turned about to face his neighbor, and the two carried on with the ducking an extravagant pantomime, portraying the hunt or the war; the music rose in the most frantic *crescendos* and savage discords; the actors, bounding about, bent over and tore the scalps from their prostrate victims, while yells and groans filled the air. It was the ancient war-dance, lacking only the lurid fire on the plumes and bloody tomahawks of the naked, painted savages.

A TRIP ON THE OTTAWA

"I wonder who the writer was that said there were two ways of travelling on a river?" mused our friend Jack, as he looked up from trying to place the point of his cane on a speck of sunshine that kept dancing about on the ground in obedience to the fluttering of the leaves overhead.

"What an absurd statement!" quickly answered a soft contralto voice. "As if there were not a dozen ways of achieving that object!"

"As usual, madame, you jump to a conclusion before hearing the whole statement. One way is to journey up, and the other to go down. And now just see the happy vantage-point we hold at this present moment. Here we are situated midway on this river, and can adopt either course we prefer. All we have to do is to take the voice of the meeting on the subject. What do they say?"

The meeting of four being addressed in this decided manner, tried to gather to itself a sense of the fact that the time for action had again arrived. The Basso, who was also the Artist of the party, growled from his bed on the grass that he was willing to do anything the rest agreed upon, but it was too hot for him to come to any decision for himself, at the same time languidly drawing his leg into the shade, when he suddenly bounded up, and searching in the grass upon which he had been reclining, tore out by the roots a small Canadian thistle, and viciously threw it over the cliff, giving utterance to a sound that caused the second lady of the party to exclaim, in a shocked voice, "Why, Frank!" while Frank, who had again taken a reclining position, assured her, with a face of child-like innocence, that he was merely trying to reach the lower D, and he thought he would accomplish it yet, after a little more practice.

The party were on the Cliff Walk, or, as it is better known, the Lover's Walk, along the face of the cliff upon which stood the Parliament Buildings at the capital of the Dominion, and the Ottawa River was the one under discussion as to the advisability of going up or down it. The three who were grouped together had a full view of a beautiful stretch of the river as it moved past them some hundred feet below where they stood, but they scarcely noticed it: in fact, they were in that happy condition that they were content simply to be conscious of the act of living and resting, and to drink in the soft breeze with every breath they drew. Not that they were any more lazy than you, my energetic friend. No; they were four busy brain-workers, and many months of continuous mental application had made them determine to enjoy their summer vacation to the full. One pair hailed from the modern Athens; the others were from busy Gotham. Chance had thrown them together, and a similarity of tastes had sealed a bond of friendship between them. One link in their chain of friendly intercourse was a mutual love of music, and by a happy coincidence they were each gifted so as to form a very harmonious vocal quartette, which was a source of much social enjoyment to themselves and others. After wandering about the country until a map of their route would be best represented by the branch of an old and very much pruned apple-tree, they at last reached the spot where we made their acquaintance, at the seat of the Dominion government, the city of Ottawa. They had viewed the points of interest, and driven over the neighboring country. The Artist had secured many good subjects; the Tenor had gathered in a quantity of information on all sorts of subjects, which he took every opportunity to inflict on the rest, and it was evident from his restless mood that he was full of knowledge yet unimparted, and insisted that the time had come for them to move on again.

"Now here we are," he explained. "We can either float down to the mouth of this river, with its beautiful coffee-colored water cheerfully entwined with sawdust and chips, or else we can take canoes and work our way up to its source. I was told this morning by a fair-haired giant of a raftsman that 'there was the biggest views ever seed up theer.' What is that you say?" the speaker asked, turning to the prostrate figure of the Basso. But, alas for his eloquence! the Basso was audibly asleep. The rest of the party, feeling this was a slight upon their company, proceeded to awake him by the aid of two parasols and one cane. When at last aroused, he was assured they had only disturbed him so that he might see the beautiful effect of the sunlight on the Chaudière Falls. He slowly sat up à la Turk, and in reply to many gushing expressions and requests that he should make a sketch of it, quietly remarked, There was too much sawdust, new boards, and saw-mill for his taste. In fact, the thing did not appeal to him at all, and he could only work with a hope of success when the subject strongly appealed to his sympathies.

"I suppose," said the leading voice, "you always respond when so appealed to?"

"Certainly," answered the Artist.

At this point a malicious gleam of delight came into the Tenor's eye as he said (apparently addressing the tree-tops): "What consummate humbugs these artists are! This morning for nearly ten minutes I saw a blind beggar appealing to the sympathies of this gifted genius, and he never responded with a cent." The Basso went through a pantomime behind the ladies' backs of punching the Tenor's head at the first convenient opportunity, and having thus relieved his feelings, picked up his sketching traps and sauntered off with the others. It was unanimously decided to go down-stream, leaving the upper portion of the river for another year's trip. When they had about reached the end of their walk, they came upon one of the many perfect pictures along this delightful promenade—a rustic stairway leading up at right angles, a piece of Gothic stonework, with luxuriant vines running over it in magnificent profusion, overshadowed by graceful elms, the whole being a rich mass of color, made up of the mellow green of the trees and delicate gray of the stones contrasting with the golden glowing brown of the sandy path. Here was evidently something of an appealing nature, for a sketching stool was promptly set up, followed by the opening of a sketchbook and a water-color box, a trio of musical voices wishing success, a flutter of bright color as the ladies passed up the stair, a wave of a pretty hand, a pantomimic action on the part of the Tenor suggestive of a fatherly blessing, a silence for a moment; then the endless music of Nature as she sings only to those who love her. Never was artist blessed with more propitious surroundings, and the sketch in his hands was beginning to repay Nature for her kind influences. Only a few more touches were needed. The brush had been filled with Indian red to put in a deep warm shadow, and was just being brought to the desired shape by gently touching the tips, when a crashing report rung out on the quiet and solitude like the bursting of everything mundane. The painter went straight up in the air several feet, the brush, full of color, was thrust as many inches down his throat, before he realized it was only the noonday gun that had been fired by an artilleryman about twenty feet over his head. As he crawled round on his hands and knees looking for his scattered colors and brushes in the grass, a listener would have thought he had at last reached to the deep bass note he had so long been in search of.

Early next morning the party boarded the steamer, and one of the ladies remarked, "It makes one feel quite at home to have the captain meet you and shake hands, as though you were visiting at his house, instead of coming on board his boat." For such was the urbanity of the gallant captain of the *Peerless* that all his passengers were his friends. The boat swung slowly out, affording one of the finest views possible of the beautiful Parliament Buildings, with all their architectural magnificence. But they are all too soon lost sight of as the boat suddenly rounds a bluff which shuts off the view, and reveals nothing but the unsightly lumber piles of the manufacturing city of Hull, on the opposite side of the river, which is occasionally called by the euphonious name of Slab City. Once more the quartette are on the move, drifting, as it were, for everything now seems so quiet and restful. On they go, past banks of

PARLIAMENT BUILDINGS.

rich foliage, green to the very water's edge, the cool-toned Laurentian range of mountains forming a background, and branches of willow marking by their brilliant and tender color where the land ended; but it could only be surmised where the water began, so cheated was the eye by the wonderful reflections. Here are several islands, beautifully wooded, and with the same delicate color over all. One of these—Kettle Island it is called—is the home of the Canadian Grace Darling—a modest, sweet-faced young girl of only eighteen summers, who, it is asserted, has already by her own unaided efforts been the means of saving seven human lives. She is very reserved about speaking of her own heroic deeds, and particularly dislikes being interviewed. The Marquis of Lorne, late Governor-General of Canada, has visited her on more than one occasion, and insists she shall receive the Humane Society's medal, which hitherto she has been in no hurry about accepting. Such heroism and modesty are indeed rare.

At short intervals the steamboat would make up to a collection of piles, with a few loose planks laid on top of them, called, per courtesy, landings. These stood about fifteen or twenty feet out of the water, with water-marks at different elevations all over them.

Although the scenery along the banks is a constant delight to the eye, the people

WAITING.

are a disappointment. They appear for the most part poor and spiritless, and judging from the tumble-down condition of their steamboat landings, must be shiftless indeed. The houses seen from the banks of the river are mere huts or shanties. No doubt there are well-to-do people living in the inland villages, who live in better style, but the general impression is one of apathetic poverty. At one of the landings the only living objects to be seen were three dogs. Two of these were collies, with their bright intelligent faces and restless action; the other, a great clumsy mongrel bull-dog, blind of one eye. They all expressed such lively interest in the approaching steamboat that our party concluded their master, mistress, and all their friends must be on board. But the captain volunteered the information that the cook was in the habit of throwing them something to eat every time the boat passed.

As the boat proceeded on her way the party became more and more enthusiastic over the beauty of the route. A little below Thurso, which the captain explained was the principal picnic resort for the people of the city, was another beautiful group of islands, so thickly overgrown and compact-looking that they had the appearance of having been trimmed like a hedge. And it required very little stretch of the imagination to form all kinds of objects out of them. As the Tenor observed, one looked like a vessel pulled up for repairs. Then there were such delightful glimpses of bays and inlets, suggesting such delicious fishing and mosquito bites! The banks gradually began to assume more and more the appearance of the river Thames, and some English passengers on board began to look for some of the old landmarks, until suddenly a large raft came into view, and called them back to the New World. On an average the boat stopped about every twenty minutes at some small village, each having its own local interest. Here is Montebello, where can be seen through the trees the seigniorial residence of the late Hon. Louis Joseph Papineau, the ex-arch-rebel, who in the rebellion of 1837 fled to the United States, and a price was set upon his head. But after a brief exile matters righted themselves with the Canadian government, and he was pardoned, and returned to his home, where he was received with open arms and loaded with honors, and he lived happy ever afterward (as they always do). Now they approach L'Original.* There is a very perceptible flutter on board. There is also a very decided improvement in the construction and appearance of the wharf. The Alto and Soprano exchange glances as they see large Saratoga trunks being deposited on the same. The Tenor feels it incumbent on him to find out what is the meaning of all this. He comes back with the information that this is the landing where passengers take the stage for the celebrated Caledonia Springs, situated about seven miles distant inland. The waters are considered very beneficial in cases of rheumatism and other kindred diseases. A company have erected a spacious hotel, and it has been dubbed the Saratoga of Canada, as here flock all the fashionably halt, the fashionably maimed, and the fashionably blind from all parts of the Dominion. At one of the smaller landings, where the boat did not usually stop unless signaled, a man was seen standing gesticulating wildly. The captain came forward and with an amused expression of countenance informed the passengers that he knew from the excited state the individual was in that a wedding party was coming on board. And his prognostication was soon verified, for as soon as the boat touched the landing a motley procession came trooping down — old and young and middle-aged, from the infant in arms to the aged couple, who, John Anderson like, were tottering down. The procession was headed by the bride and groom, the latter looking excessively uncomfortable and out of place in his "dressed-up" condition;

* Pronounced *Lo-reen-yal'*.

but the bride presented a great contrast to her new-made lord; her self-satisfaction was supreme. As the captain remarked, "If you really want to witness happiness and contentment, you must see a French-Canadian bride from the rural districts. She has attained to the height of her ambition; she is at last decked out in bridal finery." She went straight for the saloon after coming on board, and looked round a little nervously at first, then sat frigidly down on the extreme edge of the nearest bench, and cast down her eyes, as was supposed, in blushing modesty. But no! it was not modesty; it was her shoes upon which her admiring glances were directed.

The rest of her costume was commonplace, consisting of a black dress of some cheap material, which one of the ladies designated as "lustre." She wore a hat trimmed with a wreath of tawdry-looking pink and blue artificial flowers, while bows of yellow and green ribbon relieved the sombre hue of the dress. But it remained for the shoes to give the true bridal character to this somewhat remarkable toilet. They were of white kid, low cut, with huge rosettes on the instep. Her pedal extremities, which were of rather colossal proportions, were augmented by home-knit woollen stockings, which appeared just a trifle incongruous. Her husband soon joined her, and took a seat beside her, and as he sat speechless, with his wife's hand lying in his own, it was supposed he too was lost in admiration and wonder at the beauty of the slippers. A half-hour later found them in the same position, with the bride still casting loving glances at her feet. When the newly wedded pair left the boat they were met by an old man and a young girl, who, by the way they embraced the bridegroom, were set down as his father and sister. The former took the bride gently by the hand, who received them with rigid stateliness. The girl timidly ventured to kiss her newly made sister. The caress was passively permitted, not returned, and afterward deliberately wiped off with a blue cotton pocket-handkerchief. The last seen of the kid shoes they were almost invisible as their owner trudged up a steep sandy hill on a hot August afternoon.

The captain now came forward and announced to his passengers that the next stopping-place would be the last, as far as he was concerned. They would have a

ISLANDS BELOW THURSO.

little variation now in their mode of travelling, as the river for the next twelve miles was so full of rapids and dangerous shallows it was impossible for a steamboat to navigate. Therefore it was necessary to make a portage by railway to Carillon, at the foot of the rapids. The quartette thought this rather a good idea, as it would serve as another novelty in this very pleasant journey.

When they reached Grenville, the point at which they were to make the change, the Tenor, who had been missing for the last half-hour, made his appearance, and informed the other three that he had been talking with the captain, who had been giving him a description of a rafting station about two miles up on the opposite side of the river.

"Now," said he, "as we are all out for amusement, and our time's our own, why should we not stop over a day here, and make a call upon the raftsmen?"

"The very thing!" exclaimed both ladies at once; while the Artist declared his soul had been yearning for an introduction into rafting circles.

After a unanimous vote had been taken on the subject, the party bade adieu to the *Peerless* and her zealous captain and officers, and went in search of the ferry, as they had been directed. They looked in vain for the ferry-boat. There were several men grouped about the wharf, of the class one usually sees about railway stations and steamboat landings in country places—men who seem born to occupy positions with their backs against posts or walls, with their legs crossed, and their hands in their empty pockets, gazing with a far-away look of vacant stupidity on their equally empty faces. The Basso went up and accosted one of these wharf ornaments by inquiring, "Can you tell me where the ferry-boat starts from?"

"Here," was the laconic reply.

"Where is the boat?"

"There"—pointing to an ordinary-looking fishing-punt of apparently medium size.

"That?" chimed in the Tenor. "Why, we've got several valises."

"And where are my sketching traps to go, I should like to know?" came in an indignant *basso profondo*.

"Dat all right, monsieur," put in another individual, who had come upon the scene within the last few minutes. The speaker was a fine sturdy specimen of the French Canadian habitant, rather advanced in years, but of fine physique and good presence.

One of the ladies inquired, "Are you the ferryman?"

"Oui, madame."

"How many can you carry in your boat?"

"As many as want to go."

This was not very re-assuring, as by this time quite a number of people had come down from the village, men, women, and children, with carpet-bags, trunks, bundles, and babies too numerous to mention.

The Soprano, with true feminine caution, suggested to her friends the advisability of getting in at once, as the old man would certainly have to make two trips, and naturally those who got in first would start first. So they proceeded to embark on the primitive craft. The baggage was stowed away first in the bow. Then the human freight was to be disposed of. On they came, one after another, until the Soprano began to suspect she had been premature in her calculations. "I believe," said she, "the old man is going to take them all at one load." And such, indeed, was the case. And, impossible as it may seem, the load consisted of twelve human beings, besides about eight hundred pounds of baggage. "Are you not afraid to take so many?" asked one of the passengers. "Afraid! No, indeed; I could easily carry six more." This reply caused a general laugh, and served to restore confidence among some of the more timid passengers. One young man generously offered to assist the skipper if another pair of oars could be procured. But this offer was politely but resolutely refused. "How far is it to the point where you land?" was asked. "About three miles," answered the ferryman. "Three miles!" exclaimed the astonished Tenor. "One man row twelve people, besides all that freight, against the current too! He'll never do it." But he did, laughing and talking good-naturedly all the while, and when the boat drew up to the landing he appeared as little fatigued as when he started, and handed his lady passengers out as gallantly as any courtier from his beloved "La Belle France." The party proceeded by a foot-path through the woods to the hotel which had been recommended to them before leaving the steamboat. The house was new, and appeared clean and comfortable. The host was a French Canadian, who, to do him justice, tried to do his best for the accommodation of his guests, but, unfortunately for the comfort of our party, his knowledge of hotel-keeping was limited.

The house was filled with summer boarders, which meant, in Canada, tribes of children with their mammas and nurses. Not a masculine was to be seen anywhere (they knew better). When the boarders descended to the dining-room with appetites that would have done ample justice to a good meal, they were appalled by the heterogeneous mixture of babies, mothers, and nurses who had possession of every table in the room. And when at last a space was cleared by one of the waiters for the quartette, it was to sit down to soiled table linen and the refuse of food left by the last relay of babies. Meanwhile the respective mothers glared at the intruders, and passed audible remarks of a disagreeable nature anent the new arrivals. The landlady followed her disgusted guests out of the dining-room, and apologetically explained matters by saying they never had taken summer boarders before; but they were anxious to get their house paid for, and they thought it would help. "But, mon Dieu! we lose money all the time. We have thirty-five children in the house, the oldest only ten years old, and when they are not quarrelling the nurses are." The quartette, who were out for pleasure, decided to leave as speedily as possible. The good-natured landlord, willing to do all in his power for the accommodation of his American visitors, kindly put his own skiff at their disposal to go out to the rafts, and sent his clerk to act as their gondolier, which latter personage appeared very well pleased to exchange the close atmosphere of the hotel office for a blow on the river. He was an intense young Frenchman, showily arrayed in cheap store clothes, plated jewelry, and patent-leather boots, and, as the Contralto remarked, "evidently got up for the occasion." This gorgeous young creature answered to the classical name of Achille, and as he launched his boat and got into position with some difficulty, the party soon perceived that his skill and experience in aquatics were very superficial. But there was an air of importance about him as he put his oars in the row-locks that made some members of the quartette begin to think they had not done this young person justice. And if real hard work be taken as a criterion he must have been a perfect Hanlan in the art of rowing. The Artist, who was an adept in all matters pertaining to boating, and was now comfortably seated under the shade of his sketching umbrella, kept (despite the protestations of the ladies) urging the young fellow on by such exclamations as, "Go it, Achille; you'll yet cover yourself with glory." He was pretty well covered with water by this time, both from his profuse perspiration and the quantity his oars had shipped in his frantic endeavors to make good time. They had proceeded at such a rapid rate they had failed to note any of the beautiful scenery through which they were passing, until they suddenly found themselves in full view of the rafts, the object of their quest.

They were very politely received on board, and fairly delighted with all they saw. Everything was practically explained to them, from the construction of the raft to the working of it down from its native woods to the ocean. But the most interesting part to the ladies was the exploration of the culinary department, where the next day's meals were in course of preparation. The friendly cook courteously invited them to partake of the homely fare, which they gladly accepted, for after the wretched dinner they had tried to eat, this meal, served with the elegance of cleanliness, and an unlimited supply of good-will, tasted to them like a collation from Delmonico's. Moreover, it was a novelty—a luncheon on a raft. The sun was now beginning to light up the glorious Laurentians to the west of them, which suggested to the Tenor the propriety of moving on again, and they bade adieu to their jovial hosts on the raft with many good wishes and hopes of future meeting. They again took their places in the boat, and judging by the way the young man handled the oars, he had, during his season of rest, become "a sadder and a wiser man." As they were going with the stream, he took the advice of the Basso, and simply drifted down, using an oar now and then to guide their course. What a delicious half-hour it was! The sun, which was gradually sinking, made the water in the wide part of the river appear like a sheet of pure gold, without a ripple to mar its surface. The banks on either side were thickly wooded down to the water's edge, and cast such perfect reflections that it appeared as if the boat was actually drifting through the forest glade. There were several picturesque old piers built far out in the stream, for the convenience of loading the boats with lumber from the mills dur-

ing low water; for this thrifty little village of Hawkesbury is a great lumber centre, and is dependent for its prosperity upon one or two wealthy mill-owners. The quartette felt the influence of the tranquil evening and its suggestive imagery, and as if by common consent a soft strain of music sweetly floated over the water, and as they neared the landing the last chord died away just as the last ray of sunlight sank suddenly behind the distant mountains. As they landed, no word was spoken. Their minds seemed filled with a sort of reverential feeling, which was uninterrupted until they were close to the hotel, when the irrepressible Tenor broke the silence by exclaiming:

"I'll tell you what it is, Frank, that last half-hour was worth living. I don't feel half as bad as I did an hour ago about facing supper at the hotel."

"I am glad to see the waters have had such a soothing influence on you," answered the Soprano. "For my part, it would take oceans to obliterate the evil glare of that mother when I innocently usurped her baby's seat at dinner."

As there was no train from Grenville until noon next day, our travellers were compelled to accept the situation and remain where they were for the night. We will not dwell upon their sufferings during the period of their sojourn. Suffice it to say, if their dinner was bad, their supper was worse, and their breakfast next morning a little more so. As soon next day as the old ferryman would convey them, they took their departure, feeling deeply thankful that they were not in the position of the poor French landlord and his wife, who were compelled to take summer boarders in order to eke out a living. The party arrived at Grenville a good hour before the train was due, and amused themselves by looking about and watching the peculiarities of the native population, which caused them no little amusement.

By the time the train arrived the travellers were glad to resume their journey. Arrived at Carillon, the party were again charmed with their surroundings, and very much interested in the various points of attraction. They were soon on board the steamer which was to convey them down to Montreal, and by a happy coincidence they met with a party of congenial spirits, and the captain affably performed his duties as host by making them mutually acquaint-

THE FERRY.

ed. They had ample time to discuss the scenery in the neighborhood, as the boat did not leave for nearly an hour after they had embarked. On the opposite side of the river was Point Fortune, the line that divides the provinces of Quebec and

Ontario; and there, in the distance, are the grand old mountains containing much that is dear to the heart of the geologist. They are stated to be the oldest geological formation on the continent. But the great glory of Carillon is its dam and timber slides. A gentleman on board declared this dam was the largest in the world. "Phew!" came from the Artist; "that's pretty good. I was up in the Sierra Nevada Mountains about a year ago, and saw one there over a hundred feet high."

"As to that," put in one of Montreal's most popular D.D.'s, "I stood upon one once in another part of the world that was three miles across."

"Don't care," said the first speaker; "this is the largest in the world."

The discussion waxed hot. At last the captain was appealed to. "Why do they call this dam the largest in the world, captain?"

"Because there isn't a larger."

This was considered conclusive, and a general laugh put an end to the controversy.

But the quartette did not see this wonderful dam in all its glory, as it had been partially carried away by the spring freshets only a few months before. "Now," said their newly acquired friend the divine, as Carillon was gradually fading from view, "you will see between here and Lachine the gems of the Ottawa." And as they beheld the ever-varying landscape on either side of the river, with its alternate beauties of meadow and woodland, and the wonderful effects of light and shade on their old friends the Laurentians, which form an almost unbroken chain along the route, they fully realized the truth of the Doctor's words, while at intervals they would stop at some pretty little village that appeared in marked contrast to those at the commencement of their trip, nearer Ottawa City. These bore every evidence of thrift, not to say wealth. Here and there were cozy little villas, owned and occupied during the summer months by well-to-do Montrealers, and whenever they stopped, bevies of pretty girls would flock down to the landing to meet friends or exchange greetings with acquaintances on board. They were now coming in sight of the Lake of Two Mountains, where the Indian village of Oka is situated. "You ought to stop here," said the Doctor to our friends;

"there is something worth seeing, especially for you," regarding the Artist. "They have a Trappist monastery here, where, I am sure, an artist will find enough material to repay him for visiting it. Then the village itself has its interest in the fact that it has been for some years the scene of much conflict and strife between the Roman Catholic Church and the Protestants concerning the claims of the Indians. Then there is Mount Calvary and the seven chapels. Yes, you must see Oka; it is full of interest." The Tenor and Soprano felt very much tempted to remain a night at this interesting spot; but as they were under bonds to meet other friends in Quebec on a certain day, they felt constrained to push on. But the Alto and Basso realized it was their artistic duty to see the Trappists, if nothing more, of this celebrated place. So the party separated with mutual regrets, but not without arranging to come together again at no very distant date. The Artist and his wife left the steamboat amid the hearty good wishes of all on board, and started to explore this Franco-Indian village in pursuit of shelter for the night, as this was the first consideration before seeing the sights. They discovered there were two hostelries in the place kept by rival Frenchmen, and as neither of them spoke English, and our travellers' knowledge of the French language was very slight, and as there seemed no way of arriving at the respective merits of each house, the pair decided on the house on the sunny side of the street, as it appeared neat and prosperous-looking, and it had the largest sign out. The landlord was the largest man, his wife the largest woman. The lady was in hopes they might get the largest kind of entertainment. An Indian youth was at last found who condescended, for a large pecuniary consideration, to carry their valise and sketching traps up from the wharf, where they had been standing unprotected since the boat left, and had been a subject of much speculation to the juveniles, who had contrived to loosen all the straps round them, in which condition the Indian boy started to carry them. He had not proceeded many yards when first a roll of canvas, then a bunch of brushes, fell out. In vain the Artist called to him to stop; he only did that when he arrived in front of the hotel, with the empty straps in his hand; then he went back and carefully picked

OKA.

up all that he had dropped on the way, and carried them safely in his arms. The couple were shown their room, which blighted all hopes of colossal entertainment at the outset. It was small and stuffy, and immediately under the eaves, and, upon entering, it emitted that peculiar odor, common to many country sleeping apartments, which suggests equal parts of new plaster and old straw beds. They quickly deposited their wraps, and were hurrying down to seek the fresh air, when they were arrested on their way by a low sweet female voice singing a sadly pathetic melody, accompanied by a cabinet organ. The music had such a weird charm about it that our travellers were compelled to stop and listen. After a while they traced the sounds to a half-opened door leading out of the hall, where in a small, dimly lighted room could be seen the form of a young girl, apparently under twenty years of age, seated before the organ, with bent head and fingers wandering nervously over the key-board as she chanted her mournful lay. What a picture it was, and one that told its own sad story! Her listeners' eyes were suffused

with tears as they crept stealthily away. Not for worlds would they have disturbed the sightless singer, shut forever out from the light of day.

The next morning was set apart for the visit to the Trappist monastery, which was eight miles distant. The road followed the river-bank nearly all the way, and the party got the benefit of a soft cool breeze that was blowing refreshingly off the water. Altogether it was a charming drive. As they passed the humble homesteads of the habitants a general commotion would invariably ensue. Numerous pretty black-eyed children would run out, and stand open-mouthed viewing the strangers wonderingly, followed by two or three little black curs, which snapped and yelped viciously until they were looked at; then they would retreat in quick time into the innermost recesses of their dwelling-place. Added to these there was the inevitable pig, which expressed his approval or disapproval by a grunt.

The Artist's wife was enraptured by the luxuriant growth of wild flowers. Everywhere, as far as the eye could reach, it was one glorious burst of color. She had never seen such wild flowers; they were tropical in their magnificence. It was evident Nature had made amends for the brevity of the Canadian summer by loading it with her richest treasures. They had just ascended to the brow of one of the many hills when the monastery came into full view, and our friends could not help commenting on the fact that if these monks were denied all the other pleasures of the world, they had taken advantage of the one still left them. The site chosen for their habitation afforded to the eye a never-ending feast of the beautiful in nature. The building is situated on an eminence that commands the whole of the beautiful lake and the mountains from which it derives its name. The monastery itself is a large square building, solidly built of wood on a stone foundation, built at the expense of the Dominion government, which also gives an annual grant to help support the institution. This order has only been established in Canada about two years. They were driven out of France during the late political troubles there, and forbidden ever to return. They being thus cast upon the world, naturally sought protection in the province of Quebec, that great stronghold of Romanism. It is pretty generally known that these monks are the most rigorous of any order. They are also of very ancient origin: they were founded in the sixth century by the abbot of La Trappe; they were reformed in the year 1150, again in 1600.

The driver, who performed the office of guide and interpreter, soon made the attendant in charge understand that the lady and gentleman wished to inspect the institution. He was answered by a very low bow, speech being strictly forbidden unless by permission of the Father Superior of the monastery. However, he went to communicate with that gentleman, who soon came forward and urbanely welcomed his guests in good English with a French accent. He was a man about six feet in height, of good build. He was rather prepossessing in appearance, and when he spoke, his face was particularly attractive, owing to a very genial expression and a somewhat humorous twinkle in his eye. His head was cleanly shaved, all but a short close fringe of hair about an inch long all the way round. He was dressed in a long robe of cream-colored serge that reached down to his ankles, displaying low-cut shoes, and stockings of the same color as his robe. Over this robe he wore another garment, a sort of over-dress without sleeves, composed of black material of a finer grade than the serge. This latter had a sort of cowl or hood attached to it.

He was very polite to the visitors, and informed them that while he would be delighted to show the gentleman all over the establishment, it was strictly against all usage to allow a lady the same privilege. Personally, he was entirely at madame's service; but—with a truly Parisian shrug of the shoulders—madame knows we must obey orders. So madame was fain to sit in the reception-room, while her husband explored the monastery, and learned the manners and customs of its inmates; but the lady did not keep a solitary vigil, as a handsome young lay brother did his best to entertain her, although I am sadly afraid he transgressed the rules by talking so much. But, shades of good St. Anthony, was there not a woman in the case? The Artist returned to his wife ecstatic. Such pictures as he had seen! Oh, if one could always live with these Trappists, there would be no lack of subjects. After going through the dormitories and other portions of the building, he had gone out into the fields and watched the brothers at their work of reaping and gathering in the harvest, for they do all their own work, both out-doors and in, even to making their own clothes. No female element is allowed to enter their lives. As the Artist watched the picturesque groups of men performing their silent labor, still in the garb of their order, what effects, tones, values, and keys of color were evolved in his mind, as he noted the sun strike on the rich golden brown costume of the lay brothers, forming vivid contrasts to the more sombre hue of those in full orders! And how strange it seemed, all this active life going on round about him without a sound being uttered, to see them suddenly fall on their knees while the father whose duty it was would perform the office. For everything is done by rule, and whatever the occupation, it must be suspended when the bell sounds for these religious exercises. Everything was so automaton-like that it almost appeared like enchantment. Father Alban, the Superior, at length rallied our absorbed friend, by asking him if he would not like to join their order. "Yes, if you will take me in the capacity of special artist," he

DIVINE OFFICE IN THE FIELD.

laughingly replied. "Well, come and live with us a month or two, and see how you like our life." This proposition was eagerly responded to on the part of the Artist, but met with indignant glances from his wife. The worthy father, who was a bit of a wag, quietly gave her a re-assuring smile, and proceeded to give her husband a list of the rules laid down for the guidance of his household. No conversation permitted under any circumstances except by special permission of the father, and then as few words as possible must be used. Entire abstinence from meat, fish, eggs, or butter; a very spare quantity of bread, vegetables, and milk only being allowed. The brothers were compelled to rise at 2 A.M. for prayer and meditation. Here the worthy father was interrupted by the Artist exclaiming, very emphatically, "No, thanks; I won't join." His enthusiasm had been visibly dying out during

the father's recital, and the final clause provoked downright rebellion. But they compromised by the Artist asking permission to come out the next day, fully equipped with sketching appliances, and the genial father willingly promised to place himself and the brotherhood at his disposal.

When the pair again embarked on board the steamer it was one of those lovely afternoons we sometimes see late in the summer, when everything in nature seems veiled under a soft mist. They secured seats under an awning on deck, and sat enjoying to the utmost the balmy, bewitching atmosphere by which they were surrounded.

"What is that old ruin we see over there?" inquired the Basso of a gentleman near by.

"That is the remains of an old French fort, destroyed in 1745. We are now coming to St. Ann's," answered the individual addressed, "one of the loveliest spots on the Ottawa. It is crowded to its utmost capacity during the season by tourists, excursionists, and those seeking a quiet corner to rest in after the busy round of toils and pleasures of city life. It is only twenty miles from Montreal, but it might be two hundred, judging from its primitive attractions. It was here that Moore wrote his celebrated 'Boat Song.' Yonder, spanning the river from shore to shore, is the Grand Trunk Railway bridge, interesting from its irregularity of outline, which makes it appear so unlike a railway bridge."

Fortunately the boat had to wait a long time here, and the Artist took advantage of it to get the rapids and a sketch of Moore's house, which is a quaint, cozy-looking stone house with an old-fashioned high-pitched roof of glittering tin, with two tiers of dormer-windows in it, one above the other. It is still in good preservation, and looks as if it might yet shelter a generation or two more of poets. The afternoon was drawing to a close as they left St. Ann's, and our musical friend could not refrain from softly repeating,

"Soon as the woods on shore look dim,
We'll sing at St. Ann's our parting hymn."

They were now quietly drifting down to Lachine, where those passengers who do not care to run the rapids can proceed by rail to Montreal, a distance of nine miles, but very few persons leave the boat here. On the contrary, the number of passengers is generally augmented by parties who come out from the city for the special purpose of going down the rapids.

Here at Lachine the Basso and Contralto bid farewell to the Ottawa, on whose waters they have had such a happy summer holiday. They are now on the St. Lawrence. The two rivers here meet, but do not mingle. Their distinctive char-

acters are retained. Our old friend the Ottawa, with its coffee-colored water flows peacefully by the side of the brilliant-hued St. Lawrence until they reach the tide.

After leaving Lachine, all the interest centres on the rapids. The others crowd to the bow of the boat to get a good view, but our travellers take up their position in the stern, where they can watch the water rushing over the rocks, pursuing them, as it were, while they seem to be running

TOM MOORE'S HOUSE.

STEERING A RAFT THROUGH THE RAPIDS.

away from it. As they descend one steep pitch after another they sometimes fancy the waters are really going to catch them, and instinctively jump back like frightened children.

The boat has dipped for the last time, and the excitement is over. Now they are within sight of the Victoria Bridge. The giant structure is glorified by the misty gray shadows of evening combined with the reflection of the setting sun, which have for the time transfigured this useful but by no means ornamental eighth wonder of the world.

THE HOME LIFE OF THE ESKIMO

IN his preface to *Eskimo Life*, Fridtjof Nansen says: "And if in some point I should appear unreasonable, I must plead as my excuse that it is scarcely possible to live for any time among these people without conceiving an affection for them—for that, one winter is more than enough."

With the present writer, the first of his thirteen months among the Eskimos made him their debtor in gratitude, and the succeeding months kept adding to the score. Nansen came to them after his crossing of Greenland, lived as their neighbor in his own house with several white companions; he was largely independent of them; when they were in his dwelling they were his visitors. With me the situation was different. I had also come to them overland, but with no companions, no resources. I had expected a ship with food and clothing to meet me at the mouth of the Mackenzie, but the ship never came. The Eskimos are natural sceptics, and I don't think they believed that ship of mine to have any existence outside of my imagination. But that did not matter, for I was among a people who are every one's friends, communists who looked to it that I should be as well fed and clothed as themselves; for the necessities of life belong not to him who produces them, but to him who needs them. When I tried in my fragmentary Eskimo to express thanks for their kindness they were more surprised than pleased. "Do, then, in the white man's land, some starve and shiver while others eat much and are warmly clad?" To that question I said, "No," though I knew I was lying. I was afraid the competitive system could not be explained to them satisfactorily; neither was I, being the poorest among them, very anxious to try justifying it.

The general public knows a good deal about the Eskimo, but that knowledge consists mostly of things that are not so. Sober truth about them, therefore, not only looks novel but sounds improbable. One whose aims are scientific writes with the purpose of making known facts; one who writes about a little known people for whom he feels affection is naturally anxious that the facts he relates shall, in a measure, justify that affection. He hopes that between the lines of what is intended as a plain narration not unworthy of scientific uses there may appear now and then the truth that in even savage bosoms every human heart is human. That is a fact which, if understood, contributes to one's general satisfaction in life.

In many things we are the superiors of the Eskimo, in a few we are his inferiors. The moral value of some of his superiority is small—he can make better garments against cold than our tailors and furriers; he can thrive in barren wastes where a New-Englander would starve. But of some of his superiority the moral value is great—he has developed individual equality farther than we, he is less selfish, more helpful to his fellow, kinder to his wife, gentler to his child, more reticent about the faults of his neighbor than any but the rarest and best of our race. As a guest who could not pay for my keep, as a stranger whose purpose among them no one knew, I learnt these things in a winter that, for all its darkness and cold, was one of the pleasantest of my life.

It was in the latter part of December, 1906, that, driven by scarcity of food to the westward, a few of my Eskimo friends and I presented ourselves at the house of the chief Ovayuak, the most influential man in the community east of the Mackenzie River. When our sleds approached his igloo at Tuktuyaktok we could see from afar thick smoke rising, and knew a kettle of fish was boiling against our arrival; for the hospitable

Eskimos always keep a sharp lookout for the appearance of a sled on the snowy horizon. When within half a mile, a crowd of shouting people and barking dogs came tumbling to meet us, and at their head Ovayuak himself, the man whose warm house and good-will were to make the arctic winter pleasant for me, both then while it was passing and now that it is a memory.

Ovayuak is a type of the best of his countrymen. With a stature of five feet ten he has those qualities of body which make him look tall even when seen with larger men—and larger men are common among his neighbors. He has level, sparkling eyes, with the barest suggestion of the Asiatic, a clean-cut Roman nose, and a bronze complexion dark for his people, who occasionally show the pink white cheeks of the Teutonic European. As he came skipping along to meet us his round, rich voice conveyed the essence of true welcome even then, when as yet I but imperfectly understood his speech.

There was no hand-shaking. The true Eskimo does not know the custom, nor has his language any special word of salutation or farewell. But in the waste isolation he is unaffectedly glad to have strangers come to his house, doubly glad at the arrival of old friends. On this particular occasion, Ovayuak's chief emotion seemed to be surprise at seeing a white man approaching when it was well known no whaling ship was near. A few words from my travelling companion Roxy, however, explained my plans and purposes, and my welcome was as warm as that of any of the party.

A half hour later, when we were all gathered in the house around huge troughs of boiled fish, Ovayuak had many questions to ask. Why had I come to this cold country from the south, where, he had been told, it was warmer and better suited to white men, whose skin easily freezes and who quickly get tired running ahead of a dog sled? He was glad I had come to his house, and I might stay as long as I wished; he would give me the best he had to eat; his women would boil fish heads for me and sew me warm clothing. But warm clothes are not so good as a warm country where any sort of garments will do.

What was I, then, seeking? Did I want to buy the skins of white, silver, and black foxes, as the Hudson Bay traders far to the south are doing? If I had come several years ago he would have given me black-fox skins, for he had no great need of them, but now he hunts with a rifle, using smokeless cartridges instead of arrows, and he must also buy tea and tobacco. It would have been better if I had come when he was a boy, for then there were many deer and no rifles and people were never hungry. Even now he and his family are never hungry, for they stay by the seashore and catch fish; but some people go inland looking for valuable furs, stay there trapping till their dogs begin to die of hunger, and then come down to the coast to be fed on the fish he has been catching all summer. He is glad he can feed them when they come, but sorry that their hunger for white men's wares is so great that they soon go off again to hunt marten and starve. But I had not come with wares to trade for furs; he had been told I came to learn his language and see how the people lived. But why should I do that? Did not my people have a good language, just as good as his? Then why should I want his language? Of course I could learn how to hunt white whales and build snowhouses. But of what use is that? Was it not true, as the whaling captain said, that in San Francisco, where all the white men live, people do not know that white whale is good to eat, and have no snow for houses, nor need for any?

With occasional help from Roxy, who was used to my peculiar Eskimo, I endeavored to explain a thing that has often been explained with little better success to men farther south—that there are those who want to know merely for the sake of knowing; that I should go back to tell of what I had seen, but did not expect to apply my knowledge to house-building or food-gathering. But would I then be paid for telling these useless things, just as the missionary at Herschel Island was said to be paid for telling people how to talk to God? But I must not mind that he could not understand my motives, even though he tried; doubtless my reasons were good; besides, it was really none of his business

A WRECKED WHALER AT KINGS POINT

why I was there. He was glad I had come and hoped I would stay long in his house. He wanted his little boy to learn to write "tea," "sugar," "powder," and other words on paper, so that he could send letters to the whaling ships lying twenty days' journey to the westward. It would be very convenient, he thought, for an Eskimo to be able to write: "I send you three fox skins; I want tea, cartridges, and matches."

With this sort of talk, and much laughing at the simplest remarks, passed my first afternoon in Ovayuak's house. Then and later the household life made varied impressions upon me, but the most enduring are those of the unvaried kindness, the uniform courtesy, of every one through all the many days spent with them.

The typical dwelling near the Mackenzie has the ground plan of a four-pointed star. Although the main part is not excavated, the entrance passage is, and the door to the house is a hole in the floor. That feature is one of the great secrets of the comfort of an Eskimo house. These northern philosophers discovered, probably much earlier than those of temperate lands, that cold air is heavier than warm and will not rise from below up into a warm room. Accordingly, the door is left open day and night. Lying on the floor beside the opening one can reach with his fingers down to zero tem-

perature, while one's shoulder is in the comfortable warmth of the house.

The house floor is ordinarily of split logs (driftwood is everywhere abundant) and is some eight inches lower over the square middle portion of the house than it is in the star points, three of which serve as sleeping alcoves, while the fourth is partly occupied by the trap-door. In these alcoves we slept with our heads towards the centre of the house and feet towards the narrow points of the star. The covering of the house is earth over a frame of wood, the roof supported by perpendicular posts to the floor. There is one window of thin skin or seal's intestines at the peak of the roof some eight feet above the floor, but during the larger portion of the winter one depends for light far less upon it than upon the six or eight seal or whale oil lamps that are kept burning day and night. Each of these lamps, shaped like the half of a saucer, burns with a flame from four to eight inches long, and, taken together, they maintain the house at a uniform temperature of about 60°, and this with fair ventilation, for an air pipe in the roof of from four to eight inch diameter is always kept open.

Few peoples are so fond of singing as the Eskimos. Their music is ordinarily referred to, and fairly enough, as monotonous chanting, but they take more pleasure in it than we in our symphonies.

When exceptionally happy or a trifle gloomy, their resource is equally the song and drum. Of an evening when no visitor is arrived, or when he has told all the news he remembers, we take our places, sitting cross-legged each in his own sleeping-place, and join in the song. If it be a well known one, most of the grown people and an occasional youngster take part; but frequently the song is improvised by some one who feels that way inclined, and the rest join in the chorus. Usually the topic is some past experience of the singer's; occasionally

Once my uncle advised me to winter at Kingnak.
Anga-ya, anga-ya, etc.,
He is a wise one, my uncle.

I tried to catch fish, but there were no fish,
Anga-ya, anga-ya, etc.,
He is a wise one, my uncle.

I built a house, but the wood was bad,
Anga-ya, anga-ya,
He is a wise one, my uncle.

I set my traps, but no marten were caught,
Anga-ya, anga-ya,
He is a wise one, my uncle.

And so the song went on through a recital of the various hardships consequent on wintering where the uncle had advised, and ended with the statement that if any one wanted competent advice as to where to spend the winter, "Just go and ask my uncle!" All but the uncle had joined in the refrain, and when the song was over there were shouts of laughter and cries of, "Do you give your advice to everybody or only to your relatives?" "Where would you advise me to spend the winter?" etc. When the uproar died down the uncle borrowed a drum, and after beating it in silence for some time, broke into a song that was a sort of rebuttal of Ovayuak's: the wintering place had really not been so bad, but Ovayuak was then young and inexperienced and did not know how to build houses or catch fish. Such a tilt as this often furnished us amusement for a whole evening.

Although our midwinter days were merely twilight noons, we usually had the house astir by seven o'clock

INDIAN CARRIERS AND PACK-DOGS

it is a lampoon on some one present. A typical example was one I heard on the occasion of the visit of Ovayuak's uncle to our house in January. The substance of the song follows; the chorus consisted of a number of meaningless phrases and of the refrain, "My uncle, he is a wise one":

in the morning. About that time one of the women would rise on her elbow on the sleeping platform, trim afresh the lamp nearest her (for occasionally the lamps begin to burn dim towards morning), and, calling out a name, would challenge some other woman to a race in dressing and getting outdoors to the fish cache for an armful of fish for breakfast. Their talk would awaken those of us who were still sleeping, and by the time they returned to the house with their piled armfuls all of us were awake. The rock-frozen fish were thrown on the floor with a clatter to remind of cedar firewood being dumped in heaps on a farmer's kitchen floor. When the flinty, resonant hardness of our breakfast was thawed to a temperature where it was merely frozen, the skin of each fish was given a lengthwise slit from head to tail with a sharp knife. Then, getting hold of the edge of the skin with their teeth, the women stripped it off in a manner remotely resembling the peeling of a banana. The frozen fish were then placed in troughs and passed around to the rest of us who were still in bed. Each would rise on his elbows, take a fish and gnaw it after the manner of eating corn from the cob; the residuum of "insides" and backbone was left behind, as one might the core of an apple, and put back upon the food tray. This—frozen raw fish— was our invariable breakfast. In telling this I am telling of no hardship; in the long run fish frozen raw is more palatable than cooked in any form, just as most people would tire less readily of raw than fried oysters.

Breakfast finished, we would dress and turn to the day's occupation. Most of the men and two or three of the women ordinarily spent the day in fishing. In summer nets are used, but in winter the fish are caught with ivory hooks through holes in the ice. The variety most abundant is the *inconnu* of the Hudson Bay trader —a white fish ranging in weight from ten to forty pounds. Our best catch last winter was sixty-eight of these fish caught in about six hours with a single hook.

One day as Ovayuak and I sat on our snow blocks with backs to the wind, fishing, I asked him why he was not satisfied with the huge pile already stored away—more than our family of twenty-two could eat in two years. He then told me that he was a chief. And why,

ESKIMO MOTHER AND CHILDREN

did I suppose, was he a chief? Or, now that he was chief, did I suppose he would continue being a chief if he were lazy? We had plenty fish for ourselves there at Tuktuyaktok, but who could tell if the people who had gone inland after reindeer might not return any day with empty sleds, or possibly with no sleds— carrying their children on their backs because the dogs were dead of starvation? And how about the people west of the Mackenzie at Shingle Point? True, they had caught plenty fish in summer, but they catch none in winter, and they are not sensible now as they formerly were, but will haul a big load of fish a long distance to sell to the whalers at Herschel Island for a little tea, which tastes good, but does not keep a man alive. And what of the people up the Mackenzie? They depend largely on rabbits. Some years there are plenty of these, and other years, for some reason, there are few or none. Might we not some day see many sleds coming from the southwest along the coast? And may not these sleds turn out to be empty because there are no rabbits in the willows? Did I suppose that if all these people came we would have too much fish? And why was he a chief, if not for the fact that people twenty days' journey away could always say when they became hungry, "We will go to Ovayuak, he will have plenty food"? He had heard that in the white man's land a man was a chief because he was rich. But that is not the way among the Eskimos. Last winter, as I knew, Kakotok, who is a fine hunter, caught two black foxes and a silver fox. Did I suppose all the fish at Tuktuyaktok could be sold for as many rifles and copper kettles as those three skins? And had I ever heard Kakotok called a chief? Did people go long distances to his house when they were hungry? If Kakotok should say to some man, "Stefánsson is my friend, lend him a dog to help pull his sled to Baillie Island," would the man do anything but laugh? But if Ovayuak should say that same thing, would not the man reply, "Your friend may take as many of my dogs as he needs; and if he does not know the road my son will go with him"? Kakotok is no chief because he does not gather things together for the purpose of giving them away. No man who wants to be called a good man stops fishing when he has just enough for his own household. Seeing Ovayuak is a chief, how can there ever be too much fish on his fish platforms?

Thus it seems that he who gives to the needy all he has is as great a figure in the life of the heathen Eskimo as he is in the sermons of the Christian white. I lived long enough with Ovayuak to see that his kindly power over all his neighbors rested on the watchful energy with which he worked to keep himself in readiness to give when others needed help. There were not many families that did not keep the same end in view, but some had sickness among them, and others the gambler's instinct led in pursuit of fox and marten. Besides, Ovayuak had the magnetic qualities that tend to inspire confidence and that make for leadership anywhere. Among the Eskimo a man is "chief" not by formal election, but through the consensus of public opinion, much as certain men of breadth and integrity have influence among us.

Although I fished many a day at the next ice hole to Ovayuak's, I learnt few of the more interesting things about him and his people on these occasions. It is not so much that a temperature of fifty below zero is very uncomfortable, for the skin suit keeps you warm, but the wind is usually blowing a bit and the snow drifting, and this makes conversation difficult. The evening was the time for discussions, stories, and songs.

By three in the afternoon the midday twilight had darkened to a glimmer in the southwest and our working day was over. If we came home a little early we usually had a meal of raw fish on coming to the house, but by four or five a kettle of boiled fish would be ready, and this was our heaviest meal of the day.

It was after dinner one evening that I asked Ovayuak why he had two wives while no other man in the country had more than one. That was, he said, because he was a prominent man, had a big household, and many visitors continually. A few years ago his first wife, Anaratziak, had said to him: "I am becoming old now; my first daughter will soon be married; there is much work in preparing food for all your guests. Why don't you get a young wife who can help me with the housework?" That was why he married Illerok, who is young and strong. "But Illerok is not so important as Anaratziak. See how Illerok cooks the fish, puts them on a platter, and brings them to Anaratziak so she may pick out for herself and her favorite son as many of the heads and tails as she likes. Illerok does what she is told, for she is the younger wife." And never did two women get along more amicably together than these two wives of Ovayuak's. When Illerok's youngest baby was about ten months old, Anaratziak brought out some especially fine tobacco she had long treasured for the purpose and taught the baby girl to chew. Though Eskimo babies are seldom weaned till they are four to five years old, they ordinarily learn to chew (and swallow the tobacco juice) between the ages of nine and twelve months. Before whites came to northern North America they seem to have received their tobacco

RABBITS MAKE A SUBSTITUTE FOR DOLLS

as well as their Chinese pipes from Siberia across Bering Strait by prehistoric trade routes. The customs, practically universal with both sexes, of inhaling tobacco smoke and swallowing the juice of tobacco seem to be of no recent growth. No conspicuous evil results of either practice are readily apparent.

Our family seldom had an evening to themselves, for visitors were continually coming and going.

The approach of a sled was usually hailed with rejoicing, but one day the announcement brought quite the opposite result. The visitor was Direksina, from Kiglavait on Richard Island. When he was gone the next day I learnt the following facts about him:

A few years ago (I believe not more than five; one can never get definite ideas from the Eskimo if more than three years are involved) a man, whose name I neglected to make note of, was living with his wife Ekopterea and two children in a little fishing-house, for it was not yet quite time to go into winter quarters. One day, when the woman and smaller boy were a little way from shore fishing, Direksina came to the house where the man was sleeping after a hunt and shot him with a rifle; then he shot the boy who was outside playing, and came out on the ice to shoot the woman also. But the woman shouted to him that if he did not kill her she would tell everybody that he had killed her husband in self-defence. With many vows and promises the woman agreed to always tell this story. Direksina believed her and did not kill her. That evening she hitched up her dogs, drove to Ovayuak's, and told him the whole story. He took her and the boy into his house, and kept both, until last winter Ekopterea died, shortly after this visit of Direksina's.

The circumstances connected with this murder throw many a side-light on Eskimo character and views of life. Most striking perhaps (at least on first thought) was the fact that although the announcement of Direksina's visit spread gloom for the moment, yet when he actually arrived he received a welcome only a trifle less hearty than did visitors customarily. Even his victim's widow, who was the oldest and most decrepit member of the household, joked with him and told him in great detail her various sufferings from rheumatism and oncoming age. I, who as yet did not know his story, saw nothing unusual in his entertainment, and concluded for the time that I had been mistaken in thinking the announcement of his coming to have been unwelcome news.

The next day, when he was gone, I

learnt the story. "But," I asked Ova-yuak, "is it, then, not true, as the Hudson Bay trader told me, that you formerly used to kill several men each year in blood revenge and perpetual feuds? And is it not true that Taiakpanna, your next neighbor to the south, killed six men for the murder of his father?" Oh yes,

A TYPICAL YOUNG ESKIMO COUPLE

that was all true, but it happened long ago before the whalers came and the epidemics which sometimes killed ten where there were thirteen in a house. There were so many people then that there were as many able hunters in the single village of Kittegaryuit as there are men on two whaling ships; now, on the whole length of coast, five men can count the hunters on their fingers and toes. When the epidemics were gone the people began to talk and say, "We must not fight among ourselves any longer; we are too few." And then all agreed, after talking about it a whole summer, that there should be no more killing for revenge, not even though a murder were committed. Since then there has been one murder only, and Direksina will not be killed for it. When I asked why he was so well treated, even by the relatives of the murdered, the answer was characteristic: "To kill him, that might be sensible, for he is a bad man and may commit more crimes; but to treat him badly and make

him miserable, what good would that do?" It may be said, in passing, that this consideration for the feelings of others is carried to a point where we consider it a grave fault; it is found among many other "uncivilized" people. Their range of "white lies" is much larger than with us; if they once find out what you want to hear, they will tell you it, whether it happens to be true or not, their motive being the same as ours when we praise the poor handiwork of a friend, or compliment a young woman on good looks that are largely imaginary.

Later I found out that Direksina was a thief also, a liar (one who told mischievous rather than considerate untruths), and (worst of all) a "man who speaks badly of others." Except under certain restricted conditions, when the fact is pointed out as necessary information, it is a worse offence to say of a man that he is a thief than it would be to be in reality a thief. If I am about to leave my rifle on the fish platform outside a house, it is good form —it is even the host's duty—to tell me, "Do not leave it there; Direksina may steal it." But if, as a matter of gossip or news, he were to say, "It is never safe to leave a rifle on the fish cache when Direksina or his partner is around," the speech would be a very reprehensible one, and any one who made it would fall greatly in public esteem.

It may perhaps be called a general rule that the more primitive a people are the more numerous and complicated are their ceremonials. In this as in many other things the Eskimos stand high, for they dispense with a few of those formalities which even we have not yet abandoned. Marriage, for instance, has with them little of rite or ritual about it.

The complete history of a first marriage came under my observation. One

September forenoon, when ours was one of fourteen tents at Shingle Point, a boat arrived from the west bound for the Mackenzie delta. In this boat, among other passengers, was the young man Sitjak, later my travelling companion on several sled trips. In our tent at this time was a marriageable girl of fourteen, the daughter of Oblutok, Roxy's fishing partner and a man famous in distant communities for his patriarchal beard. These young people had seen each other once or twice before, but Sitjak assured me that now for the first time he thought of Pannigak as a possible wife. When the visiting boat was about to leave, Sitjak asked them to wait while he asked Pannigak's father for her hand in marriage, saying that he would like to go on eastward with them if he should be refused, but would otherwise stay at Shingle Point. Oblutok, when approached, called his wife in consultation. They agreed the match was not a brilliant one, but thought they might broach the subject to Pannigak. When asked, the girl said she had not particularly noticed Sitjak, but would go and have a look at him. In a few minutes she came back to our tent and told her parents she was not particularly struck with the young man, but would nevertheless marry him. The boat accordingly set sail without Sitjak, and from that day on he was a member of Oblutok's household.

Later in the winter this young couple furnished me with an illustration of the corresponding ease and simplicity of divorce. I had come from Tuktuyaktok on my way to Herschel Island in February. At that time food had become very scarce with Roxy and Oblutok, who were the only two men living at Shingle Point. On inquiry, we told them that at Ovayuak's house there was plenty of fish, and Oblutok at once announced his intention of going there. But this did not quite suit Sitjak, who said he was tired of fish, and would rather go up the Mackenzie, where his uncle probably had plenty of lynx meat and rabbits. He accordingly suggested that his parents-in-law should go to Tuktuyaktok, while he and Pannigak went up the river. Pannigak, however, said that his uncle's rabbits were a bit problematic, while Ovayuak's fish were a certainty; besides, she was not very fond of rabbits anyway. She would therefore go with her parents. It was forthwith agreed, with no apparent feeling on either side, that the two were no longer man and wife, since neither was willing to yield to the other. There may have been deeper reasons for this divorce than difference in taste for fish, but whenever either husband or wife

TRAVELLING WITH DOG-TEAM IN WINTER

prefers permanent separation to doing as the other wishes, divorce takes place.

The history of this marriage was typical of that of first marriages in general among these people. With them the condition seems, in a measure, the converse of that ordinarily found among us. We frequently marry for love and stay married a long time without it; theirs are "marriages of convenience" more often than ours, but are never long endured unless a strong affection develops. It is rarely a first, sometimes a second, and more often a third marriage that proves permanent. With their absolute equality of the sexes and perfect freedom of separation, a permanent union of uncongenial persons is well-nigh inconceivable. But if a couple find each other congenial enough to remain married a year or two, divorce becomes exceedingly improbable, and is much rarer among middle-aged people than it is among us. People of the age of twenty-five and over are usually very fond of each other, and the family life, when once it becomes settled, appears to be on a higher level of affection and mutual consideration than is common among us. Whether it be better to require love as the essential of the beginning of married life, as we do, or as the requirement of its continuance, as the Eskimos do, is a question which a student of society arrived here from the planet Mars might conceivably answer otherwise than in our favor.

In an Eskimo home I have never heard an unpleasant word between a man and his wife, never seen a child punished nor an old person treated inconsiderately. Yet the household affairs are carried on in an orderly way, and the good behavior of the children is remarked by practically every traveller. These charming qualities of the Eskimo home may be due largely to their equable disposition and the general fitness of their character for the communal relations, but it seems reasonable to give a portion of the credit to their remarkable social organization, for they live under conditions for which some of our best men are striving, conditions that with our idealists are as yet merely dreams.

The communism which most of us admit would remedy the worst of our social ills, "if our nature were less selfish" or "if it could be made to work," is the foundation of their every-day life; active co-operation is conditional of possible existence in their land of uncertainties, where one village may have tons of food while another's nets are continually empty; and these conditions in turn have made him who gives all he has the first man of them all.

This communism in the necessities of life has, among other things, made it impossible for the Eskimo to even conceive of "marriage problems" and "divorce problems" after the manner in which they present themselves to us. The economic factor is removed. An Eskimo wife with a baby at her breast could, if she wished, leave a husband who mistreated her, without a single thought of "How shall I support myself and bring up my child?" As long as there are food and clothing in the community, she and her baby will be as well fed and clothed as any one there. She suffers neither materially nor in social standing; neither economic condition nor public opinion binds the wife or the husband to a union that seems to either of them to have disadvantages outweighing its advantages. If discord develops, separation follows, but between congenial people there grows an affection that continually develops towards middle life and old age.

These "uncivilized" heathen communists, more interesting to the sociologist than our parlor experimenters in co-operative living, are apparently facing strange new conditions, for the traders are coming nearer and the Church of England already has an outpost on Herschel Island to the westward. These people, who are now living with a higher average degree of material well-being than any non-white people in America, under whose benevolent protection they may be, are facing economic changes that have in the past brought misfortune on their kinsmen in the east and west; the home life that stands above ours in the uniformly pleasant picture it presents and the happiness it yields will probably not long escape the influence of the missionaries whom our spare pennies support in their work of "carrying light to the dark places of the earth."

NIAGARA

WHILE hundreds of tourists visit the Falls of Niagara every season, not one in a thousand actually sees the river. But with the "freeing of Niagara," celebrated by New York State and Canada July 15, 1885, the river experienced a new birth. Hereafter, in the true spirit of this international bond, the traveller, having enjoyed restored nature at the points comprised within the limits of the International Park Survey, may explore Niagara River to where, actually freed from its high, precipitous mural boundaries, it pours the waters of our upper inland seas into the broad Ontario. Here culminates the historic interest of the Niagara frontier, as at the Whirlpool modern rock-readings tell us to seek a clew to its geological past. For of few other rivers may it be said that they have a threefold charm, appealing alike to artist, historian, and man of science.

True lovers of Niagara hope that the day is not far distant when the International Park will consist of not merely a mile strip on the American bank, but a grand double boulevard, running from Buffalo to Youngstown, and on the Canadian cliffs from the Horseshoe Falls to Queenston. As a site for country villas, Lewiston Ridge, with the unnumbered beautiful drives in its neighborhood and its picturesque historical associations, must, as the cities of western New York grow in wealth and population, become not less famous than the cliffs of Newport.

Below the cataract, the Niagara, although comparatively few tourists discover this fact, has a beauty and grandeur no less imposing than the falls themselves. Not content with its mighty plunge of 165 feet, the river goes surging and tossing downward another 104 feet in its rocky bed over the obliterated falls of a preglacial stream, the remains of a third cataract being still perceptible in the Whirlpool Rapids. At the Whirlpool the river untwists itself like some mighty serpent from its sinuous contortions in this concave prison, to pour itself an emerald-green wave into a channel at right

Photographed by George Barker.

THE RAPIDS ABOVE THE FALLS.

angles with its former course, and henceforth trends northeast with many a gentle curve.

Not until we reach Lewiston Ridge do we turn our backs on the Niagara's stupendous exhibition of power. From this height, described by Father Charlevois as "a frightful mountain which hides itself in clouds on which the Titans might attempt to scale the heavens," is a view worthy the expansive canvas of a Bierstadt. The table-land terminates abruptly in an escarpment. Beneath stretch boundless meadowlands as rich as any in agricultural England. They slope gently to the river, which, coming headlong down the gorge, with the leap and roar of the Whirlpool upon it, gradually subsides into a tranquil stream as the bold outlines of the banks above Lewiston fall away into broad smiling plains. Across the gorge is the Bunker Hill of Canada, crowned by its lofty shaft. Few monuments in the world have so imposing an effect in the landscape as the lonely form of Brock towering in the blue clouds far above the heights of Queenston.

Nestling under the shadow of her mountain is Lewiston, so named in 1805 for Governor Morgan Lewis, of New York. At the extreme north, beyond the village of Youngstown, and commanding the angle at the headland of river and lake, we descry the white ramparts of Fort Niagara, whence the gallant Pouchot, begirt with enemies, looked out in 1758, vainly attempting to discover moving among the trees the battalions of his allies from the Detroit River. Exactly opposite Fort Niagara lies "fair Newark, once gay, rich, and beautiful," presenting to the water's edge her ancient front of crumbling fortresses and gray church towers.

"Geology is a noble science," says Taine in his tour afoot through the Pyrenees. Upon Lewiston summit its theories have flourished. It was here, equally distant from the present cataract and from the outlet of the river — seven miles — that we were formerly supposed to get a comprehensive idea of the origin and progress of Niagara Falls. In his mind's eye the geologist raised a transverse barrier from Lewiston Ridge to Queenston Heights. Over this precipice, some 200,000 years ago, said he, poured the united affluents of the upper lakes. This belief concerning the remote beginning of the Niagara Gorge, so simple that the youngest child can understand it, to the great mystification of the unscientific, has been partially set aside for the more reasonable, if

Photographed by George Barker.   Engraved by Pettit.

THE WHIRLPOOL RAPIDS.

more complicated, one now favorably received by some of the leading geologists of the United States, which makes the gorge between the present falls and the Whirlpool older than the Ice Age. The only part it admits to have been excavated by the modern river is the three miles between the Whirlpool and Lewiston. Inasmuch, however, as guide-books and hack-drivers continue to quote the theory which traces the progress of the cataract back from Lewiston, it is well, in the dawning of a new era for Niagara as a place of

resort, that modern conjectures concerning its past should be more generally known.

Since the original survey of the gorge in 1841, the science of geology has made surprising progress. It has been able, perhaps, to reduce the age of Niagara Falls from 200,000 years to less than 20,000. The falls, it now tells us, instead of cutting their way up the gorge from Lewiston, began their existence, as one cataract, not more than a mile north of where they now are. If true, the value of this discovery, largely due to the protracted, patient investigation of the gorge by Dr. Julius Pohlman, director of the Buffalo Museum of Natural Sciences, will be inestimable. It will give geology a new basis of calculation. Formerly it had recourse to the stellar spaces for a standard by which to reckon the lapse of time between the Ice Age and our own. For while 200,000 years were adequate to account for all the other recent changes in the configuration of the earth's surface, the Niagara Gorge, supposing it to have been excavated throughout by the modern river, after all the essential transformations of the surrounding country had been effected, prevented the theory of any reasonable lapse of time since the arctic climate was again changed into a temperate one.

It has been too much the fashion with writers to belittle Niagara River by detailing the accidents and incidents connected with it, ignoring its magnificent natural phenomena for the sake of creating a vulgar curiosity that will impel the travelling public to visit this or that point in the neighborhood of the cataract, or rapids, as the former scene of some sensational catastrophe.

With the American, pedestrianism has become almost as favorite a mode of exercise as with his English cousin. One of the finest autumnal tramps this country affords is a walk up the gorge of the Niagara. No tour afoot in the Swiss Alps is more exhilarating. On the one hand are the organ tones of the turbulent river; on the other, the steep, weather-beaten cliffs, shaggy with forest trees, and of appalling height; and the cloud-embosomed form of Canada's hero follows the retreating footsteps, as if, weary of the vague isolation of the higher atmosphere, he would fain seek companionship with humanity below.

The whole series of rock strata composing the sides of the gorge is laid bare up the perpendicular American bank, like the layers of a well-regulated jelly-cake. A study of this rocky wall in the course of a walk from Lewiston to Suspension-bridge not only shows the varying thickness of the different strata, but gives a clear idea of the nature of the erosive process by which, according to recent surveys,. portions of the cataract recede at the rate of three feet a year. Hard layers of the Niagara and Clinton limestone alternate

with the soft shales of the same names. Beginning at Lewiston as a narrow strip, the upper stratum of Niagara limestone increases in thickness to the falls. Here the mighty force of the cataract constantly washes away the foundation of soft shale on which the limestone rests, and thus undermined, the hard upper rock breaks off.

The narrow road by which pedestrians descend from Lewiston escarpment pursues a winding, zigzag course, its passage broken by two secondary terraces. Along this steep precipice, described by Charlevois and Pouchot in their memoirs as though it were one of the most difficult passes in the Alps, was visible, until recently, the remains of an old tramway, "the first railroad in America." In the days when Lewiston and her neighbors over the river were flourishing trading posts, here began the portage around the falls. At this point all the goods in process of transportation between the lakes underwent transshipment. The heavy bales were raised and lowered on a sliding car or cradle moved on an inclined plane by a windlass. Up and down this narrow defile passed a motley procession of European traders, Americans, and Indians. To the "trois montaignes" came Father Hennepin, his portable chapel on his back, and with him that bold adventurer who threatened to make "the griffon fly above the crows"; for while there is nothing in these decaying river towns to recall the fact, we are actually in the neighborhood that witnessed the birth of America's magnificent inland commerce.

The walk up the gorge is made easier by leaving the train where the engine slows up this side of the mountain. Near by are the exposed foundations and anchors of the old Suspension-bridge. The remnants of its heavy cables flap and sway across the gorge between Lewiston and Queenston like an empty clothes line. At our left is a tunnel cut through the side of the rock. It looks like a ruined arch; but although the surrounding country is rich in tradition and history, the banks of the Niagara are not crowned with castles. Some one in the party remembers that Mr. Benson J. Lossing has a sketch of it in the *Pictorial Field Book*, and it is well to say here a preliminary reading of this careful historian vastly enhances the enjoyment of a tramp through the battle country of the war of 1812.

Near the Devil's Hole, where the railway goes into the mountain, we leave the track and mount the ridge. From the top of the cliff overlooking this awful chasm is another sweeping view of the river north and south. Peering down into the depths of the leafy gulf, it seems almost impossible to conceive in the sylvan calm of this peaceful ferny solitude that it could once have been the scene of a murderous ambuscade.

Passing the squatter sovereignty at Suspension-bridge, and pausing midway on the hanging viaduct, we have a full view of the wonderful and many times described Niagara Gorge. Great white gulls are circling over the narrow rock-bound chasm, in the bed of which flows the emerald-green river. The perpendicular cliffs, three hundred feet high, through which the stream makes its impetuous passage are still clad in the fading russet tints of maples and elms, among which the severe outlines of tall pines stand forth like black priests, mounting the gorge, up and up in solemn file, carrying us back into that remote past when first the Jesuit fathers visited the nation which gave to the river, on either side of which its camp fires burned, its musical name.

Crossing the bridge, we witness at the Whirlpool on the Canada side "the culminating act of the Niagara drama." Little known, and less appreciated by the generality of travellers, to the thinker the Whirlpool is the most fascinating spot along the river, more awful in the mysterious swirl of its waters and in the eternity of ages its past involves than the cataract itself. Compressed within these narrow limits is the drainage of half a continent. Two of the three sides are steep, rocky precipices like the rest of the river gorge. The other is a sheer slope of primeval forest, at which the water rushes with the tremendous force acquired in its swift descent. To account for this wooded declivity carries one far deeper into the fathomless ages than any possible calculations as to the period required for the falls to dig the gorge from Queenston.

Through an unwillingness to believe the commonly received theory that the concavity of this basin is due to the erosion of the water striking constantly against the bank, and believing the mysterious weakness of the northwestern end of the Whirlpool indicated traces of the buried outlet of a former river, was begun the investigation which has dispelled in so many minds the illusion that the Falls of Niagara were once at Lewiston. Having conceived the idea of an ancient stream, the present Tonawanda, carving out, in a period preceding the Ice Age, a channel as far as the Whirlpool for its destined successor, the Niagara, the new theory about the cataract is readily understood. From the Whirlpool the Tonawanda had its outlet through what now is the closed, wooded side of the basin known as the St. David's Valley. The modern river, following a shallow valley of a preceding era, quickly excavated that part of the gorge between the Whirlpool and Lewiston—how rapidly is seen by noting that the Niagara limestone, which at the point where the present falls tumble over it is eighty feet thick, has a depth of but ten and twenty feet in the lower gorge.

From the Whirlpool basin most pedestrians avail themselves of the rapid transit of the inclined railway to reascend to the upper bank.

Having recrossed the bridge and made our way to Prospect Park, the geologist of the expedition points from the parapet across the Canadian bank to a secondary ridge, now crowned by summer villas, over which, perhaps, the falls precipitated themselves before they began their backward march.

This geological tramp ended just at sundown in a supplementary expedition through the chill shades of Goat Island as the tall leafless oaks were darkling against the brilliant after-glow in the west. There are no sight-seers to disturb with their chatter at this season, and the forest solitude was unbroken, save by the rustle of the fallen leaves and acorns which we trod underfoot.

Issuing forth from beneath these late autumnal shadows at the furthest point of the Three Sister Islands, the rapids were so high that they seemed about to overflow the land.

In the fast waning twilight it was indicated how that accommodating little stream, the Tonawanda, shaped the rapids and islands that form the beautiful scenery above the falls.

The Tonawanda's waters represented no such tremendous volume as does the Niagara to-day. They were merely the drainage of a tract of land of perhaps 1500 square miles, a basin formed in the soft rocks of the Onondaga salt group lying

LEWISTON.

between two limestone ridges, one of corniferous rock, barring up the present outlet of Lake Erie, the other (northern) barrier being the upper portion of the Niagara limestone ledge over which the waters of the Niagara Falls are now precipitated. Furthermore this valley was bounded on the west by the water-shed of the Dundas Valley, in Canada, and on the east by that of the Genesee River. Flowing north in one broad stream, these waters gradually cut their way over the lowest boundary, the Niagara ridge. Exhibiting the usual tendency of water to unite in one stream, these sister rivulets, flowing over the lime-stone bed, became one river somewhere to the north of Goat Island, which then, instead of terminating in an abrupt bluff, extended northerly perhaps 600 or 700 feet further than now. From this point the Tonawanda excavated a bed due north to Lake Ontario by way of the Whirlpool and the now buried St. David's Valley.

This comparatively small volume of water was aided largely by atmospheric erosion in deepening the outlet, because the upper portions of the limestone are formed of thin slabs, while the lower part, that which now forms the edge of the falls, represent heavy, thick, almost

Drawn by C. Graham.   Engraved by Pettit.

THE BROCK MONUMENT.

indestructible masses. This cutting-down process naturally gave birth to a series of smaller channels, which again resulted in the formation of numerous little islands, the remnants of which are known to us now under the names of Goat, Luna, Bath, and the Sister islands.

With the descending frosts of the Ice Age the earth's crust in this latitude was covered with glaciers 1000 feet or more in thickness. Melting slowly in the course of a long period, the surface beneath was found to have considerably changed its aspect. During the ice period the limestone ridge that in the preceding age formed a dam from Buffalo to Canada broke away. Thus Lake Erie was destined, with the subsiding of the inland sea, to have a free outlet into the ancient Tonawanda Valley.

Before the Ice Age the basins of Lake Erie and Lake Ontario had been occupied by a series of rivers, those of Lake Erie finding their outlet through Canada into Ontario's at a point about opposite Dunkirk. Lake Erie and Lake Ontario, meantime, far overflowing their present boundaries, were one vast inland sea, which subsided simultaneously until separated by Lewiston Ridge. To have had the supposed falls start at Lewiston, it would have been necessary for Ontario to lower its level more rapidly than Lake Erie. Ancient beach marks show, on the contrary, that the two lakes fell together, their relation at first being like that now existing between Lake Erie and Lake Huron, two large bodies of water connected by a swift stream. Separated at length by the Lewiston Ridge, Lake Ontario fell slowly, with long pauses. Lake Erie, with an excess of 20,000,000 cubic feet of water a minute pouring into her for which to find an outlet, made short work of excavating the gorge between Lewiston and the Whirlpool. Here meeting the ancient Tonawanda's valley, the water naturally accepted the bed already cut for it—a fact accounting for the sudden turn the river makes here. We cannot comprehend the period of time represented by the erosion of the rock bed above the Whirlpool. The course of the preglacial Tonawanda, however, must have been broken by three

Photographed by George Barker.   Engraved by Atwood.

THE PATHWAY BETWEEN QUEENSTON AND NIAGARA.

falls as the water slowly carved the present deep gorge through the alternating layers of hard and soft rock.

The first fall was perhaps one mile north of the present cataract. The second was midway between this and the Whirlpool, all evidences of it having disappeared; while traces of the third are still seen in the Whirlpool Rapids. The force of the immense volume of water that we see to-day, pouring over the first cascade, soon obliterated the lower and middle falls, and thus the river assumed its present aspect.

Photographed by George Barker.   Engraved by Dels.

QUEENSTON AND NIAGARA RIVER FROM BROCK'S MONUMENT.

II.

From the summit of Brock's Monument —a Roman column exceeded in height only by that Sir Christopher Wren erected in London to commemorate the great fire —is a panoramic view of our whole pedestrian excursion, and one which gives a connected image of the river. From here we see not only the Whirlpool and the spray of the cataract, but all of the near towns of Upper Canada, with a distant glimpse of the historic field of Lundy's Lane. We discern the long gap of the St. David's Valley, through which, emerging from the northwest side of the Whirlpool, across the country to St. David's, flowed the ancient Tonawanda. To-day the valley of this river-bed is a highway. Under the shadow of its hoary cliffs, much like those which frown above the present Niagara, the Canada Southern Railway passes to descend into the open Ontario plain just beyond St. David's, a village two miles west of Queenston, where are seen remains of the old cliffs of the preglacial Tonawanda.

Another pedestrian excursion which is open to the sojourner at Niagara is as dear to the naturalist as is the one already described to the geologist. Its course is from Queenston along the Canadian bank at the base of the cliff to the old town of Niagara. The gentle picturesqueness of the river at this point harmonizes well with the apparently unexplored loveliness of the natural growths of ferns, vines, and wild flowers along the margin. Monarch trees overshadow the narrow footpath, shooting straight into the upper air, their roots exposed, and clinging to the shelving banks, or clasped tightly around huge bowlders, which they hold in place.

No such walk is possible on the American side, for the engineering talent which achieved the railroad along the precipice destroyed the sylvan beauty of the bank below, filling it up with stones and rocks hewn off to lay the track. Similarly on the Canadian side the once famous Hennepin, or "La Grosse Roche," near Queenston, is scarcely to be distinguished from the main bank, since the space originally separating it from the shore has been closed by débris accumulated when the cables were sunk for the old Suspension-bridge. As dense with matted foliage as any unexplored mountain cañon of the far West, this path between Queenston and the Whirlpool is as narrow as the way of life, and destruction as sure to him who steps out of it. On the one side is the river, on the other the abrupt vertical cliff. Last season the shadows of the evening twilight overtook a party of pedestrians here, and, afraid to retrace their steps, a hopeless attempt to climb the bank resulted in their being stuck fast on a rock all night. When the International Park is older there should be donkeys to carry the traveller over these roads. From this path curious eddies are noticed in the river, which all summer long is haunted by anglers who cast their flies or troll for black bass. Two-thirds of the river pursues an undeviating downward course, the other third runs backward. Lazy fishermen take a base advantage of this eddy, allowing it in the morning to carry them up-stream to the fishing grounds. At nightfall the main current takes them home again.

During a temporary stay at Newark in

Every step of the way between Queenston—so named in honor of Queen Charlotte—and Niagara is historic country. The cliff road, which skirts the high bank of the winding river, with glimpses of the American shore on the right and an unbroken view of undulating meadows on the left, should become popular with coaching parties. Acres of wheat field stretch out toward the north and west.

But a few short hours after leading his hastily summoned militia up Queenston Heights, with the cry, "Push on, York Volunteers!" Sir Isaac Brock again passed over this road, when his body, with that of his brave aide-de-camp, was brought back,

Drawn by Harry Fenn.　　　　　　　　　　Engraved by Anderson.

THORN-TREES NEAR NIAGARA.

1804, Tom Moore used every day to stroll up the road on the river-bank as far as an old oak-tree which stood midway in the path. Moved one afternoon by the sound of a woodpecker tapping at the bark over his head, he was inspired to write the ballad beginning:

"I knew by the smoke that so gracefully curled
　　Above the green elms that a cottage was near,
And I said, 'If there's peace to be found in the world,
　　A heart that was humble might hope for it here.'

the enemies' minute-guns all along the opposite river-bank firing a salute of respect. Hither from Kingston came in 1792 Prince Edward, Duke of Kent, father of Queen Victoria. Landed at Newark by a pleasure schooner, he was received by a salute of guns and entertained at Navy Hall. From thence the royal party wound their way on horseback by the narrow river road to the falls. Returning, they were entertained with a war-dance by the Mohawks, headed by Brant himself.

We approach the beautiful town of

JOHN GRAVES SIMCOE.

York, typical of the material forces that have moulded the nineteenth century, we come upon a spot of intensest quiet, in the shadow of whose ivy-mantled church tower sleep trusted servants of the Georges, Tories and their Indian allies.

The place has been overtaken by none of that unpicturesque commercial prosperity which further up the frontier threatens to destroy all the natural beauties of the river-banks.

The Welland Canal and the Grand Trunk and Great Western railway systems diverted from Niagara the great part of the carrying trade, and with it that growth and activity which have signalized the neighboring cities of Canada. "Refuse the Welland Canal entrance to your town," said the commissioners, "and the grass will grow in your streets." The prediction has been realized. St. Catharines is a flourishing neighbor, while Niagara, with a harbor in which the navy of England might ride, sees her main thoroughfares a common pasture. Cows crop the turf up to the door-steps of the brass-knockered, wide-windowed houses, and the classic goose roams at will through the town. The alleged business part of the village centres around the post-office.

The rush of business, however, is never such, even in the season of the summer boarder, as to prevent the proprietor of one of the most modern-looking of shops in the town from turning the key in the lock at high noon while he goes home to dinner.

The public business street bisects the town, and there are about five hundred acres of government land in two expansive commons lying on either side of the village, north and south. During the period of our visit a brigade of the red-coated militia of the Dominion was encamped on the breezy southern heath, just on the outskirts of the leafy colonnades of Paradise Grove, on the bluff opposite Youngstown. The unwonted bustle and stir created by the militia of the Dominion in the sleepy old town made it the more easy to summon a picture of that remote past when Niagara, then Newark, figured as a gay frontier military post.

Niagara through an aromatic pine forest, which is succeeded by an oak wood, "Paradise Grove," under whose lordly arcades picnic parties from all the surrounding country hold high revel in midsummer. Beyond is an open heath, on the edge of which stand, "outlawed, lonely, and apart," a picturesque clump of thorn-trees. One of the best known writers of the Dominion, and author of that powerful historical romance *Le Chien d'Or*, Mr. William Kirby, a resident of Niagara, traces the planting of these trees as far back as to the period of the French occupation of Fort Niagara. In one of his series of Canadian idyls the poet beautifully relates how under the oldest of these French thorns, "in a grave made wide enough for two," sleep a once gay cavalier of Roussillon, and a fair dame of Quebec whose bright eyes caused him to forget his châtelaine in Avignon.

Niagara is the Plymouth Rock of Upper Canada, and was once its proud capital city. Variously known in the past as Loyel Village, Butlersbury, Nassau, and Newark, it had a daily paper as early as 1792, and was a military post of distinction before the present century, its real beginnings, however, being contemporaneous with the war of independence. Here, within two short hours' ride of the most populous and busy city of western New

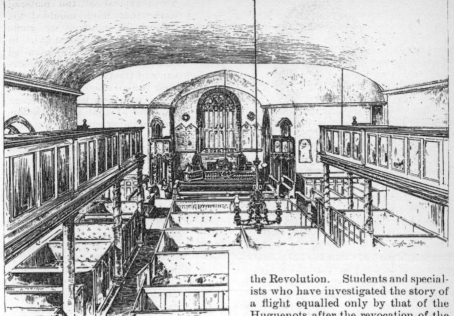

INTERIOR OF ST. MARK'S CHURCH.

Here Governor Simcoe opened the first Upper Canadian Legislature; and later, from here General Brock planned the defence of Upper Canada. While the cities of western New York, which have now far eclipsed it, were rude log settlements, at Newark some little attempt was made at decorum and society.

Guests from the "Royal" stroll frequently to the grassy ramparts of old Fort George, whose irregular outlines are still to be traced upon the open plains which now surround it. Here landed, in 1783–84, ten thousand United Empire Loyalists, who, to keep inviolate their oaths of allegiance to the King, quitted their freeholds and positions of trust and honor in the States to begin life anew in the unbroken wilds of Upper Canada.

History has made us somewhat familiar with the settlement of Nova Scotia and New Brunswick by the expatriated Loyalists. Little has been written of the sufferings and privations endured by "the makers" of Upper Canada. With the present revival of interest in American history it is singular that writers do not awaken a curiosity about the Loyalists of

the Revolution. Students and specialists who have investigated the story of a flight equalled only by that of the Huguenots after the revocation of the Edict of Nantes, have been led to admire the spirit of unselfish patriotism which led over one hundred thousand fugitives to self-exile. While the Pilgrim Fathers came to America leisurely, bringing their household goods and their charters with them, the United Empire Loyalists, it has been well said, "bleeding with the wounds of seven years of war, left ungathered the crops of their rich farms on the Mohawk and in New Jersey, and, stripped of every earthly possession, braved the terrors of the unbroken wilderness from the Mohawk to Lake Ontario." Inhabited to-day by the descendants of these pioneers, the old-fashioned loyalty and conservatism of the Niagara district is the more conspicuous by contrast with neighboring republicanism over the river.

Near Fort George, less than a century ago, stood the first Parliament House of Upper Canada—a building rude in comparison with the massive pile, the Bishop's Palace, used for a similar purpose at Quebec, but memorable for one at least of the many liberal laws its homespun representatives enacted. Here, seventy years before President Lincoln's Emancipation Proclamation, the first United Empire Loyalist Parliament, like the embattled farmers at Concord, "fired a shot heard round the world." For one of the first measures of the exiled patricians was to pass an act forbidding slavery. Few readers know that at Newark, now Niagara, Ontario, was enacted that law by which Canada became not only the first country in the world to abolish slavery, but, as such, a safe refuge for the fugitive slaves from the Southern States.

After much hesitation and perplexity, Governor Simcoe decided to fix the seat of government at Newark, where a small frame house served him for the Executive residence as well as the Parliament building. Traces of the fish ponds which surrounded it may still be detected in the green depressions of the river-bank where it stood. A landed gentleman and a member of the British House of Commons, Governor Simcoe voluntarily relinquished the luxuries of his beautiful English home and estates to bury himself in the wilderness, and use his executive powers for the service of his country in establishing the government of Canada on broad and secure foundations. We read of the first Governor of Upper Canada that he lived in a noble and hospitable manner, "without pride." His guard consisted of four soldiers, who came from Fort George, close by, every morning, and returned thither in the evening. Mrs. Simcoe not only performed the duties of wife and mother, but acted as her husband's secretary. She was a gifted draughtswoman, and her maps and plans served Governor Simcoe in laying out the towns of the new colony.

Facing Fort George and the site of the old Parliament building is a low red brick cottage where the ex-President of the Confederate States, Jefferson Davis, lived for some time as the guest of Senator Mason. Niagara was a famous resort for the Confederate leaders, and a pretty domicile on the ridge overlooking the lake is pointed out as having been the abode of General Breckinridge in 1864.

With the sweet chimes from its belfry tower pealing out across the village park, where a flock of lambs are cropping the turf up to the hedge-rows, every visitor, when first he comes in sight of St. Mark's gray buttresses, must echo Dean Stanley's involuntary exclamation, "Why, this is old England right over again!" Surrounded by a church-yard full of moss-grown tombstones, and shaded by drooping elms, the air sweet in spring-time with the scent of wild flowers, St. Mark's is the very picture of an English country church. Entering the dim, quiet interior, the legend "Fear God! honour the King!" carved on a mural tablet, greets the eye, to renew the impression of the Christian patriotism which animated the early settlers of the town. This stone is to the memory of Colonel John Butler, of Butler's Rangers, his Majesty's Commissioner for Indian Affairs, and of Wyoming Massacre memory. He was the founder of St. Mark's Church. The parish register contains this record of his death:

"1796. *May* 15.—Col. John Butler, of the Rangers. (My patron.) Robert Addison, min'r of Niagara."

ST. MARK'S CHURCH.

MISS RYE'S ORPHANAGE.

lery supported by slender pillars runs around the church, and the high square box pews are curtained in red. The neutral tints of the stained glass in the chancel windows, harmonizing well with the faded quaintness of the gray interior, are a relief to the eye in a day when every railway waiting station and tawdry cottage flares with the gaudy hues of cheap colored glass. Established in 1792, the parish has had but three rectors since the beginning. The church itself, the oldest but one in Upper Canada, was built in 1802.

Revered in Canada, it is a gratifying fact that more recent investigation has proved much of the obloquy cast upon Colonel Butler by earlier writers of American history to have been due to the heated partisan prejudice of that time.

Few churches in America can boast so many quaint and peculiar tablets as St. Mark's. One is to the memory of an officer who "served in most of the glorious actions of the Peninsular war." A gal-

The names in the earlier pages of the register represent the different nationalities which made up the motley population of a stirring frontier town—English, Irish, Scotch, French, Indians, and negroes, with a generous sprinkling of Tories from the Hudson and Mohawk. Colonel Butler's importance as the first citizen of the town is indicated from the beginning to the record of his death in the number of parents who paid him the compliment of calling their children after him. His namesakes in Upper Canada at that time were a progeny scarcely less numerous

Photographed by George Barker.

FORT NIAGARA.

Engraved by Levin.

than George Washington's across the border.

On the outskirts of the town stands a large, square, yellow, brick house, mantled in ivy and clematis. Its broad and spacious porch looks upon an old-fashioned garden and orchard. Approaching it by the country road that leads off from the town, past detached villas, the green common, and over an old stone bridge, one sees shy, curious little faces peering out through the fence pickets. For it is here, under the name of "Our Western Home," that Miss Rye, one of the most distinguished of England's women philanthropists, has established her famous orphanage. Since 1869, when the house, formerly the old Niagara County jail, was opened, over 2000 London waifs, ranging in age from 2 to 16, have found a home under this roof. Three parties of children are sent out from England annually, the cost of transportation not exceeding 12 or 15 pounds sterling for each child, this sum including all expenses from the moment of rescue in London until the girl is housed in the orphanage across the ocean. These children have been adopted by families in Ontario, and with scarcely an exception make good, industrious women.

Old Fort Mississauga, its walls,

" Thick as a feudal keep, with loop-holes slashed,"

lies to the northeast of the town of Niagara, on a bluff above the lake, and in the nooks and crannies of its ruined arches innumerable pigeons nest. Built from the ruins of the ancient town, it serves to keep in mind traditions of that bleak December's night when the 400 inhabitants of the little settlement were turned into the streets to brave the ice and snow of a Canadian winter. To England, then absorbed in a deadly struggle with Napoleon, this frontier war of 1812 was as nothing in comparison with the mightier issue at stake, but of vital moment to the pioneers fleeing from the whirlwind of fire and sword which, beginning with Newark, swept the whole frontier, to culminate in the burning of Buffalo, then the largest settlement on the Niagara border.

Exactly opposite is Fort Niagara, whose ramparts command a sweeping view of Lake Ontario, with distant glimpses of Toronto when the atmosphere is clear. The history of Fort Niagara, knit up as it is with all America's past, from before the time when the French king, dallying with his favorites, thought this region valuable only for furs, down to the imprisonment of Morgan in 1828, in the low magazine near the river-bank, yet remains to be written. Its materials are rich and abundant, but they exist in scattered records and in romantic stories handed down from generation to generation among the old residents of the frontier. During a long period it was a little city in itself, and the most important point west of Albany or south of Montreal. In the centre of the enclosure stood a cross eighteen feet high, with the inscription, "*Regnat, vincit, imperat, Christus,*" and over the chapel was a large ancient dial to mark the course of the sun.

It was in February, 1679, that La Salle, wanting to obtain supplies for his proposed ship the *Griffon*, then building at the mouth of the Cayuga, a creek a few miles above Niagara Falls, his bark wrecked, and the lake too rough for a winter's voyage by canoe or brigantine, set out on snow-shoes, with only two men as his companions, and a dog to draw his baggage, for Fort Frontenac, now Kingston. He had to travel over twenty leagues across the frozen surface of the snow, and Father Hennepin and Tonty accompanied him as far as Niagara. While there La Salle traced the outlines of the fortress, from whose lofty flag-staff now floats the emblem of the republic, but which, alternately owned by French and English, witnessed some of the most hard-fought engagements in their strife for mastery of the New World.

No regular defensive work was constructed on the site of La Salle's rude stockade of 1679 until the Marquis de Nonville fortified the tongue of land, describing it, in words equally true to-day, as the most beautiful, pleasing, and advantageous on the whole lake. Called at first Fort de Nonville, after the marquis, this name soon gave place to the more appropriate one of Fort Niagara. Many interesting characters have at different periods made the fort their abode. In 1780 a handsome house within its enclosure was occupied by Colonel Guy Johnson. It was also the home of both Butlers, father and son, as well as of Captain Joseph Brant. From here young Walter Butler marched to the Cherry Valley Massacre. Catharine Montour also, who was at both the Cherry Valley and Wyoming massacres, at one time took refuge with her two sons at Fort Niagara.

LIFE AT RIDEAU HALL

SINCE the advent of the Princess Louise as its mistress, more than usual curiosity has been manifested regarding the life at Rideau Hall, the "White House" of Canada. Before that time, if it was thought of at all, it was only as the Government House; but since a Princess dwells there, a new interest attaches itself to the place, and it is not strange if every little American "sovereign in her own right" should exercise her national prerogative, and ask all the questions she likes about "court life" at Ottawa. Much of this curiosity has already been satisfied, for from the day the Marquis of Lorne and his royal wife landed upon Canadian soil, very little of the slightest interest concerning them has passed unnoted by the press.

So popular were their predecessors, Lord and Lady Dufferin, that the places which they left were difficult to fill. Indeed, I am sure there are people in Canada to-day who believe that they took their places with them, instead of leaving them to be filled. The Marquis and Marchioness of Lorne took the wisest and easiest way—they retained their individuality, and *created* new places for themselves.

HOUSES OF PARLIAMENT.

So unaffected is the life at Rideau Hall that it shows almost a republican simplicity when compared with the ceremony and parade kept up in many of the great country houses in England. No court etiquette is observed, and only the rules of good manners are adhered to. It is the very evident desire of the Governor-General and Princess to make all those who enter their home feel welcome and at their ease. The public sees very little beyond the usual formalities surrounding the two chief personages of the Dominion. Their home life is jealously guarded from the world.

I often think, when I see the flag which always floats over Rideau Hall when the Princess is there, what a change has come into her life. "Piccadilly and green pastures"—London and Ottawa. Brilliancy, art, culture, and caste—and a crude little city, struggling in the chaos of newness and the doubt of permanency. And I fall to wondering what her feelings were that bleak November day, when she drove, just at night-fall, under the dripping and leafless trees, up to the door of Rideau Hall. Velvet lawns had been exchanged for a soaked meadow turf, and a palace for a comfortable, roomy, old-fashioned home. The life she was leaving behind her had filled her æsthetic nature, and the one to which she was coming could only have as its greatest merit, in her eyes, novelty.

It would not be very strange if she were not happy here, for if we look back over the two years she has spent with us, enough has happened to associate sorrow with Canada. The death of her favorite sister, the Princess Alice, which followed closely her coming, filled the first months of her stay with grief. Of course she was surrounded with an atmosphere of sympathy, but, after all, she was separated from those who felt the grief in all its bitterness with her. But even this was only allowed to very briefly interrupt the gayeties at the Government House. She assumed these duties, and bravely performed them in spite of the mourning of which her face attested the sincerity. Then came the shocking accident which almost cost her her life, and which has left her in a state against which a continual struggle must be made to prevent her sinking into confirmed invalidism. Of late she has been trying the effect of travel. During her absence Lord Lorne has to a great extent supported her rôle as well as his own, and during the winter just passed society has not wanted for entertainment at the Hall.

Royalty is so hedged in by etiquette, that you can only approach it through certain openings, and in Ottawa, as elsewhere, these openings do not frequently occur. Since her Royal Highness has presided at Rideau Hall, even that society which the popular voice calls "the best,"

The hospitalities of Rideau Hall which are extended to the general public may be enjoyed by observing the following rules. In Ottawa the political, judiciary, military, and clerical dignitaries have official precedence, while, under the head of "prominent citizens," clergymen, lawyers, doctors, bankers, and heads of large business firms, lumbering and mining interests, take rank with the officers of the civil

THE DRAWING-ROOM, RIDEAU HALL.

has not had as free access there as formerly. In Lady Dufferin's time the doors swung open easily and often. Of course then, as now, there was always the intimate circle of friends. This, Lady Dufferin chose from Ottawa society. Now it is chosen from England, and comprises the ladies of her household and transient guests. These, almost without an exception, have been artists. Amongst these has been the gifted Miss Montalba, who is making such an enviable reputation in England, and, indeed, throughout Europe. She left as a souvenir of her visit a bust of Lord Lorne, which is strong and masterly. It has been put into bronze, and now stands in the main corridor.

service in society, and amongst these the chiefs of departments take the lead.

To enjoy the hospitalities of Rideau Hall—that is, to get your name upon the lists—you must go and register your name in one book for the Princess Louise, and in another for the Governor-General, and you will do well to leave a separate card for each lady and gentleman making up the Governor's family. In acknowledgment of this civility, you will have your call returned by card by those for whom you have left yours, and from the Marquis and Marchioness of Lorne you will receive invitations to the various entertainments as they occur.

These entertainments have one pecul-

iarity which would impress an American
observer: they are nearly all out-of-doors,
perchance lawn tennis inaugurating the
season.   Some softly bright October day,
such as comes in perfection in our Northern climate, the gardens and lawns surrounding the Hall are brilliant with gay
people in afternoon dress.   Even the usu-

bluff which overhangs the Ottawa River.
Nearer, the fringe of trees bordering the
grounds, and looking like a procession
with triumphal banners floating in the
hazy atmosphere.   Beneath these, across
the lawn, and amid the richest and last
floral offering of summer, promenade the
guests.   The band of the Governor-Gen-

PRINCESS LOUISE, MARCHIONESS OF LORNE.

al gloom of male attire does not stand out
en bloc, as it is broken into by the uniforms of the Governor's aides-de-camp,
which gleam here and there through the
crowd.   At such a time, and upon such a
day, I can imagine with what delight an
artist—Raimend de Madrazo, for instance
—would study the scene.   Detail and accessories are all there.   Imagine this:
Vaguely showing through the autumnal
glow, over a mile away, is the background
formed by the beautiful pile of government buildings resting upon the bold

eral's Foot-Guards is stationed near the
house, and their red coats and flashing
instruments harmonize with the whole.
On the broad gallery stand groups of visitors, while through the open windows
you see a few irrepressible dancers in the
parlor.

After it is too late for lawn tennis and
croquet, the skating and toboggan parties
come, and at these young Canada is in its
element.   Then the daring of Canadian
attire reaches its climax.   No color is too
brilliant and no garment too fantastic to

THE MARQUIS OF LORNE.

be worn. The toboggan slide and vicinity fairly blossoms with the merry, romping company. Surplus dignity is thrown to the winds, along with streamers of ribbons, tassels, and bright-hued scarfs. A pretty Canadian girl never looks prettier than when clad in her cloak made of a fleecy white blanket (its gay border carefully reserved as a trimming), a red or blue *tuque* perched coquettishly upon her abundant hair, its saucy-looking tassel bobbing about at its own sweet will, and a bright-colored skirt just showing between her cloak and moccasined feet. Put now a toboggan and two or three beaux at her disposal, and she is happy. She will slide all afternoon, leaving, per-

haps, just a margin for a skim over the ice, and then scamper into the house, replace her moccasins, or skating boots, with slippers, throw aside her cloak, and dance until the stern law of etiquette, or the equally stern command of her chaperon, who, although kind and discreet as a chaperon should be, feels at last the *ennui* and the interest in the approaching dinner hour natural to her age. These afternoon parties never last later than six o'clock, and a few minutes before that time the last guest is usually gone.

"And does the Princess Louise take part in these sliding parties?"

Yes, to a certain extent, though, knowing her character, you can readily understand that she only does so *à la princesse*. I have never seen her guide her own toboggan, a feat seemingly easy enough of accomplishment when you see it done by a Canadian girl, but which, after a trial or two, the lately arrived Briton or American is very shy of undertaking.

Lately there has been built a little log-cabin under the tall natural growth of pines, well off to one side of the Hall. It overlooks the skating rink, and is divided into two rooms, into which the skaters can retire for rest, warmth, or preparation. It is very comfortable, and doubtless serves the purpose for which it was designed, if that purpose was not picturesqueness. It is so hopelessly unlike the genuine log-cabin that one expects to see a stage peasant step out from its door and soliloquize upon its platform. On this platform chairs are arranged for the Princess and distinguished guests to rest and watch the skaters when they do not care to be of them.

For the amusement of the Governor-General and his gentlemen friends there is a fine curling rink, where the lovers of "the roarin' game" very often congregate. Likewise there is a foot-ball and cricket ground for them; but as this is a pre-eminently feminine piece of literature, I decline to go outside of my province, and so say nothing about the entertainments intended only for gentlemen.

Balls are not of very frequent occurrence, but I can assure those who are interested upon that point, that when they are given, they are "perfectly lovely." You are bidden to one two weeks in advance by a card of impressive dimensions, bearing the monogram of the house, and which reads as follows:

The Aide-de-Camp in waiting is commanded by
His Excellency
The Governor-General and Her Royal Highness the
Princess Louise
to invite
Mr. and Mrs. —— ——
to a Ball on —— ——,
the —— ——, at 9 o'clock.
An answer is requested to the A.D.C. in waiting.

On the appointed night the road to New Edinburgh is lined with sleighs, and by the time the gate is reached, so dense is the crowd of vehicles that the remainder of your drive is likely to occupy more time than did that part of it from the city out. Once inside the Hall, the scene which greets you is indeed charming. Up and down the stairs, along the brilliantly lighted corridors, into the leafy shade of the conservatory, in and out of the several handsome rooms thrown open for the occasion, throng the elegantly dressed guests. The ball-room is packed to suffocation, and it is a terrible pilgrimage to make to the further end, where the Governor-General and the Princess Louise are receiving their guests. When the dancing begins, the pilgrimage becomes an impossibility, and the only thing left for you to do is to gaze hopelessly in their direction. The dressing at one of these grand balls is elegant, and, as a rule, graceful, but when compared with that seen upon a similar occasion at the White House, for instance, is inexpensive. There are handsome silks, satins, and velvets, and a few costly laces, but very few diamonds are to be seen. As a rule, the ladies are *décolletées*, but there are amongst them a good many who are dressed in "the American fashion," as the high-necked full dress is here described.

The ball-room is a large and handsome apartment, occupying the wing to the left of the entrance. The walls are tinted in a soft dark shade, which shows off a brilliantly dressed company to the best advantage. The wood is finished in white and gold, and the window drapery is crimson. On ball nights the tennis-court, in the wing to the right of the entrance, is used for a supper-room. Its walls and ceilings are lined with red and white bunting to simulate a tent. It, as well as the ball-room, was added in Lord Dufferin's administration, and at his request. About midnight the piper is heard piping along the corridor, and the supper-room is thrown open. Into it the vice-regal party lead the way, followed by five or six hundred of their guests, as only about that number can conveniently be served at once. The vice-regal party sit, and the rest stand.

Dinners are far fewer than formerly, and the diners are chosen rather more exclusively. Of course these dinners are the most ceremonious entertainments which take place. The guests enter the reception-room with the right hand bare, although they are not received by the Princess before dinner. She enters just as dinner is announced, and is escorted to the table by the gentleman who takes rank amongst the guests, the Marquis offering his arm to one of the ladies. If they are thus in company with French Canadians, they enter into conversation in French, as both speak it well and fluently. After dinner, when the company returns to the drawing-room, the Princess passes about amongst her guests, speaking to all. It is not proper to sit when the Princess does not, and whenever she has occasion to rise, the entire company does the same, and remains standing until she is again seated.

that it can easily be converted into a theatre. The platform upon which the musicians have sat for the one occasion is now, by an ingenious contrivance for enlarging it, turned into an exquisitely appointed stage. Of late years Rideau Hall has been fortunate in having within its walls most excellent amateur talent. Lady Dufferin was a most charming actress, and in the present household one of the aides-de-camp has the reputation of being the finest amateur actor in England.

SKATING RINK AND CABIN.

In these days of ceramic achievements it is quite allowable to peep into other people's china closets, so I may say something of the china displayed at Rideau Hall. Much of it is beautiful, but by no means exceptionally rare. Neither is the plate of unusual magnificence, though rich and handsome, and gold enters freely into the furnishing of the table. Of course the family plate of Argyll is not yet inherited, still, so abundant is the supply that it is hardly missed.

Of all the entertainments given at the Government House none are more popular or more enjoyed than the theatricals, and invitations to them are eagerly sought. The ball-room is so constructed

He certainly plays to perfection—that is, non-professional perfection. The ladies and gentlemen taking part in the theatricals are usually from Ottawa, and the Princess does not act. And just here I am reminded to say that the announcement that the Princess has written a play founded upon scenes and amongst the fishermen of Gaspé Bay is quite untrue. No such play has been written, or, at least, not by her Royal Highness. The theatricals are full-dress occasions, and the ball-room on these nights presents a brilliant appearance. The plays are always put upon the stage with all the elegance of which they admit, or taste or money can supply. Flowers are used in profusion.

THE BLUE DRAWING-ROOM, RIDEAU HALL.

and their arrangement calls forth the greatest admiration. New scenery has been painted, under the supervision of the Princess, and altogether the stage is a little gem.

The most public appearance of the Princess in Ottawa society is upon the evening after the opening of Parliament, when she holds a "Drawing-room" in the Senate-chamber. This reception is also a full-dress affair, and whoever wishes may attend. The Governor-General and his wife stand upon the dais at one end of the chamber, and the guests approach and are introduced by one aide-de-camp, who has had the name read to him by another from the card with which each guest is provided. As the name is pronounced, the Princess and Marquis simply bow, unless it should belong to some person of sufficient distinction, when they offer their hands and speak a few words with him. After the introduction the guests pass out by a door to the right of the dais, and so can quit the apartment without turning their backs upon royalty—a thing which is, of course, never done. The "Drawing-room" is usually over by ten o'clock. For-

merly there were afternoon receptions, somewhat similar to those at the White House, which could be attended by any one who wished. These have been discontinued, and all parties are now formed of invited guests. This change is solely owing to the increasing numbers who now yearly come to Ottawa.

Some idea of the number of guests entertained in various ways at Rideau Hall since Lord Lorne has been Governor-General may be gained by the following figures:

At dinner parties in 1879.............			904
" " " 1880.............			688
" " " 1881.............			627
At balls in 1879.....................			1000
" " 1881.....			1600
At "At Homes" each year.............			900
At skating and tobogganing parties, each			
year............................			2000
At theatricals, each year.............			1300

On New-Year's Day the Governor-General follows the custom of his predecessors in receiving all who come to wish him a happy New Year, and these receptions are quite as informal as those of the President at the White House. He is also always willing to see any one who asks to see him on business at any time, and so cordial is his manner in these interviews, and so delightful a talker is he, that occasionally his caller loses sight of business in friendly chat.

While Parliament is sitting, the Princess often occupies a chair near the Speaker on the floor of the House of Commons, an interested listener to the debate upon some important bill. · At such times she offers her hand and chats cordially with those members who approach to speak to her. She is always attended by a lady in waiting and an aide-de-camp.

She is, like so many English women, a good walker and a fair rider, and during her first winter here she could be met almost any day miles away from her home. She "did" much of the vicinity of Ottawa on foot, always *sensibly* shod and dressed, and in slippery weather carrying a cane. Almost invariably she wears a veil. It has been the subject of much comment, and the curious often complain that the public never sees her face. Her reason for wearing it probably lies as much in the fact that she suffers terribly from neuralgia as from any wish to thwart the curious gaze. Both the Princess and Marquis readily adopted winter sports, and many a merry snow-shoe tramp was organized from the Government House; and when the spring opened, and the rafts from the Upper Ottawa began to come down by hundreds, they enjoyed the grand and exciting fun of running the rapids above the Chaudière Falls, and coming down through the "slides" upon these log rafts.

From this slight glimpse into it you see that Rideau Hall is by no means a Castle of Indolence. The Princess is a busy woman, and her range of duties is a very wide one. Her artistic pursuits are, without doubt, nearest her heart, and you often see her abroad with her sketch-book, filling it with souvenirs of her Canadian home. She has a snug little sketching box, which can be whisked about from place to place as she desires it. Fortunately for one of her artistic nature she lives in a region surrounded by loveliest views, and whichever way the eye turns, it is gladdened by some picture never to be forgotten.

The Princess is a communicant at St. Bartholomew's, the little English church

THEATRICALS IN THE BALL-ROOM.

PRINCESS LOUISE'S SKETCHING BOX.

at New Edinburgh, which stands near the grounds (the rector of which is chaplain for Rideau Hall), while the Marquis of Lorne comes into the city, and is a regular attendant at "the kirk." Her Royal Highness has always taken an active interest in church affairs, and to her the little church is indebted for a fine chime of bells. The children of the Sunday-school are regularly entertained at the Hall with a Christmas tree and party. She visits hospitals, schools, and convents, and carries on all the work of a charitable lady in private life. Much of her good work is done in a quiet, unostentatious manner, which fully carries out the Biblical injunction; but a princess can not hide from the public the work of one hand, even if she can keep it a secret from the other, and so we from time to time catch a glimpse of her true, kind heart.

All of these public duties do not interfere with those of a more domestic character. She, of course, has a small army of servants. There is a *chef*, and *un garçon de chef*, and I would be afraid to say how many more *pour faire la cuisine;* there are maid-servants and men-servants

for each particular kind of work, and a housekeeper to oversee them all. But, in spite of much aid, the Marchioness of Lorne is at the head of her establishment. She does not think it beneath her dignity to go into the laundry and instruct the maids concerning their duties, or to give an occasional eye to the marketing when it is brought in. A story I have just heard about her makes her quite rival in housewifely attainments the queen of good King Stephen, who, from the "peck o' barley meal," concocted that historical pudding so well known to the student of Mother Goose. A friend of mine was lately dining at Rideau Hall, and during the dinner she remarked upon the excellence of the oyster *pâtés* to one of the ladies in waiting to the Princess. "Yes," she replied; "they were made by her Royal Highness."

The immediate household at Government House consists of two or three ladies in waiting and several aides-de-camp. The military secretary and his wife occupy a handsome house near by, where the Princess often calls informally, or takes a five-o'clock "school-room tea" with the secretary's children.

Rideau Hall in every part shows itself to be the home of an artist and a poet. An air of culture and refinement pervades it, and whichever way you turn you are delighted by some pretty conceit, or tasteful fancy successfully carried out. Here are old tapestry hangings, as rich with history and associations as color and skill. Exquisite ornaments are scattered about in profusion, but not with that riotous plenty which simply suggests money. The "blue parlor" is, to my taste, one of the most charming rooms I can recall. It is a large and handsome apartment, and is furnished upon the happy meeting ground of classical severity and elegant luxuriousness. It is essentially feminine in its taste, and you at once say to yourself, "It is the expression of the *artist*." About you you feel much of its presiding genius. Here is a panel of flowers, and here a door decorated by her brush; an unfinished study hangs in one corner, and rare paintings glow upon the walls. Sitting before the bright coal fire on a winter day, you can look out through the warmly draped windows upon a driving snow-storm, or, if you turn slightly, you can look into the fairy-land of flowers, for the conservatory opens from this room.

Next to the blue parlor is the library, a snug and rather surprising library, with none of the conventional solidity of furnishing which one naturally associates with books. It is pretty and simple, in white and green.

With the exception of perhaps these two rooms, the color throughout the Hall is crimson. Perhaps no better could be chosen. It is a stately color, and glows with a perpetual warmth which our long Canadian winters make acceptable.

Louise we knew better as a clever artist than as a princess. So we were prepared, in anticipating their coming, for a more exalted and refined life than Canadian society had yet known, and our anticipations have not been disappointed.

Two years is a short time, but it has been long enough to establish upon a substantial foundation a national academy of arts and several art schools in Canada. and what is, perhaps, still more to the point, to implant a respect for mental su-

PRINCESS LOUISE'S BOUDOIR.

I have only written of that life in which the gay world is interested; but there is another and higher life lived at Rideau Hall, and I doubt if either the Marquis of Lorne or her Royal Highness knows how wide-spread its influence is. Its spirit does more toward awakening a desire for mental improvement than anything else could. Years ago we knew our present Governor-General as a writer who did not have to call his rank to his aid to gain admittance to the literary world, and before him we had learned the character of the house of Argyll. While the Princess

periority in all departments. Like all people who are true to their tastes, and who are happy enough to have the means, they have opened and smoothed ways in which to advance those who are less fortunately placed. They have sent young artists abroad, generously patronized those already before the public, and fostered education in many ways. With this kindly spirit and good work the present Governor-General and his wife will have marked their stay in Canada with a characteristic influence which will be felt for many years to come.

BROTHER TO THE SEA

YOU see Lake Superior best, as an incident in crossing the continent, when travelling over the Canadian transcontinental railroad, and of all the various "scenic wonders" that the different cross-continental railroads advertise, not one seems to me more grand or more grandly beautiful than this. For more than half a day the cars glide along the shore, whose irregularities provide a wide diversity of scenery, in woods, among rocks, and every few minutes close beside the closed ends of the great bays which spread out into an ocean-like endlessness of water. Each time that I have made the journey it has been my good fortune to see the lake clear, smooth, and brilliant, as if it were a vast mirror that Dame Nature might have been holding up to herself. And the lake, like a huge bowl of quicksilver, has each time caught and held the brilliant scene around it—the cloud-littered shining skies, the quiet stately forests, and the towering rocks, which rise in all the forms of turrets, pinnacles, ramparts, castellated heaps, and frowning walls, now green, now red, now purple, and anon dull brown or ashen.

GRAND ARCH, PICTURED ROCKS, LAKE SUPERIOR.

Lake Superior is almost everywhere noble, grand, impressive, majestic. Its surroundings are, for the most part, far more suggestive of what one fancies the ocean should be than are those of the oceans themselves. Old Crowfoot, with his marvellous faculty for aptly nick-naming whatever new thing he saw, was never happier than when he tried to express in a phrase the impression Superior made upon his mind. The Canadian officials were bringing him on a sight-seeing tour to Montreal from the Blackfoot territory on the plains, where he ruled the wildest Indians of Canada; and when he saw the greatest of all lakes, and saw it again and then again, until he comprehended its majesty, he said, "It is the Brother to the Sea."

It is the largest lake in the world, and the largest body of fresh water. It is 380 miles in length and 160 miles across in its widest part. Its watery area of 32,000 square miles proves it to be the size of the State of Indiana, or four times as big as Massachusetts.* It is about 600

THUNDER CAPE, NORTH SHORE.

TRAP-ROCK CLIFFS, NORTH SHORE.

The lake is practically the property of the United States. The Canadians own the beautiful north shore, but very little of the lake itself. The main body of the traffic on the lake is ours by a right that cannot be questioned, for it proceeds from our vastly greater population, and from our possession of the coal supply of the continent, which gives to American vessels the cargoes with which to return westward after having floated grain and ore eastward.

Lake Superior is a capricious monster, demanding skilled seamanship and the use of powerful and stanch boats, the majority of which are comparable with the vessels in our Atlantic coasting trade. The lake is a veritable womb of storms. They develop quickly there, and even more speedily the water takes on a furious character. It is always cold, and the atmosphere above and far around it is kept cool all summer. I have been told, but cannot verify the statement, that the temperature of the water in the open lake never rises above 46° Fahrenheit. As a rule, the men who sail upon it cannot swim. The lake offers no inducement to learn the art, and, alas! those who are expert swimmers could not keep alive for any great length of time in the icy water. When I was making inquiries upon this point, I found, as one almost always does, some who disputed what the majority agreed upon. I even found an old gentleman, a professional man of beyond seventy years of age, who said that for several years he had visited the lake each summer-time, and that he had made it a practice to

feet above the sea-level; but the government charts show that in its deepest part the water has a depth of 231 fathoms, or 1386 feet, so that there, at least, the lake is more than 700 feet below the surface of the sea as well as 600 feet above it. North of Keweenaw Point, on the south side, there is a depth of 1008 feet, and great depths, above 500 feet, are scattered all about the lake. Its shore line is 1500 miles in length.

One very dignified English authority terms Lake Superior "the head of and chief reservoir for the most magnificent system of inland navigation in the world," a system which, if taken to embrace the water route from the source of the St. Louis, emptying into the head of the lake, to the mouth of the St. Lawrence, is 2100 miles in length. Curiously enough, the same plateau in Minnesota wherein the St. Louis has its beginning is also the starting-point of the Mississippi and the Red River of the North. But Lake Superior owes little to the St. Louis. It receives the waters of 200 rivers, and drains a territory of 53,000 square miles exclusive of its own area.

bathe in its waters nearly every day. It was chilly, he admitted, and he did not stay in very long. But many sailors, among them some ship and steamship

I asked one captain how long he supposed a man might battle for life, or cling to a spar in the lake. He answered, very sensibly, it seemed to me, that some

THE NORTH SHORE, LAKE SUPERIOR.

captains, confirmed my belief that few Lake Superior seamen have learned to swim, and that the coldness of the water quickly numbs those who fall into it.

men could endure the cold longer than others, and that the more flesh and fat a man possessed, the longer he could keep alive. "But," he added, "the only man

I ever saw fall overboard went down like a shot before we could get to him. I always supposed he took a cramp."

The bodies of the drowned are said not to rise to the surface. They are refrigerated, and the decomposition which causes the ascent of human bodies in other waters does not take place. If one interesting contribution to my notes is true, and there be depths to which fishes do not descend, it is possible that many a hapless sailor-man and voyager lies as he died, a century back perhaps, and will ever thus remain, lifelike and natural, under the darkening veil of those emerald depths.

The great, fresh, crystal sea never freezes over, and yet its season for navigation is very short. This is due to the ice that makes out from the shores, the points, and the islands, and closes some of the harbors. One captain told me he had seen ice five miles out from the lighthouse on Thunder Cape, and that is an island in deep water. In 1880 the season opened on April 5th; in 1888 it began on May 21st. In 1880 it closed on December 3d, and in 1883 there was navigation until December 30th. But those are extreme dates. As a rule, navigation opens in the middle of April and closes in the middle of December.

But there are two obstructions for which Lake Superior is notorious, and they rank next to the ice, and still farther limit navigation for some lines of ships. These evils are the fogs and the snow-storms, and of the two the fogs are the more numerous and the snow is the more dreaded. In the summer Dame Superior wears her fogs almost as a Turkish wife wears her veils. There is a time, in August, when the only fogs are those which follow rain; but the snow begins in September, so that the reader may judge of the sort of navigation the lake affords. The Canadian Pacific steamships (Clyde - built ships that are like our Havana and Savannah boats) are in service only between May and October, and it is the snow which curtails their season. It snows on the great lake just as it does on the plains, in terrible flurries, during the course of which it is impossible to see a foot ahead, or to see at all. Mark Twain did not exaggerate the character of these storms when he described the fate of men who were lost and frozen to death within pistol shot of their cabins. It has a way of snowing on Superior, by-the-way, as

late as June and as early as September; in a light and frolicsome way, to be sure, but it snows, nevertheless. As for the fogs, though they are light and often fleeting after midsummer, they are sufficiently frequent during the rest of the season of navigation to have given the lake a distinguished bad character in the minds of those who sail the warmer lakes, and I have had a captain tell me that he has made seven voyages in succession without seeing any lights on his route from Port Arthur to " the Soo."

But its charms outweigh all its caprices and atone for its worst faults. It is supremely charming, a vast nursery for exquisite effects, and a play-ground of beauty. Out on its broad bosom it imitates the sea exactly. There was no apparent difference in the immensities of the two bodies, and the view within the speeding circle of the horizon was that of the same deep blue field of veined and ruffled water. By day the patent log kept up its angry whistle, and the clumsy gulls, with their broken-looking wings, beat the air and sounded their baby treble in a soft shattered cloud over the vessel's wake. The sky was never to be forgotten, not soft like that over southern Europe, but of the clearest, purest blue imaginable, and yet a blue to which the sunlight lent an active living tone like that of flame diluted or transformed. On no visit did I ever see the sky free of clouds, and I cannot imagine it so, but Lake Superior fair-weather clouds, always cumuli, of course, are the softest, roundest, most feather-like vagrants that ever loafed like lazy swans in heaven's ethereal sea.

One peculiarity of Lake Superior cannot be too strongly dwelt upon or exaggerated. That is its purity, the wonderful cleanness and freshness of it, and of its atmosphere and of its borders. It must become the seat of a hundred summer resorts when the people visit it and succumb to its spell. Think what it is! A volume of crystalline water in which all Scotland's surface could be sunk like a stone—of water so clear and translucent that one may see the entire outlines of the vessels that cleave its surface, so pure that objects may be distinguished on the bottom at a depth of 20 feet; 45 feet they call it who have to do with the lake, but I was unable to see through more of it than 21 feet. Fancy such an expanse of water so clear, and then picture it bordered by 1500 miles of balsamic forests, which extend backward from the lake to distances that overreach States and provinces. Travellers accustomed to frequent transcontinental journeys look longingly forward in the summer to the time when they shall be passing the great lake, either to the northward or southward, certain that the daylight hours will be pleasant and that the night-time will be cool. Cleanliness—perhaps I should say tidiness—is everywhere the characteristic of Superior. Its famed and stately walls of rock delve straight downward into it and rise sheer above it without giving nature the slightest chance to make a litter of rocks or dirt at their feet. While other rocky shores of other waters stand apart or merely wet their toes in the fluid, these monsters wade in neck-deep, and only expose their heads in the sunlight, fathoms—sometimes 200 fathoms—from the bottom. Terrible prison walls these become to shipwrecked drowning mariners, for they extend in reaches sometimes 25 miles long without offering a finger-hold for self-rescue. Tourists who have seen the Pictured Rocks will understand this feature of the lake's boundaries.

Again, Superior's waters lend themselves to the most exquisite effects, to the most opulent coloring, by their surroundings and in themselves. Those extravagant chromatic surprises in nature which cause the Western people to rave over the charms of their most beautiful resort, Mackinac, are at the command of all who visit Lake Superior at any point around the spectacular sea. A thousand lovelier Mackinacs are there. The same charms, the same mysterious colorings, the same gorgeous effects, illuminate the view from the coal-docks of Duluth, the cottages at Marquette, the wharves of Port Arthur, the decks of the steamers that cruise among the Apostle Islands, or the canoes of tourists or half-breeds who fling their fly-lines or haul their nets in the lonesome caves and neglected harbors where nature's is the only other presence. To begin with, the Lake Superior water is always green where it is comparatively shallow. If you are observant, you will notice that it is green in your pitcher, green in your washbowl, and green in your shaving-mug wherever you put up on the shores. It is not a repellent green; it is the green of the pea-vine, of

thinned chartreuse—the lively, beautiful green of a thick cake of pure ice.

Everywhere, then, the edge of the water is of this beautiful emerald hue, showing its color against the pink sand, against the brown and red rocks, against the dark green forests. At a distance it insensibly deepens and changes into blue, but by such degrees that the indigo of the greatest depth is approached through slight changes beyond the first sky-color to the turquoise, and from that to the deeper hues. With every change in the atmosphere the views change. A strong sun will lave great fields of the water with a flood of salmon-colored light; and a brilliant moon, which at times silvers a wide swath upon the surface, will yet, under other conditions, tinge the water with a blush of pink.

Fit and true it was for Longfellow to fix in Lake Superior the mysterious climax of his legend of Hiawatha. The lake has impressed itself deeply upon whatever of religion is felt by the Indians upon its borders—and those of all the Algonquin family, whose tribes reach from the Rocky Mountains to the coast of Maine. Every here and there, upon the rocks which the Chippewas treat as altars, or in the swift currents that race between them, the red men offer gifts to the spirits which they fancy are domiciled there. As far as I have been able to comprehend their favorite legend of that Minnebajou (or Nana-bejou) who seems to have been the creator and yet subordinate to God, it was in Superior that he sought his yet enduring rest after he had constructed the present earth in the waters that swallowed a former one. There are several of his homes in various parts of the lake. And well may Superior breed mysticism in the minds of savages, for it is given to startling tricks. The mirages that are seen upon it have bestowed upon it a peculiar and distinct fame. They are known to the people of the lake only as "reflections." I have heard many sailors describe the wonderful ones they have witnessed; I would give another journey out there to see one. Men have told me that they have seen Duluth when they were 185 miles away from it—upside down and in the sky, but distinctly Duluth. One sailor said that at one broad noonday he suddenly saw a beautiful pasture, replete with an apple-tree and a five-rail fence, shining green

IN THE HARBOR AT DULUTH.

and cool before him, apparently close at hand. The effect the clear air produces by apparently magnifying objects seen upon the lake is most astonishing. To illustrate what I mean, let me tell what happened the very last time I saw the lake. I was on a tug-boat, and upon coming out of the cabin I saw ahead of me a tremendous white passenger steamship. The boats were approaching one another at right angles, and this new-comer loomed up like a leviathan among vessels, bigger than one of our new naval cruisers, high above the water as a house would look. I called attention to it, and a companion, familiar with the lake, replied,

"I wonder what boat it is; she's a whopping big one, isn't she?"

Something distracted my attention, and five minutes afterward, when I looked at the approaching vessel again, she had passed the mysterious point at which she was most exaggerated in apparent size, and had become an ordinarily large lake steamer. But that was not the end of the trick. She began to dwindle and shrink, growing smaller and smaller in size, until the phenomenon became ridiculous. In time the elastic boat had become a very small passenger propeller, and I found myself wondering whether she would be discernible at all by the time we were abreast of her. But at that the optical frolic ceased. A small screw steamer of the third class was what she proved to be.

Lake Superior was once a great deal deeper lake than it is now. All along the Canadian shore any one may see the former coast levels that now form pebbly terraces hundreds of feet above the present water. At Duluth the beautiful Terrace Drive above the city lies along a former coast line that was 470 feet higher than the present level of the lake. Perhaps the most compact picture of the first dawn of Lake Superior upon the ken of white men, indirectly through their relations with the Indians, is drawn by Washington Irving in his *Astoria*.

"It was the fur trade," he says, "which gave early sustenance and vitality to the great Canadian provinces." As the valuable furs became more and more scarce near the settlements, the capital among which was Montreal, the Indians went farther west upon their hunting expeditions. "Every now and then a large body of Ottawas, Hurons, and other tribes who hunted the countries bordering on the Great Lakes would come down in a squadron of light canoes laden with beaver-skins and other spoils of their year's hunting.... Montreal would be alive with naked Indians running from shop to shop, bargaining for arms, kettles, knives, blankets, bright-colored cloths, and other articles of use or fancy, upon all which, says an old French writer, the merchants were sure to clear at least 200 per cent." Thus came into existence a new class, called *coureurs des bois*, or rangers of the woods. They were men who had originally gone abroad with the red men on hunting expeditions, but who saw how a point could be gained upon the merchants at home by going out among the Indians or meeting them in the forests, there to peddle necessaries and ornaments from well-stocked canoes in exchange for peltries. In their track went out the missionaries; for none but an Indian ever went farther than the traders in those days, and eventually the Hudson Bay men—a still later growth—crossed the continent in advance of the solitary and devout clergy. When we have considered these actors upon the scene, and have understood that the *coureurs des bois* came to live with the red men, and created a body of half-breeds who were destined to be both white and red in their affiliations and their neutral influence, we may imagine that we can see the vanguard of the host that in time reached Lake Superior.

The first white men to see the lake were *coureurs des bois*, it is safe to say, but the first recorded visits are mainly those of missionaries of the same stock that are to-day living adventurous and solitary lives in what is left of the wilderness, now shrinking closer and closer to the arctic regions. "The Soo" was first visited by the missionaries in 1641, and they honored the brother of their king by calling the rapids the "*Sault de Gaston*." Nineteen years afterward Père Mesnard conquered the rapids with his canoe, and found himself out upon the great waters of Superior. That was in 1660, and what they then called the lake I have not learned; but in 1771, in a map published by the Jesuits, it is inscribed "*Lac Tracy, ou Supérieur*." In that map the neighboring lakes are named *Lac des Ilinois* and *Lac des Hurons*. In 1668 there arrived Père Marquette, that saintly man whose name lives anew in that of a progressive lake port, and whose memory is honored by every intelligent man in all that vast region. He was accompanied by Claude Dablou when, having brought his wasted body there to end his days, as he thought, in a brief attempt to spread the gospel, he landed at the place which he renamed *Sault Ste. Marie*, and founded there the first settlement in Michigan. Messrs. Chanart and d'Esprit (sieurs des Radison and des Groselliers) have left a record of their visit to the western end of the lake in 1661, six years before Père Allouez and a company of traders reached there, and eighteen years before Du Lhut arrived with a band of *coureurs des bois* to make the neighborhood of the city that bears his altered name his place of residence for several years. After these, by a great stride over the slow-making pages of history, we come to find the great Hudson Bay Company, and its rival the Northwest Company of fur-traders, conducting a systematized business on the north shore of the lake; while in time the American Fur Company, under John Jacob Astor's management, copied the methods of those corporations on the south side. Trading-posts grew into fortified places, trails spread into roads, and settlements around mission houses developed into villages. Then, two hundred years after its discovery, Lake Superior stood still for many years—for nearly forty years—so that its present history, solid and certain in its promises as it is, resembles the record of a mushroom.

The date of the last enlargement of the lock of the Sault Ste. Marie Canal is the date upon which to base all computations of the age of the present lake traffic and its consequences. That lock was enlarged and newly opened in 1881. Marquette, "the Queen City of Lake Superior," is an old place of former industry, but it is a mere baby in its present enterprise. Superior dates from 1852 "on paper," but from 1881 in fact, while Duluth is only a few years older. Port Arthur, the principal Canadian port, owes itself to the Canadian Pacific Railway, now about seven or eight years of age, and many of the cities of the future are not yet discovered, while of great resorts that are to be, like Munising and Nepigon, only those two are known, and they are known only to the most enterprising sportsmen.

The men of the Lake Superior region will in time form a new conglomerate, if I may use a geologist's term. The sailors of the great unsalted sea are a very nautical-looking lot of men—as spare of flesh, as bronzed and leather-skinned, as if they were from Maine; but the surprising thing about them, so far as I may trust my observation, is that they all obtained their training on the lakes. I did not find one who had ever seen the ocean, and I thought I detected among them a tone of contempt whenever they spoke of the genuine sea, as if they were of the opinion that the Atlantic is a sort of juvenile campus for playing at sailoring, whereas it requires grown men to battle with the lakes.

Along-shore one meets with a queer hodgepodge of men. On the United States side the Scandinavians are very numerous. They are highly spoken of by the Americans. They are bankers and merchants there, as well as laborers and household servants. They have spread themselves over all parts of the new field with wonderful assimilative capacity. They are a sturdy, shrewd, thrifty, and ambitious people, as a rule. They make the strangest mess of speaking English at first, and we may expect a new touch in dialect literature when writers who understand them begin to treat of them. Yet they are sufficiently important to render a knowledge of their native tongue very advantageous to Americans, and I found the general passenger agent of a great railroad in the lake region assiduously studying Swedish. There are many Welshmen in that country, but I only heard of them in the mining regions. For the rest, the people are American, with all which that implies; that is to say, some have an American tree with roots two centuries old, and some carry naturalization papers.

Over on the half-deserted Canadian side the rulers of Canada—who are the Scotch first and the English second—are conspicuous in the towns, settlements, and heavier industries. But the hunting and fishing are still so good that the red Chippewayan servants of the Hudson Bay Company still patrol the streams in canoes and traverse the winter snow fields with sledges dragged by "huskies," those ill-used Eskimo dogs whose fare is said to be "one part fish and nine parts clubbing." Gaunt and tireless prospectors, axe in hand and pack on back, walk northward among the rocks, far ahead of civilization. Hudson Bay factories are yet the stations, as the waterways are yet the only roads, once you get beyond the rails of the transcontinental road skirting the very edge of the lake.

The lake and a vast region around it is a sportsman's paradise, and a treasury of wealth for those who deal in the products of the wilderness—furs, fish, and lumber. At little Port Arthur alone the figures of the fishing industry for the market are astonishing. In 1888 the fishermen there caught 500,000 pounds of white-fish, 360,000 pounds of lake trout, 48,000 pounds of sturgeon, 90,000 pounds of pickerel, and 30,000 pounds of other fish, or more than a million pounds in all. They did this with an investment of $3800 in boats and $10,000 in gill and pound nets. This yield nearly all went to a Chicago packing company, and it is in the main Chicago and Cleveland capital that is controlling the lake's fisheries. The white-fish is, in the opinion of most *gourmets,* the most delicious fish known to Americans. The lake trout are mere food. I am told that they are rather related to the char than to the salmon. They are peculiar to our inland waters. They average five to ten pounds in weight, and yet grow to weigh 120 pounds; but whatever their weight be, it is a mere pressure of hard dry flesh, calculated only to appease hunger.

But I find that on both shores of the lake there is a growing feeling that, in spite of the millions of "fry" the Fish Commission dumps into that and the other lakes, the vast reservoirs of delicious food are being ruined by the same policy and the same methods that make our lumbermen the chief criminals of the continent. Men who have spent years on the lakes solemnly assert that not only are the annual yields growing smaller and smaller, but that the sizes of the fish caught are growing less and less. Worse yet, they assert that illicit practices, or those which should be made illicit, result in the catching and destruction of millions of fish which are too small to market. I do not believe that any man of leisure could find a more benevolent or worthy cause in which to enlist than in that of a crusade against the use of small-meshed nets in Lake Superior. I will not, on my present knowledge, say that the planting of fish fry is a waste of time and energy, but it certainly is regarded by many as ineffectual in the present crisis. Government had better direct its energy to that ounce of net-cutting that is better than a ton of fry.

At present there are trout a-plenty in

the streams that flow into the great lake through the beautiful forests which clothe that enormous tract, in which, south of Superior alone, there are said to be between 500 and 600 little lakes. Exactly like it, from the sportsman's point of view, is the region north of the lake, where the land looks, upon a detailed map, like a

is a railroad, the Duluth, South Shore, and Atlantic, which dissects this entire region from point to point of the lake along its southern coast. The best sport is found south of the railroad rather than between it and the lake.

Of the ports and lake-side cities of the "great unsalted sea," I have already, in a

THE LOCK AT "THE SOO."

great sponge, all glistening with water, so crowded is its surface with lakes and streams. In the north are caribou, and all the animals that the fur-traders of the Hudson Bay Company value. South of the lake there are no animals larger than deer, but deer are abundant, and bear are still numerous. In the fishing season a man may feast on trout, black bass, pickerel, muskallonge, partridge, venison, and rabbit; and he may, if he has the soul of a true sportsman, revel in the magnetic, wholesome qualities of the air, and in the opulent and exquisite beauties of the woods. For good sport, however, let him avoid the famous places. There are half a dozen streams near the celebrated Nepigon that are better than they have been for years, while on the south side it is better to go to quiet regions, like Munising or the streams near the Ontonagon, than to whip the more noted waterways. There

previous article, described the two leading ones—Duluth in Minnesota, and Superior in Wisconsin. They lie side by side at the western end or head of Lake Superior.

The city of Marquette, on Iron Bay, in the centre of the most picturesque part of the south shore, gets importance as a shipping port for ore and lumber, but it occupies the most beautiful site and is the most beautiful town, as seen from the water, of all those that have grown up on the lake. It has a large and busy trading district on the sandy shore of the lake, but the finer residence districts surmount a high bluff which half encircles the town. Ridge Street, 200 feet above the lake, may easily become one of the finest avenues in America, and already it numbers among its appointments some of the most artistic and costly houses in the Lake Superior region. With its drives and neighboring forests, its fishing-streams, and the beauties and pleasures offered by the lake, Marquette would naturally rank as a summer resort, but the addition of Presque Isle Park will, when the park is developed, raise it to the first rank among the idling-places in the West. This park covers a bold promontory formed of enormous piles of stone like the Pictured Rocks, which are themselves not far away. The water has eaten several caves into the foot of the sheer wall of forest-capped rock, and into one of these a boat may be rowed. The park is best seen when approached from the lake. The deep pellucid waters in the shadow of its walls form a famous fishing-field.

The greatest commercial activity around the lake is due to the mining. On the north shore gold has been found in the Port Arthur district. The quartz-bearing rock has been followed and the land pre-empted along several veins, but there has been no systematic mining. Silver has been very profitably and extensively mined, the famous Silver Islet Mine having yielded $3,250,000 worth of the metal. There are very many other mines in the district, many of which have proved failures, and a few of which are prosperous, while still others give promise of good futures.

But, either owing to the greater enterprise and capital of the Americans or to the more valuable and widely diffused metalliferous deposits, it is on the south side that most of the notable mining is found. The names "Calumet and Hecla," "Gogebic," and "Marquette," distinguishing great mines or districts, are doubtless of world-wide fame. There are seventy-three iron mines on the Marquette range, and their output for 1890 was more than four millions of tons.

TROUT-FISHING.

ORE DOCKS AT MARQUETTE, THE LARGEST IN
THE WORLD.

Open-pit mining is largely followed in this district. In the region between Ishpeming and Negaunee are a few gold mines. The richest of these is stopped by litigation, but one profitable mine is being worked. The great copper region of Keweenaw peninsula—a broad, long area of land thrust out of Michigan into the middle of the lake—abounds with copper in the form of conglomerates, or mineral mixed with rock. The census report upon the district declares that 117,800,000 pounds of this mineral yielded 87,445,000 pounds of ingot, showing the percentage of copper to be 74.24. In the census year, 1890, the amount of rock crushed was 2,137,653 tons, and this yielded 86,604,283 pounds of ingot copper. Silver is said to be found in the copper region. The famous Gogebic iron region, or range, marks the western limit of Michigan's 150-mile-wide mineral section, from which, exclusive of gold, copper, and silver, between five millions and eight millions of tons of ore is annually sent away. The logging or lumbering industry, especially on the southern and western ends of the lake, is a gigantic calling, but it is not within my ability to summarize its extent with figures.

All the commerce of Lake Superior that is sent to or from it must pass through the Sault Ste. Marie Canal, until the Canadians finish the parallel waterway, which they are building in order to be in all respects independent of us. Nature made the waters of Superior to flow into Huron by means of the St. Marie River, but in doing so they drop to Huron's level, which is somewhat lower than that of the king of lakes. They make eighteen feet of the descent suddenly by the rapids which give to the artificial waterway built to avoid them the name of the Sault Ste. Marie Canal. "Soo" and "Soo Saint Mary," or "Susan Mary," as it is often called, are Western forms the words take. Commercially speaking, this canal added Superior to the great lake system or route, connected it directly with the Atlantic and the world at large, and shortened very greatly the railroad carriage of ore and grain to the East, and of coal and general merchandise to the far West. The canal accommodates an amount of traffic which for years has been greater than that of the Suez Canal. In 1886 the freighting through the great African canal amounted to a gross tonnage of 8,183,313 tons; but it has decreased, if I am not mistaken; while the tonnage that passed "the Soo" in 1890 was 9,041,313. It is interesting to note that of this sum the proportion of freight carried by Canadian vessels was only six per cent. in

1888, and four per cent. in 1889. It is also worth while to note that of the nine millions of tons floated through the canal in 1890, about 4,500,000 were east-bound, and 2,600,000 were west-bound.

But the canal is inefficient; wofully so in the opinion of the extra-energetic shippers at the Lake Superior ports, who assert that its inability to pass the largest vessels fully laden operates to the advantage of their great rival, Chicago. The depth of water in the canal in 1890 ran from fourteen feet and nine inches to fifteen feet three inches, and during the

great commerce that strains toward development on the lake is not the "Soo" canal. That will soon be as large as it needs to be. The trouble lies in the inadequacy of the canals far to the eastward—the Welland and Lachine canals. Instead of furthering the ambition of the West, they hold it at the throat and choke it. Until they are enlarged, or belittled by larger canals, the lake commerce with Europe will continue to be greatly limited. It is true that the whaleback steamer *Wetmore* went to Europe from Superior with a load of grain, but had she been

LIGHT-HOUSE AT MARQUETTE.

first half of 1891 it varied between thirteen feet and ten inches and fourteen feet five inches. Such vessels as are now being added to the lake service draw sixteen and a half feet, and in view of the present depth of water in the canal it will be seen that they lose several hundreds of tons a trip by carrying only partial loads. The government is awake to the situation, and the new lock which it is now building, at a cost of more than four millions of dollars, will be 100 feet in width, 21 feet deep, and 1200 feet long.

The fact that the canal does more business in seven months than the Suez Canal effects in a year does not give so clear an idea of its importance as is gained from the consequences of a slight accident to the lock year before last. This necessitated closing the canal temporarily, but it cost the men and companies who use the canal a loss of about one million dollars. There were at that time 183 vessels waiting to pass out of Superior, and nearly as many going in the other direction.

The worst brake on the wheels of the

the least bit longer she could not have gone through the Welland Canal, around Niagara, and she had to dodge the St. Lawrence canals by shooting the rapids of that river. Were she to return to Superior she would have to be unriveted and pulled through the canal in two parts. Thus it was that the steamships of the Canadian Pacific Company plying on the larger lakes were brought from the Clyde.

It was a valuable experiment, that with the *Wetmore*. It demonstrated the pluck of the far Western navigators and merchants, and it accentuated the demand of the people of the entire Northwest for a practicable water route to the Atlantic. The people of the region around the Great Lakes are chafing and fretting under the chains that bind and hinder them. They demand the means of reaching the Atlantic either by the St. Lawrence or the Hudson, and they will not be satisfied with less than "twenty feet of water from Duluth to the sea." That is the battle-cry of a people with the will and persistence to achieve whatever they de-

ELEVATORS AT DULUTH, WEST SUPERIOR IN
THE DISTANCE.

termine upon. They will not long be put off. They are full of the spirit of the present revolution by which we Americans are to recover our prestige on the sea. Thus added force is found in a vast reach of new water-front, which will send upon the oceans of the world not merely men, but ships that hail from the heart of the continent.

The aim of the students of the situation is not only to keep beyond the constant reduction of railroad rates, but also to secure the carrying of the products of Asia. They argue that the Pacific Ocean currents naturally set toward Puget Sound, and put San Francisco out of the natural course of shipping, and also that the Puget Sound coast is six hundred miles nearer the north Atlantic ports than is San Francisco.

There are two sides to the contention for improved internal waterways, and I propose to present both sides, because both together reflect the influences that are building up the new West, and show the strides that have been made toward the perfection of transportation facilities.

There is a conspicuous railroad man in the West who argues that water rates will cease to influence rail transportation when the development of railroading reaches the near point toward which it is hastening. For a time in 1891 the freight rate from Chicago to New York was seventeen cents a hundred pounds, and he says that this forced the lake rate down to one and a quarter cents. He argues that when the railroads make a twelve-cent rate, as they must in time, the boats

on the lakes will not be able to earn their operating expenses.

The form of railroad progress which attracts every one's attention is that which is marked by the improvement of the palace cars through the introduction of baths, barber shops, and libraries. But the progress which affects earning capacity, and which is constantly lessening the cost of railroad service to the public, is that which comes of the improvement of the road-beds of the trunk lines by the creation of direct lines from point to point, the reduction or abolition of grades, the easing of curves, the increase in the weight of the rails, and the enlargement of locomotive power and car capacity. The outgo and the income of the railway business are found by considering the train mile and the ton mile as the units or bases of calculation. The cost of running a train a mile is the unit of expense. The amount obtained per ton per mile is the unit of income. The difference be-

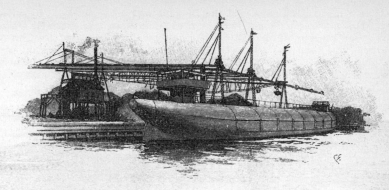

LOADING A WHALEBACK BARGE.

tween the two is the profit. The resistance, which must be reduced to a minimum, is the law of gravity. But for that a child might drag a train of cars with a piece of twine. But, as the Western railroad man remarked, "the law of gravity is like the poor, whom we have always with us, and the railroad men must see that it is not further weighted by steep grades, weak rails, sharp curves, and indirect routes. Originally railroads were laid on the surface of the ground; now they must find a level, and keep to it, as water does."

The modern railroad must also avoid all possibility of obstruction that can be avoided; and we see in the sunken track of the New York Central Railroad in New York city an example of the lengths to which the best railroads must go to obtain guaranteed freedom from obstruction. With the same aim, this railroad is to pass through Rochester upon an elevated structure, and through Buffalo on a sunken track. Yet, in spite of these strides toward the perfection of railroading, with a consequent lessening of rates, President Depew does not predict the destruction of lake traffic. On the contrary, he says that it will always be carried on. The railroads themselves find it of service; and all those trunk lines which have lake ports on their routes now either own steamers or have made contracts with steamship lines. President Depew says that although his railroad company once opposed the canals, he lives at peace with them, his argument being that the lake boats bring to Buffalo more business than the canals can handle, and the surplus goes to the railroads. Moreover, the

canals form highways through the State, and, by contributing to the prosperity of the canal towns, add to the prosperity of the railroads. Mr. Depew adds, nevertheless, that the canals are no longer formidable competitors with the railroads, as they once were. In the old days a canal-boat carried as much grain as a train of twenty 10-ton cars; but now a train may consist of fifty cars, each one carrying 25 tons. The locomotives have grown from a weight of 30 tons to a weight of 90 or 100 tons, the cars have tripled their capacity, the rails that weighed 56 pounds per yard have been replaced by 80 or 90 pound tracks; and with all these improvements has come a reduction of 50 per cent. in freight rates in the time that he has been interested in railroads.

The leading men of the lake ports admit all this; in fact, they make out a strong case for the railroads in order to emphasize the need of facilities by which those great regulators of transportation rates, the freight-boats, may meet the new conditions. Those who have made the arguments for the various lake ports show that whereas in 1868 the rail rate on grain from Chicago to New York was 42.6 cents a bushel, it was 14 cents in 1885. The water rate in that period fell from 25 cents a bushel to 4.55 cents. It has kept between 25 per cent. and 67 per cent. lower than the rail rate. The value of the waterways to the public is illustrated in a startling way by making use of the government records of the Sault Ste. Marie Canal traffic for 1889. There passed through that canal 7,516,022 tons, carried an average distance of 790.4 miles, at 0.145 cents a ton a mile. The railroads would have charged 0.976 cents, and the business would have cost the public fifty millions of dollars more if the railroads had transacted it than was charged by the boatmen.

system will be complete. It will only need enlargement to make it serve the requirements of the near future, but, even as it is, it will serve, in case of war, for the introduction of gunboats and torpedo-

A WHALEBACK DESCENDING THE RAPIDS OF THE ST. LAWRENCE.

In pressing upon the attention of the country the value of a twenty-foot waterway to the sea, the lake-port business men assert that not only did the Lake Superior traffic through the Sault Ste. Marie Canal amount to three-quarters of a million tons more in 1889 than passed the Suez Canal, but the lake business which was transacted in the Detroit River was more than 36,000,000 tons of freight, or ten millions of tons more than the total tonnage of all ocean and gulf ports of the entire coast line of the United States. In view of that fact they ask what would be the growth of this business if, instead of taking this freight out of 3000-ton ships to put it into 200-ton canal-boats, it could go directly and without change of vessels to the sea. As to the expense of the improvements that are asked for, Mr. S. A. Thompson, of the Chamber of Commerce of Duluth, asserts that in all time the Federal government has expended upon all the lakes above Niagara Falls only $28,038,590, so that the saving at the Sault Ste. Marie Canal, on the business of one lake, amounted to a return of $1 85 to the people for every dollar the government spent upon the lakes.

From the stand-point of the people of the lake ports we have not been either as liberal or as long-sighted as the Canadians, who have a well-defined system of waterways, completed by canals wherever navigation is hindered by nature. They are building a canal around the St. Mary's Falls, and when it is finished their

boats by way of the St. Lawrence into those lakes on which we are prevented by treaty from maintaining a squadron. We have upon the lakes only the old wooden sloop of war *Michigan*, and can put no other war vessels there in case of danger, unless we have the time to build them at some lake port. England, on the other hand, has fifty gunboats and other war vessels of sufficiently light draught to pass through the canals into the lakes.

It is not necessary to weigh the various plans which are offered for a national highway from Duluth to the sea. One looks toward the deepening of the canal between Oswego and Syracuse, New York, and of the canal between Syracuse and the Hudson River. Another plan leaves New York city out of consideration, and proposes direct communication between Duluth and the ocean, or the world at large, by means of a duplication of the Canadian canal system on the American border. Both these plans necessitate the building of an American canal around Niagara Falls.

The provision of twenty feet of water in the new Sault Ste. Marie lock, now undergoing construction, will make possible the employment of vessels carrying 6000 to 8000 tons, in place of the present largest-sized lake boats, which cannot carry their complement of 3000 tons. Such carriers, it is said, can cut down the present cost of water transportation fully fifty per cent. and leave a profit for the ship-owners.

In view of the enormous field awaiting development in the Northwest, and in view of the steady lowering of railway rates, the ardor with which the people of the lake ports urge the creation of an American twenty-foot water system, at least as far east as Oswego, does not seem unreasonable.

Upon the 1500 miles of the lake's shore there are living now less than 150,000 persons, and these are mainly in bustling cities like Duluth, Superior, and Marquette, in industrial colonies like Calumet and Red Jacket, or in struggling little ports like Fort William and Port Arthur. Even there the wilderness and primeval conditions are face to face with the robust civilization which is shouldering its way as capital is accustomed to do rather than as natural growth usually asserts itself. Not that it is not a wholly natural growth which we find at all points on the lake shore, for it is all in response to the inexorable laws of supply and demand. Yet the communities there have sprung into being far apart from well-settled regions in answer to these laws.

Thus it happens that to-day one may ride in an electric street car to the starting-point for a short walk to a trout stream, or one may take the steam railroad, and in an hour alight at a forest station, breakfasting there, but enjoying for luncheon a cut of the deer or a dish of the trout or the partridge which he has killed for the purpose. It is, so to say, a region wherein the wholesale fisherman with his steamboat disturbs the red man who is spearing a fish for supper, where the wolf blinks in the glare of the electric lamp, and where the patent stump-puller and the beaver work side by side.

The strange condition is most startlingly illustrated by a recent occurrence in Michigan, in the same region. Close to a watering resort which is crowded in summer by persons from all over the West, some men were cutting timber in the winter. Two brothers were among them. One hit himself with an axe, cutting open an artery in his leg. The other hurried away for surgical help. When the messenger returned, nothing but the bones of his brother were left. Wolves, attracted by the scent of his blood, had eaten him up.

It is thus that there is forced upon the comprehension the practical newness of this giant fresh-water sea, which geologists would have us believe is millions of years old, and which even history mentions in detailing the exploits of men who died in the seventeenth century. But with the youth of this new civilization have come the vigor and enterprise needed to develop industries and to rear cities of which all the people of all the States, new and old, may well feel proud.

BUFFALO

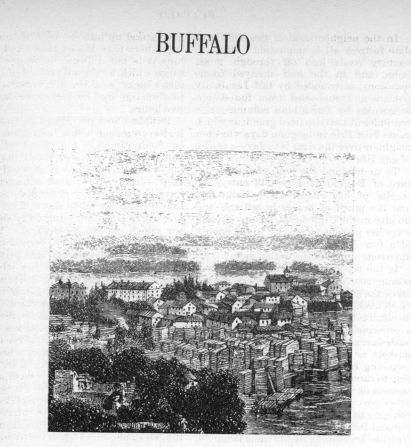

LOOKING across Niagara River from the crumbling ruins of Fort Erie, whose most frequent visitors to-day are the cows of the neighboring farmers browsing peacefully on the grass-grown ramparts, whence seventy years ago General Peter B. Porter made his brilliant sortie, one sees the granite tower of the City Hall of Buffalo rising commandingly above the surrounding miles of warehouses and factory chimneys, hooded in an atmosphere of smoke and steam.

Northward, past the high bluff crowned by the ruins of Fort Porter and the stone copings of "The Front," flows the Niagara with a constantly accelerating velocity. Parallel with it, "packed with long lines of freighted boats towed by slow - paced horses," is the Erie Canal, "the author and sure conservator of the fortunes of Buffalo."

South and westward Lake Erie spreads out in endless billows; and at the east, forming a noble background to the city, rise the Chautauqua hills and the highlands of Evans and Wales.

In the neighborhood of the old Canadian fortress all is stagnation. Peaceful country roads lead off through green lanes, and in the half-decayed frame mansions, surrounded by tall Lombardy poplars, and supported from foundation to cornice by Corinthian columns, is a reminder of that departed grandeur which made Fort Erie in by-gone days what her neighbor over the river is to-day—a centre of gay life.

To understand the past, present, or future of Buffalo as a port of entry, the results of her characteristic industries, and the pluck of her early settlers—and no city in the United States more directly owes her present prosperity to the energy of a few far-seeing pioneers—one must approach her from the harbor side.

In the foreground stands the most imposing row of bread-distributers on the lakes, the mammoth grain elevators of Buffalo Creek, nearly forty of them, making an elephantine procession a mile long, with a combined storage capacity of 9,250,000 bushels, and a transfer capacity of 3,102,000 bushels, or, in other words, the power of receiving from lake vessels and transferring to canal-boats and cars daily 3,000,000 bushels of wheat, a rate unequalled at any other port in this country. It is not uncommon to see a large lake vessel unloading and two canal-boats and two trains of freight-cars loading at the same time.

The site of the Bennett elevator, at the junction of the creek and the Evans ship-canal, is historic as marking the scene of an experiment only less interesting than the first voyage of Robert Fulton's steamboat, for it was here, in 1842, that a Buffalonian, Joseph Dart, built the first steam storage transfer elevator, on the well-known elevator and conveyer principle of Oliver Evans, in the face of the jeers of his townsmen, who predicted that he would find to his cost that "Irishmen's backs were, after all, the cheapest elevators."

The capacity of Joseph Dart's elevator was but 55,000 bushels, with a power of raising 1000 bushels an hour. To-day such an elevator as that of the connecting terminal railroad, having a capacity of 1,000,000 bushels, can elevate 19,000 bushels an hour. Watching the legs of the two towers of this huge elevator drop upon a mass of wheat in the hold of a lake vessel moored at its wharf, the machinery start, and the twelve-quart buckets dip down into the grain and rush with light-

ning speed up into the roof of the building, where they deposit their load in the bins, it is not difficult to believe that a cargo which by the old method of "Irishmen's backs" would have required a month to discharge can now be stowed away in five hours.

Buffalo Creek is interesting not only for its connection with an invention which, by facilitating the movement of breadstuffs, has a vital concern for all mankind, but as the stream—"a ford then only waist deep"—from across whose entrance some sixty years ago a few citizens, determined that Buffalo should be the western terminus of the Erie Canal, dug away the sand bar which choked its channel. Buffalo Creek Harbor was begun, carried on, and completed principally by three private individuals, who mortgaged the whole of their estate in its behalf. The river is now protected north and south by two breakwaters, but the capacious harbor thus obtained is insufficient for the growing commerce of the city, and the United States government is making an outside harbor by the construction of a breakwater designed to be four thousand feet long, fronting the entrance of the river about a half-mile from the shore. With the completion of this breakwater facilities will exist for the building of new wharves aggregating an additional five miles, making the available water-front about nineteen miles. In other words, the commerce of Buffalo Creek is destined one day to rival the gigantic traffic of the river Mersey, when the harbor of this queen city of the lakes will vie with that of Liverpool in her endless docks and warehouses.

Mr. Henry James banishes one of his characters from the Eternal City to "Buffalo" as to the wild West, forgetting or unaware that the name of this lake city is not without Old World precedent. Bosporus means ox-passage, and Oxford a ford for oxen. That the city derives its name from the river is certain, but whether the river was so called because the buffalo had at one time grazed in the shade of the basswood-trees along its margins, now lined with elevators, floaters, lumber-yards, coal pockets, chutes, and trestles, or from a mistake in the Indian title, has not been satisfactorily determined. The name of the city first appears in a treaty made at Fort Stanwix—now Rome—between the United States and the Iroquois Confederacy.

All through the summer the harbor is full of life—tugs dart hither and yon, lake vessels, big and little, receive their cargoes, huge steamers and propellers take on passengers or freight for the upper lakes, while numerous pleasure-yachts, named for sea-nymphs and dryads, steam toward the International Bridge, which opens in the centre with massive swing, and permits them to pass through on their way "down the river." Finally, and most important, stretching in all directions, are the iron rails over which the commerce of the Great West reaches the Eastern sea-board.

To win the heart of this queen city today you must court her in the rôle of a railway king. You must come as the projector of a new trunk line, prepared to lay your millions at her feet in return for a site from which to throw another iron girdle around the city, and with thousands more to invest for a commanding lot on Delaware Avenue, "The Circle," or fronting one of the many park approaches, whereupon to erect a palace of Medina sandstone, or a cypress-shingled villa rivalling those of Newport or the famous Jerusalem Road.

Never was the imperial position of Buffalo appreciated as now, when all signs point to the realization of the prophecy that she is destined to sit "like a commercial Constantinople stretching along the Bosporus of the broad Niagara, and holding the keys of the Dardanelles that shall open and shut the gates of trade for the regions east and west." A study of the globe will show why, from the founder of the city in 1797 down to the latest railway manager of 1885, eager to obtain an approach to the International Bridge, already inadequate to the demands of traffic and mooting the revival of the old scheme of tunnelling under the Niagara, every sagacious person has predicted a great commercial future for the Queen City of the Empire State. With the completion of the Northern Pacific Railroad the whole world will pay her tribute. Not only will the products of the immense wheat fields of the Red River, the coal, oil, and iron of Pennsylvania, the lumber of Michigan and the Southern States, the ores of Lake Superior, and the live stock of the great western prairies pass through her gates, but the commerce of Asia with the Atlantic States, with England, and the Continent.

In the year of Buffalo's incorporation,

1832, when there were but one hundred miles of rail in the United States, was granted the first permit to put a railroad through Erie County. Now, without the repetition of a rod, over nine thousand miles of travel are possible on the lines centring at Buffalo alone, as the starting-point or terminus of twenty different railway lines. No city, save one, owes so much to railroads as does Buffalo. Her terminal facilities are unequalled, and her transfer yards at East Buffalo are the largest in the world, with the outlying country encompassed for miles about by a net-work of tracks, approaching closer and closer as they near the city, and extending around the harbor-side to pour their freight of coal, salt, and petroleum into the lake vessels in return for a cargo of grain, flour, lumber, iron, and copper ore. Commercial Buffalo is like a portly and self-satisfied spider, supreme in the centre of her web.

The business man has his choice among six different routes to New York city. The New York Central and Hudson River; the New York, Lake Erie, and Western; the New York, West Shore, and Buffalo; the Delaware, Lackawanna, and Western; the Lehigh Valley; and the Buffalo division of the Buffalo, New York, and Philadelphia—all lead east amid the beautiful scenery of the interior of the State. Stretching away in an opposite direction toward the western prairies are the Lake Shore and Michigan Southern, the Michigan Central, the Grand Trunk of Canada, the Great Western division, and the New York, Chicago, and St. Louis, or "Nickel Plate." The remaining nine roads are local lines. Among the most important of these is the Buffalo Creek Railway, a belt freight line four miles in length, extending down on either side of the ship canal. Every railroad entering the city has a connection with this, and by the terms of the city's grant its rates are uniform to all, thus placing the railroads on equal terms.

Within the city limits railroad corporations own 2746 acres, or more than four square miles of territory. There are 436 miles of standard gauge track—more miles of rails than are contained in any other city on the globe. Within the corporate boundaries of his own town the Buffalonian could enjoy a railroad journey equal to a trip to New York over the Lackawanna, with twenty-six miles to spare.

THE COAL DOCKS.

What gives unusual interest to the marvellous railroad improvements in Buffalo since 1880, from which year dates the "new era" of prosperity, is the fact that to this construction all the newer scientific principles have been applied. The railroad kings of America have discovered that the traffic capacity of railroad lines is limited mainly by the extent of their terminal facilities, and with this conviction have been developing the terminal facilities of Buffalo most assiduously. The Lehigh Valley Railroad affords a notable illustration of a successful application of the modern theory, for although it has not a line of its own to Buffalo, but sends its coal-laden cars hither from Waverly over the Erie, the company has nevertheless expended millions in the acquisition of unsurpassed terminal facilities in the southern part of the city for the purpose of transshipping its coal, and sending it up Lake Erie and over other roads. Indeed, the opinion has been expressed that the improvements making on the Tifft Farm property—a tract of 425 acres, belonging to this road, at a cost of $4,000,000, will prove of greater value to Buffalo than any public work since the opening of the Erie Canal. These improvements consist chiefly in the turning of the city ship-canal into the farm, and so cutting it backward

and forward at right angles in huge parallelograms as to endow the city with eight additional miles of docks—an amount of water-frontage equal to all she had before—and giving the railway corporations a total of fourteen miles of water-front available for the transfer of freight from lake to rail. The most discreditable fact about the railroad growth is that, notwithstanding the exceeding generosity of the city in the matter of land grants, not one of the roads centring at Buffalo has paid her the compliment of erecting a fine railway station. Those of many New England country towns are far superior.

In no direction has the sudden broadening of Buffalo's business interests been more remarkable than in coal, both for home consumption and distribution. A few years ago the coal traffic was confined to the car-loads necessary for local use. As the city developed into a manufacturing centre the cry went up, "Give us cheap coal." This caused the opening of direct railroad communication between the Pennsylvania mines and the wholesale dealers. The Buffalo, New York, and Philadelphia, in addition to its railroad property, controls extensive coal mines and lands in Pennsylvania, from which it feeds Buffalo with a constantly increasing coal, oil, lumber, bark, and grain commerce.

A few years ago vessels started up the lakes carrying coal as ballast, in order to bring return cargoes of grain. To-day, the freights of the two shipments are day ranks as the third coal depot of America, also as the most important distributing point for anthracite coal, nearly all of which goes through the city. The bi-

ALONG THE WHARVES.

about the same. Coal as an up freightage is fully as important as the down cargo of grain. Nearly two million dollars of property is engaged, it is estimated, in carrying the product of the coal fields from this port, exclusive of rolling stock.

In the amount of tonnage, Buffalo to-

tuminous coal trade shows a progressive growth which, if prognosticated a few years ago, would have been deemed incredible. In the year 1874 the receipts were 327,467 tons; in 1884, 1,921,354 tons. Bituminous coal is largely used by the manufacturers of the city, and is one of the

LIGHT-HOUSE AT ENTRANCE OF HARBOR.

standing local grievances, on account of the soot it showers over the town. The enormous growth of the anthracite coal trade is shown by the fact that in 1874 the receipts were 472,262 tons ; in 1884, 2,451,410 tons.

Thus, were Buffalo not a railway centre, she would be known as a coal depot. Take away both these interests, and she would be reputed one of the leading livestock markets of the country. Without even this, her grape-sugar factories would endow her still with a world-wide name. Remove the grape-sugar works to the neighborhood of the Western corn fields, and she would yet be famed on both sides of the Atlantic Ocean for the greatest engineering feat of modern times—the cantilever bridge of the Michigan Central Railroad which spans the gorge of the Niagara, built in 1883 at the Central Bridge Works, now the Union Bridge Company, of Buffalo. Aside from these larger and wider-known establishments, there are over two thousand manufactories, numbering among the more important, carwheels, stoves, and engines, boots and shoes, oil refineries, malt-houses, breweries and distilleries, flouring mills, chemical works, ship-yards, agricultural implements, and minor industries without number. The mail of one large establishment last year was greater in amount than the entire receipts of the post-office in 1872.

In Buffalo, which practically controls this industry, originated the manufacture of grape-sugar. One alone of the three glucose factories of Buffalo, the American, consumes 10,000 bushels of corn every twenty-four hours, requiring as feed for a single day the average annual product of 434 acres of corn fields, or more than half the entire annual product of all the New England States, more than one-sixth of the entire product of New York, and more than 0.0022 of the total crop of the United States.

daily newspapers in judicious editorial management are unexcelled. The Buffalo *Daily Courier*, which is a descendant of the *Star*, the first daily paper in Buffalo, has had a long line of able editors, among whom was the late William A. Seaver, afterward associated with *Harper's* Drawer.

As she is to-day a highway for the commerce of the nineteenth century, so was Buffalo and Erie County at an earlier period a well-trodden pathway across which passed a motley train of pilgrims and warriors—French hunters and trappers striding to the Northwest, Cardinal Richelieu's Jesuit missionaries holding up the cross, and the Indians of the Long House to put out the camp fires of the Kahquahs and Eries. Since first her soil was

JOSEPH ELLICOTT.

An enormous capital is invested by the *Courier*, *Express*, and *Commercial Advertiser* in the printing, lithographing, and engraving business. Buffalo claims also that, in proportion to population, her

seen by white men the habitations of three distinct races have in turn occupied it; and it is less than sixty years since the second of these, the Seneca Indians, the successors of the Kahquahs, were hunting deer on the present site of the State Insane Asylum, whose symmetrical red-tiled towers, designed by Richardson, loom up imposingly at the head of Richmond Avenue.

Following North Street, one of the fashionable neighborhoods of Buffalo, which intersects Richmond Avenue at the Circle, down Porter Avenue, nearly at right angles to it—a route almost identical with the "Guide Board Road" of the period when the Indians and their English allies crossed from Canada to Black Rock to burn Buffalo—we come out upon the Front, another now favorite residence neighborhood. Here the Buffalonian gets his one "marine" view, and here, too, he has a perpetual reminder of the original owners of the soil. More than two centuries have elapsed since the smoke wreaths of the Kahquahs' lodges rose on both sides of the gorge which witnesses the nuptials of the fairest of the Great Lakes with the most powerful of rivers. They named the stream that divided their ancient domain the Onniagahra, or Niagara.

In the summer of 1687, says the local historian, the Baron la Hontan ascended the rapids of the Niagara River in his light birchen canoe to Lake Erie. His military eye taking in the commanding situation at once, he recommended the site to the French government for a fort, and marked it Fort Supposé on the map that illustrated his travels. The fort was intended as a check against the neighboring Iroquois and Seneca Indians. This, the earliest historical notice of the site of Buffalo, was more than a hundred years prior to the Holland land purchase and the laying out of the city.

"In her many diagonal streets, all radiating from a common centre, Buffalo, as I have heard, bears an intentional resemblance to Washington. But where is the Capitol?" queried one of the newer settlers lately.

It is not to the credit of Buffalo that she has as yet perpetuated by neither statue nor memorial, save in the name of a single street, his fame who not only first predicted her commercial destiny, but what is almost unparalleled in the history of cities, selected her exact site and laid out in the then wilderness at the foot of Lake Erie a city on a scale commensurate with his inspired belief in her destiny. As agent for the Holland Land Com-

SOLDIERS' AND SAILORS' MONUMENT.

A REMINDER OF HOLLAND.

pany, Joseph Ellicott, in the year 1804, completed the survey of the broad streets, diagonal avenues, and public squares, some of which are to-day included in her extensive park system, and all of which form adequate approaches to the newer suburbs of the Buffalo of 1885. To her singularly open and attractive topography it is to be regretted that she does not add that next-to-godly attribute, cleanliness.

Joseph Ellicott was the brother of Andrew Ellicott, then Surveyor-General of the United States. Fresh from assisting his kinsman to lay out the city of Washington preparatory to its becoming the seat of government, he followed the same general plan in surveying the streets of "New Amsterdam," as he proposed to call it, out of respect to his Dutch employers, the members of the so-called Holland Land Company. The chief business thoroughfare now bears the commonplace name of Main Street—one which, to all save the ears of towns-people accustomed to it, wonderfully becomes its still semi-countrified air and the non-imposing character of many of its buildings; for everywhere in her business sections old and new Buffalo jostle each other picturesquely. Had Joseph Ellicott been allowed to complete his design in the nomenclature and laying out of the main

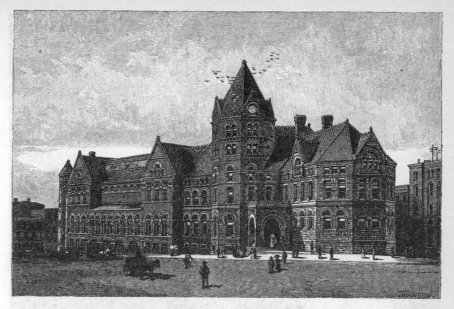

NEW LIBRARY BUILDING OF THE YOUNG MEN'S ASSOCIATION.

thoroughfare of trade, Main Street would have been Willink Avenue below "the Churches," and Van Staphorst above, for what was designed to be the site of the Capitol of New Amsterdam forms now the three blocks in Main Street bounded to the north and south by Eagle and Swan streets. Here Mr. Ellicott proposed to erect his palace, with broad vistas opening to view in all directions. The eye of the prince of New Amsterdam could have gazed at pleasure up Van Staphorst Avenue to the rising ground at the north, down Willink Avenue to the harbor, and out Vollenhoven Avenue (Erie Street) to the lake and Canada, along Stadnitski Avenue (Church Street) to the State reservation, and up Shimmelpennick Avenue (Niagara Street) past the elegant residences circling around Niagara Square, which was to be the centre of his city, straight to the setting sun. The westerly limit of this manor, extending beyond the present west side of Main Street, suggested the title of "Ellicott's bow-window" to the towns-folk. So practical a man as President Fillmore expressed just regret that the democratic spirit of that time, jealous of so baronial an establishment, cut the beautiful semicircle by running Main Street through instead of around it,

dividing the tract of about one hundred acres by North and South Division streets, since Mr. Ellicott would have left a splendid building for the display of the fine arts and a beautiful park in the midst of the city. It is a curious circumstance that the site was again selected by the visionary and famous Rathbun for his proposed magnificent Chamber of Commerce. Rathbun's dream, unlike Ellicott's, was destined to be fulfilled in part in 1884, when the commerce of the lakes and canal joined hands with the manufacturing and mercantile interests to erect, further down-town, the Merchants' Exchange. The Buffalo Board of Trade, which sunk its identity in the Merchants' Exchange, was a corporation with a noble record. To its unceasing energy and patriotism is due the promotion of many enterprises affecting deeply the commercial interests of the city and nation.

While no one would dare to advance a claim for Buffalo in the months of March and April, she has a thousand charms as a summer home. With a turn of the faucet one may drink of or plunge in the cool waters of the upper lakes. The fruit and vegetables on the breakfast table come fresh and crisp each morning from the market-gardens about the city. The fish were caught before daylight from the depths of Niagara, and the beefsteak selected from the herds waiting transportation at the East Buffalo stock-yards, where larger moneyed transactions on a cash basis take place daily than in any other quarter of the city. The roses and the lilies which brighten the morning meal were plucked in the door-yard. If the resident be a man of some leisure and fond of horseflesh, he takes an early morning turn behind his flyer around the Driving Park, one of the best and fastest tracks in the country, and famous in trotting annals as the scene of Dexter's and Goldsmith Maid's best time. The yearly meet on these grounds the first week in August brings a crowd of horsemen and racers to the city. The Driving Park Association own an elegant club-house, in the old colonial style, from the verandas of which there is a fine view over the city to the lake and the river.

The old resident who has somewhat thrown off the cares of active business visits his office summer mornings to read his letters and give directions to his clerks, then steps aboard his steam-yacht with a party of friends. After a good haul of black bass on the river, he drops anchor at Falconwood to join his neighbors and their wives, or perhaps members of his own family, whom the club boat has brought down earlier in the day, at a six-o'clock dinner. The yachts are headed up-stream just at the twilight hour, when the outlines of the Canada shore, across which tall poplar-trees throw their long shadows, are fading into indistinctness, and make their dock at the famous Fort Erie Ferry, where coaches are waiting to take the summer idlers home by way of the park boulevards.

This sketch of summer life would be incomplete without the suggestion that Lake Erie's zephyrs have so tempered the heated midsummer atmosphere that a blanket tends to promote the luxurious slumbers which follow the evening hours spent in the piazza with one's neighbors. The popularity of this form of pleasuring was voiced by the Buffalonian who said, "When I build, I shall build a veranda, with possibly a house attached."

Buffalo now ranks among the gayest and most hospitable cities in America. Her commercial growth has been traced. It would be no less interesting to note how this has reacted on private habits. Since her earliest years she has been a community of great friendliness and hospitality, of comparative simplicity in social forms, and of a singularly democratic spirit. While she is no exception to the rule that so soon as the business quarter of a town takes on the character of a metropolis, there is a tendency toward increasing decorum and stateliness in social life,

THE CITY HALL.

agreeableness and intelligence, not size of purse, are, as before she became a Mecca for capitalists, the standard of her representative families. Among the innumerable pleasant home centres of Buffalo frontier. To Mr. Marshall's efforts was due largely the organization of the Buffalo Historical Society, which has done diligent and honorable service in collecting and preserving the records of early days.

LANDING AT FALCONWOOD.

is that of the Hon. James O. Putnam, lately United States Minister to Belgium. In his high public record, no less than in his liberal culture and exceptional social qualities, Mr. Putnam's fellow-townsmen take great pride.

Buffalo has much reason to honor the literary attainments of the late Orsamus H. Marshall, the historian of the Niagara

While several private individuals have reached what Mr. Howells terms "the picture-buying stage" of development, as a city Buffalo gives no encouragement to the fine arts. Founded in 1862, the Fine Arts Academy presents a curious example of arrested development, and of the stagnation usual to art enterprises in commercial centres. The most beautiful work

ON THE CANAL.

that adorns its gallery, "The Dead Pearl-Diver," by Paul Akers (owned by his heirs), was immortalized by Hawthorne in *The Marble Faun.*

The Academy owns over two hundred paintings, among them Phillipoteaux's brilliant panoramic picture of the French revolution of '48, an immense canvas, destined to be historic, containing over a hundred figures, remarkable for fine drawing. The interest of the Jewett Fund insures the purchase of a good picture every year or two, and many have been contributed by representative American artists. Mr. L. G. Sellstedt, the able superintendent, for years has given of his time unstintingly and hopefully for the future growth of art in Buffalo.

The Buffalo Club and the City Club are the largest as well as the representative men's clubs. The Buffalo Club, whose first president was Millard Fillmore, is the older and more exclusive organization, and is to that city what the Somerset Club

DELAWARE AVENUE.

is to Boston. It also upholds the city's reputation for hospitality to distinguished men, dividing the honor in this regard with Falconwood. Ordinarily it is considered the whist centre of the town.

The City Club, for some years the only business men's exchange, numbers over three hundred members, and is an outgrowth of the newer commercial interests. It is the down-town lunching centre. While womankind is discussing the characters of the latest magazine serial, or her newest possessions in pottery and porcelain, over candle-lighted luncheon tables up-town, coal, lumber, oil, grain, and the latest railroad grant, as well as Blackstone and Chitty, furnish the divers topics of the City Club.

Buffalo is remarkable for the number of her fine amateur pianistes, and for the many musical organizations which she sustains—a development due in part to the predominance of the Teutonic element. A year ago the Philharmonic Society, a string orchestra, was started, with a subscription of $14,000. The oldest German musical organization, and one of the oldest in the country, is the Liedertafel.

In 1886, the semi-centennial year of the Young Men's Association, its new library building, designed by Cyrus L. W. Eidlitz, and intended as a home not only for the Young Men's Association Library, but for the Grosvenor (a free reference library), the Historical Society, and the Fine Arts Academy, will be finished, at a cost of nearly $300,000. As the custodian of the chief public library, and promoter of many liberal projects, the Young Men's Association has for nearly half a century been foremost in furthering the literary culture of Buffalo. In its long line of presidents are numbered the most honored names of the city. The new library building is directly in the rear of Lafayette Square. Already crowned by the Soldiers' and Sailors' Monument, with the noble façade and towers of the Young Men's Association in the background, its graceful Norman arches adorned with busts of men eminent in *belles-lettres*, art, science, and music, this square in the heart of the city will do equal honor to Buffalo and to the distinguished name it bears.

Considering that Buffalo ranks as the third city of the State, with over two hundred thousand inhabitants, and talks of numbering half a million when she rounds the century, she has little as yet to be proud of in public buildings. In the im-

posing Venetian-looking square occupied
by the City and County Hall, and in the
fair proportions of a few of the newer
structures, there is, however, much hope
for the future, architecturally speaking.

Old Franklin Square, the first village
burying-ground, now occupied by the City
and County Hall, is a historic site. In
its woods Colonel Cyrenius Chapin reluctantly surrendered the village to the
British and their Indian allies December
30, 1813, on condition that they would respect the rights of private property—a condition which they failed to fulfill; for
there is no darker chapter in the war of
1812 on this frontier than the burning of
the village of Buffalo. To-day the site
is interesting to the nation as the scene
where its President began his public career. The City Hall extends longitudi-
nally north and south in the form of
a double Roman cross, with its main façade in Franklin Street. Opposite its
Delaware Avenue front, and connected
with it by an under-ground passage, is the
jail—a massive limestone structure. The
City Hall is surrounded by a terraced
lawn bordered by granite copings, and
broken here and there by brilliant floral
parterres. Clark's Island, Maine, furnished the clear gray granite which in a rough
form composes the first story, and in finished blocks completes the two upper stories. From the observatory in the tower,
the four corners of which are surmounted
by colossal statues of Justice, Mechanic
Arts, Agriculture, and Commerce, one of
the finest views of the city is obtainable.

Inside the building, which cost less than
a million and a half, and was built " without a steal," all the municipal and county
business is transacted. To its granite
hitching-post the farmer from Willink,
Eden, or Wales, dismounting from his
rickety straw-stuffed wagon, ties old raw-
bones, and helping his wife down off her
high perch, joins the crowd of lawyers,
judges, jurymen, city and county officials,
that pours in and out of the building all
day long in an unceasing stream. The
Surrogate's Court, whither perhaps the old
couple wend their way, was the scene of
the trial of the famous Fillmore will case,
wherein the descendants of the historic
American families Jay and Clinton were
engaged as opposing counsel.

The Mayor's office now has a peculiar
fascination for ambitious country boys,
who approach reverentially the portals of
the spacious presence-chamber wherein
only three years ago President Cleveland
transacted his official duties, furnishing
the office with a pattern which tax-payers
of whatever political affinities demand
shall be copied by his successors.

Although in church architecture Buffalo
is behind the times, St. Paul's Protestant
Episcopal Church, a perfect specimen of
Early English Gothic, is the noteworthy
exception, being the most beautiful church
edifice in Western New York. St. Joseph's
Roman Catholic Cathedral contains the
celebrated Hook organ from the Centennial Exposition, as well as the finest set
of chimes in the country, from the Paris
Exposition of 1867, where they took the
first prize.

About the site of St. Paul's, the mother
parish of Buffalo, and but a stone's-throw
from the city buildings, there lingers one
of the strangest and most picturesque traditions of Western New York. What could
be more romantic or more incongruous
than to lay in the chancel of a Protestant
Episcopal Church the corner-stone of a
Hebrew city within whose precincts it was
intended to gather together all the lost
tribes of Israel ?

The year 1825 is most memorable in the
early history of Buffalo. Then occurred
the hanging of the three Thayers for the
murder of John Love, much celebrated in
song and story ; then also the reception of
General Lafayette at the Eagle Tavern.
That year pedagogue Millard Fillmore,
who boarded around among the families
of his pupils, began to be considered a rising young man ; some of the wiseacres
thought he might come to be a justice of
the peace ; others, more sanguine, did not
think the Assembly Chamber at Albany
beyond the reach of his ambition.

On the 26th of October, 1825, was celebrated the opening of the Erie Canal.
About a month before, when the community, eagerly anticipating a connection
with tide-water, was excited with visions
of prospective greatness, and ready for any
display, there arrived from New York
Major Manuel Mordecai Noah, high sher-
iff of the county of New York, consul at
Tunis, and self-styled Judge of Israel. He
came with glittering robes and insignia
of office, to establish the city of Ararat on
Grand Island, then covered with a dense
forest. Although a loyal and devoted son
of Abraham, Major Noah had not succeeded in arousing enthusiasm in his scheme

among those of his own faith. As a shrewd man of the world, an able lawyer, a successful politician, and the editor of the principal organ of the Tammany party in New York, and withal sanguine that the city would prove a mine of wealth to its founders, he had no difficulty in persuading some of his Gentile friends, among whom was the father of the late Gerritt Smith, to buy nearly the whole of Grand Island, then just surveyed and offered for sale by the United States government.

On this lonely but extensive island, between the forks of the Niagara, and lying midway between Lake Erie and the Falls of Niagara, he determined to build a city of Oriental splendor. Already, before his arrival on the scene, a flag-staff bearing the "grand standard of Israel" had been erected on the chosen site, and a stone having an inscription in Hebrew and in English

THE STATE INSANE ASYLUM.

had been prepared to dedicate with imposing ceremonies. This stone, always known in local history as "Mordecai's corner-stone," was intended rather as a memento of the founding of the magnificent city of the Jews than as the support of any particular building. In those days the luxurious steam-yachts of wealthy citizens, which now plough the rapid current of the Niagara, existed not in the imagination of the veriest dreamer; even row-boats were wanting with which to convey the crowd eager to behold the spectacle presented by the birth of an Oriental city in the depths of the forest. The brilliant and audacious Noah conceived the idea of having the ceremony celebrated with due pomp within the walls of St. Paul's Church, twelve miles from the site of his

THE MARKET.

city. To this end were invoked the willing services of all the dignitaries of the town, the military and the Masons, Major Noah the central figure appearing as the "Judge of Israel" in black, wearing judicial robes of crimson silk, trimmed with ermine, and a richly embossed golden medal suspended from his neck.

The bright September day opened with the booming of cannons. The grand procession embraced the best that the town could offer. Halting at the church door, the troops opened each way, and the pageant entered; while the band played the grand march from *Judas Maccabeus*, the corner-stone of Ararat, the city of refuge for the people who rejected Christ, was laid on the communion table of a Protestant Episcopal church, and dedicated by Hebrew ritual. The Masonic rites were performed with the typical corn, wine, and oil, the choir sang "Old Hundred," and the rector, in full canonicals, pronounced a Christian benediction.

Mordecai Noah never saw the site of Ararat, and the Hebrew race disregarded his grandiloquent proclamation and the tax levied for its building; but its corner-stone, after many curious migrations, occupies a conspicuous place in the rooms of the Buffalo Historical Society, where relic-hunters are frequently seen copying its inscription.

The old church in which these ceremonies took place has yielded to the present beautiful stone edifice of Early English Gothic architecture crowned by a graceful spire. This, with the "Old First" (Presbyterian), gives the neighborhood the name of "The Churches." They stand opposite the square originally intended for Joseph Ellicott's Capitol.

Unique as is the story associated with Grand Island's past, in its private clubs of to-day, Falconwood, Oakfield, and Beaver Island, which crown its western bluff with beautiful villas facing the Canada shore, their lawns sloping trim-shaven to the river, Buffalonians and their hosts of midsummer guests find still greater fascination. Contiguous to Falconwood, cradled by the Niagara, in itself, says N. P. Willis, "the best cradle nature could possibly form for the family of a luxurious exclusive," the "father of the greenback," the Hon. Elbridge Gerry Spaulding, spends his summers. Connected with his country-seat, "River Lawn," is a large stock-farm, famous for its thorough-bred cattle.

Adjacent to this is the farm of the Hon. Lewis F. Allen, the venerable historian of Grand Island, uncle by marriage of President Cleveland, and the pioneer stock-raiser of this region. To a few Buffalo capitalists Erie County owes largely the rapid advance of its important stock interests. Within the city limits, and adjoining the park, is a stock-farm having a herd of short-horned cattle which in numbers and pedigree are not excelled in this country or in England, where its owner employs special agents. But the already famous stock-farms of Erie County are far too numerous for even cursory mention.

Covering territory of about thirty-nine miles, an area greater than is occupied by any municipality in the United States except Philadelphia, the freeholders of Buffalo far outnumber those of any other city. So great a proportion of the laboring class of the population owning their homes gives an air of unusual thrift to the foreign quarter—a vast, closely built tract lying east of Main Street. When, on the occasion of a brief stay in Buffalo, Herbert Spencer was by his own request driven through the thickly settled wards of "Germantown," he remarked particularly upon the hundreds of one and two story cottages which line these streets, and are almost universally in good condition as to paint and window-blinds, and with every inch of the little plot of surrounding land cultivated with vegetables or flowers.

To the early influence of one man, the late Stephen Van Rensselaer Watson, a citizen whose far-seeing genius for practical affairs gave Buffalo her present comprehensive system of street railroads, is due much of the independent comfort now enjoyed by the foreign element of her population. Coming to the city in 1844, he invested largely in uncleared land on the east side. This he divided, and sold out in lots on long payments, principally to Germans, whom he aided not only with money, but with sagacious advice.

It is a significant fact that the first civilized man to settle on the present site of Buffalo was a German. Of few Northern cities can it be affirmed, as of this, that the Teutonic element constitutes nearly one-half the entire population. The Germans of Buffalo have their own press, literary and musical associations, churches, theatres, and, it is unnecessary to add, beer gardens, while in public spirit they have in one notable instance shown themselves ahead of the Americans. Not only are German names frequent on the business signs of the American quarter, but the Germans have their own long business street running diagonally out through "Germantown," and the German population has been represented frequently in city, county, and State offices.

Artists in search of models and authors making character studies will find few fields richer in local color than the German quarter of Buffalo and her two large markets. These markets are distinctive, and help to make living cheap. Each market occupies a block, and at the stalls everything, from crockery, yarn, buttons, and shining tins, to the finest cuts of beef, poultry, fish, and green truck of all kinds, is exposed for sale. In midsummer they are the market-places of flowers. Pretty young girls in fresh muslins tie their pony-carts outside, and come tripping in among the stalls to cull out bunches of mignonette, sweet-peas, and pansies, jostling against baby wagons, match venders, long-aproned butchers, white-capped Vienna roll men, and German fraus with a generous bulk of waist and shoulders.

Ever since the days when Christy's Minstrels, which originated in Buffalo, merrily sang,

"Oh, Buffalo girls, are you coming out to-night,
Are you coming out to-night,
To dance by the light of the moon?"

the belles of the city have been renowned in two continents. While the ever-increasing social obligations of a gay city life require them to be out at night more than ever, the strict regard for etiquette which now prevails in the rarefied atmosphere of Buffalo society decrees that they shall be accompanied by their chaperons. Of a city that is neither Eastern nor Western, it is natural that the best type of Buffalo womanhood should blend in her personality the salient characteristics of the women of each section of the country; in other words, she has the individuality which is inevitable from her environment. To the mental alertness of the New-Englander she superadds the fearless originality of the belle of the prairie, but without her aggressiveness or tendency to crudeness.

A vital concern for poor and suffering humanity is not characteristic of Buffalo women only, but there are few cities the philanthropic institutions of which are managed so generally by women, and who in their very positive relations toward the charities of Buffalo are, as has been remarked, "the salt of the city."

In 1832 an ambitious young merchant, Benjamin Fitch, settled in Buffalo, where he made a fortune. His subsequent benefactions to the city, amounting in all to about $300,000, entitle him to a name among the great philanthropists of America. Just fifty years after his coming the corner-stone of the Fitch Institute was laid, at which ceremony Mayor Cleveland spoke eloquently of Mr. Fitch's generosity. The old man answered, in simple phrase, "I have done but my duty."

Under the French and Gothic roof of the Fitch Institute, on the corner of Swan and Michigan streets, erected at a cost of over $60,000, there are many and divers philanthropic interests, and its illuminated clock tower is a beacon-light for the working people who pass up and down the crowded thoroughfare. Both the Fitch Institute and the Crèche are managed by the Charity Organization Society, the oldest of the associated charity systems of this country. Buffalo adopted the London method of organized charities in 1877. The Charity Organization Society, officered by the younger professional and business men chiefly, has been indirectly the source of inspiration for many of the newer movements by which Buffalo has striven to cast off her slough of conservatism.

Think of having to take care of twenty thousand babies! This is what the Fitch Crèche has done since 1879. This great public cradle is the most interesting charity in Buffalo, because the most unique. Founded on the model of the London Day Nursery to care for little children whose mothers earn their support as char-women, it has so far outstripped its progenitor as to be called the model crèche of the world.

Delaware Avenue, which "takes its rise in a jail and ends in a tomb," as a wag, sneering at its aristocratic pretensions, said, is shaded its full length of three miles with double rows of elms and maples, which arch overhead. Its beautiful houses and villas standing alone, amid broad lawns, and embowered in vines, give the long avenue the elegantly rural aspect of a suburban rather than a city street. In summer, masses of shade trees, and foliage wreathing itself over side walls and porticoes, serve to soften or conceal the architectural incongruities of some of the older

LAKE IN THE PARK.

and too elaborate houses. Its reputation as one of the finest of residence streets is likely to grow, rather than diminish, with the city. For when completed on the plan of the original survey, Buffalo Street at Niagara Falls Village and Delaware Avenue will be one long highway, and the most beautiful avenue in America. Then the City Hall of Buffalo and the proposed International Park at Niagara Falls will be connected by the same boulevard. The aspiring Buffalonian goes farther, and predicts that there will be one day a river boulevard from Buffalo to Youngstown, from Lake Erie to Lake Ontario.

Perhaps it is to offset a pardonable conceit over this nearness to the greatest of nature's wonders that Buffalo's immediate suburbs are so strictly commonplace. The city sprawls out in a north and easterly direction over an area as flat as the proverbial pancake. He who tries to drive out into the country is held fast in a net-work of railway tracks. To beautify the city within its limits by creating a continuous circle of driveways was a necessity which gave birth, in 1869, to the

park system, comprising over eight hundred acres of pleasure-grounds connected by boulevards, which together afford a drive of over ten miles.

Watching the gay and interminable procession of coaches, landaus, dog-carts, and English phaetons, with their liveried grooms, passing over the asphalt or macadamized park roads in midsummer, one has to rub one's eyes to believe that the first family carriage ever seen in Erie County, owned and driven by Samuel Pratt, rolled into Buffalo only eighty years ago. There are three large parks, the Park proper, about three miles north of the City Hall, the Parade, which is in the precincts of "Germantown," and the Front, on the banks of the Niagara. On the broad and undulating Park meadow the polo club play many of their best games, and horseback parties make this their favorite rallying point. Beneath this smooth-clipped turf, guarded by two monarchs of the forest, lie, unknowing and unknown, three hundred soldier dead, regulars of the United States army, the victims of typhoid fever in the winter of 1812. Haunted in midsummer, not by shades of these departed patriots, but by thousands of picnic parties, many of which come from the lower and more crowded parts of the city to get a breath of pure country air, the Park not alone conduces to beautify, but subserves a nobler end as a health-giving outlet and a provider of refreshing recreation at little cost.

Adjacent, sloping down to "Gala Water," freighted with gondolas, canoes, and row-boats, is the white encampment of Forest Lawn, wrapped in a silence broken only by the light tread of the squirrel or chipmunk running boldly up the side of one of the ancient oaks that abound in the well-wooded cemetery.

Among the distinguished dead who rest in Forest Lawn is the late General Albert J. Myer, whose widow is the daughter of Ebenezer Walden, the first lawyer in Erie County, and its first judge. The family mausoleum, overlooking the Park lake, is close by the Pratt Monument, also commemorative of a family prominent among the earliest settlers of Buffalo.

On that panel of the square of granite over the grave of Samuel Wilkeson which faces the harbor is chiselled:

"Urbem condidit. He built the city by building its harbor."

To tell how Buffalo and Black Rock were arrayed against each other as hostile camps in battle, each striving to be the terminus of the Erie Canal, is but to repeat an oft-rehearsed story. Buffalo, through the agency of a few resolute men, with Samuel Wilkeson at their head—who waded Buffalo Creek, and labored with the diggers on the sand bar—having succeeded in scooping out a harbor, argued with success the case against Black Rock.

In her new-found allegiance to the railway king, Buffalo does not forget her foster-mother. As a free highway the Erie Canal holds the balance of power. It regulates the transportation rates by rail, and preserves the supremacy of the great State of New York as the chief thoroughfare of commerce—a supremacy which the railways could not maintain unaided. The statistics of the past year show that the canal did as well as its rivals by rail or water, and has by no means, as has been intimated, survived its usefulness.

In the name of the rivulet which flows through Forest Lawn, Scajaquada Creek, is a reminder of the aboriginal owners of these lawns and woodlands. Another will soon be there, for under the auspices of the Historical Society is now rising a monument whose apex will be surmounted by a bronze statue of Red Jacket. This monument marks the resting-place of the recently re-interred bones of Sa-go-ye-wa-tha, the Rienzi of the Iroquois, and other distinguished chiefs of the Six Nations.

All through the earlier history of Buffalo the aboriginal lion, Red Jacket, stalks a picturesque figure. Realizing that it was the precursor of the extinction of his nation, Red Jacket was jealous of the encroachments of the white people. Naturally, therefore, although always courteous, he felt unfriendly toward Mr. Ellicott. One day the two met in the Tonawanda Swamp, and sat down together on a log. After a few moments of silence, which Mr. Ellicott knew too much of Indian custom to interrupt, Red Jacket exclaimed, "Move along, Joe." The request was complied with. After a few moments it was repeated. Red Jacket gave the peremptory order several times, until by degrees Mr. Ellicott had moved to the extreme verge of the log. Again came the mandate, "Joe, move along." "But there is no room left," was the answer. "That," cried Red Jacket, "is the way the white man treats us. He first says move along a little, then a little more. When we have moved as far as we can, he shoves us out of the world."

The Tonawanda Swamp, wherein this dialogue was held some seventy years ago, is now covered with the lumber-yards of Buffalo capitalists, for Tonawanda, the great lumber port of the Western lake territory, and Buffalo, are one lumber market to-day, with identical interests. The descendants of Red Jacket, former owners of the soil, are relegated to the Cattaraugus and Alleghany reservations, or have been "shoved" as far west on their way toward the end of the log as the distant reservations of Kansas.

Buffalo has become one of the cosmopolitan cities of the country. Germans, French, English, Italians, Swedes, Poles, Japs, Turks, and Arabs jostle each other in the crowded thoroughfares, and buy and sell in the markets. She has had her saengerfests, her great musical festivals, innumerable conventions, political, scientific, and literary, and has given the United States two Presidents and two cabinet officers.